Family Resources

THE GUILFORD FAMILY THERAPY SERIES, Alan S. Gurman, Editor

Family Resources: The Hidden Partner in Family Therapy
Mark A. Karpel, Editor

Systemic Family Therapy: An Integrative Approach
William C. Nichols and Craig A. Everett

Family Paradigms: The Practice of Theory in Family Therapy
Larry L. Constantine

Systems Consultation: A New Perspective for Family Therapy
Lyman C. Wynne, Susan H. McDaniel, and Timothy T. Weber, Editors

Clinical Handbook of Marital Therapy
Neil S. Jacobson and Alan S. Gurman, Editors

Marriage and Mental Illness: A Sex-Roles Perspective
R. Julian Hafner

Living through Divorce: A Developmental Approach to Divorce Therapy
Joy K. Rice and David G. Rice

Generation to Generation: Family Process in Church and Synagogue
Edwin H. Friedman

Failures in Family Therapy
Sandra B. Coleman, Editor

Casebook of Marital Therapy
Alan S. Gurman, Editor

Families and Other Systems: The Macrosystemic Context of Family Therapy
John Schwartzman, Editor

The Military Family: Dynamics and Treatment
Florence W. Kaslow and Richard I. Ridenour, Editors

Marriage and Divorce: A Contemporary Perspective
Carol C. Nadelson and Derek C. Polonsky, Editors

Family Care of Schizophrenia: A Problem-Solving Approach to the Treatment of Mental Illness
Ian R. H. Falloon, Jeffrey L. Boyd, and Christine W. McGill

The Process of Change
Peggy Papp

Family Therapy: Principles of Strategic Practice
Allon Bross, Editor

Aesthetics of Change
Bradford P. Keeney

Family Therapy in Schizophrenia
William R. McFarlane, Editor

Mastering Resistance: A Practical Guide to Family Therapy
Carol M. Anderson and Susan Stewart

Family Therapy and Family Medicine: Toward the Primary Care of Families
William J. Doherty and Macaran A. Baird

Ethnicity and Family Therapy
Monica McGoldrick, John K. Pearce, and Joseph Giordano, Editors

Patterns of Brief Family Therapy: An Ecosystemic Approach
Steve de Shazer

The Family Therapy of Drug Abuse and Addiction
M. Duncan Stanton, Thomas C. Todd, and Associates

From Psyche to System: The Evolving Therapy of Carl Whitaker
John R. Neill and David P. Kniskern, Editors

Normal Family Processes
Froma Walsh, Editor

Helping Couples Change: A Social Learning Approach to Marital Therapy
Richard B. Stuart

Family Resources: The Hidden Partner in Family Therapy

EDITED BY
Mark A. Karpel, Ph.D.

Foreword by
W. Robert Beavers, M.D.

The Guilford Press
New York   London

© 1986 The Guilford Press

Printed in the United States of America
Last digit is print number 9 8 7 6 5 4 3 2

Library of Congress Cataloging in Publication Data
Main entry under title:

Family resources.

(The Guilford family therapy series)
Includes bibliographies and index.
1. Family psychotherapy. 2. Family. I. Karpel,
Mark A. II. Series. [DNLM: 1. Family Therapy.
WM 430.5.F2 F19838]
RC488.5.F3335 1986   616.89′156   86-14922
ISBN 0-89862-069-4

For Denise
  who has given me more than I'd ever hoped for
and for Madeleine and Marshall
  who are patiently teaching me the real lessons of family life

Contributors

Carolyn L. Attneave, Ph.D., Sci.D. Department of Psychology, Department of Psychiatry and Behavioral Sciences, University of Washington, Seattle, Washington

Macaran A. Baird, M.D. Family Practice Residency Programs, Department of Family Medicine, University of Oklahoma Health Sciences Center, Edmond, Oklahoma

Evan Imber-Black, Ph.D. Department of Psychiatry, Family Therapy Program, University of Calgary, Calgary, Alberta, Canada

Carolyn Moynihan Bradt, A.C.S.W. Private Practice, Washington, D.C.

Jack O. Bradt, M.D. Department of Psychiatry, Georgetown Medical Center, Washington, D.C.

Margaret Cotroneo, R.N., Ph.D. School of Nursing, University of Pennsylvania, Philadelphia, Pennsylvania

William J. Doherty, Ph.D. Department of Family Social Science, University of Minnesota, Minneapolis, Minnesota

Edwin H. Friedman, D.D. Private Practice, Bethesda, Maryland

Denise J. Gelinas, Ph.D. New England Clinical Associates, West Hartford, Connecticut; Private Practice and Consultation, Northampton and West Springfield, Massachusetts

Michael D. Kahn, Ph.D. Department of Psychology, University of Hartford, Hartford, Connecticut

Mark A. Karpel, Ph.D. Private Practice and Consultation, Northampton and West Springfield, Massachusetts

Barbara R. Krasner, Ph.D. Center for Contextual Therapy and Allied Studies, King of Prussia, Pennsylvania; Department of Mental Health Sciences, Hahnemann University, Philadelphia, Pennsylvania; Department of Religion, LaSalle University, Philadelphia, Pennsylvania

Shel J. Miller, Ph.D. Harvard Community Health Plan, Boston, Massachusetts; Private Practice, Brookline, Massachusetts

Braulio Montalvo, M.A. Family Institute of New Mexico; Department of Pediatrics, University of New Mexico, Albuquerque, New Mexico

Norman L. Paul, M.D. Department of Neurology, Boston University School of Medicine, Boston, Massachusetts

Eric S. Strauss, Ph.D. Private Practice, West Springfield, Massachusetts

David N. Ulrich, Ph.D. Private Practice, Stamford, Connecticut

Johan Verhulst, M.D. Residency Training Program, Department of Psychiatry, University of Washington Medical School, Seattle, Washington

Acknowledgments

There have been a number of "hidden partners" in the creation of this book, individuals who helped to guide and sustain me throughout the project. I'll start with my "kitchen cabinet," so called because the majority of our discussions were over meals of one kind or another. Denise Gelinas, my wife, shared every moment of misery and satisfaction with me. She provided perspective, intellectual stimulation, solace and concrete support, especially during the final months of the book's completion. This was no easy task given our own growing household at that time and she has earned yet another large measure of my gratitude. Eric Strauss was an indispensible sounding-board and the only person to read and critique all of my own writing for the book before its completion. Eric knew how much his opinion counted and was, as always, exquisitely diplomatic in a way that was totally trustworthy. Harold Seewald, who is not a therapist but by now knows as much about therapy as many practicing professionals, was immensely helpful in repeatedly enabling me to differentiate my own and the book's inherent priorities from the confusing currents of personal ambition, professional politics and the intimidating power of the Fashionable. Harold helped me to remember who I am and what this book had to be about. Dave Todd and I discussed the progress of the book at our monthly breakfasts. Dave provided encouragement, intellectual stimulation and, on occasion, recommended readings. One final honorary member of the kitchen cabinet is Jeanne Gelinas, who helped out at home during a particularly stressful period, thereby freeing me to get "over the hump" in completing the book. This was nothing new but it was and still is greatly appreciated.

If there is one individual without whom this book might not have been written, it is Ivan Boszormenyi-Nagy. Ivan introduced me to family resources and provided the concepts, language and validation to explore them. More than any other clinical theorist, Ivan has struggled to reveal and detail the hidden structure of positive family relationships, the "conjunctive forces" of family loyalty, fairness and trust. Ivan's analysis and approach, his influence and his example have significantly shaped my thinking, my therapy and my closest

ix

relationships, all I might add for the better. My interest in this specific area and, more broadly, in scholarship itself has also been influenced by four individuals (including two whom I never met). They are: Martin Buber, Jules Henry, Barbara Krasner and Harold Raush.

A varied group of individuals helped in other ways. Monica McGoldrick graciously helped me navigate the logistical, professional and political waters of editing a book for the first time. Harold Raush served yet again as an excellent conceptual and stylistic consultant. Seymour Weingarten of The Guilford Press was what I would consider an ideal publisher—interested and available without being intrusive or impatient. Alan Gurman, editor of the Guilford Family Therapy Series, offered the kind of help I needed when I needed it. He did not try to impose his own biases and he respected my choices when we differed. Charles Roppel of the California Department of Mental Health also deserves a word of thanks. When I tracked him down (through of all things an article in *Vogue* magazine), he promptly and graciously sent a wealth of information on the health effects of social support, part of an ambitious public health project that he has supervised. Finally, thanks to Mary Kasper and Colleen DeCoste for "reference librarian" services, and to Kathy Fortin for congenial and efficient typing when I really needed it.

Mark A. Karpel

Foreword

> "Don't oppose forces, use them.
> God is a verb,
> Not a noun."
> R. Buckminster Fuller

The field of psychotherapy is in the midst of a revolution. Absolutes give way to relative truth; problem definitions are negotiated with and by participants; context becomes paramount; static labels lose out to concepts of transition; content is less significant than process. This is consistent with an increasing mistrust of authority, of the "expert," in most areas of our culture. As nuclear accidents proliferate, as technical and political snafus crowd the front pages, we laymen (and we are all laymen in many vital areas) want a greater voice in our destiny. Yet the world is complex, and we need guides and helpers even as we reject other people's certainty.

Mark Karpel has done a world of good for the field of family therapy and for families and individuals in emotional pain. His insights into the importance of family strengths in the results of therapists reverberates through this book and lightens the load of both families and therapists.

The humbling and freeing belief that a family's strengths are as important in outcome as a therapist's skills can produce a marvelous alchemy. This belief increases the family resources that can be brought to bear on a crisis, and the therapist's skills are augmented by including a powerful new respect for the family and its members.

A simplistic grasp of this valuable and even radical understanding of family problems and resources could set up a confusing and destructive either/or position. As Imber-Black contrasts a "deficit" model with a "resource" model and Karpel speaks of the dangers of viewing families as "dysfunctional and entrenched" it might seem morally inescapable to throw out concepts of pathology and deficits and dysfunction entirely. What a dangerous position that would be, since people seek out healers (and third party payers pay) because of illness.

Fortunately, Karpel has brought together a highly sophisticated group of family therapists who write about their use of family resources in treatment. It becomes abundantly clear that these contributors dance skillfully between an awareness of dysfunction and the possibilities inherent in the family. This delicate oscillation enhances hope, self esteem, and adaptation.

With the spirit present in these pages, one can use a deficit model and find strength, just as one uses a resource model and acknowledges dysfunction. "Entrenched" becomes the questioned concept, and these contributors provide many examples of attitudes and interventions that change dis-ease into health.

W. R. Beavers, M.D.
Clinical Professor of Psychiatry
University of Texas Health Science Center
Dallas, Texas

Preface

It's easy to lose sight of a family's resources in treatment. That is assuming that we recognize their presence in the first place. Family members themselves may be the last to point them out to us, if they are intimidated by the unfamiliar context of family therapy and too ready to accede to our supposedly greater wisdom, or if their stress and frustration have led to a kind of tunnel vision in which deficits and stalemates obscure successes and resources. If we are relatively new to family therapy, we may be preoccupied with demonstrating our own expertise to our clients, colleagues, supervisors, and perhaps ourselves, by identifying patterns of pathology that we have earnestly assimilated in training. ("There's a symbiotic relationship. That's triangulation. Father's peripheral and mother's undifferentiated.") If we attend workshops and conferences to broaden our understanding of families and family therapy, we may be distracted from the resources of particular families by an emphasis on the skill and virtuosity of the experts whose secrets we have come to learn. If our experiences in our own families have been painful and remain unresolved, we may develop blind spots for certain resources or even find it difficult to see any, whether in client families or our own. It's unlikely that we would have received any specific training in the area of family resources, whatever our professional training and "discipline of origin." Nor can we look to the language of individual and family therapy, which, if anything, seems almost to conspire against recognition of family resources.

This book represents one attempt to correct for some of these biases. Its purpose is to help therapists, primarily but not exclusively family therapists, to recognize the existence of family resources, to identify resources in client families, and to help them utilize these resources in order to further the goals of treatment. The conviction that lies at the heart of this book is that *every successful intervention in family therapy rests as much on the resources of the family as on those of the therapist.* This may seem an obvious and noncontroversial statement, but it is remarkable how easily the resources of the family are overshadowed and forgotten, in both the literature and practice of family therapy, by our emphases on the therapist's virtuosity and the family's pathology.

The concept of family resources is admittedly more visible in recent family therapy literature and this appears to reflect a convergence of several trends. At the broadest cultural level, there has been a dramatic shift over the past 20 years in popular attitudes toward the Family. In the 1960s, we seemed to discover ever more subtle and pervasive ways in which families tried to destroy their members and, at least in some of our rhetoric, we shunned them as laboratories of hypocrisy and alienation. More recently, we seem to have rediscovered the virtues of family life, the rootedness, intimacy, support, and meaning it can provide. The Family has been rehabilitated and as of this writing is being used to sell everything from telephone companies to political candidates. A less global trend involves a growing emphasis on health as opposed to pathology, both in medicine and in various approaches to psychotherapy.

More specifically, in the field of family therapy the concept of the family life cycle, with its stress on *normal* crises of family development, has provided a tremendous impetus toward de-pathologizing family problems. By addressing the ways in which different families cope with both natural and unexpected stresses, the family life cycle framework has also drawn our attention to the different resources they mobilize in these efforts. Similarly, a recent explosion of interest in "normal" families has steered us away from pathology and to the patterns and characteristics of nonclinical families. Finally, recent interest in ethnicity as a factor in family therapy has helped to demonstrate the sheer diversity of healthy family styles, provide a cultural context for what might have appeared pathological, and thrown light on the particular strengths, and weakness, of different cultural styles and adaptations.

For these and other reasons, it is no longer unusual to find passing references to family strengths or resources in the literature or at conferences devoted to family therapy. However, in spite of somewhat greater visibility, the concept of family resources remains surprisingly abstract and elusive. Many references to family resources can legitimately be characterized as lip service of the type we pay to "truth" or "democracy"; others are more thoughtful and substantial but are diminished by being isolated, unconnected to one another and falling short of a "critical mass."

This book is intended to provide both critical mass and specificity regarding family resources. Its purpose is to underscore the importance of family resources, both in day-to-day living and in the particular context of family therapy. In an effort to counteract the vagueness that has characterized this area, its guiding principle will be *specificity* and *concrete detail*.

The book presents a cross-section of experienced family therapists describing how they currently think about and work with family resources in family therapy, whether as solo practitioners or with colleagues, cotherapists, or teams. An effort has been made to examine the role of family resources in family therapy from a number of different perspectives. The therapists who describe their work here represent a range of approaches to family treatment. This is not intended to provide a lock-step comparison of different "schools" of family therapy but simply to recognize and illustrate some of the surprisingly different ways in which different therapists are already working with family resources. An effort is also made to look at different loci of family resources (i.e., nuclear family, sibling relationships, stepfamilies, and wider networks). Finally, family resources are examined within the context of different kinds of stresses and crises that families may experience.

Each contributor has been asked to discuss his/her work within the context of four major questions:

1. How do you conceptualize family resources?
2. How do you identify family resources?
3. How do you utilize or promote family resources in treatment?
4. What common errors can therapists make that may overlook or even diminish family resources?

Each has been asked to illustrate these points with specific case examples from their clinical experience.

The book is divided into four parts. Part I offers a theoretical overview, presenting some of the questions raised by a resource orientation in family therapy and examining both the obstacles to our recognition of family resources and the theoretical, clinical, and research efforts that have contributed to their increasing visibility. Part II examines different models and methods for working with family resources. Five family therapists describe how they conceptualize and make use of family resources in family therapy.

Part III explores family resources in varying relational contexts, specifically, sibling relationships (Chapter 7), core networks (Chapter 8), remarried families (Chapter 9) and the family's relationship with the therapist (Chapter 10). Finally, Part IV considers the role of family resources in families coping with stress and trauma. One danger in thinking about family resources involves seeing families in glowing, idealized terms. These and other chapters in this volume are especially important in that they demonstrate both how flawed and compromised resources can be in real life and how resources can survive and regenerate even in a context of misery, deprivation, exploitation, and despair. These chapters explore how families, and the therapists who work with them, can use resources in the face of incest (Chapter 11), serious illness (Chapter 12), divorce (Chapter 13), physical abuse (Chapter 14), and death (Chapter 15).

When I invited contributors to participate in this volume, I chose not to set the definition, limits, or terminology to be used concerning family resources, preferring instead to let each contributor respond to the concept in his/her own terms. Readers may note that various authors define the concept somewhat differently and may use different terminology, most notably either "family resources" or "family strengths." While this sacrifices some degree of unanimity or consistency of vision across chapters, the fact is that such unanimity does not now exist and I saw no compelling reason to try to impose it at this point. If a consensus does emerge over time, it will be because certain terms and meanings make most sense and work best. My own views on these questions can be found in Chapter 6.

My hope is that this book can contribute to a process of growing awareness on several levels. By first identifying family resources as a legitimate focus of theoretical and clinical investigation, it may become easier for therapists to recognize and utilize such resources in their daily practice, thereby helping families in treatment to identify and draw on their own family resources.

Mark A. Karpel

Contents

PART THREE

Beyond the Parent-Child Nexus

Family Resources

PART ONE

Overview

CHAPTER 1

Questions, Obstacles, Contributions

Mark A. Karpel

In the growing literature of family therapy, the concept of family resources is increasingly "in the air." After nearly 30 years in which the family field has been largely preoccupied with spelling out the fine points of family pathology and marveling at the magic of the masters, we are beginning to recognize that there is more to family life than pathology, pain, and power. In family treatment, we are more aware that the therapist is not alone in possessing resources that can strengthen, reconcile, buffer, and heal.

Family theory has long been able to identify patterns that weaken families and diminish the quality of daily life, patterns that impede individual growth and lead to the breakdown and cutoff of close relationships. We have described patterns that impair coping with both inevitable and unpredictable stress; obstruct resolution of unavoidable conflict; increase misery, bitterness, and despair; and foster individual symptomatology and relational insecurity. Considerably less effort has been expended to identify patterns that strengthen families, patterns that improve the quality of daily life, promote individuation *and* mutual care, buffer against the disorganizing effects of stress, and facilitate the resolution of conflict.

These strengthening patterns exist, whether we as therapists notice them or not. They are as much a part of family life, *in all families*, as are those patterns that we have identified as pathological, a realization that becomes more and more obvious in recent family therapy literature. But if the notion of family resources is more fashionable today, it remains highly abstract, blurred, and elusive. If there is a common denominator to most recent references to family resources, it is their brevity and lack of specificity. They most often take the form either of passing allusions to family resources as phenomena that presumably we all understand or of paeans to incontestable values that presumably we all share. As a colleague once commented, "It's a feel-good topic."

Mark A. Karpel, Ph.D. Private practice and consultation, Northampton and West Springfield, Massachusetts.

If our understanding of family resources is to move beyond that designation, above all else it will require greater specificity. Passing references in the literature or at professional presentations to "respecting the family's own resources" leave a host of essential questions unanswered.

QUESTIONS

How do we begin to think about family resources? What do we mean by the term? Is humor a family resource? Is clear hierarchy? Loyalty? Individuation of members? Caring? Money?

If in fact families do have resources, resources for what? Survival? Individual growth? Coping with stress? Quality of life?

Where are resources "located"? Are they properties of individuals, artifacts of dyadic relationships, properties of systems, or of the interface between the family and larger systems (such as extended family, community, ethnic group, or professional helpers)? All of these?

Are some family resources always helpful to all families in all situations, or is the value and utility of a pattern completely dependent on context, so that what helps one family at one stage of life facing one type of problem may be unhelpful or even problematic for another family in a different situation?

How do we understand the relationship between presenting problems in family treatment and family resources? Are the latter tools for managing and resolving the former, or can the presenting problem itself be seen as an expression of one type of family resource?

How do family resources enter into family therapy? How does the therapist identify resources in a particular family? Having identified them, how does he/ she intervene in ways that respect and make use of them? Would a therapist who is cognizant of family resources operate any differently from one whose primary focus is pathology?

In the chapters that follow, the contributors to this volume present their own efforts to address these questions. This chapter involves an examination of the context of family resources in the field of family therapy itself. We begin with some of the factors that have made it difficult to recognize family resources and conclude with the theoretical, clinical, and research efforts that have contributed to their increasing visibility.

OBSTACLES

Why has it been so difficult for family therapists to recognize the existence and the importance of family resources? The answer lies in a convergence of factors—historical, practical, theoretical, and cultural—that have together served to obscure the importance of family resources, either by distracting our attention elsewhere or by redefining the meaning of what we see. Perhaps the most inevitable of these factors involves the thrust of the clinical context.

The Thrust of the Clinical Context

Clients come to therapists because they feel "something is wrong." They are in pain of some kind, or feel they have lost control of some aspect of their lives. They sense that something is missing from their lives, or feel they are stuck and want something changed. They come because they are unhappy in some way and the purpose, the definition of therapy (or of any healing context) is to try to understand and, it is hoped, to do something about what is "wrong." Framo (1981) has expressed this fact of life and addressed both its limitations and dangers in family therapy:

> Since family therapists usually see families and couples when they are under stress and behaving at their worst, therapists often get distorted views of the positive sides of the relationships. Besides, most people think of therapy as a place where one talks about what goes wrong rather than what goes right. (I have observed couples being intensely hostile to each other during treatment sessions, and then, as soon as they leave the office walking away arm and arm). Finally, under the intensive scrutiny of the therapy microscope, almost every individual, family or couple can look sick. (p. 139)

The degree to which this factor becomes part of our unexamined premises and self-definitions is suggested by Kingston's (1983) wry observation that:

> It is interesting to compare someone going into a family to solve a problem with someone going into an industrial or commercial organization for the same purpose. We call the former "family therapy." But we do not call the latter "industrial therapy"; we call it "consultancy." (p. 209)

So, to be fair to ourselves, we need to remember that we are being asked on a daily basis to "fix" something that is "wrong." It's only natural then that, to some degree, we develop a way of thinking about and a language for this. The central question, however, is whether skill at identifying "what's wrong" is sufficient. The thesis of this book is that it is not. A therapist's failure to move beyond this focus and identify resources in the individuals and families seeking treatment, whether in other areas of their lives, in smaller or wider circles of relationship, or even in the heart of what they present as "what's wrong," can limit that therapist's ability to facilitate positive change and can diminish the family's ability to use its own resources.

It seems safe to assume that if the thrust of the clinical context were the only factor impeding a recognition of family resources they would not have remained overlooked for so long. Without question the most potent obstacle to the recognition of family resources has been the search for pathology.

The Search for Pathology

The effort to identify, elaborate, and categorize pathology has been the dominant and enduring preoccupation of virtually all forms of individual as well as family therapy. The family field can rightfully claim that it did not invent this search for pathology on its own, that it was a hand-me-down, "received wisdom" from the tradition of individual psychotherapy in general and from early psychoanalytic theory and practice in particular.

Psychoanalytic Theory and Practice

Psychoanalysis, which "begat" family therapy, was itself "begat" by 19th-century medicine. Thus it inherited and passed along a strong focus on the individual (as opposed to any larger social system), a therapeutic model based on "diseases" (with symptoms, syndromes, diagnoses, and prognoses), and an emphasis on cure rather than prevention. Psychoanalytic theory, by limiting itself to the experience of an individual, essentially denied the relevance of the family itself as anything other than *the locus and source of trauma*. Underestimating the significance of current relational dynamics for an individual's seemingly irrational symptoms, psychoanalytic theory was even less likely to appreciate the potentially positive and healing properties of these relationships. Correspondingly, it inflated the significance of the therapist, who was conceived of as essentially the sole change agent in an individual's life.

A further consequence of the psychoanalytic stress on an individual's internal experience was a devaluation of the *reality* of the individual's life and an overevaluation of the importance of fantasy and internal perceptions. Masson's (1984) critique of classical psychoanalytic theory, in which he has asserted that Freud's own psychological discomfort led him to abandon his early "seduction" theory of *actual* child sexual abuse as the cause of psychiatric disorders in favor of the Oedipal theory, which posited the individual's having *imagined* such activity, is only the best publicized of several similar challenges from within the psychoanalytic community. We cannot appreciate real relational resources from within a sealed world of individual fantasy and feeling.

By far the most powerful and harmful legacy of psychoanalytic theory has been its emphasis on pathology. Essentially a revisionist argument directed at Enlightment and Victorian notions of the nobility and perfectability of "Man," psychoanalytic theory identified previously unrecognized and far less noble determinants of human behavior. It identified the power of sexuality and aggression and pointed to a potential core of irrationality in all humans. But psychoanalysis did more than simply chart the topography of the psyche. Reflecting a larger cultural shift precipitated by the horrors of World War I on the naive optimism of the "Gilded Age" that preceded it, Freud and his early disciples presented their discoveries in a spirit of disillusionment and pessimism that has deeply affected vitrually all later elaborations of their work. In Haley's (1979) ironic but accurate description:

> Psychodynamic theory tends to orient a therapist into a negative view of people. Since it is the darker side of people that is repressed, including fear and hostility and hatred and incestuous passion and all that, it is the unpleasant aspects of

people which the therapist dwells upon. When the only therapy technique available within the theory involves making interpretations to bring this repressed material into awareness, it forces a focus on hostile and unpleasant aspects of people. (p. 33)

Psychoanalytic practice served to reinforce the limits of psychoanalytic theory. Seeing only one member of a family made it virtually certain that a therapist would be denied the opportunity (i.e., spared the inconvenience) of seeing beyond one person's constructions of his/her experience. Deprived of the reality of a client's relational context, the therapist is largely incapable of assessing real resources in that context and is more likely to interpret what might have been "intelligible" (Laing & Esterson, 1964), adaptive behaviors as irrational and pathological, thus reinforcing the theory that dictated the "blinders" in the first place. Furthermore, by proposing to help an individual independently of or perhaps, unwittingly, even at the expense of other family members, psychoanalytic treatment increased the likelihood that unconsulted and uninformed family members might behave negatively toward the client and therapy. This might then reinforce both the client's and therapist's partial perceptions of family members and, more seriously, possibly endanger resources of loyalty, caring, and fairness.

To summarize, psychoanalytic theory focused on one person's perceptions, favored an examination of internal experience as opposed to real life, filtered its findings through a deep pessimism about human nature and a strong emphasis on pathology, inflated the importance of the therapist, and minimized the significance of the client's real current relationships, including their potential strengths and resources. The practice of seeing only individuals served to reinforce the limits of the theory, deprive possibly adaptive responses of their intelligibility and context, increase the likelihood that family members might behave negatively toward therapy, and endanger resources within the family.

Contributions from Other Social Sciences

The climate for the recognition of family resources has not been significantly more benign in other forms of therapy and in the wider field of the social sciences. Most forms of individual therapy, even those that appear to be most unlike psychoanalysis, have adopted many of its biases without examination. Hence, the enormous popularity of "guilt" in mental health discourse, compared with the relative unpopularity of loyalty as an alternative description of identical patterns. It is simply easier for many practicing therapists to see "guilt" where one might with as much justification see loyalty. The same is true for "dependency," a buzzword so powerful that it has seeped beyond the boundaries of the mental health field into the culture at large. No one wants to be seen as dependent. The distinction between infantile and mature dependence (Fairbairn, 1952), the latter of which characterizes the ways in which even mature, individuated partners need one another (Karpel, 1976), is trampled in our panic over dependency. Furthermore, this leaves unaddressed the whole concept of *dependability*, one of the most precious qualities in any intimate relationship. It would take months, if not years, to sift through the references for dependency in mental health literature; it is questionable whether one could locate any for dependability.

Describing the field of sociology in America, Jules Henry (1965) has noted remarkably similar trends:

> . . . the American makes conflict into a God; and although sociology swells its chest with a thousand "conflict theories," it has none on compassion. Because, in the chesty American view, which sociology continues to express in a supine and opportunistic way, conflict is the source of all progress. Life without conflict seems stale to the American elites; and compassion, which is a low-paid motivation, has been relegated to the fringes of the low-paid segments of the culture, and has never been a subject for research. (pp. 197–198)

In addition to conceptual blinders and perhaps laziness, there may also be a political–institutional context to our myopia for family resources. In a conference entitled *The American Indian Family: Strengths and Stresses* (Hoffman, 1980) Red Horse observed "most professionals, including American Indian researchers and practitioners are captive audiences to titled programs and over time acquire a very limited perspective on Indian family life—a perspective dominated by "fundable" problems, such as alcoholism, child abuse, or remedial education." (p. 4)

Family Therapy

While family therapy has managed to discard many of the impediments of Freud's thinking and his method, it has been least successful in avoiding the search for pathology. Family therapy emerged simultaneously in different parts of the United States from research into the "etiology" of schizophrenia (Guerin, 1976), one of the most puzzling and riveting of human disorders. This was a field of study in which "the schizophrenogenic mother" represented an influential explanatory concept, one that in restrospect we can see as biased, blaming, and pathologizing. The early efforts of family researchers and theorists added similarly biased, blaming, and pathologizing concepts such as "pseudomutuality," "pathological symbiosis," "mystification," "double bind," and "collusion." In Guerin's words, between 1950 and 1954 when the family movement was "largely underground," "research was being done that was based on a view of the family as the unit of emotional dysfunction" (1976, p. 4).

Family therapy vastly increased our ability to understand individuals and families by introducing the critical idea of context. However, the thrust of most early family formulations was *to better understand and spell out the roots and persistence of pathology*. The concepts developed in that effort have retained a powerful hold on how we conceptualize what we see in families. In Minuchin's (1982) words, while . . . every family has elements in their own culture which, if understood and utilized, can become levers to actualize and expand the family members' behavioral repertoire . . . we therapists have not assimilated this axiom. Though we pay lip service to strengths of the family, and talk about it as the matrix of development and healing, we are trained as psychological sleuths. Our instincts are to "search and destroy": pinpoint the psychological disorder, label it and eradicate it. (pp. 262–263)

Walsh (1982) has expressed a similar view:

It has been said that a normal family is one that has not yet been clinically assessed. Clinicians are experts in diagnosing pathology and tend to focus on what they know best. . . . We are set to look for evidence of family dysfunction; therefore, we may fail to see evidence of family strength. (p. 36)

Obviously there has been progress in the last 10–15 years, especially on the part of many senior therapists in the field who seem independently of one another to be emphasizing pathology less and family resources more. However, family therapy as currently practiced on a daily basis, even with the best of intentions, is still often characterized by assessing *damage* done, assigning *blame*, and looking for *outside* resources (primary among which is the therapist). The family field has been remarkable for the sophistication with which it has begun to spell out the specifics of pathological patterns—for example, the function of symptoms as triggers in both homeostatic and deviation-amplifying cycles; it has a long way to go in extending this sophistication and specificity to the study of family resources.

The Search for Perfection

If a major obstacle to the recognition of family resources has been our inherited tendency to pathologize what we encounter clinically, then a related impediment has been our tendency to *idealize* in the same situations. Both when we categorize (different levels of functioning; different forms of adaptation; different family structures) and when we conceptualize change (the post-family-therapy family), we run the risk of conjuring unrealistically perfect pictures that are no less dangerous for our ability to perceive family resources than is our fixation on pathology.

A recent development in family theory, while tremendously helpful, may actually serve to obscure family resources unless approached with a particular caveat in mind. This involves the emerging interest in "healthy," "optimal," or "normal" families (e.g., Kantor & Lehr, 1975; Lewis, Beavers, Gossett & Phillips, 1976; Olson, Sprenkle, & Russell, 1979; Riskin, 1976; Walsh, 1982a, 1982b). These efforts to transcend a focus on pathology have made an important contribution to family theory by trying to spell out characteristics of well-functioning, nonclinical families and, in so doing, have helped lead us to the notion of family resources. But we need to remember that even chaotic, disorganized, abusive, and multiproblem families have resources. Looking at "healthy" or "optimal" families can help us understand those qualities or patterns that strengthen families so long as it does not contribute to an idealization of some families that leads us to see others as *resourceless*.

The Cultural Context

Thus far, we have examined obstacles to the recognition of family resources that have operated largely within the world of mental health professionals. However, just as individual symptoms exist within the context of family relationships, the professional world of psychotherapy exists within a larger cultural context, and changes in that context have had a profound effect on the biases and preceptions of family therapists.

During the 1960s and '70s in America, that is, the period in which family therapy came of age, there were a number of sharp and powerful changes in broad cultural attitudes. Most significant for this discussion were those changes concerning relationships, especially the family, and the place of individuals in regard to them. While there is always the danger of oversimplification in making such broad generalizations, it seems safe to say that during the late '60s and early '70s one felt a pronounced tendency to blame families (and especially parents) and to celebrate what was called "autonomy." It hardly seems a coincidence that at about the same time at which early family researchers were identifying the role of families in creating and maintaining individual symptomatology, the organs of pop psychology (popular magazines, movies, talk shows, self-help books) were sounding a similar note. As America moved rapidly toward a youth-oriented culture, there developed essentially a backlash against "The Family," with harsh light thrown on the ways in which families can entrap, cripple, and even destroy their members. This view of the family is perfectly evoked in a bitter little poem by Phillip Larkin (1974):

> They fuck you up, your mom and dad,
> They may not mean to, but they do.
> They fill you with the faults they had
> And add some extras, just for you.
>
> But they were fucked up in their turn
> By fools in old-style hats and coats
> Who half the time were soppy–stern
> And half at one another's throats.
>
> Man hands on misery to man,
> It deepens like the coastal shelf.
> Get out as quickly as you can
> And don't have any kids yourself.

Certainly these biases were strongly felt within the professional psychotherapeutic world. In both the psychoanalytic and family therapy fields during these years, an enormous amount of attention was focused on "individuation" or "differentiation." In both fields, one sensed the strongly felt bias toward efforts to struggle free from oppressive, enslaving relationships with, however, very little attention paid to how to reengage in more positive kinds of relationships (Karpel, 1976). This time period also witnessed the brilliant, minute, and furious dissections of family pathology of R.D. Laing and his colleagues (Cooper, 1967, 1971; Laing, 1965, 1969; Laing & Esterson, 1964). The following excerpts from two of these works convey some of the intensity of this bitter critique of the family:

> The bourgeois nuclear family unit . . . has become, in this century, the ultimately perfected form of nonmeeting. . . . The family—that system which . . . obscurely filters out most of our experience and then deprives our acts of any geniune and generous spontaneity. . . . "Bringing up" a child in practice is more like bringing down a person. . . .The power of the internal family, the family that one can separate from over thousands of miles and yet still remain in its clutches and be strangled by those clutches. (Cooper, 1971, p. 17–18)

> A family can act as gangsters, offering each other mutual protection against each other's violence. It is a reciprocal terrorism, with the terror of protection—security against the violence that each threatens the other with, and is threatened by, if anyone steps out of line. (Laing, cited in Simon, 1983, p. 24).

While the tone of these excerpts may be extreme and the content framed within the particulars of the antipsychiatry movement, the sentiments and biases expressed can be found all through psychotherapeutic literature from this period.

In retrospect, what seems to have been at work here was a simple substitution of blame. After years in which mental health professionals and the culture at large had sympathized with normal-appearing members of the family and accepted their definitions of the "mad or bad" (Laing & Esterson, 1964) member, there was a dramatic shift of sympathy to the (now relabeled) "Identified Patient," with the corresponding attitude of blame directed at the rest of the family. A recognition of this shift clarifies that, while the concepts and theories developed from either of these positions may have had great validity, they were marred by the absence of a *balance of compassion.*

Corresponding to this cold eye being cast on the family was a rather rosy view of what in retrospect looks like good old-fashioned American individualism. Perls's (1969) "Gestalt Therapy Prayer" ("I do my thing; you do yours. I am not in this world to live up to your expectations . . ."), with its renunciation of interpersonal accountability, was only the most obvious expression of an attitude that later gave rise to what has been called the "Me Decade" (Wolfe, 1976). This attitude, both within the psychotherapy establishment and beyond, extolled emotional separation from family, a dedicated regime of "self-actualization," and a (short-lived) oversell of the healing effects of brief, intense experiences with strangers (such as encounter and T-groups). This was the atmosphere in which family therapy matured, an atmosphere that was hardly likely to alert therapists to the resources of family relationships, even where they had few personal issues of their own, which was not always the case.

Therapists' Attitudes

Why do some people become therapists? Why do they become family therapists? There are probably more answers to these questions than there are therapists, including such factors as: expressions and compromises of family legacies, significant mentor relationships, a desire to be of service, the gratifications of status, and innate interpersonal sensitivity. But another set of factors for many therapists involves their early experiences and roles in their own families and their struggles to resolve the "unfinished business" remaining from those experiences. This leads us to wonder about what the functions of therapy are for the therapist and what biases the therapist brings into treatment from his/her own family of origin.

The danger, of course, and in many cases the reality, is that the wounds and blindspots of one's own family experiences may subtly if not flagrantly shape the direction of treatment. When therapists are working through (or acting out) their own family-of-origin issues, they may be significantly less likely to appreciate and promote resources in the client families with which they work. Lewis *et al.* (1976) address this danger when they discuss the convergence of personal and professional obstacles:

> As one example of this focus on the pathological, the mental health clinician has available to him much more data regarding families of schizophrenics than he does of healthy families. In addition, . . . mental health clinicians as a group are very likely to come from somewhat dysfunctional families. If this is so, they may have an unusually difficult time in conceptualizing realistic family treatment goals, both from the impact of their training and their own personal experience. (p. 4)

Therapists can use the tools of therapy to reconcile themselves with cutoff family members, to rework early suffering and damage, to transform enmeshed, imbalanced, or polarized relationships into caring, individuated ones. They can use their tools for different ends as well. Unreworked negative experiences in the therapist's family of origin may do more than make him/her less likely to notice family resources; it may encourage him/her to unwittingly work against them.

Therapists may try to manage their emotional turmoil by getting "one up" on the family (that is, both their own and their client families). They may take the position of a disengaged outside observer who sees the foolishness and automatic behavior of family members (but not his/her own) and operates from on high like a puppeteer. Therapists often unwittingly identify with certain family members and can end up negatively stereotyping and scapegoating those client family members who remind them of persons in their own families with whom their relationships are most conflicted. They then run the risk of trying to "rescue" a family member from those persons whom he/she needs most deeply. Therapists, like clients, can benefit from the complementarity of identity by which one partner in a relationship is able to experience himself/herself as competent and confident in contrast to the other's weakness and need for help. When this is acted out in treatment, therapists are unconsciously threatened by clients' growth and progress and so may unwittingly discourage clients' development of their own resources. This is also a danger when therapists have few or unsatisfying relationships in their current personal lives and come to depend on their clients to meet their own needs for intimacy and affirmation.

Limits of Language

Even when cultural trends and therapists' personal biases do not conspire to obscure family resources, the arcane language of present-day family therapy may achieve the same results. The language of therapists has never been well suited to uncovering family resources. Psychoanalytic terminology made it easy to see weakness and deficit, and hard to see strength and skill. Terms such as "repression," "fixation," "narcissism," and "oral sadism" could hardly help the therapist trying to appreciate family resources. Family therapy, while at least trying to develop a language that allows us to appreciate context and pattern in relationships, has done little better in helping us to think and speak about family resources.

In a witty essay on the language of family therapy, Luepnitz (1984) illustrates this point:

> The jargon of family therapy contains words from three basic groups. It is probably heaviest on computer and cybernetic language: "input," "output," "feed-back," "analog," "program" (as a verb). A second major group comes from business: "contract," "role-*negotiation*" "*executive* subsystem" and "emotional *investment*." A third group derives from the physical sciences: "homeostasis," "pathology," . . . A small category of words—perhaps the most unnerving—is that of military metaphors: "maneuver," "ploy," "strategy," "blasting," etc. (p. 38)

Like most of the social sciences, family therapy seems to labor under an inferiority complex about its failure to generate and validate the kind of "hard," "scientific" data of the physical sciences. Luepnitz cites a graduate school dean who "suggests that the attempt by social sciences to sound authoritative by using hard-science words be called physics envy" (p. 39). Cybernetic terminology, which has become quite chic in family therapy (Luepnitz refers to it as "cybernetic baroque") has, for the most part, taken us even further from the reality of family resources. Again, from Luepnitz:

> . . . cybernetic language . . . has nothing to do with emotion. (Try speaking about "dyads" and "isomorphs" when you're angry.) . . . Another problem with our cool, "no-fault" language is that it removes us from the pain people feel, and perhaps limits rather than enhances our possibilities for healing. (p. 40)

What is true here for feeling is also largely true for family resources. As family therapists we can recognize the validity of cybernetic formulations and still be frustrated at a seeming discontinuity with the deepest and most important aspects of family relationships. If psychoanalysis obscured family resources by stressing pathology and the individual, family therapy has done so by sharing this preoccupation with pathology and by using a language of *general* systems that is largely devoid of human warmth, feeling, and integrity. If cybernetic theory is to remain a viable tool for understanding families, it will need to evolve into (paraphrasing the European left) a "cybernetics with a human face." There may actually be some movement occurring in this direction. Recent elaborations of cybernetic theory, such as the "second cybernetics" (Hoffman, 1981), which examines how living systems transform themselves in spite of homeostatic tendencies, may in fact help us understand some aspects of family resources more easily.

The Magic of the Masters

There is one last significant factor within the family therapy field that has served to obscure the natural resources of families in treatment. It involves our fascination with the virtuosity of the therapist. All approaches to healing develop heroes. Family therapy seems in this regard to be no better or worse than the rest. It is certainly true that, from its inception, the family therapy field has produced an impressive number of "masters," theoretical pioneers and highly skilled, intuitive therapists, who have developed devoted disciples and participated in a continuous series of workshops, seminars, and conferences. These "road shows" have had a significant impact on the development of family therapy and its ability to attract adherents from the larger world of practicing clinicians. Like the use of videotape, which has probably been utilized more extensively in the family field than in any other, these workshops have often been a double-edged sword. Both in their use of videotape and in their conferences, these individuals have been more willing than many therapists in other fields to open up their work for observation. But in the process, a mentality has developed that focuses largely on the skill of the therapist, with the family becoming almost incidental.

This dovetails nicely with a pathology orientation since a match is made between a highly resourceful therapist and a family whose resources are negligible. The family is like a crippled person who has to jump a hurdle; there is simply no way they can surmount their problems on their own. The therapist introduces the magic ingredient (insight, personal integrity, imagery, redirection, paradox) that enables them to move. Obviously, there are exceptions to this characterization as well as cases where these assumptions are present but a good deal more subtle. Nevertheless, our delight with the "magic" of these masters in the family field is undeniable, and this is precisely the problem.

Just as stage magic involves *distracting* the observer from the means of accomplishing an effect, so our focus on the artistry of the therapist *distracts* us from the resources of the family. How do family members help the therapist "accomplish his effects?" What does the therapist have to work with in working with them? What do they contribute to the therapy? Recognizing family resources reminds us that the family is more than a lump of inert clay waiting for the shaping touch of the artist's hands. Families bring their strengths along with them into therapy, and if the therapist is wise she/he will look for and make use of them. From this perspective, the family is less like a crippled person facing a hurdle than like an athlete, with particular skills and strengths, working with a coach who can guide and develop those strengths in the interests of the athlete's own goals.

In spite of the obstacles described here, the concept of family resources has in fact become increasingly visible in recent years. What follows is an examination of theoretical, research, and clinical literature that has contributed to this progress.

CONTRIBUTIONS

Relatively little has been written that explicitly addresses the concept of family resources. There is, however, a significant body of literature that can contribute to an effort to understand them. The contributions to this literature can be roughly divided into five major groupings:

1. Social science models of family functioning, especially those concerned with social support and the family's adaptation to stress.
2. Research projects on how families see family strengths and on how families process information and respond to their environments.
3. A body of work on family enrichment and family life education.
4. Recent conceptual frameworks in the family therapy literature that pave the way for a greater appreciation of family resources, such as growing interest in the family life cycle, ethnicity, and normal family process.
5. Implicit and explicit conceptualizations of family resources in various approaches to family therapy.

Each of these groupings are briefly reviewed. Since terminology used to refer to family resources varies with different investigators (the reader may find terms such as "family strength," "family strengths," and "family resources"), an effort is made here to respect these varying preferences.

Social Science Models

Social scientists who study the family have attempted to describe the factors that contribute to family strength, often as part of larger efforts either to analyze overall family structure or to understand the processes of family coping with stress.

Early Models

One of the earliest of these attempts was Angell's (1936) study of families coping with the Depression. Angell identified two factors: family integration and family adaptability. Family integration referred to unifying forces in family life, such as affection, common interests, and a sense of economic interdependence. Family adaptability referred to the family's ability to meet challenges and vary its repertoire of response. The two dimensions run through virtually all later attempts to define family resources, most notably Olson *et al.*'s Circumplex Model (discussed below).

Cavan and Ranck (1938) and Koos (1946) identified other resources, such as family agreement about its role structure, subordination of personal ambitions to family goals, the family's ability to meet the physical and emotional needs of its members, and goals toward which the family can move as a group.

Family Problem-Solving Effectiveness

Closely related to the study of family stress and coping, sociological inquiries into factors facilitating family problem solving have identified a wealth of "antecedents" of such behavior (Klein & Hill, 1979). There is no way to do justice here to the intricate models proposed by Tallman (1970) and Aldous (1971), among others. However, some of the variables one encounters in both models include: self-esteem, supportiveness of affect structure, freedom from pressure to conform, and the number and variety of alternative solutions proposed. Tallman has also cited the degree of belief in mastery over nature, legitimacy of authority and of distributive justice beliefs, and esteem for other family members, while Aldous has noted the utility of playfulness, tolerance for uncertainty, and acceptance of individual differences and disagreement (Klein & Hill, 1979).

Social Support

One avenue of theory and research with considerable applicability for the concept of family resources has examined the family as one type of social support system. The social support literature attempts to describe how people function as supports for one another in natural social systems. It tries to spell out the specific functions served in these groupings both in everyday life and in special circumstances of stress and crisis and to document the effects of such support or of its absence. Social support has been defined in a number of different ways. House's (1981) definition, based on a summary of the literature, included the most often cited components. Social support was defined as an interpersonal transaction involving one or more of the following:

1. emotional concern (liking, love, empathy),
2. instrumental aid (goods or services),
3. information (about the environment), or
4. appraisal (information relevant to self evaluation). (p. 39)

Caplan's (1974) description of social support systems covers similar ground and evokes some of the lived experience of its members:

> . . . the characteristic attribute of these social aggregates that act as a buffer against disease is that in such relationships the person is dealt with as a unique individual. The other people are interested in him in a personalized way. They speak his language. . . . Above all, they are sensitive to his personal needs, which they deem worthy of respect and satisfaction. (pp. 5–6).

Caplan has described the ways in which family members help one another, by offering concrete assistance or financial help, by directing and bringing members to external resources, by providing feedback about how they present themselves, by helping them with the "worry-work" of confusing, distressing experiences, and by offering advice and guidance. He paid special attention to the family's role in buttressing the individual's identity "during the confusion and uncertainty of crisis and transition by reminding him of those elements, particularly his abilities and strengths, about which he is temporarily in doubt or which he has entirely forgotten" (1976, p. 30). Caplan (1976) has also stressed the "haven function" of families:

> All this adds up to the family being a group in which each member has the possibility of being understood and dealt with as his own unique self, and in which his idiosyncratic needs are recognized, respected, and satisfied to the degree that this is possible within the limits of available resources.
>
> It is these aspects of family life that make the family a sanctuary or haven, namely a place where it is safe to relax and be oneself, where despite continual changes, the other people are well known, where one can speak one's own language and be readily understood and, most important, where one can set aside the burdens and demands of the outside world for as long as both the person and the family consider appropriate. . . . this most significant in protecting its members from [physical] morbidity. (pp. 28–29)

Nothing could be more commonplace than the widely held assumption that relationships are good for people; nothing could be more startling than the accumulating clinical and epidemiological findings that confirm this view. Over the past 20 years, a growing body of scientific research has repeatedly demonstrated a significant correlation between the presence of supportive relationships in a person's life and his/her physical and psychological health. The findings from a handful of these studies are summarized below, divided roughly into three clusters: deterioration in physical health, depression and psychiatric hospitalization, and mortality (Califorrnia Department of Mental Health, 1982).

Deterioration in physical health
• Pregnant women under stress and without supportive, confiding relationships were found to have *three times the number of complications* experienced by women undergoing similar stress levels without such relationships (Nuckolls, Cassel, & Kaplan, 1972).

• *Twenty-eight percent of widows,* compared with only *4.5% of married women,* matched for age in an Australian study, complained of blurred vision, chest pains, shortness of breath, infections, and headaches, as well as nervousness, nightmares, panic, and depression (Maddison, 1968).
• Men who were forcibly unemployed but reported high levels of social support showed *significantly fewer symptoms of illness and depression* and had *lower elevations of cholesterol* than did men who reported little social support (Gore, 1978).

Depression and psychiatric hospitalization
• In a study of women experiencing severe life stresses, those women who reported not having a confidant were *ten times more likely to be depressed* than were women undergoing similar stresses but reporting one confiding relationship (Brown, Bhrolchain, & Harris, 1975).
• Men and women who had friends and a confidant had *significantly lowered psychological and physical symptom levels* than did those without such relationships (Miller & Ingham, 1976).
• *Rates of psychiatric hospitalization* were found to be roughly *five to ten times higher* for separated, divorced, and widowed persons compared to married persons (Carter & Glick, 1970).

Mortality
• For widowed men age 55 and older, the death rate from *heart attack* and *arteriosclerosis* was found to be *40% higher* within the first 6 months of widowhood than it was for married men of the same age (Young, Benjamin, & Wallis, 1963).
• Death rates for single, widowed, and divorced men (ages 40–69) were found to be *significantly higher* than for married men, among both smokers and nonsmokers. The highest death rates were for single smokers. The death rate for divorced nonsmokers was only slightly lower than for married smokers among men (Morowitz, 1975).
• Socially isolated persons were found to have *two to five times* the overall risk of dying of those persons who maintain supportive relationships, independent of traditional risk factors such as smoking, drinking, exercise, and obesity (Berkman & Syme, 1979).
• Mortality rates among infants who are deprived of mothering, even while getting adequate physical care, were found to be substantially higher than among infants not so deprived (Spitz, 1965).

While there is little question as to the correlation between relationship, or social support, and health demonstrated in these studies, there is less agreement concerning the mechanism by which such benefits are conferred. One popular hypothesis is that relationship increases coping ability and thereby "short-circuits" the illness response to stress (Cassel, 1976; Satariano & Syme, 1980). In Minkler's (1980) words: "social ties may act in a supportive manner by providing resources for coping with life problems, and this in turn may increase the individual's resistance to disease."

Family Stress, Coping, and Adaptation

One of the most interesting and potentially productive lines of inquiry into family functioning has involved efforts to understand how families cope with stress. The models that have emerged in this area offer elegant and clinically useful formulations of the elements and processes of family coping patterns and lead directly to the recognition of family resources.

The foundation of recent work in this area is Hill's ABCX Model (1958) of family coping and crisis. In Hill's formulation: "A (the stressor event)—interacting with B (the family's crisis meeting resources)—interacting with C (the definition the family makes of the event)—produces X (the crisis) . . . " (p. 141). What in retrospect may seem a fairly obvious formula served to highlight two areas that had previously been largely overlooked—the family's definition of the event and their resources for coping with it. Their definition of the event involves family values and previous experiences with stress and may vary from seeing such stresses as challenges to be met to experiencing them as disastrous and uncontrollable events. Family resources are seen as "the family's ability to prevent an event or a transition in the family from creating a crisis or disruption" (Burr, 1973, cited in McCubbin & Patterson, 1983b, p. 9). These factors, once introduced, seemed to help explain why different families presented with very similar threats or losses responded and fared so differently.

More recently, the Double ABCX Model, which emerged from studies of war-related family crises (McCubbin, Boss, Wilson, & Lester, 1980; McCubbin & Patterson, 1981, 1982, 1983a, 1983b), extends Hill's model in several ways, most significantly by tracking family process not only leading up to but following the development of a crisis. In this framework, stressors are seen as "a life event (e.g. death, purchase of a home, parenthood, etc.) impacting on the family unit which produces, or has the potential of producing, change in the family social system" (McCubbin & Patterson, 1983b, p. 7). Stressor events produce tension that calls for management. When this tension persists, family stress emerges:

> Family stress is defined as a state which arises from an actual or perceived imbalance between demands (e.g. challenge, threat) and capability (e.g. resources, coping) in the family's functioning. It is characterized by a nonspecific demand for adjustment or adaptive behavior. (p. 10)

Coping is seen as "those actions which make it possible for the family to understand, shape and master the environment, as well as themselves" (Melson, 1983, p. 158).

As in Hill's framework, a family confronted with a particular stressor, say the diagnosis of a serious illness in a child, reacts to that stressor with its resources and within the framework of how it perceives that event. VanMeter (1980) has pointed out that, although "the objective resources of a family might be adequate to meet the hardships or difficulties of the change, if the family defines the event as insurmountable, the likelihood of strain or crisis is much greater" (p. 319).

When the family's efforts to manage the stress produced are unsuccessful, a crisis develops. McCubbin and Patterson have extended Hill's analysis beyond the point of crisis by essentially recapitulating the ABCX Model, now in response not to the initial stressor but to the crisis itself. The family now experiences not only the original stress but a "pile-up" of demands:

> There appear to be at least five broad types of stressors and strains contributing to a pile-up in the family system in a crisis situation: (a) the initial stressor and its hardships; (b) normative transitions; (c) prior strains; (d) the consequences of family efforts to cope; and (e) ambiguity, both intrafamily and social. (McCubbin & Patterson, 1983b, p. 14)

In the family described above, these might involve: (a) the emotional stress of the diagnosis on all family members and hardships such as frequent visits to doctors and hospitals; (b) the ongoing stresses imposed by the adolescence of the ill child and a younger sibling; (c) prior family strains related to the demands of an elderly grandparent living nearby; (d) financial and emotional strains introduced because the mother has quit her job to care for her son; and (e) ambiguity about changed sibling roles (should the younger brother now take over the older brother's chores?), family interaction (should the parents and younger brother go on an outing or weekend trip without the older brother or should all stay home?), and social interaction (how much should family members tell others about the illness?).

The model is fundamentally concerned with family adaptation. McCubbin and Patterson have divided the family's response to the stressor into phases of "family adjustment" (a short-term response, often inadequate to the demands of the stressor) and "family adaptation" (more fundamental forms of "restructuring" and "consolidation," called for by the disorganizing effects of the crisis and its demands for significant changes in order to restore equilibrium).

Specifically, with regard to the topic of family resources, the authors have differentiated between family members' personal resources, the family system's internal resources, and social support. Personal resources "refer to the broad range of characteristics of individual family members which are potentially available to any family member in time of crisis." These are divided into financial, educational, health, and psychological resources, with psychological resources including self-esteem and mastery ("the extent to which one perceives control over one's life chances . . ."). Family system resources are defined in fairly general terms, involving "family cohesion and adaptability" and making reference to Pratt's (1976) "energized family," characterized by flexible role relationships, shared power, and member autonomy. Social support was seen as involving emotional support (leading family members to feel cared for and loved), esteem support (leading family members to feel valued), and network support (leading family members to feel they belong to a network of mutual obligations and understanding) (McCubbin & Patterson, 1983b, pp. 16–17).

The ABCX Model, and the more elaborate Double ABCX Model, provide a sophisticated framework for tracking family process in response to stressor life events. In a sense, they constitute subspecialties of the family life cycle in that they attempt to describe the predictability of change. The framework may well have significant clinical utility since most clients seeking treatment are experiencing some degree of stress or outright crisis.

The model's contribution to family resources is threefold. First, it is concerned not with disorders and syndromes but with how families cope with inevitable life stress. In this sense, it both normalizes family problems and implicitly defines the family as an active agent of its destiny. Second, by dissecting the factors and phases of family coping the model forces our attention to the resources that families mobilize in response to stress. Finally, although the authors do not include the C factor—the family's definition of the event—as a family resource, they identify in this what many would consider a critical family resource for coping and survival.

Family Research Models

In the growing body of literature on "nonlabeled" or normal families, there are studies of how families see themselves, how they perceive and respond to their environment, and how they are seen by investigators.

Family Resources as Families See Them

Fisher, Giblin, and Hoopes (1982) asked a number of nonlabeled families to describe what they considered to be healthy families. Their respondents (largely white, well-educated, Catholic or Mormon) agreed on the following description:

> A healthy family is one in which family members develop an attitude of camaraderie and mutuality. That is, members are generally reciprocally accepting, supporting and caring of one another. They honor their agreements and commitments with one another. . . . differences are respected. These characteristics are achieved through open and direct communication. Family members are encouraged to express their feelings and thoughts which are attended to and valued by other family members. These behaviors result in family members feeling secure, trusting, and positive about and in the family. (pp. 283–284)

Interestingly, when this description was compared with how family therapists saw healthy families in an earlier study (Fisher & Sprenkle, 1978), the authors noted significant differences regarding "cohesion" aspects of family functioning. In particular, families tended to rate factors such as unity and togetherness much more highly than did therapists, who favored instead factors related to tolerance for differentiation and communicational skills. Fisher *et al.* noted, for example, that in rankings of these factors families ranked "loyalty" 9th while it was ranked 29th by family therapists.

In an unrelated study (McKeon & Piercy, 1983), family therapists, priests, and ministers were asked to rate the relative importance of family strengths. All three groups agreed on the importance of togetherness, individuation, leadership, order, flexibility, and clear communication. Family therapists tended to emphasize flexibility and individuation while ministers favored structured order and togetherness; priests stressed order, falling between the two other groups on the importance of individuation and togetherness.

When college students were asked to describe their views of family strengths (Beam, 1979), they stressed togetherness, a religious orientation, shared recreational activities, satisfaction with their communication with parents, and the perceived value placed on strong families by other groups. When a self-selecting sample of "strong families" were recruited to respond to a questionnaire through newspapers around the country (Stinnett, Sanders, & DeFrain, 1981), the five characteristics they noted most highly were love, religion, respect, communication, and individuality. Also cited were: doing things together, consideration, commitment, sharing, and a positive example set by parents.

Finally, as part of its preparation for the White House Conference on Families, the Delaware delegation initiated informal discussion groups with 25 families throughout the state. All of the families were both self-identifying and seen by others outside the family as "strong families" (Nelson & Banonis, 1981). The two elements most frequently mentioned in defining a strong family involved seeing the relationship as greater than the individual, and members supporting one another through both good and bad times. Other characteristics of strong families included: love and commitment, a strong marriage, members feeling welcome to discuss problems, a willingness to sacrifice for each other, doing things together as a family, and understanding and respect for children.

Lewis, Beavers, Gossett, and Phillips

In one of the most ambitious studies of healthy families (Lewis et al., 1976), families with no identified emotionally ill member were presented with a series of tasks to perform and were filmed, observed, and rated on interactional scales. Families with a psychiatrically hospitalized adolescent were studied in a similar fashion. Noting that no single quality adequately differentiates these two groups and that healthy families exhibit a great deal of variety in "style and patterning," the authors nevertheless believe that an analysis of structure and function yields intragroup commonalities that set the two groups apart. They presented these variables as a series of polarities or alternatives:

- affiliative versus oppositional attitudes in the family
- respect for own and others' subjectivity versus disregard for the unique in self and others
- openness, directness versus distancing, obscuring or confusing mechanisms
- firm parental coalition versus "tattered" parental coalition
- understanding of varied human motives and needs versus rigid control orientation
- spontaneity of interaction versus repetitive, stereotyped interaction
- initiative versus passivity

- unique, impressive individual characteristics versus bland "plain vanilla" qualities. (p. 100)

Amplifying on several of these variables, Lewis *et al.* note the importance of "tolerance for individuation," observable in "the ability of individual family members to express themselves clearly as feeling, thinking, acting, valuable and separate individuals and to take responsibility for thoughts, feelings and actions," in "respect for the unique experience of another" and in "the ability to hear and respond to others" (p. 57). They point out that "successful individuation" provides a "powerful base from which to solve problems and learn from others" (p. 67). They stress the importance of a strong parental coalition that allows parents to separate from their own parents and to maintain strong generational boundaries vis-à-vis children. Empathy, and respect that "encourages openness and increases the possibility of new and useful input into family negotiations" (p. 67), are considered especially important.

Two additional factors that correspond to family resources and are noted by Lewis *et al.* involve the family's "transcendent value system" and its relationships with its social surroundings:

... clinical work suggests that . . . a functional transcendent value system is necessary to handle object loss capably. If family members have an extended identity that reaches beyond their own bodies and those of loved ones, they are not so dependent on meaning derived from a particular person who is irreplaceable. (p. 70)

The ability to have meaningful encounters and relationships in the broader environment must be emphasized as a part of healthy family systems. These relationships, reaching into the wider community, are sources of stimulation to the family structure, putting "life" into the system. They strengthen the ability of the parents to accept their own aging and the developing autonomy of their children with equanimity. (p. 70)

In recognizing the need for an empirically based framework for normal family patterns, in developing research procedures for generating such a framework, and in identifying and explicating the operation of specific health-related patterns, Lewis and his colleagues have made a significant contribution to the understanding of family resources.

Kantor and Lehr

Kantor and Lehr (1975) ask how families deal not with crises or with the relatively exotic context of family therapy but with everyday life. Using naturalistic observation and nonclinical families, they are interested in description based on observation, not judgment. From their observations and descriptions they derived an elaborate and intriguing model of how families manage the "givens" of family life, such as time, space, energy, affect, power, and meaning.

They conclude that the families they have observed fall into one of three different types: open, closed, and random. Open families value sensitivity to one's own and other's feelings and the needs of individual family members. Closed families value stability and unity in the family group. Random families value exploration and spontaneity in the interests of creativity and self-actualization of family members. Kantor and Lehr see these family types as determining the family's response to everyday events by serving as a "reference frame through which both external and internal events can be processed and ultimately through which change can legitimately occur" (p. 119). Part of the value of this model for family resources is that it breaks the tyranny of the ideal type, the assumption that there is one desirable way for a family to function, with the implicit corollary that all other ways are undesirable:

> Many therapists have made the mistake of thinking that there can be only one homeostatic ideal for all social systems. . . . Many family practitioners make the same mistake, attempting in their therapy to restore families to a state of tranquility that may never have existed and may not even now be desired by family members. In our own research and clinical experience, we have noted that different family systems espouse different equilibrium–disequilibrium ideals. (p. 117)

Kantor and Lehr refer to "enabling" families much as other investigators do to "healthy" families. In their discussion of such families, among other characteristics, they stress flexibility, meaning both an ability to adaptively change course and a flexible distribution of roles:

> Not even enabling families manage to stay on course all the time. All families experience disablement at least some of the time. When disablement occurs, families are faced with the necessity of having to take corrective action. Family enablement is thus directly related to the effectiveness of a family's repair strategies in taking corrective action. We believe that an enabling family is capable of employing strategies associated with other types as well as its own . . . so that all members may actualize their typal inclinations. . . . Furthermore, . . . we believe that an enabling family is flexible in the distribution of its player parts. (p. 233)

In one highly abstract passage, Kantor and Lehr refer to what boils down to fairness:

> We believe . . . that an enabling system is one which maintains a distance regulation balance so that no one subsystem or member is consistently and systematically denied actualization of its typal goal. . . . an enabling family spreads the demands around so that no one family subsystem or member is singled out for repeated sacrifice to the whole. When a just and enabling balance of subsystem sacrifices is achieved, each member can become psycho-politically free to cooperate with his or her family even though it may require a temporary sacrifice of individual goals. Since all families cannot help but obstruct the bid of each subsystem for maximum actualization at one time or another, such cooperation is absolutely essential to preserving family enablement. (pp. 231–232)

Like many attempts to understand families outside the framework of pathology, Kantor and Lehr's work is noteworthy as much for the effort it represents as for the particular concepts it generates. Simply by asking how "normal" families manage the givens of daily life, they avoid the standard search for pathology and direct our attention instead to more commonplace, everyday matters and thus to a more benign and realistic view of the family.

Reiss et al.

Another research effort that began by asking how families experience and respond to their environments involves the work of David Reiss and his colleagues (Oliveri & Reiss, 1982; Reiss, Gonzales, & Kramer, in press; Reiss & Oliveri, 1980). Reiss began this line of research by asking how families with a member diagnosed as schizophrenic processed information. He used a variety of problem-solving tasks in a laboratory setting and compared these families' responses to those of two control groups—families with "delinquent" members and nonlabeled families. The initial focus on problem-solving behavior shifted over time to an interest in how these different groups of families perceived the laboratory setting itself. This led to a model of "shared construing" in families, that is, an assumption that all families have a "paradigm" or "set of shared assumptions" about the fundamental nature of the social worlds" (Reiss & Oliveri, 1982, p. 96).

Later work with nonclinical families led to the formulation of three dimensions along which characteristics of family paradigms were seen to vary. "Configuration" refers to the family's levels of belief that "they can discover and master the basic rules in a new setting" (Reiss, *et al.*, in press, pp. 3–4). The authors point out that this dimension refers not to a family's problem-solving skills but to their sense that problems are solvable. "Coordination" refers to families' levels of belief that "they must . . . face ambiguous situations as a unified group rather than as individuals." "Closure" refers to the family's levels of receptivity to new and unexpected information and events in its social environment. "Delayed closure" reflects the family's "openness to new information and . . . their ability to change their problem solutions in accord with new data." "Early closure" denotes a tendency to see all new information within the confines of past experience and to reach conclusions about how to respond as quickly as possible. The authors assume that high degrees of configuration, coordination, and delayed closure facilitate successful problem solving. They point out that the three dimensions are independent of one another as well as social class, family composition, intelligence, and reported participation in therapy of any kind.

Each of these dimensions would appear to tap potential family resources. Configuration corresponds to Hill's "C variable," the family's definition of the stressor event and their ability to master it. Coordination resembles concepts of family cohesion and mutual support. Delayed closure corresponds to concepts of family adaptability and flexibility. In a study of families' responses to the hospitalization of a family member, Reiss *et al.* (in press) make this connection to family resources explicit: "The family's problem-solving styles may be regarded as a precious set of resources assisting the family to deal with the enduring stress and uncertainty of chronic illness" (p. 3).

In one jarring finding of this study, Reiss *et al.* note that "high coordination in families . . . predicts death in chronic renal patients" (p. 13). In other words, renal patients whose families scored high on measures of coordination were likely to die earlier, rather than later, in treatment. In an effort to explain this finding, the authors hypothesized that, while an extremely close family's ability to coalesce around a member's illness in its early stages may be adaptive, in chronically ill patients this may render the family dangerously vulnerable. The family may respond with "an extreme coping mechanism, the reorganization of the family itself" (p. 22), that is, the exclusion of the ill member. The authors further suggested that these patients essentially accept such exclusion with resignation, which leads to earlier death. Obviously, replication of these results is paramount, as the authors noted. However this finding, if confirmed by subsequent research, is consistent with the recognition that particular strengths carry with them particular weaknesses. Furthermore, it reminds us of the dangers of approaching family resources in a naive and simplistic way.

Like Kantor and Lehr, Reiss and his colleagues contribute to our understanding of family resources not only by their conclusions but by nature of the questions they pose for study. Instead of asking what is wrong with a particular family or how families with a particular type of identified patient are deficient, they ask how families in general perceive their social environment and their place within it and how these family paradigms influence their response to those environments.

The Circumplex Model

One highly ambitious body of research that attempts to integrate many of the lines of inquiry already described involves the Circumplex Model (Olson, McCubbin, Barnes, Larsen, Muxen, & Wilson, 1983; Olson, Russell, & Sprenkle, 1979, 1980, 1983). This research brings together concepts derived from the family life cycle, sociological models of the family, and literature on family stress, coping, and adaptability in a large-scale empirical effort to understand how nonclinical families cope across the life cycle. The authors administered research scales, designed to assess family type, family resources, family stress and changes, family coping strategies, and marital and family satisfaction, to members of over 1,000 families, with at least 100 couples or families at each of seven stages of the family life cycle.

The Circumplex Model presents a typology of families based on the two basic dimensions of family adaptability and family cohesion. A third dimension, communication, is seen as facilitating movement on the other two dimensions. Both dimensions are divided into four levels. For example, ranging from low to high on the Cohesion dimension, families are seen as either disengaged, separated, connected, or enmeshed. Similarly, on the Adaptability dimension, families are described as either rigid, structured, flexible, or chaotic. Thus, a four-by-four matrix yields a total of 16 possible family types (rigidly disengaged to chaotically enmeshed). The authors further distinguish between Extreme, Mid-range, and Balanced family types. Extreme families are those whose scores fall at the extreme ends on both dimensions; Balanced families, those whose scores are in the middle range on both dimensions; and Mid-range families, those with middling scores on one dimension and extreme scores on the other. Being balanced, in the authors' words, "means a family system can experience the extremes on the dimension when appropriate but they do not typically function at these extremes for long periods of time" (Olson, McCubbin, Barnes, Larsen, Muxen, & Wilson, 1983, p. 59). The four Balanced family types are assumed to be most conducive to healthy family functioning:

> Balanced families will have greater resources (marital and family strengths) across the family life cycle. . . . because of these resources, Balanced families will be less vulnerable to stress and will deal more effectively with it. . . . Balanced families will also use various coping strategies to deal with the stressor events. Lastly, Balanced families will generally have higher levels of marital and family satisfaction. (pp. 16–17).

In describing their focus on families, the authors propose the following:

> . . . family strengths characteristic of "normal" families at various stages of the family life cycle are identified and described. . . . family strengths used by families who encounter less stress are described. These strengths can be seen as buffering these families from stress or as resources that help them cope more effectively with the stress they do encounter at various stages. . . . specific family strengths that seem to help families function more effectively at each stage of the life cycle are identified. (pp. 19–20)

Specifically, the authors conceptualize "family resources" as including both "marital and family strengths." Family strengths include family pride, which "focuses on the positive aspects of respect, trust and loyalty within the family," and family accord, which involves "the family's sense of competency, especially in dealing with conflict" (p. 39). Other family strengths identified are parent–adolescent communication and congregational activities (degree of family involvement in church activities). Marital strengths include various "content areas" in marriage such as communication, sexual relationship, conflict resolution, and role relationships.

This research also attempts to "identify attitudinal and behavioral strategies used by families in response to problems or difficulties." "Internal" coping strategies include reframing, family members' belief that they can solve their own problems, and "passive appraisal," a more "inactive, 'wait-and-see' attitude" (p. 41). External coping strategies include acquiring social support (from friends and relatives), mobilizing to accept help (from professionals and community agencies), and seeking spiritual support (from church, ministry, or prayer).

By now, many of the strengths described here are familiar: family pride, communication, cohesion, confidence in one's ability to solve problems, willingness to draw on external resources. The emphasis on congregational activities, while hardly unique, is more prominent in this research than in that of many other investigators. Each of the family resources mentioned here is measured with specific scales designed to tap these areas. This provides an empirical base for a theoretical framework that significantly resembles those of other authors and investigators. It remains unclear, however, to what degree these particular resources are singled out *because* there are scales to measure them. Where this is the case, we have the benefit of empirical data but run the risk of inflating the relative importance of these resources and overlooking others less susceptible to measurement at this time. Nevertheless, the work of Olson and his colleagues represents an ambitious attempt to provide an empirical base for many theoretical assumptions made about normal families, the family life cycle, family stress and coping, and family resources.

Family Enrichment and Family Life Education

Otto's (1963) paper entitled "Criteria for Assessing Family Strength" can be said to mark the opening salvo of a growing movement dedicated to building family strength by means of education, experiential workshops, and enrichment programs. Closely related to the human potential movement and representing an extension of its values and techniques into the sphere of family life, this movement stresses the importance of individual family members being able to develop their own potential, of open communication, and of emotional sharing in family relationships.

In this paper, Otto developed a list of family strengths based upon information derived from open-ended questionnaires and tapes of couples' groups discussing family strength. His list included:

1. Ability to provide for the physical, emotional, and spiritual needs of the family
2. Ability to be sensitive to the needs of family members
3. Ability to communicate effectively
4. Ability to provide support, security, and encouragement
5. Ability to initiate and maintain growth-producing relationships within and out of the family
6. Capacity to maintain constructive and responsible community relationships
7. Ability to grow with and through children
8. Ability for self-help and ability to accept help when appropriate
9. Ability to perform roles flexibly
10. Mutual respect for the individuality of family members
11. Ability to use a crisis or seemingly injurious experience as a means of growth
12. Concern for family unity, loyalty, and interfamily (i.e., extended family) cooperation

In 1975, Otto defined family strengths as:

> . . . those forces and dynamic factors in the relationship matrix, which encourage
> the development of the personal resources and potential of members of the family,
> and which make family life deeply satisfying and fulfilling to family members.
> (p. 16)

One distinctive approach to family enrichment is that of Bernard Guerney
and his colleagues (Guerney 1964, 1982; Guerney, Guerney, & Stollak, 1971/
1972; Guerney, Guerney, & Stover, 1972; Guerney, Stollak, & Guerney, 1971).
Relational enhancement (RE) represents a blend of humanistic values with
Rogerian and behavioral principles. It endeavors to teach relationship skills to
individuals, in a group setting, that they can then apply in their own intimate
relationships and teach to the significant others in those relationships. Its goal is
"to increase the psychological and emotional satisfactions that can be derived
from . . . intimate relationships and, in addition, to thereby increase the psychological and emotional well-being of the individual participants" (Guerney, 1982,
p. 1).

Guerney's views on relational resources are evident in his description of
enhanced relationships:

> "Enhanced" relationships are those in which the participants have developed a
> greater capacity, within and by virtue of the relationship, to better understand
> themselves and each other. . . . The components of interpersonal understanding
> . . . are *honesty* and *compassion* [author's italics]. (pp. 12–13)

> An empathic relationship . . . promotes . . . the feeling of being secure in the
> relationship and being relatively free of anxiety due to the fear of loss of love or
> fear of the termination of the relationship, . . . a feeling of general well-being,
> happiness and confidence. It seems to raise a person's self-esteem and ego-
> strength, and to promote confidence in his ability to earn the respect and affection
> of other people in general. This in turn seems to make it much easier for people
> either to live with or to overcome, what they may previously have regarded as
> serious deficiencies in their personal make-up. (p. 15)

Guerney stresses the need to balance spontaneity with empathy and honesty
with compassion, describing the latter as "sympathy, mercy, tenderness toward
another, and the willingness to try to protect others from distress" (p. 13).
"When spontaneity is tempered by empathic relationships . . . , the individual's
own life satisfaction are enhanced" (p. 18). The RE program teaches participants "modes of communication," (such as expressing feelings honestly and
clearly and empathic responding), by means of didactic lectures, modeling, and
role play. In doing so, it teaches and attempts to enhance the resources of
mutual respect and self-respect in relationships.

The conception and implementation of RE reflect clear values concerning
family resources and their implications for the role of helping professionals.

Guerney takes a strongly antipathological position, stating that "the orientation of the professional employing the education model is not toward finding out more about *deficiencies* or poor habits and *remedying* them; rather, it is toward *setting goals* and *reaching* them" (p. 21).

Following this premise, Guerney asserted that, except in rare cases that involve "biochemical" disorders, the term "therapy" is inappropriate:

> Nonbiological techniques that have usually gone under the name of *psychotherapy* are in reality highly unstructured, unsystematic education. Because such methods do not necessarily deal with illness, or even abnormality, it is inappropriate to call them *therapeutic*. [author's italics] (p. 6).

Instead, Guerney proposes that professional helpers describe their activity, as he does, as education. This is probably a more radical redefinition than most family therapists would care to make, but it is a logical extension of the antipathological critique that many share with Guerney. He emphasized that the proper function of what is usually referred to as therapy is not to fix problems but to teach skills that individuals can use as they see fit:

> In the case of traditional methods of providing help, the participants are dependent on the skill of the professional to solve their problems. . . . [RE] imparts a skill to the participant that they can continue to use for a lifetime. (p. 23)

This is one of a number of ways in which Guerney seeks to limit reliance on professionals and to maximize resources of participants and natural intimate relationships. Another involves his emphasis on encouraging participants to pass along the skills they have acquired to others in close relationships:

> The RE approach makes it feasible . . . to use the principals in the relationship as psychotherapeutic and relationship change agents for each other. (p. 7)

> When intimates learn skills that are therapeutic in nature, we believe they can have extremely beneficial effects in helping each other to work through intrapsychic conflicts as well. (p. 3)

Finally, Guerney states that:

> We believe that the beneficial effects of empathy coming from a paid professional or paraprofessional is much weaker than the effects of empathy from someone, such as a friend, a parent, or a spouse, with whom one has a more natural, genuine, important, constant, and enduring relationship. (p. 16)

In its focus on relationship enhancement rather than pathology, its preference for an educational (i.e., nonclinical) context, its definition of the characteristics of enhanced relationships, and its effort to delimit the role of professional helpers and to maximize the therapeutic potential of intimate relationships, relational enhancement makes a distinctive contribution to the recognition and activation of family resources.

The most impressive gathering of work in this area has been that of Stinnett and his colleagues (Stinnett, Chesser, & DeFrain, 1979; Stinnett, Chesser, DeFrain & Knaub, 1980; Stinnett, DeFrain, King, Knaub, & Rowe, 1981; Stinnett, et al. 1982). Beginning in 1978, these individuals have convened yearly conferences on family strengths, "National Symposia on Building Family Strengths," and edited the proceedings in successive volumes. Stinnett (1979) defines family strengths as:

> . . . those relationship patterns, interpersonal skills and competencies, and social and psychological characteristics which create a sense of positive family identity, promote satisfying and fulfilling interaction among family members, encourage the development of the potential of the family group and individual family members, and contribute to the family's ability to deal effectively with stress and crises. (Stinnett et al., 1979, p. 2)

He goes on to list what he considers to be six qualities of strong families:

1. Appreciation ("psychological strokes," "building each other up")
2. Spending time together
3. Good communication patterns
4. Commitment
5. High degree of religious orientation
6. Ability to deal with crises in a positive manner

The family enrichment literature is sometimes marked by an idealized and somewhat bloodless view of family relationships in which harmony and joy seem to predominate. In addition, it is often limited by the particular ideals of the human potential movement (i.e., democratic and collaborative structures are more likely to be seen as optimal than hierarchical ones). In keeping with its implicit philosophy, the movement has been somewhat more oriented to education (in schools, churches, and neighborhood organizations), experiential exercises, and workshops than to direct clinical work. For this reason, its impact has been less strongly felt in family therapy than in these other areas. Conversely, this marks a legitimate contribution to work on family resources precisely because it involves a *nonclinical*, i.e., normal or healthy, context.

Conceptual Reorientations in Family Therapy

Over the past decade there have been three conceptual reorientations in the family therapy field that have had particular significance for the recognition of family resources. Each has emerged independently of any particular treatment approach, although each has, to varying degrees, influenced the theory and practice of a number of different approaches. Each has moved beyond a focus on pathology and closer to a recognition of the existence and therapeutic potential of family resources.

The Family Life Cycle

Family theory began with the analysis of family structure (the predictability of pattern) and only in the last 10 or 15 years has began to integrate a framework for family development (the predictability of change). Spurred on by a growing awareness of the individual life cycle (Erikson, 1959; Levinson, 1978) and by sociological frameworks for family development (Duvall, 1977; Rogers, 1960), the family life cycle began to make a significant impact on the literature of family therapy in the early 1970s (Haley, 1973; Minuchin, 1974; Solomon, 1973). Carter and McGoldrick's (1980) book gave added depth and legitimacy to the subject. In their preface, the authors identified the significance of the family life cycle framework for family resources:

> It is our purpose to explicate as fully as we can the very complex processes of normal family development . . . and to reduce the tendency of therapists, focused as we are on problems, to rely on narrow definitions of pathology. (p. xxi)

The family life cycle framework is inherently normalizing. The concept of normal crises of family development alerts us to the fact that all families face predictable and unavoidable periods of stress and transition. It increases our ability to understand symptoms as expressions of this stress and of the temporary disorganization/reorganization that accompanies it. Finally, it reduces the risk that we will see symptoms as indicators of idiosyncratic family pathology. One dividend of this conceptual reorientation is a reduction in the distinction that therapists can make, sometimes subtle and sometimes explicit, between their clients and themselves. When we recognize that we're all "in the soup" of family life together, it's more difficult to see ourselves as paragons of health and our clients as bereft of resources.

The family life cycle framework makes us more aware that all families face similar tasks at each stage of development. The ways in which they respond will contribute to a better or worse resolution of these challenges, and this resolution will have significant bearing on the degree of difficulty they experience in subsequent stages. This leads us to consider why some families are so much better in meeting the challenges of particular stages, and which brings us to family resources. As soon as we can conceive of the family as an active, problem-solving organization, we can begin to ask what tools or assets the members bring with them to the job. Finally, there may be a significant connection between what the family achieves when the tasks of a stage are well handled (Carter and McGoldrick's "second order changes") and what we refer to as family resources.

Ethnicity

The fact that ethnicity has become a "blip on the screen" of family therapy is largely due to articles, workshops, and a comprehensive volume edited by McGoldrick, Pearce, and Giordano (1982). While a handful of earlier papers on the topic existed in family therapy literature, these authors have been primarily responsible for identifying the importance of ethnicity for family therapy, for gathering statistical, sociological, and anthropological data on the subject, and for soliciting and collecting in one volume papers by a number of family therapists on different ethnic groups and their characteristic participation in family therapy.

Defining an ethnic group as "those who can conceive of themselves as alike by virtue of their common ancestry, real or fictitious, and who are so regarded by others" (Shibutani & Kwan, 1965, p. 23, cited in McGoldrick, 1982), McGoldrick views the relevance of ethnicity for family therapy as an extension of the contextual emphasis of family theory:

> Just as family therapy itself grew out of the myopia of the intrapsychic view and concluded that human behavior could not be understood in isolation from its family context, family behavior also makes sense only in the larger cultural context in which it is embedded. (p. 4)

This suggests one of the major contributions of the study of ethnicity to the understanding of family resources. Ethnicity provides *intelligibility* to some of the behavior of families and the individuals within them, both within the family therapy setting and in the life outside therapy that they recount sometimes to the puzzlement, misunderstanding, and critical judgment of the therapist. The framework of ethnicity reminds us that there are considerable natural differences in the values, perceptions, styles, and rituals of different ethnic groups and that what, out of context, may appear pathological may in fact be culturally normative. In teaching us to look for and respect cultural differences, an appreciation of ethnicity encourages us to further understand and respect more specific, idiosyncratic differences among families. When our categories are limited to functional and dysfunctional and, further, when they are biased unbeknownst to us toward particular cultural expressions of what is functional, we have little choice but to view a wide array of adaptive styles and culturally normative behavior as pathological. *Any concept or framework that breaks the tyranny of one ideal model of family life is inherently resourceful for families and for family treatment.* Parenthetically, McGoldrick has pointed out that an awareness of ethnic differences can provide intelligibility not only between clients and therapists but between spouses in ethnic intermarriages.

A second contribution of ethnicity to an awareness of family resources involves the fact that, in beginning to distinguish ethnic differences, we become more aware of the particular strengths (and related weaknesses) of different styles and adaptations:

Every culture generates characteristic problems for itself. These problems are often consequences of cultural traits that are conspicuous strengths in other contexts. For example, WASP optimism leads to confidence and flexibility in taking initiative, an obvious strength when there are opportunities to do so. But the one-sided preference for cheerfulness also leads to the inability to cope with tragedy or to engage in mourning. (McGoldrick, 1982, pp. 10–11)

Thus we are automatically led to recognizing the adaptive, or *resourceful*, and maladaptive features of different ethnic cultures and, by extension, of the particular families who compose them.

Finally, ethnicity itself can be seen as a resource. McGoldrick has pointed out that ethnicity can confer a sense of belonging and identity as well as contribute to positive personal self-esteem, as when one feels proud of belonging to one's own ethnic group (e.g., "black is beautiful"). Also, the ethnic neighborhoods in which many families reside typically offer at least some of the social support that promotes family coping and individual health.

Normal Family Processes

A third conceptual reorientation in family therapy that leads us closer to a consideration of family resources involves the study of "normal" or "healthy" families. Numerous investigators have approached this topic from a variety of different perspectives, among them Rapoport (1962), Riskin (1976), Kantor and Lehr (1975), Olson *et al.* (1979), Lewis *et al.* (1976), Reiss and Oliveri (1980), Kleiman (1981), Hansen (1981), and Walsh (1982b). Walsh's *Normal Family Processes* (1982b) provides a comprehensive look at recent theory and research in this area.

The obvious virtue of these studies is that they recognize the limitations of theoretical frameworks based on dysfunction and pathology. They investigate "nonlabeled," or nonclinical, families in an effort to understand how these families function, how they "organize their resources and . . . accomplish their tasks" (Walsh, 1982a, p. 9). Walsh cites Offer and Sashbin (1966), who pointed out that the term "normality" usually implies one of four major meanings: (1) normality as health (an absence of pathology), (2) normality as utopia (ideal or optimal functioning), (3) normality as average (midrange on a normal distribution curve), and (4) normality as process (natural development along universal lines). Much research has focused on the first two of these meanings, and there is certainly a fair degree of overlap between the factors identified in these studies and what we consider family resources. The difference, as stated earlier, is that, in designating certain families as healthy or normal, we may overlook the resources of what might then be seen as dysfunctional families. With this caveat in mind, however, by looking for alternatives to a pathology orientation and by examining the patterns and characteristics that appear to be common to non-labeled families, investigators of normal families have helped to pave the way for a greater awareness of family resources.

Family Therapy Models

Different approaches to family therapy have always emphasized different pathological patterns. One approach might focus on weak generational boundaries and another on "more of the same" problem solving, while a third directs the therapist's attention to destructive entitlement. The same is true for family resources. Different models of family therapy emphasize different kinds of family resources. However implicit, these assumptions concerning family resources can contribute to our recognition and utilization of such resources in family treatment.

With this selective purpose in mind, the assumptions of a handful of family therapy approaches are briefly examined, in no particular order, in the remainder of this chapter. Discussion focuses not only on concepts that highlight particular family resources but on the stance of the therapist as well. For example, are problems seen as normal consequences of common stresses in living or as signs of ominous disturbance? Are client families seen as sharing the same human dilemmas as the therapist or examined with a wholly different lens? Does the therapist trust the family's ability to be instrumental in their own progress and to grow and solve problems without his/her assistance? These questions address how the therapist "approaches" the family and highlight preconceptions about family strengths, the meaning of symptomatology, and the nature of the therapeutic partnership.

Structural Family Therapy

Salvador Minuchin and his colleagues (Montalvo, Fishman, Aponte, Rosman, Liebman, Baker, Stanton, and Todd among others) have developed an approach to family treatment that is active, pragmatic, and socially conscious. Minuchin is responsible for introducing an enormous number of people, nationally and internationally, to family therapy and systems concepts. This is at least in part related to Minuchin's own charisma, caring, and creativity as well as to the simplicity of structural theory. For example, Minuchin refers to the need for a "family map," "a powerful simplification device, which allows the therapist to organize . . . diverse material" (1974, p. 90).

It is significant that Minuchin's *Families and Family Therapy* begins with an extended interview with a "normal" family and with a vignette concerning an elderly woman living alone. The woman becomes increasingly distraught after the apartment in which she has lived for 25 years is robbed. She moves to a new apartment but becomes increasingly paranoid, with referential and persecutory delusions. She is given tranquilizers by one psychiatrist and referred by another for hospitalization, which she refuses. A third therapist (presumably Minuchin or a colleague) explains to her that she has "lost her shell—the previous home where she had known each object, the neighborhood, and the people in the neighborhood." They discuss how she can "grow a new shell" quickly. He recommends putting up all her old pictures in her new apartment, shopping only in a small number of stores (even going repeatedly to the same checkout counter), seeing her friends from the old neighborhood, and keeping her worries largely to herself.

The vignette is instructive since it illustrates several elements of Minuchin's approach. The woman's symptoms are viewed in a normalizing life cycle context and in a real social context. Instead of a psychotic patient, we see a woman who has presumably functioned well in the past and who is now disoriented by frightening changes. The therapist's job is to help restore her previous adjustment. Her needs for continuity and familiarity are seen as normal. Social support and other environmental resources are utilized. A charming and reassuring metaphor frames recommendations that mobilize the woman to become active in her own recovery.

The themes of resources and normality run through structural family therapy. In the following excerpts concerning resources, from early and later works, one sees the evolution of a framework from one still influenced by pathology-based dichotomies to one in which the strengths in all families are recruited:

> In average families, the therapist relies on the motivation of family resources as a pathway to transformation. In pathological families, the therapist needs to become an actor in the family drama, entering into transitional coalitions in order to skew the system and develop a different level of homeostasis. (Minuchin, 1974, p. 60)

> In every family there are positives. Positives are transmitted from the family of origin to the new family, and from there to the next generation. Despite mistakes, unhappiness, and pain, there are also pleasures; spouses and children give to each other in ways that are growth-encouraging and supportive, contributing to each other's sense of competence and worth. (Minuchin & Fishman, 1981, p. 268)

Themes that do not change involve a view of the family as needing to adapt to normal crises of family development and possessing the potential for a wide variety of responses that may become temporarily unavailable:

> Families involved in unresolved conflicts tend to become stereotyped in the repetitive mishandling of interpersonal transactions, with the result that the family members narrow their observation of each other and focus on the deficits in the family. When they come to treatment, they present the more dysfunctional aspects of themselves. . . . the family therapist should not respond to the family as if their presentation of the dysfunctional stereotypes were the whole of the family. The dysfunctional components are merely those segments of the full family potential that are, at this point, most available to the family organism.
>
> If the therapist is an enthusiastic psychopathologist, he will respond to the morsels of pathology that the family presents and be misled into observing only the less competent parts of the family organism. If he expands his focus of exploration, however, he will find that the family has alternatives that can be mobilized. (Minuchin & Fishman, 1981, p. 277)

In particular, the structural approach stresses the importance of firm but flexible boundaries between different individuals and subsystems within the family and between the family and the larger systems with which it interacts. The assumption is that such boundaries, for example, between parental and children subsystems, allow for contact and closeness while protecting individuality and difference, and provide a flexible organizational structure that allows different subsystems to develop and fulfill their functions most efficiently in the family.

The primary resource that is stressed in the structural approach, however, is flexibility—"a sufficient range of patterns, the availability of alternative transactional patterns, and the flexibility to mobilize them when necessary" (Minuchin, 1974, p. 52). The therapist *assumes* the existence of this untapped repertoire of response and attempts to catalyze the family's access to it. The notion of untapped reservoirs of knowledge and response brings immediately to mind the work of Milton Erickson.

Ericksonian Approaches

Milton Erickson was arguably the most original and profoundly influential clinician in America. His near deification may strike some as excessive, but there is no question of his genius and originality. The intuitive power, range, and inspired improvisation of his clinical work appears to have been coupled with a deep respect for individuals' vulnerabilities and defenses. Erickson's approach was highly pragmatic, symptom focused, and directive.[1]

The elements of Ericksonian treatment most relevant for a consideration of family resources involve: (1) the assumption of a reservoir of untapped knowledge in every individual, (2) the therapist's effort to utilize whatever clients bring with them into treatment, and (3) the therapist's respect for vulnerability and defenses. As Rosen (1982) has pointed out:

> . . . if Erickson and his followers have any "religious" guide or belief, it must be in the wisdom of the unconscious. He believed that people can be guided by and trust their own unconscious minds to determine what is best in a particular moment and in general. (pp. 464-465)

Erickson told clients repeatedly that "your unconscious contains a vast storehouse of learnings, memories and resources" (Lankton & Lankton, 1983). Haley contrasted this with the popular psychoanalytic view of that time:

> Insight therapy was based upon the idea that the unconscious was a place full of negative forces and ideas which were so unacceptable that they had to be re-

---

[1]Directive, that is, in the sense that he felt certain about which changes would be desirable for a client and tried to maximize his infuence toward effecting these changes. The use of *indirect* methods toward these ends constitutes a hallmark of Erickson's approach.

pressed. According to that view, a person needed to watch out for his or her unconscious ideas, and to distrust the hostile and aggressive impulses striving for expression. Erickson took the opposite view and accepted the idea that the unconscious was a positive force which held more wisdom than the "conscious". If a person just let his unconscious operate, it would take care of everything in a positive way. (Zeig, 1982, p. 20)

In other words, the therapist is primed to *expect and look for* resources within the client, instead of perceiving the client as deficient and in need of an infusion of external resources (such as the therapist's wisdom).

More remarkable than this assumption of untapped, but tappable, resources within all individuals is the Ericksonian principle of "utilization." Simply put, this reflects Erickson's willingness to *accept* any behavior that a client brings into treatment. This might involve compulsions, phobias, word salad, self-hatred, and, most importantly, all forms of resistance:

> If they bring in resistance, be grateful for that resistance. Heap it up in whatever fashion they want you to . . . . But never get disgusted with the amount of resistance . . . . Whatever the patient presents to you in the office, you really ought to use. (Erickson & Rossi, 1981, p. 16)

One aspect of Erickson's genius was his ability to envision and utilize the power inherent in these patterns to advance the goals of treatment. Again, this stance *predisposes* the therapist to ask himself/herself: How can we use what this client has to offer? What is the *therapeutic potential* of what they present in treatment?

Finally, Erickson understood his clients' reluctance to be aware of certain facets of their experience and the increased risk that they might resist attempts to make them consciously change in these areas. Unlike therapists who try to interpret unconscious material with little consideration for how this might affect a client (and, at the extreme, become themselves unconsciously engaged in a game of one-upmanship), Erickson would try to communicate metaphorically with clients. In some cases, he would use hypnosis to promote selective amnesia. This was done in an effort to respect clients' vulnerabilities and defenses, to let them "save face," and to reduce the risk that ill-timed and threatening interpretations would prevent change. Therapists who are insensitive to these vulnerabilities and eager to prove their own perceptiveness may inadvertently diminish clients' self-respect. Erickson's respectfulness and acceptance of the client makes this much less likely.

The person who introduced Erickson to a wide audience, especially among family therapists, was Jay Haley. Erickson's influence can be seen in Haley and Madanes's strategic family therapy.

Strategic Family Therapy

Like Erickson, Haley and Madanes's approach to treatment is pragmatic, symptom focused, and highly directive. Their emphasis is less on description and analysis of dysfunction than on how to bring about change in families. For this reason, their primary contribution involves assumptions about and techniques of therapeutic change rather than theoretical elaboration of family structure. As Haley has stated in *Leaving Home* (1980), "This book is not about how to raise children correctly; it is about how to do something for them when they have gone mad" (p. 8). Above and beyond the originality of Haley and Madanes's treatment techniques, one of Haley's most important contributions in this vein involves his insistence that therapy *do something*, that treatment be directed to accomplishing what clients want accomplished as quickly as possible. In his repeated insistence that "theory should guide a therapist to *action* rather than reflection" (1980, p. 10) and his ironic critiques of treatment that leisurely pursues sweepingly ideal goals, Haley reminds therapists of their basic accountability to their clients, a reminder that is inherently respectful of families.

Haley's orientation, like that of Minuchin, with whom he worked for many years, and Erickson, with whom he studied, is a normalizing one. Problems are viewed within the context of the family life cycle and symptoms are defined as problems in living, not psychiatric disorders. This redefinition of the nature of the problem is especially striking in those cases that typically involve the most ominous psychiatric diagnoses (schizophrenia, anorexia, psychosis, and suicidal depression). One common aspect of treatment in these cases involves weaning the family from a sometimes elaborate and confused network of "helpers" whose participation reinforces a psychiatric definition of the problem.

Strategic family therapy assumes that symptomatic behavior results from a confused hierarchy or other "mal-functioning" organizational structures in families. Accordingly, the therapist's goal is to help the family restore a clear hierarchical organization. In the therapy of "eccentric" young people, for example, this involves the therapist's encouraging the parents to take charge of the adult child's behavior. What is important here is again the depathologizing context of this approach (especially in the face of very extreme symptomatology), the mobilization of the personal and relational resources of the parents to interrupt destructive patterns, and the goal of treatment—to facilitate the young person's eventual independence from the parents' home—being a very normal development.

More recently, strategic theory has followed Madanes's (1980a, 1980b, 1983) emphasis on protectiveness as a powerful determinant of symptomatic patterns. While Haley and Madanes's discussion of protectiveness often stresses its more extreme and self-destructive expressions, the recognition that family members care enough to try to protect others in the family is another step toward a resource orientation. In this context, Madanes's (1980b, 1983) "pretend" techniques offer an intriguing avenue for gaining access to otherwise potentially overlooked family resources. Basically a refinement of paradoxical interventions, this approach involves suggesting that family members "pretend" to act out interactional patterns that relate to the therapist's hypothesis of the protective function served by a particular symptom. Because of its similarity to children's commonplace use of "make-believe" in play, this technique makes it possible for even small children to participate in therapy in the treatment room and at home in ways that might be precluded by a rigid format of verbal discussion among adults.

Systemic Family Therapy

A highly original and influential approach to treatment, now referred to as "systemic" family therapy, was first developed by the Milan group in Italy (Selvini Palazzoli, Boscolo, Cecchin, & Prata, 1974, 1977, 1978a, 1978b, 1980a, 1980b) and elaborated in the United States and elsewhere by Hoffman (1981, 1983), Papp (1980), Tomm (1984a, 1984b), and VanTrommel (1984) among others. The systemic approach represents an attempt to develop a therapeutic method based on the "circular, cybernetic epistemology of the Bateson group" (Hoffman, 1981, p. 285). Its importance for family resources is more related to the therapeutic stance it recommends than to any particular theoretical constructs for family resources. However, its therapeutic method is based on a view of families as natural problem-solving groupings and of symptoms as often ingenious attempts at solutions to particular problems. As Hoffman (1983) has pointed out, "Many of their interventions can be seen as attempts to encourage the family to experiment with adaptive mutations that are within its repertory, but previously not permitted or perceived" (p. 39).

Applying concepts developed by Maruyama (1968) and others, the systemic approach assumes that families, like all other living systems, are characterized not only by processes that maintain constancy but also by processes that promote fundamental change and transformation. This perspective moves beyond the classical family systems notion of homeostasis, which in essence suggested that family process was powered by a need to prevent change and growth. Symptoms were seen as operating in the service of this need to maintain the status quo, and resources for change therefore had to come from outside the family. From the perspective of the "second cybernetics," symptoms are seen as serving both the homeostatic and transformational tendencies of the system. In Hoffman's words (1981),

> The symptom is only the most visible aspect of a connected flow of behaviors and acts as a primary irritant that both monitors the options for change, lest too rapid movement imperil someone in the family, and also keeps the necessity for change constantly alive. (p. 166)

This transcendence of the static and narrow emphasis on homeostasis in early family theory in favor of recognition of the family's inherent "capacity for transformation" (Selvini Palazzoli *et al.*, 1978a) constitutes, by itself, a noteworthy contribution to our awareness of family resources. This is especially true in the redefinition of symptoms from signs of individual or family dysfunction to efforts to solve vexing dilemmas, protect family members, and explore possibilities for change and growth.

Systemic therapists stress the "co-evolution" and "circularity" of all family patterns thus rejecting a mechanical view of "linear" causation. Because no individual or subsystem is seen as independently "causing" anything, the therapist's "enemy" is never a particular person or persons but "the game itself." This enables the therapist to avoid blaming family members for their situation, which is again depathologizing. This is typical of systemic therapy in that principles of treatment that appear to stem from either abstract theoretical concerns or immediate strategic considerations in fact contribute to a therapeutic method that respects and utilizes resources in treatment.

The emphasis on "positive connotation" in systemic therapy provides a good illustration of this. Essentially devised as a strategic means of justifying counter-paradoxical messages (e.g., "Don't change"), positive connotation involves the therapist's framing not only the symptom but the particular contributions of all family members as positive or helpful in some way. So, for instance, an anorectic daughter might be complimented for giving her maritally dissatisfied parents a crisis that allows them to defer an impending, feared separation and to join together out of shared parental concern. A well-behaved brother might be credited with trying to keep things stable in the midst of the uproar over his sister's condition. The parents themselves might be praised for keeping their complaints directed at one another instead of at members of their families of origin whom they may have felt mistreated them but whom they feel loyalty-bound to protect. Characteristically, the therapist might then caution the family not to change any of these patterns "at this time" as it might endanger them to do so.

Positive connotation may have evolved as a solution to certain technical difficulties in paradoxical treatment. However, familiarity with systemic treatment indicates that families respond powerfully not only to the therapist's successfully avoiding a trap in treatment and to the shock value of this "reverse psychology," but to the resources of caring, loyalty, and concern that are identified by such interventions.

Systemic therapists strategically side with the homeostatic tendency of the family by restraining from change instead of pushing for it as expected. Thus, like Erickson, they express acceptance and respect for the family *as they are at present*. A further resemblance to Erickson involves their effort to *utilize* whatever families bring with them into treatment and to use resistance in the service of therapeutic change. A concerted effort is made to tailor interventions to a particular family by identifying and utilizing its "inner language," values, and pressing concerns. This willingness to "speak their language" also conveys to the family respect and appreciation of their unique qualities. Prescribing rituals for the family to enact in some cases, rather than simply discussing observations, is intended "to unite the participants in a powerful collective experience," introducing "the basic idea of union, cooperation, and complementarity to the common good" (Selvini Palazzoli *et al.*, 1978a, p. 96).

Finally, the systemic approach has insisted on the necessity of looking at the total therapeutic system, that is, the system formed by therapist(s) and family, rather than focusing on the family and ignoring the therapist's contribution. The reliance on teams of observers behind a one-way mirror reflects this insistence and strengthens the "observer" side of the therapy team's participant–observer function. As Hoffman (1983) has stated, "The therapist is never conceived to be 'outside' or 'above' the group or situation treated" (p. 39). This represents an important development in the evolution of family treatment. If the therapist can more easily be seen as part of the problem in treatment, perhaps families will more easily be seen as part of the solution.

Contextual Therapy

There may be no approach to family therapy as explicitly concerned with family resources as is contextual therapy. Conceived by Ivan Boszormenyi-Nagy (hereafter referred to as Nagy) and elaborated with various colleagues (Boszormenyi-Nagy, 1972, 1976; Boszormenyi-Nagy & Krasner, 1980; Boszormenyi-Nagy & Spark, 1973; Boszormenyi-Nagy & Ulrich, 1981), the contextual approach focuses on issues of fairness and trust in families. Like other pioneer family therapists, Nagy's entree to the family perspective involved the treatment of schizophrenia. This led him, as it did many others, to the concepts of fusion and individuation. His antipathological, resource orientation was evident at that time (the early 1960s). While most other investigators were focusing on the pathology of fusion and the effort to extricate clients from it, Nagy (1965) tried to describe the *relational structure* of *nonfused*, dyadic relationships. His later work, in a sense, extended this interest in nonpathological relationships to the family as a whole.

Contextual theory and therapy address the following questions: What is the relational structure of "balanced" family relationships? What are the "conjunctive" forces that bond family members together in spite of inevitable competition and hurt? What kinds of patterns promote individuation and mutual care among family members? How can destructive patterns of exploitation, cutoff, and suffering, often passed along for several generations, be reversed? The contextual framework is alone in explicitly addressing the ethical, or fairness, dimension of family relationships. It assumes that family members cannot help but be influenced by the degree of fair give-and-take among them. What is expected of each? What is provided for each? What do they *deserve* by virtue either of their efforts to help others or of the ways in which they have suffered? What do they *owe*, by virtue of what others have done for them or of what they have done to harm others? Fairness is seen not as a perfect state of static parity but as a mutual willingness to *consider* one another's claims and, to whatever extent possible, to *act* in ways that would repair unfairness. Thus, fairness, or ethical balance, depends on the ability of family members to express their *claims* to one another, to *acknowledge* the legitimacy of others' claims when this is apparent to them, and in whatever way possible to *act* to correct unfairness.

More than any other approach, contextual therapy has emphasized the importance of *loyalty* in family dynamics, thus recognizing a powerful potential resource where other frameworks might see only guilt or fusion. The contextual approach stresses the importance of intergenerational *legacies*, felt imperatives relating to the facts of one's birth and life circumstances (for example, the expectation that one will sacrifice all leisure to manage a family business or follow in the career of a parent or older sibling whose life was cut short by illness or accident). In so doing, it identifies forces with claims of their own that can complicate individuals' efforts to balance multiple claims from others (e.g., husband or wife and children). However, legacies can also serve as valuable resources for family unity and pride, individual self-respect, and initiative (think of the legacies portrayed in Alex Haley's *Roots*).

Especially important is the contextual emphasis on *trust* and *trustworthiness*. Trust, so often desired and so often despaired of in people's lives and in therapy, is seen as a natural consequence of the degree of trustworthiness of the individual's most important past and present close relationships. The importance of action, *actualized trustworthiness*, is central. One of the most valuable contributions of contextual therapy is its presentation of a methodology—trustbuilding—for repairing unfairness and strengthening both trust and trustworthiness. In this method and in the concepts of fairness, dialogue, repair, loyalty, legacy, trust, and trustworthiness, the contextual approach explicitly identifies and attempts to promote family resources.

Family Systems Therapy

An approach often associated with contextual therapy in compendiums of family therapy but one that is significantly different in theory as well as method is Murray Bowen's family systems therapy (1971, 1978). Both approaches make extensive use of "coaching" (seeing individuals in treatment to help them change family relationships) and emphasize "unfinished business" in the family of origin. However, family systems therapy places a much greater emphasis on helping individuals to extricate themselves from relational binds and to overcome the disorganizing effects of the "family emotional processes." Bowen's theory is normalizing to the extent that all individuals are seen as struggling with the same life forces, such as individuality versus togetherness (Bowen, 1971) and intellectual versus emotional functioning (Bowen, 1978), regardless of symptomatic patterns and diagnosis.

In family systems theory, the major threat to the family is "emotional reactivity," seen as fueled by and fueling anxiety, which decreases the ability of individuals to react intellectually (i.e., nonemotionally) to situations and which encourages greater degrees of fusion and triangulation in the system. The fundamental resource in the face of these forces is the *individual*. Family systems therapy relies heavily on coaching individuals to resist the pull of fusion and triangulation, to "define a self" in the midst of these forces, to prevent emotional functioning from overcoming intellectual functioning, and to withstand the disorganizing effects of anxiety. "Differentiation of self" is seen as a fundamental family resource since more highly differentiated individuals are seen as "more adaptive to stress, . . . less vulnerable to symptom development, . . . and have a greater prognosis if they do get sick" (Kerr, 1981, p. 247). The term "solid self" is used to refer to "that part of the individual that is not negotiable under pressure from the relationship system. . . . it permits [the individual] not to be totally at the mercy of emotional processes from the group to think and act in certain ways" (Kerr, p. 247)

Family system therapy seeks to change relational patterns and thereby eliminate symptomatic expression *through* individuals who participate in the system. The therapist encourages the development of particular family resources by allowing individual family members to take an active role in changing negative patterns instead of having them sit by while a powerful outside agent attempts to do so.

"Emotional cutoff," the avoidance of unresolved family relationships, is viewed negatively in family systems therapy. This implies some benefits of continuing relationships with these family members, although such benefits are asserted more than they are delineated in this approach. They are somewhat more explicitly addressed in a number of approaches that utilize the client(s)' familial and social relationships.

Resources in Relationship: Family of Origin, Sibling, and Network Approaches

These three approaches to therapy bear mention here because they explicitly identify specific sets of relationships as resources for individuals, couples, or families in treatment. Therapists who work extensively with family of origin (Framo, 1976, 1978, 1981; Kramer, 1985; Williamson, 1981) guide their clients' efforts to resolve "unfinished business" with their family of origin: (1) as a way to promote their individual growth, (2) as a means to resolve the destructive effects of acting out these patterns in current marital and family relationships, and (3) because members of the family of origin are seen as present and potential resources for the individuals involved.

Most therapists employing this method base their interventions on the assumption that conflicts derived from experiences in the family of origin become projected and acted out in current marital and family relationships. They further assume that, in Framo's words, "dealing with the real, external figures loosens the grip of the internalized representations of these figures and exposes them to current realities" (1981, p. 138). While the theories employed may be somewhat different from those of Bowen and Nagy, there are significant similarities in the actual therapeutic context and conduct of sessions with members of the family of origin. This applies to sessions spent preparing for conjoint meetings, the actual conduct of such meetings, and the uses to which material derived from such sessions is put in subsequent treatment.

While often more implicit than not in discussions of this approach, the inherent values reflected involve differentiation of self, continuity of care, self-awareness, and relational maturation. These are the individual resources both sought after and promoted in such an approach. As the title of one of Framo's best known papers suggests, this approach focuses explicitly on the family of origin as a "therapeutic resource"; the recognition that mutually satisfying relationships with members of one's family of origin constitute living resources outside of therapy is implied, if not always spelled out, in such an approach.

An interesting variant of the family of origin approach is one that focuses on sibling relationships in particular. Stephen Bank and Michael Kahn, who are primarily responsible for defining this focus (Bank & Kahn, 1975, 1982; Kahn & Bank, 1981), make clear that they see siblings as resources for one another as children, adolescents, and adults, in daily life and in treatment. Describing the functions that siblings often serve for one another, Bank and Kahn point out that:

> Siblings give reflected self-appraisal. . . . Sibs turn to each other for protection when parents are disorganized. Siblings can, and do, form cohesive defensive groups when one is attacked by an outsider. . . . they can activate "rescue squads" requiring differentiated roles within the sibling pack. (1975, pp. 317–318)

And elsewhere:

> The process by which one child sees himself in the other, experiences life vicariously through the other and begins to expand on possibilities for himself by learning through a brother's or sister's experience is a powerful phenomenon. Identification is the "glue" of the sibling relationship. (pp. 319–320)

> [Siblings] provide a safe laboratory for experimenting with new behavior where new roles are tried on . . . . Siblings provide an "observing ego" for one another that can exert an effective and corrective impact upon, and for, each other. . . . they can teach each other skills, lend each other money . . .
> We are impressed with the ability of siblings to negotiate and bargain effectively with each other in a manner that would be instructive for most warring married couples!
> In the delicate set of family checks and balances, siblings can protect one another from parental–executive "abuse of power."
> Siblings together can negotiate with more strength against the parents than one of them acting alone.
> Siblings are the guardians of each others' private worlds.
> Siblings serve as a bridge for one another between their world and that of the adults. (pp. 321–324)

In the particular context of therapy, Bank and Kahn (1982) indicate a variety of ways in which siblings can provide a valuable therapeutic resource in the treatment of adult clients, whether in individual, marital, or family therapy. Efforts can be made to change old patterns of relationship between siblings, thereby offering them a real new source of support, a different experience of themselves (as relationship and identity change together), and a successful experience in facing and changing old patterns that, in some cases, may provide courage to attempt changes in similar relationships with parents. Siblings may be included as "consultants" who can sometimes offer information, observations, or experiences that may provide either valuable confirmation of a client's repeatedly disqualified experiences or a catalyst for understanding and loosening up previously entrenched and intractable patterns. Finally, siblings can be included in "sibling rallies" to provide concrete support for a client having difficulty. Bank and Kahn point out that these rallies are "like miniature network assemblies which orchestrate help around crises" (1982, p. 322), thereby leading us to the last of the three approaches indicated above.

Network therapy, pioneered by Ross Speck and Carolyn Attneave (Attneave, 1969; Speck & Attneave, 1971, 1973) and elaborated by many others (among them Erickson, 1975, 1984; Garrison, 1974; Hurd, Pattison, & Llamas, 1981; Pancoast, 1981; and Rueveni, 1975, 1979), incorporates systems concepts, social support theory, and tribal values (Attneave's heritage is Delaware Indian on her mother's side). In Erickson's words (1984):

> Fundamentally, social network intervention is based on a value orientation that assumes that individuals are inherently problem-solving and desire the resources and skills to act in a problem-solving manner and . . . want an expansion of connections and clusters and thus, new information, resources and the possibility of support. (p. 196)

Erickson identified different applications of the network approach, such as curative groupings, network meetings, and created networks. The first refers to the effort to gather all potential helpers together in hopes of strengthening support for clients on an ongoing basis. Network meetings are described as more time-limited and treatment-oriented meetings that expand membership to include all caregivers and other potential helpers, with the goal of functioning as a "problem-solving and resource-generating cluster" (p. 194). Created networks are self-help groups organized around a particular kind of transition or loss such as divorce or death of a spouse.

Caplan (1976) described some of the specific functions served by support networks as:

- Collectors and disseminators of information about the world
- Sources of ideology
- Guides and mediators in problem solving
- Sources of practical service and concrete aid
- Havens for rest and recuperation
- Sources and validators of identity
- Contributors to emotional mastery

As Erickson pointed out, "The notion of the network as a storehouse of resources is held in common in some way in all network practice" (1975, p. 489). Like approaches that utilize family of origin and siblings, network therapy defines particular sets of relationships as resources both in daily life and in treatment.

Symbolic–Experiential Family Therapy

More than any other widely known family therapist, Carl Whitaker has, for many people, come to represent spontaneity, irrationality, self-disclosure, unpredictability, and whimsy in family treatment. While this popular image is warranted, it may eclipse the premises upon which it is based. Whitaker believes in growth, in an inherent thrust toward health and development in all individuals and families. For example, in discussing what is so often referred to as "flight into health," he says:

> I do not define a crisis, intervene in it, and then initiate the ending. I expose the growth effort of the family and accept their impulse to break away from me as a healthy move and one that I believe in. I assume they'll go on growing. I believe the family's flight into health is not just a defense. (Neill & Kniskern, 1982, p. 294)

This belief in the family's capacity to grow is visible in nearly every aspect of Whitaker's work, as when he recommends the technique of "redefinition of symptoms as efforts for growth" (p. 298), or when he reassures us that "the family will utilize what it wants and is perfectly competent in discarding what is not useful" (p. 299), or when he recommends the therapeutic use of frustration as an enzyme for accelerating growth.

Whitaker believes that this natural growth effort can become stalled or stifled (whence the many references in his writings to the dangers of becoming "stagnant" or "drying-up") and that it is the job of the family therapist to catalyze and liberate this impulse:

> Therapists must decide for themselves and with each individual family whether they will work on the level of symptom relief or whether they would prefer to invest the time and struggle to demand the maximal growth of the family in all directions possible. (Neill & Kniskern, 1982, p. 285)

Whitaker's unorthodox therapeutic stance is related to this belief in the family's often stifled potential and to a cagey intuitiveness regarding the need to avoid traps for the therapist. His willingness to "act crazy" in therapy reflects his belief that spontaneity, creativity, and playfulness are "lively" (i.e., expressions of life) and that the therapist teaches this by modeling them with clients. His therapeutic style also reflects his conviction that the therapist must do therapy *for himself*, for his own growth, and that "if the therapist enjoys himself, the patient will grow" (Neill & Kniskern, 1982, p. 300). In this sense, Whitaker goes further than most family therapists in implementing the family systems truism that, if one person behaves a certain way in a relationship, it requires others to change their behavior. Thus, in Bowenian terms, Whitaker takes a strongly differentiated stance, saying in effect, "I refuse to play Savior to your Cripple. I will care about you but I will be sure to take care of myself." Whitaker's unpredictability in treatment also reflects an awareness of potential traps and a natural agility in avoiding them. In this sense, he resembles some of the more strategic therapists, such as Haley and Erickson, who have influenced him. Whitaker uses his unpredictability to become a moving target, to keep clients off balance so as to avoid being bogged down and paralyzed by their protective efforts to nullify his influence.

Many of Whitaker's assumptions about healthy family patterns resemble those of other approaches presented thus far—a strong generational boundary, flexibility of role distribution, freedom to differentiate along with family unity. He frequently asserts that the family's role flexibility should ideally be such that any member can temporarily function in any role:

> The four-year-old son can "mother" his own father; the 40-year-old mother can be a little girl to her son or her daughter and this flexibility is available in response to . . . the impulse or creative moment taking place within the family. (Neill & Kniskern, 1982, p. 284).

Whitaker also stressed the importance of family pride or "family nationalism," which is compared to "a team with high morale" (Whitaker & Keith, 1981, p. 200).

Two more original contributions involve an emphasis on the therapeutic function of family and the utility of a playful, or "as if," stance:

> The healthy family . . . is . . . therapist to the individuals, rotating the security blanket and serving as goad when needed by persons and subgroups. (Whitaker & Keith, 1981, p. 190).

> A basic characteristic of all healthy families is the availability of this "as if" structure. . . . The healthy family knows the difference between murder and play murder, between sexual play and intercourse. (p. 190)

By an "as if" structure, Whitaker refers to the ability of family members to play at certain roles or feelings, for father and daughter to play at sexiness without becoming sexual, for spouses to play at murderous anger without murdering. This playfulness allows family members to express strong and potentially destructive feelings without destructive consequences. Like humor, the play that is so central to Whitaker's approach detoxifies potentially threatening or terrifying feelings and experiences. Put another way, this type of playfulness increases *tolerance* for such feelings in oneself and in others:

> The culture thinks of a healthy family as one with a lot of positive effect. We agree. We also think that children hate and ought to know that they are hated. (Whitaker & Keith, 1981, p. 192)

This tolerance, or acceptance, of intense hatred, of passion, of extremes in deviant behavior, is a hallmark of Whitaker's approach.

In each of these aspects of Whitaker's approach, one senses an appreciation for the basic human struggle and potential of both therapist and client and the normalizing and healing message this conveys. There is a recognition, *made explicit*, that client and therapist are no different, both wrestling with the same dilemmas, both capable of the same extremes. Both can be playful or crazy and, if crazy, maybe more creative. Even Whitaker's standing metaphor for family therapy is a normalizing one. The therapist becomes like a grandparent, that is, parent to the parents who are trying to parent their own children. Somehow one senses in Whitaker a man who has met misery and chosen delight and who offers his clients that same choice.

Virginia Satir

Among well-known family therapists, Virginia Satir is most closely identified with the human potential movement. Placing a primary value on the ability of individuals to grow and to actualize their full potential, Satir views families as "laboratories" that can create more or less fully realized human beings (1967, 1972). An excerpt from *Peoplemaking* (1972) conveys the flavor of this orientation:

> Over the years I have developed a picture of what the human being living humanly is like. . . . a physically healthy, mentally alert, feeling, loving, playful, authentic, creative, productive human being; one who can stand on his own two feet, who can love deeply and fight fairly and effectively, who can be on equally good terms with both his tenderness and his toughness, know the difference between them, and therefore struggle effectively to achieve his goals. (pp. 2–3)

Satir's work is guided by an effort to identify patterns of interaction between people that promote such personal growth and to develop ways of teaching these patterns to large numbers of families and individuals. She identifies four major factors that she feels contribute to such patterns: (1) individuals' feelings of self worth, (2) clear, direct, specific, and honest communication between people, (3) open and flexible rules in human systems, and (4) an open and hopeful linking between such systems and the surrounding society.

Satir's major contribution to an understanding of family resources involves her repeated emphasis on self-esteem not only as a "product" of family interaction in children but more importantly as a critical ingredient in the parent's efforts to create a satisfying and growth-enhancing family life:

> I am convinced that the crucial factor in what happens both *inside* people and *between* people is the picture of individual worth that each person carries around with him . . . (1972, p. 21)

Integrity, honesty, responsibility, compassion, love—all flow easily from the person [with high self-esteem]. He feels that he matters, that the world is a better place because he is here. He has faith in his own competence. He is able to ask others for help, but he believes he can make his own decisions and is his own best resource. Appreciating his own worth, he is ready to see and respect the worth of others. He radiates trust and hope. . . . He accepts all of himself as human. (p. 22)

She further identifies the ways in which honest, direct, and clear communication and rules that are flexible and responsive to change promote such feelings of self-worth in family members.

Each of the four mutually reinforcing factors identified by Satir constitutes an important family resource. Her decision to move beyond strict clinical work to reach a much wider audience through large workshops and books written for nonprofessional readers both expresses and furthers her adherence to a growth-oriented, nonpathological orientation. Also, in her particular emphasis on the relational preconditions and consequences of individual self-esteem, she has thrown light on a critical family resource, long overlooked or dismissed by other theorists.

Integrative Family Therapy

Fred and Bunny Duhl have developed an approach to family therapy (1979, 1981) that integrates values, concepts, and techniques from a variety of approaches. The Duhls operate from a humanistic framework that values individual growth and a high degree of communication and intimacy in families. Their approach to treatment is eclectic and pragmatic ("We tend to use whatever tool will do the job with respect" [1981, p. 486]). What makes them relevant to this discussion is the significant and explicit emphasis they place on family resources. They assert that: "The therapist is better as orchestrator of [the family's] resources than as the single resource for the family" (1981, p. 499).

Their theoretical framework stresses the significance of individuals' vulnerabilities and the defenses they marshall in order to protect themselves as fundamental to symptomatic patterns. These defenses are elaborated into "automatic patterns" of behavior and interaction, often in such a way that one person's defense triggers the other's vulnerability and vice versa, contributing to escalating cycles of attack and counterattack. From this standpoint, the Duhls place special emphasis on the value of flexibility and receptivity to novelty:

The presence of novelty . . . , with its tendency to make the familiar strange and thus lead to new options, is a strength, a major resource in families. The more that families have the ability to generate or welcome novelty or disorder as an element in the process of change, the easier is the therapist's task. (1981, p. 498)

If receptivity to novelty is a major family resource, for the Duhls novelty itself is a critical component of therapy or any other effort at change:

. . . in order for change to take place, that which is automatic and familiar behavior, maintained by a set image, must be made strange.

In order to do this, therapists and change agents introduce novelty in some form or fashion. (1981, p. 511)

In addition, the Duhls stress humor and "safety" as resources and facilitators of change. Humor is identified with an ability to gain distance on familiar patterns and threatening experiences and to view these situations with novelty. Safety is "the feeling experienced when you know that one's boundaries will be respected, that you are regarded by others with caring, and that you have sufficient information about an event or person to predict possible futures" (p. 506), a description that corresponds in some ways to what is often meant by the term "trust." They correctly point out that: "Too little is written about safety as a prerequisite for change, for risk, and for growth" (1981, pp. 506–507).

The Duhls are explicit about the need to identify family resources in family therapy and for the therapist to draw out and rely on these resources instead of trying to replace them and having the family rely on him. In their emphasis on the importance of safety, flexibility, and novelty, they go beyond simply asserting the need for this and offer one way for therapists to go about it.

Psychoeducational Approaches

Psychoeducational approaches to family therapy have emerged from work with what have traditionally been considered major psychiatric disorders such as schizophrenia and depression. Falloon and Liberman (1983), Anderson (1983), and Kopeikin, Marshall, and Goldstein (1983) have described applications of this approach to the treatment of schizophrenia and Anderson (1984) has applied the approach to the treatment of depression. The psychoeducational approach is significantly different from other models of family therapy, in its method of treatment, its attitude toward "labeling" of the identified patient, and its utilization of family resources. Anderson's description of the psychoeducational approach to families with a member diagnosed as schizophrenic exemplifies some of the distinctive features of this model.

Anderson (1983) begins by describing schizophrenia as a "core psychological deficit" that increases an individual's vulnerability to internal and external stimuli. Following the research of Brown, Birley, and Wing (1972) on "expressed emotion," Anderson hypothesizes that intense emotional reactions by family members to the identified patient are likely to precipitate increased symptomatology and, when patients return home after hospitalization, to increase the likelihood of relapse. In particular, intense overinvolvement and intrusiveness or angry, critical, and rejecting responses are most often associated with increased risk of relapse. Thus, "patient vulnerability and family turmoil . . . are thought to interact to a patient's disadvantage in a spiraling manner" (Anderson, 1983, p. 101). Treatment employs psychotropic medication and family intervention to address both sides of this interaction.

Unlike most other family approaches to schizophrenia, the psychoeducational approach assumes that the patient has a bona fide illness. It approaches families not as the cause of that illness but as concerned and sympathetic parties who are bewildered and severely stressed by the extreme and seemingly inexplicable behavior that accompanies it. In Anderson's words, "most families are not destructive, just anxious" (1983, p. 111). The acceptance of schizophrenia as a real disorder is central to the psychoeducational approach and to its unique utilization of family resources. This acceptance allows the treatment team to avoid blame and decrease defensiveness on the part of family members, to provide information and support, and to increase tolerance, a valuable family resource:

> It is believed that labelling has advantages that outweigh its disadvantages. When a family member is behaving in a deeply disturbing way, a view of him or her as ill makes it more likely that the family will be able to continue to provide support during those times when the person is unable to function at full capacity. Furthermore, an illness label decreases the tendency to assign negative and emotional meanings to symptoms. If the family can believe that the patient is neither malingering nor attempting to communicate a malicious message, there is likely to be decreased anger at the patient and at the treatment team. (1983, pp. 104–105)

Given the thrust of much family theory over the past 30 years, which has been to view schizophrenia as a relationally mediated expression of collusive scapegoating in families, this decision to accept the label of schizophrenia is a daring one and one that reflects the compassionate pragmatism of this approach. It allows the treatment team to approach the family as they would a family with a member suffering from, say, diabetes—that is, with genuine sympathy and a willingness to provide information and support. Part of the elegance of the model is that, in doing so, it simultaneously works to reduce those expressions of familial overinvolvement and frustration that appear to contribute to relapse. In this sense, the approach is reminiscent of Bowen's in its effort to reduce family members' anxiety and reactivity to the patient's behaviors.

Important features of the approach include: initial sessions directed at joining with the family as soon as possible after the patient's admission to the hospital; a day-long educational workshop for several families once during the hospitalization; "highly structured, low-key" family therapy sessions before and after discharge; and possibly more extended family therapy. Each of these aspects of treatment reveals an appreciation and utilization of family resources. Initial sessions are directed not at ferreting out the subtle processes by which family members induce the patient's symptomatology, but at helping the clinician to understand "the problems and resources of family members," and beginning to "establish the legitimacy of needs other than those of the patient" (Anderson, 1983, p. 102). The clinician is receptive to how difficult the patient's behavior has been for the family and respectful of their ability to cope thus far on their own; she/he begins to enlist "family members' concerns and involvement in constructive attempts to help themselves and the patient" (1983, p. 102).

Perhaps the most unusual feature of this approach is the day-long educational workshop given for several families of patients. The workshop serves several purposes at once. It provides family members with information about schizophrenia, thereby reducing confusion and mistaken assumptions and conveying respect for their ability to understand and help their relatives by "opening the books" of professional expertise in this area. It avoids blame and defensiveness by sympathetically approaching family members as individuals trying to cope with a confusing and highly stressful situation. It sets the groundwork for later therapy by emphasizing the role of stress in triggering relapse and the need to reduce stress at home, for example, by decreasing expectations when the patient first returns from the hospital and by moderating the type of emotional responses that contribute to relapse. Finally, it reduces some of the isolation and stigma of the condition and provides social support by bringing together several families who are all living with similar problems. Subsequent family treatment is aimed at helping family members implement the principles presented in the workshop, reducing anxiety, increasing family members' ability to react helpfully to the patient, and assuring that their own needs and responsibilities toward spouses and children are not overlooked.

Once the goal of effective functioning outside the hospital is met, the family is offered two options for treatment: "more traditional family-oriented treatment to resolve long-term family conflicts or unfinished business" or "periodic supportive maintenance sessions of gradually decreasing frequency" (Anderson, 1983, p. 112). Here as in earlier phases of treatment one sees in this approach an awareness of the family's legitimate need for some sense of control, a respect for their ability to steer their own course regarding treatment, and a willingness to help them cope with an acute crisis and then allow them to rely more on their own resources in the future.

WHERE ARE WE NOW? MIDCOURSE CORRECTIONS AND CONUNDRUMS

The obstacles and contributions discussed in this chapter suggest some trends in the theory and practice of family therapy that influence our ability to recognize and utilize family resources in treatment.

There has been a greater appreciation of context, exemplified by the family life cycle framework and interest in ethnicity. Both developments encourage therapists to approach families with a more *sympathetic understanding* of who they are and what they are struggling with. Research on the processes of family coping promises to make a similar contribution to clinical practice but has not yet achieved the same degree of visibility as these other frameworks.

There has been a softening of the "helper–helpless" distinction between therapist(s) and family members. Here two unrelated lines of work have, in a sense, converged. There has been a somewhat greater tendency to see client families as resourceful in various ways and, most likely related to growing experience with live supervision and the use of teams, a greater willingness to see the therapist as sometimes "stuck" or part of the problem.

As the sophistication of family theory increases (including theories of change), it becomes easier to approach client families with greater respect and less rigid, pathology-based models. This is not to assert that the practice of family therapy at large has changed significantly, which is beyond the scope of this observer, but that models are now available that make this more readily possible. The evolution from a reliance on the concept of homeostasis, with its implied limitations and blame, to that of co-evolution and transformational tendencies, provides one illustration of this point.

These conceptual changes allow the therapist to see the family as both less and more unique at the same time; less unique in that their problems may reflect not so much their idiosyncratic relational pathology as various aspects of the human condition that they share with other families, and more unique in the therapist's appreciation of the particular values, themes, and resources within the family.

All of this may serve to temper the occasional arrogance of those of us who want to feel that we "know it all" in a profession in which we can know so little for certain; it may encourage us, therefore, to approach families with greater respect, curiosity, and receptivity to their needs, values, and strengths.

One final and significant trend in the evolution of family theory and practice has been from the psychiatric and psychoanalytic focus on the individual as the focus of pathology through family therapy's early focus on the family as the focus of pathology to the present disaffection with the pathology framework, a widespread and noncontroversial sentiment. Somewhat more controversial is the question that practicing therapists now need to answer for themselves: What is the *alternative* to the pathology framework?

If the therapist no longer sees his/her mission as being to identify and repair pathology, how does she/he understand what she/he is about? How do the definitions, methods, and goals of therapy change? What, then, is the role of the therapist and the nature of the therapist–family relationship? In the chapters that follow, a number of exprienced family therapists offer their own responses to these questions.

REFERENCES

Aldous, J. A framework for the analysis of family problem solving. In J. Aldous, T. Condon, R. Hill, M. Strauss & I. Tallman (Eds.), *Family problem solving: A symposium on theoretical, methodological, and substantive concerns.* Hinsdale, IL: Dryden Press, 1971.

Anderson, C. A psychoeducational program for families of patients with schizophrenia. In W. McFarlane (Ed.), *Family therapy in schizophrenia*. New York: Guilford Press, 1983.

Anderson, C. Depression and the family. Paper presented at the Seventh Annual Family Therapy Network Symposium. Washington, D.C., March, 1984.

Angell, R. *The Family Encounters the Depression*. New York: Charles Scribner, 1936.

Attneave, C. Therapy in tribal settings and urban network intervention. *Family Process*, 1969, *8*, 192–216.

Bank, S., & Kahn, M. Sisterhood–brotherhood is powerful: Sibling sub-systems and family therapy. *Family Process*, 1975, *14*, 311–339.

Bank, S., & Kahn, M. *The sibling bond*. New York: Basic Books, 1982.

Beam, W. College students' perceptions of family strengths. In N. Stinnett, B. Chesser, & J. DeFrain (Eds.), *Building family strengths: Blueprints for action*. Lincoln: University of Nebraska Press, 1979.

Berkman, L., & Syme, S. Social networks, host resistance, and mortality: A nine-year follow-up study of Alameda County residents. *American Journal of Epidemiology*, 1979, *109*, 186–204.

Boszormenyi-Nagy, I. A theory of relationships: Experience and transaction. In I. Boszormenyi-Nagy & J. Framo (Eds.), *Intensive family therapy: Theoretical and practical aspects*. New York: Harper & Row, 1965.

Boszormenyi-Nagy, I. Loyalty implications of the transference model in psychotherapy. *Archives of General Psychiatry*, 1972, *27*, 374–380.

Boszormenyi-Nagy, I. Behavior change through family change. In A. Burton (Ed.) *What makes behavior change possible*? New York: Brunner/Mazel, 1976.

Boszormenyi-Nagy, I., & Krasner, B. Trust-based therapy: A contextual approach. *American Journal of Psychiatry*, 1980, *137*, 767–775.

Boszormenyi-Nagy, I., & Spark, G. *Invisible loyalties: Reciprocity in intergenerational family therapy*. New York: Harper & Row, 1973.

Boszormenyi-Nagy, I. & Ulrich, D. Contextual family therapy. In A. Gurman & D. Kniskern (Eds.), *Handbook of family therapy*. New York: Brunner/Mazel, 1981.

Bowen, M. Family therapy and family group therapy. In M. Kaplan & B. Sadock (Eds.), *Comprehensive group psychotherapy*. Baltimore: Williams & Wilkins, 1971.

Bowen, M. *Family therapy in clinical practice*. New York: Jason Aronson, 1978.

Brown, G., Bhrolchain, M., & Harris, T. Social class and psychiatric disturbance among women in an urban population. *Sociology*, 1975, *9*, 225–254.

Brown, G., Birley, J., & Wing, J. The influence of family life on the course of schizophrenic disorders: A replication. *British Journal of Psychiatry*, 1972, *121*, 241–258.

Burr, W. *Theory construction and the sociology of the family*. New York: John Wiley & Sons, 1973.

California Department of Mental Health. *Friends can be good medicine*. Resource Guide, Lisa Hunter, 1982.

Caplan, G. *Support systems and community mental health*. New York: Behavioral Publications, 1974.

Caplan, G. The family as a support system. In G. Caplan & M. Killilea (Eds.), *Support systems and mutual help: Multidisciplinary explorations*. New York: Grune & Stratton, 1976.

Carter, E., & McGoldrick, M. The family life cycle and family therapy: An overview. In E. Carter & M. McGoldrick (Eds.), *The family life cycle: A framework for family therapy.* New York: Gardner Press, 1980.

Carter, H., & Glick, P. *Marriage and divorce: A social and economic study.* American Public Health Association, Vital and Health Statistics Monograph. Cambridge, MA: Harvard University Press, 1970.

Cassel, J. The contribution of the social environment to host resistance. *American Journal of Epidemiology,* 1976, *104,* 107–123.

Cavan, R., & Ranck, K *The family and the depression.* Chicago: University of Chicago Press, 1938.

Cooper, D. *Psychiatry and anti-psychiatry.* London: Tavistock Publications, 1967.

Cooper, D. *The death of the family.* New York: Vintage Books, 1971.

Duhl, B., & Duhl, F. Integrative family therapy. In A. Gurman & D. Kniskern (Eds.), *Handbook of family therapy.* New York: Brunner/Mazel, 1981.

Duhl, F., & Duhl, B. Structural spontaneity: The thoughtful art of training in integrative family therapy at BFI. *Journal of Marriage and Family Therapy,* 1979, *5,* 59–76.

Duvall, E. *Marriage and family development* (5th ed.). Philadelphia: Lippincott, 1977.

Erickson, G. The concept of personal network in clinical practice. *Family Process,* 1975, *14,* 487–498.

Erickson, G. A framework and themes for social network interventions. *Family Process,* 1984, *23,* 187–198.

Erickson, M., & Rossi, E. *Experiencing hypnosis.* New York: Irvington Press, 1981.

Erickson, E. *Identity and the life cycle.* New York: International Universities Press, 1959.

Fairbairn, W. *Psychoanalytic studies of the personality.* London: Tavistock Publications, 1952.

Falloon, I., & Liberman, R. Behavioral family interventions in the management of chronic schizophrenia. In W. McFarlane (Ed.), *Family therapy in schizophrenia.* New York: Guilford, 1983.

Fisher, B., Giblin, P., & Hoopes, M. Healthy family functioning: What therapists say and what families want. *Journal of Marital and Family Therapy,* 1982, *8,* 273–284.

Fisher, B., & Sprenkle, D. Therapists' perceptions of healthy family functioning. *International Journal of Family Counseling,* 1978, *6,* 1–10.

Framo, J. Family of origin as a therapeutic resource for adults in marital and family therapy. *Family Process,* 1976, *15,* 193–210.

Framo, J. In-laws and out-laws: A marital case of kinship confusion. In P. Papp (Ed.), *Family therapy: Full length case studies.* New York: Gardner Press, 1978.

Framo, J. The integration of marital therapy with sessions with family of origin. In A. Gurman & D. Kniskern (Eds.), *Handbook of family therapy.* New York: Brunner/Mazel, 1981.

Garrison, J. Network techniques: Case studies in the screening-linking-planning conference method. *Family Process,* 1974, *13,* 337–354.

Gore, S. The effects of social support in moderating the health consequences of unemployment. *Journal of Health and Social Behavior,* 1978, *19,* 157–165.

Guerin, P. (Ed.). *Family therapy: Theory and practice.* New York: Gardner Press, 1976.

Guerney, B. Filial therapy: Description and rationale. *Journal of Consulting Psychology,* 1964, *28,* 303–310.

Guerney, B. *Relationships enhancement: Skill-training programs for therapy, problem prevention, and enrichment.* San Francisco: Jossey-Bass, 1982.

Guerney, B., Guerney, L., & Stollak, G. The potential advantages of changing from a medical to an educational model in practicing psychology. *Interpersonal Development*, 1971/1972, *2*, 238–246.

Guerney, B., Guerney, L., & Stover, L. Facilitative therapist attitudes in training parents as psychotherapeutic agents. *The Family Coordinator*, 1972, *21*, 275–278.

Guerney, B., Stollak, G., & Guerney, L. The practicing psychologist as educator. An alternative to the medical practitioner model. *Professional Psychology*, 1971, *2*, 276–282.

Haley, J. (Ed.) *Advanced techniques of hypnosis and therapy. Selected papers of Milton H. Erickson, M.D.* New York: Grune & Stratton, 1967.

Haley, J. *Uncommon therapy: The psychiatric techniques of Milton H. Erickson, M.D.* New York: Norton, 1973.

Haley, J. Ideas that handicap therapy with young people. *International Journal of Family Therapy*, 1979, *1*, 29–45.

Haley, J. *Leaving home.* New York: McGraw-Hill, 1980.

Haley, J. The contribution to therapy of Milton H. Erickson, M.D. In J. Zeig (Ed.) *Ericksonian approaches to hypnosis and psychotherapy.* New York: Brunner/Mazel, 1982.

Hansen, C. Living-in with 'normal' families. *Family Process*, 1981, *20*, 53–76.

Henry, J. *Pathways to madness.* New York: Random House, 1965.

Hill, R. Generic features of families under stress. *Social casework*, 1958, *49*, 139–150.

Hoffman, L. *Foundations of family therapy.* New York: Basic Books, 1981.

Hoffman, L. A co-evolutionary framework for systemic family therapy. In B. Keeney (Ed.) *Diagnosis and assessment in family therapy.* Rockville, Maryland: Aspen Systems Corporation, 1983.

Hoffman, F. (Ed.), *The American Indian family: Strengths and stresses.* Isleta, NM: American Indian Social Research and Development Associates, 1980.

House, J. *Work stress and social support.* Reading, MA: Addison-Wesley Publishing Co., 1981.

Hurd, G., Pattison, E., & Llamas, R. Models of social network intervention. *International Journal of Family Therapy*, 1981, *3*, 246–257.

Kahn, M., & Bank, S. In pursuit of sisterhood: Adult siblings as a resource for combined individual and family therapy. *Family Process*, 1981, *20*, 85–95.

Kantor, D., & Lehr, W. *Inside the family.* San Francisco: Jossey-Bass, 1975.

Karpel, M. Individuation: From fusion to dialogue. *Family Process*, 1976, *15*, 65–82.

Kerr, M. Family systems theory and therapy. In A. Gurman & D. Kniskern (Eds.), *Handbook of family therapy.* New York: Brunner/Mazel, 1981.

Kingston, P. Power and influence in the environment of family therapy. *International Journal of Family Therapy*, 1983, *5*, 209–226.

Kleiman, J. Optimal and normal family functioning. *American Journal of Family Therapy*, 1981, *9*, 37–44.

Klein, D., & Hill, R. Determinants of family problem-solving effectiveness. In W. Burr, R. Hill, F. Nye & L. Reiss (Eds.), *Contemporary theories about the family (Vol. 1).* New York: Free Press, 1979.

Koos, E. *Families in trouble.* New York: King's Crown Press, 1946.

Kopeikin, H., Marshall, V., & Goldstein, M. Stages and impact of crisis-oriented family therapy in the aftercare of acute schizophrenia. In W. McFarlane (Ed.), *Family therapy and schizophrenia.* New York: Guilford, 1983.

Kramer, J. *Family interfaces: Transgenerational patterns.* New York: Brunner/Mazel, 1985.

Laing, R. D. Mystification, confusion and conflict. In I. Boszormenyi-Nagy & J. Framo (Eds.), *Intensive family therapy: Theoretical and practical aspects.* Hagerstown, MD: Harper & Row, 1965.

Laing, R. *The politics of the family and other essays.* New York: Pantheon Books, 1969.

Laing, R. & Esterson, A. *Sanity, madness and the family.* London: Tavistock Publications, 1964.

Lankton, S., & Lankton, C. *The answer within: A clinical framework of Ericksonian hypnotherapy.* New York: Brunner/Mazel, 1983.

Larkin, P. *High windows.* New York: Farrar, Straus, and Giroux, 1974.

Levinson, D. *The seasons of a man's life.* New York: Knopf, 1978.

Lewis, J., Beavers, W., Gosset, J., & Phillips, V. (Eds.). *No single thread: Psychological health in family systems.* New York: Brunner/Mazel, 1976.

Luepnitz, D. Cybernetic baroque: The hi-tech talk of family therapy. *The Family Networker,* 1984, *8,* 37–41.

Madanes, C. The prevention of rehospitalization of adolescents and young adults. *Family Process,* 1980a, *19,* 179–191.

Madanes, C. Protection, paradox and pretending. *Family Process,* 1980b, *19,* 73–85.

Madanes, C. *Strategic family therapy.* San Francisco: Jossey-Bass, 1983.

Maddison, D. The revelance of conjugal bereavement for preventive psychiatry. *British Journal of Medical Psychology,* 1968, *41,* 223–233.

Maruyama, M. The second cybernetics: Deviation-amplifying mutual casual processes. In W. Buckley (Ed.), *Modern systems research for the behavioral scientist.* Chicago: Aldine, 1968.

Masson, J. *The assault on truth: Freud's suppression of the seduction theory.* New York: Farrar, Straus and Giroux, 1984.

McCubbin, H., Boss, P., Wilson, L. & Lester, G. Developing family invulnerability to stress: Coping patterns and strategies wives employ in managing family separations. In J. Trost (Ed.), *The family in change.* Vasters, Sweden: International Library, 1980.

McCubbin, H. & Patterson, J. *Systematic assessment of family stress, resources, and coping: Tools for research education and clinical intervention.* St. Paul, MN: Family Social Science, 1981.

McCubbin, H., & Patterson, J. Family adaptation to crisis. In H. McCubbin, E. Cauble, & J. Patterson (Eds.), *Family stress, coping and social support.* Springfield, IL: Charles C. Thomas, 1982.

McCubbin, H., & Patterson, J. The family stress process: A double ABCX model of adjustment and adaptation. In H. McCubbin, M. Sussman, & J. Patterson (Eds.), *Advances and developments in family stress theory and research.* New York: Hayworth Press, 1983a.

McCubbin, H., & Patterson, J. Family transitions: Adaptation to stress. In H. McCubbin, & C. Figley (Eds.), *Stress and the family.* (Vol. 1). New York: Brunner/Mazel, 1983b.

McGoldrick, M. Ethnicity and family therapy: An overview. In M. McGoldrick, J. Pearce, & J. Giordano. (Eds.), *Ethnicity and family therapy.* New York: Guilford Press, 1982.

McGoldrick, M., Pearce, J., & Giordano, J. (Eds.) *Ethnicity and family therapy.* New York: Guilford Press, 1982.

McKeon, D., & Piercy, F. Healthy family functioning: What family therapists, priests, and ministers say. *International Journal of Family Therapy*, 1983, *5*, 190–202.

Melson, G. Family adaptation to environmental demands. In H. McCubbin & C. Figley (Eds.), *Stress and the family* (Vol. 1). New York: Brunner/Mazel, 1983.

Miller, P., & Ingham, J. Friends, confidants and symptoms. *Social Psychiatry*, 1976, *4*, 51–58.

Minkler, M. People need people: Social support and health. Paper presented at "The Healing Brain II" Symposium, San Francisco, California, 1980.

Minuchin, S. *Families and family therapy*. Cambridge, MA: Harvard University Press, 1974.

Minuchin, S., & Fishman, H. *Family therapy techniques*. Cambridge, MA: Harvard University Press, 1981.

Morowitz, J. Hiding in the Hammond report. *Hospital Practice*, August, 1975.

Neill, J., & Kniskern, D. (Eds.) *From psyche to system: The evolving therapy of Carl Whitaker*. New York: Guilford, 1982.

Nelson, P., & Banonis, B. Family concerns and strengths identified in Delaware's White House Conference on Families. In N. Stinnett, J. DeFrain, K. King, P. Knaub, & G. Rowe (Eds.), *Family strengths 3: Roots of well-being* (Vol. 3) Lincoln: University of Nebraska Press, 1981.

Nuckolls, K., Cassel, J., & Kaplan, B. Psychosocial assets, life crises and the prognosis of pregnancy. *American Journal of Epidemiology*, 1972, *95*, 431–441.

Offer, D. & Sashbin, M. *Normality: Theoretical and clinical concepts of mental health* (1st and 2nd editions). New York: Basic Books, 1966, 1974.

Oliveri, M., & Reiss, D. Family styles of construing the social environment: A perspective on variation among nonclinical families. In F. Walsh (Ed.), *Normal family processes*. New York: Guilford, 1982.

Olson, D., McCubbin, H., Barnes, H., Larsen, A., Muxen, M., & Wilson, M. *Families: What makes them work*. Beverly Hills, CA: Sage Publications, 1983.

Olson, D., Russell, C., & Sprenkle, D. Marital and family therapy: A decade review. *Journal of Marriage and Family*, 1980, *42*, 973–993.

Olson, D., Russell, C., & Sprenkle, D. Circumplex Model VI: Theoretical update. *Family Process*, 1983, *22*, 69–83.

Olson, D., Sprenkle, C., & Russell, C. Circumplex Model of marital and family systems: I. Cohesion and adaptability dimensions, family type, and clinical applications. *Family Process*, 1979, *18*, 3–28.

Otto, H. Criteria for assessing family strength. *Family Process*, 1963, *2*, 329–337.

Otto, H. *The use of family strength concepts and methods in family life education*. Beverly Hills, CA: The Holistic Press, 1975.

Pancoast, D. A method of helping natural helping networks. In G. Erickson & T. Hagan (Eds.), *Family therapy: An introduction to theory and techniques* (2nd ed.). Monterey, CA: Brooks-Cole, 1981.

Papp, P. The Greek chorus and other techniques of paradoxical therapy. *Family Process*, 1980, *19*, 45–57.

Perls, F. *Gestalt therapy verbatim*. Moab, UT: Real People's Press, 1969.

Pratt, L. *Family structure and effective health behavior: The energized family*. Boston: Houghton Mifflin, 1976.

Rapoport, R. Normal crises, family structure and mental health. *Family Process*, 1962, *2*, 68–79.

Red Horse, J. American Indian families: Research perspectives. In F. Hoffman (Ed.),

The American Indian family: Strengths and stresses. Isleta, NM: American Indian Social Research and Development Associates, 1980.

Reiss, D., Gonzales, S., & Kramer, N. Family process, chronic illness and death: On the weakness of strong bonds. *Archives of General Psychiatry*, in press.

Reiss, D., & Oliveri, M. Family paradigm and family coping: A proposal for linking the family's intrinsic adaptive capacities to its responses to stress. *Family Relations*, 1980, *29*, 431–444.

Riskin, J. 'Non-labeled' family interaction: Preliminary report on a prospective study. *Family Process*, 1976, *15*, 433–439.

Rogers, R. Proposed modifications of Duvall's family life cycle stages. Paper presented at the American Sociological Association Meeting, New York, August 1960.

Rosen, S. The values and philosophy of Milton H. Erickson. In J. Zeig (Ed.), *Ericksonian approaches to hypnosis and psychotherapy*. New York: Brunner/Mazel, 1982.

Rueveni, U. Network intervention with a family in crisis. *Family Process*, 1975, *14*, 193–204.

Rueveni, U. *Networking families in crisis*. New York: Human Services Press, 1979.

Satariano, W., & Syme, S. Life change and disease in elderly population: Coping with change. In J. McGough, L. Keisler, & J. March (Eds.), *Biology, behavior, and aging*. New York: Academic Press, 1980.

Satir, V. *Conjoint family therapy*. Palo Alto, CA: Science and Behavior Books, 1967.

Satir, V. *Peoplemaking*. Palo Alto, CA: Science and Behavior Books, 1972.

Selvini Palazzoli, M., Boscolo, L., Cecchin, G., & Prata, G. The treatment of children through the brief therapy of their parents. *Family Process*, 1974, *13*, 429–442.

Selvini Palazzoli, M., Boscolo, L., Cecchin, G., & Prata, G. Family rituals: A powerful tool in family therapy. *Family Process*, 1977, *16, 445*–453.

Selvini Palazzoli, M., Boscolo, L., Cecchin, G., & Prata, G. *Paradox and counterparadox*. New York: Jason Aronson, 1978a.

Selvini Palazzoli, M., Boscolo, L., Cecchin, G., & Prata, G. A ritualized prescription in family therapy: Odd days and even days. *Journal of Marriage and Family Counseling*, 1978b, *4*, 3–9.

Selvini Palazzoli, M., Boscolo, L., Cecchin, G., & Prata, G. Hypothesizing–circularity–neutrality: Three guidelines for the conductor of the session. *Family Process*, 1980a, *19*, 3–12.

Selvini Palazzoli, M., Boscolo, L., Cecchin, G., & Prata, G. The problem of the referring person. *Journal of Marriage and Family Therapy*, 1980b, *6*, 3–9.

Shibutani, T., & Kwan, K. *Ethnic stratification*. New York: Macmillan, 1965.

Simon, R. Still R. D. Laing after all these years. *Family Therapy Networker*, 1983, *7*, 23–25.

Solomon, M. A developmental, conceptual premise for family therapy. *Family Process*, 1973, *12*, 179–188.

Speck, R., & Attneave, C. Social network intervention. In J. Haley (Ed.), *Changing families*. New York: Grune & Stratton, 1971.

Speck, R., & Attneave, C. *Family networks*. New York: Pantheon, 1973.

Spitz, R. *The first year of life*. New York: International Universities Press, 1965.

Stinnett, N. In search of strong families. In N. Stinnett, B. Chesser, & J. DeFrain (Eds.) *Building family strengths: Blueprints for action*. Lincoln: University of Nebraska Press, 1979.

Stinnett, N., Chesser, B., & DeFrain, J. (Eds.), *Building family strengths: Blueprints for action*. Lincoln: University of Nebraska Press, 1979.

Stinnett, N., Chesser, B., DeFrain, J., & Knaub, P. (Eds.). *Family strengths: Positive models for family life.* Lincoln: University of Nebraska Press, 1980.

Stinnett, N., DeFrain, J., King, K., Knaub, P., & Rowe, G. (Eds.). *Family strengths 3: Roots of well-being.* Lincoln: University of Nebraska Press, 1981.

Stinnett, N., DeFrain, J., King, K., Lingren, H., Rowe, G., VanZandt, S., & Williams, R. (Eds.). *Family strengths 4: Positive support systems.* Lincoln: University of Nebraska Press, 1982.

Stinnett, N., Sanders, G., & DeFrain, J. Strong families: A national study. In N. Stinnett, J. DeFrain, K. King, P. Knaub & G. Rowe (Eds.), *Family strengths 3: Roots of well-being.* Lincoln: University of Nebraska Press, 1981.

Tallman, I. The family as a small problem-solving group. *Journal of Marriage and the Family,* 1970, *32,* 94–104.

Tomm, K. One perspective on the Milan Systemic Approach: Part I. Overview of development, theory and practice. *Journal of Marital and Family Therapy,* 1984a, *10,* 113–126.

Tomm, K. One perspective on the Milan Systemic Approach: Part III. Description of session format, interviewing style and interventions. *Journal of Marital and Family Therapy,* 1984b, *10,* 253–272.

VanMeter, M. Seeing dependency as strength from generation to generation. In N. Stinnett, B. Chesser, J. DeFrain, & P. Knaub (Eds.) *Family strengths: Positive models for family life.* Lincoln: University of Nebraska Press, 1980.

VanTrommel, M. A consultation method addressing the therapist–family system. *Family Process,* 1984, *23,* 469–480.

Walsh, F. Conceptualizations of normal family functioning. In F. Walsh (Ed.), *Normal family processes.* New York: Guilford, 1982a.

Walsh, F. (Ed.), *Normal family processes.* New York: Guilford, 1982b.

Whitaker, C., & Keith, D. Symbolic–experiential family therapy. In A. Gurman & D. Kniskern (Eds.), *Handbook of family therapy.* New York: Brunner/Mazel, 1981.

Williamson, D. New life at the graveyard: A method of therapy for individuation from a dead former parent. In G. Berenson & M. White (Eds.), *Annual review of family therapy, (Vol. 1).* New York. Human Sciences Press, 1981.

Wolfe, T. The me decade. *New Yorker,* August 23, 1976.

Young, M., Benjamin, B., & Wallis, C. Mortality of widowers. *Lancet,* 1963, *2,* 454–456.

Zeig, J. (Ed.), *Ericksonian approaches to hypnosis and psychotherapy.* New York: Brunner/Mazel, 1982.

PART TWO

Models and Methods

CHAPTER 2

Resources for Healing and Survival in Families

Edwin H. Friedman

John W, a hard-driving real estate manager with no particular sophistication about psychology, biology, or pathology, was told that his aches and pains were due to a rare form of cancer that required an operation with a 20% chance of survival. His instantaneous response was, "I want to be one of the 20%." Without waiting to consult his wife, his brother (a physician), or his own staff, he arranged for the recommended surgical procedure. One month later he was back at work lamenting that he had to spend an hour and a half each day traveling back and forth for his radiation treatments, and wanting to know if they could double the dosage of his chemotherapy so that he could get better faster.

"John," I asked, "Did you ever hear about the U.S.S. Cruiser *Indianapolis*?" He said he hadn't.

"It went down in the Pacific," I added, "after delivering the atomic bomb to the Marianas. Hit suddenly, without warning, and before a 'Mayday' message could go out, the rapidly sinking craft left 800 men in the water faced with sharks, a scorching sun, and no sustenance. Every now and then one would swim away and give himself up to the sharks. How do you explain it?" I asked. "What went into survival out there?"

"Those guys who swam away," he answered, "they didn't have no future."

It is the thesis of this chapter that a major resource for survival in families is the horizon level of its members. In any crisis, those who tend to let only the horizons they can actually see define their "condition" generally have far less chance for survival than those whose horizons are images projected from their own imagination. Further, since horizons depend on the head, the head of a body or the "head" of a family, survival in any family often has more to do with the functioning of its leader than with any outside expert's knowledge of

Edwin H. Friedman, D.D. Private Practice, Bethesda, Maryland.

pathology or technique. In this regard, clarity may be more important than empathy.

These conclusions do not rest on my experience with John W alone, but rather on 25 years in the same community observing which families, and who in which families, survive. The vantage point of these observations has been in part 20 years of work with families in a nonsectarian setting, but it was originally an overlapping 20 years as a congregational rabbi. The importance of the latter is that members of the clergy receive a slant on life that is not necessarily available to members of the other helping professions and that puts into question many of the conventional assumptions about what goes into healing and survival. Clergy have the continual opportunity to become close with families that are not deeply troubled for long periods of time (sometimes it spans a generation). This "intimacy with the normal" enables us to become "familiar" with many families who experience major crises and who change significantly without relying on the helping establishment. On the one hand, this kind of experience raises the question of whether it would have made a difference if such families had sought outside help in the first place, since it appears to have been resources natural to the family that promoted its healing. On the other hand, it also raises the question, when families do heal after seeking outside help, of whether it was the "expertise" that mattered rather than the way in which their own natural resources were released.

This long-term intimacy with the normal also affords clergy the opportunity to note that many of the factors that are conventionally blamed for troubled families' troubles (e.g., distance, differences, fusion, enmeshment, broken home) often are present in "normal" (i.e., untroubled) families. And that puts into question the widespread assumption that such conditions are automatically pathogenic. It would appear that, like bacteria, viruses, carcinogens, and some genes, the conditions can't do it alone.

For myself, a quarter century of "intimacy with the normal" has led me to the following conclusions: first, families have their own resources for healing and survival, and where they benefit from outside expertise, it has less to do with the knowledge the therapist has injected into the situation and more to do with what he or she tapped, catalyzed or promoted within the family, often unwittingly. As I have observed and trained counselors and therapists from all the healing disciplines, I have come to recognize that the crucial factor in their effectiveness is neither their specific degree nor their theoretical orientation, but the capacity or desire of the healer to promote family resources. Second, I would thus conclude today that, to the extent that any type of healing depends on the functioning of the healer, no matter how it is packaged, it is faith healing. The importance of this conclusion is that it leads logically to the notion that, in order for the self-reliant, nonanxious family attitudes and thinking that maximize healing to operate at their best, they also must be present in the healer.

This chapter is divided into two major parts, one theoretical, one clinical. In the first section I will discuss what I consider to be the three most important variables in a family's capacity to draw on its own natural resources, no matter what the "dis-ease." And, in the second section, I will describe how two families with different types of survival crises were helped to heal through the application of the principles enumerated in the first section, by encouraging patterns that were sometimes almost totally different from one family to the other.

THREE VARIABLES

There are three interdependent variables that maximize a family's ability to draw on its own natural resources: (1) their capacity to view the hostility of an environment as proportional to their own response to the threat; (2) the richness (variability) of the family's repertoire of responses; and (3) the family's ability to produce a *leader*, meaning someone who can define him or himself while maintaining a non-anxious presence. As mentioned, these three variables are interdependent; their presence promotes one another, their absence inhibits one another.

The Concept of a Hostile Environment

There is a general tendency among families and among therapists to assume that the harmfulness of an environment is simply proportional to the strength of its noxious components. Such linear, cause-and-effect thinking is appropriate in certain cases (e.g., exposure to radiation) but when it comes to family relational crises and many conditions of ill health, another, often crucial, variable also exists; the organism's own response to challenge. When that response is ignored, either–or thinking develops, resulting either in an attitude of helpless victimization toward the hostile environment, or all-out efforts to escape from it. However, when the organism's response is emphasized, not only can the toxicity of an environment often be neutralized, but a second result can be transformation of the organism itself. Indeed, actual modification of that environment becomes a third possibility. Victim attitudes that measure the harmfulness of an environment only by the strength of its toxicity preclude these other two vital, evolutionary possibilities! They also minimize the possibility that resources natural to the family will be tapped.

To clarify, hostile environments can be divided into two categories: those where the human response is irrelevant, and those where it can make a difference. Category I hostile environments are absolutely hostile; the organism contains no resources that would enable it to adapt. For example, a land-based animal locked in an unbreakable tank of water or a "fish out of water" cannot survive. Likewise, a human organism near ground zero in a nuclear explosion, by its nature, cannot withstand the heat, the shock, or the radiation.

The vast majority of survival crises that human beings experience with regard to relationships or their health, however, belong in Category II, where the response of the organism is a variable in its own survival. Included in Category II are such hostile environments as plagues, epidemics, economic depressions, gas

shortages, slavery, prejudiced communities, "Jewish mothers," traumatic experiences, ghettos, ship sinkings, miserable marriages, lousy bosses, some genetic
defects, exposure to germs and viruses, and many cancer and heart conditions.
Even what we refer to as "stressful environments" often have more to do with
the organism's response than with the impact (pressure) of the enviroment itself.
There is a marked tendency among human organisms to assume that when they
are in an extremely hostile environment *ipso facto* they are *in extremis*. But in
family life, death—"extinction"—is rarely only a physical phenomenon.

Some who survived the Nazi extermination camps have provided important
evidence of how much of a difference the human response can make. Here was a
hostile environment that came as close to Category I as could be found in earthly
experience. First of all, it was totally hostile by the nature of its harmful
components. After all, it was an environment designed for nonsurvival! As if
that were not enough, fate, "dumb luck," seemed to rival the all-determining,
unintelligent selection forces that have shaped evolution.

Day-to-day survival, for example, could have depended on such un-influence-
able factors as whether the number tatooed on one's arm was odd or even, or
whether a totally unrelated order to a work detail withdrew one's lot from the
deadly numbers game altogether. On the other hand, the momentary whim of a
captor could also have determined one's future forever.

In an environment of such random permutations, it is easy to fall "victim,"
and so the matter of survival came to be called *selectzia*, as if to say a "natural"
(i.e., environmental) selection process totally beyond the influence of the organism was in charge. The truth of the matter, however, is that even "the natural
selection" processes in the evolution of our species were affected by the repertoire of an organism's and/or a species' responses.

So, too, the concentration camp survival literature (e.g., DesPres, 1979) has
often shown that even in that close-to-Category I environment the response of
an organism could influence the possibilities of survival (see below, p. 77). It
did not guarantee survival; what can anywhere? But it could make a difference
where a difference was possible. As small as the crack in the door of fate was,
some saw it and some didn't. Indeed, some apparently looked for it and some
did not.

One way to preserve the importance of the human response variable, yet also
allow for differential in luck or other determinative factors in an environment, is
to think of all these forces as dials on an amplifier that can vary the mix. This
avoids the opposite alternatives of automatic victimized capitulation on the one
hand, or simplistic mind-over-matter solutions on the other. In some circumstances the dial marked "chance" is low, and in some situations it is all the way
up; so also the dial marked "physical," that is, environmental determinants. But
there is still the dial for the "human response to challenge." It also can be tuned
low or high, and in Category II hostile environments often the final "mix" is
dependent on its fine tuning. This is, in fact, the essential difference between
Category I and II; in Category I the tuning of this dial doesn't matter. Category I

thinking, therefore, by its nature inhibits a focus on a family's own resources for survival.

Society and Category I Thinking

What makes it especially difficult for therapists to encourage families to conceptualize hostile environments in terms of Category II is the Category I thinking in society at large and the thinking structure of much of our own profession itself, which is perhaps symptomatic of the larger system.

Two examples of Category I thinking in society are the responses to the threat of carcinogens or recombinant DNA. In both situations the concern is overwhelmingly in the direction of the hostility of the environment, with little focus at all on the response and, therefore, the resources of the organism.

In some ways the almost frantic searching for carcinogens in the environment resembles the hysterical hunt for communists in the 1950s. It is as though the carcinogen has replaced the communist as the focus of society's anxiety. Witch hunts are always Category I thinking at its worst. They are always characterized by emphasis on subversive forces that will take us over to the exclusion of the internal strengths that can nullify the foe. In the anxious '50s, anyone who urged Category II thinking, who said, "Put emphasis on strengthening our defenses, educate our minds to our history and heritage and focus less on the enemy alone," was a still small voice indeed.

Today, also, many factors beyond the presence of the "enemy" must go into which members of any family become "victims" of cancer or cholesterol. This does not mean that such substances are not dangerous, any more than that a communist would not, if given the opportunity, subvert a democratic nation. It is rather a matter of which overall focus is more likely to promote survival: measuring the hostility of an environment as an isolated quantity, or as a ratio that includes the organism's response. It is, of course, possible to say that eliminating the enemy (even the "intimate enemy") may be classified as a response of the organism, but such outward focus alone often brings with it an internally destructive phenomenon: an autoimmune response (see below, p. 72). As Walt Kelly's Pogo used to put it, it is often a case of "we have met the enemy, and they is us."

Similar Category I thinking pervades much of the anxiety that exists today concerning the possibility that recombinant DNA techniques might produce new organisms hostile to human beings for which there is no remedy. Less anxious scientists have pointed out, however, that the fact that an organism is inherently toxic to human beings does not automatically endow it with the capacity to be necessarily lethal. It must also have the capacity to bind itself to the cell wall and defeat the immunological response which always contains a pool of unrealized resources.

In family relationships, also, as long as individuals focus primarily on the toxicity of their relatives' behavior and remarks instead of on what makes them vulnerable, they will fail to realize that it is far healthier to work on their own "cells" as a way of nullifying the "insult," or the "hurt." And as mentioned above, such responses will accomplish more than self-protection; they will also tend to modify the "noxious" behavior.

Therapists and Category I Thinking

Unfortunately, the structure and thinking characteristic of the therapeutic establishment mirrors society's general tendency to conceptualize hostile environments in terms of Category I. Incidentally, it may be precisely this lack of differentiation from society at large that explains why psychotherapy has not been more successful in inducing fundamental change. One can never expect the change agent, therapist or therapeutic establishment, to function effectively if its own anxiety is at the same level as its "client."

The emphasis in the therapeutic field tends to be on diagnostic categories or "conditions" (of the individual or of the family) as if these "slices of life" can exist frozen in space, like so many slices of tissue isolated from the response of an organism to its own situation, no less as part and parcel of it. As can be seen in Table 2-1, the world of psychotherapy has become its own "complex." It is not only possible to specialize in any item on this list, but, by taking from each column, to "deepen" one's expertise further. But complexity should not be confused with depth.

Were it necessary for therapists to have that much knowledge no one could promote healing at all. Indeed, the concern with expertise as defined primarily by knowledge of a condition subverts the healing force, for it maintains or even elevates the basic anxiety level of many therapists as they are led to constantly perseverate after the latest insight or technique.

Classification is necessary for orderly thought, but classifying the human phenomenon by condition can have seriously limiting effects. It is a meaningless concept in the context of healing when it is isolated from the response variable, thus diverting attention away from the family's natural resources.

TABLE 2-1
Psychotherapy's Data Base

Problem	Theoretical school or technique	Family member	Background
Abortion	Psychoanalysis	Wife	Appalachian, etc.
Adoption	Freudian	Husband	Black
Aging	Jungian	Mother	Chinese
Anorexia	Adlerian	Father	German
Asthma	Lay	Son	Greek
Conflict resolution	Sullivanian	Daughter	Hispanic
Communication	Ericksonian	Grandparent	Irish

TABLE 2-1
Psychotherapy's Data Base

Problem	Theoretical school or technique	Family member	Background
Depression	Behavioral therapy	Youngest child	Italian
Grief	Skinnerian	Oldest child	Jewish
Living with:	Wolpean	Middle child	Mexican
Preschoolers	Gestalt	Only child	Puerto Rican
Latency phobias	Transactional	Adopted child	Spanish
Schoolage phobias	Rogerian		Vietnamese
Adolescents	Group		Lower class
Leaving home	Eriksonian		Middle class
Learning	Family therapy		Upper class
disabilities	Systems		
Marriage	Structural		
Blended families	Strategic		
Single parent	Art therapy		
problems	Biofeedback		
Divorce	Cognitive therapy		
Marital stress	Dance therapy		
Inter-marriage	Effective parenting		
Pain	Hypnosis		
Personality	Massage therapy		
Schizophrenia	Milieu therapy		
Boarderlines	Object relations		
Obsessives	Pharmacotherapy		
Hysterics	Play therapy		
Phobias:	Sensitivity training		
planes	Techniques of:		
trains	Stress management		
being alone	Handling shyness		
Psychosomatic	Loneliness		
ailments	Intimacy		
In the head	Growth		
In the gut	Creativity		
On the skin	Acupuncture		
Sexuality:	Traditional acupunc-		
Impotence	ture		
Premature ejacula-			
tion			
Frigidity			
Vaginismus			
Homosexuality			
Substance abuse			
Drugs			
Liquor			
Food			
Children			
Suicide			
Violence			
Women's issues			

The data base of psychotherapy, as illustrated in Table 2-1, has turned therapists into pathologists rather than healers. It is also a focus on weakness rather than strength, that is, *resource*. When it comes to healing and survival, however, knowledge of pathology is probably far less important than the capacity of a family to produce a leader, and technical savvy is probably less significant than reducing chronic anxiety, in the healer as well as in the family.

And all of this does not begin to mention the additional fact that, within families themselves, diagnostic, that is, "condition," thinking also limits the flowering of a family's own natural resources because it fuels the fire of blaming another family member, or one's background. An even more powerful understanding of how focus on resource rather than on pathology can lead to fundamental healing in the most hostile of environments follows from the recent success in reversing malignancy in lukemic cells by treating cancer as immaturity rather than pathology (Sachs, 1986). Since as cells mature into the stages of differentiation and specialization they cease proliferating, several research teams have asked whether cancer cells would do the same if they were made to "grow up." After determining the growth factor (specific proteins) these cells were lacking, these researchers have found that if the missing proteins are replaced, the cells do indeed stop proliferating and the malignant condition immediately ceases to exist. The analogy to families is astounding. There is, after all, no such thing as acting out children in a system led by mature parents, and where chronic problems do exist "in" children, when the parents can be enabled to defocus the child and the pathology in the system, and work instead on their own differentiation, the malignant proliferation to their offspring will usually come to a halt. Actually, the analogy can be carried to an even more profound parallel. For once the proliferation of immaturity ceases within any given family "colony of cells," the process by which acting out children "metastasize" that immaturity into the other organ(-ization)s of society, also automatically comes to a stop. This same analogy can be made to many other chronic family problems also, of course, particularly alcoholism.

The Response of the Organism

In his essay "Despair and The Life of Suicide," the literary psychoanalyst Dr. Leslie Farber (1966), opened with a quote from the existential philosopher Gabriel Marcel: "The fact that suicide is always possible is the essential starting point of any genuine metaphysical thought." From the perspective of this essay I would say that the fact that an autoimmune response is always possible is the beginning of any serious consideration of an organism's role in its own survival. If capitulating victim-like to a hostile environment prevents a family from utilizing its own resources for survival, the exact opposite response can have a similar effect.

In recent years more and more attention has been focused on the fact that an organism's own response to threat can do it in. Dubbed the autoimmune response, it occurs when a body's system of defenses, far from capitulating to a hostile environment, overreacts to such an extreme that it loses the ability to distinguish self from nonself and begins to attack the very self it is there to protect.

As Lewis Thomas (1974) has aphoristically put it, often what we have to fear is not the enemy but our own "Pentagons." With family survival as with national survival, both extremes, the hawk response and the dove response, are forms of surrender, surrender of the self, and either extreme reduces a family's capacity to draw on the full range of its resources. It is important to emphasize, however, that in an autoimmune response we are not dealing simply with an inappropriate response or overreaction, with the "mere" danger of self-fulfilling fantasies, as in a paranoid preemptive strike (e.g., during a marital separation). Biologically, the autoimmune response involves the disintegration of the organism's own fabric of existence. Comparable emotional phenonema occur when one winds up totalitarian in the effort to combat totalitarianism, or becomes rigid in the effort to combat another family member's rigidity, or selfless (or manipulative) in an adaptive effort to preserve a relationship one considers vital to one's "self"-preservation. We are thus not talking here about some overlay of behavior that prevents the true self from emerging, some defense mechanism that has perverted personality; rather we are encountering, paradoxically, the *internal erosion of a self's own integrity* caused by its very effort to preserve that self.

The concept has more in common with the notion of "tragic flaw" than "Achilles' heel," for the latter suggests simply a weakness or unprotected spot (as the fable goes) and fails to capture the pathetic grandeur of the concept embodied in "tragic flaw"—that what in the past may have worked to elevate now not only ceases to be effective but serves to bring down. In families the emotional autoimmune response occurs when continued striving for more togetherness, a quality normally needed for family survival, serves to destroy the family. One example is the families who could not leave Europe in the 30's despite the mounting threat because the threat itself made it more difficult for them to separate from one another, although "breaking up the family" was the way to optimize the survival of some part; similar were those families that "pulled together" while they were in hiding when that very togetherness maximized the possibility of their being discovered. (Parents or marriage partners who respond anxiously to distancing in other family members by trying for more togetherness often create similar self-destructive situations.) It is also possible, of course, that families fail to be clear-headed about oncoming danger because their already existing stuck-togetherness foreshortens their horizons.

Beyond the specific histology of the autoimmune response, the fact that such a paradoxical event can occur biologically or emotionally (and they may be more deeply related than we would care to believe) has deep philosophical import for human existence. First, autoimmune phenomena suggest that human survival in a hostile environment is a far more complicated matter than just refusing to lie down and die. The avoidance of Category I thinking turns out to be only half the problem. As we shall see, survival depends less on a specific response than on the richness of a family's repertoire of responses. Second, for several reasons explored below, the autoimmune response suggests that *anxiety* is the emotional phenomenon that most precludes a family's capacity to draw on its repertoire. Third, the possibility that the biological and the existential varieties of response are connected emphasizes the relationship between survival and integrity.

Repertoire of Responses

The fact that self-protection as a response to threat (apparently the exact opposite of Category I thinking) can be as victimizing as actual surrender aids in establishing parameters for helping families draw on their own natural resources for healing and survival.

The key is not the specific response of a family but the breadth of richness of its repertoire. Here an analogy may be drawn to the major 20th-century emendation of Darwinian theory, the concept of genetic variability, which states in essence that the richer the gene pool of a species the more chance it has for survival. The more varied the genetic resources, the more the odds favor that some portion of the species will be able to adapt to a wider variety of hostile environments. The emotional analog for the survival of families, not necessarily related to their actual genes, of course, is that the more varied any family's repertoire of responses the wider the range of crisis it can survive; in the process, the more opportunity it has to grow. Indeed, the richer the repertoire of a family's responses for meeting crisis the more likely it is that each crisis is turned into an opportunity for the family's own evolution, as dormant, perhaps hitherto unrealized, resources materialize.

One reason this is true is that symptom and response are far more connected than is generally realized. No family gets the problem it can handle. This always appears to be an after-the-fact state of things but was in fact built into why that family has that particular symptom. For it is almost always the response of the nonsymptomatic family members that determines whether any initial presymptomatic behavior is to become or remain chronic. Not all families respond with the same degree of anxiety to similar abnormalities. Changing a family's response to symptomatic behavior therefore always involves unhooking them from the very ways of thinking that were part of that symptom's natural manure. Where this can be accomplished, not only does the symptom itself often respond, but it is like pulling a cork, as other responses, often unpredictable and by the nature of the case totally inconceivable in advance, flow forth almost naturally, once the blockage has been removed.

In emphasizing the richness of a family's repertoire of responses, however, the intention is not to convey mere *flexibility*. The concept has more to do with *resiliency*, for there are families who are "flexible" because they do not know any other way to do it. Sooner or later that tendency to be automatically adaptive will catch up with them. A prime example is unreasonably reasonable parents who try to understand thier cursing, arrogant, selfish, boorish child rather than defining themselves to its invasiveness. The rigidly flexible family is victimized by environments that require it to take stands.

Either way, the factor that is most likely to narrow a family's repertoire of responses is its level of chronic anxiety.

Anxiety and Survival

The classic model of autoimmune behavior is the horseshoe crab, a terribly undifferentiated creature. Its head and its body are one. It is a cul-de-sac in evolution, functioning in the same way now as it has for millions of years. It is possible to inject a substance into such creatures that is not by nature harmful to the organism's makeup and observe the crab respond by totally destroying itself within half an hour.

One can argue that if a substance can by its nature trigger an autoimmune response then we might as well call it inherently harmful to the organism. For that terribly undifferentiated creature, the horseshoe crab, yes. The biology of the situation makes it automatic—that is, Category I—and there's the rub. For the human organism, however, whose place in evolution has brought with it the potential for a much wider range of responses to hostile environments, a response rarely has to be automatic. Thus when an autoimmune response does occur in the human animal or human clan, whether it is biological or existential, this type of self-disintegrating reaction always represents an evolutionary regression at the least, and a step toward undifferentiation at its worst.

Metaphorically, if not actually, the horseshoe crab's autoimmune response is a model of anxiety. For the family organism, likewise, its capacity to avoid such regression, to draw on its own resources (to make use of the full repertoire of its responses), is always inversely proportional to the level of its anxiety. Moreover, a sustained level of high anxiety not only produces temporary regression; it will probably work to wither the resources available. In other words, reducing family anxiety is not merely in the service of enabling everyone to be more clear-headed about their condition. Rather, anxiety has the capacity to erode the internal fabric of a family's being. Chronic family anxiety not only diminishes a family's capacity to utilize resources that might otherwise be available; continued disuse always runs the danger of total atrophy.

Yet it is an even deeper phenomenon than that; for immunology is not merely about systems of defense that an organism "uses"; it has to do with the essential *integrity* of the organism itself. This relationship between immunology and self has far-reaching consequences for etiology and healing in both physical and emotional illness.

Biologically, it could mean that not only diseases like multiple sclerosis, lupus, rheumatoid arthritis, or allergies may be autoimmune phenomena, but that perhaps any "dis-integrative" disease, including cancer and coronary "conditions," could have an autoimmune (i.e., loss-of-integrity) factor in its development and continued manifestation. With families, this emphasis on integrity, which is not the same as unity, sharpens the perspective on how denial, marital fusion, and other enmeshed forms of stuck-togetherness can be viewed as autoimmune responses of that type of organism. For they fit the basic criteria of biological autoimmunity: triggered by threat, designed to protect, but ultimately perverting one natural resource into a force that blocks other resources (whether hormones or perceptions) from coming to the rescue.

Immunology and Integrity

While families differ from one another in the potential variability of their responses, few draw on the richness of their repertoire to anywhere near the extent to which they are capable. It is possible, after all, to have a Category I view of that repertoire itself, that is, to assume that the resources a family has used to a given point are all they have. Such an attitude helps foster the notion that the family is therefore determined by that "condition."

The basic question for family therapists, therefore, is, what will optimize the fruition or the broadening of the family's repertoire? The answer, I believe, has to do with the promoting of self-definition and the reduction of chronic anxiety, which are often reciprocals of one another. The latter will be explored below in the discussion of the third major variable—leadership. For the moment the focus will be on the former, self-definition.

The reason a family therapist's efforts to promote self-definition will work toward the natural development of the family's own resources is in part due to the fact that self-definition and anxiety are inversely proportional and in part because undifferentiated togetherness inhibits the imaginative (horizon) capacity. Most basically, however, these efforts work in that direction because integration of the self and immunology are intricately connected. The autoimmune response is defined medically as the loss of the capacity to distinguish self from nonself. The other side of that definition is that for an immunological system to function well in any organism (individual or family) there probably needs to be some degree of well-integrated self to begin with.

What is being suggested here is not only the possibility that immunological responses may never be solely biological phenomena, but always to some extent existential, but also that the connection between the biological and the existential has to do with their relationship to self-integrity. There is some natural evidence for this related to the evolution of our species.

First, it would appear that it was only with the development of an immunological sytem that the protoplasm on this planet could have evolved into discrete entities in the first place. In other words, without the development of immunological systems, the existential category of self would be meaningless. Second, any advance in the development of higher organisms would also probably have been prevented without an immunological system, since when microorganisms lacking an immunological system become too close they have a tendency to disintegrate, that is, to lose integrity.

The "enmeshed" or "fused" family (one that lacks self-definition) produces the same results. One example is the wife who is chronically ill, emotionally or physically. With emotional illness she may be phobic or hysteric, in an out of institutions, exhibiting constant failure of nerve to ever leave home. With physical illness she may have operation after operation to repair nonvital parts of her body and may always be listless and fatigued. In all such marriages the husband is too close! Either there is not enough emotional space between them of the kind produced by self-definition or she has not enough self to tolerate its lack. They are close but, despite their closeness, are not able to tolerate being together. The immunological system thus is not only necessary for defense, but it appears that it also makes possible love, that is, connecting.

It is precisely these two widely different aspects of the immunological phenomenon, its crucial part in promoting separateness as well as in enabling togetherness, that emphasize the role of integrity, and give to the autoimmune response (the failure to distinguish friend from foe) such philosophical import. It is therefore instructive to note at this point that many who wrote about their survival in the concentration camps seemed to have managed some balance between the discrete and the connected (DesPres, 1979).

Three major factors have often appeared in the survivors' accounts. They are extraordinarily similar to what seems to work for survival in families:

1. A healthy self-concern that kept a prisoner from losing self in the group and perhaps missing an opportunity here and there to do something for his or her own daily survival, e.g., noting a piece of bread in the hand of someone who had already died.

2. Not cutting oneself off from the group either by withdrawal or through a selfishness that did another in—stealing bread from someone who was still alive. The group would make sure such an individual was on the next list for the gas chambers.

3. A commitment to survive; in other words, a response that saw the hostile environment as a challenge.

But, how does the relationship between immunology and integrity apply to the family itself as an organism? The answer to that question lies in the third major variable in a family's resources for survival, in its capacity to produce a leader. For leaders function as the immunological systems of their families, in that their presence or absence affects the repertoire of a family's responses.

Leadership

The third major variable in family resources for survival is leadership. So crucial is this factor that without it all efforts to promote nonvictim thinking, or prevent an autoimmune response, may be useless. For leadership is itself a therapeutic modality. It is true that an anxious leader could accelerate an autoimmune response on the part of the entire famly (Jonestown), or that an overfunctioning leader, anywhere, who fosters collapse and dependency is hardly promoting integrity. But by definition that is not leadership in the sense intended here. The type of leadership that promotes a family's resources occurs when a family member has the capacity to maintain enough distance from the surrounding emotional whirlwinds so as to be able to keep clear his or her own life's goals (maintain his or her own *horizons* and integrity), can continue to articulate them and follow them despite the family's crisis, and can, as a result of this capability, maintain a *nonanxious presence* in the system. Once again, there is a reciprocity to these various factors since the capacity to maintain a nonanxious presence helps the maintenance of horizons and integrity, while the latter increase the ability to stay out of the anxiety.

It is my own view that the capacity of any family or work system to produce this natural resource, the emergence of a well-defined head (unlike the horseshoe crab), is the major variable in its survival, and is often the major determinant of whether or not the disappearance of a symptom means fundamental change or an intermission in a recycling process. Families in which no member is capable of taking a stand will defeat the best efforts of the most experienced therapist. They are like watch springs that seduce one into thinking that each turn is energizing the system that much more, and then, suddenly, after one more turn, the whole thing unwinds, and it becomes necessary to start the entire effort all over again. (This is of course particularly descriptive of alcoholic families).

Where family therapists can identify the family member with the most leadership potential as defined above and encourage and support that member to lead (again as defined above), almost all other therapeutic techniques, no matter what the symptom, pale in potential. Not all families contain this resource to the same extent, of course, but in many situations it is latent, or merely fearful to emerge.

Why is leadership a therapeutic modality? I believe the answer lies in the very nature of protoplasm. It is simply a biological fact that swarms, herds, flocks, indeed all forms of social organization, need direction to function effectively. The same is true in work systems where the capacity of any member of any hierarchy to function in well-defined manner is determined primarily by the character of one or two people at the top. It is far more than a trickle-down phenomenon, however; no organism functions well if its "head" is poorly defined. What counts is not how the manager manages the players but how he or she manages him or herself.

Elsewhere (Friedman, 1985) I have discussed in greater detail many of the effects of well-defined leadership on the health of a personal family or work system. The notion is far more complex than administrative techniques and has biological, existential and philosophical ramifications for the nature of the hundreds of different forms of symbiosis (literally: living together) found in life on our planet.

For the thrust of this chapter, however, with its focus on family resources, it should be noted here that focusing on leadership is a focus on a family's strengths, not its weaknesses, on (the potential variability of) its own responses, not its "condition," on its integrity and the integrity of its members, not unity.

It is true that the exact opposite type of sytem can appear to work for survival also: a family can become enmeshed in a unified consensus, as a leaderless school of fish, in which the emotional system produced by the inner relationships makes each member the other's radar, and all move as one automatically. Within certain ranges this can work for a family also, but the family that always swims together is also more likely to sink together because the overall lack of differentiation means a narrowness in its repertoire of responses.

It is also important to emphasize that leadership as defined here is more than a matter of modeling. The goal is not to get other family members to emulate the leader; in fact, often they work to sabotage him or her precisely when the leader is doing what is ultimately best for the family, for example, not catering to their symptoms, not participating in their denial, or recognizing that another's most basic need may be not to have their needs fulfilled! Ultimately, the leader's promoting effect on the resources inherent in other family members is due to the effect his or her integrity has within the overall emotional system. It is change on that level that affects the other members, not whether they follow in the leader's footsteps! This is a very fundamental level of communication, bypassing the unconscious. In family emotional systems, communication is often "heart-to-heart".

The depth of this systemic effect can perhaps best be illustrated by the manner in which a leader's nonanxious presence can modify chronic anxiety throughout a family. Such an illustration has an added advantage since it will also bring sharply into relief the fact that reducing family anxiety is one of the major ways to unblock natural family resources.

Chronic family anxiety, as compared to anxiety over a specific problem, at times seems to function like electricity and at times seems to have the nature of explosive gas fumes. In either case, by defining himself or herself, and maintaining a nonanxious presence, the leader's functioning can channel that potential energy into healing directions.

Anxiety and Electricity

The reason for comparing anxiety to electricity is that both seem to have some of the same properties: an invisible force that is given to surges of power and can be seen only through its effects. What is also true about electricity, of course, is that there must be two poles to maintain its potential. The same seems to be true about anxiety: All chronic conditions in families require feedback. It is therefore not possible for only one family member to remain chronically anxious. When any member of a family can define himself or herself the circuits of the anxiety currents are broken, and, when he or she can maintain a nonanxious presence, that family member begins to function as an electrical transformer that has consequences that are even more fundamental.

In electrical circuits it is possible to raise or lower the power by means of a device called a transformer. In a 100-to-1 step-up transformer, for example, current can go in at 110 volts (household current) and come out at 11,000 (which will make it cheaper to transport). Of course, at the other end of the line, after it has been transported, one would need a step-down transformer. There are family members who regularly act as the step-up transformers for all the anxiety in their system. Any anxious current that enters them at 110 will feed back into the system at 11,000.

We have all experienced that phenomenon in families, either our own or our patients', and we know the effect can be "like lightning". But similar extraordinary effects can occur if a family member can, by maintaining a nonanxious presence, be a step-down transformer in the system, seeming to let all the anxiety currents go right through them without being touched by or absorbing the anxiety. This is one of the most difficult tasks in the world. Anyone can remain nonanxious by not being present, but that will not modify the system! However, where a family member can remain nonanxious while also remaining present, it will do more to release natural family resources than can be accomplished by a therapeutic outsider.

Therapists, and their supervisors, can of course also potentiate anxiety in a family, creating one long anxiety grid, as anxious supervisors respond anxiously to anxious therapists, who respond anxiously to their anxious clients, who are responding anxiously to members of their family. Any therapeutic endeavor, therefore, that can help a family member become more of a nonanxious presence in the system promotes a family resource at the most fundamental level; in addition it helps release other resources. When that natural resource is developed in a family member who is already the leader, it is more effective, but, when it is developed in a previously leaderless (undifferentiated) family, it creates a family leader.

Anxiety and Gas Fumes

Lest it appear, however, that families need a strong, take-charge person to accomplish anxiety reduction, it is important to note that chronic family anxiety also behaves like volatile gas fumes that hang heavy over a specific location. It is therefore important to point out that one can lead a family by trying to loosen it up, by refusing to get caught in its seriousness. This is another, if apparently opposite, way of remaining self-defined and will also serve to reduce chronic anxiety, and release natural family resources. (Compare these opposite approaches in the two clinical examples in the next section.)

Families that evidence such seriousness are as if surrounded by the volatile fumes of anxiety. Any small incident can create a flare-up. They will always assume that it was the incident that created the problem, but in truth it is the way they relate and think that gives any incident its inflammatory power.

On the other hand, if one family member can successfully stay out of the family "seriousness," while remaining present, changes can be made in this "noxious atmosphere," and the anxiety fumes will disperse. (This, incidentally, would seem to be the real value of paradoxical responses, their playful effect in loosening up serious systems, rather than the reverse psychology or therapeutic double-bind effect they have on the family member at whom they are directed.) Then the sparking incidents of life that are necessary for creative existence (and the full employment of the family's resources) can occur without igniting a crisis. Here especially, successful "therapeutic intervention" depends on the richness of the therapist's repertoire, which should not be confused with being "eclectic," and has more to do with the therapist's own integrity.

Summary

To review the major concepts of this section, the most fundamental healing occurs when a family heals itself. This is most likely to occur when the family's own resources are brought to bear on the problem. It is least likely to occur when families go to one of two opposite extremes regarding any crises: surrendering to the inevitability of the condition, thus disregarding the importance of their own response, or, reacting in what has been termed an autoimmune response, producing a defensive reaction of such proportion that the fabric of the family's existence disintegrates.

The families that have the best chance of mobilizing their own resources for surviving crises are those with the broadest repertoire of responses. To bring that to the fore it is necessary to counter the family's chronic anxiety, which always serves to narrow a family's response spectrum. To accomplish this, the therapist first must be able to manage his or her own anxiety, thus maintaining a rich spectrum of his or her own responses. Then he or she may encourage the family in a similar direction, usually by supporting a family leader, defined as any member who can remain focused on horizons beyond the immediate condition while trying to maintain a nonanxious presence within the family system.

TWO CASE EXAMPLES

In this section, two case examples, both composites of several clinical experiences, will be presented to illustrate the principles described earlier in this chapter for promoting the family's own resources for survival. One involves the survival of a marriage, and one the survival of a mother–child relationship, if not their own existential survival as well. It may be important to note that the principles apply equally whether the crisis is physical or emotional, and whether what is at stake is a relationship or life itself. Often the two go together. This should not be surprising; the family, as stated, is an organism, and whether a relationship fails to survive because of an emotional cut-off or because of death, in either case its demise can often be attributed to either the lack of family resources for survival, or the failure to promote their influence.

Both case studies contain significant similarities and differences. In each situation only one member of the family is motivated to seek change. In each case, as stated, the health of the motivated member is in jeopardy, and, having tended to focus on the condition of the other rather than on her own resources, each woman is beginning to feel hopeless and enervated.

In both situations, also, the effort is made to turn the motivated family member into the leader as defined earlier, one who can define self and maintain a nonanxious presence through a combination of challenging the organism (stimulating its immunological system to function); focusing that person on their own being (in part by broadening their horizons), and reducing their chronic anxiety, in large part, by helping them differentiate themselves from multigenerational forces. Once again it should be stated that the three processes contribute to one another, but, whereas in the first case the emphasis is directed toward the client's basic ability to take charge of a situation, in the second it is the nonserious, the mischievous side of the woman that is drawn out. These cases are metaphors; such opposites have been purposely chosen to point up the fact that, while their personalities (strengths) are different, what they have in common is a potential natural resource.

Case Example 1: Jill Johnson

Jill Johnson had a totally uncontrollable 15-year-old son. He had been adopted in an interracial marriage that broke up within 2 years of the child's being brought home. Her husband married again, and, after an unsuccessful effort to take his son away (arguing that the same-race parent should be the custodial parent), tried thereafter to have little to do with him, no less Jill. He made support payments randomly and distanced whenever Jill sought his help.

A social worker, she was bewildered that her son defied all the well-known prescriptions for child rearing. Parents should be loving, Jill was loving; parents should be sensitive, Jill was sensitive; parents should be understanding, Jill was understanding. Her response to her failures was to read more books or seek more counseling.

All efforts to reason with her son failed. If anything, he seemed to react to reasonableness with more violence and lawlessness. He would take mother's car any time he wished, cut school at a whim, and make the most out of his winsomeness by conning many of the girls in his school, as well as a whole host of counselors, into thinking he needed compensation for all the rejection in his past.

Efforts by authorities to punish him rarely had lasting effect. When Ms. Johnson came in for help she was almost literally worn to a frazzle. She had lost 25% of her weight the previous year, knew she was not functioning well at her work, had developed some gastrointestinal symptoms, chronic bronchitis, and tennis elbow, and admitted that at times she had seriously considered suicide.

She opened by listing all the terrible things her son had done and all her own good efforts to improve him. Her comments were wrapped in assurances that she was basically kind, sympathetic, and sincerely anxious about what would become of him.

THERAPIST: Ms. Johnson, I am more worried about you than your son.

MS. J.: I don't have time to think about me. He never gives me a moment's peace.

THERAPIST: Look, I could give you a whole slew of techniques for trying to get control of this situation, but frankly they won't work till you're fed up. And I don't think you're fed up enough yet.

MS. J: Tell me how to get there.

THERAPIST: You have to make your own life more important so you'll know what you have been giving up.

MS. J: I know you're right but I have trouble keeping that in focus. Besides, all the counselors I have seen keep telling me I have to understand him.

THERAPIST: Well maybe you just haven't been understanding enough.

MS. J: I think I've been too understanding.

THERAPIST: Have you ever thought of giving him up for foster care?

MS. J: Frankly, I have, but it seems so cruel. He's already been rejected three times. But it's killing me.

THERAPIST: At least you will leave a good name behind you. I'll bet the eulogy will be glowing, and they can put some very nice epitaph on your tombstone. So it won't really have been in vain. If there is another world you'll probably get your reward there.

MS. J: I don't want to wait. I want it here.

THERAPIST: Then you need insensitivity training.

MS. J: What kind of therapist are you?

THERAPIST: You know, every one of these uncontrollable kids I've ever seen that have their parents dripping with anxiety about whether they are going to destroy themselves . . . they're like cats. They always land on their feet. The only destruction associated with them is what they leave in their trail.

MS. J: That's true; he does always survive.

THERAPIST: I had another situation like this, involving an unbelievably sassy 16-year-old who was threatening to run off to Florida when her parents finally started to take stands. Their perpetual fear was that she would wind up in white slavery. I saw her for a session alone. She was so brazen that I told her parents not to worry about that slavery stuff: she'd be cracking the whip in a week.

MS. J: I have to tell you that several times I just wanted to smash him, turn him over to the authorities, or move away and just leave him. But every time I get to thinking that way, I remember what a dirty deal life has dealt him.

THERAPIST: Suppose his greatest need is not to have his needs satisfied?

MS. J: I'd never thought of it that way.

THERAPIST: Is he winsome, you know, charming?

MS. J: Boy, can he turn it on!

THERAPIST: What do you think would happen if you "rejected" him?

MS. J: He'd make out, I guess.

THERAPIST: Well I don't really mean *reject* him; what I am after is something he and frankly many counselors he would come into contact with afterward might perceive as rejection. Suppose you made your life come first, and gave him choices to adapt to you or live elsewhere? This would mean defining your position every chance you get about where you stood, what you were willing to do. In other words, focusing on you, rather than trying to change him. Where you have been walking on eggs, stomp on them.

MS. J: I love it. That's the way I used to be, but this thing has undercut my confidence.

Ms. Johnson has been challenged and her horizons lifted. Future sessions were spent supporting her efforts to focus on herself in the face of her son's reactivity to these efforts, and despite the anxiety of other helping professionals.

Jill Johnson turned out to be an oldest of 8, a position generally given to taking charge. Her family had been part of the great settling of the American Mid-West, and she was descended from several generations of robust pioneer women. She was the only one to leave her home or to obtain a graduate degree. As far as she could tell, her decision to leave was motivated by a desire to escape the narrowness of her parents' world. And she saw her concern to always show concern as somewhat of a rebellion against the constant mind-over-matter approach of her family of origin, although, she said, as a therapist she was tough with other parents. She thought this inconsistency went back to the loss of her brother, who killed himself at 19. He had been close to her, and she had always hoped that her son would be the replacement to give her mother.

For the next 6 months the frontier-woman side of Jill Johnson was encouraged. This could range from taking positions with her son about what she would do about herself if her son misbehaved to simply informing him of her opinions. At all cost, however, she was to avoid getting into a contest of wills, that is, argumentative conversations in which each was trying to change the other. The differentiating partner and potential leader in any relationship must be warned that, when one family member begins to take the lead, others will up the ante by repeating exactly that type of behavior that was prone to make the differentiating partner anxious in the past. However, if he or she can manage to stay loose during such a period, the other's behavior will tend to wane without feedback to support it. Unfortunately, sometimes other members of the helping professions will step into the breach because of their anxiety, thereby undercutting the therapeutic power of self-definition in a family, and thus hindering change. This is exactly what had been happening in the past few years, and precisely what happened again while Ms. Johnson was being supported to define herself and maintain a nonanxious presence.

For example, Ms. Johnson took a firm position with her son that she did not like him coming in all hours of the night. She did not put it on the basis of what was good for *him*, but rather that unpredictable, middle-of-the-night sounds threatened *her* sleep, and that she intended to lock all doors and windows after a specific hour. He tried to argue with her about what he had a right to do, but she "declined the lists," unlike before, and just continued to frame her position in terms of her own needs. He immediately stole her car and took two teenage girls to Florida with him. Ms. Johnson persevered, however, and did not pursue him.

A week later he was back at school. The counselor called immediately to say mother could come pick him up, assuring her that "there had been no drugs or sex." Instead of rushing over she responded that if he knew how to get to Florida he knew how to get home. The counselor, aghast, said "But this is a cry for help." She politely hung up.

As it happened, she had been thinking of changing her door locks, and son came home just as the locksmith was doing his job. Immediately he said aggressively to his mother, "Why are you doing this to me?" Ms. Johnson told him that his assumption was a conceit; she was not really thinking about him at all. Next she read him a list of rules that he would have to obey if he stayed there. He responded predictably that there were some he could follow, but he wasn't sure about some of the others. She answered, "You don't understand, these are not for bargaining. They are the conditions under which I am willing to have you live with me. You can't bargain with me about them, because you don't have anything I want."

He called his father and asked if he could live with him. Father agreed, but within 2 weeks son had returned home and taken the car again. This time Ms. Johnson preferred charges. To her shock, the court social worker went to bat for her son and got him off. Ms. Johnson was encouraged to go directly to the judge and explain this dilemma, in which she was trying to get her son to face his responsibilities to society but mental health professionals were preventing this growth experience from occurring. The judge understood immediately and had him sentenced to a special prison-school for a year.

At first it appeared that Ms. Johnson had at last found some professionals who understood her priorities. The school staff supported her efforts to be strong and were strong with the boy themselves. During this period of institutionalization, Ms. Johnson was encouraged not to let it be a time of cut-off but to continue the relationship by letter, phone and visits. She was warned, however, to be wary of his efforts to charm her back. Above all, therefore, she was to keep defining herself and stay in touch with the boy. Soon she came to realize that she really didn't want him back unless he could absolutely prove himself to her, and that she was in no hurry for him to get out. It was also enlightening to her that without responsibility for him she could take stands more easily.

But as Jill Johnson continued in this stance, the counselors at the school began to push her to weaken and take a more "understanding" attitude. She had learned, however, not to try to explain her attitude, and continued on her course. Son steadily improved and began to devote more time to his studies. Progress, however, is always a jagged line with regressions along the way. One such regression occurred when Ms. Johnson, in a session with the counselor present, told her son outright that she was not sure she would take him back because, frankly, she was not sure she was good for him. Later that week son ran away with another boy. Mother was informed anxiously by the school but did nothing to look for him. He was back in a week. When mother came down for the next visit she asked no questions about the exploit. And when, on a brief drive around town, son kept pointing out places he had been during his side trip, mother showed no interest. By the end of the weekend son was depressed (not a bad sign at all), and told mother he had to go to his room for the rest of the day. She politely told him she hoped he would feel better soon and headed back home. On her way out the chief counselor said to her, "I'm afraid your son needs intensive therapy." Somehow managing to maintain her composure, she responded, "How much more intense does it have to get?"

As Ms. Johnson stayed on course, her son's development was parallel. His acting out virtually disappeared. He devoted more time to his studies, and whereas at first he seemed resentful of his mother's racial difference, he now seemed to exhibit pride. In addition, leadership qualities never before exhibited by him also began to emerge, and he took to counseling and warning his fellow students about their behavior.

During the year, Ms. Johnson was also encouraged to further involve her former husband in the project. Usually such men will distance from all efforts that are couched in anxiety or pressure, but will respond most unwittingly if the overfunctioning mother will simply report factually what is happening.

At the end of the year the parents had become cooperative to the point that Mr. Johnson agreed to find a residential school near him that was *not* for problem children, and, through continued coaching, she was able to promote healthy directions in all three parts of this triangle.

Case Example 2: Mary Windsor

Mary Windsor, having just turned 40, dragged her husband in for marriage counseling. He was apparently having an affair, though he denied it completely. They had two daughters, one of whom had just left home and was engaged to a drifter. The other was a barely passing senior in high school seeking only her Prince Charming. Throughout the session, Mr. Windsor offered no information voluntarily, answered all questions with an economy of words, and always responded to his wife's complaints either by turning them back to her, or with such bewilderment that he left her feeling she was fighting a phantom. His demeanor was always polite and clouded in a pipe-puffing calm. He never took a position. When asked if he had any complaints about the marriage other than the fact that his wife had complaints, he answered, sincerely, "No." Efforts to engage Mr. Windsor in any kind of meaningful way were totally unsuccessful. He always had good excuses to account for his time regarding her inquiries about his possible affair. Mary, for her part, seemed always on the verge of rage, frustrated by his passivity and what's-all-the-bother attitude.

The session was a metaphor of their marriage in which she had become the activities director, the cheerleader, his pacemaker. A highly energetic, petite blonde, Mary was the kind of woman who would be described as full of life, but it was ebbing out of her.

Two years previously, after unsuccessful marriage counseling that had urged her to be more adaptive to her husband's needs, a small malignant tumor had necessitated the partial removal of both breasts. She had tried cosmetic surgery, but the partial mastectomy had clearly affected her self-image. They had not had sex since then, but her husband kept assuring Mary that her disfigurement had not affected his sexual desire in the least. If she wanted to know why he did not make sexual advances himself or repulsed hers, he would point out, again calmly, that her perceptions were inaccurate. At one point Mary had suggested he move out and find some other woman to take care of him. He had responded simply that he was happy in the marriage; she was the unhappy one. In no way would he leave.

Two years after that first session, Mary had obtained a top management job with a major mortgage banker, despite the fact that she had never finished college and had had only a very small amount of work experience when she began. Her husband, who had moved out 10 months previously, was showing genuine romantic initiative for the first time since their courting days (although Mary doubted he had shown much initiative then either). Mary, who in the meantime had enjoyed a torrid, amorous relationship with another man for over a year, was preparing to let him go and let her husband try again. In addition, both daughters had also shifted their horizons from men to self-fulfillment, although their behavior and attitudes towards life were almost never discussed in mother's therapy.

Here is how those 2 years went. As a family therapist interested in tapping the family's own resources, I generally consider it a waste of time to work with unmotivated members. Not only is their presence unuseful and boring, it sops up time and energy, thus at the least diluting family resources present elsewhere. Sometimes their behavior is absolutely sabotaging of the efforts, obscuring the horizons of the more motivated members (the potential leaders) to move in resourceful directions. I believe progress can usually be made faster by coaching the most motivated member alone. "Family therapy" is thus not distinguished from individual therapy by how many people are in the room but by where the focus is placed, on the individual's own "personality" or on their position in the system.

The more motivated member is generally the one who calls, generally the one who articulates the problem, and always the one who is more capable of defining his or her position in a nonblaming way. It is not always readily apparent, however, which partner is more motivated, and there are exceptions to these criteria, as, for example, when a husband makes the initial call in order to please his wife. Therefore, to validate my initial clinical impressions I often tell the couple I would like to see each partner alone once, because "sometimes people think more clearly if they are not in the presence of their spouse." Generally, I try to see the one whom I perceive to be the *un*motivated partner first. This is done in order that I may have solid information with which to encouarge the partner I perceive to be more motivated and so that we can "launch the mission immediately."

In that first session with the less motivated one I just shoot the breeze, do not expect to get anywhere, and slip in the challenge that, if they think their spouse has changed a great deal or has become more troublesome recently, things will probably get worse. I "assured" Mr. Windsor that he had only seen the tip of the iceberg. What I wanted to convey to him most clearly was that I would not join the conspiracy of others who had constantly encouraged her to adapt to him. I am careful in these sessions not to appear that I am out to change this unmotivated family member (which would only increase his or her distance) and tend to say that since he or she does not seem to see much value in counseling sessions, maybe I should see his or her partner alone—but "feel free to call me if you ever want to come back." Unmotivated partners usually readily agree to this "release," in part because they really do not want to come, and in part because they think that by not attending their spouse, who then attends alone, will be kept in the identified patient position. It rarely occurs to such family members that as a result of an approach that taps the partner's (or parent's) resources for survival, they will themselves remain "in therapy" whether or not they actually participate in the sessions.

The passive–aggressive partner in any relationship only has power when other family members make their functioning and fulfillment dependent on his or her behavior or responses. That is probably the major reason the latter are quick to drop out of therapy. They assume that their nonaction will preserve the status quo. Unmotivated people will not change through insight—they must be motivated by pain in the situation. To bring about such a situation the overfunctioning spouse must be taught how to shift the pain, and nothing produces that shift like self-definition and the refusal to take responsibility for the other's anxiety.

Where the motivated partner can be supported to go as far as he or she can in the direction of seeking their own salvation—*but without cutting off*—the pressure that is put on the other, unmotivated partner, even though nothing is done directly to them, is enormous. Elsewhere I have discussed this concept, designed to remove the leverage of the person who is vested in the self-serving status quo, as leadership through self-definition (Friedman, 1985).

Some will hear this as manipulating and unsympathetic but it is precisely those "sympathies" that play into the manipulative hands of the passive member and gravitate the family toward its weakest direction. The capacity of any system to ensure its own survival as well as that of all its members is far greater when each has been given the choice to remain or quit, rather than continually trying to change one another, for the latter enervates their resources.

Projecting horizons beyond her condition was not hard for Mary. It had been her initial effort to establish personal goals for herself several years previously that had promoted marital problems in the first place. Similarly, there seemed little need to challenge her. Her confrontation with her own mortality that resulted from the cancer, as well as its daily reminder in the mirror, provided that stimulus.

Controlling her own reactivity to her husband seemed another matter, however. She understood the necessity of making him less important to her and of resisting the urge to get back at him with quick quips (which he made difficult by giving her so many reasons for getting back at him), but she often found she just couldn't resist. Blessed with a sharp wit and an almost poetic sense of irony, she found it almost impossible not to express the delicious returns that came to her head. At times this inability to remain focused on her own horizons depressed her immensely. As Mary saw it, what kept her most reactive to her husband's reactivity to her was her tendency to assume the worst. Her thoughts would always cascade in anxious directions.

Since Mary was a youngest rather than an oldest child and came from a family of adaptive rather than self-reliant women, she was not encouraged to try to overcome her anxiety by mere dint of taking charge, which would have been most unnatural for her. She had a lot of spunk, had been the *enfant terrible* as a child, and enjoyed being outrageous, so the mischievous side of Mary was promoted instead. This was done with regard to her husband's affair, his general passivity, and her relationship with her mother, an important source, as we shall see, of her chronically anxious thought patterns.

For example, she found that she had great difficulty not thinking about her husband's affair and not trying to prove its existence. It is very difficult for anyone to "do" *nothing*; one must do *something*. It was therefore suggested that she encourage it! Mary began to tell her husband to feel free to stay away evenings, made suggestions for gifts and exciting romantic places, and, once, when the woman whom she thought was the "other woman" called, Mary greeted her with friendly warmth, suggesting that they get together and compare notes. (Click!) Mary's husband kept denying anything was going on, but also stopped doing little things to flag her attention about it, and almost never seemed to go out in the evenings anymore (although weekend absences continued).

Encouraging an affair also breaks up its triangular quality, which often provides most of its excitement. Unmotivated marriage partners are hardly going to give up their "addiction" anyway, and generally can't go "cold turkey" on their paramour. In fact, often when they are pressured to, they wind up doing more thinkng about the relationship than when they are encouraged to enjoy it. It is self-differentiation on the part of the motivated partner that will get them thinking about their spouse.

Similar playfulness was promoted in Mary's relationship with her mother. Multiple generational transmission is almost always the source of chronic anxiety. Mary could remember that her mother had always been a "worry-wart," was plagued by a pessimistic attitude toward life, was a constant complainer, and always saw the glass as "half empty" compared to Mary, who vowed not to be that way and always insisted a glass was half full. One result, of course, was that Mary, in the denial necessary to preserve this illusion, wound up just as anxious.

Women whose mothers are complaining, pessimistic, "half-empty" people generally alternate between distancing from their mothers or perpetually trying to reassure them, sometimes to the point of madness. Mary's mischievous side was once more appealed to. Would she be willing to write a letter to mother, whose own mother had died when she was 2, whose father had beaten her, whose oldest child was divorced, but who had also lived a long healthy life, was really loved by her children, and competently ran her late husband's business? The following note was sent the next time mother complained:

Dear Mother:

I have gotten to thinking how unfortunate your life has been. Nothing has ever worked out well. You lost your mother at 2, your father beat you, both your children have severe marriage problems, and neither spends as much time thinking about you as you would like. It's almost as though you're star-crossed. I don't believe in these things but maybe you should start taking to reading horoscopes. I just can't understand why anyone should be so cursed. It's almost as though you did something wrong as a child for which you are being punished.

Your concerned daughter

Mary's mother responded somewhat predictably by saying that she didn't think her life had been so bad at all, tickled pink that her daughter had shown all this concern. As is usual in such situations, she also ceased complaining so much to her daughter, who, when mother lapsed into the former attitude, reminded her that things could only get worse.

Generally, this type of change in a mother–daughter relationship will free daughter greatly from mother's chronic anxiety and give daughter more distance from her own anxieties as well. Sometimes it actually turns mother into someone to lean on.

Shortly after this, Mary, who had begun to work, also began to seek a man. She had reduced her thoughts about her husband almost to zero. He had obviously increased his about her though, since his passivity and withdrawal had turned into criticism, which is always a form of pursuit. He objected to her working, her staying out late, and her general insensitivity. She told him things would probably get worse.

Then Mary met a man who fell desperately in love with her. After at first being overwhelmed by all this adoration, she settled back into just enjoying it, and also made sure to let her husband know what was going on, calling her paramour by name. Husband began to make overtures, but, as soon as Mary reciprocated, he withdrew again. After several rounds of this, Mary told her husband "she wanted to live with Bill." Mr. Windsor moved out. The final straw was an evening in which her husband broke a date, after appearing to be genuinely motivated to increase the romance between them, because some friends were throwing him a birthday party. Suspecting it was more than that, and knowing exactly where it would take place, Mary "dressed to kill" and followed suit. Arriving at the restaurant, she found, as she knew she would, her husband, several male friends, and several female companions. Walking directly up to the woman she was sure her husband was having an affair with, Mary told her she could have him. The (other) woman protested that she was only trying the help the poor man because he was so depressed by his marriage. "Him upset by the marriage?" Mary responded. "It nearly cost me both my boobs." And, in the kind of triumph usually reserved for the end of movies like "The Graduate," she vanished into the night, her husband's best friends trailing behind with explanations.

For the next year Mary continued to rise in her corporation, taking exams that gave her special credentials, while her husband, her daughters, and even her parents took turns playing saboteur. One daughter became preanorexic and the other was picked up for drunken driving; her father developed mysterious coronary-like episodes (which her mother kept informing her of); and her passive husband began threatening to shoot her and her paramour. Mary was urged not to take any of this too seriously, but to employ her resource of the mischievous to stay in touch nonanxiously with all of them, thus modifying their behavior.

For example, Mary told her preanorexic daughter that there were other kinds of foods with less caloric content, and whenever possible took her daughter's dish away before she finished her diminishing portions. And she bought her husband the fanciest water pistol she could find. At the same time she went out of her way to inform each family member that, if they thought she had been thinking about them less recently, things would only get worse.

Eventually the members of her family recovered from whatever was ailing them and each began to pursue his or her own life's goals. About 6 months after these crises Mary permitted her husband to move back, defining clearly her own plans for the future, totally convinced that her family's survival depended on hers, not the other way about.

CONCLUSION

In the year 198 (going back in history by a factor of 10) the amount of information that existed in the world could be put on one shelf in your library. Today, 10 times that number of years later, the amount of information available is not 10 times greater, but a billionfold. Now suppose we go forward by a factor of 10 to the year 19,850. If the same methods of storing information are continued the total amount will outweigh the planet! Nor, can we safely say, will our species ever catch up. For even though the memory capacity of computers had doubled every 2 years since the first microchip was introduced, this merely accelerates the information expansion because every additional bit from the moment it is added immediately increases the frequency of cross-pollination from field to field.

Amidst such exponential circumstances, how can any therapist who bases his or her healing initiatives primarily on information ever feel adequate? Specialization? That merely changes the direction as one must struggle to keep up with knowing more and more about less and less. Some have chosen a way out of this dilemma by adopting a kind of therapeutic know-nothingism. Information is irrelevant—what counts, says the advocates of this view, is the therapist's art, his or her charisma, savvy, skill. But if successful therapy is to depend primarily on the personal qualities of the healer then how will we learn from one another?! Families, after all, are about generations, about what can be transmitted.

Another way out is to say that not all information is equally important, and to develop criteria for the selection of which information should be stored. With this approach one does not have to keep up with everything. From this perspective therapeutic effectiveness is based less on the quantity of information at hand than on the principles of selection. Information still remains important but it is put to the service of the therapist's own lead.

This essay has been an effort to supply such criteria of selection by asking what has worked for healing and survival in the human species since its origins, and no matter what its subculture.

REFERENCES

DesPres, T. *The survivor.* New York: Oxford University Press, 1979.

Farber, L. *The ways of the will.* New York: Basic Books, 1966.

Friedman, E. H. *Generation to generation: Family process in church and synagogue.* New York: Guilford Press, 1985.

Sachs, L. *Growth, differentiation, and the reversal of malignancy, Scientific American,* 1986; *254,* 1.

Thomas, L. *The lives of a cell.* New York: Viking Press, 1974.

CHAPTER 3

Family Strengths: Obstacles and Facilitators

Braulio Montalvo

Effective therapists seem to have no consistent framework for intervention when searching for ways to mobilize strengths in the family. They move from systems thinking to individual thinking and from individual thinking to systems thinking. They are open to the way in which the family reacts to them and they shift theoretical lenses as needed. Sometimes they see family members as related waves, sometimes as unrelated particles. In the same family they sometimes treat the identified patient as the victim of the family, sometimes the family as a victim of the patient. Sometimes they address the family as a unified camp and at other times as a set of subsystems. It is the fact of perceptual shifting, their deciding who and what will be foreground or background, that permits clinicians the freedom to search for family strengths.

Guiding their search, there seems to be one common notion among therapists of all ideologies—a keen sense of homeostasis as obstacle. But beyond the notion that if you create a change here it will be resisted by the people over there, most system considerations seem to be rather tidy cybernetics after the fact, not of much use in the therapist's untidy business. Untidiness may come in the shape of a unit with no handles, like a mother and father who see no problem, who can barely reflect on any imperfection in their family, while their teenage son has tried to self-destruct with some kind of drugs. Encapsulated in its dissatisfactions and its concealed festering fury, such a family can come across as a steel ball with no handle to grab hold of. A therapist may mumble to the mother that he feels like swordplay, or like doing karate, or that he has an odd urge to dance right now. Looking at the timing of such comments, we see that they punctuate a moment when the mother or father blanked out once more, denying again any pain or any thoughts pertaining to the obvious problems of their son. Whenever they stonewall or close down, the therapist takes off with "irrational" images depicting an interactionalizing of anger.

Braulio Montalvo, M.A. Family Institute of New Mexico; Department of Pediatrics, University of New Mexico, Albuquerque, New Mexico.

This therapist recognizes a rigidly closed system and is working to lance an abscess. He is acting like the antibiotic against tuberculosis. His confusing ramblings are solvents for destroying the capsule surrounding the microbe, hoping that the white blood cells can then rush to get that pneumococcus before it eliminates the whole organism. These interventions sometimes work like laser surgery, cutting underneath without immediately lacerating the tough outer shell. Implicit systems notions exist that elicit and guide these kinds of interventions. We need to know more of them in order to tap family strengths. Those notions generate the use of darting outrageous remarks, puzzling non sequiturs, and incisive aggressive wisecracking while not necessarily focusing the therapist on what brought the family in. They are an art form for loosening rigid defenses, compelling a kind of insidious family reorganization.

Another set of useful ideas is oriented around the asymmetries of certain relationship seesaws. Those ideas lead to parking or jumping on one side of a key coalition, consistently taking sides in a relationship until the system overheats and tilts, and something gives. There are other work-guiding analogues. Therapists differ on how they conceive the disrupting of the symptom and the underlying forces, as well as in their skills for integrating both levels. For a supervisor, the important consideration is to stay out of the way to permit the unfolding of such approaches while watching for immediate and long-range outcome. Therepists will try all kinds of moves to loosen things up, to create flexibility and a search for change where stereotyped adaptation prevails. After that they count on homeostasis as an ally and not as an obstacle. They count on homeostasis to set in to protect the change. It is easy to observe, however, that an approach to change that has evolved from, say, severe psychosomatic conditions is not easily adapted and transposed to working with encysted schizophrenic processes or vice versa—at least not with the same profit. There is something specific to syndromes, the family configurations sustaining them, and the range of therapeutic modes most likely to induce modification. All these are still waiting for precise observational study and research.

In the meantime, many therapists continue to rely on the best technical invention in family evaluation and therapy—compositional shifts. By seeing the family not just as a total system but as a set of interlocking subsystems (in different subgroups) you get "part-to-whole" understandings and new ways of working for change. We owe this concept to McGregor, Ritchie, and Serrano (1964), early anatomists of the family long before family therapy became a noisy messianic movement. Their way of seeing promotes a practical perspectivism—a concern with finding ways of reading the family through the fit or lack of fit of different viewpoints of the participants who belong to different coalitions. With McGregor *et. al.*'s lenses we assemble unaccustomed combinations and get a more dynamic, evolving entity than would be suggested by using only Claude Bernard's concept of homeostasis. The family does not adapt by returning to the exact state it was in before a perturbation, but, as Dubos and Escande (1979) remind us, the organism adapts, but often by changing. Families seen through compositional shifts teach us that useful adaptation is not merely homeostatic adaptation. To watch the flow of who sides with whom about what is to see the heart of family process and to discover its strengths.

The absence of this concept of compositional shift leads to the misutilization of the family approach and handicaps the search for family strengths. This can be seen in people abusing the concept of family dynamics. They do family evaluations that tell the court who is a better parent, who gets custody of the child, without meeting all parties and observing interactions between them. Legal and professional controls seem to be required because this has to do with dividing families and uniting families, and family diagnosis is not so highly developed, so theoretically and practically refined, as to be the last word in such decisions. People who honestly understand the power of compositional dynamics do not do evaluations that tell a judge who is going to get the child without even seeing the family in different subsystem arrangements. Yet the misusers of the family approach see the mother and father and get a report from them separately. They see maybe a child or two, here and there, and seldom see the total family. They do not actually see a child reacting to the father. Instead, they reveal the mother's thoughts about how the child reacts to the father, and then do a King Solomon report unrelated to actual family strengths.

There are many places in which to look for family strength. The concept shows up when seeing how families deal with adversity. It frequently appears when a youngster sees a member of the family coping in the midst of uncomfortable circumstances, personal loss, grief, economic hardship, illness, and other oppressive situations. The concept of family strength seems tied to behavior in the face of the inevitable as perceived by the youngster, who learns from it how to fashion a stance toward the world. In this sense the idea of family strength is involved with attitudes and images that become a special legacy for dealing with difficult situations. At other times the idea is used to depict a lingering sense of being part of a positive coalition, which is born in the family and later becomes a cornerstone of security for handling the demands of the environment.

This chapter leaves unexplored these rich areas and deals instead with ways in which therapists elicit strength by bringing out among family members certain emotions and sequences of conduct necessary for solving problems. Attention is paid here to strength as the ability to resist the organizing pull of the "weak" or incapacitated family member. It is the ability to take charge, sheltering and guiding a despairing member to interrupt self-destructive patterns. It is the skill to reform interpersonal boundaries among three generations without severing ties, or to display measured impatience at the spouse level in order to modify behavior jeopardizing health in the child. It is the use of cumulative indignation as a means of recalling a deviant member, awakening his/her sense of duty. It is the ability to block patterns of spellbinding that restrict important protective action. Finally, it is the ability to exercise the imagination and the possibilistic premise to satisfy unmet needs and arrest pathology.

These strengths are explored here through brief case examples, emphasizing ideas and attitudinal features in the therapist as technical mobilizers. They are the tools employed by the therapist attempting to elicit strengths. These include searching for available hidden strengths in the family using the anachronistic set; orienting parents to arrange conflict of principles in order to deter self-destructive action in a youngster; and fashioning tasks to establish unity between disconnected members and release new opportunities for intervention. We also see the building of impatience to unbalance relationships between spouses and to force revision of inadequate patterns of health care, as well as the shaping and amplification of the indignation response and the blending of extrafamilial and intrafamilial influences to make an irresistible demand for change. We examine the use of malice and of changes in the composition of the family unit to break cognitive spells between spouses that endanger the protection of the child. We examine as well the defining of the past, present, and future to establish fantasy exchange and sponsor new beginnings. The discussion concludes with comments on broader considerations that tend to act as obstacles or facilitators in the professional's efforts to mobilize or support family strengths.

CASE EXAMPLES: ELICITING STRENGTHS

Active Search for Family Strengths

The significance of the bias for family strength is well displayed in the work of Ken Covelman. An adolescent girl of about 17 becomes paralytic 7 weeks after her 18-year-old brother both wrecks a car and drops out of school. Of course he comes back home and sits there incapacitating himself, doing nothing socially. The mother has a history of depression, which started after her husband left her in what turned out to be a temporary separation. She was about to react to the son's failure to stay in school when she was intercepted by the daugther's dramatic symptom eruption. The husband, who of course had returned at some earlier point—perhaps pulled by his wife's depression—is very concerned for the daughter. He joins his wife, keeping her on top of the daughter's situation. These serial failures to leave home by two adolescents help pull the husband even further into the family but in such a way that he crystallizes into the system to reinforce his wife's role as a busy caretaker for the crippled daughter.

The girl's paralysis undergoes all kinds of clinical examinations. She is in a body cast for a while and, after more neurological workups it is determined that there is nothing wrong organically. The family then seeks therapeutic help. It's about 3 months into the girl's paralysis when they first meet the therapist. Covelman starts with a tentative assumption of family strength. He talks as if the family can survive without symptoms, and explores the limits of what the family can tolerate as it attempts a change. He firmly conveys to the mother, father, and daughter that these behaviors that make mother busy have definitely been helpful to her, but he wonders rhetorically, without expecting an answer, whether she still needs them. Covelman tries to utilize a barely detectable sense of being drained and exploited on the part of the mother. The children are grown, yet she cannot take off toward her new tasks, her second adolescence.

She cannot even pay attention to her returned husband if the kids cannot leave the nest. Since the husband's idea of helpfulness is to point out that he is able and willing to help his wife in dealing with the daughter, the issue becomes how to keep addressing the hidden capabilities in this family while circumventing their defenses.

This husband cannot be made to feel guilty for trying to help his wife without incurring a great deal of resistance. Covelman proceeds to congratulate the man on his ways of trying to help his wife. He exonerates him from any possible feeling of guilt, specifying that, indeed, his wife did need that kind of help at the beginning, but stressing again that perhaps that is no longer necessary. If anything, she needs now to be helped by being pulled away from the excessive demands of the daughter. Otherwise, the daughter will not make much effort to begin to move on her own. His wife now has to convince the daughter that she no longer needs her daughter's help in this way.

The girl becomes increasingly anxious, sensing that a dismantling of the defenses could be in the offing. The husband, in a decisive shift, begins to support his wife as she attempts to retreat from the daughter. The daughter gets upset but begins to consider the possibility of moving. In a matter of months she is in a walker and after that she restores herself to actual walking and moving around. For Covelman the organizing hunch here is the idea that the severe psychosomatic symptom, the paralysis, is an interprotective move, a rescue operation taking the mother away from possibly collapsing into another depression. She is having to face her son's failure on top of the previous separation from her husband. The symptomatic eruption in the girl simultaneously rescued and protected the mother and the brother, who was about to get some heat for his failure to leave home. It may have also satisified the daughter's intense competition with her sibling. He is a rival who now shows up with a dramatic, conspicuous failure that is about to take all attention away from her. A ready-made means of escape from her own individual difficulties in leaving and joining her peers had certainly been provided by the brother.

In this case the assumption of family strength is rendered effective by the therapist's aplomb in his use of the notion that the symptoms were helpful but anachronistic. He operates as if family strength is available but manifesting as resistance, instead of willingness to change. By offering the parents and daughter a kind of justification for whatever behaviors they were producing, he allows the family enough self-forgiveness to help it move in a different direction. Had the father felt he had contributed to making things worse, or the mother that she was an accomplice in the process of incapacitating her daughter and son, this family would have been entrenched in a nonchanging, guilt-defending position.

Conflict of Principles

A 13-year-old deaf mute was gesturing at stabbing himself repeatedly. In school, teachers picked up the signals and became alarmed because he finally stabbed himself in the hand with a sharp pencil. Within a week he also tried stabbing himself in the neck artery with real application of pressure. At home, the parents discovered him late one night as they went down to the kitchen, pushing at his stomach with a kitchen knife. When asked what was happening, he explained that he was lonely and that nobody liked him. He despaired in school. He was in a special school for the deaf. Somehow, he had been lost in the shuffle and was having enormous difficulties contacting other children or feeling liked by adults. For a year, he had been in that school struggling to find a place for himself in both the peer and the adult world without any success. He had complained to his mother, and she immediately went to the school. On two or three occasions, she went there imploring them for help. She was specific: she asked for counseling. She wanted some kind of systematic effort made to have her son meet some other youngsters. None of this was answered. In the family session, she is frustrated and defeated because she has not been able to move anyone to help her.

Behind the youngster's gestures we find a removal of key interpersonal props in his social context, all of them occurring in such a way that he becomes devastated. A year before the self-stabbing he began to get very lonely. The father had become involved with a new business, a bar, that had absorbed all of his time. He was seldom home, meeting with the family on weekends only. About that time the mother, too, had to go to work. The loss of this interpersonal security for the young man occurred precisely at the moment when he needs it most. He was floundering in the world of peers, and in his own job, doing schoolwork.

The therapist, Sam Scott, meets with the mother, the father, and this young man, in a family with no other siblings. In sign language, he begins by asking the son what he would most like in the world. The youngster signs back, "Great Adventure." Great Adventure is an amusement park, the desire of many adolescents, physically and metaphorically. Wanting "Great Adventure" means wanting a place where fun is continuous, an antidote to depression. After finding out from the boy that he did not like what was happening to him in school—he didn't like having no friends, he didn't like to be around there—Scott puts the parents in charge in an effort to mobilize them. They are to ask the youngster what he thinks will happen when he dies. Finding that the kid is honestly blanking out on them, Scott suggests to the parents that they tell the youngster what will happen after he dies. To further stimulate them and to orient them, Scott asks the youngster himself how many people will attend his funeral, who is going to be there, and so on.

Soon enough the parents get the gist of Scott's approach and begin to carry the task themselves. These are eager, concerned parents who want to help their son but need initial modeling and direction from the therapist. The father addresses the boy directly, explaining that he will have to buy a suit and new shoes. He goes into exquisite detail about how the boy's face will have to be made up. Through all this, the young man is reluctant but sincerely attentive. The mother continues right after the father and explains to the youngster what goes on in the funeral parlor. She talks to him about the casket and gives an elaborate description of how they take your blood out when you die. This is signed by pointing to her own arms, to her veins, to the blood emerging and going out into a receptacle. The youngster doesn't like that at all. He doesn't like it either when father explains that he will have to have a suit and, most terribly, a haircut.

In every respect, the parents demonstrate their deep knowledge of what will be against this adolescent's principles. They stretch the sequence, soberly presenting to the young man all the revolting details of what will take place after he dies. Going forward to the consequences of the destructive wish, but on a safe imaginal plane, they are draining from the wish some of its compulsion. In the meantime, Scott monitors their display of family strength, carefuly calibrating the response of the parents, watching for what needs less or more amplification. At some point, for instance, the father is about to smile, and Scott quickly conveys that this is nothing to laugh about. The parents return immediately to the appropriate affective wavelength. The atmospherics are fine tuned. The parents walk a thin line between mocking and honestly presenting the consequences of taking one's life. This control of the mood in the room makes the exchange authentic and enables the parents to reach their youngster.

It soon becomes possible for Scott to see that the young man is responding to more than a self-destructive urge from within because life is no fun. The young man is responding as well to the immediate interpersonal situation of his mother. She has lost security through the husband's absence and her inability to shake the school. By threatening to kill himself, he was providing his mother with clear and strong ammunition to recall her husband and to handle the unbudging personnel in the school. She can now jolt the school into action in a way that she previously could not.

The uncamouflaged basic strengths in the family that permitted the therapist to be of help are seen when Scott asks the young man, "Why didn't you do it?" The youngster answers that his parents "didn't want me to." There was enough in the family for Scott to work on. Building on that foundation of caring, he could get the parents to shelter the son by creating for him a productive conflict of principles. The session ends with the father telling Scott, "I will put on my spurs," conveying that he is ready to fight the school and demand that more be done for his son. The father firmly says to the youngster, "You are going back to school." The youngster signs back painfully, "But I have no friends there." And the father answers, "I don't want you near those guys. You stay away from them." The boy had already been home for weeks brooding on his own strangeness, on how deviant he had become. He was out of the mainstream. The father pushes him back into the mainstream, and the father's stern communication turns out to be effective perhaps because it conveys, "I would even punish you if you let yourself be hurt by those rejecting youngsters around you." These parents stand by the youngster as he returns to school. It is a dangerous period, with everyone wondering whether it is premature. The father steps in and pushes the school around, insisting that more be done for the youngster, supporting his wife's earlier pursuit.

Three years later this isolated boy has some relationships, not only to peers, but to a skill. He has become very involved with computers and looks happier than ever.

Reforming Boundaries

Andy Fussner's work illustrates well how releasing certain strengths among a few participants can bring new possibilities for improving overall relationships in the family. The new possibilities often offer a new perspective on the symptom and make for a fuller understanding of the forces that go to work in shaping and sustaining it. A young girl of about 11 has been vomiting on and off for weeks. Her mother intervenes, trying to help her, but at some point the repetitious vomiting and the girl's severe but seemingly groundless fears, mainly that she will not grow up, that she might die, begin to exasperate the mother. After one particular vomiting episode, the mother becomes punitive and pushes the girl's face in the vomit. By the time they bring the girl to psychotherapy, the mother really feels that she's losing control.

The father is a concerned person, a Vietnam veteran who lost his first wife to a severe illness. His daughter was then about 4, and he moved her to his parents' home. They became his support in caring for the girl. Some years later, he met his current wife, the new mother for his daughter. Fussner learns that this new mother has frequent headaches and sometimes is incapacitated for 2 or 3 days at a time. This all rings too familiar to the girl, who had lived through similar episodes shortly before her mother's death. Fussner also observes that the mother is feeling very upset upon seeing how distressed and explosive the father becomes toward the girl's symptom. He notices a chain of stress: the girl vomits; the father gets furious; the mother feels intimidated instead of supported in her efforts to help the girl, and becomes even more punitive and ineffectual.

Concerned over the urgent fear of death in the girl and the mother's acute helplessness with both the girl and her husband, Fussner concocts a task. He requests that the mother take the girl into her lap every night to tell her stories. The stories are to be fashioned in such a way that the girl will delight in how, when she's big, she will have her own children to whom she will tell stories, making them happy. The mother is to describe in detail and with pleasure what it means to be a grown-up woman. She needs to impress upon the girl how she will enjoy taking care of her own children. The father is to be sure the TV is off and that they have calm privacy. The creative task works. The girl begins to look forward to these peaceful moments of closeness and soft nurturance from this woman who used to pursue her in anger over the vomiting. The father has no trouble becoming supportive of the mother during her time with the girl. He used to be worried about his daughter and wife—their relationship and their respective symptoms—to the point that it was affecting his work. He now feels relieved.

It is quite clear that the task is not just counteracting the fear of death, the fear of growing up in the girl, but is doing so by breaking a chain of stress between three people. The girl now visualizes for herself the possibility of reaching a stage that up to now she thought impossible. We have a bonus of unexpected developments. Because the girl can now trust and talk to her mother, she can reveal herself to her. In her mother's lap she explains one day that when she goes to grandma and grandpa they tell her, "She's not your Mommy and she will never be." With this discovery the mother moves to her husband, discusses the issue, and they decide together to close the boundaries between them and the grandparents. Had Fussner not intervened to modulate the establishing of the new boundaries, they would have been drawn too completely, closing the door totally on the grandmother and grandfather. This would have been very unfortunate for everyone, particularly for the girl, who looked to them as strong substitute parents. It would have been difficult for the husband, who would have had to turn against his own parents after they so supported him during his tragedy. All this was avoided because Fussner modulated the couple's anger, facilitating an atmosphere of forgiveness and reconciliation. This fostered unity between the three generations as a strength worth preserving.

The resolution of the girl's symptoms could have been achieved by simply having her new mother display strength as nurturer, providing special closeness and security while interacting around the stories. The change would have crystallized just through the father's becoming less furious, replacing tension with his obvious capacity for pleasure in seeing the closeness now developing between his wife and daughter. That alone would have changed a fundamental stress-inducing sequence in this family. But the change goes beyond that because a totally new perspective on the case is suggested by the revelations from the girl. They bring to the fore the importance of the current relationship between her grandparents and her mother and father. They teach that the symptom is not only or even mainly due to the loss of the first mother and the fear of loss of the new mother. The symptom is more than a recapitulation of loss. It obeys, as well, the contemporary distress the girl feels in trying to get close to this second mother while being pulled back by her loving grandparents. New work possibilities on the three-generational issue of family unity come forward only when the girl feels nurtured enough and close enough to mother. She can then dare to depart from her coalition with the grandparents and reveal the powerful divisive directives she's been receiving.

Impatience for Imbalance

A case of Karlotta Bartholomew's reveals how the family may need to unleash special emotions as strengths in order to arrest certain pathological developments. A severely diabetic youngster was not yielding to his medical regimen. It had been determined by the physicians that the youngster did not have the discipline to carry on his own routines of self-medication and that his loving family could not support him in the necessary self-care so important in dealing with his disease. The father had enormous difficulties displaying any kind of aggression. He could not request anything, not only from the son, but especially from his wife. He had allowed his wife to be captured by the idea that, since her son was so sick, she was totally licensed to be even more indulgent than she ordinarily was. The end result was a youngster who could violate all the tenets of self-care, neglecting his injections and his nutritional mandates. He was producing and mismanaging crisis after crisis. Sporadic pleadings from the mother to the son would evaporate the moment the youngster cried or displayed any sort of discomfort over taking control of his insulin.

Bartholomew chose an unbalancing strategy by steadily parking herself very deliberately on the side of the father (Minuchin, Rosman, & Baker, 1978). She pushes the father to question what the wife is doing. A stressful set of motivational and preparatory steps leads the father up to this questioning. Bartholomew stubbornly urges him to become impatient and intolerant, to see his wife as someone who lets the boy "get away with it," who cannot push the son, who could perhaps let the youngster die. Can he be intense enough to help his wife not to be so indulgent as to jeopardize the life of their son?

Observing the apparent one-sidedness of this stage, one wonders how Bartholomew can move herself into the stance of unfair provocateur without being kicked out. The reason is that the auspices of the intervention are clear. She can incite the husband into being aggressively demanding of his wife because earlier on she connected with the mother's desperate search for extraordinary measures to help her son. She thus earns the wife's consent to begin moving the husband against her. By the time the more pushy and extreme procedures are in motion, the husband obligingly gets furious at the wife any time she indulges or forgives the youngster's delinquencies over his health. And the wife doesn't defend himself from Bartholomew's prodding the husband because she senses the urgency of the endeavor as a necessary response to her emergency situation.

In this system the change in the youngster comes by provoking and releasing aggressive strength in the executive system. It is based on the building of impatience between the husband and wife. The risks are clear. Unleashing that strength could produce a scared wife, perhaps a wife ready to leave her husband. It could also result in having her join even more indulgently with her son. Yet, it seemed that only if the therapist could summon her own aggressiveness in pushing the husband could he be sufficiently tenacious and demanding of his wife. The husband had to find strength to face the risk of losing his wife if she fought off his demands. The wife had to feel that it was out of honest concern for her youngster, rather than as a subordinated response to the husband's demands, that she stopped indulging her son. These risks surface only as the therapist builds intolerance toward behaviors that had been patiently accepted as customary, even though they were taking a toll on the child's health. It was clear to Bartholomew that the family's ability to put up with such things, their patience, could be a strength later. It would be necessary after a change was achieved. The youngster would attempt to take over his body and fail. Then the parents would have to patiently hold fast, allowing for errors without relaxing standards.

Indignation Plus

An example of a clinician drawing out family strengths can be seen in the work of Paul Riley as he deals with a man who has been making a living by pushing and using drugs. Observing the third session, one sees this man seated fairly close to Riley while across from them is the wife with a young child in her arms. Next to her are her parents. Through gesture and other nuances Riley is monitoring the interaction of the addict and his family. Whenever the addict is eager to say something, he glances at Riley, who states quite soberly that he is to remain quiet. "You will now listen to her."

Then, turning to the young wife, Riley asks, "How many times have you waited until midnight with your baby for your husband to arrive? How many times?" The woman hesitates, painfully bringing out that 2 or 3 nights a week she waits and waits. She adds that it's difficult to do that waiting while also feeding her child. Riley goes on, "How often does he go beyond 11:00?" The woman explains again that it also happens on Saturdays and Sundays. It is frequently past 11:00. Riley elongates every response from this woman, carefully exploring her worries, her need to be heard, and her fears. He wants to bring out all her specific concerns for her safety, for her child, for the addict's safety, for his showing up in time to see the baby before she puts him to sleep, and so forth.

The addict wants to say something, but again Riley sternly says, "Now you will listen." He turns to the man's father-in-law: "How many times have you been worried that he has been killed on the street or picked up by the cops?" The father-in-law pours out a litany of worries, of endless fears and shame. Riley is relentless. "How many times have you gone out to look for him even when you were falling asleep?" The father-in-law tells how many times. The addict, of course, now wants to speak even more, but Riley stares him down: "You will listen to him."

Riley's interventions are magnifying effective feedback from those in the family suffering the harsh consequences of the addict's behavior. Almost no room is left for explanation from the addict. Quite clearly Riley sits on him. It is obvious that he knows something about this kind of family. He is ready for the rapid deployment of rationalizations and excuses that the addict can expertly produce. He is working from the premise that the confrontational strength of the family can emerge only if he organizes and controls the situation to ensure that the addict hears and sees in a different way the impact of his conduct on others. In the past, the addict has been successfully avoiding, evading, conning his way out of every demand in his dire reality. After each family member has discharged a list of complaints, fears, worries, then and only then Riley turns to the man, who appears shaken by all this.

Riley seems to work on the assumption that this man's skin is thick, and that the intensity of the family's indignation is still insufficient to elicit productive guilt and a sense of interpersonal duty. Just when the observer feels the gloomy feedback may be too much, Riley adds the last straw. He asks the addict, "What about that attempt to push you out of that corner? What about the threat on your life if you keep selling from where you're selling?" From there on, the addicted man is allowed to bring out the dangers he faces as he tries to sell drugs in a territory that has now been staked out by other competing interests. The timing of the question links the previous complaints from the family members to this new external pressure. By artfully mobilizing the inside pain of the family members and the outside forces of the black Mafia in the neighborhood, the therapist gets the man to see and feel that his family is about to drop him as the world of drugs is about to kill him. The dangers he is facing as a pusher on the streetcorner plus the danger he is facing in exhausting the indulgence of his wife and in-laws stop being separate and discrete domains. They are now one strong, total necessity, a compelling reality calling on him to abandon his way of living.

The technical mobilization of strength in this family was based on the skill of the therapist in helping the family to articulate and escalate its indignation with sufficient intensity. This meant coordinating the family to complain in a new, nonsuperficial way, and in an insistent, prolonged fashion. They were helped to go beyond displeasure and to show their strong wishes to protect themselves and to protect the addict from the consequences of his addiction. Crucial to the therapist's strategy was his ability to engineer the display of mood and complaints, and to perceive a potential liability as an asset. The black Mafia threatening to take this man's place in the community was seen as an advantage that could be employed to further intensify the demands on this man to reconsider his life. Certainly, the family had tried before on its own to use its injured dignity to pull back and shape up their deviant member. But it took the orchestration and amplification of the therapist, blending two forces into one, to bring about significant change.

Breaking the Spell

Among the most intriguing ways therapists elicit strength from family members are those in which the therapist must play on the architecture of time and thought. In 1972 one such moment was documented in a videotape, "The Construction of a Workable Reality" (see Montalvo, 1973). In it, Ron Liebman was at work "discovering" a problem that was blocking family strength. The "problem" was an elaborate interpersonal product whose construction required the induction of instrumental amnesias not only in the family participants but in himself.

That phenomenon is often at work in the shaping of dangerous situations, as in a case Barbara Bryant handled recently with a father who abused his daughter sexually. The daughter was a very young child with a young mother. Much work went into getting this young mother to appreciate the magnitude of the abusive act. This was extremely important for Bryant because the mother was not at all alert to the father's contact with the child. A young preschooler, the child had to sit in the father's lap, approach him, touch him, caress him. When he was watching TV, she would come into bed with him and so forth. There was a whole array of such "innocent" situations about which Bryant wanted the mother's eyes and ears to sharpen. She worked on getting the father to make some kind of admission or acknowledgment that he has indeed done things to the little girl. She wanted the wife to become more protective, more alert. She wanted the wife to focus not only on her child but on her husband and his limitations. The man admitted in the session, in front of Bryant and his wife, that he does such things. His wife now knows the man is capable of feeling tempted when the little girl is around, sitting in his bed, taking a bath, or whatever.

The therapist, as in many situations like this, realizes she cannot rely simply on intrafamilial forces. She cannot relax her vigilance one iota. So she shifts the composition of the unit seen. In an individual session with the wife, Bryant seizes the opportunity to explore further the woman's puzzled look. She draws out the information that at home the husband makes statements like, "You don't really know if that happened, you know," and the wife becomes honestly confused. Coming out of such exchanges the wife gets a blurred perception of her own thoughts. She is no longer sure what she thinks about her husband. In the session, the husband can openly acknowledge a behavior with the wife right there—but he does so fully confident that by working on her before and after sessions he can twist her perceptions. He is confident of his command of her cognitive processes. He knows he can erase, or at least create severe doubt about, his involvement with the child, even after his admissions in front of her. The "instructions" to the cooperative wife outside the sessions have been, "What I say there, in front of those people, really doesn't count." The husband and wife both play upon time and context in such a way as to make it less likely that the wife will become vigilant and protective toward the young child. They have prepared a scenario for the wife's conduct in which *he* has control. His acknowledgement of deviant behavior is then treated by the wife as if it were false, maybe made only for the sake of the therapist. Or maybe it did not happen at all.

This is the essence of what must be taken into account when dealing with situations shaping special dangers—the situations of battered women who get battered again, abused children who get abused again, and so forth. In the past, the field of mental health has dealt with this by simply declaring that the wife is displaying denial, which understates the elaborate interpersonal process at work. It is the time-honored process of subordination and control, of cultivating a special vulnerability to an induction, that permits a participant, in this case the wife, to recode certain information on cue. The instructions to recode can be pre- or postevent.

Many cases of repeated abuse in which we wonder how another person managed to be there have been explained through the simple business of "being an accomplice." But more is involved than just being an accomplice. Selective utilization of denial under the strength of instructions from somebody else is also involved. The "somebody else" is usually a powerful figure to whom the person is already tied. This interpersonal situation is really like the crash of Flight 90 (Trivers & Newton, 1982). The copilot sees ice on the wings of the plane before takeoff, but he is dazzled by the confidence and risk-taking behavior of this pilot, who is hierarchically slightly above him and on whom he depends. His attention is so ruled by the pilot that he does not stop him. There is no hiding the fact that the pilot commands the attention of the copilot because of the copilot's need for approval, but there is also something beckoning about the display made by the pilot—the risk-taking behavior, the aplomb, the self-reliance that he exudes—that makes the relationship danger-prone because it influences the copilot to abandon his own strength, his judgment.

To break such a reciprocal spell, the therapist must have individual sessions with both parties separately before putting them together. Then he/she must work with them together also. The woman in this example was becoming progressively less alert, dismissing her own thoughts. She continued to allow her husband to abuse their little girl again. Obviously, her complicity was not a simple personality act, but the result, at the very least, of a gruesome-twosome arrangement in which she would lose her independent strength. And the therapist might have joined in and made it a fearsome-threesome had she not been the alert, sharp person that she is. Such amnesiac effects are organized to shift not just the wife's, but the *therapist's* reading of reality, permitting the husband to prevail. Power seeking is at the bottom of this, as is the search for counterfeit love. In order to restore the strength of the participants in the family to break the spell, therapists must have a good share of malice and forethought, particularly malice. It is extremely important to be skeptical and awake to the manipulations between spouses, their implicit directives as to how to react to certain behaviors in certain contexts. Whatever is said in the session is being coded, or decoded and recoded, to meet the requirements of larger, more fundamental dramas in which the participants play. In this case, the mother's active effort to protect her daughter was a family strength that could only be released by recognizing and challenging such spellbinding.

The Possibilistic Premise

In family work it is important for supervisors to support the therapist's attempts to help the family find and use its own arrested capabilities. A practical way of doing this is to provide a live supervision where the supervisor is cryptic, and does not barge in or call a lot to confuse the therapist (Montalvo, 1973). This format permits the therapist to be inventive and allows him/her to recover from mistakes. At its best, it helps to prevent them. This supervision allows itself to disturb phenomena, but modulates the degree of dislocation and anxiety that ensue as relationships are reorganized. It aims at helping the therapist orient the family to new possibilities and fresh beginnings.

A brief example can be given from a transformation ceremony used by Peter Urquhart 15 years ago. A harassed mother says that her delinquent 13-year-old is a liar and cannot be trusted. Urquhart simply asks the youngster, in front of his mother, very gently, whether he is telling the truth *now* about wanting to do something [fishing with the mother's boyfriend]. The youngster mutters, "Yes," and Urquhart remarks softly, "That is good enough for me; I'll take your word for that." He becomes a kind of character witness for the child, implying he can be allowed a new start, maybe a new identity. The mother–son relationship is mildly dislocated. The mother immediately responds to Urquhart, telling him how "bad" the kid has been in the past, insinuating that Urquhart is being conned. Urquhart listens very respectfully and says, "Well, he is saying *now* that he wants to try things . . . and I want to believe him."

Urquhart's entry is the clear, steady way he says "now," providing a special way of defining the past, present, and future. He is aware of what the mother brings, but he declares that to be information "over the dam," attending instead to the person's new efforts. The youngster gets a fresh chance in front of the mother, and the mother's attempts to put him and the therapist back in place, the automatic, homeostatic correction that we always see in families, becomes an opportunity. Urquhart adds, "We'd rather do this because I don't know, after all, what he is feeling." What Urquhart means is "I have no x-rays, I would rather start by not judging. Allow me *not* to go with how he is defined by you."

Think of an agitated, overintrusive, clairvoyant, but benevolent type of mother, and you see how this elementary request works to shift her. Later, Urquhart asks the youngster to tell his mother what he wants. The boy almost inaudibly says, "a room." He has no room psychologically and physically. He has been doubling up with his sister in cramped quarters and has not dared to ask, protecting his mother from looking bad. The mother is very poor, and realistically it is hard for her to deliver. She looks scared and unable to display her strength. Urquhart calms her: "Look, he is saying 'Is it possible?'!" The tone is reassuring, and the thought implies that man doesn't live by bread alone, but by possibilities as well. Urquhart actually relieves her. The mother goes on to entertain the possibility that she could give a room to this youngster. As Urquhart moves them to a brief talk with each other, the youngster says, "I could hang some posters up," revealing how much that room has meant to him. For a long time the room has existed in his head. Before the mother can get off this track and back to the reality of their situation—"You know I live in the projects"—Urquhart has her stay in there long enough to spark her imagination. She playfully joins her son in decorating the fantasy room ("No single bed? No twin bed? . . ."). Brief as the moment is, she emerges as a giver of considerable resources, while the kid receives a room that is yet to be.

This happened to a boy who wasn't sure that he could competently extract necessary things from his mother, and didn't want to expose her presumably limited supplies. Later on, Urquhart enriched his intervention by becoming a hard-nosed advocate. He shook the housing authority and assisted with other important reality-based errands. That family lived for 6 months or so without a real room for the boy until the housing authority came through, but the youngster had already begun to abandon his compensatory delinquent behavior.

Any therapist in this situation could have become only an errand runner instead of sponsoring the imaginary for the real. The temptation was to assist directly and immediately with this woman's urgent "no room to give" reality instead of working for a magical exchange between her and her son to decorate that imaginary room. Well-timed live supervision made the difference. The supervisor, Jerry Ford, sensed that something vital was about to happen and spoke to Urquhart the moment the mother began to say, "You know I live in the projects." Ford simply said to Urquhart "Please do not become an expert in the housing authority at this moment." This kept the therapist on course as the family found its own strength.

OBSTACLES

This section leaves the specific case anecdote and comments on obstacles to the development of strength mobilization. Obstacles are usually found in the way the family is organized and the mechanisms it characteristically uses when dealing with problems. But obstacles can be found as well among the background considerations and general notions orienting the work of the helping therapists. Without attempting to be comprehensive, a few of the notions are presented here. These include: reliance on spirals; ideological constraints on the therapist's use of blame when relating to the marital skew; reliance on ethnicity as a central factor; the gift of self-view; the notion of the indispensable three generations; the fascination with metaphor; and the overestimation of family strength based on *under*estimation of the family's link to surrounding resources.

Reliance on Spirals

One way in which systems thinking becomes an obstacle to the discovery of family strengths is by inducing false confidence. For instance, a beginning therapist can become overconcerned with kicking off and then relying on a positive spiral. A positive spiral develops when you facilitate a situation in which someone who has been on a collision course toward a spouse, or someone else, shift gears and becomes friendly. They tend to get a friendly contribution from the other side, and you hope that the trading of positives will continue for a while, presumably by itself. Unfortunately, that kind of relying on the momentum of an interpersonal cycle to bail people out seldom works by itself. In real life you need responsibility, commitment, vigilance, and monitoring of exchanges. You cannot be comfortable and spontaneous with a positive exchange for long periods. A positive spiral should not be trusted. To the extent possible, the participants must awaken to exercise choice, to monitor and steer the spiral. This applies even when people must choose not to steer because when they attempt to steer, the spiral instead steers them.

Systems thinking is a temporary and incomplete intellectual prop. It can underestimate the importance of the person as a locus of action choice, as more than a participant in complementarity patterns or the beginning or end of feedback loops. It also threatens to become a facile and abstract determinism that overestimates what you can actually do by disrupting or enhancing the current maintenance of the symptom, the contemporary forces holding behavior in place.

Ideological Marital Skew

A feminist ideology need not present an inevitable problem to the therapist unless he/she finds no way of utilizing this creatively and with a sense of balance. Then you have a handcuffed therapist unable to hold accountable a woman who may well be overinvolved with her children while her husband rests easy in a peripheral position. The therapist may be more concerned with blaming the man who flees from his wife or acts uninvolved with the children than with shaking the woman to shake the man who allows her to become depleted, exhausted, and exploited in dealing with the children strictly by herself. Similarly, that therapist may not feel free to attack the man for letting the woman rob him of all opportunities to deal with the youngsters. To help the woman "take on" the man you may need to use both interventions flexibly.

Most unable to release and encourage family strengths are the "born-again" feminists who now attack only the woman, instead of the man, for allowing herself to operate as if the man is crippled and cannot be engaged in caretaking duties. Born-again feminists' therapeutic flexibility is limited by their fear of being seen as sexist in the interaction. This scenario merely represents one instance of the danger that strong ideological positions may limit the therapist's flexibility in treatment.

Ethnic Factor

The ethnic factor, too, can be employed as an obstacle to the mobilization of strength in families. During the last 30 years a variety of therapists have managed to be helpful to people and families from different ethnic groups without having to become experts in the ethnic background of the participants. Pending the arrival of evidence to the contrary, We take the position that the discovery of my Puerto Rican–ness, or my Italian–ness, either as therapist or family member, doesn't necessarily help much with being effective in drawing upon family strengths. It may be of some indirect or associated value—in increasing self-esteem—but it is not central to the therapy. Like the supercompetent Samurai image of the therapist—which should not be bought unless we also allow him/her to be Inspector Clouseau as well—the feel for ethnic considerations is only one more aspect of a multifaceted process.

By and large, it seems to be the therapist's skill in touching the nonethnic, universal aspects of the family that allows him/her to act as a catalyst for family strengths. The ethnic factor offers no royal road to family strengths. The ethnic factor is secondary to how to do therapy, how to become collaborative with the family and make sense to them. Beyond knowledge of how members deal with each other, what therapists find useful to know is something about the pattern of institutional utilization the family has. They watch how family members deal with each other, then with school, employment, health resources, and the like. That's all. That knowledge is best obtained by observing carefully and, most importantly, by letting the family teach you. The knowledge obtained by specialized study of ethnic backgrounds of the participants does not seem to be the same. Beyond openness and respect for the family's background, nothing else seems necessary.

The Gift of Self

A curse now loose in the land is the view of the therapist's "self" as indispensable to the explanation of change. This notion indeed has some value, but *not* when it assumes that all the issues of differentiating intrafamilial processes or recognizing problematic families are insignificant by comparison. That leads to grandiose claims that the gift of self can be used to repair everything, and that the family only looks this or that way mainly because of the therapist's doing. We could, as well, be impressed by how families homogenize therapists, making different therapists look the same. The issue is still how we can help families draw on their strengths and weaknesses to get over their problems. Well-designed observations and research on how to do that are still needed. To learn about family strengths the field may have to move again to differentiating processes in families that lead to certain behaviors, that maintain them, that eliminate or reduce them. The emphasis has to move back to *families* and away from therapists, although therapists can be important catalysts in the process of eliciting or inhibiting family strengths.

Three Generations

An unhelpful idea gaining currency in family work is that three generations are always involved, *and* needed, in order to unleash enough family strength to make or solve a problem. Yet complex problems continue to be resolved by therapists who do not bring in the whole family. They do not share the assumption of extraordinarily permeable boundaries between generations. They work well by having each parent handle his/her own family of origin, keeping that primary unit (the second generation) primary, and only sporadically using the whole family if necessary. The evidence is that families solving problems in a three-generational mold were very rare in the beginnings of this country. The elderly didn't live that long. What we had more of were lateral social networks. Hareven (1982) reminds us that the family always had boarders, a man that worked the fields or the stables, a blacksmith, or a miner, somebody who was staying in the family without being part of the central group. Boarders were entangled in family problems more than were grandparents. The three-generational Waltons constitute a myth, a recent development, perhaps preparing us to deal with the army of the elderly who now constitute almost half of the population.

The Needed Symptom

Another notion preventing us from finding and building strength is that the symptom will be there as long as the family needs it. This idea is often thrown around by honest therapists who have done their best at trying to shift a system and a symptom and couldn't get either to budge. It can be an accurate observation. The symptom hangs in there as long as the family needs it, waiting for some changes in other parts of the system. As soon as those are completed, the symptom is shed. More generally, however, when it is said that the symptom will be there as long as they need it, you could also be talking of a therapist so deluded into working on "deep" levels that he/she is becoming indifferent to helping the family get over what ails it.

Metaphor

Another popular impediment to the discovery of strength in family members is the notion that the therapist's use of metaphor is a sufficient condition for change. Yet people can joust, can power struggle through metaphors in a metaphoric manner, and still keep the situation the same. Too much emphasis can be placed on the development of metaphors. This is a powerful and fundamental idea, but it does not account for therapy. The metaphor is a communicational bridge, and the therapy may or may not happen through that bridge even after it is clearly and creatively established. The bridges are simply a way of mediating messages—and no more.

Consider the proverbial story of the youngster who is in a constant, powerful, hostile, defiant relationship with his father, who is a heart surgeon. The clinician tries to arrange an encounter that he/she hopes will find common ground between them. He/she gets the father in as friendly a mood as possible and brings him over for a session in which the boy works on his car. The boy likes to tinker around with the engine, but he has never met his father's expectations. While the son is working on the engine, trying to make it work, the clinician subtly notes, "He, too, likes to work with what makes things tick, makes things go." The father looks down and curtly says, "Yeah, I would like to see him do that when the motor is running." The putting down of the son and the sense of, "You can never be as good as me," prevails. The father is in metaphor and the son perhaps too, and so maybe is the clinician. But they come out on the other side pretty much exactly as they went in.

Neglect of Psychosocial Aspects

A sociopolitical context that tends to overestimate what the family can do by relying on its own strength is now being created in a retreat from more than 40 years of overwhelming findings associating mental health problems and poverty. The obvious fact that mental health problems also occur among the economically advantaged—and that children from impoverished homes in certain samples do manage to eventually escape poverty after 35 years—is now used to dismiss the enormity of that association. The tendency is to act as if poverty is for everyone merely a set of temporary rough spots providing at most an exacerbating factor. In this way the influence of psychosocial circumstances depleting and undermining family strength are pushed into the background, highlighting again personality features and organic dimensions. A gross social Darwinism is exposed here, endorsing numbness toward family suffering and at times even the romantic belief that poverty, if anything, strengthens and ennobles the most deserving families. According to this argument, those families that cannot endure the demoralizing effects of entrapment in chronic poverty are just the natural and inevitable losses of a basically sound social order.

The aggressive neglect of psychosocial variables creating or worsening illness and the accompanying professional flight into organicity and personality produces more unnecessary institutionalization, and its equally irresponsible twin, the denial of necessary institutionalization. Philadelphia, for example, like other big cities, closed its big general psychiatric hospital. The ostensible argument was that it was just warehousing people. The job could be better done, while saving lots of money, by the private sector's outpatient services and their arsenal of modern medications. To encourage a propitious atmosphere for these developments, outpatient services were paid significantly more than inpatient services. But the private sector did not exactly rush to the rescue. Professor Max Silverstein estimates that 75% of the numerous street people in that city are disabled and destitute ex-patients, now roaming the town abused and neglected. The serious psychosocial work of prospecting for strengths, of finding and assembling whatever remnants of a debilitated family existed around these people, and the job of creating artificial families when necessary, has not been done. Emergency room and board and medication as solutions may have prevailed. Now the cry is back: make another hospital. The possibility of creating halfway houses, small group homes, semi-closed wards, and other more community-based institutions, founded on an appreciation of family strengths, is not even heard. That easily happens when psychosocial and familial dimensions become secondary.

To make the support of family strength a primary issue it seems important to also resist the thought in the current sociopolitical context that a generation of men and women may have to be sacrificed to structural unemployment. It seems important to resist the idea that the disruption in the vulnerable family's interior—the child abuse, the spouse abuse, the worsened marital split, the violence, the depression, the alcohol and drug use—is necessary social entropy to be handled as it arises, by developing shelters and using more psychiatrists, psychologists, and social workers who will employ delayed and exotic repairs, such as family therapy.

Family therapy as one way of dealing with psychosocial problems is an inward-looking idea. It overemphasizes what family members do to one another and obscures what's done to them by their social and economic environment. To deal with family strength, the therapist must develop formal understandings, and preventive use, of interinstitutional processes, of how what happens in the job or in the school spills over into the mood and welfare of the family. The model of the bounded family, without windows to the socioeconomic context, should no longer exist. As Dick Auerswald said 20 years ago (personal communication) "It really never did with the poor." The point, however, is that the model could exist. Families need not be conscious of windows unless they feel vulnerable to dangerous drafts coming through them. The tools to control those drafts are available. Striner's (1976) plan for manpower training programs appears capable of realistically eliminating unemployment as a fundamental stressor of families once and for all.

FACILITATORS

Integrating Approaches

The most promising work in the use of the family approach is that which facilitates the development and growth of strength in families. There is more exploratory integration of what were once separate and discrete approaches. There is very good work employing learning and behavior principles within a family framework. Everything that was learned for the control of phobias and anxiety states and psychophysiological problems is being combined with understanding of sequences in the family that promote or deter certain behavior. Other promising combinations blend hypnosis, a fairly well-developed tradition, with family interviewing, which is a more recently developed tradition (Covelman, Scott, & Buchanan, 1983; Haley, 1973; Ritterman, 1983). Therapists making these blends are not encumbered by the immobilizing view of the family as an awesome sea of simultaneous transferences of equal and delicate intensity. They are at ease deciding the extent to which the participants are to become background or foreground in different subsystems. They are more effectively organized around the practical in the management of conflict resolution, mostly through forms of mediation and negotiation techniques. They are centered on how to equip participants to deal with each other in such a way that they settle their differences instead of avoiding them.

Since attempts to modify another's personality still tend to twist easily into attempts to fully control that other's personality, this focus on resolving differences can be expected to remain perennially complex. Between people as well as between nations, this most human "controlling" tendency, like original sin, drains strength and foments trouble. Therapists have moved to looking anew at how to get participants to somehow collaborate, dealing with the situational and mood dimensions that must be changed, the opinions and beliefs about the other that must be modified. More therapists have become realistic, going for installing a plain *modus vivendi* between participants rather than aiming for self-actualization and self-growth in each and every one of the family members. One feature seems common to all new promising developments. Sacrifice and compromise are being rediscovered as here to stay and *not* always as the makers of pathology, or as insults to the self.

Observing and Recording

Among the most significant developments facilitating the discovery of family strengths is a renewed interest in the most ignored contribution of family therapy—the tradition of observability and recording. By insisting that the behavior of the therapist and of the family stays watchable and can be video-taped, a manner of documenting cases has become available that may allow for a variety of process and outcome studies in the future. This means holding fast until the tradition of observability and recording starts to be used as a sensible tool for examining procedure and for ensuring that we know what we are doing and improve the next time. One long-range promise of interactional process observation lies in the possibility that, by studying people at war, whether a husband and a wife, parents and youngsters, or representatives from two different countries, we may learn more about the strengths involved in negotiating differences during power realignment. We may learn how power sectors unbalance and rebalance themselves with no severe or dangerous dislocation. We may learn more of the context and process of negotiation, of confidence building, confidence undermining, and confidence rebuilding. Studying the context of violent exchange alone has not led us to understand how people induce cooperation.

The tradition of observability and recording confirms already that not all family members can be lastingly helped just by learning meditation and stress decompression techniques. Not everyone can be helped by revising central mechanisms, implicit cognitive processes, and philosophic outlooks—just because those guide behavior. Individuals can learn how to mitigate their anxiety, but still keep intact the larger patterns of getting themselves into impossible unbeneficial situations—and not just in the family. A significant issue being revealed by observing and recording is that relationships between the boundaries of the inner world and the outer world call for different techniques, which must supplement and complement each other. As long as people remain able to engineer themselves into stressful broader circumstances, their being technically skillful in the management of their own anxiety will not be optimally helpful. Their margin of freedom of choice for action is restricted by the external circumstances, the systems they are in or get into, and how these systems are managed by the persons.

The family remains one of the most significant systems converging on the person. It is a system still in need of a professional field that can think more about basic documentation and less about junior metaphysics. It needs antidotes against the recycling superstition that anything goes, everything may be helpful, scientific proof doesn't matter, and facts do not exist except as sociocultural and history-bound interpretations. Observing and recording will not help this kind of extreme contextualism to fade away. Flooding the field with contributions grounding the concept of family strengths could do it.

ACKNOWLEDGMENTS

My thanks to Marcia Vitiello for her editorial assistance, and to Ken Covelman, Sam Scott, Karlotta Bartholomew, Pete Urquhart, Barbara Bryant, Paul Riley, and Andy Fussner for sharing their work.

REFERENCES

Covelman, K., Scott, S., & Buchanan, B. *An integrated approach to severe vaso-occlusive crises in sickle cell disease using family therapy and self-relaxation.* Paper presented at the Annual Conference of the National Sickle Cell Disease Program, Eleventh Annual Postgraduate Conference, 1983.

Dubos, R., & Escande, J. *Quest: Reflections on medicine, science and humanity.* New York: Harcourt Brace, 1979.

Haley, J. *Uncommon therapy: The psychiatric techniques of Milton H. Erickson, M.D.* New York: Norton, 1973.

Hareven, T. American families in transition: Historical perspectives on change. In F. Walsh (Ed.), *Normal family processes.* New York: Guilford Press, 1982.

McGregor, R., Ritchie, D., & Serrano, A. *Multiple impact therapy.* New York: Grune & Stratton, 1964.

Minuchin, S., Rosman, B., & Baker, L. *Psychosomatic families.* Cambridge, MA: Harvard University Press, 1978.

Montalvo, B. Aspects of live supervision. *Family Process*, 1973, *12*, 343–359.

Montalvo, B. Interpersonal arrangements in disrupted families. In F. Walsh (Ed.), *Normal family processes.* New York: Guilford Press, 1982.

Montalvo, B. Observations on two natural amnesias. *Family Process*, 1976, *15*, 333–342.

Ritterman, M. *Hypnosis and family therapy.* New York: Josey Bass, 1983.

Striner, R. *Regaining the lead: Policies for economic growth.* New York: Praeger, 1976.

Trivers, R., & Newton, H. The Crash of Flight 90. *Science Digest*, 1982.

Whitaker, C. Psychotherapy of the absurd: With special emphasis on the psychotherapy of aggression. *Family Process*, 1975, *14*, 327–343.

CHAPTER 4

Trustworthiness: The Primal Family Resource

Barbara R. Krasner

What [the problematic person] wants is a being not only whom he can trust as a person trusts another, but a being that gives him now the certitude that "there *is* a soil, there *is* an existence. The world is not condemned to deprivation, degeneration, destruction. The world *can* be redeemed. *I* can be redeemed because there is this trust." (Buber, 1965b, p. 183)

CONCEPTUALIZING FAMILY RESOURCES: A MULTILATERAL STANCE

Trustworthiness requires a mutuality of commitment (Schoeninger, 1983, p. 47). It also requires the capacity to stand over against the proposition that any one side, one person or one group can ever function as the whole of *any* relational situation (Cotroneo & Krasner, 1981, p. 41).

Peter, 26, is a third-year medical student (Figure 4-1). Yesterday he took a 6-week leave of absence from school. He says:

> Family stuff is interfering with my work. Of course, medical school *per se* is a crazy place to be. But the real issue is my mother. It's almost February now and she's still calling me about Christmas. Gift-giving is a big thing in my family but we haven't exchanged gifts yet. She has a knapsack for me but none of us go home for holidays anymore. Holiday gatherings have been strained and artificial since my sister died.
>
> Kathy died 6 years ago when she was 32. None of us seemed able to talk about her death or even her. In fact we don't seem to have anything to talk about

Barbara R. Krasner, Ph.D. Center for Contextual Therapy and Allied Studies, King of Prussia, Pennsylvania; Department of Mental Health Sciences, Hahnemann University, Philadelphia, Pennsylvania; Department of Religion, LaSalle University, Philadelphia, Pennsylvania.

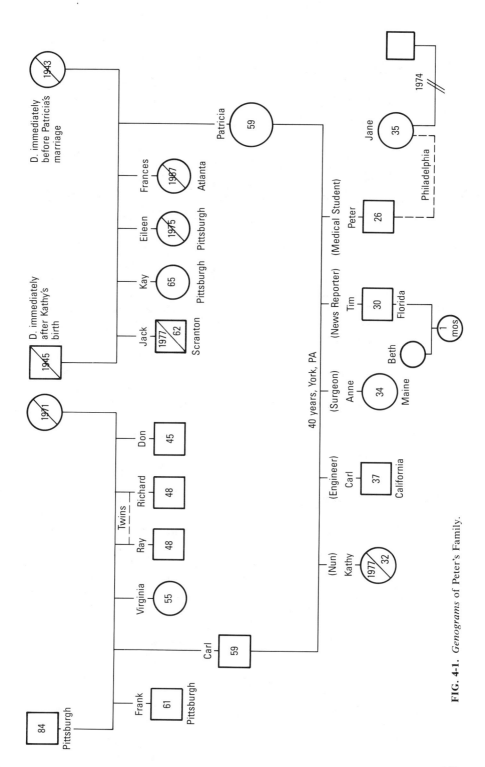

FIG. 4-1. *Genograms* of Peter's Family.

anymore. This year was the first time that I didn't go home either. But whenever we call each other, my mother keeps asking when I'll visit her. This last call was more than I could take. I feel depleted and depressed. I need a reconnection with my source of strength. I need some kind of program that helps me with relationships. I can't be with people if they're going to swallow me up. I need to know what it means to live as a man.

That was 4 months ago. Peter arranged for two therapy sessions weekly for the 6 weeks following his initial visit. He returned for two meetings 6 weeks after that. Currently he has plans to reenter therapy with a possible shift in focus from family to peer relationships. In a period of approximately 4 months, he has been able to find the energy and resources to reconnect with his parents on new terms, to rework his "go-between" relationship with his older sister, to contact one of his brothers and together tap into the resources and commonalities of their childhood friendship, to face more deeply into the mourning process over the loss of the family's eldest child 6 years earlier, and to return to medical school.

Within weeks after therapy sessions with each of his parents, Peter was able to stabilize his relationships with two friends, one male and one female, and to pursue solitary hobbies like writing and baking. His current energy level is high and his depression has receded. He is functioning well in medical school, and seems more resilient in the face of the day-to-day traumas and assault of medical school life. The strategies and mechanics of his own suicide, so carefully planned shortly before he entered therapy, seem to have fallen by the wayside. By his own report, his suicidal fantasies are currently being replaced by escape fantasies, primarily that of dropping out of school. Peter defines the switch as less destructive, as an improvement, and as a relief. He is currently exploring plans to specialize in psychiatry, though he is wary of the interviewing process. The interviewing context is highly competitive, he says, and threatens to impinge on his lack of resolution around his sexual identity.

Peter continues to struggle with issues of sexual identity as he has done from the time that he was a little boy. The struggle is intensified by his long-held, fairly absolute, and polarized perceptions about who men and women are and can be. For him men (that is, his father) are logical, rational, pragmatic, and managerial; women (that is, his mother) are emotional, irrational, whimsical, and seductive. The apparent accuracy of Peter's perceptions of who his parents are was to be documented later in therapy by his parents' self-described versions of their roles, transactions, and behaviors in past and current family life. Their partial inaccuracy was to be documented in the process of a contextual assessment of what each of them would like for each other and for themselves.

Peter's ability to make decisive choices about his sexual identity and preferences is further undercut by a convergence of parental inhibitions and religious moralism. Raised in a tradition-bound Roman Catholic family, his siblings and he were forbidden to talk about science or politics in the presence of their parents, much less about sex. The basis of these proscriptions seems to have lain more with the mother's felt inadequacies about the subject matter and with the father's collusive attempts to protect her than with ideological "rights and wrongs." Whatever the underlying motives, the children apparently bonded together in confrontations with their parents at the dinner table, and seem to have drawn some strength and support from each other. On the other hand, the family was split by the religious conversion of three of the children when Peter was only 10. At that time Anne, Tim, and Peter converted to "fundamental Christianity."

The conversion, which each of the three young people eventually reworked, may have served many functions. It may have been a strenuous attempt to recreate a source of reliable parenting. It may have been viewed by the youngsters as an alternative or surrogate for rigid, inaccessible, and judgmental parents. It is also likely that it was meant to force some differentiation between the younger children on the one hand, and on the other their mother, father, and elder siblings, who seemed to have functioned as a power alliance cloaked in the garb of a parenting team. In any case Peter's background and past are characterized by a legacy of absolute rights and wrongs, and by irrefutable goods and bads that are embodied in his parents and in his former church alike. Under the circumstances, his capacity to make choices of his own vis-à-vis sexual identity— or in any area of his life that he fears might be censured by parenting sources—is clearly inhibited. In contextual terms, his entitlement to a life of his own as well as a capacity to make choices that are discretely *his* have been stultified by his unreworked loyalties (see Boszormenyi-Nagy & Spark, 1973, Chap. 3).

For the moment Peter has withdrawn from an active sex life in an effort to reconsider his current options and directions. A search for intimacy that neither rebuffs nor engulfs, neither repulses nor consumes, carries a high priority in his life. To test an intimate relationship one more time, however, seems like a staggering demand, for he lacks the courage to surface his own claims in any relationship. In fact he's not sure that he knows how to identify his own terms or how to present them. So at this stage anyhow it may be wiser, he believes, to withdraw than to fail.

Peter's present capacity to risk trust in a relationship is radically constricted (Krasner, 1983, pp. 39–40). He cannot tolerate the possibility that still another person may demand more from him than they're willing to give him. Moreover, his perceived failure of trustworthiness in parent–child relations binds him to his father and mother through negative loyalty ties. That is, whether or not he sees his parents, Peter feels misused, even betrayed by them. Their treatment of him, as he defines it, remains the negative measure of what he expects and guards against in other relationships. It also remains the basis of how he treats other people.

Peter remains essentially unfree to make *any* peer commitments in depth and continuity, whether sexual or platonic, for his life still belongs to his legacy. He may be free to achieve (i.e., to go to medical school) precisely because it allows him to replicate his part in entrenched family patterns of one-sided giving. Paradoxically, though, his very capacity to perform may diminish whatever residual capacity he may have to risk trust in relationships. His amply demonstrable competence *ipso facto* may be leaching him dry. Medical school or any intellectual or professional pursuit may be providing Peter with an avenue of escape. It may be functioning as a buffer zone that protects him from facing mounting resentment and rage over how severely his personal terms have been (or have felt) repudiated, or, in fact, from the necessity of *ever* having to surface his terms. One-sided giving, then, characterizes Peter's personal and budding professional life.

The act of receiving in his context is simply too threatening, too replete with risk for him to attempt to require a balance of give-and-take. For to receive implies indebtedness; and indebtedness opens up further possibilities of being exploited; and further exploitation threatens an even more disabling loss of trust. Put in terms of contextual family therapy,[1] Peter's capacity to take pleasure from relationships is largely linked to the balances of fairness and unfairness, and trustworthiness and the lack of trustworthiness in his family of origin. His current state of depression and depletion may have brought him to a crisis of maturity. In the long run, his felt estrangement from his sources of strength may be read as a gift, an opportunity for a careful reassessment of his context—done through a dialogical stance. Peter's freedom to risk receiving in peer and professional relationships can be most directly won through "going home" to *test* the relational premises by which he is shaping his future and life.

Unfaced family injuries, their implications and unintended consequences, and their replication in the workplace and community are probably the most onerous, enervating, and demotivating forms of human bondage. The mistrust and injustice that emanate from interpersonal injuries—real and imagined—are probably the source of people's most intense intellectual, emotional, and spiritual pain. The pathology that results from containing conflict among caring people, that is, keeping it under wraps, is probably the single most formidable obstacle to attaining a genuine condition of forgiveness and the freedom that that implies. The slavish tendency to please people rather than to risk hurting them by saying what we need and want ranks among the most destructive and trust-demolishing of any human tendencies.

The foundations of trustworthiness in family and community are subtle and profound, for birth itself is their cornerstone and, with it, transgenerational and

---

[1]In brief, contextual therapy is a complex and sophisticated modality based on a dialectical, multipersonal paradigm of ethical balance and imbalance in significant relationship. The school was founded by Ivan Boszormenyi-Nagy and codeveloped by numerous therapists including Geraldine Spark, Barbara Krasner, and Margaret Cotroneo. It is a trust-based therapy. The crucial dimensions of the contextual approach incorporate the variables of the human condition and include: (1) fact (destiny), (2) need (individual psychology), (3) power (communication, transactions, and alliances), and (4) merited trust (balances of fairness or injustice). Contextual therapy identifies and utilizes unrecognized resources and residual trust that exist between and among relating partners. In the process, the contextual practitioner acknowledges pathology, but his/her efforts are not delimited by it. A heretofore neglected facet of therapeutic investigation and application, the dimension of merited trust is contextual therapy's major contribution to psychotherapeutic knowledge.

intergenerational consequences. Just as parents become responsible for the survival of their helpless infants, children soon become accountable to the people who alone among all others gave them life. In the beginning a will to reciprocity is rooted in existential ties. A parent cannot help but exert a lasting, irreversible influence—positive and negative—on a child, with all its attendant implications for posterity. A child cannot help but inherit the consequences of the past's endowments and be intrinsically loyal to them—for good or for ill—for every child is born into a family legacy where he/she is bound to experience disappointment and pain. Every parent has exacted undue and unfair demands from a helpless child at one or another time.

Injury and exploitation are givens of every parent–child relationship. There is simply no way for people—in this or in any other significant relationship—to be cast into a long-term involvement without encountering conflict and collisions in their life priorities. It is not the fact of injustice, disappointment, and pain, then, that is intrinsically destructive between the generations. The question before us is whether family members can eventually choose to reassess the meaning of these facts in terms of maturity rather than from the long-internalized perspective of helpless and overpowered children. Is there anything new that Peter, at age 26, can grasp about his parents' relational realities that were beyond him even at age 19? What fresh insights and freedom of options and action can be won when he readdresses his parents' contexts and lives, this time with adult ears and eyes (1 Cor. 13:10–11)?

The process of reassessing the nature of our parents' positive and negative contributions to our existence raises demanding questions (Krasner, 1983, pp. 43–44):

- Can family members find the courage to grasp each other's reasons for what was given to them and for what was denied?
- Can adult children come to grips with their parents' potential and limits without finally being contained or defined by them?
- Can adult children find ways to tell their family members about their own relational perceptions without having to coat them with veneers of idealization or deprecation?
- Can people take the mass of their deep-held anger, resentment, and guilt and begin to reshape it by addressing its causes and sources?
- Can family members mobilize the residual trust that flows from the past into redemptive options and action for posterity? Or, by omission, will they choose for a peace that is no peace, and so repeat their parents' destructive transgressions?

In sum, must adults settle for a stagnant existence essentially defined by power tactics, timidity, and blame, or—in the midst of fear and disappointment—can people commit to a process of identifying, mobilizing, and utilizing hidden resources that can turn their hearts and minds to trust (Malachi 3:24)?

Like the rest of us, Peter can ill afford to stay stuck in a predisposition to scapegoat his parents for real or imagined injuries—without also acknowledging *their* version of how they contributed to his life. Nor can he afford to overlook *how he and his life interests have contributed to them and their life interests.* For despite his longing to be free of his parents' hold over him, Peter, like all children everywhere, is dynamically invested in their well-being. In a parallel vein he also needs to *know* factually that his parents have decisively invested in him.[2] A family's actual capacity to plumb the depths of each other's contributions and care, however, is typically masked by well-entrenched barriers and defenses. Peter's family members, for example, tend either to dismiss each other's terms and criteria for relating, or to cut off from each other in wounded and retributive withdrawal. From Peter's side his family's apparent inattentiveness to him and his own hurt withdrawal from them have already trapped everyone in a relational corner—though presently Peter is most aware of his own dilemma and binds.

If cutoffs and rebuffs are really the only legitimate options of commitment and exchange between Peter and his family then the costs in relational injuries may simply outweigh anticipated benefits and returns. In fact, they may demotivate everyone from reaching toward each other. More simply put, under the circumstances the price of potential pleasure to be derived from relationship may have become too dear for Peter even to make a bid. Moreover, if he is really unable to exculpate his parents for the destructive consequences that their lives and actions have had for him, he may be unable ever to exculpate himself (Boszormenyi-Nagy & Spark, 1973, p. 35). And distance, evasion, and blame may become his only relational alternatives. Indeed, if he can find no reason or way whatsoever to tender esteem to his parents, he may discover that *he* is lacking a solid and reliable base from which to esteem himself.

For Peter life has become unbearably chaotic and purposeless, and at the moment he cannot find a way toward order and meaning. So he has decided to begin a process of reappraisal and reassessment—within the limits and possibilities of his time, energy, inclinations, and the immediacy of educational demands. Fundamentally he has entered a process of rebalancing what he owes and what he deserves. In what measure is he obliged to significant others? In what measure is he entitled to free choices and pleasures solely for himself? And by what criteria can he judge the degree of his entitlement vis-à-vis the degree of his indebtedness (Boszormenyi-Nagy & Krasner, 1980, pp. 770–772). Some of the answers that Peter is looking for are embedded in the questions that he is surfacing as he struggles toward more viable modes of relating (Controneo & Krasner, 1981, p. 45). "What do I owe and to whom?" he is asking. "What do I deserve and from whom?" "What relationships do I need and want?" "What relationships am I bound to retain whether or not I need or want them?"

Neither family nor friends nor pastors nor teachers have ever directly posed questions of entitlement and indebtedness to Peter in this or in any way. Directly

---

[2]The phrase "ethical engagement" is used to designate a dialogical involvement among people who have contributed to each other's well-being, particularly parents, children, and siblings.

or indirectly, though, each has made demands on him and communicated to him what he owes and what he *should* do. In point of fact, his life is ruled by "shoulds." Like most people, he is overburdened if not crushed by obligations but knows little of what he deserves. To consider responsibilites and freedom at one and the same time is a new thought process for him, one that he is tempted to avoid. In his context considering oneself before others (or, perhaps, even at all) is viewed as selfish in the most pejorative sense of the word. It is seen as characteristic of the "me generation," a stance to be eschewed and disdained. Still, he has exhausted all other routes. He has futilely waited for consideration that once in a while, he had hoped, might be offered solely on his terms. He has consistently anticipated that the quality of other people's commitments might be as reliable as his own. He has isolated himself to an extreme, and has entertained fantasies of suicide. Were there any options left?

Peter's tendency to idealize relationships has functioned as still one more setup for loneliness, disappointment, and failure. Take what happened at Christmastime that, along with his mother's phone call, seemed to be the very last straw. Over time Peter has discovered a soulmate in Jane, a fellow medical student who lives nearby. Here, finally, he thought, was a person with whom he could share himself—and she would understand. With Jane every intimacy seemed an option, though she was still involved with another man. Together they decided to go to New England to visit his sister Anne and her close woman friend. Another female couple was there when Jane and he arrived. Peter was aware that he was the only male present in the group but that seemed to be okay. After all, he was with a sister who had helped him through so many family battles and who seemed to be a source of healing for so many jagged wounds. And he was with Jane. "The first day I felt at home," Peter said.

> It was a situation of intimate security. But then sitting around one night, we got to talking. We're all interested in music, and the conversation settled on the topic of a concert that was being given exclusively *by* women and *for* women—with absolutely no exceptions. I raised a question about the fairness of that. I tried to have them at least understand how that rigid a policy simply ran over me. I tried to have them comprehend, especially Anne and Jane, that if I were sensitive and intuitive enough and caring enough to have as a really good friend, what could justify my having to be excluded from that concert? I know how women have been hurt, but when they behave in kind to men, where does that leave people like me?
>
> In any case, it was like talking to a wall. Anything else that I said seemed to polarize us even more. I finally left the room in tears and spent a lot of time crying that night. There was nothing left to do. All I wanted was for someone to say that this was an interim period in society, that eventually healing could take place. All I wanted was for someone to see my face—without imposing one more mask on me. But it didn't happen. Things got awkward and tense. I couldn't handle any more pain. I haven't called Anne since we got home; that's unusual for me. Jane and I haven't talked about it either. I may have lost a soulmate too. I don't know what to expect from her now. When we first met, I wanted to rescue her from everything that she'd been through. I had the gift of asking all the right questions. But now there's a part of me that needs to be rescued too.

At this point in his life journey Peter is half a dialogue bursting to begin. His first therapeutic task, then, is to implement his readiness to rework his isolation and self-isolating ways.

Peter's readiness for dialogue *ipso facto* provides direction to the therapist, who, like others before her, views dialogical meeting as both the starting point and the goal of therapy.[3]

> It is very important, of course, that the therapist not place the demand for responsibility in dialogue upon the patient before he is ready for it. That is why the reconstruction of the capacity for dialogue must go hand in hand with the methodological attempt to loosen and dismantle the complex defense mechanisms in the psychic realm of expression as fast as the recuperating self permits. (Friedman, 1975, p. 262)

But almost from the beginning Peter was drawing on reserves of trust whose vitality was observable even if its sources could not be documented. Between sessions, he took action. He tested new options against his friends, tried spending more time alone, called his parents and sister, identified more of what he wanted to be different, saw his own collusion in maintaining destructive relating, and came to the next therapy meeting with sturdy questions of his own. Memories were awakened, doubts were surfaced, explanations were demanded, and challenges were made. Peter was coming alive. Given these indications, the therapist was prepared to help him pursue answers to some of the following questions. Can he move beyond his own psyche to inquire into other people's realities and life interests as *they themselves* define them? Can he move beyond his most reactive behavior to a point of surfacing his *own* terms for relating? Does he *know* his own terms, that is, what specifically *he* wants? Can he muster the courage to *test* the conclusions he has drawn about a relationship, or does he *choose* to proceed on untested monological premises? Can he differentiate between when people are actively rejecting him, and when they are simply functioning within their own personal and interpersonal limits?

How do past injustices, actual and perceived, affect the status of his current relationships? When last has he directly surfaced his regrets over the injuries and disappointments that estrange him from a close relative or friend? When last did he elicit or simply tolerate someone else's assessment of the causes of *their* estrangement from him? When last has he risked saying what he wants, and received a caring response? Can he identify how *his* behavior (inadvertently or directly) tends to rebuff people whom he'd like to befriend? Can he identify the merit that still exists in a formerly significant relationship that is currently stagnant? Can he identify what still holds him to an estranged relationship?

---

[3]See Friedman (1975, pp. 256, 262). *Healing through Meeting* is the title that Martin Buber gave to the posthumously published book by the Swiss psychoanalyst Hans Trub (*Heilung aus der Begegnung*). Friedman wrote that in *Healing through Meeting*, Buber pointed to Hans Trub as the man who broke the trail as a practicing psychotherapist in the recognition and realization of the therapeutic possibilities of dialogue.

Does he draw a negative satisfaction from perceiving himself as victim? Is he using a relationship to avenge himself of injuries that belong to someone else (revolving slate) (Boszormenyi-Nagy & Spark, 1973, pp. 65–67)? Does he see a realistic pathway toward reclaiming a relationship that is still founded on pockets of residual trust?

In great measure or small, residual trust is the keystone of the dialogical process—and hence the chief resource of human relationships. It is the long-term consequence of one person's *actual* care for another person. It is the fuel that empowers people to risk relating *after* they have suffered injustices and estrangements. It is the summation of a "ledger sheet" that records the merit *between* people. It is the token of a once-warranted faith that witnesses to the fact that assets in relationship are at least as significant as debits. It is the recognition that one person's investments in another may be limited or marred but, for all of that, are still worthy of consideration. It is the understructure of relationship, that is, the rudimentary resource of individual and interpersonal growth. Residual trust is the *sine qua non* of fairness or justice *between* person and person. It is the dough in the bread of relationship, kneaded by the energy and efforts of visible and invisible hands. In sum, residual trust lies at the heart of every redemptive investment in the dialogical process.

In the beginning trustworthiness takes root through parents' unilateral, perhaps unconditional, investment in their offspring. Eventually trustworthiness becomes multilateral through the filial capacity to *acknowledge* the merit of parental investments. Early on, from the time that they can read their parents' wishes, children enter the process of establishing their own ledgers of merit. They develop responsive actions, behaviors, and ways of warranting their mother's and father's trust. They also receive their parents' "feeding" in varying ways, rejecting and accepting what is offered without awareness of the impact. Even babies are active in building up or tearing down trustworthiness long before they can consciously acknowledge the merit of parental investments.

Whatever their words, dependent and adult children alike are intrinsically loyal and reactive to what they have been given. Who lives for them, who wants them, who is available to them, and who has made material, relational, and spiritual investments in them are fundamental factors in a youngster's attitude toward the world. Moreover, the presence or absence of parental contributions is irrevocable, irreplaceable, and nonsubstitutable for their children. These contributions are subject to interpretation and always benefit from dialogical exploration between parent and child. But whether or not they are ever addressed, their impact and consequences exist in the lives of untold, even yet-unborn generations. The dynamic ties between the generations are established at birth, and outlast physical and geographical separations. Most significantly, perhaps, they influence the degree to which progeny can eventually be free to commit themselves to building trustworthy relationships outside of their original contexts (Boszormenyi-Nagy & Krasner, 1980, p. 768).

At base, then, trustworthiness evolves from a mutuality of commitment. It also evolves from a multilateral stance. It requires a capacity to stand over against the proposition that any one side, person, or group can ever function as a measure of the whole of *any* relational situation. It is always a product of at least two people, and can never be reduced to the psychological universe of either one of them. It is characteristic of mature, nonexploitative relations of any kind. It helps people control their exploitative tendencies in close relationships. It serves self-interest through retaining the resource of a given relationship, *and* through functioning as a resource for relationship. Caring for another person's needs can enhance personal satisfaction through establishing a basis for equitable balances of empathy and love.

Retaining a trustworthy relationship is in the reality interests of all participants. A sustained capacity to consider and to respond to another person involves long-term balances of fair give-and-take. Trust-based relationships help people accept periods of transitory unfairness, and result from mutual commitment and actual exchange. On the other hand, a chronic failure of trustworthy relating reinforces the likelihood that people will be cynical, manipulative, exploitative, and unfair—if only to protect themselves. Without some manifestation of trustworthiness, there can be little will to risk investing in new relationships or in sustaining old relationships. And so there can be no further development and accrual of residual trust. Without the motivation that is nurtured by the resource of trust, there can be little justification for dialogue or for hope for the healing that comes of meeting (Friedman, 1975, pp. 262–263).

IDENTIFYING FAMILY RESOURCES: DIALOGICAL QUESTIONS

> A soul is never sick alone, but always a betweenness also, a situation between it and another existing being. (Buber, 1969, pp. 142–143)

The family is a meeting place for the converging currents—genetic, personal, and interpersonal—of thousands of individuals and hundreds of generations. It is the fundamental forum for early human injuries and injustices, lost hope, deep disappointment, profound disillusionment and even exploitation, hurtful estrangement, and relational stagnation. It is also the fundamental forum for receiving early nurture and care, sustained protection and consideration, life-giving interpersonal exchange, deep-rooted loyalties, paradigms for learned patterns of give-and-take, investments of parenting that give birth to hope and energy to aspirations, a socialized basis for trustworthy response, and justifiable reason for risking trust. The very passion—positive and negative—with which people tend to view their "close" relationships is evidence enough to underscore the tenacity of the family's enduring hold and sustaining meaning for its members.

Disappointed family expectations themselves are expressions of meaning, albeit meaning that is presumed to be lost. Were Peter and his mother once friends? Why, then, does their relationship feel like a battleground now? Did Peter function as his family's therapist from the time that Kathy died? By what justification, then, can he now discard that task? By what right can he suddenly demand that, in his adult life, *they* now offer him a new kind of care? By their very nature family disappointments can blind people to the residual trust that still exists between them. One person's presumption that another person has actively "rejected" him is an untested premise at best. At worst it obscures each person's potential to identify the resources that manage to endure beneath the traumas of the process of estrangement.

One of life's more painful paradoxes may lie in the fact that it is generally easier for people to cite problems and pathology in relationships than to identify their resources. This issue is compounded by a contextual definition of resources. Here what may be a resource to one person can also function as a stumbling block to another person. Intimacy, money, humor, status, and religious or moral values can all be described as two-edged swords. Fundamental religion, for example, may represent the only remaining structure of "parenting" for a woman who has lost her entire family in the Holocaust. As such, it is a resource that may keep her from despair. Religion may also be a roadblock and a source of despair for the young if, for example, it converts free inquiry into a taboo (Krasner, 1981–1982). Or consider humor or money, whose effects can be salving or bruising, an invitation to easy exchanges or a wall against accessibility. It is precisely the two-edged nature of every relational commodity that makes it impossible to define a given offering as a resource *per se*.

It is only mutuality of commitment conveyed through trust-based dialogue that might rightfully be defined as an ongoing resource. Martin Buber put it this way: "I have no teaching," he wrote. "I only point to something. I point to reality. I point to something in reality that had not or had too little been seen. I take him who listens to me by the hand and lead him to the window and point to what is outside" (Friedman & Schilpp, 1967, p. 698). Contextual theory and therapy have followed Buber's lead. Here the process has no content except what the client and his context bring. "There are no concrete objective descriptions of the trustbuilding resources that exist between people, and certainly no prescriptions" (Boszormenyi-Nagy & Krasner, 1986). Conviction and courage are required instead. The therapist is obliged to direct his/her attention to signs of vulnerability, rejection, and evasion between a person and his/her significant relationships. "These are the signs of relational failure that become especially significant when they are presented unilaterally" (Boszormenyi-Nagy & Krasner, 1986). It is in the midst of these failures that a therapist can begin to identify the still, small voice of residual trust.

The ability to recognize and utilize trust resources requires an autonomous self as well as a will to reciprocity. It requires, even demands the inner strength for self-assessment as well as the courage to hold accountable those people for whom we care. It requires a capacity to make personal claims and, when indicated, to hold to them in the face of hostile, opposing messages. It requires an ability to tolerate short-term injury and exploitation in the interests of continuing a merited relationship. It requires a decision to disclose hard-won convictions, and to run the risk of having them challenged and reshaped. It requires the will to test the possibilities of a given relationship, to identify its intrinsic limits, and to learn to differentiate a person's limits from his/her intentions to reject. It also requires the maturity to abandon the self-defeating game of comparative victimization.

However burdensome the task, the ability to help other people identify, mobilize, and utilize trust resources requires Peter to begin with himself. The capacity to tap into a family's trust base has to begin with self-reflective questions (Krasner, 1983, p. 43):

- Who is trustworthy in my own family and life?
- When I think about family and community, do I think in terms of trust-worthiness, fairness, and resources? Or do my thoughts and feelings dwell mainly on pathology, unfairness, and mistrust?
- Have I failed my family, or have they failed me? How?
- Can anything be done to transform these real and felt failures? To whom can I turn to assess and rework them?
- Are my expectations of myself and of others realistic?
- Do I test my assumptions or do they typically stay locked up within me? What will the costs of testing them be?
- When I'm unsure of what I want, can I say so? If not, why not?
- To what degree do I retreat to moralisms and ideologies when I lack firm personal and relational ground?
- When people are violent, can I still hear their side?
- When people are judgmental, can I still say my side?
- What kinds of criticism evoke shame in me?
- Who in my context knows and accepts me for who I really am?

Hard questions characteristically yield healing answers. Trusting enough to test our truths with people from whom we're estranged may produce trauma. It is also likely to produce new degrees of freedom—whether we're well received by them or not. Asking for what he wants can be as caring an act on Peter's part as a knee-jerk if begrudging response to one more of his parents' demands. In any case, Peter was clear about his resistance to more commands to care for his parents when he first came into therapy—even though both of them are ill.

Peter's mother suffers from angina, lung cancer, and asthma. By his own early report and by his father's confirmation, she is also relationally crippled. In addition, if his mother and father were not actually alcoholic, at the very least they drank too much. Initially Peter doubted that his mother could be of any help to him, given her suffering and needs. Her own parents had died before she turned 20. Her father was a "drunk" and beat her mother. Family myth has it that Peter's father has regretted their marriage since the year after it took place. His mother describes herself as "God's plaything, a creature afflicted and lost." She seems less in touch with how she has afflicted others, though—especially when she felt denied her children's affection. "All she wants is more of me," Peter complains. "It's worse since Kathy's death. Until then Kathy was the family healer, our mother's therapist."

Peter's father suffers from leukemia as well as from alcohol misuse, but he still manages to get things done. He's the buffer between his wife and their children. He maintains his job as a salesman. He manipulates what personal space he needs by being "on the road" for his work. Aside from expressing regret over his marriage, he shares little of himself with his family. Peter speaks of his father, with an edge of derision, as a one-dimensional man. "We all think he's a wonderful denyer."

> The night that the call came to let us know that Kathy had died, Father relayed the message to Tim and me and never spoke of it again. There was no expression of feelings, no consolation of us, nothing! On second thought there was something. That evening I looked out the window and saw my father standing motionless, alone, just staring at the water in the pool. He stayed a long, long time. Someone to console him, put their arm around his back? No one for any one. In our family we're all alone.
>
> People are alone in my father's family too. They see each other often but they're of German immigrant stock: Work and food are their major coinage of exchange. My father was close to his mother but mocks his father, who's still alive. They've had a hard time together; they all seem devoid of emotion. Everyone's bright, bantering, belittling. In fact, abrasive humor is the only real sign of affection among the five brothers. They also have a sister who's a nun. Anyway I don't talk to my brothers much either. If I do, it's always a superficial exchange. When it comes to my father, talk about the car is the usual topic. I pay for my education; he pays for the car. He'll call up to talk about functional things like insurance. It never gets much deeper than that.
>
> I guess distance is our only safeguard. Kathy left home for the convent when she was 18. Carl, Anne, and Tim all live far away from our parents, maybe to protect themselves. Up until Christmas, I thought Anne and I could talk. I suspect that it will be alright again but for now I don't know where we stand. Typically we're in touch by phone at least once a week—but so far this week neither one of us has called.

Peter's relational paradigm of one-sided giving to his family, to friends, and even to professors at school is no longer functioning beneficently for him. He feels exploited, depleted, isolated, bereft of consolation. What's worse, old injuries keep resurfacing. He sees his family as a chronic source of pain and is doubtful that they can ever be anything more. On the other hand, he is out of touch with how *he* colludes in maintaining destructive family patterns and imbalances of fairness. Peter's problems seemed overwhelming to him at the beginning of therapy, and therapy itself provided him with still another dilemma.

As he entered the therapeutic process, Peter necessarily came face-to-face with the dilemma of how to harness his feelings. On the one hand, he wanted nothing more than to be "done" with his family, to be buffered from the trauma of what they do and of who they seem to be. On the other hand, he wanted nothing more than to help his parents, to bring surcease to their chronic suffering, conflicts, and sadness, to make it alright for them, *and* to live a life of his own. In a primal prototype of filial response, he was caught between the poles of caring for his own well-being and for the well-being of people who are highly invested if enmeshed with him; between his self-interests and genuine interests in his parents and siblings. Or, in contextual terms, he was caught between the dialogical poles of self-delineation and self-validation (Boszormenyi-Nagy & Krasner, 1985).

Like the rest of us, Peter's dialogue with his world is bi-level. He draws purpose, integrity, and meaning from investing in himself: that is, from gaining personal satisfaction, from making self-serving decisions, and from shaping life according to his own terms (self-delineation). Paradoxically, though, he can be dynamically free to pursue his own vested interests *only* if he identifies options and eventually acts on options for investing in the well-being and life interests of significant others as well (self-validation). There are adults, of course, who seem to be totally self-centered. Contextual theory describes such people as destructively entitled. In developmental and in justice terms alike, they either have felt or have been so decisively deprived of their rightful due that they are "free" to take what they can get, as they can get it—without regard to the consequences of their behavior for anyone.

Short of desperate extremes, though, men and women are dynamically obliged to consider the consequences of their actions and choices for people about whom they care. From the beginning, the young seem impelled to please their parents at the same time that they are taking and testing. However inadequate or insufficient their efforts over his lifetime and even of late, Peter's family members have indeed expended energy in offering him care. For example, his father calls regularly to discuss insurance payments for Peter's car. It takes little imagination to conclude that car insurance may be his father's only safe entry to Peter's adult life. The topic of car insurance may also serve to provide a thin thread of commonality between father and son because it is the only area in which the father is presently making an active contribution to his son's current context and life. Of late his father is also concerned about the cause of Peter's need for therapy.

Peter is perplexed over the apparent narrowness of his father's expressed concerns for him. He wonders what keeps them from having more in common. Why haven't they been able to move into an adult-to-adult relationship? Why hasn't his father been more forthcoming in his initiatives toward Peter? For that matter, what has blocked Peter from taking initiative with his father? In any case, something still exists. Peter's father is still making legitimate if frustrating offers of concern. For his part, Peter remains essentially indebted, that is, unfree to travel his own path without some way of manifesting a reciprocal concern. Put in other words, it is unlikely that a child who has been fiercely loyal to his/her family's legacies and expectations (by definition, every child) can suddenly metamorphose into an adult who knows how to be indifferent to his/her family's neediness and pain.

The pain that people suffer in their relationships with each other must be as old as life itself. Religion, like psychology, has struggled to identify the sources of that suffering and to offer options for health and healing. It may be that the primal scream for healing through meeting was first heard when God called out, "Adam, where art thou?", a cry that eventually was met with "man's" fearful and ambivalent response: ". . . I was afraid because I was naked, and I hid myself" (Gen. 3:10). In religious terms, the basis for dialogue has been established through the offer of covenantal relationship: "They shall become my people and I will become their God" (Jer. 32:38–42). Covenant presumes at least two partners, however unequal or unmatched they may be. Convenantal relationship also presumes a justice base. It has been argued for thousands of years now that the impulse toward justice is intrinsic to the human situation, that it is essentially inborn (Deut. 10:18–20). It has also been argued that justice begins to be actualized when people recognize its dialogical criteria and find the resources to act on them.

The Decalogue, or Ten Commandments, for example, is one side of a dialogical effort, that is, a set of terms that argues for free and responsible human beings to incorporate equitable criteria in their lives and contexts (Deut. 5:6–6:9). A human being's decision to respond to those terms, in a personally unique integration of spirit and letter of the Law, is his/hers alone. Like any other set of convictions or guidelines the Decalogue can be parentified. It can be converted into a literal, absolute, and incontrovertable demand. Or it can be the basis for personal response; an offer to be considered, debated, tested, and acted upon—because it yields a reasonable and caring way and a promise of just return. Undergirding these efforts to establish viable guidelines for fair human behavior is God's prior offer and actual delivery of care (Exod. 20:2).

It is precisely the delivery of care that is the common thread between religious reality and psychotherapy. Each of these modalities has a vision of human potential that offers viable paradigms of healing and the conviction that people can be healed. Moreover, it seems likely that psychology has drawn deeply from religious scripture and tradition. Bakan (1965), among others, has argued for the linkages between Freud's work and the Jewish mystical tradition. Other approaches, like Jung's (1958), clearly draw from the insights of religious tradition. Contextual theory converges with the insights of Martin Buber's philosophical anthropology, which carries the convenantal paradigm into inter-human terms.

Martin Buber argues that the justice of the human order can be rebalanced in the I–Thou relationship where "deep calls to deep" (1965a, p. 204). In clinical terms it has been aruged that the distribution of justice can be reworked when people can reassess the balances and imbalances of fairness in their relationships on a periodic basis—that is, when they can discover sufficient trust to join in a dialogical assessment of the assets and debits, the burdens and benefits, and the healing and injury that lie between them (Boszormenyi-Nagy & Krasner, 1980, p. 771). To wit, can each relating partner jointly consider and reconsider the balances of personal freedom and personal responsibility in their own lives and contexts?

The balances of entitlement and indebtedness are given conditions of existence, and a contextual measure of human commitment and devotion. For example, Peter was born to his parents and nurtured and tended by them. He is indebted to them and needs to find ways to repay them in intent if not in kind. On the other hand, he is entitled to live his own life. Here a collision is inevitable between him and his parents at some point in his life. Such a collision can be translated into an experience of mutual rejection, or it can be transformed into a new balance of give-and-take if Peter can differentiate between what he wants (self-delineation) and what he *chooses* to give of himself to his parents (self-validation).

Dialogue is based on these two sequential phases: (1) self-delineation, the phase in which people surface their own claims and state what they want; and (2) self-validation, the phase in which people consider others and offer them care, actions that earn them "right," if you will, to define the degree to which they are free to live with the fewest possible encumbrances. The dialogical phases of self-delineation and self-validation are the instruments by which the degrees of justice in context can be identified and balanced again and again. What's *fair* between Peter and his parents has much to do with how each of them can balance self-serving claims and offers of due consideration to significant others.

From the beginning moments of their work together, the therapist acknowledged Peter's long-term care and concern for his family *and* surfaced evidences of their long-term concern and care for him. She acknowledged the crippling effects of his felt depletion and injuries, and the realities of his loneliness and felt isolation. Early on, she also indicated that Peter stood at a crossroad. Sooner or later he would have to make a choice about how to interpret his feelings. Would they eventually be used to validate *only his* injuries and pain? Or would they also be used as valid indicators of real and perceived injustices that exist between him and the people to whom he remains loyally attached as well?

Will Peter use his feelings to justify his estrangement from his family, that is, to underwrite his disappointments in who his parents are? Will his sense of being overwhelmed by his family's neediness (psychology) freeze into a permanent state of injuries and injustice (relational ethics), and solidify into an inflexible rationale for ethical disengagement? Will he choose to protect himself from the sources of his injuries and, in so doing, cut himself off from the sources of his healing? Will he trap himself in the self-pitying confines of self-imposed monologue and so lose the validation he can have confirmed only in the dialogical process? Buffered from the merit of their valid truths and trust, will he unilaterally impute causes, motives, and blame to his family—and victimize them as he feels they have victimized him? Will his self-protectiveness ultimately reify into the keystone of a lifetime's solipsistic stance?

Will Peter's secondary if currently intense loyalties to the therapist (an accidental relationship at best) serve to undercut legitimate options for dialogue with the people still committed to him and to whom he remains committed—in spite of his anger and frustration? Can he recognize the built-in limits of the therapeutic relationship? That is, regardless of caring feelings, the therapist's ledger with him existentially can never be ethically analogous to that of his family's; that, perforce, her investment in Peter excludes a mandate of long-term commitment. Will his evolving dialogue with the therapist triangulate his family, however unintentionally, and serve to rob its members of the chance to articulate *their* valid claims and sides? Or, conversely, can Peter use therapy to help him find the trust and courage to test his world from the perspective of a dialogical stance? Can he eventually afford to read his feelings as manifestations of injustice rather than as indictments of someone else's limits? Or will he finally choose to consign himself to a world in which feelings are used as ends unto themselves?

"Feelings," wrote Martin Buber, "are a mere accompaniment to the metaphysical fact of the relation which is fulfilled, not in the soul, but between the I and Thou" (Buber, 1937, p. 81). In the first instance, Buber seems to argue, it is not a change of feelings that is required but a turning, a change of heart and stance.[4] His emphasis here can be linked to at least two factors. The first is Biblical religion, which, for Buber, pointed "the way." Despite their myriad distortions of living reality, Jewish and Christian interpretations of relationship have continued to emphasize commitment, devotion, loyalty, and service in the world rather than feelings. A second factor is psychology. "Buber charged Freud with being a 'simplificator,' one who places a general concept of reality in place of the ever-renewed investigation of reality" (Katz, 1975, p. 416). He also charged psychology, the Jungian in particular, with promulgating a new religion at the same time that it protests that psychology is a science and nothing more. He claimed that the new psychology makes the error of "mystically deifying the instincts instead of hallowing them in faith" (Buber, 1952, p. 137).

The passion that Buber invests in dialogue clearly reflects his own rarely stated religious commitment:

> Only he who himself turns to the other human being and opens himself to him [who] receives the world in him. Only the being whose otherness, accepted by my being, lives and faces me in the whole compression of existence, brings the radiance of eternity to me. Only when two say to one another with all that they are, 'It is Thou,' is the indwelling of the Present Being between them. (1965a, p. 30)

The realm of the "between" was so absolutely compelling for Buber that he wrote, "A man can ward off with all his strength the belief that 'God' is there, and he tastes him in the strict sacrament of dialogue" (1965a, p. 17). "The sphere of the interhuman," he said, "is one in which a person is confronted by another. We call its unfolding the dialogic" (1965b, p. 75).

---

[4]See Krasner and Shapiro (1979, pp. 14–16). *Tshuvah*, or turning, is the outcome of a personal assessment and accounting of the condition of one's soul in the context of the convenant (*Hesbon Ha-Nefesh*). Assessing and accounting imply the option of return to an original order of existence that is both healing and redemptive. Personal unity (Deut. 6:4 ff.) and interpersonal justice (Deut. 16:20) provide the foundations of such an order and, dynamically, may be gained and regained through the process of addressing and reworking individual and relational imbalances and breakdowns.

What unfolds is neither in one of the two partners nor in both taken together—it unfolds and emerges in the "between." The happening is therefore not psychological but objective, with a reality of its own which can be accessible to the individuals who truly meet. While accessible it cannot be confined, delimited or reduced. (Katz, 1975, p. 422)

What Buber termed the objective reality of the between, contextual theorists call the ethical dimension of reality.

True meeting between parent and the dependent or independent child is never simply psychological. It is also always ethical, that is, the parent–child relationship is rooted in the soil of earned merit. The ethical dimension of reality is an existential link between them that is unbreakable and is accessible to both of them. Parent and offspring can misunderstand, wound, and undercut each other. They can tear down all visible evidence of trust between them but their linkages remain. It is these linkages that function as the reservoir of residual trust. Liking, approving of, or agreeing with each other is not the primary basis of their invisible attachment. Rather it is caring, given and received—and documented in the predetermined facts of begetting, pregnancy, and survival—that provides the cornerstone for their mutuality of commitment and the mortar for building a sturdier foundation. Fully turned and radically open to the other, the parent and the child who truly meet are strengthened by their course (justice) and lent courage by their source (residual trust).[5]

Residual trust can never be confined, delimited, or reduced. It lies latent in the substream of enduring relationships, waiting to be tapped. First, however, it needs to be identified. It is most readily identified in the midst of the lingering devotion and of the amorphous commitments of family members who are irrevocably linked by ties of root and legacy. It is never to be found in some pure or idealized feeling state. To the contrary, residual trust is typically to be mined in the depths of volatile passions and in the midst of forbidding injustices, pathology, and mistrust.

MOBILIZING FAMILY RESOURCES: HEALING THROUGH MEETING

PETER: We're making a big difference in my family, you and I.

Peter was aware of the nature of contextual work if somewhat alarmed by the prospect of the dialogical process. First of all there was Kathy, and she was

---

[5]See Heschel (1949, p. 620). Heschel argued for a personal and interpersonal paradigm of being and relating founded on the existential options of justice and care: "The prophets discovered the holy dimension of living by which our right to live and to survive is measured. However, the holy dimension was not a mechanical mechanism, measurable by the yardstick of deed and reward, of crime and punishment, by a cold law of justice. They did not proclaim a universal moral mechanism but a spiritual order in which justice was the course but not the source. To them justice was not a static principle but a surge sweeping from the inwardness of God, in which the deeds of man find, as it were, approval or disapproval, joy or sorrow."

dead. So what could he do about it? He still dreamed about her often. He was 6 when she left for the convent. He remembers holding her hand at the beach when he was a little boy. She never seemed angry, he says, unlike their mother, who always seems angry and moody. A year and a half before she began to die, Kathy was helping Peter decide what to do with his life. "She was an endearing, caring person," he recalls. Peter was away at school when Kathy's health got worse. "My parents lied," he says.

Peter was 19 at the time and in his first year of college. It was February when Carl, his elder brother, called. Carl informed him that Kathy's health was seriously slipping. She was constantly in pain, hallucinating, on morphine by then. "She taught me how to touch people," Peter remembers. "We said our good-byes right before she died in July. 'I'm grateful for your touch; it means so much to me,' she said." Kathy and Anne were also reconciled before Kathy died. Yes, Peter still wants to talk to his family about Kathy. He wants to know why he wasn't told the truth. He wants them to know what happened to him in the aftermath of her death. He wants to know what happened to them. He was, he says, very immature at the time. He felt frightened and trapped as the youngest child, but that was nothing new. He had hidden from his parents since high school began.

In the first place, his father never seemed to respect Peter's deepest beliefs. The family just didn't seem to take his pain seriously. He found some peer acceptance in high school among intellectual kids. He was good at gymnastics but was still ridiculed a lot by male peers in gym class. Even in first grade he felt judged for preferring jump-rope over ball games. His parents "freaked out" when he made a black friend. Peter recalls that then, like now, his mother typically cut off when she didn't like what he'd done; and she rarely made apologies. His, Peter says, is the security of ambiguity. In college, he didn't date at all but he had a lot of women friends. He wasn't interested in "magazine beauty" in women. He was interested in the "spark of the soul" in them. He felt the need for male friends too. He found himself looking for attractive men, but he didn't find any friends. After college Peter won a scholarship to Europe and left the country, but he still worried a lot. He wasn't exclusively gay, but he was confused. Was it, Peter wondered, morally wrong?

He tried to be conventional and mainstream but found himself unhappy. It reminded him too much of his mother's love. It was "strangling." In his adolescence he had spent a lot of time sitting with his mother, who complained about his father. "But you . . . ," his mother had said. Peter backed off and tried to let her know that he was not her lover. She was unhappy, though, especially with his father, and sometimes she had a point. Perhaps he reflected his mother's complaints, or maybe they were his own. In any case, Peter viewed his father as untrustworthy. He knew little of him except that his father was resigned to a "wrong marriage choice," was a good photographer, and told a lot of stories about his experiences in the war. The notion of asking his father to help Peter learn more about him was intriguing.

Peter initially resisted the idea of bringing his mother and father into therapy. He just wasn't ready to "take off his clothes" in front of them. He simply was not prepared for an abrupt disclosure or announcement of his struggle with his sexual identity. The therapist assured him of his right to privacy. She also stressed his right to decide the therapeutic agenda, should his parents agree to attend. If either of them was to be invited, he was clear that it had to be his father first. He was reluctant to address both of his parents together, and saw his father as a priority. Somehow facing him was less frightening than taking on his mother now. Besides, there were a lot of old scores that Peter needed to understand.

A session was spent setting priorities about which issues Peter wanted to address. By the fifth session, he had called and invited his father to a meeting. His father immediately agreed. In fact, on learning of Peter's leave of absence from school, his father seemed freer to call—three times that weekend. Was Peter okay? Was there something that his father could do? He indicated his willingness to do *anything* that Peter might ask. Even prior to therapy sessions ever taking place, father and son had moved from the topic of insurance to a mutually assuring stance.

Peter opened their joint session by saying how little he knew of his father. He also quickly established the fact that he didn't want to spend their time together talking about his mother. With Peter and his father present in the same room, sitting face to face, new elements about each of them and about their relationship were immediately disclosed:

1. They talked in triangles.
2. Peter allowed his father's presence and style to silence him. He stepped back from an actively inquiring role, and gave up all of the initiative that had made the meeting possible.
3. Peter's father, invisibly delegated to fill the relational void, simply held forth—and pontificated.
4. Neither father nor son risked testing each other's premises. There were no interruptions, no challenges, certainly no open disagreements. Each waited politely until the other had finished. It was as if the two men were acting on separate stages.
5. They seemed to trust neither themselves nor each other enough even to interact.
6. Nevertheless, they also seemed committed to each other's well-being and desperate to find a way toward something new.

The two men seemed to have no experience as a dyad, in a one-to-one dialogical exchange. There was always a third person and her problems and crises to come between them: "Mother is ill, disappointed, or upset," or, "Anne seems terrible alienated; she still stays away from us all." Peter's questions of his father, how he really feels or what he really needs or wants, were quickly and deftly deflected: "You do what you have to do," his father said without apparent feeling and by unreflective rote. "Some things never change; you just learn to adjust." Or else his father talked in abstractions and Peter simply withdrew. In their first few moments together, Peter had looked for an opening, for a pause in his father's flow of words—but there was none. So he exchanged the option of dialogue for a defensive stance of "deference and respect."

Twenty minutes into the hour, the therapist asked why Peter had withdrawn, given up, abandoned the dialogical process. Hadn't the client and therapist jointly planned a forum, strategies, and methods so that Peter could at last surface his priorities, interests, questions, and claims? Hadn't they carefully worked out an approach that might finally lead to a hope that he would be heard by his father, and hear his father in return? Was there a loss of courage? Had Peter changed his mind? Why was he so rapidly reduced to silence? Could he find no way to interrupt his father or just to slow him down? Could he see no merit in his father's speaking style and habits? Could he find no way to identify his father's authentic if wayward attempts to protect himself, his wife, and his son?

Peter was startled. No, he wasn't aware that he had withdrawn and fallen silent. Yes, he was overwhelmed by his father's flow of abstractions. Yes, it was very hard to slow his father down. To his memory, he had never even tried it. No, he didn't know how to interrupt his father. His father's respectful style obscured Peter's disappointment and rage, and functioned as a stumbling block to real exchange and care. For his part, Peter's father was doing what he knew best: He filled the void between family members when life got tense and frightening. Early on though, he reflected, he had made a mistake "in trying to control my wife." He laughed ruefully when the therapist asked if he had accepted a "zoo-keeping role." "I guess that's true in a way. My stance with the children had always been, 'Don't worry, I'll take care of it.'"

Over time, Peter's father had let caretaking and protectiveness become a form of compulsive busyness—the kind of busyness that tries to deny his own and other people's despair. It was true that his marriage was bad and his wife problematic. But didn't his children deserve something more? As Peter's father defined it, his go-between function helped save the children from their mother. If he could manage to contain her anger, resentments, and blame, why not? Why burden the children with her problems and tendencies to dump them on anyone who would listen? They surely deserved to be spared from their mother's drunkenness and roller coaster moods. "But somehow in all of that," Peter's father said, "something seemed to go wrong. What happened that kept my children from staying close to each other and me?"

PETER: But what about you, father? What about your hopes, your wishes, your feelings? What about you and me?

FATHER: Why, I thought you knew, Peter, that you've always been my favorite. I think I've told you that before. Ours has always been a privileged relationship. Don't you yet know that it's you to whom I most readily turn? There's nothing I wouldn't do for you in the past. There's nothing that I won't do for you now. Just tell me what you need.

PETER: But that's part of the problem all by itself, I've spent my lifetime being concerned about everyone around me, just as you have. I can't take that anymore. I even used to think that our relationship depended on my finding a way to solve your marriage problems. I guess I'm aware that somehow I've been important to you—but I need something more now. I need you to know who I really am. I need to know that you can learn what I think is important to me. I need to know that you get something from life that doesn't depend on mother.

The meeting ended. Peter and his father ate together and talked for a long while later in the day. It was the first time in Peter's adulthood that they had been able to share time alone. They tried to cultivate the fragile ecology that typically exists between the man who is father and the man who is son. They knew that their newly discovered will to dialogue had only just begun. Certainly nothing radical had shifted, but something *had* happened. Somehow both of them were clearer about the reality of each other's care. Later in the week Peter's parents telephoned him. "It was nice," he later reported, "not to have a horrendous emotional reaction to their call." Residual trust was beginning to surface from its latency of so many years. Resentment, guilt, and defensiveness were not the only way.

Peter's father's patterns of relating might be severely limited in the ways he chooses to live, but he can still hear his son. A connection between them remains. What's more, Peter's mother had finally sent Peter his Christmas gifts. For the first time in a very long while, she sounded really animated over the phone. Peter doesn't know what his father chose to share with her about the therapy session—nor does he intend to ask. In fact, he is trying to talk separately to each of his parents over the phone rather than to both of them together. Now that he knows how family members tend to triangulate each other, he wants to extricate himself. There's a long way to go. Still, things promise to be different. He feels good to know that he didn't have to be so defensive when his parents called this time. He just didn't feel so scared. It was also nice to skip the banal formalities with his father. It was especially nice not to have to talk about insurance and the car.

Peter was fast discovering that the consummate triad consists of father, mother, and child. Factually and dynamically, it is literally impossible to address a youngster and one parent as if the other parent were of no import. People try and fail. At one or another time, in subtle or blatant forms, they get involved in allying themselves one against the other. After a while, each member of the parent–child triad is responsible for pitting one person against another instead of building trust. Over time each of them is well served to assess their own discreet parts in unjust relating, and in creating a deteriorating situation. For example, how have the three relating partners become destructively enmeshed? Do power alliances of two against one become a daily game? Will the consequences of a legacy of split loyalty (in which a child offers his/her love to one parent at the cost of betraying the other) infinitely repeat themselves in all of the offspring's future relationships? To what degree can fairness be a real option for any of them unless one of them decides to risk a challenge? Has the family environment developed enough of a trustworthy basis for each of the two parents and their adolescent or adult child to develop a dyadic friendship, one that can respect age, filial, marital, and gender-appropriate roles? All of these questions came into play when Peter began to addresss his parents as two separate, discreet, and unique human beings.

One of the major developmental tasks of dialogical relating has to do with an offspring's capacity to differentiate between a false responsibility for rectifying the skewed condition of his parents' marriage, and an authentic adult responsibility to establish fair balances of consideration between him and *each* of them. In the former instance, an offspring can find himself helplessly caught in a hopeless and permanent triangle. In the latter instance, an offspring can earn merit by reconnecting with each parent, and free himself to live his own life *despite* his parents' inability to get along with each other. Finding fair options for relating to his mother and father, however destructive or limited each or both of them may be, inevitably has a liberating effect on the "child" who can still offer care.

For as long as he can remember, Peter has assumed the burden of "saving" his parents' marriage. Why did they stay together? He wasn't really sure. Maybe for reasons of money, religious fidelity, health. They had been married now for over forty years. What did each give to the other, and what did each get in return? Not much, he suspects; but they provide company for each other now. Did they contribute to each other's lives in ways he couldn't see? He didn't think so but didn't know much about that either. What Peter does realize is that his wish to help his parents make a life together became a self-assumed mandate early on. Or could it be that they somehow delegated the task to him as well? He is the youngest child, after all, and may be his parents' last symbolic try at establishing commonality. In any case, the mandate became a paramount effort and the effort became a compulsion. Could he ever be free to live his own life if his parents stayed stuck in despair? When it finally seemed apparent that he had "failed" in attempts to rescue them, Peter suffered a loss of self-esteem, he suffered for them, and he suffered an even greater loss of trust in a patently unfair world. Only now was he reconsidering the possibilities. Perhaps something of a different nature could still occur.

A couple of weeks after Peter's meeting with his father, his focus began to turn to his mother. If his father and he could rebuild a connection-in-common, could he manage a shift with his mother too? Hearing his father talk had made him feel less lonely, less cut off. It had also reminded him of the good times he had once had with his mother. Only recently had he remembered her packing surprises in his lunch bag. She really had spent a lot of time and energy on him and Tim. He was less frightened to take his own needs into consideration now. It seemed that little could be lost by testing out the situation. His father had said how glad he was that Peter had chosen a family path for therapy. Peter felt hopeful too. This past weekend a fourth-year medical student had committed suicide. It reminded Peter of how close he himself had felt to death. He's upset about it like everybody else, but amazed in a way too. He's moved far from suicidal thoughts. How could it have been a real option such a short time ago?

By the following week Peter had phoned his mother. The exchange was superficial but friendly. When he asked her to a therapy session her first response was fear: "I don't want a therapist to listen, and then to go and commit me." But it didn't take long for her to agree. "I'd like to come down," she said. "I'll do anything that you want." Like any parent who is deeply invested in her young, Peter's mother was afraid of being judged. However, she was more afraid of losing her son permanently, and certainly interested in reclaiming him—on different terms if necessary.

Peter began to list priorities between him and his mother. First of all he wanted to talk about Kathy instead of continuing to pretend that she simply had never existed. What's more, since Kathy's death he's conceived of his mother as an aging and dying parent about whom he has to care—without expecting much of a return. He was worried about her emotional neediness too, and her press to please everyone all of the time. She could never say "no" to anyone, including him. In his "religious days," Peter couldn't say what he intended to his mother either. She knew that and once accused him: "You're afraid to stand up to me!" "I have a horror of upsetting father, of seeing him in an emotional state," Peter said. "With mother it's different. I expect to get more from women. Even now, we can talk about a lot of things. Mother and I haven't even met yet, but our relationship is already beginning to regain some of its old vitality."

"Maybe father voices over mother too," Peter mused, "the same way he still manages to voice over me." The possibility that his father's behavior might have destructive consequences for his mother was underscored by the negotiations about his mother coming to a therapy session on her own. After she had agreed to be present, his father asked when "our appointment" was scheduled—despite the fact that Peter had asked to see each of them separately. "Mother, of course, can't make the trip alone," his father said. "It's over a hundred miles. Yes, there is a train but you know about her heart. She's still in pain from her bout with the shingles and she's struggling with cataracts too. I'll just sit in the waiting room and stay out of the way." Did his mother think she could travel alone? She told Peter that she has no problem with the idea at all. Was Peter worried about her safety while she was on the train? He didn't think so; he thought she'd be alright. Would he be more confident if she consulted her physician? That might be a good idea. He would ask her if that would help.

Peter was reluctant to confront his father on the matter. His father "lacks the language" to say what he means. In any case, it was probably inappropriate, just a way of setting up one more triangle. After all, it was for his mother to decide. On the phone the other night, she was anxious about Peter's father's behavior too. She has long leaned on her mate in ways she could never lean on her dad. Her husband was available and reliable in ways that her father never had been. Long ago she had joined the children as a competitor for her husband's parenting. Peter's father may have his limits; still, he often seems to have been the only adult there. "He'll override me," she said, but Peter encouraged her to fight for what she wants. His father yielded once his mother stated her strong preferences. He was still worried about her. More to the point, her decision threatened old

# #

patterns that existed between them. What losses did he suffer if she began to function independently? How competitive with her was he for the attention of their son? How much did he depend on his wife's depending on him?

Peter met his mother at the train. She greeted him with "I did it." He greeted her with relief. In the session his mother was eager, voluble, alert, articulate—far from the emotional cripple that father and son had described. "We've had trouble," Peter began, "giving each other what we each have to give. I guess I thought that being independent meant I had to stop taking anything from my parents." "I came down today," she replied, "because Peter needed me." The intergenerational gauntlet had been run. Parent wants to conserve the family; son wants to press beyond it. Neither is possible in a pure or simple form. At best each family passage creates a developmental crisis, a natural conflict between the generations. Mother and adult child are locked into a face-off steeped in colliding entitlements. Neither can change the direction or priorities of their stages of life, but both can influence the balances of just consideration that exist between them.

Too often therapists are forced to witness the consequences of grieving offspring who have lost the chance for direct exchange between themselves and a parent who's died: their entitlement to pleasure muted; constricted in their give-and-take with others, particularly spouses; unable to offer what they never received. A word, an act, one last offer of tenderness from offspring to parent might have changed the balance. A touch, an acknowledgment, one final word of gratitude or even regret from parent to progeny might have transformed the legacy for generations to come. One last chance to connect—just this one time—with adult heart and mind. Possibilities to right the ledger with a dead parent continue to exist in indirect ways but none that can reopen dialogue. If people can find courage to trust enough to risk again with parents, rebalancing can occur before the final and fleeting impetus of dying and death. If people can define transgenerational conflict as more often normative and resource-based than pathological, reconnecting is more likely to heal, benefit, and free than to injure, burden, or exploit.

Peter and his mother had rejoined, this time on adult terms: two selves present to each other with directness and immediacy—each with merit and legitimate claims of their own. The residual trust between them supported their efforts. They clashed, but neither submitted nor resisted, apologized nor attacked. Each acknowledged his and her own contribution to the breakdown between them. Each surfaced how they felt injured and ignored. They incorporated other family members in their exchange without surrendering their own perceptions, and worked hard to leave out blame. There were no triangles this time delimiting their freedom, but two sets of perceptions looking for a bridge. "He's had a rough time with me," Peter's mother said.

> I wanted to be a model mother but I just didn't know how. I wanted to let him grow up; but how do you let go of worrying about what he needs? I'm jealous of his older sister Anne. They're very close, you know. I have two and a half givers

and two takers in the family. Anne's a taker. She was that way even as a baby. I took care of her, bathed her, dressed her, played with her. But when her father came home at night, she ran into his arms. When they're little, you know, they step on your toes. When they're big they step on your heart.

In Peter's mother's view Anne not only preferred her father but "took over" her younger brothers too.

Anne seems to have rebuffed attempts to reconcile, at least by her mother's report. After Kathy's funeral, Anne had taken a big step. "Let's let things go," she is reported to have said. "I was so very grateful then," her mother recalls. "We hugged, we held each other, we cried. And then something went wrong. I don't really know what happened. Anne's a self-sufficient person, I guess. Its clear that she doesn't need me." Then there was the day that Anne graduated from medical school. "I told her how proud I was of her," her mother went on. "'You've made it all by yourself,' I said. She never said a word."

In part, Peter's mother's estrangement from Anne is based on parentification (Bakan, 1965). From Anne's first year of life, her "preference" for her father made her mother feel unwanted. In part, the estrangement is built on power alliances, that is, Anne's influence over Peter and her mother's competitive resentment. In part, her mother's intensity about Anne is clearly linked to her earlier relations, which always seemed to result in loss—her father's violence, her mother's helplessness, their deaths before she was 20. As she sees it, her tragic legacy of loss has continued through her daughters: "Anne turned her back on me," she says, "and won my husband and two sons. And I lost Kathy to the nuns."

Two events marred Peter's mother's memories of Kathy. The first had to do with her birth, the second had to do with her death. When Kathy was born, her sister-in-law Virginia "took her to the altar and dedicated her to God." "Aunt Virginia was a staunch Catholic," Peter relates, "and authoritarian too. She gave Kathy away." At the time of Kathy's death, her mother had to compete with nuns again.

They took over and were so cold and decorous. I felt my tears were judged. The day we buried her was the worst day of my life. She had never been left alone. I just wanted to get a chair and go back to sit with her. None of us has ever talked. We have never shared our grief. I just remember this bunch of nuns. To them Kathy was getting a good break; she was going to God. I didn't want them to look down on me but I got to the point that I hated them. I also hated God. I quit going to church. I went to a priest. I asked him not to holler at me for hating God, but how could it be? Kathy was doing his work in his world and still he snatched her up.

The priest asked me if I thought that I was the only one in this world who ever hated God. That shocked me; I didn't know what to do. I just don't want her forgotten. In my mind she's always there. My husband cried a lot when we lost her, and then he vowed never to cry about Kathy's death again. My oldest and my youngest children were my very best—and they loved each other too. I think that this guy [Peter] thought Kathy was his mother.

Peter's mother's life, as she saw it, was in everyone's hands but hers. She felt particularly defined by her husband—of whom she sometimes still managed to speak with humor and grace.

> My husband can best be described as a modern, old-world man. On the one hand, he has to be head of the family. On the other hand, he's always been ready to accept the responsibilities of a father. In fact he accepted them too well. He would play with Tim and call him endearing names like "brown bear," and he would take long walks with Peter. He would tell them how much he loved them, and I always felt left out.
>
> I'm schizophrenic when it comes to my husband. For example, I can go out with the girls [friends] and have a wonderful time. They let me know that I'm fun and tell me that I'm bright. They treat me with respect and sometimes ask for my advice. Then I come home to him and never know what to expect. So I slink down and act moody and unhappy. It's like I'm two separate people. I don't know if I want to try anymore. How many times can you risk being hurt?

Peter's mother's responses, when it came to her children, were appreciative, competitive, regretful. "Tim and Peter were the only two I really had time for. Peter was so beautiful, too beautiful to be a boy. He should have been the daughter; Anne should have been the son. She played softball, watched football with her father, and knew how to talk to him." Throughout the meeting Peter had been patient if involved. Now he became momentarily annoyed, and then forthright.

PETER: I don't like hearing that I should have been a girl. I've heard it all my life. How much, I wonder, has that added to all my trouble in learning how to be a man? I don't like being defined by you. There's no way anyone can replace all that you've done for me. But it makes me angry when you try to keep me from other people.

MOTHER: [interrupting] I would never do that.

PETER: I always felt forced to choose between you and Anne. You demanded to know who I loved more, her or you. That wasn't a fair thing to do to a 10-year-old kid.

MOTHER: [protesting] But I felt she was taking over you and Tim. The only way to win with Anne was to make her leave the house. Even then she'd write to your father at work. I know how hard I've tried with Anne.

PETER: It's not Anne that's the problem. Look at what happened whenever we brought people into the house. If Carl or Tim brought women home, you were always incredibly jealous. What were we supposed to do?

THERAPIST: Could it be that your mother always seems to lose in a three-way exchange?

MOTHER: Yes. Kathy and her aunt, Kathy and the nuns, my husband and Anne, Anne and the younger boys; the list goes on and on. I always seem to lose what I want in any threesome I'm in. What do I do wrong that lets others get their way?

The session ended in a welter of emotions: mother and son crying and laughing, overwhelmed by the weight and the promise of the hour's events. Legacies had been surfaced, hard issues had been raised and joined. Fears of addressing each other were demystified. Destructive patterns and fresh options for relating had been noted. Two people reconnecting, reworking perceptions and expectations, intuiting each other's private if not separate contexts, beginning to grasp each other's terms and sides. Again latent trust had begun to emerge between two human beings whom fate, through birth, had cast into each other's lives.

Over the next few weeks Peter noted changes taking place in different ways. First of all he spoke to Anne. Things were awkward between them. Early on she had counseled Peter not to tell their parents that he was in therapy. Now she warned him not to impose the gains of his therapy on her. He and Anne could still be friends, Peter observed. What was clearer now, though, was how much their past friendship had rested on a common definition of their parents as adversaries—especially their mother. Peter wondered if there were resources that could shift the balances of unfairness here. Or would their parents remain unintended pawns between them? Could brother and sister build a trust-based relation that could transform their conflicting loyalties into a common future that would be more decisively their own?

Peter was more closely in touch with his own needs and wants now. He was clear that he didn't want his parents to relate to each other at his expense. He was just as clear that he didn't want to continue to relate to Anne—or to anyone—at his parents' expense. He was freer to make new choices. He would find a way to tell Anne what he wanted to do. He was confident that, given their friendship, she would find a way to hear. Peter's entitlement to make decisions of his own had grown in direct proportion to his efforts at reconnecting with each of his parents—on his terms as well as on theirs. That entitlement accrued and provided a reservoir of trust resources that allowed him to risk investing in relationships anew. He no longer counted on automatically losing himself to other people when he and they didn't agree. He no longer had to be defined in someone else's image or by one-sided terms. Peter was very hopeful. After all, look what had happened with Tim.

Tim had called to tell Peter about his new job. He was to write short news stories for a denominational press. "You're an accomplished interviewer," Peter told his older brother, "I have a lot to learn from you." Tim was startled at Peter's words. "You have it backwards," he said. "You're the one who's becoming a psychiatrist. I'm the one who has to learn from you." "Whether or not I become a psychiatrist," Peter replied, "I'm still a person with needs. I've felt lonely and cut off from everybody, including you, since high school. We were close then but I stopped turning to you. You seemed distant and bored, with no time for me."

"It was amazing," Peter said. "Tim was interested in me. We talked about my issues in high school and how some of them are still unresolved. He even came after me for how I had distanced him. He's good at saying his piece without a lot of regard for how other people take it." Tim had said, "You've always seemed like you wanted to go it alone, as though yours was a private kind of suffering that you didn't want to share." "Can you believe it?" Peter mused. "Tim wants me to be a part of his life."

> I guess I should have known it. Tim and Carl are the only ones who really seem able to live their own lives. On the other hand there seems to be a tragic gloom that hangs over Tim. I wonder if it affects an infant *in utero* if its mother is always crying and sad? Tim's had no qualms in saying his truth. He was the only child who shouted at Mom. Sometimes she would go after him with a lighted cigarette when he wouldn't say he loved her. Other times she would lock herself in her room. Then Tim would cry, "I just want to hear you say you love me." In any case, I see a real promise of friendship for Tim and me. He and Beth even plan to spend some time with me in June. It makes me realize that I'm not sure about Carl yet. He's older and lives far away. He tends to be superficial too, and I guess I never know what to say. It annoys me when he asks about my girlfriends, and insists on calling them "chicks." Even with him, though, I guess I'll find a way. This family stuff comes out at every turn. It reminds me of I Ching.

At Easter Peter, Tim, and Beth, who was 8 months pregnant, went "home" to spend 2 days. The gathering went well; conversation flowed and was more one-to-one. Their mother wasn't excluded this time, and their father was emotional—just plain glad and grateful that their children had decided to try again. The family was even able to talk about Kathy some. "Something else new happened," Peter related. "Tim and Beth invited our parents to visit when the baby is born. Mom is going to do that even though she's scared of planes. I'm looking forward to being an uncle, and I'm sure that the baby will favor 'our side.' " The first night with their parents was almost perfect; the second night a little more strained. Their mother and father had drunk too much wine. "We were all embarrassed but no one said a thing," Peter recalled. "Tim and I talked about it later. The next time will be different. At least we want them to know what we think."

In terms of his life with his peers, Peter is still struggling with uncertainties about intimacy and sexual identity. He and Jane have continued to see each other over the winter and spring. They explored the parameters of their relationship. Could it be platonic or could sexual intimacy eventually evolve? They have felt close and loving, and enjoy a lot of interests in common. Recently, though, life together has gotten unbearably rocky. Jane seems resentful of Peter's sexual withholding and feels as if he always needs to control. Peter is hurt by Jane's accusations, and confused over her chronic volatility. They decided to use a therapy session to investigate how to reestablish the closeness they once felt. Here again, though, the issue was more one of commitment than of feelings. They had been unable to establish a viable contract that could support responsible continuity of relationship. In addition, they were hard put even to surface their own claims and terms. Jane's is essentially a spousal expectation of Peter; Peter's a brotherly one of Jane. There is no question of their genuine affection for each other, but, still, there is a mismeeting. There simply is no option through which to rework their colliding intents.

In the session Peter and Jane eventually recognized their dilemma and, momentarily at least, could transcend their tendencies for disappointment and blame. Jane was willing to continue the friendship if Peter could promise to consider sexual intimacy as a goal. "It seems like too much to lose," she said. Peter preferred not to make a promise under pressure. He just wasn't sure what he wanted, or what he was able to do. He did know, however, that he couldn't live his life right now at someone else's pace. He was weary of giving offered by a fist in a velvet glove. He was also weary of "maternal" women who used their emotions to manipulate people, and to avoid having to say what they want. He didn't want to lose Jane's friendship. He understood that his decision might be based on a need to protect himself from his mother, or to replicate the relationships with his sisters. He was truly regretful, but finally decided to choose for himself. The session together had clarified their situation but not reconciled it. Jane and Peter had hoped for something different, some definite direction for the future, but they recognized their limits and were glad, at least, to have had their say. They made plans to part, with an agreement to give each other space and to take some time to think.

Over the past 3 months Peter has also begun to rework how he relates at school and, when he can, to choose for himself there too. He's felt a lot of resentment at physicians who act and speak in front of patients as if the patients aren't present. Instructors on medical rounds often discuss the implications of a person's injury or disease in front of him/her, with little consideration or regard for the person's terror or sensitivities. It dismays Peter, and makes him mad. Up until now he's hung back until after everyone has gone, and taken time to assure and console the patient. He still does that sometimes. He has also begun to address the offending physicians directly, and to challenge other professors as well: "Is it necessary to do that? Can it be done in another, more caring way?" "Is this recent test a fair assessment of what students actually know?" Peter seems freer to take some initiative when skewed or loaded questions are being raised. Also, he's actively interviewing for a residency in psychiatry. There's no more talk of dropping out of school.

Peter's life goes on, and the quality of his life deepens as he maintains a dialogical stance. His trust base has deepened, his isolation lessened. Reality has forced its way into his vision and ideals. He is newly able to take risks, to test the world around him. His anxiety has lessened. He is hopeful and playful too. He has used therapy well and could do so precisely because he operates out of an ample reservoir of resources with whose existence he had lost touch. He listens well, can hear nuances, and recognized his own terms and priorities early on, even when he couldn't articulate them. Most of all, perhaps, he's found the freedom that comes of telling the people he loves who he is and what he wants. He's earned the merit that comes of risking the courage to mean what he says and to say what he means. He's discovered that to make a claim or request for himself can be an expression of giving, a contribution to his friends' and relatives' well-being, instead of a selfish act. Peter has begun to learn about the freeing aspects of choice (Deut. 30:19), and in the process of choosing, he has reconnected with his family's sources of trust.

REFERENCES

Bakan, D. *Sigmund Freud and the Jewish mystical tradition.* New York: Schocken Press, 1965.

Boszormenyi-Nagy, I., & Krasner, B. R. The contextual approach to psychotherapy: Its premises and implications. In G. Berensen & H. White (Eds.), *Annual Review of Family Therapy* (Vol. 1). New York: Human Sciences Press, 1981.

Boszormenyi-Nagy, I., & Krasner, B. R. *Between Give and Take,* A clinical guide to contextual therapy. New York: Brunner/Mazel, 1986.

Boszormenyi-Nagy, I., & Spark, G. *Invisible Loyalties: Reciprocity in Intergenerational Family Therapy.* New York: Harper & Row, 1973.

Buber, M. *I and thou* (R. G. Smith, Trans.) Edinburgh: T. & T. Clark, 1937.

Buber, M. *Eclipse of God.* New York: Harper & Row, 1952.

Buber, M. *Between man and man.* New York: Macmillan, 1965. (a)

Buber, M. *The knowledge of man* (M. Friedman & R. G. Smith, Trans.). New York: Harper & Row, 1965. (b)

Buber, M. *A believing humanism: Gleanings.* (M. Friedman, Ed.). New York: Simon and Schuster, 1969.

Cotroneo, M. & Krasner, B. R. A contextual approach to Jewish–Christian dialogue. *Journal of Ecumenical Studies,* 1981, *XVIII* (1), 41–62.

Friedman, M. Healing through meeting: A dialogical approach to psychotherapy. *American Journal of Psychoanalysis,* 1975, *35,* 255–267.

Heschel, A. J. The mystical element in Judaism. In L. Finkelstein (Ed.), *The Jews.* Philadelphia: Jewish Publication Society of America, 1949.

Jung, C. G. *The Collected Works of C. G. Jung.* (R. F. C. Hull, Trans.). Bottingen Series *XX.* New York: Pantheon Books, 1961, Vol. 11.

Katz, R. L. Martin Buber and psychotherapy. *Hebrew Union College Annual,* 1975, *XLVI,* 413–431.

Krasner, B. R. Religious loyalties in clinical work: A contextual view. *Journal of Jewish Communal Service,* 1981–1982, *LVII* (2), 108–113.

Krasner, B. R. Towards a trustworthy context in family and community. *Journal of Christian Healing,* 1983, *5,* 39–44.

Krasner, B. R., & Shapiro, A. Trustbuilding initiatives in the rabbinic community. *Conservative Judaism,* 1978, 33 (1), 6–21.

Schoeninger, D. W. Notes on restoring trust. *Journal of Christian Healing,* 1983, *5,* 45–55.

CHAPTER 5

Toward a Resource Model
in Systemic Family Therapy

CONCEPTUALIZING FAMILY RESOURCES

A family was sent to family therapy by a school guidance counselor because their 8-year-old son said he "wants to be a girl." He was behaving in ways that were upsetting to his parents and teacher. A report from the school counselor arrived before the first appointment. As most such psychological reports do, this one focused on symptomatology and likely etiology. The parents were framed as having many deficits. Fears and weaknesses were highlighted. Veiled hints of child sexual abuse were suggested with no evidence. Parental reticence to be involved in treatment was discussed as resistance. In short, a reality composed of written words had been woven focusing on blame, shortcomings, and out-of-context symptoms.

The systemic therapist encountering this family, or any family, has a many-faceted task to accomplish, including: formulating systemic hypotheses, engaging family members, conducting a relevant interview, designing effective interventions, and, in this particular case, accounting for and perhaps negotiating the family's relationship with a complex larger system that views them negatively (e.g., the school). For the systemic therapist, all of these tasks are done within a larger contextual frame that views families as essentially resourceful, and only secondarily and temporarily as in need of therapy or other outside input.

The systemic therapist's viewpoint is that all families are problem-solving entities. Any existing family has solved thousands of problems, utilizing the resources of individual members and the unique collective resources that result from relationships in dyads, triads, the whole family, and family members plus others. Through a trial-and-error process over time, families become adept at handling a wide range of life's exigencies. Patterns develop that are often routine

Evan Imber-Black, Ph.D. Department of Psychiatry, Family Therapy Program, University of Calgary, Calgary, Alberta, Canada.

and out of awareness. Explanatory metaphors emerge for "why things are the way they are." In short, families are drawing on their own resources, or figuring out ways to utilize the resources of others, almost continually.

At various points in any family's life cycle, however, the family may be called upon to meet new demands, experience an overload of stress due to the convergence of too many difficulties (including physical, emotional, social, and political), or be unable to solve a problem from within their own frame of reference. At this moment, the family has not suddenly become bankrupt in terms of its own resources, although its assets may be temporarily frozen or creating no interest. Individual strengths may be blocked by organizational constraints, within both the family and the wider context with which the family interacts.

When a therapist enters the sphere of any family, she is faced with a fundamental choice that will guide subsequent action, and serve to influence profoundly the co-created therapeutic reality. This choice involves adopting a deficit model of family functioning or a resource model of family functioning.

A deficit model of family functioning assumes appropriate knowable norms for family organization and interaction (e.g., two-parent family as most optimal). Whatever deviates from these norms is in need of repair. The focus is on weaknesses, static, knowable traits, and diagnostic labels. Therapy is seen as that which puts something into the family that the family is missing.

A resource model of family functioning assumes a family is continually generating its own norms in an interacting context of history, culture, ethnicity, social class, politics, interpersonal relationships, and individual quirks. The therapist searches for strengths, and attempts to remain respectfully curious and open to difference. Diversity is welcomed. Therapy is seen as that which facilitates the family's creative capacity to solve problems, to effect healing, to generate development, and to gain new knowledge, first with the therapist and then without the therapist.

This fundamental choice underpins all that follows, and all that follows will feed back to and reinforce this fundamental choice. Assuming a resource model of family functioning orients the therapist's general attitude and obviously organizes what and how one sees.

The therapist continually examines for the *meaningful context* in which behavior, thoughts, feelings, and actions *make sense*, rather than appear aberrant. This positioning of herself as participant-observer in a widening circle of connections buttresses the therapist against the pull of a deficit model, which tends to reduce and atomize.

The therapist appreciates the notion of complementarity in relationships and frequently scrutinizes stated attributes from this perspective. Thus, for example, while a family may designate a father as "strong" and a mother as "weak," the therapist is searching for strength in the mother's "weaknesses," or for what might emerge in the mother if the father appeared less "strong." Thus, complementarities rather than static qualities inform the resource model.

Every family is understood to have a wealth of idiosyncratic resources that the therapist can learn about and utilize, rather than ignore or dismiss. The first of these is religious, cultural, and racial identity as manifested by this particular family at this particular time in history.

A very religious Mormon couple came for therapy with two grown daughters who insisted they were no longer Mormons. The family fought constantly about this, until the oldest daughter began to appear severely depressed, resulting in the referral for family therapy. As therapy began, however, it was evident that engagement was very difficult, especially with the father. Clearly, therapy was not a comfortable or familiar way to solve problems. The girls began insisting that a Mormon cotherapist was necessary for their parents to feel understood. Three sessions appeared to have little effect, until the decision was reached to respect the spirit of the daughter's request, and to bring in a Mormon consultant. This session was extremely effective. The therapist listened attentively while the consultant explored religious issues with the family and then carefully connected these to relationship issues. The successes of the prior sessions became evident and were acknowledged by the family. The family confirmed that they would enjoy seeing the Mormon consultant again, but that their therapist was doing very well with them. In the next session, arguments over religious practices were dismissed by the family as no longer being of central concern.

In this brief case example, a resource model was employed. Rather than viewing the family as resisting, or the girls as trying to sabotage treatment or disqualify the therapist, the family's views about themselves (e.g., "We are a Mormon family") were respected as a resource and utilized as such to further progress in therapy.

A second area of resource includes all of a family's "inner language," that which identifies them to themselves and others as a family. This includes words and phrases with special meanings, positive myths, metaphors, imagination and rituals, special foods, family jokes in particular, and a sense of play and humor in general. A therapist using a resource model identifies aspects of the family's inner language and utilizes this when appropriate (see major case discussion, p. 157). A therapist's interventions that is grounded in the family's inner language may, in fact, enhance the family's repertoire in this domain.

A mother and daughter were seen in therapy following the daughter's precipitous return from college due to what appeared to be a psychotic episode. The girl had been hospitalized, put on high doses of medication, and carried the label "paranoid schizophrenic." Therapeutic work aimed at delabeling and centering the girl and her mother in the midst of a developmental crisis was quite successful. However, the mother complained that she was still frightened of her daughter and so "handled her with kid gloves." At these moments, the girl often took advantage of the situation, and the danger of a new escalation certainly existed. The family had a lovely flair for the dramatic and a fine sense of humour. A ritual was designed to further the process of normalizing their relationship of mother and emerging young adult, rather than custodian and patient. They were instructed to go shopping together, which they heartily enjoyed, and to find the most elegant, most expensive pair of kid gloves possible. When they returned home, the mother, with the daughter watching, was to soak the gloves in a bowl of water and put the bowl, gloves and all, in the freezer. She was then instructed to continue to treat her daughter with kid gloves when she needed to, but only *after* she had removed the gloves from the freezer and let them thaw out. Mother and daughter performed the ritual with great care and lots of laughter. The daughter continued to grow in responsible action and the mother stopped being afraid of her or of making inappropriate demands on her. The kid gloves stayed in the freezer and became part of the family's inner language.

A third area of resource, which may overlap with the others, involves *individual and family commitments*, loyalties, a sense of connections. This is a more difficult arena of family resource to articulate as it is often in this arena that members experience great difficulties, pain, and suffering. Any extended family, for instance, is an intricate web of commitments and loyalties involving feelings, beliefs, and actions. The primary task facing any new couple is the complex act of balancing commitments to each other, two sets of parents, and new children. We live in a time and place where individuals often experience more than one marriage, stepparents, and stepchildren, interethnic, interreligious, and interracial relationships, high geographic mobility, socioeconomic shifts, dramatic role changes within a generation, and the like. Human beings will frequently and unwittingly distort themselves in order to maintain labryinthine mazes of loyalties. A resource model recognizes that this area is fraught with potential dilemmas, while affirming that human connections in the family, commitments and loyalties within and among the generations, are the major source of human healing.

A fourth area of resource involves the family's *capacity to interact with the outside world* in a way that preserves and enhances its own integrity. This includes involvement with the entire nonfamilial world, such as work, neighbors and friends, and, in particular, large public sector systems such as schools, hospitals, welfare, courts, and clinics, which increasingly affect family life.[1] Families develop "rules" for dealing with the "outside world" just as they develop "rules" for family relationships. Since the therapist is, indeed, part of the outside world, each family will approach a therapist in its own unique way. For some families, this may include a long and unhappy history of dealing with the outside world. In these cases, in particular, a resource model examines the family in its wider social ecology, and "researches" with the family ways in which the family understands its own *survival* in the face of what it experiences as a hostile world. Here, the therapist takes care to enter in a way that enhances the family's abilities to cope with the outside world (the discussion of "neutrality" on p. 160 elaborates on this). What has been seen in the past as "defiance" or "being unworkable" may, in fact, be reframed as a family's plan to protect itself, which then becomes an unfortunate part of an escalating war between public sector helpers and a family. Affirming such a resource to the family may be the *first* step in establishing a different, more viable relationship with the outside world.

---

[1] For a more detailed discussion of family interaction with public sector systems, the reader is directed to Imber Coppersmith (1983a, 1983b, 1985).

The four major areas of resources discussed here—religious, cultural, and racial identity; inner language; commitments and loyalties; and interactions with the outside world—are intended to be suggestive of others and by no means complete. These are arenas to orient one's journey with the family, but a resource model implies an openness to discoveries.

In a resource model, interaction with the family is grounded in examining for and affirming competencies, even when those competencies may seem unusual. By showing frank and open interest in the family's view of itself, its struggles, its interpretations of its own history, its attempts to deal with a debilitaing "symptom," the therapist communicates a resource model to the family analogically. Reframing and more elaborate positive connotation (discussed in greater detail below) are major tools in a resource model, as the therapist seeks to communicate in words her own understanding of family members' resourcefulness.

Finally, respect for family resources is demonstrated in the therapist's response to the family's response to an intervention. In a resource model, the therapist remains open and curious, seeking to discover what the family did with new information, whether this information came as an opinion, a letter, a task, or a ritual. The actual performance of an event according to some instructions remains far less important than how the family members processed the intervention and utilized it as a catalyst for their own creativity and inventiveness. Here, the therapist needs to listen and observe carefully, for as change happens she/he may no longer be needed. A resource model communicates itself in action by designing "follow-up rather than therapy in 2 or 3 months" or by terminating, often by mutual consent.

IDENTIFICATION OF FAMILY RESOURCES

A resource perspective is implied in the patterns of systemic family therapy. It is my intent to demonstrate this, and then to suggest more explicit avenues for implementing a resource model within the systemic framework.[2]

Presession Team Discussion

The identification of family resources begins in the presession team discussion of any family to be seen in therapy. The intent of the team is to generate hypotheses for the conductor of the interview. Hypotheses are undecidedly not diagnoses. They are open, flexible, changeable in the face of information from the family. Thus, the therapist enters the therapeutic domain as one who will invite interaction with the family and who will remain open to encountering points of view that may not fit the hypotheses originally generated.

Further, as more is known about the family, the team works to develop *systemic* hypotheses, or those hypotheses that link family members together

---

[2]For a complete description of the systemic model, the reader is directed to Tomm (1984a, 1984b).

from a perspective that positively connotes the present family system. In order to do this, one is working, either implicitly or explicitly, from a resource point of view, as family members are designated as protective, loyal, behaving in the service of connectedness, helping other members out, attempting to rebalance old hurts, joining themes from previous generations, and the like. One is definitely not looking for deficits during this process.

For example, in the case cited earlier of the family whose little boy was upsetting everyone by saying he wanted to be a girl and behaving in what people deemed to be inappropriate ways (see p. 148), the presession hypothesizing focused on how this behavior might be protective and to whom, what kind of message the boy was giving and to whom, who was being distracted from more pressing concerns, and so forth. Hypotheses were also generated regarding the family's relationship to the school and the boy's possible role in this. Decidedly absent were gloomy views of the family as "abnormal," "impaired," "incompetent," "poorly organized," and the like.

Initial Interview

Following the presession, the therapist conducts the interview, primarily utilizing circular questions. Here, a resource model can inform the kinds of questions asked and the manner of asking. The questioning and responding process identifies family resources to the therapist *and* identifies family resources to the family in a number of ways.

Interviewing to Elicit Resources

In most circular questions, a family member is asked to comment either on the relationship between two or more other members, or on the family process in general, or on various family members' beliefs and actions. Several phenomena occur during this process that tap resources. The respondent is asked for observations, and thus is put in the position of articulating awareness about relationships that often remain out of awareness. Other family members who are listening are learning about themselves through the eyes of one of their own members.

Connecting the Family to Others

Many circular questions are designed to connect the family to others, to obviate a sense of isolation that permeates many families. Such questions orient the family to resources they may be ignoring, either within the family or outside. In this area come all of the questions about extended family, friends, and social relationships. Included are such questions as "What do you think your mother would say about this?" (and various other relatives), and "How would you compare your family to other families you know?" (along some particular dimension or theme). The latter question is often effective in evoking a family's sense of its own uniqueness. Such questions have the effect of centering the family in a wider context, allowing for more ways to see an issue and potentially more solutions. Frequently, empathy becomes more available as members hear each other's struggles from other contexts.

A couple was seen for a consulting interview. Each had been married before, and they were planning marriage now. However, since setting the wedding date, they battled constantly, and had cancelled the first wedding date. The interview began with the man remarking "Things are down the toilet." All attempts by the consultant to talk with them resulted in their constant refocusing on their war with each other. They saw only the two of them, isolated and battling. Finally, the consultant asked the following question: "Suppose the two of you did have a wedding—who would you invite?" This one question opened a 30-minute discussion in which the man and woman each reconnected with people and themes from their families or origin, prior marriages, and grown children, and during which their own resources as a couple reappeared, including empathy, warmth and understanding.

Exploring Alternative Beliefs and Perceptions

Certain questions are designed to explore opposite beliefs or perceptions. Often a family's view of itself or its members has narrowed, selectively omitting a range of possibilities that previously existed. Such questions may reawaken or evoke a more complex sphere of interaction. For example, with the "battling" couple just described, one may ask: "When is the last time you had fun together?" "What do you think he likes best about you?" "Which of you is the best fighter?" (implying some good things about fighting). "Who is good at making up? Who enjoys the making up?" (implying the connection between fighting and good times that follow). "If you did decide to leave each other, what do you think she'd miss the most about you?" All of these questions are designed to recontextualize the relationship as one where interactions other than fighting occur, and where "fighting" might have other meanings.

Hypothesizing about the Future

A particular line of questioning explores the future and hypothetical situations. Such questions tend to draw upon resources of imagination and creativity, while evoking a capacity to examine the present in the light of a possible future. Questions such as "How do you think things will be 5 years from now?" (for various people and relationships, along various themes) highlight degrees of connectedness in relationships, and issues of commitment. While there are exceptions, future-oriented questions often tend to generate a sense of hope, operating to remove the family temporarily from a more dismal present context.

Hypothetical questions that rearrange relationships frequently allow people to discover contextual constraints. For example, the question "Suppose your daughter left home next year—what effect would that have on the relationship between you and your husband?" may lead to the discovery of a desire for greater closeness that is somehow blocked by the present triadic organization, or to the discovery of a desire for greater distance whose expression is prevented by the current arrangement, or to the discovery of some other contextual constraint.

Future-oriented questions can also provide a measure for a family's sense of its own resources over time. For example, a series of future questions were asked in a first interview with a family with a "hyperactive" boy. The parent's view of his future and theirs was quite bleak, as they predicted his delinquency, dropping out, needing their care, and the like. Similar questions asked near the end of therapy were responded to with a sense of optimism for all concerned.

Focusing on Difference and Connectedness

Finally, all manner of circular questions and responses, whether triadic questions, ranking questions, or future hypotheticals, among others, focus simultaneously on two crucial phenomena in family life, *difference* and *connectedness*. Questions are asked in such a way as to promote allowance for the expression of differences. The therapist, through neutrality toward persons and ideas, through respect and compassion, sets a tone that invites the expression of differences without a fear of judgment or criticism. At the same time, the therapist interviews the family in such a way as to impart a sense of connectedness to a common history, to a valued heritage, to familiar themes, to a preferred future.

Postinterview Team Discussion

Following the interview *per se*, the team meets again to hypothesize based on information generated in the interview, and to make a decision regarding whether or not to utilize an end-of-session intervention, and, if so, what it should be. Here, a resource point of view again emerges. Positive connotations may be developed that connect the family quite explicitly to some of its resources. The family's inner language is examined and utilized as sources for possible interventions, including rituals that may draw on the family's language, symbols, metaphors, sense of humor, and sense of the absurd.

Interventions are designed to "go with the system," thus communicating respect for the family and its resources. Many interventions ask the family to make decisions, rather than the therapist making decisions for them. For instance, a ritual may be designed asking family members to decide who should come to the next session. Or, an intervention task may be given and the family asked how long they will need to complete the task in order to set the next appointment. Such decisional elements of interventions imply a belief in the family's knowledge of itself. They have the pragmatic effect of contravening unnecessary struggles in the therapeutic domain, and as a result enhance the actualization of latent resources.

Intervention

In the case of the boy who said he wanted to be a girl (see p. 148), several elements emerged in the interview that led to an intervention based on a resource perspective. The parents appeared very reluctant to discuss anything in front of the children. This was respected and the children were asked to leave for awhile. What emerged was a situation in which the parents had spoken to no one about this problem, and were, in fact, isolated from family and friends. The family was totally naive to therapy or other professional involvements, and would not have come if the school had not sent them. The issue was not spoken about at home either, except when fights erupted between the father and son. The mother and father were quite distant most of the time, except when fights between the father and son provoked the mother to enter and mediate, after which she spent time with her husband. The boy's problems, which also included a fascination with fire, coincided with the father losing his job and becoming a full-time househusband, who cooked and took care of the children while his wife worked all day. Most striking was the parents' great reluctance, bordering on terror, to discuss the issue in front of the children, stating they believed "talking about problems can often make things worse." Although they allowed the boys to enter when the therapist asked if she could talk to the boys with the parents listening, the session became quite frozen, and the boys either refused to talk or answered with non sequiturs.

An intervention was designed with several elements:

1. The therapist began by positively connoting the parents as very concerned parents, who were careful with their children and with how things were talked about in front of their children.

2. The therapist then stated: "In most situations, we find that it is useful for families to discuss sensitive issues among the members but we don't know if this is true in your situation." Here the therapist acknowledges that, while she has professional expertise and knows some things about families, she doesn't know all about their family, and that they are the experts on their family. Thus, this intervention is designed to draw on resources. The team thought that either the family could decide it would like some assistance in discussing sensitive issues openly, or it could figure out other ways to solve the problem. As will be seen, the family, in fact, developed a third alternative.

3. A ritual was assigned to assist the decision. The parents were asked to discuss the advantages and disadvantages of discussing sensitive issues. They were asked to examine the effects of these advantages and disadvantages on each family member, on each possible dyadic combination (e.g. husband–wife, mother–son, father–son, two brothers), and on the family as a whole. Further, they were asked to decide who should come to the next session, based on this discussion. At the next session, a decision would be made regarding whether or not family therapy was indicated, based on their discussion. The session was set for about 3 weeks away.

4. Finally, the parents were invited to come to the next session with any

questions they might have about therapy: what it was, what they might expect, and so forth. In this portion of the intervention, the therapist framed them as consumers of a service and entitled to knowledge about that service.

The whole family returned for the next session looking very different. All entered and all were eager to talk. The parents reported changing the ritual rather profoundly. They talked briefly to each other and quickly decided that it was silly not to talk to their sons, and so included them in the discussion. The subject shifted from the advantages and disadvantages of discussing sensitive issues openly to an actual discussion of these issues for the very first time. The boy began relating his behavior to dissatisfactions he was experiencing in the family and was quite articulate about them. The father said he discovered a lot about how he was expecting his two sons to be identical, and that he realized this was not possible. The husband and wife reported spending some enjoyable time together. The boy had ceased his symptomatic behavior. The family said they saw no need for therapy at the present time and agreed to come to a follow-up in 3 months. At the follow-up, the family reported no problems they could not handle, and no return of symptomatic behavior, and a mood of greater openness and relaxation prevailed.

The intervention respected the family's sense of readiness and timing, and in so doing, tapped the family's own resources for solving problems.

THE POTATO AND THE KIWI FRUIT: MOBILIZING AND UTILIZING FAMILY RESOURCES

In the following section an entire 10-session therapy is discussed with a focus on a resource model as underpinning systemic practice. Issues of neutrality, collaborative teams, questions, interventions, and stages of therapy are highlighted as these affect family resources.

A family was referred for family therapy by a dietician due to an "eating disorder" in the 12-year-old daughter. The referral source had seen the girl for several months with no change, and conceptualized the problem as "anorexia." She anticipated continued contact with the girl, but felt family therapy was indicated. The family consisted of: father, Bob, 33; mother, Sue, 30; a 12-year-old daughter, Sandra; and an 8-year-old daughter, Ellen.

Initial Interview

Exploration of the family's view of the problem in the first interview included many aspects of a resource perspective. In the opening moments of the interview, the family indicated that the mother saw the problem as a huge problem and the father seemed to vacillate between seeing it as more minor and being quite concerned. All agreed that the mother was the most worried and upset. In addition, the mother took the most action about the problem. She and Sandra struggled daily over Sandra's eating. However, the struggles only occurred at dinner, the one meal when the father was home. While the mother and Sandra fought, the father generally left the room and watched television.

When the therapist tried to talk to Sandra, she cried and wouldn't respond verbally. She appeared much younger than her stated age. The therapist then reframed the problem as Sandra "having favorites to eat" and Sandra smiled, wiped her tears, and said "Yes, french fries, bread, and milk." All agreed that, if left alone, Sandra would be content to eat french fries, bread, and milk. This reframing of an eating disorder as "having favorites" became a major theme in this therapy, standing metaphorically for issues of autonomy and tolerance for difference.

Further exploration revealed that, while Sandra was a bit underweight, she really did not have the classic symptoms that are agreed upon to be "anorexia." She simply refused to eat anything except her favorites, and had, in fact, behaved this way since infancy. However, all family relationships were now permeated by a focus on Sandra's eating. It was the main topic of discussion among all dyads.

Ellen, dressed in velvet, was framed as a "good girl who will eat anything!" Ellen refused to answer most questions. She would smile sweetly and reply "I don't know." Thus, the girls existed in a complementary relationship that constrained both their behavior and others' views of them.

Relationships with extended family also focused on Sandra's unique style of eating. Her mother's mother believed it was a severe problem. Sue talked to her mother often about it, and her mother frequently sent her books and articles about "anorexia." Sandra's father's mother believed it was a minor problem and advised her daughter-in-law to leave Sandra alone and that she would begin to eat on her own. Loyalty issues appeared quite salient, and the parents' positions vis-à-vis the problem began to make more and more sense in light of extended family relationships. Sandra's mother's high degree of worry and activity appeared to maintain a crucial connection to her own mother. Her father's vacillation made sense as he appeared to be trying to please both his wife and his mother, who disagreed with each other. Likely, the relationships manifested vis-à-vis Sandra's unique eating style were metaphorical for long-standing relationship issues between the family and extended family.

Time was devoted to exploring the family's relationships to the outside world, especially professional helpers. It emerged that the family had a long history with professionals. Sandra was born with a congenital heart defect that required surgical correction at age 11. There was, in fact, never a time in the life of the family when professionals were not engaged with it.

MOTHER: She was born with a congenital heart defect. I was 17 at the time the doctor came and told me the baby had a heart problem and then said "Don't worry about it."

The mother's tone as she spoke was one of frustration and near contempt. Her initial involvement with a professional left her feeling unsupported and misunderstood. In the face of this, she drew closer to her own mother. During the discussion of Sandra's heart problem, it became apparent that the family had lived with a decade of uncertainty regarding Sandra remaining alive. Her heart was now repaired, but the family still dwelled in this uncertainty. A portion of the interview given over to future predictions yielded the startling information that both parents believed Sandra would die in a few years if a solution were not found now. The mother believed this most, but the father agreed, explaining that he believed she would slowly eliminate foods and stop eating altogether. While the girl was not in any immediate danger, the capacity of the system to escalate, and the present inability to envision her future life due to the precariousness of her childhood needed to be taken quite seriously.

Following Sandra's recovery from open heart surgery, her mother sought help with the eating problem. The family doctor counseled ignoring the problem, thus unwittingly joining the position of the father and father's mother. Finally, the mother insisted and a dietician was brought in, who framed the problem as very serious, thus unwittingly joining the position of mother and mother's mother.

All direct involvements with professionals were the province of the mother, a very common situation. Such involvement tended to support the ongoing nature of a system in which the mother was most involved in the problem and the father was more aloof.

Discussion with Sandra about the dietician revealed that she regarded the dietician with derision.

THERAPIST: What happens when you see the dietician?

SANDRA: I just listen to a lecture [*tone of contempt*].

THERAPIST: What does she tell you?

SANDRA: She talks a lot about kiwi fruit! She tells me to eat kiwi fruit and I hate it!

Sandra emerged each week from the dietician's office with a list of two new foods to try. She handed this list to her mother, who then made a special trip to the store to purchase the items, thus involving her more in Sandra's unusual eating style and further omitting the father. Mother and daughter would then spend the week struggling over these new foods.

Finally, a portion of the interview was devoted to exploring prior solutions. This exploration communicates respect for the family as a problem-solving entity. The family had tried all manner of solutions, including bribery, punishment, force feeding, and seeking outside help. All attempts, however, were mitigated by a theme of "push her–back off" that reflected the positions of various members of the system.

Mobilizing family resources came from a number of vantage points in this session.

Neutrality

The therapist adopted a position of neutrality. Neutrality toward persons and ideas is a core concept in systemic family therapy that often promotes the actualization of family resources. Since the therapist is not critical, judgmental, or sidetaking, the family can gradually be less fearful and closed. Unable to discern *exactly* what the therapist thinks they should do or how they should be, the family is facilitated in its own search for how to organize without a symptom. A therapist utilizing neutrality attempts to see behavior in context. Here it is important to note that neutrality is not coldness or aloofness in therapeutic style. Neutrality is not a cavalier acceptance of symptomatic solutions. Nor is there anything inherent in a neutral position that prevents a therapist from affirming family resources. Indeed, from a neutral position, a therapist is more likely to remain open to the expression of resources that do not fit a preconceived notion of how all families should be.

All of this family's prior experiences with professionals had involved unwitting sidetaking and either explicit or implicit criticism. Here the therapeutic stance of neutrality allowed the father to become more active and involved and removed the stigma of blame from the mother. Neutrality provided the family with an *unexpected* relationship with a professional, one that differed from previous notions of help. The therapist maintained a stance of openness and curiosity in the relational domain, refusing to be drawn into the alliance patterns. She was careful neither to minimize the problem and thereby join the father and his mother, nor maximize it and thereby join the mother and her mother. The therapist maintained neutrality toward other ouside help, implicitly communicating that the family knew best for itself.

Initial Hypothesizing

This approach relies on hypothesizing about patterns among people rather than about static, individual traits or characteristics, which frequently focus the therapist on deficits. Intersession hypothesizing conceptualized Sandra's symptom as supporting and supported by a system whose overarching pattern was escalating complementarity. Sandra's mother, her mother, and the dietician believed Sandra had a serious, life-threatening condition, in need of immediate attention. Sandra's father, his mother, and the physician believed in backing off and that Sandra would eat normally in time. From time to time, the father would briefly join his wife's position, but would take no action, since to do so would make him disloyal to his own mother. Each position encouraged an exacerbation of the other. Escalating complementarity pervaded both the family system and the family–professional system.

It was further hypothesized that loyalty issues were salient and that Sandra was now in a position where she could not get spontaneously better, since to do so would be to side with her father and her father's mother, nor could she get better due to outside help, since to do so would be to side with her mother and her mother's mother.

Collaborative Team

Initial work with the family was done with a collaborative team (Roberts, 1983).[3] Such teams enhance a resource perspective. Since collaborative teams rely on mutual strengths of colleagues, they are more likely to focus on the strengths in families. When a resource point of view is part of the team's norms, then team members tend to mitigate against the emergence of deficit-model thinking. Thus, while some initial comments may focus on deficits, a more contextual and complementary conceptualization quickly emerges. Multiple punctuations of a given set of events are available. With a collaborative team, a therapist feels less personal "ownership," and so is less likely to push an idea on an unwilling family, and is more likely to remain open to a family's response. A team can be utilized to juxtapose two or more perspectives, thereby facilitating the family's own thought and decision-making process. Finally, with a resource model, it is hoped that the family can take credit for any changes that occur. This is more likely to happen when the therapist is receiving a sense of credit from a collaborative team.

In this case, the team developed the hypotheses described above, and the interventions described below.

Interventions

Two interventions were given at the end of the first session. Both involved family resources. The first was an "Odd Days–Even Days" ritual (Selvini Palazzoli, Boscolo, Cecchin, & Prata, 1978). Framed as an "experiment," the parents were asked to alternate days in dealing with Sandra's eating. Each was encouraged to approach the issue in his/her own unique way, thus communicating that each had something to contribute to the solution of the problem. This ritual had the immediate effect of engaging the father in the therapeutic endeavor, which no outside helper had previously attempted. Further, it affirmed that the mother's involvement was also needed.

The second intervention was quite unusual and was built on the family's inner language. This was a family whose entire existence presently centered on food and eating. The family was thus requested to bring dinner to the next interview.

---

[3]The collaborative team in this case consisted variously of Dr. Karl Tomm, Laurie MacKinnon, Alan Parry, Marija Bakaitis, Karine Rietjens, Joanne Schultz Hall, and Dr. Gary Sanders. Of the 10 sessions, the first six involved a team. A collaborative team is especially useful when one is experimenting, as in this case. However, systemic work and a resource perspective are viable for the sole practitioner.

Special instructions were given, requesting that Sandra and her father go shopping and get the items on the dietician's list, plus any "favorites" that Sandra would like the family and the therapist to eat. Her mother and Ellen were asked to make preparations. The family members all giggled at the prospect of the father going shopping and agreed to bring the dinner.

The In-Session Meal Ritual

The in-session meal ritual in systemic therapy from a resource perspective has been experimented with by myself and others in cases of "eating disorders." The ritual differs from a structural meal session in a number of ways. First, the family is asked to bring the food, rather than the clinic ordering food. In this way, the family is, in fact, able to bring a part of its daily ritual, eating together, to the therapeutic domain. General and specific instructions for buying and preparing the food are given. Often these instructions designate the system as presently organized. Sometimes, the instructions may be an experimental shift in organization. Family meals define membership. The in-session meal ritual places the family in the position of opening its boundaries to include the therapist as a "guest for dinner," thus temporarily shifting the helper–helpee complementarity. The therapist then conducts the session like any other systemic session. She/he does not criticize or instruct. This is probably the most powerful aspect of the ritual. A family with an eating problem likely comes to the meal session expecting criticism and advice. When the therapist remains neutral, the family is confronted with the unexpected, and is more likely to search for its own resources.

The in-session meal may be considered a gentle paradox, as family members discuss an eating problem while eating.

Family Session

The family took the task quite seriously. They arrived with china plates and a roast, salad, pickles, vegetables, and lots of buns, chosen by Sandra as her "favorite." A much more relaxed atmosphere prevailed and Ellen became quite willing to talk. Much of the session focused on a discussion of "favorites" and "disliked" foods in an attempt to put all members on the same level, and to further the reframing begun in the first session. Questions highlighted similarities between the sisters regarding the issue of food—for example, both hated pickles and salad dressing. Sandra allowed that the list of things she would eat was actually longer than first described. The therapist adopted a playful stance regarding Sandra's favorites, asking 'Where is the best place in town to get french fries?", connoting her as a "french fry gourmet." Questions focusing on which sister was "better at refusing certain foods" served to further detoxify the symptom, and raised the confusing notion that one might be very good at doing something considered very bad. Sandra insisted that she was much better than

Ellen at having her way, that she was, indeed, the "expert." What became apparent during this discussion was that Sandra's definitive expressions regarding what foods she would and would not eat were her only presently allowable expression of strong opinions. Likewise, her mother's countering Sandra with her own views about food were the main arena for the mother to express strong opinions. Thus, the "food fight" was valuable in a family where other strong opinions and expression of difference were presently unavailable.

During the session, Sandra caught the drift that she might be losing her special status, and she made attempts to reaffirm it. These attempts were parried by humor by the therapist.

SANDRA: I sat a long time at the dinner table.

MOTHER: Yes, she sits and sits.

THERAPIST: Really? What's her record at the dinner table? Five hours? [*Implying* that anything less was really no "big *deal*"].

MOTHER: Oh, no! I'd say much less.

SANDRA: An hour and a half! [*Very proudly.*]

THERAPIST: An hour and a half! Sort of European style leisurely dining! [*Laughter from the parents.*]

During the meal, the Odd Days–Even Days ritual was explored. All agreed that "Sandra ate better on her father's days." Her mother appeared greatly relieved to have him involved and not at all upset by her own inability to effect any change.

It should be noted that, during this meal, Sandra did, indeed, eat in unique ways. She refused most of what the family ate and consumed six buns and two cartons of juice. Attempts by the mother to get her to eat (it was her night in the Odd Days–Even Days ritual) were refused by Sandra.

Intervention

A ritual was designed to intensify the reframing of "favorite" foods and "disliked" foods in a way that suggested that Sandra simply was at the far end of a continuum that included the entire family. Each family member was assigned a day. On that day, the person was to tell the other three a food he/she especially disliked. The three were to get together and prepare that food in a new way that they thought might be palatable. That evening at dinner, the three were to work on convincing the person to eat the food. The family was asked to repeat this ritual so that each member had three turns before the next session.

The ritual implicitly called upon several resources. Family members were asked to join in new combinations not generally found in this family. All were asked to use their imaginations, both in preparing the food and in convincing the person to eat it. Members had to focus on other members beside Sandra.

The mother was to receive support in her efforts to get Sandra to eat. The ritual also supported the family's present resource of expressing strong opinions in the domain of food and eating.

Feedback to the Intervention

The family returned and reported that it had been more trouble to get Ellen to eat than Sandra. They stated that their mother and Sandra had ceased struggling over food, and had had a more ordinary mother–daughter fight over the state of Sandra's room. At this juncture, the mother began to complain more openly about feeling unsupported generally by her husband. This was the first expression in therapy of a strong opinion directly in the relational domain. Sandra stated she would be shocked if her father supported her mother, and that she always expected him to side with her. Up until this point, the therapy had centered on Sandra and her eating. Any attempts by the therapist to investigate other areas had been blocked. The family appeared more ready to look at other issues. However, as the therapist proceeded, the parents refocused on Sandra, insisting that she still ate "abnormally."

Marital and Extended Family Focus

At this juncture, it was decided to more thoroughly investigate the development of this family through time, including the marriage and extended family. It was discovered during this session that (1) the couple married quite young (17 and 20); (2) the father's parents objected strenuously to the marriage because Sue was pregnant with Sandra and was of a different religion; (3) the couple established and maintained great distance from the father's family; (4) the mother's parents were worried about Sue marrying so young and having a baby; (5) Sue and her mother established a special closeness after Sandra's birth that focused to a great extent on Sandra's eating; (6) the couple had great difficulty expressing differences and resolving conflict; and (7) both Sue and Bob believed that when there was conflict, Sue always "gave in." The session in which this information was generated was quite tense. Clearly, the therapist had walked to the edge of the family's tolerance for relational issues.

Positive Connotation

At the end of this session, the following positive connotation and opinion were offered:

"We think that you, Sandra, have taken on a really big job in this family. In terms of some of the unusual ways that you've decided to eat, we think you've taken on a really big job. The first thing that you do by eating in unusual ways is, of course, you worry your mother. She spends 50% of her time worrying about you. Now, what happens when your mother worries about you is that her mother worries about her, O.K. Now we know that your mother left home pretty young, at 17; she really left home, maybe, too soon; maybe she didn't get finished being mothered by her own mother, O.K. Now, one of the things I think you do when you eat in unusual ways is that you help your mother to stay close to your grandmother. [At this, the mother nods affirmingly.] We think, too, you've taken on a big job in terms of your dad's family, O.K., because when your folks got together in the first place, your dad's parents weren't too happy about that. And when that happens, for a lot of couples, O.K., when their parents don't think they should get married in the first place or they didn't approve of mother, that's a very hard problem to resolve, O.K., and a lot of people resolve it the way I think this family has resolved it, which is to stay distant, O.K., to stay a little more cut off from your dad's parents. Now one of the things that happens when you eat in unusual ways is, of course, your parents get very upset, but your dad's parents, they don't think it is a problem. They've said that, that they think you'll grow out of it, and I think that when they say that, which is a very different view than your parents' point of view, that that maintains the distance, that helps maintain the distance between this family and your dad's family, which is a way that they have of solving this problem about what to do about their feeling about your mom and dad as a couple.

"I think, third, part of the big job that you've taken on is that at some point in time, and probably pretty unconsciously, that you came to the conclusion that your parents hadn't really gotten married yet, O.K., and I want to explain to you what I mean by that. Lots of times when a couple gets off to a funny start, kind of a hard start, when their own parents don't think it's such a good idea for them to get together in the first place, they're worried about it, or they disapprove of it—couples like that are in a hard situation, O.K., because they want to be a couple with each other, but they also want to stay loyal to the families that they come from. So, how do they stay loyal to the families that they come from if those families don't think they should be a couple in the first place? Well, one way to do that is to not get fully married to each other and we think that, maybe that's what you think about your parents. And so that part of the big job that you've taken on is to work with them to help them get more married to each other. [Sandra is rapt throughout this discussion of her parents' relationship and her role in it.] Now, how have you done that? Well I think gradually, very gradually over 10 years, you've taken on the job of teaching your mother how to stand up to your father. [Here, the mother chuckles.] Every day you have struggles with your mother, you keep trying to teach her how to stand up to your father so they can get closer, they can be a couple, they can get more married in that way. Also, though, we think that you think that your father needs a hand in fighting with your mother and so every night you stand in for him and you do it for him. So these are some of the things that we think are the big job that you've taken on in this family by the unusual ways that you've decided to eat.

"Now the difficulty is that I think, Sandra, that you've recognized that in order to do this job and to do it until it feels finished, that right now you can't grow up, that right now you can't move ahead, become a teenager, begin to move away from the family and so it's necessary to continue to eat in unusual ways. We suspect, O.K., that right now, for the time being that Sandra is going to continue to do this big job until she's convinced that she doesn't need to do it anymore. Now, we don't know what it will take to convince her and so we'd like to meet with just the two of you [parents] in about a month to discuss that issue."

This particular positive connotation and opinion contained many elements. While the opinion was lengthy, it should be noted that the entire family listened with great interest and attention. It suggested a link between Sandra's actions and a whole host of family relationships and issues. Even problematic relationships, however, were connoted with words and tone as people doing their best under present circumstances. What might be seen as "overinvolvement" or "disengagement" were highlighted as solutions to very difficult problems. The possibility of overt conflict in the couple was framed as positive, as that which draws people closer.

Response to the Positive Connotation and Opinion

Often a positive connotation and opinion will mobilize family resources in unexpected ways. While the positive connotation, *per se*, is a comment on one view of the family's resources, families often respond by rejecting the explicit content while changing dramatically in the relational domain. What is especially important is that the therapist remain open to the ways that the family has utilized and responded to the intervention.

In this case, the parents returned as requested in a month. At this time, both soundly dismissed every aspect of the positive connotation and opinion. They offered a great deal of evidence to contradict the views that had been given. The father was more active than at any prior time in the therapy and stated: "The real problem is that my wife and I just haven't worked together on this. That's what we want to do now. We've never tried that before. That's what we need your help with."

This was a crucial turning point in the case. The family's resources had, indeed, been mobilized. The positive connotation seemed to generate new behavior and new observations of one another. The parents noticed aspects of Sandra's development that were previously unseen, and they highlighted her as an adolescent and not "young." New commitments were forming between husband and wife. A new relationship was being negotiated with a professional helper, one where the parents viewed themselves as consumers with rights to define parameters of the helping endeavor.

The therapist and team approached this turning point with deliberate efforts to enhance the change process. As the parents explained their reasons for rejecting the positive connotation, the therapist admitted her error, framing the parents as clearly knowing their situation best. The therapist and team then split. The therapist agreed to form a "partnership" with the parents in the endeavor they were requesting, while the team insisted that this would not succeed due to all the reasons given in the opinion in the previous session. The parents left redoubled in their determination.

A Note on Therapeutic "Partnerships" and Family Resources

In the case being discussed, the parents made an explicit bid for a shift in the therapeutic relationship. While this does not always occur, it is important to remain cognizant of those times in therapy when the helper–helpee complementarity can become less distinct. Here, the family owns more and more of its own changes and the therapist becomes a reflector and affirmer of family resources. Generally, this period in therapy is brief, occurring as change unfolds or when therapy is near an end. The therapist may coach the family, while still remaining neutral toward the family's actions. Or the therapist may simply do "follow-ups" in which the family reports on its own work. The formation of such "partnerships" and the acknowledgment of a shift in the relationship to one marked by greater symmetry is especially important with families whose prior experiences with helpers have been marked by disqualification of the family's experience of itself.

Sessions 7, 8, and 9

The next three sessions were short, often fairly boring in content, but very exciting in terms of the family's changes. The parents worked together for the first time, as they had insisted they wanted to do. In so doing, they provided Sandra with a way out of the loyalty bind previously discussed. She would not improve spontaneously, nor with the aid of a helper, but in a third way, via cooperation with caring parents. They devised their own simple behavioral plan with no input from the therapist. It included time lines, specific discipline, expectations, and the like. Sandra quickly began to follow it. By the ninth session, she was eating quite normally. Lest anyone think she became repressed, however, it should be noted that in the ninth session, Sandra stated firmly "I hate sauces! I will always hate sauces!" A girl who previously only ate french fries, bread, and milk, now ate nearly everything but sauces, and, of course, kiwi fruit!

The parents drew closer during this period. As they worked together regarding Sandra, they began to share other aspects of life as well. The mother, who had been a bit overweight, lost 15 pounds without mentioning to anyone that she was dieting.

Sandra grew up more and more each session. She came to the eighth session with her hair styled, having decided on her own to get a permanent. She came to the ninth session wearing nail polish and talking about shopping malls and earning money to spend.

In the ninth session, the mother announced that she had fired the dietician: "I showed her the plan Bob and I drew up and she ignored it and gave Sandra her own plan. I thought it was just too confusing so I told her we would handle it ourselves." Clearly, the family's relationships to outside helpers had undergone an important redefinition. The family felt greater confidence in their own decision making, and relied less on the opinions of others when these did not make sense to them.

At the end of the ninth session, the therapist suggested a follow-up appointment in 2½ months' time. This long a break serves to communicate confidence in the family's capacity to continue their development without therapy. The following ritual was given to the family:

"We'll meet again in about 2½ months. At that time, I'd like to suggest that we have a meal together again [here Sandra broke into a grin and Ellen said, "Oh, good"]. This time I'd like everyone to participate in selecting the foods. Perhaps you can go back to finding some favorites, or preparing some things that people don't like in new ways so that they'll eat it. Don't get too elaborate. It doesn't need to be a banquet."

The intent of this ritual was to draw the family together in what essentially was a celebration of their work together. A second meal was suggested in order to mark the changes with an event where the changes would be obvious to all. The instructions were an implicit comment on the greater freedom and flexibility now available in relationship options, in contrast to the earlier instructions that highlighted covert dyads. Suggesting that they bring favorites and disliked foods prepared in new ways recapitulated central themes of the entire therapy.

The Second In-Session Meal

The family came with a diverse meal to which all had contributed. Notably present was Sandra's favorite, french fries. Rather than china, the family brought paper plates. Rather than the mother functioning as sole caretaker of all matters relating to food, everyone participated in preparing and serving. Most striking was the difference in Sandra's eating. She willingly ate some of everything. Her mother did not focus on Sandra's eating, as she had at the first meal. Sandra continued to look more grown up, and came to the session with her ears pierced. The therapist asked some questions about earlier issues:

THERAPIST: [*to Sue*] Do you think your mother is still worried about her?

MOTHER: Oh, no. She was visiting recently, and she just remarked about how good Sandra looked.

THERAPIST: Is Sandra's eating a topic of discussion between you and your mother?

MOTHER: No, we have plenty of other things to talk about now.

THERAPIST: [*to Bob*] How do you think things will be going in 5 years? Do you think you'll be discussing Sandra's eating, or do you think it'll be a thing of the past?

FATHER: Oh, it'll be a thing of the past.

THERAPIST: [*to Sandra*] What do you think?

SANDRA: I think it'll be a thing of the past.

The family went on to discuss their anticipation that Sandra would go to college and to law school. The contrast to the first session when they predicted her death was cogent. The discussion of the future was filled with humor, good-natured teasing, and optimism. The mother expressed her own plans to look for work outside the home. Normal problems of growing up were anticipated with both Sandra and Ellen.

Termination Ritual

At the end of the meal, the therapist said to the family: "You've brought food to me a couple of times, so tonight I want to give something to you." Here the more symmetrical relationship existing at the end of therapy was highlighted. The therapist then took a potato and a kiwi fruit out of a bag and placed them on the table. Sandra laughed.

THERAPIST: You know what that is.

SANDRA: [*with disgust*] Kiwi fruit. [*all laughed*]

THERAPIST: And you know what that is.

SANDRA: [*brightly*] Potato!

THERAPIST: Why do you think I brought these?

FATHER: [*teasing*] Because Sandra likes both?

SANDRA: No way, I hate kiwi! [*all laughed*]

THERAPIST: Well, first of all, they're not to eat. Obviously, the potato wouldn't be too good to eat like that, huh?

SANDRA: [*interjecting*] We could cook it!

The therapist then continued: "I brought them, I guess, in terms of some of the things we've been working on. I remember way back in the first session when we got together, Sandra said the dietician wanted her to eat kiwi fruit and she hated it. I asked how it was and she said 'Yucch, awful!' But potatoes have been something that all along you really liked. And you still do, hmmm? [Sandra replied "Yes."] So, it seems to me that the potato and the kiwi fruit represent the things that you like and the things that you really don't like. O.K., as well I think, as I thought about, it's one way to think about the difficulties that the family got into, where some things got pretty stuck around preferences, likes, dislikes, kind of normal things getting out of hand. Some things got pretty out of hand so that your relationship [mother and Sandra] really suffered, and the two of you [mother and Sandra] were struggling over this.

"So, I brought this, not for you to eat, but for you to take home and what I'd like you to do with these is for Sandra and Ellen, with your folks around, to take them and put them in a big plastic bowl, fill the bowl with water and put them in the freezer. Put them in the back of the freezer, so you'll have them. They will be there, O.K. Now, the reason I want you to do that is I think there will be times in the life of the family of the future when the family may be unsure how to solve a particular problem. It might be difficult to decide if something is a big problem, whether something is simply a matter of personal preference, expression of individual development, or whether what's going on is a serious problem for an individual, a problem for two people, a problem for the whole family. When you find yourselves in that kind of quandary, what I would like to recommend that you do is take the potato and kiwi fruit out of the freezer, let them thaw out, and have a family discussion as to whether it is a problem the family can handle on its own, whether you need a hand with it, whether it is just a matter of things being individual preferences or whether it is individual growth and development that the family is experiencing with her [Sandra] getting older, her [Ellen] becoming a teenager, the two of you aging as a couple. [Parents laugh.]

For instance, Ellen may decide to become very stubborn. She may decide to imitate Sandra, or she may decide to do something more original than that, or Sandra may decide to go out with some boys her parents do not like [Sandra laughs with delight], or the two of you may be unable to resolve an issue, or there may be some struggles with extended family—things that are normal for families to go through. So, what I am recommending is that at those times any one of you could initiate thawing out the potato and the kiwi fruit and that that is a sign to have a family discussion and to make some decisions, maybe make some new decisions. The two of you are good at that from what I experienced. You came in and told me how you wanted to work. You developed a plan. You carried it out. So, then afterward you can freeze it again and that will be yours for as long as you want it."

Here, the family thanked the therapist, took the potato and the kiwi fruit and left. At 6-month follow-up by mail, the family was doing well and there was no symptomatic behavior.

This termination ritual dealt with family resources in a number of ways. It utilized and underscored the family's inner language. It reframed all of the difficulties around Sandra's unusual eating as that which will now provide opportunities for the family to handle problems. Future problems were cast in the frame of normal, developmental, expectable, and solvable. Family connectedness was highlighted, while individual initiative was also maintained. Humor permeated the entire ritual. Therapy was terminated with symbols of the entire therapy remaining with the family "in the back of the freezer," thus available, but not necessary in a daily way.

COMMON ERRORS

It is difficult to develop, hold, and utilize a resource model. The reasons for this difficulty can be found first in the larger context of giving and receiving help in our culture. We are, in fact, embedded in a deficit model. Families are implicitly and explicitly encouraged to look outside themselves for appropriate norms. Rather than assuming that the presence of a problem is an opportunity for the discovery of resources, the presence of a problem is taken to imply weakness and the presence of more problems. The presence of problems is assumed to require the entry of specialists. Frequently, the family is fragmented through interaction with helping professionals. Resources are diminished rather than enhanced.

Broad generalizations are made about categories of people that overlook strengths and resources. For instance, single-parent families are most often examined for what's missing, rather than for the strengths that emerge in this configuration. Families with handicapped members are more often criticized for the handling of their handicapped children than acknowledged for their coping. Too often professionals assume they could be "better parents," particularly with low-income, less formally educated families.

In the public sector human service system, the norm is to identify more and more problems, and to provide more and more directive assistance or intervention. The eroding effect on families' sense of their own resources is overlooked. It is not unusual to encounter families who have seven or 10 different professionals engaged in an ongoing way with "correcting" the family. A mother may be sent for training in "parenting skills" by a professional who ignores the impact of this intervention on the parental dyad, and pays no attention to the cultural norms of parenting in this particular family. A single parent may be told her children need "Big Brothers" and "Big Sisters," disqualifying both her own position as a nurturing adult and her more natural support network as potential sources of adult interaction for her children. Families are natural ecologies. Like other ecologies, they can be enhanced by interventions that are executed with care, respect, and congruence, or they can be damaged by interventions that ignore or disconfirm systemic givens.

The family therapist wishing to adopt a resource model must be aware of several potential traps that draw him/her into a deficit perspective. The first entails the *propensity to provide more and more "help" people*. Since the wider helping context supports this direction, the family therapist must often swim upstream. As one provides more and more "help" to a family, the family becomes less and less able to rely on its own resources. Here an escalating complementarity is generated, since as the family shows itself as less able, the therapist enters more and more, and the family demonstrates greater helplessness, and the therapist offers more assistance, and so on.

A second complementary pattern that interferes with a resource perspective is that in which *the therapist is seen as all-knowing and all-giving* and the family is always the recipient of this knowledge, always the receiver of care. The therapeutic arena is one that is predefined by society along the complementary lines of helper and helpee. A resource perspective attends to ways to prevent rigidity in this complementarity, making deliberate efforts to introduce greater symmetry at appropriate moments.

The whole area of *labeling* is one that requires attention from a resource model. Family therapists frequently receive cases in which an identified patient has been labeled by other professionals. Frequently, the family is also invested in the label. A resource-model practitioner can make two errors regarding labels. The first is to accept the label, and ignore all of the constraints on creative solutions that labeling engenders. Labels do impose limits on expectations and on development. They lead us to think in terms of static categories and to deny emergent possibilities. Labels preceded by "chronic" engender pessimism and hopelessness.

The second error, however, is to simply reject the label and thereby disqualify colleagues or get into struggles with the family. Rather, a resource perspective implies acknowledging the label as part of the system initially and exploring all of the beliefs regarding the label, highlighting the constraints inherent in labeling through a discovery method (e.g., "If he goes through life believing he is hyperactive, what effect do you think this will have?", "Suppose you were to pretend that he doesn't have a condition called hyperactivity, but that he is a normal boy who does naughty things—what would you do differently?", etc.), and developing relevant reframings. At the same time, family therapists need to continue to develop an epistemology that renders diagnostic labeling for essentially social phenomena obsolete.

An area where a therapist may easily overlook family resources is in regard to *interventions*. All interventions are handled by families in their own unique way, and not according to some prescribed formula. If a therapist expects a particular response to an intervention, she/he will miss opportunities to confirm the family's own creative response. Thus, once an intervention is given, based on hypotheses and a particular strategy, the therapist needs to adopt a position of receptivity to the family's response. This may then lead to new hypotheses, change in the direction of therapy, decisions to terminate, and so forth.

Termination is an area where family resources can either be overlooked or utilized. If a therapist continues to see a family long after a change process has begun, the family likely receives the message that they are unable to go on on their own. If a therapist insists on holding on, finding new problems to investigate, worrying more than the family is worrying, then family resources will be undermined. A therapist must attend to the sometimes subtle signals that a family is ready to terminate. Occasionally, the therapist may need to highlight resources and capabilities to the family that enable them to leave therapy. For families who have had a lot of prior unsuccessful therapy, it is as important to exit in a new way as it is to enter in a new way initially. For instance, if a family is used to remaining in therapy until a therapist gets frustrated with them, it is crucial that a new ending be experienced that puts the family in charge of the decision. If the family believes it is always dependent on helpers, then an ending needs to include an experience whereby the family gives to the therapist. Rituals of termination in therapy may enhance resources for some families (as in the case discussed above).

A final area that is, in fact, a land mine for the family therapist involves *the family and other larger systems*, such as schools, welfare, probation, and hospitals. Unless one enters this labyrinth with care, it is extremely easy to contribute to inadvertent triangles that deplete family resources. One needs to assess and intervene in families and larger systems while maintaining a resource perspective with both. That is, it does little good and may, in fact, do harm to adopt a resource perspective with families while adopting a deficit perspective toward colleagues from larger systems. To do so contributes to symmetrical struggles over "who knows best" and introduces no "news of a difference" within the wider context. When the entire ecosystem is examined with a resource model in mind, then contributions can be mutually affirmed, interprofessional suspicions can be minimized, and limited "partnerships" can be negotiated that affirm distinct areas of knowledge.

A FINAL NOTE ON CONTEXT AND RESOURCES

In the final analysis, a resource model is an attitude, a set of beliefs. While this attitude can be fleshed out by a set of techniques, as this chapter has attempted to do, like any set of beliefs the resource perspective must be nurtured in a context that highlights the resources of therapists and trainees. Human beings tend to see strengths in others when they are maintaining a sense of their own strengths. People celebrate the empowerment of others when they are feeling empowered. Training designs and therapy working contexts that highlight weaknesses or ignore existing competencies will generate deficit-model practitioners. Training designs and therapy working contexts that affirm diverse life experiences, build on existing strengths, confirm creativity, encourage experimentation, and build structures that share responsibility for both successes and failures will generate resource-model practitioners.

ACKNOWLEDGMENTS

The author expresses deep appreciation to Dr. Richard Whiting. His colleagueship nurtured many of the ideas in this chapter, particularly the material on rituals. Thanks also are expressed to Dr. Karl Tomm and the staff of the Family Therapy Program, where most of the therapy described in this chapter was conducted.

REFERENCES

Imber Coppersmith, E. Families and public sector systems: An assessment model. In B. Keeney (Ed.), *Assessment and Diagnosis in Family Therapy*. Rockville, MD: Aspen Publications, 1983, *4*, 83–99. (a)

Imber Coppersmith, E. Families and Larger systems: Interviewing and Interventions. *Journal of Strategic and Systemic Therapies*, 1983, *2*, 38–47. (b)

Imber Coppersmith, E. Families and multiple helpers. In D. Campbell & R. Draper (Eds.), *Applications of Systemic Family Therapy*. New York: Grune & Stratton, 1985, pp. 203–212.

Roberts, J. *The third tier: An ignored dimension in family therapy training. Family Therapy Networker*, 1983, *7*(2), 30, 60–61.

Selvini Palazzoli, M., Boscolo, L., Cecchin, G., & Prata, G. A ritualized prescription in family therapy: Odd days and even days. *Journal of Marriage and Family Counseling*, 1978, *4*(3), 3–9.

Tomm, K. One perspective on the Milan Systemic Approach, Part I. *Journal of Marriage and Family Therapy*, 1984, *10*(2), 113–125. (a)

Tomm, K. One perspective on the Milan Systemic Approach, Part II. *Journal of Marriage and Family Therapy*, 1984, *10*(3), 253–271. (b)

CHAPTER 6

Testing, Promoting, and Preserving Family Resources: Beyond Pathology and Power

Mark A. Karpel

CONCEPTUALIZING FAMILY RESOURCES

Over 20 years ago, in one of the first published works to explicitly address family resources in the field of family therapy, Otto (1963) remarked:

> Professional people as well as lay persons often describe a family as being a "strong family" or refer to "family strengths." Closer examination, however, reveals considerable confusion and lack of clarity about the meaning of family strengths, and we have found that most families are themselves not too clear about what they consider to be their own strengths. . . . A search of the literature reveals that family strengths are more often implied than defined or described. (p. 329)

While some progress has occurred since that statement was made, the observation still largely holds true. In addition to the cultural and historical reasons cited earlier for the persisting ambiguity of family resources (see Chapter 1 of this volume, pp. 4–21), one major factor may well be the sheer generality of the concept itself. At its worst, trying to discuss family resources can be like asking what's good for people. One hardly knows where to start. For this reason an analysis of family resources begins with an effort to define the term in a more specific and manageable way.

Mark A. Karpel, Ph.D. Private practice and consultation, Northampton and West Springfield, Massachusetts

Resources for What?

In this chapter, the term "family resource" or "family resources" refers to *those individual and systemic characteristics among family members that promote coping and survival, limit destructive patterns, and enrich daily life.* Before elaborating on the elements of this definition, we can briefly address what we do *not* mean by family resources.

In specifying "individual and systemic characteristics," we mean to exclude such concrete, material factors as family finances, physical aspects of the family's household, transportation, and neighborhood. These physical aspects of the family's economic and political environment may significantly affect coping, survival, and daily life, but they broaden the concept of family resources unmanageably. Similarly, this definition is meant to exclude resources as usually meant in the external sense, that is, social service agencies, local support groups, and specialized services. From this standpoint, a family's ability to *make use* of such community resources would fall within the area of discussion; the presence of such community resources would not. Furthermore, in discussing family resources we do not mean to imply "normal" or "healthy" families. Even families with severe and chronic problems, families that would qualify in most research designs as "dysfunctional," nevertheless may possess resources that can be drawn on in the context of particular stresses.

Finally, a distinction should be drawn between two important but quite different facets of a resource orientation in therapy. One facet involves the therapist's attitude toward what the family presents in treatment. Milton Erickson's term "utilization" (Erickson, 1960, 1965; Erickson & Rossi, 1981) perhaps best describes a therapeutic stance that attempts to accept and make use of whatever clients present most powerfully in treatment. Erickson himself, his followers, and the systemic family therapists have been especially creative in their efforts to utilize clients' behavior, including their compulsions, fears, symptoms, challenges to the therapist, and attempted resistance, in order to further the goals of treatment.

Obviously, compared with a primary mission to identify pathology, this stance increases a therapist's ability to identify and utilize resources. But what a therapist can make use of and what is inherently resourceful for families are not necessarily the same. Therapists may be able to use the force of a compulsion to alter and eventually eliminate a compulsion. They may even be able to conceptualize a positive element within the context of the compulsion (i.e., creating a symptom that functions to prevent a threatened separation). But this is far different from asserting that compulsive symptoms are inherent resources in family life. Even with the qualifications of context in mind—ethnicity, type of family structure, stage of family life, and particular life stress—there appear to be particular patterns that are, in most cases, for most families, enabling and strengthening. These are family resources. We can now examine the elements of the definition given above.

Promoting Coping and Survival

Families face a multitude of stressors[1] throughout the life cycle. These may be predictable and unavoidable stressors such as the birth of children and the death of an elderly parent. Or they may be unexpected stressors—unemployment, difficulties surrounding childbirth, geographic separation from social support systems, separation and divorce, the unexpected death of a family member. Family resources constitute an important part of the family's repertoire of responses for meeting the demands of stressors and preventing a stressor event from escalating into a crisis (McCubbin & Patterson, 1983). Pediatricians who have seen different families respond to the chronic illness of a child, or ministers, rabbis, and priests who have attended and followed families after the death of a family member, can attest to striking differences in how families react to these stressors, in the particular resources they bring to bear and in the responses and accommodations that emerge from their efforts to resolve the stressors.

Limiting Destructive Patterns

Hand in hand with the power of family resources to promote coping is their ability to limit possible destructive patterns. At first glance, this may seem an unexpectedly negative way to conceptualize resources. Yet this aspect of family resources is particularly compelling and serves to guard against the danger of seeing resources in one-dimensional, Pollyanna-ish terms, as though all we need to do is to encourage people to be "nice" to one another. There is destruction aplenty in many families, whether from external stressors or from the various ways in which family members can attack, demean, neglect, and diminish one another when vulnerability is high and personal and relational restraints are low.

Family resources serve to limit destructiveness in a variety of ways. By helping families cope more successfully, they limit the potential harmfulness of external stressors, thereby preventing further crises and "pile-up" of stress (McCubbin & Patterson, 1983). They may also thereby speed recovery from stress or crisis experienced by the family. In this sense, family resources are analogous to *resistance*, not in the clinical but the *immunological* sense, in that they enable the organism to fight off environmental threats, and, when such threats do compromise health, they speed recovery and prevent more serious damage.

Limiting destructive patterns is a hallmark of family resources when the threats to family members are generated from within the family as well. The most common examples involve the ability of individual family members to

---

[1]This discussion follows McCubbin and Patterson's (1983) distinction between stressors—"events, transitions and related hardships [producing] tension which calls for management"—and stress—"a state which arises from an actual or perceived imbalance between demands (e.g. challenge, threat) and capability (e.g. resources, coping) in the family's functioning" (p. 11).

resist the pull of more destructive patterns in another member. Thus the ability of a spouse the resist the alcoholic's "invitations" for a coalcoholic marriage, the ability of parents to exercise appropriate parental leadership over an acting-out adolescent, and the ability of children to refuse to be triangulated in the parents' destructive marital impasse all reflect patterns that can potentially limit destructiveness in families. Therapists have long recognized this. When a Bowenian therapist coaches a client to be less reactive in family triangles, or a contextual therapist encourages a client to consider the limits, as well as the extent, of what he/she owes a family member, or when a structural therapist tries to block a recurring transaction that violates necessary boundaries, they are all responding to a recognition that individuals, by their actions and interactions, can have a greater or lesser ability to limit the destructiveness of patterns generated from within the family.

Enriching Daily Life

If resources were defined only as aids to coping and limits on destructiveness, the implied world view would be a bleak one, the implication being that life is simply an endless struggle against a more-or-less inimical environment. While recent and current world events remind us that this can in fact be the case, for the large proportion of families in late 20th-century America, life is more than a "vale of tears." However, it can be difficult to discuss the quality or richness of daily life without lapsing into either the mystical or the pop platitudes of TV talk shows and self-help books.

Perhaps we can simply remember that, for the most part, people want to enjoy life, to experience satisfaction and pleasure in their relationships and their work, to care for others and know that they are cared for, to feel pleasure and involvement in life, to feel healthy, to have "bright moments" (Kirk, 1973). Just as the relationship between physical health and immunological resistance is reciprocal, so is that between quality of family life and the ability to cope with stressors. In fact, consideration of family resources may recast somewhat the claims often made for the preventive benefits of family therapy. Most often these benefits are presented as though the mechanism by which they occur involves the treatment's efficacy in eliminating the original source of a symptom so that new symptoms in other family members are unneccessary. For example, a child's rebelliousness or somatic complaints may have served to distract and unite her otherwise antagonistic and dissatisfied parents. Treatment that can successfully extract the child from this pattern and help the parents improve their relationship is thought to eliminate the need for further symptomatology. It may well be that an additional (or alternative) mechanism of prevention in family therapy involves strengthening family resources so that the family's "immunological resistance" to stress, disorganization, and destructive patterns is enhanced.

When we examine the resources that families bring to bear in stressful situations, we observe that some of those resources reflect characteristics of individuals while others involve characteristics of relationships. For this reason, we will discuss both *personal* and *relational* resources in families. Some of the most important personal resources in family life involve, among others discussed, self-respect, protectiveness, affection, and hope. Among the most important relational resources are rules that regulate interaction, particularly rules regulating patterns of respect, reciprocity, reliability, and repair. These terms have an old-fashioned, even outdated ring. However, while lacking a contemporary, "high-tech" sheen, they are nevertheless properties of relational systems and significant factors in the family equation.

Personal Resources

Self-respect

When couples join to create a family, they bring with them both the resources and the limits they have inherited from their experiences with their own upbringing. Among the many assets, talents, and personal qualities that an individual can bring into a marriage and family, none is more important than self-respect. It is remarkable how little has been written in the literature of family therapy concerning patterns of respect. Until now, discussion of respect has been largely limited to incidental observations, usually of its apparent absence in a particular client family. The level and quality of respect expressed in a family is a critical family resource, one that promotes effective joint efforts at coping, limits destructive patterns, and enriches daily life. A person's ability to treat his/her spouse or children or parents with respect depends most fundamentally on his/her ability to experience self-respect.

Self-respect involves the personal experience of seeing oneself as worthwhile, deserving, "O.K." While not prominent in the lexicon of psychotherapy, it overlaps with terms more familiar to the ear of the mental health professional. Self-respect is closely related to Bowen's use of "differentiation of self," to Boszormenyi-Nagy's "entitlement," to psychoanalytic notions of "ego integrity," and to as popularized a term as "assertiveness." Virginia Satir (1967, 1972) stands out as one theorist who gives self-esteem a central place in her conceptual framework and approach. Obviously, an individual's capacity for self-respect derives largely from the ability of those who helped form his/her character, in childhood and adolescence, to demonstrate respect in their interactions with that person. Thus, respect and disrespect are shaped and bequeathed across generations.

Self-respect suggests personal security. So much of the pain that family members inflict on one another stems from their insecurities, their sense of being vulnerable and threatened, and the defenses (and "offenses") they develop for protecting themselves, often at great cost to themselves as well as others. Self-respect reduces the likelihood that family members will have to misuse one another to achieve temporary relational security (for example, aggrandizing oneself by belittling another).

Self-respect implies an ability to perceive others in close relationships with a minimum of distortion stemming from painful early relationships. It suggests a sense of entitlement that reduces the likelihood that current relationships will have to be sacrificed in the service of persisting, exorbitant loyalties in other relationships. Relationally, this amounts to what, in turning a cliche of pathology on its head, we might refer to as "finished business."

Similarly, self-respect makes it easier to resist the pull—the manipulation and blackmail, the triggering and traps, the desperation and demands—of family members who, at a given point, may be acting out the vulnerabilities, the costs, and the ghosts of other relationships.

A woman in her mid-30s confronts her husband of 10 years and the father of her four children, whose drinking has increased significantly over several years. Unlike spouses who cannot set limits on the drinking partner and whose families can be devastated by the effects of alcoholism, she tells him that he has one year to stop drinking. If he has not done so by then, she will leave him and take the children with her. Her husband knows that she loves him and knows that she means what she says. He stops drinking and remains dry.

High vulnerability makes us easily threatened, especially by those on whom we depend most for our sense of identity and self-esteem. The personal security that accompanies self-respect makes it more likely that an individual will be able to face and acknowledge the legitimate claims of other family members.

In each of these ways, the self-respect of individual family members limits possible destructive patterns and makes conjoint efforts at coping with stress more likely to succeed. For each of these reasons and because it reduces the likelihood of repetitive patterns of self-created misery, self-respect contributes to the quality of daily life in the family as well.

This discussion is not meant to imply an idealized view of self-respect. We do not mean to suggest a dichotomy between "highly" and "poorly" individuated persons. Most people feel secure in certain areas, with certain people, on certain turf, and not others. The point is that, wherever and however it can be discerned, self-respect can potentially serve the interests of a family, even if it simply means a wife hesitantly but defiantly calling for a restraining order one time on an abusive partner, or a couple for once resisting their adult son's attempt to control all of their lives with his often-repeated threats of indirect self-destruction unless he is granted his latest exorbitant demand.

If self-respect makes it more likely that family members will not allow themselves to be mistreated, protectiveness is one personal resource that makes it more likely that they will not allow others to be mistreated.

Protectiveness, or Caring in Action

After a long history of "bad press" in the mental health literature, protectiveness is beginning to be rehabilitated. Henry (1965) has pointed out our historical devaluation of protectiveness:

All cultures and all families institutionalize norms of protectiveness, and the tendency of our culture to lose them is expressed in the fact that while psychiatry is preoccupied with overprotectiveness, it has shown relatively little interest in understanding protection. There are many works on the overprotective mother and a whole folk ideology has developed around "momism," but there are no works on underprotectiveness and no folklore. (p. 23)

More recently, family therapy has begun to pay more attention to protectiveness and to diminish some of the stigma previously attached to it. Family approaches as otherwise dissimilar as contextual therapy, systemic family therapy, and strategic family therapy converge in their appreciation of the protective functions served by many symptoms. Without losing sight of the high price individuals may pay for unwittingly protecting other family members, we need to remember that an individual's willingness and ability to protect members of his/her family is a fundamental personal resource that makes family life possible.

Protectiveness can be expressed in highly unexpected and imperfect ways:

A woman in her mid-20s, diagnosed as having a major bipolar affective disorder, says she thinks that her mother may have suffered from a similar illness. As small children, she and her sister were often beaten by their mother, who was a single parent. However, she recalls that, by a certain age, her mother ceased beating them but would instead periodically lock both girls out on a landing. From there, they would go to a neighbor upstairs who looked after them until their mother would fetch them home a few days later. She remembers both herself and her sister understanding that their mother now recognized some imminent change and did this to protect them; she recalls that both felt grateful to their mother for this.

A 16-year-old girl is hospitalized after experiencing a psychotic depression. Her father, an unusually brutal man, regularly beats her older brothers and has gone so far as to destroy one son's precious and painstakingly repaired automobile with a backhoe. In spite of his abusive behavior, this man is genuinely concerned about his daughter and understands how his behavior affects her. On at least one occasion after her return from the hospital, he steps into her room with words to the following effect: "Okay, now look, I'm gonna go beat up your brother but I don't want you to get nervous about it, O.K.?"

Protectiveness highlights the degree to which, for any personal resource to positively affect family life, it must somehow impinge on the world of action. An individual may possess different personal resources to varying degrees, but the only way in which those resources can contribute to family life is through that individual's action. When a parent gives up a long-awaited day of private relaxation to spend time with a child, when a spouse refuses to tolerate abusive and self-destructive behavior in a partner, or when parents refuse to give up hope on actively seeking a medical cure for a seriously ill child, they have mobilized personal resources into real action. Even when a person seems not to have acted but where possibly destructive actions have been restrained by affection or tolerance or gratitude, personal resources have been mobilized into action. Because family members must care about one another in order to act in these ways and because their caring will be wasted unless expressed in some form of action, protectiveness expresses the fundamental personal resource of *caring in action*.

Hope

Hope implies a belief in possibilities, and personal involvement in a particular outcome. As Henry (1965) has pointed out, hope operates as a kind of meta-resource, in its absence diminishing and in its presence enhancing our ability to identify and use other resources.

> Hope actualizes resources that are latent; if I have hope for my child I can become active in his life, but if I am without hope . . . whatever possibilities I might have for helping my child are never actualized—my resources are not made available to him. What a parent is to his children, what energy and enthusiasm he can awaken in them, is related to his hope. (pp. 292–293)

Hope is essential in any effort to cope with stressors or crises, and despair, hope's abandonment—in the face of crisis seriously threatens the survival of the family unit.

Tolerance

Tolerance, that is, an individual's ability to accept difference or otherness, is a valuable quality in family life precisely because family members live so closely together, "cheek by jowl," as it were, and because without tolerance differentiation is made vastly more difficult. Tolerance is, in a sense, what family therapists encourage when they coach family members to be less automatically reactive to particular forms of emotional triggering by others in the family. Tolerance as meant here also refers to a "live and let live" attitude that one senses strongly in Whitaker's work with families, a capacity not to be threatened or "bent out of shape" by individual differences and personal idiosyncracies. There is of course a risk that family members will be too tolerant of the behavior of others in the family, as implied in earlier examples. The counterweight that best assures that this will not occur lies in the self-respect of other family members.

Affection

A personal resource that we often, mistakenly, take for granted in family life is affection or fondness. Affection involves appreciation, not so much in the sense of gratitude for care given as in appreciation of a work of art or a job well done, that is, delight in a person's particularity. It is closely related to but much less complicated and confounded than what we call "love." Colloquial phrases such as "being tickled by," "getting a kick out of," or "getting off" on someone suggest its meaning more clearly. While the origins of affection might be debatable, its consequences are more clear-cut. Affection makes a myriad of potentially difficult interactions go more smoothly. Like humor, affection greases the wheels of interactions that might otherwise be difficult or abrasive. Affection motivates us to take care of one another and, most importantly, increases our tolerance. How often have parents experienced a rush of exasperation at a child only to find a potentially hostile outburst quelled by a wave of affection for the child? How often have sulking children, denied some momentarily desperately important excursion, been able to give up their resentment when a parent can tickle their feelings of affection with humor or sympathetic teasing? Like other personal resources discussed thus far, affection makes family life easier and more pleasurable on a daily basis and can be identified and utilized in therapy.

Humor and Playfulness

Humor is one of the most underrated of personal resources in virtually all relationships, whether family, work, friendship, or therapy. Humor can make potentially threatening or abrasive interactions go more smoothly. Humor "disarms," that is, it encourages us to relax defenses; it allows us to accept information or perceptions that might otherwise be experienced as threatening or attacking. Perhaps this is because humor metacommunicates that the other person accepts and cares for us, that the matter at hand is not one that makes us "not O.K." or could lead to our ultimate rejection. This type of humor, affectionate rather than hostile, communicates that the other person is laughing with us, not at us.

Humor is integrally related to distance in the sense of perspective or acceptance. It should not be surprising, then, that Cousins (1979) has identified humor as a critical resource in coping with serious illness and promoting health. Perhaps one reason why humor is so valuable in therapy involves its almost magical ability to decrease the "toxicity" of certain feelings, such as shame, and its power as a tool for interrupting and reframing highly charged emotional impasses. A sense of humor in individual family members is one good prognostic sign for family therapy.

Relational Resources

Relational resources denote patterns and characteristics of relationships. But how do we begin to think about the kinds of relational patterns that can serve the functions we have delineated for family resources—promoting coping and survival, limiting destructiveness, and enriching daily life? In what might seem to be an act of conceptual revenge, we can enlist the aid of classical, pathology-based family theory. One of the core concepts many of us were trained to use in the early years of family therapy was that of "rules." Rules were seen as being unwritten, unstated, and often unconscious. Family members could not tell you what their rules were but they would be observable in the process of the family; all family members knew when a rule had been broken. Significantly, as many of us used the term then, rules served largely pathological functions—thwarting individuation, perpetuating triangulated relationships, prohibiting communication in areas vital to the family. Typically, these early analyses of *how* rules functioned were quite accurate while their assumptions about the kinds of functions they served were limited and biased toward pathology.

Relational resources can be seen as often involving rules, but instead of being rules that limit individuality and perpetuate pathology, they are rules that limit destructiveness and make living together easier and richer. The most important of these relational resources involve rules concerning *respect, reciprocity, reliability,* and *repair.* Two other relational resources that have been discussed more extensively by other investigators (see Chapter 1) but merit a brief mention here involve the family's flexibility of response to challenge and family pride. These can be said to roughly correspond to Angell's (1936) original formulation of family adaptability and cohesion.

Relational resources need not be thought of as applying solely to whole families. They can be identified in any relationship, that is, any dyad or subsystem within the family or in relationships between family members and members of the extended family. For example, Bank and Kahn's (1975, 1982) work on sibling relationships has identified resources between and among siblings that do not necessarily exist between children and their parents.

Respect

One of the most glaring omissions in the literature of family therapy involves the virtual absence of any serious discussion of respect. Perhaps, along with other terms that are critical to family resources, such as tolerance, affection, loyalty, and hope, respect has been considered too old-fashioned or insufficiently systemic. Yet it seems clear that rules that govern the expression of respect and disrespect in families are as real and as recursive as any other rules, that the interactional loops and spirals that can be identified around symptomatic behavior can also be identified around the expression of respect for other family members and the limits placed on expressions of disrespect.

Certainly Boszormenyi-Nagy's references to "filial piety" (Boszormenyi-Nagy & Spark, 1973) suggest concern for some form of respect from children to parents, although here the emphasis is primarily on the actions by children that fulfill existential obligations to their parents who, literally, gave them life. Others, such as Attneave (1980), Lewis, Beavers, Gossett, and Phillips (1976), Otto (1963), and Van Meter (1980), have noted the importance of respect in their discussions of family resources.

For respect, what does and what does not transpire are equally important. Respect involves interacting with others in ways that communicate that they are valued, that their experience, their feelings, their contributions are seen as important and legitimate. This attitude is communicated in words, in gestures, and in action. At times, when frustration or anger or vulnerability are high, it may call for an active effort not to hurt the other person by blaming, belittling, or retaliating. This is where restraint becomes so critical.

Disrespect is corrosive in families. It eats away at the self-respect of individual family members and poisons interactions between them. In attacking individual vulnerabilities, it encourages more powerful defenses, which often involve emotional remoteness and/or retaliatory attacks on the vulnerabilities of the other(s). Disrespect thwarts coordinated problem-solving because individual initiatives are more likely to be belittled, thereby nullifying their potential contribution and further reducing the likelihood that they might be offered in the future. In families in which interactions are characterized by chronic disrespect, one usually experiences a hardened feigned indifference along with barely concealed rage and vengeful vulnerability. One thinks, for example, of the marital interaction portrayed in *Who's Afraid of Virginia Woolf?* (Albee, 1962).

It is a truism that respect begins "at home"—that is, the ability to respect another is partly dependent on a capacity for self-respect that in turn depends on the quality of respect received from significant others in one's upbringing. It is also true that respect is *earned*, that is, to some degree respect is a natural response to a person who demonstrates and, by his/her actions, deserves respect. This points up both the personal and relational, rule-governed nature of respect. Over the course of countless minute and critical interactions between and among family members, invisible limits (norms, in a sense) evolve that exert a powerful influence over individual behavior. These limits on disrespect can be strengthened, maintained, eroded, and repaired over the course of the family life cycle. They can be threatened or damaged by particular stressors and crises and they can be restored by the actions and reactions of individuals.

The power of respect to limit destructive patterns is obvious. By enhancing the self-respect and therefore individuation of family members, respect also enhances the quality of daily life and promotes coping and survival.

Reciprocity

Reciprocity refers to fairness of give and take among family members. Boszormenyi-Nagy has identified the importance of fairness both as a family resource and as a central dimension of family life (Boszormenyi-Nagy & Spark, 1973; Boszormenyi-Nagy & Ulrich, 1981). He reminds us that, in assessing the degree of reciprocity in a particular family, we must distinguish between our own particular conceptions of fairness and those of the family in question. There is a distinction, in other words, between assuming that we can set the *terms* of fairness (how spouses should divide child care, what children's chores should be) and observing whether the terms that exist are considered fair by family members and whether there is some effort to adhere to them. Reciprocity means that, within the family's particular definition of fairness and within the limits and demands of available resources, no family member suffers prolonged and unredressed deprivation. Obviously, reciprocity depends on the particular actions of individuals, but in this context we are more interested in the relational rules that govern such actions.

Reciprocity increases trust. It allows us to feel secure, "well held," and cared for. In being responded to, we are more able to be responsible toward others. When family members feel that their own needs and entitlements will not be overlooked, they are freer to consider and act in the interests of others. For these reasons, reciprocity promotes coping by encouraging family members to be willing to make sacrifices for one another and for the family as a whole without feeling unrecognized or used for their efforts. Reciprocity contributes to the quality of daily life by promoting a "generous economy" (that is, one in which family members are more inclined to do for one another) and by affirming the contributions of family members. It limits destructive patterns by minimizing the likelihood that individuals will feel exploited by others and then respond by withdrawing or retaliating. It further reduces the likelihood that they will carry that sense of exploitation into other relationships and try to regain fairness by getting others to "pay" for what they have experienced.

Reliability

If reciprocity tests whether efforts to do for others will be recognized and returned, reliability tests something even deeper. Reliability, in this context, refers to the ways and the degrees to which we can depend on others. This can mean something as simple (but not trivial) as, if a parent says she/he will be somewhere at a certain time (for example, to fetch a child after school), whether or not she/he in fact shows up. Or it can mean something as basic as whether we can trust our parents to care enough about us to protect us if we are endangered, to comfort us if we are suffering, and, most fundamentally, not to abandon us. Reliability depends on action to confirm promises; it concerns what individuals do more than what they say they will do. In the most insignificant and repetitious interactions of daily life and in the most rare and critical moments of crisis and choice, reliability—*the demonstrable effort to be as dependable as possible within a given context*—shapes the integrity of family relationships and the ability of individual family members to trust.

Reliability is critical in family life because it assures and demonstrates *continuity of care*, without which family life is a sham. To speak of its contribution to the richness of family life is difficult, for without it there can hardly be an ongoing family life in any real sense. Reliability is essential for the survival of the family; it promotes coping by promoting trust. It limits destructiveness by preserving a web of secure connections among family members and preventing escalating spirals when members feel betrayed or abandoned. Like respect and reciprocity, it is self-reinforcing. Each individual's acts of reliability encourage reciprocal actions from others.

Most therapists have certain unforgettable examples of unreliability culled from the stories of their clients' lives—the mother who abandons her latency-age children to a physically and sexually abusive boyfriend, with full knowledge of his having raped her daughter at the age of 3; or the father who pimps his latency-age daughters to friends and colleagues and is personally involved in sadistic sexual abuse with them. For an especially chilling and poignant description of family life without reliability, we have Colin Turnbull's (1972) observations of the Ik, a small tribe in eastern Africa whose society has collapsed in the face of starvation. In one scene, he describes a gentle young girl who is considered mad by the members of her community.

> [Adupa] . . . thought that parents were for loving, for giving as well as receiving. Her parents were not given to fantasies, and they had two other children, a boy and a girl, who were perfectly normal, so they ignored Adupa, except when she brought them food that she scrounged from somewhere. They snatched that quickly enough. But when she came for shelter they drove her out, and when she came because she was hungry they laughed . . . as if she had made them happy. . . . She kept going back to their compound. . . . Finally they took her in, and Adupa was happy and stopped crying. She stopped crying forever, because her parents went away and closed the *asak* [an entrance to the household compound] tight behind them, so tight that weak little Adupa could never have moved it. But I doubt that she even thought of trying. She waited for them to come back with the food they promised her. When they came back she was still waiting for them. It was a week or ten days later, and her body was already almost too far gone to bury. Her parents took what was left of her and threw it out, as one does the riper garbage, a good distance away. (pp. 131–132)

Repair

Repair involves efforts to make up for emotional and relational damage done. Rules governing repair are, in a sense, metarules in that they prescribe what must be done when rules are broken. When family members have actively harmed or mistreated one another, dangerous cycles of retaliation or withdrawal can ensue unless an effort is made to repair such damage. In this sense, relational repair resembles the withdrawal of the fuel rods powering a nuclear reactor to prevent a chain reaction from taking place.

Repair generally involves a verbal or nonverbal expression of regret or apology, a stated or implied acknowledgment of injury, and an admission of error or regret. Such initiatives facilitate the critical, complex, and largely ignored process of forgiveness (Cotroneo, 1982) in close relationships. Forgiveness allows the individual who feels wronged to "give up the grudge." This dilutes what can otherwise be a powerful obstacle to family members being able to utilize the resources inherent in these, and other, relationships. In this way, repair is a critical family resource in limiting potentially destructive patterns and, like the other relational resources discussed thus far, promotes coping and survival and enriches daily life.

Flexibility

Flexibility refers to the family's ability to vary its response to a situation or environment. It denotes both a range of possible responses and a capacity to experiment, change, or select from those possible responses. There is virtually no theorist or researcher who has investigated family resources who has not included flexibility as a central resource for families. Its value for coping and survival is obvious, as is its critical importance in the specific context of family therapy.

Family Pride

Whitaker and Keith (1981) have referred to family pride as "family nationalism" and compared it to "a team with high morale" (p. 200). The comparison is an apt one. Family pride reflects a shared sense of delight and value at being part of this small social system. It corresponds in a sense to a kind of group self-respect. It conjures a benign Us-versus-Them distinction in which *we* are valued without diminishing or being threatened by *them.*

It may reflect intergenerational legacies, as was powerfully expressed in the book and later television presentation of Alex Haley's *Roots* (1976). It is often expressed in stories that are told at family gatherings of moments in the family's history that are selected, perhaps embellished, even extensively revised, but that say in effect: "We're Kamens or Parkers and we're hot shits." Family pride contributes to and is one of the sources of personal pride or self-respect. When family members go off to form new families, personal pride promotes family pride.

Loops of Interaction

Recent family theory has introduced the notion of "loops" of interaction. Although less obviously pathologizing than early formulations of family rules, the particular loops of interest have been those that perpetuate symptomatic behavior. Hoffman (1981) has pointed out how the therapist can intervene to interrupt such loops, thereby altering one aspect of a perhaps otherwise quite rigid pattern of symptomatology.

Consideration of the rule-governed relational patterns described above suggests that these relational resources also involve loops of interaction and that these loops are, to some degree, self-reinforcing, that is, that the active expression of behavior associated with these rules by one family member encourages more such behavior from other members. In this sense, we believe that these relational resources function by means of rule-governed *resource-amplifying loops* of interaction, and furthermore that family therapists can not only interrupt symptomatic loops but in some cases promote resource-amplifying loops. More is said concerning this in the discussion of trust building later in this chapter.

The Interplay of Personal and Relational Resources

If we consider the relational resources presented above, we can better appreciate the "fit" between personal resources and relational resources. In each of these cases, the family's ability to utilize a particular resource is significantly affected by three factors, all of which influence one another. If we take relational repair as an example, these factors include (1) each individual's *capacity* to repair (i.e., freedom from "unfinished business" that makes repair appear extremely risky or shameful); (2) family *rules* prescribing repair; and (3) *active efforts* on the part of individuals to initiate and collaborate to repair.

Whether or not damage will be repaired depends, first of all, on the individual family members' capacity to initiate and respond to repair (that is, to evaluate their own behavior and its impact on others, to acknowledge harmful actions, to apologize or "make up," and to respond to these initiatives by others with understanding and forgiveness). Family rules prescribing repair serve to increase family members' motivation to do so. Furthermore, repair can only take place if family members put their motivation and capacity into action. Finally, *active* efforts to initiate repair strengthen the rules that prescribe it and increase the likelihood that other family members will behave similarly.

PROMOTING FAMILY RESOURCES

In order to set the context for a discussion of interventions from a family resource perspective, we need to say a few words about family therapy itself, the role of the therapist, and therapeutic priorities as seen from that perspective.

Family Therapy

As family concepts and approaches have achieved greater acceptance, the use of the term "family therapy" has both expanded and contracted. One can find the term being used to refer to a host of treatments whose only relationship to family therapy involves a passing reference to "family dynamics" or to imply that only a particular school or set of approaches constitute "real" family therapy.

In the following discussion, "family therapy" will refer to treatment in which three criteria are met: (1) that the therapist conceptualize problems as being *between* people, as opposed to simply within them; (2) that the goals of treatment include *changing relationships* as opposed to simply changing an individual; and (3) that the therapist view his/her ethical responsibility as extending to *all persons* in relationship to the client(s) who will be significantly affected by therapeutic interventions (this is in contrast to viewing oneself solely as responsible to one or two individuals seeking treatment). When these three criteria are met, whether the therapist meets with a large extended family or with one individual, whether the concepts employed involve "recursive cycles" or "differentiation of self," whether interventions involve restraint from change or family sculpting, we can say that family therapy is being practiced.

The Role of the Therapist

How does the conceptual shift to a resource orientation change our understanding of the therapist's role, the family's role, and the "fit" between the two in family treatment? In a pathology framework, either implicitly or explicitly, the therapist is seen as bringing resources to a "deficient" or "dysfunctional" family. The therapist imparts knowledge of esoteric interpersonal patterns, offers superior solutions to nagging problems that the family has failed to solve, or forces a halt to repetitive symptom-maintaining cycles. There has always been something of the "white man's burden" about this attitude on the part of the therapeutic establishment, as if client families were seen as impoverished, somewhat backward populations who could be uplifted and enriched by a superior culture. In Whitaker's words (Neill and Kniskern, 1982), "Each of us is a missionary trying to find a heathen to save so we can bribe our way into heaven." (p. 374). It is not surprising, then, that family therapists can find themselves trapped in a "savage war of peace."[2]

When we reconceptualize family treatment from the perspective of family resources, we recognize that both therapist and family bring resources with them into treatment, just as spouses bring their own resources into their marriage. The same condition that maximizes resources in couples' relationships—that is, *mutual respect*—also maximizes the resources that therapists and families bring together in treatment. Therapists are most likely to be able to recognize and make use of family resources when they approach families with curiosity, respect, and self-respect, attitudes that facilitate growth and accomplishment in virtually all relationships.

The family's resources, in the context of family treatment, provide a *foothold* for therapeutic intervention. They are analogous to the solid ground that supports the weight of a building erected upon it. Working with families in which resources are extremely limited or obstructed is more like trying to build in a swamp. There is no footing and foundation timbers are simply drawn into the mud. This is one reason why certain techniques or approaches which are helpful with some families have so little impact on others. It also illuminates the surprising invisibility of family resources. Where they are lacking, we see pathology; where they are present, family resources are as easily overlooked or taken for granted as the ground upon which we stand.

In many ways, the best model for the ideal fit between therapist and family resources in treatment comes from Erickson's concept of the hypnotic relationship (Erickson & Rossi, 1981; Haley, 1967, 1973; Lankton & Lankton, 1983; Zeig, 1982). From the perspective of family resources, *a successful therapeutic*

---

[2]Take up the White Man's Burden/The Savage War of Peace/Fill full the mouth of famine/And bid the sickness cease (Kipling, 1940).

collaboration exists when family members allow the therapist(s) to create a context in which they become more able to use their own resources. When a family therapist successfully reframes a particular pattern or symptom, the family has allowed the therapist to utilize their capacity for conceptual flexibility; they have given the therapist access to the family's imagination. When a therapist coaches a family member to behave differently, that individual allows the therapist to elicit his/her potential to act differently, that is, his/her flexibility of response. When a therapist can defuse tension and hostility with humor, the family allows the therapist to tap their own capacity for humor and apply it to the particular charged situation.

Therapeutic Priorities: Testing, Promoting, and Preserving Resources

The concept of testing is critical to a resource orientation. Frequently, individuals and families assume that certain resources are either unavailable or nonexistent. This is especially true in polarized, stagnant, or cutoff relationships in which one or both partners assume, after years of repetitive negative interactions, that the other is either unwilling or unable to meet their needs. Such needs might be for the other to accept their individuation without retaliation, to hear their side of the relationship, or to acknowledge the injurious consequences of previous actions. A single-parent household may assume that the noncustodial parent is essentially indifferent to the children's lives, especially when unresolved marital issues color the parenting relationship. Or, other agencies may assume that parents are incapable or unmotivated to protect their children from various dangers.

In each of these situations, the therapist can explore the possibility of actually testing these assumptions by designing ways to approach the individual or couple or family so that they have an opportunity to respond to the challenge posed. The therapist helps the family members involved to assess not only the risks and costs of making such an attempt but the risks and costs of not doing so. Fundamentally, it is the client(s) who must decide whether the costs of the present situation and the possible benefits of such an effort outweigh the risks and costs of the effort. If they choose to try to test such resources, the therapist can help them plan the timing, the "turf," and the focus, extent, and stages of such an effort. This is always done with an eye toward maximizing the chances of success, minimizing the risk of destructive outcomes, staying close to the client(s)' idiosyncratic core issues and goals, and representing the interests of the other persons involved as well. Some of the case examples that follow in this chapter illustrate the process of testing more concretely.

In a sense, all interventions from a resource perspective test resources, but some can more accurately be said to promote them. These are cases in which potential resources are identified by a therapist and efforts made to somehow increase their power in the relationships at hand, whether by making family members more aware of them, by removing obstacles that limit their influence, or by reinforcing their expression in daily life.

When families are seen as dysfunctional and entrenched, therapists can feel freer to wade in, using all their force and wile to provoke change. This increases the risk that valuable family resources may be negatively affected by treatment. A resource orientation begins with the Hippocratic Oath to, first of all, do no harm. In practice, this means making an effort to be aware of valuable family resources and intervening in such a way as to preserve them.

Family Resources and the Presenting Problem

The presenting problem provides a starting point from which the therapist can think about and explore resources in a particular family. Family resources can be identified in relation to the presenting problem in three different ways.

Resources Inherent in the Presenting Problem

With a loosening of the grip that pathology has exercised over our attempts to understand family process, it becomes easier to identify resources in the heart of the presenting problem itself. This is commonly the case when therapists identify the loyalty and concern that underlie the efforts of identified patients to protect family members through their symptomatic patterns. It is one of the targets of treatment approaches that reframe the meaning of symptoms in more positive ways, such as systemic and contextual therapy. For example, contextual therapists look at the "volatile passions" (see Krasner, Chapter 4 of this volume) that exist in negative, polarized relationships as indicators of potential resources since they are evidence of a lingering need to be understood and accepted and a persisting hope to effect such healing.[3] The therapist looks for the positive forces that contribute to problematic patterns in an effort to preserve them, to call them to the family's attention, and, if possible, to redirect and/or strengthen them.

Alternatives to Problematic Patterns

Family resources can also be identified in existing or potential alternatives to problematic patterns. If a relationship between parent and child is described as a negative, conflictual one, are there in fact any exceptions to this pattern? If a parent is seen as irresponsible and uninvolved, is there evidence to the contrary, or can more responsible behavior be elicited? If a family is self-described as joyless and depressed, are there small, unnoticed oases of liveliness, or can they be promoted? This is the intent of treatment approaches that seek to draw on the family's ability to mobilize alternative interactional or problem-solving sequences, such as structural and some strategic approaches. The therapist looks for evidence of the "flip side" of a symptomatic pattern, which can be built on in treatment.

[3]For a particularly striking example of resources inherent in presenting problems, see Gelinas (Chapter 11 of this volume), who identifies potential resources in several of the major factors contributing to the initiation and perpetuation of incest in families.

Resources in the Relational Context

Even when it is difficult to identify family resources in the presenting problem itself or to discern existing or readily activated alternatives, the therapist can explore the relational context of the presenting problem for resources that might be brought to bear in efforts to resolve it. This might involve particular individuals or subsystems within the family or in the wider relational context (extended family, neighborhood, or school), or values and rituals that exist in other areas of family life. This is the rationale of approaches that move beyond the "rigid triad" in many family symptomatic patterns to involve family members more peripheral to the presenting problem and therefore, it is hoped, more flexible and responsive to efforts to change it. Given these three options for *where* the therapist looks in order to identify family resources, we can examine *how* he/she goes about it.

Identifying Family Resources

There has been less written about identifying family resources than about conceptualizing them and promoting them in therapy. This may be because identifying resources in treatment is normally such an intuitive process. When first encountering a family, therapists are bombarded with a wealth of impressions and information (more often apprehended than comprehended) concerning the existence and levels of various family resources. Often, these impressions play a significant role in both our prognostic expectations and our personal reactions to specific families, although without a language and a deliberate effort to be aware of them, they may affect us more subliminally than directly. In this context, it should be remembered that in reality the therapist can never assess the resources of a particular family in a vacuum, that is, as unaffected by his/her participation, but only *in relation to himself/herself*. The family's ability to use the context created in the treatment room, to trust and call forth their own potential, will depend significantly on the atmosphere of safety, trustworthiness, respect, and challenge created together with the particular therapist involved.

Among the ways in which therapists can try to identify resources in client families are the following.

Attendance: Recruiting Resources

Family members and therapists may differ on who they feel should be included in family sessions. Families rarely offer to make too many individuals available to the therapist; they often propose, from the therapist's standpoint, too few. This is true when therapists simply want to better understand the patterns of pathology in a family; it is even more true when they want to be able to identify possibly unrecognized or untapped family resources. The categories of individuals whom families are most likely to exclude from treatment include separated or divorced parents (especially noncustodial parents), grandparents, and siblings of the identified patient (especially grown siblings living out of the home). These individuals are often dismissed by those seeking treatment as being either unaware of any problems or destructive, uncaring, and unavailable. If the therapist automatically accepts such a narrow definition of the relevant or workable system and agrees to limit the treatment to those individuals offered at the outset, she/he runs the risk of overlooking individuals and relationships that might make a critical difference in treatment.

The therapist can start, either in an initial telephone contact or in a first meeting, by sketching out his/her own rough genogram of the family. Some therapists find it useful to have the family research and complete the genogram themselves or to develop it conjointly with the therapist, but these techniques are not necessary for the purposes intended here. Acquiring identifying data that make clear the network of current and past family relationships and that are summarized in schematic form by the genogram serves to alert the therapist to individuals who might be able to be of service to the family and to the therapist's effort to help them.

Beyond inquiring about members who are not present or offered for sessions and questioning family members' perceptions of the involvement, interest, and availability of such individuals, the therapist can try to include them in the therapy process. Where resistance to this effort is minimal, it can often be accomplished on the initial telephone contact with the therapist. However, where the degree of risk or resistance felt by those initiating treatment is high, the therapist may chose to wait and discuss it further in person in the initial meeting. She/he need not necessarily insist on conjoint meetings. For example, when a painful divorce contributes to an explosive and destructive relationship between former spouses, separate individual meetings may be arranged with them.[4] What the therapist wants and needs is to form his/her own impressions of the often denigrated excluded members and of any possible contribution they might make to the goals of treatment.

Precisely because family members often narrow their views and therefore their expectations of one another, particularly when under stress or in crisis, the therapist has to be especially mindful to question the limits and accuracy of such perceptions. If she/he does not, she/he may pass up at the outset a major opportunity to reveal a different side of the presenting problem, a different perspective on its meaning, or simply a valuable ally in treatment.

Case Example. A couple in their mid-30s request family treatment for problems involving their two daughters, ages 2 and 4. They are particularly upset about the older girl, whom they describe as uncontrollable with her mother and difficult with her father. This girl reportedly refuses to do anything requested by her mother without whining, crying, tantrums, and repeated urgings. She destroys her own and her sister's toys. She refuses to stay in her car seat when the

---

[4]For a more detailed discussion of how to include family members for evaluation, see Karpel and Strauss (1983).

car is moving or in her stroller when shopping with her mother, in this case climbing out, laying on the floor in the store, and screaming if her mother tries to continue her shopping. The 2-year-old is much better behaved but is more and more beginning to mimic her older sister.

The mother, who is doing most of the child care, is extremely tense and irritable, with significantly elevated blood pressure. The maternal grandmother lives in the home and cares for both of her granddaughters while their parents work. She is described by the parents as an "adult whiner," very much like the problematic daughter, and the mother feels tormented by these females generationally on either side of her. In a first meeting with the parents, both spouses dismiss the grandmother as a necessary nuisance who interferes with their parenting efforts and models undesirable behavior for the children. In this couples session the therapist lays the groundwork for the next meeting, a family meeting to include both parents, both daughters, and the grandmother. The parents are surprised by this request to see the grandmother, but agree with little coaxing.

One striking aspect of the girls' presentation is that, despite the fact that one is twice the age of the other, they appear and are treated by their parents as if they are twin 2-year-olds. Their identification is so strong that the younger girl has begun to copy a speech defect in her older sister caused in the latter's case by a congenital malformation. Both in the whole family meeting and in a separate individual meeting, the therapist works to form an alliance with the grandmother, soliciting her views on the family and commiserating with her frustrations and dissatisfactions. In a follow-up meeting with the parents, the therapist begins to test the possibilities for change by recommending very small changes. In the expectation that later work will require more assertiveness by the mother, both with her daughters and her own mother, he encourages the parents to invite the grandmother out to a special dinner with them to show their appreciation for all her help with the girls and the household. He further suggests that the parents try to encourage somewhat greater age differentiation between the girls, for example, by commenting to the older girl that she can do certain things because she is a "big girl" or a big sister.

When the couple return for the next meeting, they report that the grandmother was visibly touched by their gesture of gratitude and that the dinner went well. Incidentally, they report that the grandmother, with whom the mother had discussed some of the previous session, has been more active than either of them in implementing the age differentiation that the therapist had recommended.

Here is a situation in which the therapist could easily ignore the grandmother altogether or see her only as the parents do, essentially as one of the villains of the piece. If this occurs, the therapist *and the family* lose whatever potential resources the grandmother might bring to the process of change. They may even draw forth a powerful opponent to change if she feels that her side is devalued and her interests threatened. Instead, simply by extending his sympathy and curiosity to one more family member the therapist was able to enlist a valuable therapeutic ally.

Observation: Looking for Resources

The family "tells" the therapist much about the existence and levels of family resources by how they present themselves and interact in early meetings. What do their behaviors and interactions reveal about individual family members' levels of self-respect and respect for one another? How do they seem to feel about belonging to this family? Are humor, playfulness, and affection expressed? Do family members take care to protect one another in this somewhat threatening new context or turn on one another, exposing weaknesses and leveling blame? Is there evidence of tolerance for difference and disagreement? Do any of these qualities seem to be absent in certain relationships (e.g., between parents and identified patient), but present to varying degrees in others (e.g., within siblings groupings, between parents and other children, or between the identified patient and a grandparent)?

For example, in one family, a supposedly callous and vicious adolescent identified patient exhibited an almost maternal level of affection, involvement, and protectiveness toward a younger brother in family evaluation sessions, smiling encouragingly at his efforts to speak, nonverbally reprimanding his behavior when out of line, and defending him against criticism by other siblings. Is there some evidence of hope, or does this seem a hopeless, dispirited group? In most cases family members indicate some measure of involvement, caring, and hope simply by showing up for such meetings. Therapists need to remember this and, on occasion, to express this awareness directly to the family.

The Family Tells Its Story: Listening for Resources

Family resources become evident not only in how family members behave and interact with one another but in the anecdotes and incidents they share. These anecdotes often make indirect statements (sometimes intentional, sometimes not) about the levels of various resources by describing how family members have treated one another and how they have responded to problems either in the past or around the current crisis that brings them to treatment.

In their descriptions of how they have reacted to and managed their current problems as well as earlier stresses, the family can reveal a considerable amount of information concerning its flexibility and range of alternative responses, its rules concerning respect, reciprocity, reliability, and repair, its pride in itself, and its members' levels of protectiveness, tolerance, humor, affection, hope, and self-respect.

Case Example. A couple with two daughters, ages 13 and 12, request family treatment in relation to what they describe as the older daughter's rebelliousness and quarrelsome behavior. There is a significant degree of conflict between the mother and this girl. In a family evaluation session, they disagree constantly and easily escalate to the point of shouting and near physical confrontation. In an individual meeting with the daughter, the therapist is exploring what might change if she and her mother were to stop fighting. In this context, for the first time she reveals and the therapist hears the "flip side" of this relationship. The therapist asks the girl to complete a sentence with whatever pops into her mind. The exchange is recorded on a videotape of this meeting:

THERAPIST: If you and your mother never fought anymore, your mother . . .

DAUGHTER: I think my mother would always be in a good mood. [*Brightening up and smiling with affection.*] I love her in a good mood.

THERAPIST: You do?

DAUGHTER: Yeah, she's so much fun when she is in a good mood.

THERAPIST: Say more about that.

DAUGHTER: I don't know, like you know when she's in a good mood when she's wearing jeans and a sweater. And she'll bring you to the Arcade and give you some money or bring you to the Mall or bring you out to eat and you'll just have a great time with her.

THERAPIST: *You* will?

DAUGHTER: Yeah, I will.

THERAPIST: What is it that's different when she's in a good mood?

DAUGHTER: I don't know, like when I do something she never takes it seriously. She'll take it as a joke.

The degree of warmth and affection expressed in this exchange was quite unlike all previous observations and descriptions of this mother–daughter relationship. It indicated that such feelings were not deeply buried by old issues or current conflicts. In fact, evaluation revealed a relatively strong family struggling with normal issues of renegotiating independence and differentiation for the first child approaching adolescence. These issues were complicated in this case by the traumatic loss of the mother's beloved younger brother in Vietnam 15 years earlier when his jeep suddenly hit a mine. The older daughter was strongly identified with this young man by other family members and herself (even wearing his fatigue jacket to one therapy session). The girl was constantly described as reckless and impulsive, although her behavior was extremely restrained by any adolescents standards. The mother's absolute panic over losing this girl, blocked by formidable defenses against feelings of loss, was expressed then as a desperate, urgent anger and a secondary fury that she could not prevent what she experienced as an imminent disaster. Thus, the mother's anger was reinterpreted by the therapist as a desperate attempt to protect her daughter, given her own past experience of loss; the daughter's resistance was interpreted as an effort to convince herself and her mother that the world was not terrifying and malevolent and that she could move out into the world socially and physically without undue danger.

As part of the feedback to this family following the evaluation, the therapist asked for and was granted permission by the daughter to show this excerpt from the videotape of her individual meeting to her parents. This was done at the end of the session. Both parents were visibly moved, the mother crying and shaking her head in disbelief and pleasure. She later communicated that she felt this had enabled her to be much more patient and less reactive in subsequent interaction with the daughter. The incident provides one example of a therapist's listening for, seizing on, and magnifying resources that might otherwise be overlooked and unutilized.

Questions: Surfacing Resources

In addition to observing the family and listening to its story, the therapist can ask questions designed to surface family resources. These may be general questions, applicable to virtually all families, or highly specific questions in response to a particular situation in a particular family. For example, one general question that is helpful with most families involves asking each family member *who they worry about most*. This often has the effect of changing the affective tone from one of tension, anger, or blame to one of sympathy and concern. It can be especially revealing, as suggested earlier, when a supposedly selfish and indifferent identified patient expresses his/her worry over a parent's health or the parent's marriage or a sibling. This is one example of questions that explore the "flip side" of problems as presented. Another general example, which can be asked with all families, is what the family members' favorite, and least favorite, times are at home. Answers to such questions may provide a counterpoint to the picture of conflict or alienation presented by the family. These questions ask, in effect, regarding problematic patterns: Is that all there is? Is this the whole picture, or is there another side?

More specific questions can be designed in particular cases to look for exceptions to the problematic patterns described. For example, in the case described earlier, if the teenage daughter had not volunteered positive information about her mother, the therapist might have asked if she ever felt good about her mother or had fun with her. The therapist must be careful not to push this exploration to the point where family members feel their experience of the problem is being minimized or rejected. With this proviso, such questions may open up an overlooked side of the presenting problem or of the context in which it exists.

Questions directed at past problem-solving efforts may identify resources that the family has been able to mobilize and found helpful in previous stressful situations. Such questions also communicate to the family that the therapist assumes that they have resources of their own and that she/he is as interested in this side of their family as in their problems.

Assignments: Gauging Resources

One final method of assessing family resources involves "assignments," specific therapeutic recommendations that provide information about how the family will engage in treatment and that, it is hoped, further the goals of treatment as well. Assignments can be given with the straightforward expectation that they will be followed and prove helpful. More strategically, they can be given either in the expectation that they will be disobeyed (in order to secure an opposite result) or in order to facilitate changes not directly related to the content of the assignment (encouraging parents to spend more time together by directing them to discuss certain aspects of a child's problem).

Thus assignments can be used early in treatment as a way of gauging resources either that the therapist thinks she/he has tentatively identified or that may appear virtually nonexistent. Such assignments are most often used to assess the family's ability to develop alternative patterns of interaction. In the family with two small daughters described earlier, the therapist's first recommendation, that the parents try to encourage greater age differentiation between the 4- and 2-year-old girls, revealed that the father and grandmother were able to accept and implement this change; the mother's statement that she had been "too busy" suggested that she had greater difficulty changing her behavior in this area. Assignments given early in treatment can function both as tools for assessment and as initial attempts to facilitate change.

Case Example. Meeting a family with a teenage son and daughter, the therapist was struck by an unusual degree of depression, alienation, and conflict for all family members, along with a virtual absence of positive family feeling and a remarkable amount of difficulty talking to one another and to the therapist. The parents presented complaints about the children, who would shrug their shoulders and say little. There were signs of severe marital problems that the parents would not discuss. They stated several times that talking generally "did no good," and the children's near silence certainly lent support to this view.

In view of this stalemate, the family's dispirited, hopeless air, and their extreme difficulty talking, the therapist decided to see if it would be possible to generate alternative patterns in a concrete, nonverbal fashion and in an area less charged than that of the presenting problem. He accepted their view that talking did no good, at least as things stood at this point, and explained that, instead of talking, he would recommend things for them to *do* differently in order to see if it were possible to make changes, and that at the start this would not involve any of the problem areas they had raised. He then recommended, having ascertained that they already owned a camera, that they engage in a "silly picture contest." This would involve the children and the couple, at first operating as separate teams, taking silly pictures of each other, separately and together, and then taking pictures of all four together, and together deciding which were the "winning" pictures.

The therapist's hope was to temporarily sidestep the charged and impacted stalemate, to accept their reluctance to "talk," to see if some spark of family togetherness and play could be generated, and to inject a light note of humor into the situation. When the family returned, they reported that only the children had followed through with the assignment. They brought in five or six pictures they had taken, and all family members agreed that it was a picture in which both children uncharacteristically "looked happy" that they liked best. The family's response to the assignment reinforced the therapist's sense that it would be extremely difficult to engage the parents in efforts to change, but that there was at least a spark of liveliness and engagement on the part of the children that could be mobilized in treatment. Discussion of the picture of the children "looking happy" brought the first smiles into the therapy room and prompted them to talk a bit about why it was so hard to be happy with each other.

Mobilizing Family Resources

Clinical intervention from a resource perspective does not necessitate radically different techniques. Much of what therapists have traditionally done in a variety of approaches can be knowingly used in the service of promoting family resources and may have been unknowingly used in this way by practitioners using a pathology framework. In the following discussion, a number of such techniques and approaches are described and illustrated with case material. The purpose of this discussion is not to introduce innovative techniques, but rather to demonstrate how familiar therapeutic approaches can be deliberately used to promote family resources in family treatment. Many are in fact fairly common-place and routine, and this is fitting. What matters here is not the genius of the therapist, but the potential within the family. It is important for therapists to understand that there are relatively simple and straightforward interventions that can maximize the family's ability to resolve their own problems.

Reframing

The term "reframing" refers to the therapist's effort to enable family members to think of a particular pattern or problem in a different way. The therapist may propose a shift in how one looks at any of a variety of aspects of that pattern: its temporal or relational context, the motivation of individuals involved in it, its function, and its meaning. Reframing may be used to accomplish different ends. Like psychoanalytic interpretation, which it resembles, it may be intended to foster insight. In other cases it may be used to make alternative patterns of interaction easier to enact or to make it much more difficult to persist in problematic patterns. From a resource perspective, it is probably most often used to identify resources that are *inherent* in the presenting problem itself, as in the use of statements that throw light on patterns of loyalty, concern, and protectiveness in what would otherwise look like destructive or self-destructive behavior.

Case Example. The parents of a 16-year-old boy request family treatment as summer approaches. The boy, who is the youngest of three children, is expected to return home shortly from a prep school in another state. When he returned the previous summer, the ensuing conflict was, in the mother's words, "a horror," and they hoped to avoid a repetition this time. When he came home, he would apparently lay around the house, doing nothing to help out and making no move to pursue activities in which he expressed interest. He and his father fought frequently, with the consistent result that the mother would come to her son's defense and the cycle would conclude with an emotionally bruising marital fight. The boy was described as apathetic, disorganized, and perhaps even in some vague way impaired.

Discussion revealed that, several years earlier, the father had had a long secret affair, virtually under the mother's nose. Her eventual discovery of the affair led to a 1-year separation, after which they agreed to reconcile. They had now been reunited for a couple of years, but the affair was very much unresolved, the mother being still angry and mistrustful of her husband, and the father guilty and resentful of his wife's unwillingness to forgive and forget. Although there were clipped references to this impasse, it was neither discussed nor fought over overtly at any length. The boy presented as bright, flippant, cooperative without being self-disclosing, and clearly not impaired cognitively in any way.

The available family members (mother, father, son, and one older sister, also home for the summer) were gathered and given, essentially, the following feedback from the therapist: "You've come here because of your concern over Andy's frequent conflicts with Dad, which lead to fights between Mom and Dad, and over his not getting things done. You wonder whether he just doesn't care or perhaps is somehow incapable of organizing himself. I am convinced that neither of these is true. Andy is reasonably bright, has a working memory, and is fully as capable of organizing himself as anyone else is. And, if anything, he may care too much. In order to understand the reason for these problems, we have to look at a major event in the family's past—your father's affair—and its aftermath. This event was extremely disruptive. It led to a separation and reconciliation, but what kind of a reconciliation is a question on everyone's minds. Where do all of you, especially the parents, go from here? You can't go back to the way things were before the affair, but you seem equally unable to put it behind you and go on from there. So it remains unsettled, undigested, unresolved, and presents an awful, insoluble dilemma.

"This is where Andy comes in and he deserves credit for coming up with a fairly ingenious solution to this impasse. He has managed to behave in such a way as to give his parents a more 'urgent' problem to focus on and so distract you from your dilemma, but also to give you an area in which you can express anger toward one another, albeit on a safer, less threatening issue. Your mother may be unwilling to stand up for herself with your father, but she'll stand up for Andy. Your father feels too guilty to get angry at your mother for 'holding onto' the affair, but he can get angry at Andy, and at your mother for defending him. It's easier for you to fight about Andy than to fight about the affair. So Andy's behavior keeps the focus off the affair, but it also 'keeps the pot boiling.' After all, look at where you are right now and how you got here."

The therapist complimented Andy on the loyalty and willingness to sacrifice that this solution expressed. He pointed out how little Andy benefited from his "selfish" laziness and emphasized the high price he paid: a poor relationship with his father, inability to do any of the things he wanted, and the image of a boy who needed his mother to protect him. They were warned of the dangers if Andy or any of the others should change their behavior at this point and encouraged to continue behaving as they were for now while the issues were "explored" further. "Andy, you should continue to provoke Dad, act like you can't plan or remember anything or take care of yourself. Dad should continue to hassle Andy about all of this, i.e., to keep the focus off the affair. And Mom should continue to protect Andy from Dad's anger and pick up any slack in what Andy leaves undone as a way of thanking him for his willingness to act like a failure." The family seemed initially shocked by this interpretation but, to the therapist's surprise, readily accepted it and protested not the reframing but the recommendation to continue enacting the cycle. The therapist refused to be convinced that any change would be wise at this point.

The following week, the parents reported that things were very different at home. Father and son were no longer fighting; the son had mobilized on his own to register for a summer course he had wanted to take, and the parents requested help with their own stalemate. Throughout the parents' continuing marital therapy and as of a follow-up contact 3 years later, there was no return to the previous problematic cycles involving the son.

In this case, reframing the presenting problem in a way that connected it to a major unresolved issue in the family and surfaced the son's involvement and need to be of help led to a surprisingly rapid change in behavior on the parts of all three members of this triangle, interrupting the pattern that made the boy part of the problem. It is impossible to tell whether the therapist's restraint from change was, in retrospect, unnecessary or served to add power to the reframing and avoid resistance that might have met a direct encouragement to change. In any case, it should be noted that the *therapist* did not interrupt the cycle. He simply reinterpreted it in a way that motivated family members to interrupt it. The resources utilized here included the boy's willingness to sacrifice himself in an effort to solve a family dilemma, the parents' concern and protectiveness (expressed here as an unwillingness to allow the son to continue to sacrifice himself and suffer in this way), and whatever residual trust and hope existed that the marital impasse might, after all, be soluble.

Widening the Resource Pool: Bringing Reinforcements into Treatment

This intervention, often but not exclusively associated with various family-of-origin and network approaches, actualizes a therapeutic conviction in the potential ability of individuals in the client's closest relationships to serve as resources for them, both in therapy and in everyday life. The particular resources drawn on may vary. Individuals may be enlisted for functional and emotional social support, especially in times of crisis. Siblings, parents, or other relatives who share a history together may be brought in to provide information about subjects in which a client is confused, anguished, or stuck. Individuals with whom a client has painfully polarized or cutoff relationships may be invited into treatment in a effort to remove obstacles and increase mutual concern and availability.[5]

Widening the resource pool in this way is probably most often used to facilitate *alternatives* to problematic patterns and to mobilize aspects of the *relational context* that can dilute, counterbalance, or quarantine them. It frequently serves to strengthen both relational and personal resources. Finally, widening the resource pool expresses the therapeutic conviction that resources should be *tested* before being dismissed. Clients who have given up on various individuals as potential resources are often surprised to find how willing such persons are to be of help in some way. (For an example of widening the resource pool see the case example on pp. 222–230.)

Leaving Family Members in Charge

This is a broad category of interventions, all of which involve the therapist's resisting the urge to step in and take over responsibility for some aspect of the family's current situation and instead encouraging them to take responsibility for it themselves. The operative therapeutic principle here is that, whatever needs to happen either in treatment or in the family's life at this point in time, it is better for the family, rather than the therapist, to do it. Obviously there are occasional exceptions (for example, a therapist's trying to mediate a marital impasse rather than having a child saddled with that responsibility). But as a rule of thumb, this principle helps to correct for therapists' tendencies to assume too much responsibility in the therapeutic partnership, thereby diminishing the family's responsibility, mutual reliance, and pride in accomplishment.

This class of interventions may involve various aspects of problem-solving (especially around the presenting problem), a host of case management issues (especially where therapists exercise broader authority, as in cases of residential treatment for children or inpatient hospitalization of parents), and the terms of the therapeutic partnership itself. This is especially true where issues of termination are involved. Therapeutic approaches that respect families' decisions about readiness to terminate, rather than engendering feelings of insecurity, dependence, and failure, are generally more respectful and protective of family resources. Setting up follow-ups, rather than more therapy, or letting families end treatment when they feel they have resolved a problem to their satisfaction with the understanding that they can recontact when and if they choose (a "family practitioner" or "sequential treatment" model) rather than prescribing continuous long-term treatment, represent efforts to put this orientation into practice.

[5]For examples of bringing siblings and network members into treatment, see Kahn (Chapter 7) and Attneave and Verhulst (Chapter 8), respectively, in this volume.

This category of interventions is broad enough that it may involve virtually any and all of the family resources discussed earlier, whether they be inherent in the presenting problem, an alternative to problematic patterns, or recruited from the wider relational context of such problems.

Case Example. A woman is referred for family evaluation by her private psychiatrist, from whom she has sought help for a germ phobia and related compulsive rituals. The family consists of mother and father, both in their late 40s, and their two daughters, ages 17 and 20. Some years earlier, the father left his lifelong job in industry to become a Lutheran minister. He was finally ordained and hired by a congregation, and the family moved into the church parsonage, whereupon the mother's symptoms developed and escalated. She washes her hands "100 to 150" times daily. She finds physical contact with all people, including family members, "painful" and so no longer hugs or touches her daughters and has all but eliminated her sexual relationship with her husband. Both parents are recovered alcoholics. Both daughters have had varying degrees of social and academic problems. The father and daughters are furious with the mother over her behavior, but do not feel they can blame her for a condition over which she has no control; the mother at times feels isolated, "up against The Big Three."

Given that this extremely insecure and unassertive woman opposed her husband's move into the ministry, that her symptoms appeared with the family's move into the parsonage, which she detests ("my prison"), and are "80% improved" when she leaves for any length of time, one can see an intense symmetrical power struggle, enacted in terms of his calling and her compulsions, neither of which can be questioned or blamed. Thus the major challenge for this family is to rebuild trust to the point where these conflicting needs can be renegotiated in a more cooperative and honest way. As it turned out, the father later offered to leave the active ministry if it would make his wife happier; she soon after reported being miraculously healed of her compulsions by Jesus.

An incident involving one of the daughters early in treatment provided an opportunity for the therapist to let the family solve a problem instead of accepting their request that he do so. At the start of one family meeting, they reported that the younger daughter was frequently absent from school with vague and insubstantial physical complaints. They requested additional sessions for her individually. The therapist knew that both daughters felt somewhat abandoned by both parents, the father to his parish responsibilities and the mother to the misery of her compulsions. He knew also that the older daughter was extremely afraid to go back to college, where she had been unhappy, and that the mother dreaded attending her husband's church on Sundays because she was jealous of his relationships with parishioners and felt disliked by them.

Instead of agreeing to try to solve the daughter's problem with more therapy, the therapist turned the request around, asking if the family was able to somehow provide the courage to help one another face the things they feared in life. The mother said that she felt the same way about church as her daughter did about school. She seemed relieved to no longer be the only fearful one, as each family member shared their own fears about various social situations. They were asked if they could do anything to help the daughter and said they would talk it over.

At a subsequent meeting, they reported that the daughter had attended school every day. The family had decided to institute a temporary, rotating buddy system in the mornings, with a different family member getting up with the daughter, reassuring and encouraging her on her way to school. Both mother and daughter reported special pleasure in the mother's involvement in this project. For the family, it signaled a step out of the mother's withdrawn self-preoccupation; for the mother, it offered a vehicle for participation in the family outside of the "cripple" role she had assumed and a specific, concrete way to be helpful to her children.

For a second example of "leaving family members in charge," see the case example on pp. 207–210.

Removing Obstacles/Releasing Resources

This is again a broad category of interventions. It includes therapeutic efforts from a wide range of models which employ a variety of specific techniques; what these efforts share is their attempt to remove obstacles that inhibit or diminish resources in relationships and to make these resources more accessible to the participants. Often when families come into treatment, therapists can discern caring and longing for closeness blocked by bitterness or mistrust (and in some cases, even that anger or mistrust blocked by an individual's low self-esteem or vengeful refusal to admit such feelings). Therapists may see a deep sense of loyalty and protectiveness concealed by a surface show of defiance, hostility, or indifference. They may find a capacity for tolerance limited by an individual's vulnerability or insecurity; feelings of affection and gratitude made seemingly inaccessible by a need to protect someone else. A family member's ability to show respect and appreciation for another may be severely limited by unfinished business in other relationships; an individual's capacity for self-respect may be stunted by his/her excessive obligations or basic misconceptions about other family members. As these examples suggest, interventions of this type can affect all of the three arenas of family resources (inherent, alternative, and contextual) and virtually any of the personal and relational resources discussed above.

Case Example. Mrs. Cowell is a 42-year-old twice-married, twice-divorced mother of six children. The five children from her first marriage range in age from 7 to 21 years old. There is only one son in this group, Gene, who is 16 years old. There is also a 5-year-old son from the second marriage. Living in the home are Mrs. Cowell and all the children except the two oldest daughters, who are both extremely involved with the family and with later family treatment. Mrs. Cowell was hospitalized on an inpatient psychiatric unit with severe anxiety, depression, and somatic complaints. Her symptoms suggested an inability to cope with a variety of situational stresses. Neither of the children's fathers was currently involved with them, which left her to try to function as a single parent for four children in the home. She had moved away from her own family of origin and had no current external support of any kind. The family was on welfare and lived in "the projects," a high-crime neighborhood. As Mrs. Cowell became more overwhelmed, the children fought more among themselves and experienced a range of school and social problems, creating more pressure on her.

There was a great deal of conflict between Mrs. Cowell and her 16-year-old son, Gene. Following a violent quarrel between Gene and one of his sisters when he was 11 years old, he had been sent to live with his father and paternal grandmother. He had returned to the family 1 year earlier and since dropped out of high school, now doing little besides watching TV and flirting with illegal activity with other neighborhood boys. Mrs. Cowell was unusually critical of this son, describing him as lazy, contributing nothing to the home, and abusive with the two youngest children.

Observations of the full family together and discussions with Gene and other siblings revealed a somewhat different picture. Except for his 5-year-old brother, Gene was the only male in the family. All older siblings agreed that the two youngest children were virtually undisciplined by the mother, especially since her depression had intensified. They felt that Gene's attempts to impose some order were well intentioned and fairly appropriate, although understandably imperfect given his having lived without any siblings for 4 years (until 1 year ago). They felt Mrs. Cowell consistently rejected these efforts, leading him to withdraw in anger and indeed "do nothing" around the house, fueling further criticism from her.

In an individual meeting, Mrs. Cowell was able to recognize the impossible position that Gene had come to occupy. She was further able, to the therapist's surprise, to see how she had come to use Gene as a target for long-standing feelings of anger and bitterness involving his father. Following this session, Mrs. Cowell explained all of this to Gene, apologized, and agreed to try to work out how he could participate in the family as neither a parent nor a good-for-nothing but as a responsible older sibling.

The obstacle that was removed here was the mother's "revolving slate" (Boszormenyi-Nagy and Spark, 1973), her transference of anger and resentment from her ex-husband to her son, which prevented her from seeing him separately from his father and made her blind to his real efforts to contribute to the family and especially to her. Her continual criticism made him feel that it was pointless to try to help and led him to withdraw into angry, and self-destructive, negativity. Removing this type of obstacle often permits a natural trust-building process to unfold. Here, the mother was able to recognize and acknowledge Gene's efforts to help. Finally being recognized and affirmed in this way, he became more active in helping out at home and clearly more of an emotional support for his mother. Both now described this as a positive relationship. Gene's ability to be of real help to his family and to be recognized for it may have helped him pursue his own interests actively as well. Three months later he decided to join the Marines, hoping to qualify for embassy guard duty overseas, a decision that for him reflected a desire to "make something" of himself, and to make himself and his family proud of him. Before he left for boot camp, he took all of his savings (around $300.00) and bought his mother a fur coat for Christmas.

The following case demonstrates several of the approaches discussed here, including leaving family members in charge, removing obstacles/releasing resources, and trust building.

Case Example. Mr. and Mrs. King request family therapy for problems involving Mrs. King's son, Eric, from her first marriage. Eric, 10 years old, is described as angry, depressed, and extremely passive. He has engaged in some stealing (from his mother), has temper tantrums, is extremely sensitive to feeling left out, and seems to repeatedly provoke anger from other family members, especially his mother. Eric is the younger of two children, the older being his 15-year-old sister, also from his mother's first marriage. Mr. King has three grown children from his first marriage. The couple has been married for 6 years. Eric sees his now-remarried father in another state three or four times a year.

While conflict is described between Eric and his sister as well as both parents, quite clearly the most charged relationship is that between Eric and his mother. He can elicit feelings of fury from Mrs. King in a variety of ways—by "doing nothing" (that is, moping obviously around the house), not doing his schoolwork, and not practicing his music lessons. Their relationship has settled into a cycle of conflict and frustration. Eric does something that annoys Mrs. King, who expresses her annoyance or frustration, leading initially to more passive–aggressive behavior on Eric's part but eventually to an explosion of anger on both sides. Both parents work long hours, extending into many weekday evenings and limiting the amount of time spent together in the home.

Mrs. King reports that Eric has been like this "since the day he was born." She had separated from Eric's father several months before Eric's birth and feels, in retrospect, that she was significantly depressed from the time of that separation until she met Mr. King 4 years later. The pregnancy and birth were both difficult and Mrs. King had little family support during this period. She had medical complications following the birth and remembers being sick and depressed when she came back home with Eric. She reports that he was an extremely difficult baby and that, unlike her first child, this made her feel she "couldn't do anything right" as a mother. She describes his having been colicky for 1 year, screaming for hours and being inconsolable at these times. When held, she says he would arch backward and put a hand against her neck to push away.

Citing this history, they wonder if his current fits of temper are perhaps "internally triggered." Significantly, however, there is no evidence of such behavior outside the home. The boy's schoolwork clearly does not reflect his abilities, but there are no reports of behavior problems in school. On evaluation, he impresses the therapist as a normal 10-year-old boy, with no serious psychiatric disturbance but marked feelings of resentment, apathy, and low self-esteem. The therapist consults a child psychiatrist, a child psychologist, and a pediatrician to be sure he has not overlooked any important biological or developmental factors and concludes with them that the boy's behavior as an infant most likely reflected a mixture of constitutional factors and the mother's significant depression at that time.

Meeting with Mr. and Mrs. King, the therapist shares his sense that the conflicts between Eric and his mother began with and are a direct continuation of the patterns established during Eric's infancy. Every one of Eric's provocations communicates a "silent reproach" to Mrs. King: "You don't give me enough. You are bad to me. You don't love me. You're a bad mother." Mrs. King's responses convey her anger at being held accountable in this way along with her inability to free herself from it. It is as though she is saying: "Stop it. I'm doing my best. It's not my fault. You're a bad child." Mrs. King knows that she avoids and overreacts to Eric, but by now his behavior has made it even harder for her to love him. Thus in every encounter, whether over a homework assignment or a TV program, the unspoken but somehow understood subtext is about whether Mrs. King is a bad mother or Eric an unlovable child. This view is shared with the parents. There are significant indications of marital problems in this case as well, but the couple are clear that this is not their reason for seeking treatment and it is not open for discussion. Because the boy's problems do not appear integrally related to the marital relationship, the therapist decides to accept Eric's relationship with his mother as the focus of treatment, waiting to see where this will lead.

Mrs. King's reaction to the therapist's feedback is powerful. She cries when she thinks of her son's infancy, remembering how miserable that period was for both of them and how she wishes it could have been different. Mr. King wonders whether it might be helpful for her to see the therapist for a few meetings in order to work through her grief over this period. The therapist opts instead to try to redirect this back into the family. He describes the initial goal as involving an effort to break out of the vicious cycle that has evolved between Mrs. King and Eric. He asks that she set up a regular weekly block of time, from 1½ to 2 hours, for her to spend with Eric, doing whatever he wants, within reason, and that she tell him about the new arrangement. He also recommends that she find two occasions during which she can grieve over Eric's infancy *with Eric*. He suggests she do this either alone with Eric or with Mr. King present for support. He makes clear that these are opportunities for her to express her feelings of grief over how hard these years were for both of them. The only caveat is that she in no way communicate that any of this was Eric's fault.

When the couple come back a week later, Mrs. King reports that she and Eric had their first block of play time. It made her more aware of how distant and awkward they were with one another when they weren't fighting. In spite of this mutual discomfort, the time went fairly well. Her awareness of the need to implement the grieving discussion during the week made her aware of the fact that there was no unstructured "together" time between her and Eric. All of their time together was spent either in structured activities or with her nagging or chastising him. She had been able to take advantage of a passing reference to pregnancy with Eric to discuss her own pregnancy with him. This wound up being a light and fairly nostalgic talk. At the end she told Eric that she loved him and, to her surprise, he said he loved her too. She remarked that there was virtually no precedent for such a clear, open exchange of affection between them.

The following week, Mrs. King reported that she had finally forced herself to discuss Eric's infancy with him at the last possible minute, that is, the night before the session. Before he went to sleep she went into his bedroom with baby pictures of him (the pictures being her own idea). She was herself surprised, incidently, that in most of the pictures Eric was smiling; she said that she had honestly not remembered him ever smiling as an infant or toddler. Eric at first resisted the discussion by acting infantile, but Mrs. King persisted and, on her urging, he settled down and listened. She talked about how hard it had been for both of them and described some of the reasons why it had been that way. She cried, expressing her wish that it could have been different, that he deserved better. Eric began to cry, grabbed his mother and hugged her, and for a time they held each other and cried. Mrs. King said "I love you" and that "you are just the kid I wanted." Later in the therapy session, the couple discussed Eric's resistance to schoolwork; the therapist recommended having Mr. King become more involved in this area for a time. He also suggested that Mrs. King select one of the early pictures of Eric or Eric and herself and, without saying anything about it, frame it and put it on her bureau.

The following week, Mr. King began by saying that he found himself resentful of the suggestion that he help out more with Eric regarding schoolwork. He related this to his own dissatisfaction with certain areas of the marriage and what he described as a "what about me" feeling (i.e., his own entitlement). At this point, the couple discussed and asked for help with the marital relationship. When they chose to terminate 4 months later there was improvement along with continued problems in both the mother–son and husband–wife relationships. The couple had not been able to change as much as they had hoped in the marriage, but were more accepting of limitations at least for the present and less likely to blame and distance from one another because of them. Eric still tested his mother often and Mrs. King still blew up and retaliated occasionally, but both parents felt that there was a definite change in this relationship. There were more obvious spontaneous expressions of warmth between mother and son. Eric did considerably better in school despite the fact that neither parent was any longer supervising his schoolwork.

An incident that occurred the night before the last session expresses something of the change. Mrs. King disciplined Eric for some misbehavior and he responded by throwing a tantrum. She was infuriated and remembers being tempted to "smash" him. Instead she grabbed his collar and yelled "This is what you're doing to me. You're trying to get me to fight. You're saying 'Come on, fight with me!' I don't want to fight with you. I don't want this!" Eric became teary, leaned against her, and again both held each other and cried. He said he didn't want to fight either. Mrs. King said that it had been a powerful moment for both of them and that she felt "great" about having been able to head off the usual retaliatory cycle and grim finale.

In this case, the sheer intensity of the conflict between mother and son pointed to the resources of caring that were present but thwarted in the relationship. One simply does not invest that much energy in relationships that are unimportant; in order to be hurt that much by perceived rejection and disapproval, one must badly need and expect acceptance and approval from the other person. The therapist identified this resource and helped the family members to release it. They were able to build on some measure of residual trust to create a "beachhead" of mutual acceptance, approval, and declared attachment that served as a counterweight to destructive interactions. The therapist resisted the temptation to "fix things" himself and instead directed the mother to her son. In this way, she was able to grieve over the period of her son's infancy *with him* and thereby to demonstrate her caring *to him*, to provide information and perspective on their relationship, and to relate in a different and more positive way than previously. This set a cycle in motion that built trust and trustworthiness and allowed for *safer* and hence greater expression of caring and attachment. There could be no clearer example of the healing power of this "beachhead" of trust in a context of mutual anger and disappointment than the incident described at the end of treatment. In this one incident we see the mother's effort to restrain her rage and, in the midst of her fury, not to attack but to plead for a truce, and we see the son's restraint in response. Thus we can see protectiveness or caring in action and the evolution of relational rules limiting destructive interactions and promoting repair.

Coaching One Person

"Coaching," a term most often associated with family systems therapy, refers to an approach to treatment that is, in fact, practiced by a wide range of family therapists. The therapist acts as a consultant to one individual in a marriage or family and serves to guide his/her efforts to change certain aspects of the relationships in which she/he participates. In some cases, other family members are seen and perhaps even coached separately by the therapist; in others, the therapist may never have met these other individuals but tries to proceed as much in their interests as in the client's. Thus coaching typically promotes *personal resources* that may then mobilize *relational resources*. For example, the therapist may help the client build self-respect, reduce reactivity to relational "triggers," take charge in a crisis, or generate alternative patterns of participation in interactions; often this generates relational changes, such as more expressed caring and affection, higher levels of tolerance for difference, greater reciprocity and reliability, or easier and more rapid repair. As these examples suggest, coaching is probably most often used either to generate *alternatives* to symptomatic problems (such as helping individuals resist the pull of destructive interactions) or to change the *relational context* of a particular problem (for example, by enabling an individual to initiate a reconcilation that reduces the urge for vengeful, self-destructive behaviors).

Case Example. A couple, both in their early 40s and married only 2 years, requested treatment for problems involving the wife's 18-year-old daughter from a previous marriage. The oldest of four children, the daughter had been diagnosed as having juvenile diabetes at age 11. The mother complained that her daughter was belligerent and provocative in the home, to the point of punching holes in doors when angry, strewing the basement with garbage, and sneaking her boyfriend into her bedroom at night despite her mother's insistance that she not do so. The daughter was also verbally abusive to her mother. She relied on her mother to provide the supplies necessary for her insulin injections, but consistently mismanaged her condition and had reportly done so since its discovery. Significantly, such mismanagement had only resulted in hospitalization one time when she was 11 years old. She currently worked part-time in a local restaurant. The parents had asked her to leave home but she refused. They felt, with good reason, that she was unable either to leave home or to live peacefully there. The family was obviously experiencing difficulties around the "launching" of this oldest child. Plans had been made for her to attend college nearer to her biological father, but she refused to go. She was obviously trapped, perhaps by loyalty conflicts involving her parents, perhaps by fears of greater independence; she was responding by digging in her heels at home and abusing both herself and her family. She refused to attend therapy under any conditions.

The stepfather felt his wife needed to be firmer with her daughter but, due to his newcomer status and lack of previous experience with children, did not feel entitled to press the point. The mother also felt that she should probably be firmer, but a mixture of fear and guilt made this more difficult for her. As is common in such cases, the mother felt blackmailed by the threat of her daughter's more seriously mismanaging her diabetes. Furthermore, the daughter's explosive and abusive outbursts reminded her of her own near-violent father; she was intimidated and would "cave in" to avoid such scenes. Finally, the daughter's diabetes was diagnosed soon after the mother separated from her first husband and was for some time preoccupied with going back to school and launching a career, all of which contributed to a feeling on the mother's part that she was somehow responsible for all of her daughter's problems.

The therapist accepted this family as it was presented to him, with the mother as most concerned and motivated, the stepfather as her supportive backup, and the daughter as nonparticipant. He offered to see the parents together in order to help the mother explore ways to change the terms of her relationship with her daughter and to help the stepfather provide emotional support and a sounding board in her efforts to do so. He agreed that they were "not in control" of their own home at this point, but pointed out how helpless and out of control the daughter's behavior was as well. He commiserated about the risks of being firmer with the daughter but pointed out the risks to all of them if things were allowed to go on as they had been. He asserted that the only way to interrupt this cycle would be for them to employ effective action that backed up their verbal protests to the daughter about her behavior. He recommended a stance that combined demonstrable affection and availability with firm limits on disrespectful and destructive behavior. Different tactics for implementing such a stance were discussed but none definitely chosen in the first session.

The second session, however, showed that the mother was ready for such an approach, that her own self-respect, her concern for her other children and her husband, and her concern for this daughter's future could be mobilized to overcome her guilt and fear. She reported that when she once more found that the daughter had smuggled her boyfriend into her bedroom overnight, she told her that she could no longer live at home. The daughter, to her surprise, acquiesced quietly and found an apartment for herself, increasing her hours at work. The mother informed her that she was now totally in charge of her own syringes and any other matters related to her diabetes. The daughter ignored this communication by twice leaving angry notes complaining about her mother's failure to leave her something required for her treatment. With great difficulty, her mother ignored both notes. No further such requests were made; the daughter apparently accepted the necessity of managing her diabetes herself and did so.

Now that she was out of the home, discussion focused on ways of continuing to be available without diluting the strong stands that had been taken. For example, in view of daughter's legitimate need for transportation on one occasion and in lieu of allowing her to take her mother's car as she had done without permission in the past, her mother was encouraged to offer to drive her where she needed to go. This provided an opportunity for some light conversation and implicit reconciliation, as well as a powerful message about the rules and benefits of more respectful relating.

In a third session, the couple reported that when the daughter's television had been stolen (quite probably with the cooperation of her boyfriend), the step-father was able to be helpful in recovering it. In two follow-up sessions over the next month, both parents reported minimal but positive contact with the daughter, who remained in her own apartment, working to support herself, managing her own medical status, seemingly less unhappy and clearly more considerate and sensitive with them.

Challenging

Challenging, as used here, refers to a number of interventions, both with individuals and larger groups, that temporarily heighten discomfort and even despair. This might involve telling a client or clients that one does not believe they can change or warning them not to in view of possible greater dangers. It might entail creating a manageable crisis or heightening despair by detailing the specifics of a bleak future if things cannot change. Many therapists are uncomfortable with such interventions because they feel they are manipulative or dishonest. In fact, there are numerous clinical situations in which more straightforward approaches are virtually certain to fail, that is, to leave clients entrenched in misery and therapists frustrated and annoyed. This is especially true where resistance is high, most clearly signaled when clients *tell* the therapist that they cannot change. However, precisely because these interventions either directly or indirectly suggest *deficits,* rather than resources, they need to be used more carefully and selectively. What the therapist wants is to goad or shock or provoke in order to elicit resources that she/he feels are latent in the client or family, not to engender real hopelessness and defeat. While particular forms of challenge, such as positive connotation and restraint from change, may make use of resources *inherent* in presenting problems, challenge is most often directed at generating *alternatives* to symptomatic patterns.

Case Example. Mrs. Frank, a woman in her early 40s, requests therapy for herself, her husband, and the three of their five sons, ages 16 to 24 years old, who are still living in the home. The 17- and 19-year-old sons are both abusing alcohol and drugs. The 17-year-old refuses to attend school; the 19-year-old has had a psychotic break that forced him to drop out of college. He has been treated for some time with lithium. Both boys spend much of their time watching TV at home, doing little around the house, either ignoring or arguing with their mother and sometimes stealing from her. Mr. Frank is an alcoholic who is verbally abusive and physically threatening to his wife and sons when drinking. He has, in essence, lived apart from the family for over 6 years, spending long periods of time with another woman and her children. Despite the fact that all family members know of this "second family," it is never discussed and the separation is not defined as such. Earlier it was simply presented as father being "on the road" for work and more recently, since a geographical move, as a temporary separation necessitated by father's work. Mr. Frank comes and goes as he pleases. Mrs. Frank has protested this state of affairs but never acted decisively to change it. She contacted a lawyer a few years earlier, but could not bring herself to follow through with initiating divorce. She attends AlAnon and urges therapy and alcohol counseling on her husband and sons with no success. She is herself the daughter of an alcoholic father. All the members of this family present in treatment as feeling guilty, hopeless, confused, and stuck.

After several sessions the father drops out of treatment, followed by both sons. The third son is willing to attend, but a decision is made to meet individually with the mother for several sessions. Earlier, the therapist had related both sons' problems to the confusion and stalemate in the parents' marriage and to both parents' inability to break their addictions, his to alcohol and hers to her husband. Mrs. Frank expresses some resentment with the ways her husband and sons treat her, but, like many children of alcoholics, she has learned to make do with little, tolerate much, and never give up trying to save the other person. Accordingly, she dwells on their good points (which are legitimate and obvious in spite of their treatment of her), admits and berates herself for her own inability to set firmer limits, and weakly defends her tolerance by pointing out that her husband has never beaten her.

Mr. Frank is currently coming into the house drunk late at night and waking the household with angry, accusatory tirades. An attempt to straightforwardly encourage Mrs. Frank to take more assertive action in her own and her family's interests fails. She says she knows what she should do but cannot bring herself to do so yet. Her "yet" allows her at least the hope that one day she might, and thereby makes it easier to bear her current failure to act. At this point, the therapist ends the session by saying that in fact she can't and won't do anything more to stand up for herself because deep down she doesn't believe that she deserves to be treated better. All she really deserves is not to be beaten.

The following week, she returns and begins by describing how shocked and angry she had been the week before. She remembers "white-knuckling" the steering wheel of her car after the session. She reports that her husband came in drunk again, waking everyone up and harassing them. She called the police, who intervened, and afterward she took out a restraining order forbidding her husband to enter the home. The boys seemed to be rallying somewhat and displaying a bit of hope and family pride by organizing a tag sale to raise money and by painting and cleaning one of their bedrooms. One week later, she reports that the two older boys have both found jobs and the younger of the two is investigating a possible return to school. She has reconnected with two long-cutoff siblings and at work has pushed for and been given a promotion.

This woman saw herself as an assertive, modern woman. She had a capacity to defend her own and her sons interests, a capacity that was blocked by her long self-identification as a caretaker and by the rationalization that someday she would act. The therapist declined to participate in this rationalization as she had expected, that is, patiently talking with her until she got the nerve up to act. Instead, he challenged her view of her own assertiveness, reflected an unflattering view of the low self-esteem her nonaction bespoke, and made it more difficult to rationalize her current nonaction. This challenge mobilized a surprising flurry of assertive, self-respecting action across a range of areas, some of which had never been discussed in treatment, and this action triggered other resources of family pride, hope, and initiative in her sons.

The following case demonstrates the use of two different treatment approaches concurrently with a couple. In essence, the husband is approached from a challenging, strategic direction while the wife is coached in a straightforward, compliance-based approach.

Case Example. Ann and Bob, both in their late 30s, request marital therapy. The presenting problem is their failure to conceive a child. Ann had become pregnant once before but the child was stillborn (1 year ago). Since then they have been unable to conceive. There are no diagnosed medical problems, but Ann feels that the tension in their relationship and Bob's subsequent avoidance of sexual relations are clearly making things more difficult.

Although Bob complains about Ann being unrealistically romantic, both spouses agree that Bob is basically the problem. They present themselves as a conventional, old-fashioned couple. Bob is the boss; he does little around the house, although both work full-time jobs. He is critical of Ann, frequently irritable, and occasionally demeaning in his frustrated outbursts. Ann resents this treatment but has great difficulty standing up for herself. She feels that she doesn't know how to fight back and usually withdraws instead when angry at him. Although she makes her unhappiness known, she also makes it clear that she would not consider leaving her husband. She tries to get Bob to help out more, to be more affectionate, to take her less for granted, all with no sign of success. Bob freely admits that "the biggest problem is my inability to show affection," along with his automatic resistance to doing anything she asks of him. In discussing goals, both wish he could be more affectionate and more cooperative, but convey their pessimism about this change really occurring.

What this marital description fails to convey is the therapist's immediate impression of two likable, lively, playful, and caring people. They had found one another relatively late in life, she after years of living alone and he after being left by his first wife. The therapist felt that Bob was deeply attached to Ann but, as reported, did not show this. Clearly, both partners had been traumatized by the loss of their first child. Bob admitted that he wanted a child but was terrified that, if Ann lost another, she would completely fall apart. He also admitted that his first wife's infidelity had devastated him and made him more mistrustful. Bob's family history revealed that, an only child, he saw his mother as overly critical, domineering, and "degrading" toward his father, who "just took it," staying with her "out of duty." His mother was also agoraphobic and on occasion developed somatic symptoms apparently to avoid social situations that made her uncomfortable.

At the end of the evaluation, the therapist gave essentially the following feedback to the couple: "You've both specified the changes you would like to see in Bob but you have both expressed pessimism about any of these changes happening. I think you are right. These changes will not happen. Not because Bob is selfish or anything like that. He doesn't mean for it to be like this or want it to be like this but there isn't a damned thing he can do about it. It seems to me that Bob has learned two very powerful lessons in his life, more powerful even than what you mean to him, Ann. First, he's learned what a woman can do to a man if he lets her take control. He learned this mostly from his parents and then had it reinforced in his first marriage. The lesson is that if you give in to them, *in any way*—with your feelings, by helping around the house, whatever—they'll take over. When you've learned a lesson like that, you can't separate a woman's reasonable, harmless requests from *disaster*. I think I know what you are both feeling. How unfair it seems that a lesson learned so long ago should be carried into this relationship and cause so much conflict. But that's how it is and there is nothing we can do about it. Some people spend their whole lives living out these lessons. It's clearly not Bob's fault that he learned this lesson, but there it is nevertheless.

"I said there were two lessons. The second, which I think he learned from his mother, is *avoid what you fear*. That's what she did. She avoided the outside world, which she feared. Bob avoids what he fears, which is *women*, not women *per se*, not a one-night stand or a casual relationship, but real closeness with a woman, because of Lesson One. So, as much as you can when you're married, he avoids this closeness. And again there is nothing he can do about this. Ann asked if she was expecting too much. From Bob, yes, much too much.

"Bob has suggested that maybe Ann is unrealistic, too romantic, and just expects too much, not just from him but from any close relationship. There is no way to answer this. I have a vague suspicion that he's right, but we'll probably never get a chance to find out. It's sort of like asking if someone starving in the desert might be an overeater. So what's to be done? The first and hardest lesson is for you, Ann, to recognize that you can do *nothing* about changing Bob. You have to *give up* totally on being able to change him. But it's not all hopeless. Sometimes just facing these things can help and you could use some help in learning how to accept him as he is."

The therapist recommended that Ann come in by herself weekly with this goal in mind and that Bob come in once a month, not to change anything, but just to "get an update" and "keep in touch." Bob seemed taken aback by the therapist's description of his hopeless condition and expressed reservations about whether he agreed to that extent. Both agreed to continue as suggested. Bob was offered a choice of coming for the first individual appointment in 2 or 4 weeks. He chose 2. He was warned that he might not like Ann's really giving up on him but he'd just have to accept it anyway.

The feedback given in this meeting was used to "set the trajectory" of the treatment, sidestepping the temptation to try to apply *direct* pressure to the areas in which resistance was highest and establishing a context in which *indirect* pressure could be applied, by challenging the husband and separately coaching the wife to be more assertive and thereby to apply further indirect pressure at home. Ann's first individual session, framed as "learning to live with Bob as he is" was in fact directed toward a different approach to encouraging him to change. This involved coaching her to behave in ways that: (1) stopped protecting Bob from the impact of her giving up on him, and (2) transformed direct into indirect pressure for change. Ann was encouraged not to ask anything of Bob and not to fight about his behavior, but to refuse to be treated disrespectfully and to "transform requests into regrets." So, for example, instead of nagging Bob to pick his clothes up off the floor, she would say: "For the moment there I was going to nag you about your clothes on the floor but then I remembered what the therapist said and I know I can't change you." These statements would be delivered with an air of sadness and stoical emotional resignation. At her next individual meeting, Ann reported having used this approach three times. Twice Bob became furious. The third time he said nothing but initiated sex for the first time in months. He had also been slightly more helpful to her around the house.

Bob began his first individual session by saying that he still just couldn't accept that it was impossible to change. In fact, he said, he had restrained himself from some irritable snapping and put-downs with Ann since the last meeting. He also reported that he had found himself dealing less explosively and demeaningly with a subordinate at work. He said he felt sure Ann wouldn't leave him and admitted that "it would destroy me" if she did. He said he was pleased with the sessions and that the biggest revelation for him was how much like his mother he had been acting. The therapist allowed that there were some encouraging signs here but held to his earlier pessimism about the prospects for real change.

The therapist continued to help Ann apply the approach they had worked out to the particulars of daily life. When Bob, whose one household responsibility was to do dishes, blithely left them for her, she deliberately did not make him a lunch for work, as was usual. When he angrily demanded to know why, she said: "I don't make lunches for guys who don't do dishes." When his aggressive and dangerous driving (about which she'd complained for years) upset her one day, instead of trying to get him to slow down, she quietly asked him to pull to the side of the road. When he did, she got out without a word and walked the rest of the way home, ignoring his demands and then pleas for her to return to the car. If he had been behaving badly and later asked what was wrong, she'd say "You know and I know and there's nothing we can do about it." She reported that Bob was angry and upset with her new behavior but was also more genuinely apologetic, and one time asked her please to stay with him.

Six weeks after the original feedback of the evaluation, Ann announced that she was pregnant. The therapy continued for another six sessions. During this time, Bob reported feeling that he was making headway in being less critical and explosive. He noted Ann's greater assertiveness and said that at least once it had helped him cool down more quickly. He described feelings he'd had of love and appreciation for her one night while she slept but hadn't shared these with her. When he remarked at one point again that she'd never leave him, the therapist agreed that this was probably true. A more likely scenario, he said, was that she'd stay but that Bob would gradually lose everything that made the relationship special to him as she became more unfulfilled and unhappy and resigned. It is indicative of the resources that the therapist sensed early on in this case that Bob was deeply affected by this Ghost of Christmas Future scenario.

In subsequent meetings, both Bob and Ann described their pleasure at his changes. Ann felt he was being unusually attentive and available, partly in relation to her pregnancy, but she also felt "something extra." Bob brought himself to tell her how he'd felt that night looking at her in bed. He was cooking and washing at home. His critical behavior had all but disappeared and, when it did occur, he would apologize spontaneously. In Bob's last meeting, we agreed that he had in fact shown he could change his behavior. The question was whether he could keep it up. Several months later, the couple wrote to announce the birth of their daughter.

Supporting Available Methods of Coping

In some cases, especially those involving a crisis of some kind, therapists may feel that their first responsibility is to help stabilize the family, reducing anxiety and fear, limiting potentially destructive responses, and preventing further damage, whether or not more extensive therapy will follow. In these cases, therapists may help the family utilize resources that are already visible and available but often underutilized due to the family's confusion, uncertainty, and, in some cases, tendency to rely on external resources, engendered by the crisis. This is analogous to the psychoanalytic notion of supporting defenses in individual treatment. Instead of seeking to elicit new ways of handling stress, the therapist helps the family to make better use of their own familiar ways. In some cases, this may even dictate temporarily utilizing and thereby perpetuating problematic patterns if it is felt that this can help prevent more serious damage in the long run. These interventions almost always draw on resources in the *relational context* of the presenting problem in an effort to alleviate distress, diminish symptomatic expressions, and head off a more serious crisis.

Case Example. A 77-year-old woman is referred for evaluation related to a complaint of depression. She is seen with her 65-year-old husband and 25-year-old granddaughter, whom she and her husband have largely raised as their own child. She is described as having experienced episodes of mild depression throughout her life, although her symptoms over the past 3 years are considerably worse. She has been active professionally throughout her life and is clearly experiencing losses in recent years in her ability to concentrate and remember. She has some periods of confusion, although she presents as more than usually agile and intact cognitively for her age. She has been examined by her family physician, a neuropsychologist, and a psychiatrist, who began a trial of antidepressant medication.

The referral for family evaluation comes in relation to the psychologist's hunch concerning family conflicts. In fact, there is a significant degree of conflict between the husband and granddaughter. The husband suffers from a painful neurological condition, requiring multiple surgeries; he is often irritable, markedly intolerant of his granddaughter, and impatient with his wife's bouts of crying because she can't tell him why she's crying. The granddaughter is an intelligent and sensitive but extremely isolated, suspicious, and unhappy woman. Having been abandoned by both her mother and father, her grandparents are her only real family. She alternates between living with them and travelling rather aimlessly on her own. When she is living with them, she and her grandfather argue often, he resenting her tactless and passive–aggressive efforts to run the household and she stung by his criticism and apparent resentment of her being in the home. The grandmother occasionally mediates between them with little real success.

Family evaluation identified these patterns but indicated that they were most likely a small factor in the woman's depression. More significant were the losses she experienced with aging and, secondarily, her husband's well-meaning but unhelpful demands that she explain why she is crying. All efforts to help the husband and granddaughter make peace were unsuccessful. After three or four meetings the therapist opted for a more limited and pragmatic approach. Asked when she felt most depressed, the woman realized that it was always in the late afternoon. Asked if anything usually helped her feel better, she said sometimes talking with a friend or playing cards with her husband. She did not call friends herself because she did not want to burden them with her problems and rarely asked her husband, as he always read the newspaper at that time.

The therapist did the following: He encouraged the woman to call her one best friend, to let her know about her difficult late afternoons and that an occasional telephone call then would be appreciated. He encouraged both spouses to be more aware of this especially difficult time period and to make a point of doing things together as much as possible during it. He tried to explain to the husband how someone might in fact *not* know why they were crying and to encourage him not to demand an explanation but to offer sympathy as he might if she had a headache or fever. Finally, he apprised the granddaughter of her grandmother's high-distress time period and encouraged her to keep her company when this was feasible, but not when her grandfather was already with her.

The family returned 2 weeks later. The husband told the therapist that he'd done some research and that he, the therapist, was wrong about people crying "for no reason." But he had not challenged or criticized his wife about her crying since the last meeting. They spent more time together in the late afternoon, the husband agreeing to read the paper later on after dinner. The wife still felt depressed but had had no major crying spells and found the late afternoon somewhat easier to handle. They announced that they saw no reason for further sessions and terminated.

Trust Building

Trust building is a treatment approach most explicitly articulated and elaborated by contextual therapists (Boszormenyi-Nagy & Krasner, 1980; Boszormenyi-Nagy & Spark, 1973; Boszormenyi-Nagy & Ulrich, 1981) but probably employed more intuitively by a number of therapists. It involves an effort to facilitate dialogue between individuals in close relationships, dialogue in which they can examine actions, events, and long-term patterns that have diminished trust on one or both sides. This might involve a grown daughter talking with a parent who had physically or sexually abused her during childhood or a couple trying to rework a stressful period in the marriage in which both parties felt the other had failed to support them. It requires that at least one party take responsibility for planning and initiating such a dialogue, and that both parties try to present their own claims and be willing to acknowledge what they see as the legitimate claims of the other. This means that both parties present their sides of the relationship—their experience of what has transpired, their sense of the fairness and unfairness of that experience, and their sense of what they deserve now from that relationship—and try to "put themselves in the other's shoes" as well, to listen for the legitimacy of those claims and consider their own obligations in the relationship.

Trust building relies on dialogue, that is, verbal discussion, but its heart is action. It depends on action taken to initiate dialogue and can generate actions that change long-term relational patterns. The acknowledgment provided in such dialogue and the actions that flow from it provide the concrete basis for greater trust between the participants. This is what contextual therapists mean by "actualized trustworthiness."

Trust building has a positive snowball effect. One person's willingness to consider the other's claims makes the other more likely to try to consider that person's claims. One person's demonstrated investment in the relationship makes it easier for the other to express caring. When trust is increased, a variety of other personal and relational resources become more available. In this way, trust building may be the best example of a *resource-amplifying loop* of behaviors that can but needn't be initiated in the context of therapy. Individuals who have never and will never meet a therapist may initiate such dialogues on their own, often, for example, when someone close to them is dying. Within the context of therapy, these dialogues may either be held together with the therapist or privately outside of treatment, with the therapist helping one party to prepare, interpret, and follow up on them. Trust building serves primarily to change the *relational context* of presenting problems.

Case Example. A 39-year-old professional woman is in individual therapy because of her inability to relax and her self-described pattern of making exorbitant demands on her husband and teenage children. Essentially, she refuses to ask for help with whatever she wants done but periodically explodes in outbursts of resentment, accusation, and self-righteousness. Her feelings at work are similar, but there she does not allow herself the freedom of such outbursts. The therapist meets with all family members. The husband and children confirm the mother's descriptions but feel she exaggerates the severity and destructiveness of her outbursts. They make clear that such outbursts do occur, but also that it is rarely difficult to tolerate them. They know that this is how she is and don't have too much trouble living with it. They are willing to participate in treatment as needed but support the mother's request for individual therapy for herself. The therapist agrees, retaining the option to include them in treatment later on if this seems desirable.

The woman's life history reveals a childhood with an alcoholic mother and a largely absent father, the parents divorcing when she was an adolescent. Her mother's intense neediness, emotional turmoil, lapses of reliability related to her drinking, and seeming unwillingness to hear whatever displeases her from her daughter, together with her father's essential unavailability throughout her childhood and adult life, have led her to be mistrusting of close relationships. She is virtually unable to ask for care or to let herself be taken care of in any way. She nurses a life-long grudge of which she is only dimly aware but that is repeatedly expressed in her outbursts at her husband and children. Her therapy leads her to make efforts to rework relationships with both her still-living parents. Basically, she is encouraged to make claims on both of them, to test the possibility that perhaps they can and will respond to her needs instead of assuming that they can't or won't, being silently angry and distant with them because of this and directing these feelings of anger instead at her children and husband.

Her efforts with both parents require weeks of preparation and take place at different points in her treatment. She is asked to consider what she wants changed, whether she wishes to meet with each in a therapy session or outside it, what physical conditions (timing, place, etc.) and ways of presenting agendas seem likely to increase chances for a successful outcome, what risks, costs, and benefits could ensue from such efforts, and what costs accompany the status quo. Buoyed by the success of her initial effort to take more control and thereby be less resentful and more available to her mother, she decides with much ambivalence and fear to confront her father.

She is puzzled and hurt by her father's failure to be "there" for her both in her childhood (when he was away from home much of the time) and currently. She remembers in particular one terrible period when she was newly divorced and a single parent with very little money. Her father knew of her situation but never offered to help. She feels he avoids anyone when they are ill or needy. She fears that fundamentally he has never really cared for her. She notes that he has never given her a present of any kind, although he has in recent years helped repair some things around her house and babysat for her children with his new wife. She tried once before to talk with him alone but apparently, being threatened by this, he made it impossible for her to do so. Throughhout her adult life, she has dreaded her father's visits, fearing his criticism and working for days to make things perfect in what she sees as a vain attempt to avoid it. In essence, she feels that her father doesn't love her, and has never before and will not now respond to her needs, and for these reasons cannot be trusted. She fears that any attempt to discuss this with him will further lead him to run away or disown her for good or will be met with a superficial, cheery (and unbelievable) denial, which would only confirm her worst fears.

She decides to approach her father during a summer visit. He agrees to talk with her this time. She finds to her surprise that she is able to say everything she had hoped to in this discussion, with her father willing to listen and asking questions of his own. His answers reveal a man surprisingly oblivious of the consequences of some of his actions, but clearly caring and concerned about his daughter; they also provide useful information about her. He is not glib and facile; he does not run away. He is surprised and deeply regretful at much that she raises. He admits that he avoided the home because of his wife's behavior when his daughter was growing up, but seems never to have realized that his children might also have felt abandoned. He has perceived her distance and reticence as proof that she didn't love him. During the difficult period she describes, he felt that she was unwilling to ask for help in her usual defiantly independent style and if that was how she wanted it, so be it! This feedback was especially striking for her since it confirmed a picture of her relational stance that had slowly gained force since the start of treatment, and it demonstrated that stance's potentially negative consequences in her life. Her father was genuinely pained by hearing her experience of the relationship. To her surprise, he thanked her for taking the trouble to discuss it with him. Before he left, to her shock, he bought an expensive appliance she needed and presented it to her as a gift. In a follow-up meeting, she said she felt "at peace with my father for the first time."

In this case, resources were tested. The daughter demonstrated trustworthiness by caring enough to try to improve the relationship, by being willing to listen to her father's side, and by making clear the fear of hurt and rejection she had to overcome in order to approach him. She took the risk that her father might be able to respond to her needs. He was, and he demonstrated this in several ways: by listening and acknowledging her side, by being willing and able to reveal his own, and with the concrete vehicle of the gift, both as "peace offering" and symbolic token of continuing involvement and availability. An anecdote this client shared several weeks after this discussion suggests the "ripple effect" that can take place in other family relationships when one relationship is changed in this way. The client's brother had warned her against trying to talk with their father, seeing him as "a lost cause." Soon after her talk with her father, the brother called her, expressing amazement and asking what had gone on between herself and their father. Their father had apparently sent a letter to his son that was unprecedented in its warmth, self-disclosure, and passionate statement of caring.

The following case example illustrates several techniques, including coaching, widening the resource pool, removing obstacles and trust building. Excerpts from a videotape of two conjoint sessions are presented in order to illustrate the process of trust building more concretely.

Case Example. Bobbie Tyler is a 33-year-old divorced mother of four children. She lives with the three daughters of her only marriage, ages 4 to 10 years. Two years earlier, while still married and living with her husband, she was admitted to a psychiatric inpatient unit severely depressed and following a suicide attempt. Bobbie was the oldest of her mother's five children. All but Bobbie were children of Mr. Cook, whom Bobbie's mother had married, left, and later divorced. Bobbie had little information about her own father. She had been told that "some man had dragged my mother [as a teenager] into an alley and raped her." Mr. Cook began sexually abusing Bobbie at about age 5. Bobbie reports that her mother discovered this when Bobbie was 7 years old but did nothing to prevent it and, in fact, walked out, leaving all the children with Mr. Cook, when Bobbie was 10 years old. Her sexual abuse continued on a weekly basis until Bobbie became pregnant and was sent away to deliver her stepfather's baby at the age of 15. She gave the child up for adoption and was able to prevent a resumption of the abuse. She married Mr. Tyler in her early 20s, discovering a couple of years later that he regularly cheated on her and had been prosecuted but not convicted on a statuatory rape charge involving a 12-year-old girl.

Bobbie made good use of her brief hospitalization, taking steps to separate from and divorce Mr. Tyler, who continued to cheat on her and was emotionally abusive as well. Following discharge from the hospital, she was followed in individual treatment, which she also used well. Two years later, she was no longer depressed. She was beginning to be involved in a nonabusive relationship with a man. She had enrolled in college and made the Dean's List, an extremely important accomplishment for her given a family history in which no other siblings had gone past high school and in which her own high school years had been disrupted by the birth of her stepfather's child.

As other areas of her life became more stable and satisfying for her, Bobbie began to talk more about her relationship with her mother. They were still in contact, talking together once a week. However, they had never discussed her mother's having left the children with Mr. Cook, knowing of their sexual and physical abuse at his hands. In fact, her mother refused to discuss anything about Bobbie's childhood or the past. Bobbie also had a strained and conflicted relationship with her halfsister, Joan. Bobbie complained to Joan about their mother; Joan defended her. Their relationship had alternated between periods of conflict, uneasy peace, and cutoff over the years. With the therapist's coaching, Bobbie decided to try to change her relationship with her mother. She wrote a letter asking if her mother would be willing to talk with her about her childhood. Her mother's response was devastating; she absolutely refused and criticized Bobbie for "blaming everyone else for how you've screwed up your life." Joan let Bobbie know that she had "no right" to question their mother about the past, and Bobbie described the latest quarrels with her sister to the therapist.

At this point, the therapist asked if Bobbie would be willing to bring Joan in with her for a couple of meetings in order to see if changes could be made in that relationship. She agreed, as did Joan. The therapist helped Bobbie prepare for these meetings by clarifying what she wanted to accomplish in them and how *she* would start them off. He also warned that after a long individual therapy, she might find herself uncomfortable because he could not simply be her advocate in these meetings but would have to be sympathetic to both of them. If anything, he might have to be especially sensitive to Joan at the start in order to establish that he saw himself as an advocate for a better *relationship*, not simply for Bobbie's side of it.

The therapist met with the sisters for four meetings, agreeing to Joan's condition that they not discuss their mother. The first two sessions were video-taped, and excerpts from these sessions follow. The therapist wanted to test whether both women could express their own complaints and claims to one another and listen and respond to the other's side as well. It was hoped that this process of dialogue could remove some of the obstacles that had made their relationship so difficult, thereby building mutual trust and freeing them to be more available as supports for one another. The process was in fact essentially the same as that which would have been attempted had Bobbie's mother agreed to talk with her. The sisters' discussions in these two meetings began with recent conflicts, and gradually expanded to include the trust-demolishing and unre-worked experiences of their childhood with Mr. Cook.

Early in the first session, the therapist asks Joan what she's most angry about.

JOAN: I think it's that for 3 years I've tried to be as much of a sister as I possibly could. Bobbie and I were never close when we were younger and we were never close when we were teenagers or young adults, but in the last 3 years I think I've tried to help her in many ways. And I think that Bobbie just feels that it's owed to her. I guess that's what the problem is. [to Bobbie] You said to me one day that you wouldn't be in the predicament you were in right now if it wasn't for us kids.

THERAPIST: [to Joan] Do you know what she meant by that?

JOAN: Yeah, she was trying to tell me that my father was threatening to rape me so therefore she let him . . . do his thing.

The sisters are at a stalemate. Joan, the more verbal, states her own position and describes Bobbie's. They cannot agree on what each deserves from and owes the other. Joan rejects Bobbie's claim that Joan owes her something because of what she suffered as a child; Bobbie rejects Joan's claim that Bobbie owes her anything for her efforts to help in recent years. Neither feels heard by the other. The therapist begins to test their abilities to hear and acknowledge the other's claims by asking Bobbie if she feels Joan has in fact tried to help her. He then asks Joan if she can see how Bobbie might feel that someone owes her something in relation to her childhood, leaving aside for the moment who that should be. Bobbie acknowledges that Joan has in fact been helpful and asks her how she can show that she appreciates this. Joan responds that Bobbie could give her a call if she's sick, listen to her problems, and advise her when she's having problems. Bobbie responds that when she has tried to do this in the past, Joan has "done nothing but put me down." The therapist encourages Bobbie to describe a specific incident if possible.

> You called me one time and you sounded in pretty bad shape so I got a babysitter and went up to the house and you were in very bad shape. And we talked and I tried to give you some advice and all of a sudden you didn't want to hear any of my advice and you told me I only went up there to gloat and to see someone suffering. You didn't ask me to come but you sounded like you needed somebody so I did.

Joan asks if she was drunk then; Bobbie says yes. When the therapist inquires, Joan says she doesn't remember this but believes it really happened. She admits that this changes the picture somewhat, that she would "walk away from a reaction like that" herself, thereby acknowledging that Bobbie has tried to help her and that her own behavior may have driven Bobbie away. Each new acknowledgment in this dialogue builds trust and lays a foundation for discussing more threatening and painful subjects. Joan's statement that she believes Bobbie's view of the incident even though she doesn't remember it indicates the residual trust that still exists in the relationship.

Joan soon shifts the conversation to an earlier exchange between them. At that time Bobbie had admitted that she had been aware of the one time Mr. Cook "went after" Joan (unsuccessfully) and had not intervened. Mr. Cook apparently beat all the other children but only sexually abused Bobbie. A good part of this and the next meeting was spent discussing this incident, with Joan essentially accusing Bobbie of not having protected her and Bobbie defending herself. This is striking in view of the drastic difference in extent and severity of sexual abuse experienced by the sisters and by Joan's directing these accusations at her sister when she has never confronted her mother in this way. In fact, this throws light on the primary obstacles in this relationship. In their inability to hold the responsible parties accountable for their suffering (the father who sexually and physically abused them; the mother who abandoned them), they are left directing their anger and blame at each other and, like mirror images, rejecting the other's accusations.

The therapist takes this opportunity to share his hunch that "a lot of the bumping heads in this relationship is that you folks are paying dues for other people. There is a sense in which both of you are owed a lot and unfortunately don't have a lot of places to look for who can make it up but each other, and it's hard to ask each other when each of you needs so much." Joan, who has maintained a chatty, casual air thus far, becomes visibly upset and begins crying. She is clearly someone who is uncomfortable with tears and with the past and tries to recompose herself. After much urging by the therapist, she shares the sense of recognition and pain elicited by the therapist's statement:

> [*crying*] The fact that we seem to be paying dues for other people. . . . I'm her whipping post for my mother. [*to Bobbie*] I am, Bobbie. You tell me what you won't tell her in the same ways so I hear it and get frustrated and upset. And I guess that, uh, you're probably my whipping post for, uh, childhood.

Joan provides a clear picture of the mutual revolving slates that have come between these sisters. Later in the course of conversation, she surprises the therapist by saying that she never felt guilty about her sister's situation as a child and, if anything, resented her. She describes how Bobbie "had everything, the best food, new pajamas, new socks."

JOAN: (*to Bobbie*) You didn't have to turn yours inside out to wear them the next day. That kind of stuff. And I know my brothers felt the same way, like she was the queen and we got treated like garbage.

THERAPIST: I think that's an understandable way for a child to look at it. Has she talked to you about what it was like on her side being the kid who had those special favors with those special strings attached?

JOAN: Yeah, she said she hated them.

BOBBIE: And do you believe it?

JOAN: No, I don't believe that at the time you hated them. Because you used to gloat.

THERAPIST: How do you mean, gloat?

JOAN: Oh, I remember one time when she and my father sat and ate steak and my father made us watch them eat it.

BOBBIE: Does that mean I gloated?

JOAN: You were smiling. You looked like you were enjoying it as much as he was.

The session ends on a positive note but this accusation is left hanging. It provides a context for the earlier description of Joan as an adult, drunkenly accusing Bobbie of "gloating" over her misery when Bobbie came over to help her.

The second meeting 1 week later begins with both sisters agreeing that they have at least settled some of the disagreements of recent years. Bobbie then comes back to Joan's accusations about gloating and not protecting her from Mr. Cook. In the course of the discussion, Bobbie tries to address Joan's accusations and to present a bit more of her side of things. Both sisters make comments that reveal new thoughts and views having been triggered over the previous week by the last session. Bobbie begins by describing how hurt she feels that Joan still sees her as having gloated or enjoyed Joan's misery as a child. Joan responds, "I'm just being honest about what I thought. But you know, the one thing I was thinking about is the fact that I was 15 before I realized what he was doing to you."

Joan goes on to describe an incident she witnessed when Bobbie returned home after delivering the baby and Mr. Cook was again pressuring her sexually. In fact, Joan has the ages wrong. Bobbie would have been 15, and Joan 10, at the time. But this memory over the past week and her bringing it into the session mark another step in the process whereby both sisters are able to exonerate each other of responsibility for their suffering in childhood.

JOAN: I walked in on that conversation and it stuck in my mind. It was the first time I ever saw her being put through any mind hassle, misery sort of thing. Because he always had these things in private with her. We never saw any of it before that.

BOBBIE: [*bitterly*] So that changed your opinion a little bit.

JOAN: [*quietly*] Yeah.

Bobbie then raises Joan's accusation from the past meeting that she did nothing to protect her when Mr. Cook approached her. She clarifies that the "blackmail" was his threat to "break up the family." Bobbie reports he would say, "You think this is bad. How would you like to go to an orphanage, and have no brothers and sisters." The therapist asks Joan if this changes the picture at all for her.

JOAN: Well, that one night, maybe if she'd attempted to do something, maybe he would have gone on with his blackmail, which was to divide the family. [*to Bobbie*] You know, if you got up and made a stink or something . . .

BOBBIE: [*emphatically*] I hadn't thought of making a stink that night. I had thought of going into the kitchen and getting a butcher knife. But I didn't know how to do it without having to pay for it after.

Joan tries to dismiss this by saying that all of them thought of this at times. The therapist presses, however, since this represents at least a sign of the protective concern Joan had wanted from Bobbie. Joan says she hadn't known her sister had thought of this and believes that she did, again underlining residual trust. She then asks if Bobbie was trying to keep the family together or was afraid for her at the time. Bobbie replies, "Both. Everything was in there. Killing him would have protected you but it would have broken up the family. You know, I even thought, 'If I can wait another 3 or 4 years, I can kill him and then I can be in charge of my brothers and sisters 100%. I'll be old enough.' But I wasn't old enough then. We would have been split up."

Sometime later, the therapist comes back to Joan's resentment that Bobbie didn't protect her.

JOAN: Well, I did think about that during the week, though, and I was pretty gutsy when I was a kid. Maybe she thought that wasn't an important enough issue.

BOBBIE: [*shocked*] What? Him going after you? Yeah, it was. But I just didn't know what to do about it.

Later in the meeting, Bobbie begins to share her own sense of having been isolated and unprotected:

> I don't really think there's any forgiving to be done between the two of us. I can understand where she could resent me or feel some kind of bad feeling, even for just that particular instance. I felt like that a long time. I was living through this thing all by myself. I had three brothers and a sister who never did a damned thing about it. But they were kids and I was a kid. I don't know whether she still feels the same way. I am just starting not to feel the same way.

Bobbie is groping for a way to articulate the gradual change in perspective that she is experiencing.

BOBBIE: A lot of times I say that my life in the past makes me act like I act now, right? But it's not really what was going on between Joan and I then. I do look at all of that differently now, the resentment. When I used to see it, I saw it as being *now*. I didn't see it as we were children and things were the way they were because we were children and we couldn't do anything about it.

THERAPIST: And that's starting to change?

BOBBIE: Yeah, now I know we were children and we couldn't do anything about it.

JOAN: And I know the one thing I've realized, and I think maybe Bobbie has too, is the fact that in order for that whole situation to be maintained by the sicky, he had to divide us and even the gloating was fabricated. He put it there, so that we would stay separated long enough that he could do his own thing. I did think about that a little bit and know that he used to put you in situations where we'd all be angry. He'd have you sit while he beat us, and you wouldn't get hit. And he'd give you treats that we wouldn't get, so the guy wasn't stupid.

BOBBIE: I thought that exact same thing this week. He created that situation. He built it. I felt like he made me play a part in their abuse and I felt like you still felt that way too, on top of it.

THERAPIST: Still blamed you for it.

BOBBIE: Yeah.

JOAN: No, even then, it wasn't that I thought *you* were beating me. It was always him doing it. It's just that whenever I thought of him, I thought of you too. Except when it came to food because you used to gloat about that. But I don't blame you. I didn't like the idea of taking the bones out of the garbage can either. [*Bobbie gasps*] We used to do that all the time, by the way.

BOBBIE: What?

JOAN: Yeah, after you guys had your steak, we'd get 'em out of the garbage can before anything too bad got on 'em and rinse 'em in water.

Joan introduces a detail that powerfully captures some of her experience of childhood. She goes on to identify some of the factors (age differences, their mother's absence, and Bobbie's parentification) that made it easy for her to confuse Mr. Cook's and Bobbie's individual responsibility for her suffering.

JOAN: Don't forget, you were the mother image to us. I was 5 years old. You always seemed much bigger and older than the rest of us to me. And it looked like a team. And I'm sure you weren't sitting there saying "I wish he were beating me." [*Bobbie starts to shake her head in disagreement*] Oh, come on. I wouldn't. I'd feel bad for the rest of you but I'd still be glad that I wasn't getting it.

BOBBIE: See, but I knew about how all of you felt about me. If he had been beating me, I at least would have had brothers and sisters.

The therapist asks if Bobbie had known about the bones. When she indicates that she hadn't, he asks what her reaction was when she heard it just then.

BOBBIE: [*Emphatically*] Sick.

THERAPIST: You didn't know it had been that bad? [*Bobbie shakes her head no*]. Does she know how bad it was for you?

BOBBIE: I don't know.

JOAN: I think I do, since you started talking about it.

BOBBIE: Well, when you say things like you just said. [*Joan tries to explain but Bobbie stops her*] Look, you made a legitimate remark. I mean, somebody would have to be crazy to want somebody to beat them. What you don't know is the fact that I wish he had been beating me. I would have rather been beaten and had brothers and sisters than sat there eating that steak and had nothing, had nobody.

The separate experiences of both sisters become vivid in this exchange, one sadistically tantalized but deprived of decent food, the other set apart and against her brothers and sisters, isolated. There is no denial, no deafness to the other's experience. They can see beyond their old views of the other's role in their own suffering to a realization of the particular suffering of the other. Later in the session, Bobbie makes a statement that contrasts this experience of being heard and validated by the other with the experience of impasse that existed earlier.

Well, I know it's only been these two times that we've talked that either one of us has ever given to the other side. Because I remember the last time we talked. I asked you right out how did you feel about me when we were kids. [*to the therapist*] And she told me, and it was devastating, and as many times as I said "but, but, but, but" she wasn't listening at all. [*to Joan*] You never cracked once. [*both grin*] But this is a whole different thing now.

At the end of this second session, Joan offers to give up her condition that they not discuss their mother but insists that there be no videotaping. In the final two meetings, Bobbie discovers what she has long suspected—that her mother is also an incest victim, and that Bobbie's biological father, the supposed stranger who raped her mother, was a trusted family friend with whom her mother had been sent to board as a teenager. By the fourth meeting, Joan agrees that Bobbie does have a right to try to discuss all of this with their mother. She says she will not stand in Bobbie's way but insists that Bobbie no longer complain to her about their mother, to which Bobbie agrees.

Following these meetings, Bobbie reports a much more positive relationship between Joan and herself. For example, Joan, who has extensive experience in the working world, coaches Bobbie on how to prepare for an important job interview. When Joan marries 1 year later and discovers afterward that her husband is physically abusive, she leaves and moves in temporarily with Bobbie and her children. Bobbie reports that she feels freer and better following the meetings. She also describes surprising changes in her relationship with her mother, including her mother's spontaneously, and without any prompting, initiating a conversation for the first time about Bobbie's childhood and her own. Whether these changes reflect direct communication between Joan and their mother, or a delayed response to Bobbie's letter, or a less direct "ripple effect" from changes in the Bobbie–Joan side of the triangle is not known.

Several months after these sessions are held, the therapist asks for both sisters' permission to use the videotapes in teaching at professional agencies. They agree, but specify that they want to view it themselves first. Accordingly, the therapist and both sisters view the edited tape together. At one point, watching Bobbie describing her childhood experience, Joan says, "You must have really loved us to go through all that." Bobbie later says that this was something she had been waiting a lifetime to hear.

A FINAL CONSIDERATION: NEUTRALITY AND PERSONAL CONVICTION

If we turn away from a preoccupation with what is "wrong" or "bad" in families, we find ourselves directly facing the question of what's good. Practicing therapists who want to step beyond the constraints of the pathology model will have to answer this question. They can do so intentionally or they can do so by default but, to paraphrase a family therapy truism, they cannot *not* do so. When this question is left unanswered, we run the risk of automatically following procedures that stem from pathology models. In some cases, we may burden our clients and embarrass ourselves when we come across contradictions between our professed values and our unexamined methods of practice.

The already widespread critique of the pathology framework has left a kind of vacuum in family theory and therapy. The progression neatly parallels the so-called death of God in 20th-century Western culture. Having cast off "sin" (pathology), we are left with a void, and the prime contenders for its replacement are individualism and science. The most widespread, if largely implicit, value in family therapy as practiced on a daily basis probably involves some variant of self-actualization of individual family members. This is a core value for most therapists, regardless of orientation. A more well-defined and explicit alternative to the pathology framework involves what has been called neutrality, epitomized by the "circularity" of recent cybernetic formulations (Hoffman, 1981).

In the framework of neutrality, we see a scrupulous effort to discern pattern without assigning blame, often coupled with an extreme relativism that holds that *what is* in families is neither good nor bad but simply pattern and construct, changeable and changing. There is something appealing about this effort to view human relationships with the kind of dispassionate observation usually applied to biological and physical phenomena. However, there is a real confusion concerning the meaning or extent of such neutrality. Selvini Palazzoli, Boscolo,

Cecchin, and Prata (1980) have defined neutrality as a pragmatic stance that avoids alliances with particular family members so that "the therapist is allied with everyone and no one at the same time" (p. 11), but many therapists may take it to have a much broader meaning. Is it possible to practice therapy without personal values about what is good (adaptive, strengthening, and healing) for people? If so, how are goals formulated and, more importantly, why bother? This is the point where neutrality, in the broadest sense, and personal conviction collide.

Therapy, by its very nature, demands some set of beliefs about what is desirable for people and, whether therapists acknowledge their values or not, they cannot remove them completely from treatment. We are presented with countless situations (protective concerns involving children; relative entitlements in divorce; a secretly adopted child's right to know) in which our values are unavoidably implicated, regardless of how well we try to consider the values of the family members involved as well. But the question of values poses dilemmas for the therapist. A therapist with no sense of what is good for people has no way to evaluate whether one course of action is any better than another; a therapist with inflexible notions of what is good for people may overlook clients' differing values or try to impose his/her own.

If there is a solution to this dilemma, it involves a mixture of conviction and humility. We need to know what we hold valuable about human life and relationships and then let our clients (and intimates) teach us what we don't know—exceptions and qualifications as well as unexpected expressions of those values, and differing life experiences and values that may contribute to the evolution of our own. For example, it may well be desirable for individuals to try to rework relationships with cutoff family members, but there may still be situations in which a "moratorium" is indicated. We may value a parent's responsibility to protect his/her child from danger but come to recognize that, in some cases, giving that child up for adoption represents his/her best effort to do so.

Thinking about family resources leads us inevitably to the question of the therapist's personal convictions and their role in treatment. It is a question that practicing therapists need to answer for themselves.

REFERENCES

Albee, E. *Who's afraid of Virginia Woolf?* New York: Atheneum, 1962.
Angell, R. C. *The family encounters the depression.* New York: Charles Scribner, 1936.
Attneave, C. In F. Hoffman (Ed.), *The American Indian Family: Strengths and Stresses.* Proceedings of the Conference on Research Issues. Phoenix, Arizona, April, 1980.
Bank, S., & Kahn, M. Sisterhood–brotherhood is powerful: Sibling sub-systems and family therapy, *Family Process*, 1975, *14*, 311–339.
Bank, S., & Kahn, M. *The sibling bond.* New York: Basic Books, 1982.
Boszormenyi-Nagy, I., & Krasner, B. Trust-based therapy: A contextual approach. *American Journal of Psychiatry*, 1980, *137*, 767–775.

Boszormenyi-Nagy, I., & Spark, G. *Invisible loyalties: Reciprocity in intergenerational family therapy.* New York: Harper and Row, 1973.

Boszormenyi-Nagy, I., & Ulrich, D. Contextual family therapy. In A. Gurman & D. Kniskern (Eds.), *Handbook of Family Therapy.* New York: Brunner/Mazel, 1981.

Cousins, N. *Anatomy of an illness as perceived by the patient: Reflections on healing and regeneration.* New York: Norton, 1979.

Cotroneo, M. The role of forgiveness in family therapy. In A. Gurman (Ed.), *Questions and answers in the practice of family therapy* (Vol. II). New York: Brunner/Mazel, 1982.

Erickson, M. The utilization of patient behavior in the hypnotherapy of obesity: Three case reports. *American Journal of Clinical Hypnotherapy*, 1960, *3*, 112–116.

Erickson, M. The use of symptoms as an integral part of hypnotherapy. *American Journal of Clinical Hypnotherapy*, 1965, *8*, 57–65.

Erickson, M., & Rossi, E. *Experiencing hypnosis.* New York: Irvington Press, 1981.

Haley, A. *Roots.* Garden City, N.Y.: Doubleday, 1976.

Haley, J. (Ed.), *Advanced techniques of hypnosis and therapy: Selected papers of Milton H. Erickson, M.D.* New York: Grune & Stratton, 1967.

Haley, J. *Uncommon therapy: The pychiatric techniques of Milton H. Erickson, M.D.* New York: Norton, 1973.

Henry, J. *Pathways to madness.* New York: Random House, 1965.

Hoffman, L. *Foundations of family therapy.* New York: Basic Books, 1981.

Karpel, M., & Strauss, E. *Family evaluation.* New York: Gardner Press, 1983.

Kipling, R. *Rudyard Kipling's verse.* Definitive Edition. New York: Doubleday, 1940.

Kirk, R. *Bright moments* [Album]. Atlantic Records, 1973.

Lankton, S., & Lankton, C. *The answer within: A clinical framework of Ericksonian hypnotherapy.* New York: Brunner/Mazel, 1983.

Lewis, J., Beavers, W., Gossett, J., & Phillips, V. *No single thread: Psychological health in family systems.* New York: Brunner/Mazel, 1976.

McCubbin, H., & Patterson, J. Family transitions: Adaptation to stress. In H. McCubbin & C. Figley (Eds.), *Stress and the Family*, (Vol. 1). New York: Brunner/Mazel, 1983.

Neill, J., & Kniskern, D. *From psyche to system: The evolving therapy of Carl Whitaker.* New York: Guilford, 1982.

Otto, H. Criteria for assessing family strength. *Family Process*, 1963, *2*, 329–337.

Satir, V. *Conjoint Family Therapy.* Palo Alto, CA: Science and Behavior Books, 1967.

Satir, V. *Peoplemaking.* Palo Alto, CA: Science and Behavior Books, 1972.

Selvini Palazzoli, M., Boscolo, L., Cecchin, G., & Prata, G. Hypothesizing–circularity–neutrality: Three guidelines for the conductor of the session. *Family Process*, 1980, *19*, 3–12.

Turnbull, C. *The mountain people.* New York: Simon & Schuster, 1972.

Van Meter, M. Seeing dependency as strength from generation to generation. In N. Stinnett, B. Chesser, J. Defrain, & P. Knaub (Eds.), *Family strengths: Positive models for family life.* Lincoln: University of Nebraska Press, 1980.

Whitaker, C., & Keith, D. Symbolic–experiential family therapy. In A. Gurman & D. Kniskern (Eds.), *Handbook of family therapy.* New York: Brunner/Mazel, 1981.

Zeig, J. (Ed.). *Ericksonian approaches to hypnosis and psychotherapy.* New York: Brunner/Mazel, 1982.

PART THREE

Beyond the Parent–Child Nexus

CHAPTER 7

The Sibling System:
Bonds of Intensity, Loyalty, and Endurance

Michael D. Kahn

The voice of the woman at the other end of the phone sounded strained: "I'm calling for myself and . . . well . . . also for my brothers. . . . But they don't know I'm calling a therapist. . . . It's that our father is dying, he has had Alzheimer's disease for 6 years and now he has pancreatic cancer. Our mother died 12 years ago [*the words were now rushing out, the woman speaking seemed on the edge of panic*] and my brothers and I are all that there is left of our family. We have a lot to sort out with each other. Do you think we could get to see you right away?"

This phone call, received by me as the entry point for three adult siblings into family therapy, underscores the bond that siblings[1] in the contemporary world can feel for one another. Brothers and sisters today often depend, need, love, care for, and concern themselves with each other's lives, even more than in previous generations. Such positive bonds may develop because of the pain and fear that results from the illness or death of fathers and mothers, or because of the more gradual but inevitable disappointment that all children experience with their parents, or because of a life-long emphasis on mutual caring. Siblings, to paraphrase the caller, are often what constitutes the ongoing sense of family.

That there continues to be an erosion of other meaningful points of lasting connection in American society cannot be denied. This includes a widening geographical scattering of the nuclear family, a dropping birth rate (fully 30% of college-educated women between the ages of 25 and 35 now say they never expect to have children), a high divorce rate, shrinking family size, and a

---

[1]Siblings, an underused term meaning full brothers and sisters, often conjures up images of children. Throughout this chapter, I describe the relationship among child, adolescent, and adult siblings and therapeutic strategies used with varied age groupings throughout the life span.

Michael D. Kahn, Ph.D. Department of Psychology, University of Hartford, Hartford, Connecticut.

veritable wholesale transformation of what was the American landscape and what were time-honored personal landmarks. Given these changes, it's increasingly difficult for two generations of any American family to find meaningful, reliable, stable, and consistent ways to relate to one another.

While the traditional structure of families is certainly "here to stay" (see Bane, 1976), the enormous shift in value structures, in terms of the nature of work, women's roles, allocation of resources from children to married couples themselves, more extended and specialized education for adults, greater tolerance of variation in life styles, and the increasing technological complexity of the postmodernist world, forces a shift from vertical alliances in which parents give care to their children and children give loyalty and devotion to parents to more horizontal alliances within the sibling subgroup itself. Siblings increasingly have to fend for themselves, to make their own decisions, to determine their own fates. This change, which we are growing accustomed to seeing in siblings who have reached young adulthood (20–25 years of age), seems to be reaching downward to younger and younger siblings (14–20 years of age), accelerating whenever a crisis strikes the parents' lives, such as divorce, or fragmentation of the family occurs, forcing siblings to rely more on one another and less on their parents. [For a fuller exposition of these changes, see an earlier work, *The Sibling Bond* (Bank & Kahn, 1982)]. While other horizontal relationships such as friendships and marriage may come and go, the sibling relationship always remains. There is no way to formally sever the sibling relationship, no "sibling divorce" ritual. The divorce rate among married couples today varies between 40% and 50%, but only 3% of siblings (Cicirelli, 1982) ever permanently discontinue seeing one another. Even if adult brothers and sisters seldom make the effort to spend prolonged time with each other, they "know" the sibling is "out there," available if a crisis strikes or if comfort is needed. Brothers and sisters provide life's longest lasting intimate relationship for one another, outlasting the relationship with parents by 20–30 years. The sibling connection remains as a touchstone even after each child has grown up and moved away from the nuclear family. To not have a sibling (only 10% of American adults are only children, but the percentage is slowly increasing) is to be without an important resource throughout the life span (Kahn, 1983).

This point was recently underscored by a married couple, both only children, who were forced to change their will for the third time, finally appointing the wife's aging parents as guardians for their three children. Without brothers and sisters of their own, they had selected their married friends to be their children's guardians. Each of the couples they had previously chosen as guardians then became divorced, necessitating a change in the will each time, since, with the rancor that accompanied each divorce, it seemed an unfair burden and an impossibility to gauge which person from each of these successive couples to entrust with the responsibility for the care of their children. Frustrated by the idea of using other couples, and without brothers and sisters to turn to, the couple selected the wife's parents, who, although well into their 70s, were the only immediate family resource that was available.

MYTHS AND REALITIES OF SIBLING RELATIONSHIPS

Throughout this book, the primary theme that has been emphasized is the strengths that are inherent in family systems. Can siblings really be considered a reliable family resource? For all of the usual praise for "sisterhood" and "brotherhood" that sprinkles the English language, the word most frequently associated with that of siblings has a negative onus—"rivalry." Clinicians who up to now have lacked formal training in, or knowledge about, sibling dynamics are just as subject as the next person in thinking that brothers and sisters will inevitably fight, quarrel, or bicker with, and maim, envy, hurt, distrust, retaliate against, harm, or deceive each other. This has resulted in a real deficit in clinical techniques for working with siblings in which positive feelings among sibs are expected.

Certainly it would be naive to suggest that harsh events never occur between siblings, but it is equally naive to *assume* that they always do, and that family therapists should never count on sibs to come to each other's aid. While a previous publication, *The Sibling Bond* (Bank & Kahn, 1982) goes into great detail documenting the sources of sibling discord and distrust that do occur, it is useful to briefly describe in this text some of the myths and realities of sibling discord that have helped prolong the bias against using siblings as a therapeutic resource.

Biblical

Cain and Abel, Joseph and his brothers, Jacob and Esau, and Absalom, Amnon, and Tamar are only the most prominent of Old Testament Biblical tales that recount the struggle of siblings to dominate and take advantage of one another. While themes of unity among tribal groups and married couples abound in the Bible, brothers, particularly, often attempt to dominate and deceive, often by unfair means, in order to curry parental favor. Such legends take a long time to die. A recent book for parents about sibling relationships warned menacingly in its title, *Raising Cain (and Abel Too!)* (McDermott, 1980), just how trying and treacherous the sibling relationship is still supposed to be. The popular television series *Dallas*, with the infamous but cunningly attractive older brother J.R. struggling against his well-meaning but naive younger brother Bobby in the family business, is after all just a modern-day replay of the old Cain and Abel theme.

The Legacy of Primogeniture and Birth Order

The inherent rights of firstborn children to property and power over their laterborn siblings became a legal fact in the Middle Ages, and a psychological force even after such rights were deemed archaic and nonbinding by the end of the 19th century. Such notions have been passed down to us through the works of Shakespeare and in such contemporary birth-order devotees as Walter Toman

(1976). Olders, with their head start on winning parental favor, are purported to have a leg up on their junior siblings, which creates smug, power-oriented satisfaction in the older siblings and envious resentment in their younger brothers and sisters. Primogeniture and birth-order suppositions ignore the equalizing effects that parental crises create in children's lives, the more egalitarian spirit of our own times, and how supportive and nurturing sibs can be, regardless of birth position. Yet the abuse of the power position by an older sibling is a recurring theme we all hear, particularly when parents are no longer present to monitor their children's interactions.

Psychoanalysis

Psychoanalytic literature, it has been pointed out (Kahn & Bank, 1980; Neubauer, 1983; Santiago, 1973), and psychoanalytic practice have up to now developed primarily a negative view of the sibling relationship. Whether it be from the tradition of Freud (1905/1953) and Adler (1959) or through such contemporary contributions as Mahler (1968), the sibling has often been presented as an obstacle to adequate psychological separation and individuation. American psychoanalysis, in particular its biologically deterministic wing, is so committed to refuting interpersonal dependency as having any virtue that siblings are at best mentioned as annoying encumbrances, but more usually are totally ignored. Fortunately, the object relations group of American and British psychoanalytic theorists views dependency in the interpersonal context more positively, as having both survival and psychic organizing value, and even to be of biological necessity. Siblings are still only fleetingly mentioned, but with the continued efforts by family system therapists of analytic persuasion to incorporate object relations theory into clinical practice (Framo, 1970; Kahn, 1986; Kantor, 1980; Mallouk, 1982; Sander, 1979; Stierlin, 1977), sibling interaction and the dependency it inevitably includes will undoubtedly be increasingly emphasized.

Sexual Attraction: The Children of Oedipus

Bluntly put, one glaring reality is that, under certain conditions of family unhappiness, adolescent brothers and sisters can become sexually embroiled. Sibling incest is the most frequent type of incestuous relationship, occurring, it is estimated, at least five times as often as the most cited variety, father–daughter incest. Paradoxically, it is also the least often detected, since the sibling incest taboo is fairly weak, violating neither the generational or dependency bond deemed so vital in other family relationship subsystems (Meiselman, 1978). Sibling incest often goes under the name of "play" or "fooling around." Actual sibling incest occurs clandestinely whenever parents remain oblivious to the emotional turmoil their children may be in. The guilt and fear over parental reactions often contribute to it remaining secret.

Some sibling incest may even be used by the children as a way of forestalling psychological collapse, where holding one another or exciting each other appears a better alternative than feeling totally dead or being totally ignored. Conversely, even though there may not be actual incestuous behavior, brothers and sisters from some ethnic groups are often made to feel uncomfortable by their parents when they are in each other's presence as they reach adolescence and if parents conclude there to be insufficient parental supervision. Such sexually anxious parents fear that their sons and daughters will become intimate. The fear of sexual impulses, gradually internalized by the children, may later be projected onto anyone else from outside the family who shows sexual interest (e.g., "Don't you go near our sister!").

Whether sexual feelings between siblings are ever acted upon or are only feared, become conscious or remain unconscious, sexual development during adolescence, unless dealt with openly, contextually, and in a sensitive manner, may become a real impediment to adolescent and adult brothers and sisters ever learning to trust and rely on each other.

Parental Tactics: Divide and Conquer

The family therapist who decides that it may be clinically valuable to engage siblings to cooperate and help each other, and then expects them to be mutually nurturing and dependable, may run head-on into a system where parents have for many years sown the seeds of discord and strife. There may be many reasons for this: (1) one child may be a scapegoated victim whom the others shun; (2) the parents may be emotionally overwhelmed, picking on and blaming the kids, so that their children feel terror and panic that spills over into aggression toward each other; (3) each parent's childhood may have contained so much sibling rivalry and aggression that they expect little else to occur between their own children; (4) the children may have had little meaningful psychological or physical access to one another, such as occurs with broad age-spacing; (5) one child may genuinely be the parent's favorite, whom the others resent; (6) a child may be overendowed or underendowed with special abilities, creating some large disparity between the children's abilities, and therefore a corresponding lack of meaningful identification between them; and (7) children in a family may often divide up into separate warring camps, some on Mom's side, some on Dad's, if their parents are openly unhappy. The children may become captive proxies, if their parents need them to take sides.

Siblings are unlikely to get along in such circumstances, until the parents are able to extinguish their own hostilities, or subordinate their own needs for the sake of the kids. Therapists need to know whether such preconditions exist before they plunge in with good intentions and expect the children to have a mutually cooperative, common point of view.

Aggression: What Is It?

Aggression, as we are all too painfully aware, is a basic human trait (Lorenz, 1966). Indeed, ours may be the generation that witnesses the ultimate expression of that trait, a nuclear holocaust, unless some more powerful means of checking such an instinct can be determined. Given the inherent nature of aggression in the human species, why should we not see some evidence of it in sibling interaction? However, it is important to discriminate between unchecked aggression, in which brothers and sisters may be out to "get each other," and the many variations of aggressive behavior between kids (one group of parents put it succinctly, "Why are our kids always fighting?"). In some families parents seem to have an uncanny ability to overlook the aggression that does occur between their children, even when it reaches the bloodletting level, while in others parents have a too-quick readiness to interfere the moment their kids begin to argue. The standards for aggression, carried from each parent's sibling history, often determine whether or not a therapist is called upon to intervene.

Whether or not aggression flows from parental neglect, or the tactics of divide and conquer described in the previous section, such feelings and behaviors are often expressed by siblings as an outlet for the vicissitudes of their developmental growth. Aggression in this sense serves many socially useful purposes. Some brothers and sisters first practiced the ability to dominate and to feel powerful by physically punching or wrestling with their sibling(s). Later, verbal taunting and the art of the "put-down" are often first directed at a sib, who then must learn how to respond in kind in order to save face. And all clinicians know full well that the anger and rage directed at a brother or sister is often a displacement of feelings away from the more feared, real object of anger, a parent. Aggression can also be a way of provoking a reaction from another, an essential antidote in otherwise lifeless or depressed families. Finally, aggression by young children (ages 2–4) falls under the rubric of agonistic behavior, which is developmentally important but often misunderstood by parents. Agonistic behavior in all mammals is directed toward outer objects, creating cycles of activity and reactivity. Sibs will tease, punch, poke, prod, and cajole each other, for sometimes no other reason than they, simply put, are available.

The hitting or taunting between siblings is therefore always more than simple "aggression," and needs to be discriminated by parents and clinicians as to its true nature no matter what particular form it may take.

Family Stressors

Any events in the history of a family may shake the foundation of sibling relationships. Children who occupied meaningful psychological space and played a role in the family during the period when things went well may feel quite alienated from those children who are born later, developing under difficult circumstances or, psychologically, at a different point in time. Such siblings may feel themselves to be quite different passengers on the same family voyage. Obvious events that impair sibling closeness are divorce, severe illness in a parent, chronic or terminal illness in one sibling, severe emotional difficulties in one or more children that seem unresponsive to treatment(s), death, remarriage, drastic economic downturns, geographical moves, and devastating social and historical events such as war. Although some parents may have successfully cultivated closeness between their children before events turned sour, other families are not so fortunate. By the time these families reach the therapist's office, too much hurt may have accumulated, misunderstandings may have become frozen, and images of each other as alienated strangers may have hardened (see *The Sibling Bond* (Bank & Kahn, 1982) for a fuller exposition of these concepts). If siblings are at the late adolescent or young adult stage when disaster strikes, other priorities (e.g., college, careers, spouses; Kahn, 1983) may prevent them from putting in more than token appearances at family therapy sessions.

WHEN AND HOW SIBLINGS BECOME CLOSE

Facilitating Factors

Having discussed all of this, and bearing in mind that some therapists may have their own personal sibling "blind spots," under what conditions can brothers and sisters be counted on to be useful and helpful therapeutic resources? Although rivalry, aggression, and alienation between siblings certainly exist, my clinical work over the past 20 years attests to the fact that it is just as feasible that siblings are helpful as that they are, in certain families, harmful. The nature of the complex, technologically frenetic latter part of the 20th century seems to heighten dependency, not reduce it. The sibling bond today is, in fact, much closer than several generations ago, in the era 1900–1920, when larger families and an earlier leaving of home were the rule. Incredible as it may seem to us, to leave home in the mid-19th century at 11 or 12 years of age was the norm and was not exceptional (Kett, 1977). Today, leaving home seldom takes place before 18, and then only gradually, while for some it may not occur until 24, 25, or even 30 years of age.

With smaller families, an average family size of two children, and a closer age range between siblings, an individual has a much higher chance of bonding and attaching to his/her brother or sister in a psychologically meaningful way. The gut sense that *it is the sibling that is family* is certainly driven home when one has spent one's entire life with that person, sharing secrets, space, experiences, possessions, play, alliances, and important information. Such closeness fulfills one of the major conditions that make siblings good resources for helping, which we have called "high access." High-access siblings are also more likely to identify with each other, feeling themselves to be fellow travelers on the same family ship. "You are like me and I am like you" is the sense such sibs have for each other. Strong and positive mutual identification, in which each child internalizes part aspects of the other, forms the inner glue of such relationships.

A second major condition that promotes the possibility of siblings being a helpful resource occurs when parents have taken obvious pains to cultivate a feeling of warmth and closeness between their children. Culturally cherished notions of mutual loyalty, cooperation, dependability, noncompetitiveness, humor, compassion, shared histories, and respect are more than just token values given lip service. They only occur in sibling relationships when parents day by day, year by year, put effort into facilitating these values in their children. In families where parents work at ensuring that their children have formed such values, parents create a legacy that the children learn to value as a touchstone, a genuinely felt value structure that generates feelings of warmth, affinity, and comfort for life. Without such efforts, just being thrown together in the same bedroom while growing up and told to "not fight" may ensure nothing but chaos. When therapists see some evidence of these values having been cultivated by the parents in their children's lives [unlike some theorists, most notably Boszormenyi-Nagy & Spark (1973), I do *not* assume that loyalty is an inherent and always potentially positive force in family systems],[2] it augers well for aiming interventions at the sibling subsystem with the expectation that the children will work cooperatively on therapeutic goals.

The last major condition under which siblings seem to become close is, paradoxically, when life circumstances have become severe. Brothers and sisters often turn to one another in the early and middle childhood years if their parents leave, emotionally withdraw, die, divorce, or in general are unable to tend to the care and nurturance their children need. Even if siblings may not appear to have consciously appreciated each other, in a pinch most people will say, "When things got rough, better to have had my brother or sister around than no one at all." Family and individual therapy sessions with scores of children and adults who have suffered a myriad of devastating events such as the Holocaust, a parent dying, severe poverty, enforced separation from the parents, war, being placed in institutional settings, and the like, underscore how much brothers or sisters come to depend on one another during such trying times. One soft-spoken man, who grew up in a tough and impoverished New York City ghetto where he was constantly faced with the physical danger of being beaten up and harrassed by other kids in the neighborhood, could, and always did, rely upon his three brothers for protection and support. Today, 30 years after moving away from the neighborhood, he still states, "When I'm in trouble, I don't count on my parents, I don't count on my wife, I don't count on my friends, I count on my brothers."

In another family, who lived in Poland before World War II, a girl and her younger sister were, along with all the other Jewish families in the village, rounded up by the Nazis and then sent to the extermination camp at Auschwitz. There, the two girls were separated from their parents (whom they never saw again), but the older sister vowed to keep her younger sister alive at all costs, to never let her out of her sight, to fulfill the expectation her parents had spoken to her just before they were separated. They had said "Protect your younger sister, no matter what happens." Throughout her 2 years of imprisonment she remembered her parents' words, and kept a constant vigil by her sister's side. The older

---

[2]See the later section on loyalty (pp. 244–248) for a distinction between intense and more moderate forms of loyalty. When siblings or any other family members experience little emotional satisfaction with one another, it is unlikely that they will turn to each other for help in a subsequent emotional crisis.

girl often interceded on her sister's behalf whenever guards or fellow prisoners became cruel or abusive. Keeping her sister alive became her own *raison d'être*, a way of keeping her parents' precious spirit alive, a driving force that kept her going amid all the brutality around them. Forty years after being liberated from the death camp, this woman and her sister were still extremely close, speaking to each other daily on the phone, living near one another, making sure their husbands respected the mutual bond they shared, and inculcating their own children with the legacy that brothers and sisters should always remain close, faithful, and dependable.

While this latter case example is of a more extreme nature than what most siblings experience, the underlying principle is nonetheless seen in many less extreme situations; under stress and difficulty siblings will often turn to one another for protection, nurturance, solace, and vital companionship. However, an important proviso is that, in order for there to be this close bond, the parents need to have sown the seeds of such caregiving values before there is a rupturing of connection with their children. Without such a sufficiently vitalizing precondition by emotionally responsive parents, siblings will often come to attack, disturb, or emotionally withdraw from one another when circumstances turn severe. Once such alienation occurs, therapists and others may be unable to reverse the trend, particularly if the siblings are old enough to leave home and exercise their option to come together only on infrequent holidays.

The Foundations of Close Sibling Bonding

What forms the bases for close and positive sibling relationships that as clinicians we might see, or can build on to help bring out the best in potential among brothers and sisters? Clarifying to family members some of the psychological dynamics of sibling relationships can often be a helpful intervention. It is hoped that therapists can use these patterns as cultural templates, pointing out under which conditions these occur and under what conditions they might not occur. These foundation areas can be viewed either as having descriptive value, in which the therapist emphasizes and clarifies what he/she notices in the family, so that everyone in the family can more clearly comprehend what is "under the surface," or as goals for facilitative change maneuvers. Siblings in dysfunctional roles can be utilized to fulfill productive new satisfying roles in the family through the therapist's directing them to behave differently.

A point not to be underestimated is that there are few required norms by which siblings in Western society have to abide. It is precisely because of the elasticity of norms for sibling interaction that clinicians and personality theorists, until the 1970s, were loathe to specify how to deal with sibling dynamics.[3] However, these foundation areas have, in my experience, proven to be useful

---

[3]The *Index of Psychoanalytic Writings* (1975) does not even mention siblings; most personality tests, with a few notable exceptions such as White (1976) and Aldous (1978), do not deal with the influence of siblings on personality development.

pathways for creating meaningful change in families. As can be seen in the case examples that follow, these concepts can be utilized regardless of whether family therapy or individual therapy is the primary treatment modality.

Loyalties

Intense loyalty ties between siblings are not temporary alliances, broken or resumed at a moment's whim; they are enduring patterns of relating that take years to develop and that often take precedence over other commitments. Intense loyalty, that which Royce called "the willing and practical and thoroughgoing devotion of a person to a cause" (1916), is often forged in the flames of a crisis and is called to a test when new difficulties make themselves felt. Less intense loyalty is often promoted by parents who urge their children to be kind and loving to one another.

As loyal siblings grow into maturity, their memories of their positive bonds often bring pleasure, humor, and genuine good feeling to them, or serve as reminders, as with the sisters who survived the Holocaust, of values worth maintaining in life. Therapists need to probe what the degree of loyalty might be between siblings; they need to ask whether the kids have had high access, whether they prefer each other's company, if they had been through tough times and had a way of sharing these experiences so that each understood how those events had impacted the other. Loyal siblings often do not readily reveal their bond to an outsider. It somes requires sensitive probing by a therapist to ascertain whether sibling loyalty is just as strong as or even stronger than, loyalty to a parent.

Case Example 1: Julie. Julie was a 23-year-old graduate student who had two older brothers, one of whom had been labeled as emotionally disturbed when a teenager, had done poorly in school, used lots of drugs, and eventually became a sometime rock musician with no visible means of self-support. Julie's prim and proper parents, well-to-do financially, turned the brother's care over to a succession of therapists, with no family therapy attempted. Julie had always been admonished not to get "too involved" with her brother, warned not to smoke pot with him, and not to emulate any of his other interests. The parents, perplexed and burdened by their son's unhappiness, had little energy left over for their daughter, whom they were content to see as a "good girl," always quiet, a little moody, a high achiever. Julie felt ingenuine and a "fake" when with her parents. Only after Julie initiated her own therapy was she able to tell an outsider (the therapist) of the tremendous loyalty she felt for her brother; she identified with him, depended on him for the nurturance her parents didn't provide, had ritually smoked pot with him ever since she was 13, and eventually decided to become a therapist to "help people like my brother." Starved for affection, Julie found that being with her brother gave him comfort and solace as well. Exploring the dynamics of her sibling relationship in individual therapy helped Julie to understand how these patterns had generalized into much of her way of functioning, and how much of a substitute object of attachment her brother had been.

Family therapy with Julie's parents present was begun on a very selective basis while the individual therapy continued. The brother refused to attend, thereby helping perpetuate the myth that he was always "uncooperative, disappointing, and a troublemaker." Although the parents kept insisting on seeing their son as the "bad" child, and Julie as the "perfect" child, it gradually became evident why the parents had maintained such a split view. The parents were emotionally impoverished as children. Julie's father, in the face of being neglected, had determined he would be a success "at all costs"; the mother had been alcoholic and claimed she was never able to handle any "stress," forfeiting all parental responsibility to the father, and contributing to Julie's own feelings of neglect. The brother became a lightening rod for family tension while Julie became the idealized, emotionally constricted child. Julie and her brother eventually became recognized by her parents as people with similarities and shared problems rather than children with profound differences; Julie began feeling more authentic and more integrated in her family without forfeiting her loyalty to her brother. Loyalty was now understood as arising from a context of neglect over several generations.

Case Example 2: Sam. In another family, Sam, 24 years old, the youngest of four brothers, was attempting to establish himself in the family business his grandfather had established. His wife of 2 years, Renee, with whom he was in couple therapy, couldn't understand why Sam, who had been accepted into dental school, insisted on sticking with his brothers. All Renee heard from Sam was how each day in the office the brothers ridiculed, sniped, dumped, and in general heaped abuse upon their "kid brother," who in their eyes needed, "just as we did, to learn the business from the bottom up."

Renee, a registered nurse, had just spent a stressful year ministering daily to her sister, who had finally succumbed to cancer. She had an older sister with whom she barely spoke, from whom she received little sympathy, and whom she blamed for being "uninvolved" with the family. Drained by her ordeal with her family, Renee urged Sam to get out of his family business, save both of them additional emotional hardship, and sever his relationships with what seemed like abusive siblings, just as she had with her other surviving sister. But Sam seemed so convinced that he could make his brothers respect him and reward him, the therapist decided to schedule several sessions with all three brothers (the fourth brother could not attend, being out of the country on an extended business trip), under the condition that Renee eventually be allowed to view the videotapes.

In the first two sessions, it became quickly apparent that there was enormous loyalty between the brothers, promoted by their father (the president of the company), who had remained powerfully in the background. The brothers interrupted, yelled, and insulted each other, but then softened their barbs through jokes, laughter, stories, and a certain style of macho, self-deprecating humor that took the biting edge off their sarcasm. To Renee, depressed by the terrible circumstances in her own family, it all seemed bewildering and over-whelming. The sibling dynamics of Sam's family, competitive, aggressive, hyper-masculine, were foreign to the softer, more depressively oriented Renee, who was accustomed to her sisters. The therapist was able to point out these differ-ences in going over the tapes with Renee, and Sam began to understand his own sibs better. Eventually the brothers were able to express to each other that they indeed loved one another, that they shared a legacy of a powerful, well-intending, but nevertheless autocratic and emotionally unavailable father, who had "sacrificed his life for the business."

In sessions, the older brothers softened their style, agreed to consider differ-ent ways to treat Sam, provided he met certain "conditions" (hard work, punctuality, noninterference by "the wives," etc.). Over the next few months, as couple therapy progressed fairly well with a greater understanding of sibling dynamics, Sam was able to demonstrate to Renee that his loyalty to his brothers was his way of staying connected to his family and that he wanted their respect, which his parents seemed unable to provide. He simultaneously became suffi-ciently differentiated and able to devote more time to his wife in spite of the ever-present, voracious demands of the business. Therapeutic change occurred only when both subsystems, the sibling and the marital, were worked on simultaneously, and where neither took precedence over the other. Loyalty to Sam's brothers was not sacrificed for the "sake of the marriage."

These two cases of sibling loyalty emphasize the following therapeutic guide-lines:

1. Sibling loyalty, as an operating force in family systems, usually becomes apparent only under stress, when other systems demand that the individual make a decision regarding his/her priorities.

2. Sibling loyalty is not always quickly and easily revealed to those outside the sibling subsystem. It may have developed as a counterpoint to the unavail-ability of parents and therefore be accompanied by a certain modicum of guilt. Family therapists will sometimes need to first bring the siblings together out of the earshot of spouses or parents in order to determine the real nature of their bond, and then subsequently arrange to delicately bridge the gap between all these subsystems.

3. Sibling loyalty may be apparent in childhood and adolescence, but is a more powerful dynamic than that which occurs when brothers and sisters have no choice but to spend time with each other (such as in families where there are few adults and few other children available for play and nurturance). Sibling loyalty is evident when the individual has a *choice* of whom to play or be with, and therefore is more clearly put to the test in late adolescence and adulthood when the freedom to associate or not associate with a sibling is entirely up to each individual.

Caregiving and Caretaking

Some siblings are thrust by circumstances into having to provide care, even of a life-sustaining nature, to one another. The author has already described some examples in which care is given, but we need to discriminate between caregiving and caretaking. Caretaking is one-way caring, typically when one child is instructed to provide supervision for younger siblings, and it may be resented by either the caretaker or those who are in his/her charge (typically older sisters get stuck with this role). Caregiving, on the other hand, is reciprocal, with each sibling receiving mutual benefits and neither resenting having an undue burden. If Cinderella had had a younger brother, she would undoubtedly have been assigned a caretaking role for him, along with her other chores, whereas Hansel and Gretel were certainly each other's caregivers.

Caretaker siblings are often parentified children, sometimes depleted by their junior-parent role, but sometimes gathering ego strength and a life-long satisfying identity from that role (some therapists or therapists-to-be, such as Julie, described in Case Example 1, derived their first taste of successful intervention when they were children and tried to intervene on behalf of a problematic brother or sister). Some caretakers, as they reach adulthood, attempt to receive parity from their siblings for the sacrifices they previously made, and attempt to switch from caretaking to caregiving roles. While loyalty is an underlying motive force, driving and regulating a person's actions, caregiving and caretaking are actual behaviors, which may or may not be inspired by loyalty.

Case Example 3: Barbara. The opening paragraph of this chapter described a woman who called a therapist prompted by the desperate urgency of her father dying. When she arrived, Barbara, 27, was accompanied by her two brothers, Jim, 24, and Phil, 21. Barbara had been assigned a caretaker role for her two brothers when their mother died of cancer 12 years earlier. At the time, the children were 15, 12, and 9 respectively. Barbara, being the eldest and a girl, was immediately looked to as the one who would take over her mother's responsibilities. She not only cooked the meals and made sure her brothers stayed out of mischief, but silently kept a vigil over their emotional welfare. By the time she left for college, Barbara was apprehensive but reassured in the knowledge that her brothers had received adequate nurturance from her, and kept in constant touch with them throughout the college years. It was then that their father began showing serious symptoms that eventually were diagnosed as Alzheimer's disease. By the time they were 25, 22, and 19, the siblings realized their father was deteriorating rapidly. To add to his miseries he also then developed pancreatic cancer. Forced into early retirement, at times he showed drastic cognitive changes. Barbara had married, and was torn between her loyalties to her new family and concern for her brothers and ailing father. Unfortunately, the families of origin on the mother's and father's side were of little help. Frightened by the diseases, they only complimented the children for their "courage" and kept their distance.

During this difficult and trying period Barbara and her husband decided to build a new house and she invited her brothers to join in this project. This allowed her to give them a common endeavor of optimism, a rallying ground for interaction against the background of despair from which they all suffered. Barbara unconsciously began receiving caregiving from her now-adult brothers as recompense for all she had done and was still struggling to provide. Their free help during the first summer had gotten the house-building off to a splendid start. When she called the therapist, there was a new crisis brewing. Who would spend time with the dying father? Who would watch over him daily, to ensure he would not hurt himself? Could Jim, the next-eldest, be spared the onerous role of full-time caretaker?

The first session explored the legacy of misfortune and brought out the extent of the dilemmas facing all three siblings. Jim, after his college graduation, had remained home and at 24 had already turned down two good job opportunities to be with his father. Phil, 21, had kept to his role as the "baby," spending semesters out of college traveling, going to Europe over his summers, and fearing being "trapped." Barbara, even as she had rallied her siblings to the session, was confused about shuttling back and forth, about whether to relieve the brothers and take over the care of the father or to stay away. In the seven subsequent sessions, Barbara was able to express her concern about once again resuming the role of caretaker while Jim and Phil struggled over their own priorities. When the brothers realized that Barbara, strong and indomitable as she seemed to be, nevertheless also needed caregiving, they began to reassess their own roles vis-á-vis their sister. They agreed to take turns helping their Dad, with Phil becoming more available and resuming school nearby. For the first time in 3 years, Jim felt he could leave home without guilt, and he took a job that still allowed him to come home on weekends. Barbara was assured by both brothers that she would be looked to for advice, but that they were now all aware of the heavy burden their sister had shouldered for 12 years. She felt she would no longer be taken for granted, and, loyal as she was, would no longer remain the silent caretaker. All three siblings also took heart from the idea that collectively they could approach their parents' siblings and demand more support. The caregiving ethic seemed to gather momentum as therapy ended with each sibling more confident that they were "getting," and not just "giving."

Identification

One of the major reasons why siblings can feel an affinity for one another is that they often identify themselves as being similar. Identification can be one-way or bilateral. When both siblings feel they are "identical," we view this as pathogenic or "fused," with each sibling stuck, unable to move without the other, as if they were Siamese twins. Of course, the psychological force called "twinning" (Kohut, 1977) can be an asset, providing comfort and the knowledge that one is not alone in the world. We have all been fascinated by biological identical twins and the extent to which they seem able to read each other's thoughts, confuse outsiders, and feel magically interchangeable. George Engel (1974) has written of the tremendous comfort he derived from having a twin brother and how they formed their own tiny secret society, with a secret language (they called one another "Oth" for "Other") that allowed each to feel powerful and unique during their childhoods. While twins are a special case—approximately 1 out of 86 births are fraternal twins, 1 out of 225 being identical twins—other nontwin siblings can also feel similar, although in lesser degrees. This varies depending on circumstances—age spacing, gender, appearance, changes in life events, and the like. Therapists in general should become sensitive to the dynamics of twinning, when it is destructive, preventing individuation, and when it is life-giving, providing comfort.

When identification is one-way (one sibling feels very similar, the other more neutral or even quite different), it is more likely to be temporary, occurring at a time when one individual needs a psychological anchor, a guide for psychological organization provided by the example of a close brother or sister. During adolescence this can be viewed as hero worship, and the process can extend into the important years of young adulthood. When identification is bilateral, or two-way, it is more likely to remain throughout life. In such instances neither sibling feels compelled to pull away, and each remains a vital and integral force for the other. For example, in the sculptor Alberto Giacometti's life, his brother Diego became the embodiment of his art. The younger brother Diego was the face that Alberto always sculpted, the assistant who finished the older brother's work, the ever-present partner who was critic and inspirational craftsman to his more famous sibling. One observer noted, "They were inseparable. They lived like man and wife. They understood each other so well they hardly needed to talk. It is hard to imagine them without each other" (Brenson, 1984).

Clinicians need to understand when identification is an asset and when a liability, when it can be called upon to provide the motive force for siblings to support one another and work together, or when it is necessary to get them "unstuck." Table 7-1 gives an overview of the major patterns of identification between siblings, ranging from feelings so close that there can be a lack of self-differentiation to such distance that there is total estrangement. (The full range of identification patterns is included, not just the positive ones, in order to give a symmetrical view of sibling relationships.)

Whatever forms of interaction siblings might be having, determining the nature of the identification process helps the therapist to determine how much resistance or cooperation siblings will muster for one another. Parents can exert their authority to help their children change, spouses can always invoke the "*quid pro quo*" to prod each other to be helpful and cooperative (Lederer & Jackson, 1968), but unless adult brothers and sisters feel at least some partial identification, therapists are unlikely to find that such siblings will even bother to come to the office for family therapy when asked. However, younger siblings often willingly participate in family therapy. They can, given their still undefined personality characteristics, have their premises about their siblings challenged, and can often begin to realize that a sibling they "hate" or feel totally estranged

TABLE 7-1
Patterns of Identification between Siblings

	Degree of identification	Process of identification	Type of relationship
Lack of Self	Close	Twinning	Fused: "We're just like each other. There is no difference."
		Merging	Blurred: "I'm not sure who I am. Maybe I can be you."
		Idealizing	Hero worship: "I admire you so much that I want to become like you."
Vitality	Partial	Loyal acceptance	Mutually dependent: "We're the same in many ways. We'll always need and care for each other in spite of our differences."
		Constructive dialectic	Dynamic independent: "We're alike but different. This is challenging and creates opportunities for both of us to grow."
		Destructive dialectic	Hostile dependent: "We're different in many ways. We don't particularly like one another, but we need each other anyhow."
Estrangement	Distant	Polarized rejection	Rigidly differentiated: "You're so different from me. I don't want to depend on you, and I never want to become like you."
		De-identifying	Disowned: "We're totally different from one another. I don't need you. I don't like you, and I don't care if I never see you again."

Note. Reprinted by permission from S. P. Bank and M. D. Kahn, *The Sibling Bond* (1982). Copyright 1982 by Basic Books.

from may be a victim of a contextual process that has affected them as well. To hate another is often to disavow this same characteristic in oneself. To not want to understand why someone is the miserable wretch one holds them to be is to deny and disown similar traits in order to obtain smug satisfaction at feeling superior. Family therapists can help change such rigid perceptions by uncovering the family process that may have set children in the same family into opposite roles of being "haves" and "have-nots."

HOW TO MOBILIZE SIBLINGS TO BE HELPFUL

Throughout this chapter, I have stressed some of the influences that pull siblings together or push them apart. However, becoming sensitive to sibling dynamics involves focusing on—not just on the family or individual children, but also the therapist. In order to know how to proceed with families around sibling issues, the therapist needs to understand his/her own sibling history. For all of the reasons that have been indicated, most people in our culture know very little of the interior of their brother's or sister's lives and their own role as a sibling, and this includes therapists as well. Just when siblings can begin to understand each other, during late adolescence, they leave home, rarely reuniting except at moments of crisis or on family holidays when they typically meet in the parents' home and become "the kids" again. Of course, there are also therapists who come from some ethnic groups (see McGoldrick, Giordano, & Pearce, 1983) who have powerful but covert prohibitions against becoming "too close," which mitigates against forming warm and satisfying connections. Therapists who are firstborns, who need to feel powerful, or who come from families that do not emphasize closeness or dependency are less likely to look for satisfying sibling connections even when the families they work with present this possibility.

Removing the Sibling Bias of Therapists

Therapists are therefore like everyone else, often naive, underinformed, or closed off from sensitivity to their sibling dynamics. A thorough review of the therapist's sibling history has been of inestimable value in the author's supervision of therapists. In group or individual supervision, therapists are encouraged to reconsider the nature of their sibling relationships (and even to reconnect with their sibs) and to understand how readily "frozen images"[4] from childhood can carry over into adult life. Since neither personality theories or theories of therapeutic change focus on sibling dynamics, most therapists have remained uninformed and unsupervised about sibling dynamics. Gaining a fuller perspective, whether it be around the therapists' family of origin or through case supervision or some combination of both, involves asking particular questions such as: How many brothers and sisters do you have? What was the birth order? What coalitions existed? Who were (are) the favorites? How much access to one another did (do) siblings have? What were the roles each sibling accepted? What critical events drove the siblings together or pulled them apart? Was loyalty to a brother or sister a compelling force? Did identification with a sibling play a crucial role at various stages in the developmental life cycle? Was there any caretaking? Jealousy? Rivalry? Did one sibling have to constantly rescue another?

I have had many experiences in which asking just such questions revealed information never before disclosed. (A not uncommon example is the death of a young brother or sister, whom no one has spoken about for years.) This includes

---

[4]A frozen image is the indelible characterization of another person that remains unchallenged when there is neither ongoing meaningful contact or reinterpretation of that impression by some neutral outsider. Adult siblings often carry frozen images of each other, based on fond memories or memories of hurtful events. The impressions from childhood and the incomplete understanding of contextually based processes form the foundation for these images.

therapists who may have spent as much as 5 years in their own personal individual psychotherapy, but never touched upon their sibling issues. One reason, aside from the general cultural one, is offered by Kohut (1971), who has speculated that many psychoanalysts are overly entitled firstborns whose grandiose self permits little of the egalitarian feelings that are necessary in order to acknowledge the worth of sibling relationships. Supervisors clearly need to be sensitive when noticing sibling bias or indifference in their supervisees.

Mobilizing Brothers and Sisters

Young Children

When asking young children to participate in therapy, the therapist often runs head-on into resistance. This varies depending on the age and circumstances of each family, but the following guidelines seem to be productive in obtaining initial cooperation. With families of young children, I will expect the parents to bring in every child. I then work on seeing how cohesive a sibling group the children are, pointing out similarities and differences or common patterns of identification, for example: "You and your sister seem to have the same way of dealing with your mother." "When your father gets angry, do all of you scatter and stay out of the way?" "What happened when your brother got into trouble?" "How come she is the one who always gets into trouble in this family?" "When your brother was born did you feel pushed aside?" If these questions resemble the triadic style of the Milan school of circular questioning (see Penn, 1982), it is no accident, since the horizontal vector of each child's relationship to every other child in the family always includes considerations of parental influence in the background (and is therefore always triadic). Questions that only focus on the parents' influence on each child are dyadic and follow a vertical vector.

An important dimension to consider with *all* age groups of siblings is the sameness–difference continuum discussed previously under the section of patterns of identification (see pp. 248–250). When any relationship is at the extremes of being either too fused or too disengaged, it will be problematic, conflictual, or unsatisfying. Since a relationship in which siblings can experience satisfying elements of both sameness and difference is the most desirable (called a "positive dialectic"), therapeutic efforts are always undertaken with the achievement of such a relationship as a goal. When siblings reach the point of having a positive dialectic they can be very supportive, encouraging, playful, and creative with each other. Therapy at this point is relatively calm and problem-free; the therapist can ask for cooperation and get it, can crack a useful joke and have an appreciative audience, can use play materials or fantasy and find it is catalytic and not destructive, and, with very young children, experience a noncompetitive, nonrivalrous atmosphere.

On the other hand, obtaining a positive dialectic with young siblings who are initially too close and enmeshed involves the following steps, which may meet initial resistance:

1. Start emphasizing their differences. Convey the notion that each child is at a different developmental stage and supply appropriate information to underscore such points (e.g., "Your 5-year-old sister would like to be as strong as you but she'll have to wait until she is 7 years old like you are now.").

2. Guide the parents to begin differentiating their children. Block the tendency to "lump" the children together. Address birth order considerations and developmental landmarks (e.g., "Your oldest is like another parent in this family, she listens so well," "Even though your two oldest play so well together, it must make your oldest son furious that his younger brother always keeps up with him.").

3. Use prescriptions to differentiate the children (e.g., "I want you, Johnny, to talk to your parents about staying up 30 minutes later than your sister, because you seem to need less sleep.").

4. Explore the roots of sibling fusion in each parent's family of origin.

5. Probe whether the children's fusion stems from a mutual need for attachment and contact they are unable to get from their parents.

6. Discern whether the entire family system is too enmeshed, and what contextual and emotional forces seem to fuel this.

Case Example 4. In one family, the overwhelmed, full-time working divorced mother appointed her 10-year-old daughter as babysitter for the younger children, 7- and 5-year-old siblings. Even though the oldest daughter was praised by her mother for being "mature and responsible," she related more like the younger children when she was "off duty," fighting with them, whining for favors and privileges, and constantly tattling on the others, who retaliated in kind. The mother, feeling guilty about making her daughter the overresponsible caretaker, was, in spite of appointing the older child as babysitter, treating all the children as if they were one homogeneous group, refusing to discern which child was responsible for a problem. She bent over backward to give all the children the same "fun" experiences, related to them as one age-undifferentiated set of kids, and never spent time alone with any child.

In family therapy, Ellen, the oldest child, was able to relate how deprived she felt and how, in effect, she was getting even less care than her younger sibs (in effect, negating the age differences between them). The mother, herself an oldest daughter who had cared for her younger siblings, was helped to recall her own deprivation. Once Ellen was given an opportunity to be more alone with her mother and to have the yoke of caretaking lifted from her, she became, over the following 3 months of family therapy, truly more mature and responsible. The mother's tendency to lump the children together was worked through as therapy became a means for her to, as she said, "finally get attention."

Conversely, siblings who are too disengaged (disowning is an unlikely phenomenon to have been completed in young children) need to be brought into a more closely aligned, symmetrical relationship to achieve a positive dialectic. The following strategies are helpful:

1. Start emphasizing their sameness. Point out their common experiences, similar histories and how each has learned from the other (e.g., "Your sister may have a different way of talking, but she sounds like she and you have been through the same things in this family.").

2. Block the tendency for assigning blame or scapegoating by the parents (e.g., "You know, Johnny always seems to get the rap in this family. Sally can't be such an angel, especially hanging around the same house as her brother.").

3. Use prescriptions to join the children more closely together. Stop the momentum that carries them further and further apart (e.g., "I want you to talk to both kids when one of them has done something to really bug you. I'm sure the other must have also had a hand in it.").

4. Explore the roots of sibling disengagement in each parent's family of origin.

5. Probe whether the children's disengagement stems from angry, conflicted, or powerfully destructive issues in either child.

6. Discern whether the entire family system is too disengaged and which emotional and contextual forces fuel that process.

Adolescents

The same central issues of sameness and difference, driving siblings either too close together or too far apart, can operate anywhere in the life cycle. Intervention with adolescents therefore follows the same general rules as were indicated for younger children with some additional features appropriate to the different life stage they are in:

1. It is often desirable to see adolescents separately from their parents. This does *not* mean "sibling therapy," detached from its parental context. It does acknowledge, however, that adolescents covet privacy and treasure their emerging capacity to build psychological walls toward their parents. The sibling system is an ideal place for teenagers to experience that privacy. Seeing them as a separate group often unleashes a torrent of information they would never disclose in front of their parents. In such an atmosphere words and feelings, sometimes brutally frank, emerge and can be dealt with *before* parental loyalty and power makes everybody clam up.

2. Adolescent siblings seen as a separate subgroup can rehearse what they will do once they are subsequently seen together with their parents. The therapist can help coach them and role play what might otherwise be too tentative a series of moves.

3. Explaining developmental changes can help adolescents understand why there have been sudden shifts in their previously cozy coalition or why parents, once so tolerant, have become uptight, vigilant, defensive, or punitive. Adolescents can often feel caught in a double bind of conflicting loyalties between their siblings and their parents. The therapist can be a vital intermediary between the two groups, explaining context and content to dispel the confusion that now reigns.

4. The hot spots of adolescent development, such as sex role changes, pubescence, independence, body image, autonomy, the wish for transcendental experience, and the need for a stable identity, all send ripples through each child and across the family. The therapist also needs to be sensitive to how such issues may be used by parents to deflect away from their own problems. Symptoms (e.g., anorexia, bulimia, alcohol dependence) may develop because normal developmental issues are inappropriately handled by the family, or are needed as an unconscious outlet for some undisclosed concerns in either parent. The therapist can move the focus away from the adolescents and onto the parents provided the siblings don't run away from each other in phobic concern, or collapse into an undifferentiated mess out of guilt, panic, or confusion.

5. Therapists can help adolescents become more age appropriate and flexible in caretaking, role scripting and extrafamilial activities. They can help one child to go on excursions, another to begin babysitting, another to change his/her way of dressing, and so on. Although no therapist wants to play "Fairy God-mother," we all can orchestrate and arrange events to change otherwise stuck systems.

Case Example 5. In one family the father, himself an emotionally neglected but materially spoiled younger child, seemed lackadaisical about enforcing rules with his 13-, 15-, and 17-year-old children. Remarried, his second wife seemed loathe to discipline his children (a common pattern), and kept her opinions to herself. Since the couple had a 2-year-old of their own, both the father and stepmother had the "perfect excuse" for not enforcing rules with the adolescent children. In sessions with the adolescents, the therapist quickly learned about the father's background, his considerable pot smoking, his neglect as a child, his difficult first marriage. The kids were able to effectively and quickly point out how their own difficulties with each other, school, and peers mirrored and amplified problems their biological mother (whom they rarely saw) and father had had.

Over the next 6 weeks, sibling and entire family (including the biological mother) sessions were held concurrently. The mutual recriminations among the siblings subsided and they began supporting the therapist's efforts to track the interplay between each generation's lives. Bickering, name calling, acting out, and pandemonium created in the home by the kids were now called to account in the twice-weekly sessions, and new rules in therapy transferred to become rules at home. The children's parents were more cooperative and the formerly silent stepmother was welcomed for the astute person everyone had always suspected she was.

Adults

Again, all of the previously cited tactics can, depending on circumstances, be applied to adult siblings. However, married adult brothers and sisters face differing problems, not the least of which are the priority and attention given to the events and people in their nuclear families. Spouses can be quite jealous of brothers-in-law and sisters-in-law, so the therapist must tread delicately if the sibling subsystem is to be engaged. The following guidelines can help:

1. Take advantage of family holidays, when siblings converge, to deal with conflictual events (advocates of Bowen's school of family therapy are always trained to anticipate Thanksgiving, Christmas, Passover, etc.).

2. Understand in what ways adult siblings identify, and whether they feel the same or different, before bringing them together. Disowning or disengaged siblings may either refuse to come to sessions or may covertly sabotage the change efforts by their brother or sister who is in therapy. Bringing adult siblings together for sessions (see Kahn & Bank, 1981) is always a delicate process. Strategies must be worked out in advance to ensure they neither insult each other nor renege on promises to help out.

3. More disengaged siblings can be protected from such abuse or abusing by being asked to come in for only one time as "consultants," to provide historical information. They can be defined as part of the collective "memory bank," particularly when parents have died or are no longer articulate.

4. Adult brothers and sisters can unfreeze "frozen images" and "frozen misunderstandings." The family therapist can, as no other trained professional, help discern the historical and contextual factors that may have driven the siblings apart, and that were left unspoken once everyone left home.

5. Secret experiences (e.g., sibling incest) and suppressed bitter memories (e.g., the death of a brother or sister) can be focused on in a supportive way. More adequate mourning or resolution can be arrived at than was true in childhood.

6. Sibling rallies, in or out of the therapists' office, can be orchestrated, particularly if there looms a pending crisis (e.g., parents divorcing, being hospitalized, becoming seriously ill). More egalitarian roles, rather than those dictated by birth order or gender, can be arrived at.

7. The imminent death of a parent, as does no other event, churns adult brothers and sisters into turmoil. The family therapist can instruct the siblings in dealing with each other fairly during such crises, in how not to take advantage of each other, and in trying to buffer the hurt that inevitably flows from a parents' will and last testament, no matter how nobly it might have been intended.

THE ERROR OF SIBLING ENGAGEMENT

I hope that this chapter has been as instructive to the reader as to its writer. Although I have been focusing on sibling relationships for more than 20 years, it never ceases to amaze me how little our culture emphasizes sibling engagement, closeness, and dependency. In our individualistic, competitive, and aggressive pursuits of achievement and identity, the sibling system is celebrated all too seldom, in spite of our use of catchy slogans like "brotherhood" and "sisterhood." The error we have all committed is not to have considered siblings as important resources, in spite of so many brothers and sisters feeling love and affection toward each other. There seems to be, on the basis of clinical experience, few occasions in which bringing siblings together can hurt, if for no other reason than valuable information can be ascertained. Expectations of how much help brothers and sisters will actually give each other, however, have to be measured on a case-by-case basis, depending on all the circumstances with which people are dealing. Just knowing that a brother or sister is out there, available in some way, is almost always reassuring and can sometimes be life-saving. To help or be helped by a brother or sister is one of life's sweeter experiences; putting it in the words of the famous poster from Father Flanagan's Boys' Town, which depicts an older brother carrying his younger sibling, "He ain't heavy, he's my brother!"

REFERENCES

Adler, A. *Understanding human nature.* New York: Fawcett Publications, 1959.

Aldous, J. *Family careers: Developmental change in families.* New York: John Wiley, 1978.

Bane, M. J. *Here to stay: American families in the twentieth century.* New York: Basic Books, 1976.

Bank, S. P., & Kahn, M. D. Freudian siblings. *Psychoanalytic Review*, 1980–1981, *67* (winter), 493–504.

Bank, S. P., & Kahn, M.D. *The sibling bond.* New York: Basic Books, 1982.

Boszormenyi-Nagy, I., & Spark, G. M. *Invisible loyalties: Reciprocity in intergenerational family therapy.* Hagerstown, MD: Harper & Row, 1973.

Brenson, M. The other Giacometti. *The New York Times Magazine*, March 11, 1984, *6*, 44–93.

Cicirelli, V. G. Sibling influence throughout the life span. In M. Lamb & B. Sutton-Smith (Eds.), *Sibling relationships: Their nature and significance across the life span.* Hillsdale, NJ: Erlbaum, 1982.

Engel, G. L. The death of a twin: Mourning and anniversary reactions: Fragments of 10 years of self-analysis. *International Journal of Psychoanalysis*, 1974, *45* (1), 23–40.

Framo, J. Symptoms from a family transactional viewpoint. *International Psychiatry Clinics*, 1970, *7*, 125–171.

Freud, S. Fragment of analysis of a case of hysteria. In J. Strachey (Ed. and Trans.), *The standard edition of the complete psychological works of Sigmund Freud* (Vol. 7). London, Hogarth Press, 1953. (Original work published 1905)

Index of Psychoanalytic Writings (Vols. 1–14). New York: International Universities Press, 1975.

Kahn, M. D. Sibling relationships in later life. *Medical Aspects of Human Sexuality*, 1983, *7* (12), 94–103.

Kahn, M. D. Towards the integration of individual and family therapy. In S. Sugarman (Ed.), *Individual and family therapy: Critical issues at the interface.* Aspen, CO: Aspen Press, 1986.

Kahn, M. D., & Bank, S. Response to Rosenberg: Sibling psychotherapy: An important subspecialty of family therapy. *International Journal of Family Therapy*, 1980, *7* (3), 151–154.

Kahn, M. D., & Bank, S. In pursuit of sisterhood: Adult siblings as a resource of combined individual and family therapy. *Family Process*, 1981, *20* (1), 85–95.

Kantor, D. Critical identity image: A concept linking individual, couple, and family development. In J. Pearce & L. Friedman (Eds.), *Family therapy: Combining psychodynamic and family systems approaches*. New York: Grune & Stratton, 1980.

Kett, J. *Rite of passage: Adolescence in American—1790 to the present*. New York: Basic Books, 1977.

Kohut, H. *The analysis of the self*. New York: International Universities Press, 1971.

Kohut, H. *The restoration of the self*. New York: International Universities Press, 1977.

Lederer, W., & Jackson, D. *Mirages of marriage*. New York: Norton, 1968.

Lorenz, K. *On aggression*. London: Methuen, 1966.

Mahler, M. S. *On human symbiosis and the vicissitudes of individuation*. New York: International Universities Press, 1968.

Mallouk, T. The interpersonal context of object relations: Implications for family therapy. *Journal of Marital and Family Therapy*, 1982, *8* (4), 429–442.

McDermott, J. *Raising Cain (and Abel too!)*. New York: Wyden Books, 1980.

McGoldrick, M., Giordano, J., & Pearce, J. K. (Eds.). *Ethnicity and family therapy*. New York: Guilford Press, 1983.

Meiselman, K. C. *Incest: A psychological study of causes and effects with treatment recommendations*. San Francisco: Jossey-Bass, 1978.

Neubauer, P. The importance of the sibling experience. A. Solnit, R. Eissler & P. Neubauer (Eds.), *The psychoanalytic study of the child*, 38, pp. 325–336, New Haven: Yale University Press, 1983.

Penn, P. Circular questioning. *Family Process*, 1982, *21*, 267–280.

Royce, J. *The philosophy of loyalty*. New York: Folcroft, 1916.

Sander, F. *Individual and family therapy: Toward an integration*. New York: Jason Aronson, 1979.

Santiago, L. *The children of Oedipus: Brother–sister incest in psychiatry, literature, history and mythology*. Roslyn Heights, NY: Libra, 1973.

Stierlin, H. *Psychoanalysis and family therapy: Selected papers*. New York: Jason Aronson, 1977.

Toman, W. *Family constellation: Its effects on personality and social behavior* (3rd ed.). New York: Springer, 1976.

White, R. *The enterprise of living: Growth and organization in personality*. New York: Holt, Rinehart & Winston, 1976.

CHAPTER 8

Teaching Mental Health Professionals to See Family Strengths: Core Network Interventions in a Hospital Setting

Carolyn L. Attneave
Johan Verhulst

Most conventional training in working with the mentally ill is still based on an individual model. Especially in medical settings, the training is one in which pathology is assessed rather than healthy residuals and potential strengths (Leighton, 1983). This develops an opacity to the perception of the client's strengths and often results in only temporary or partial improvement. Inpatient settings are particularly vulnerable to this since they offer a refuge to individuals from their social stresses, and at the same time are concerned with stabilizing the individual's capacity to cope once released. "The revolving door" is a phrase that describes the repeated admissions, often for the same or similar problems, that occur in many such facilities.

In a plan to interrupt this cycle, the Inpatient Service at Harborview Community Mental Health Center in Seattle began a program that not only focused on the family and social support system of the patients, but also provided effective and sometimes dramatic training in the benefits of exploring areas that lie beyond the reach of individual psychotherapy and clinical programs aimed exclusively at stabilizing medical pathology. The key concepts were first introduced to the nursing staff in an inservice training program, and then shared with other staff, including psychiatric residents and clinical psychology interns. The program was then instituted as a routine procedure each week, at which time all

Carolyn L. Attneave, Ph.D., Sci.D. Department of Psychology, Department of Psychiatry and Behavioral Sciences, University of Washington, Seattle, Washington.

Johan Verhulst, M.D. Residency Training Program, Department of Psychiatry, University of Washington Medical School, Seattle, Washington.

members of the treatment team participated in or observed one or more sessions with the patient, the family, and the core network of people involved in that patient's life. This replaced the usual discharge planning session that had been held by the chief therapist or nurse and the patient's next of kin. If possible, one session was scheduled soon after admission, and a second preceding discharge. This enabled the staff to make use of information gained while the patient was in residence.

CASE EXAMPLE

The Setting

The setting in which this case example occurred was the inpatient ward for brief voluntary hospitalization (3–21 days), which served five community mental health centers in the metropolitan area. Patients received a wide spectrum of services, including medical evaluation, group and individual therapy, and the benefits of separation from their immediate environmental pressures in a fairly pleasant open ward. One feature was a continuous series of classes on the characteristics of psychoactive drugs, including side effects and typical action, in order that patients could manage their medications more effectively. Half or more of the admissions were via the emergency rooms of hospitals, while a few cases originated from psychiatrists or other clinicians in private practice. The remainder were referred at a time of decompensation from the other community mental health centers in the region, since they did not have inpatient facilities.

The overall objectives of the ward staff were to stabilize the patient's condition, and to return him/her to the natural environment with sufficient support to function using the available resources. Inability to do this could require formal commitment procedures for longer hospitalization elsewhere. As a university teaching site, medical students, psychiatry residents, and psychology interns were part of the staffing, along with a permanent cadre of nurses, a pharmacist, a social worker, psychiatrists, and a consulting clinical psychologist. Planning for discharge began almost immediately upon admission, and it was established routine to have at least one family conference in which discharge planning was discussed, and family questions and answers could be handled informatively.

One of the psychiatrists and the consulting psychologist were experienced family therapists, and began utilizing these family conferences for therapeutic gains as well as merely an informational exchange. In so doing, they routinely included the inner core of persons identified by the patient as significant, rather than limiting the persons present to the usual legal–biological family members. The groups thus assembled ranged from five or six to 20 or more and often included extended family (parents and siblings of adults), various live-in partners as well as legal spouses, step- and foster children as well as natural siblings, and close friends of any of the participants.

This "core network" is smaller, and different in composition, than the large assemblies of 50, 75, or 100, persons assembled in Crisis Network Interventions, described by Speck and Attneave (1973) and Rueveni (1979). The purpose is to bring together the persons most intimately connected to the life of the patient, in order to both understand the patient's context and make realistic plans for the future that will include and be understood by them. In most instances the patient can be relied on in discussions with staff to select the persons to be invited. Although staff may need to encourage the inclusion of close persons who may be seen as negative influences, this is usually possible if the therapist assures support and suggests that mutual understanding may be achieved. As the process proved its usefulness, early scheduling of the first core network meeting permitted more than one session, and additional persons or subsets of the core could be met with in follow-up sessions.

If able and willing, the patient did the contacting of the persons included during visiting hours by telephone. Only if specifically requested by the patient would the staff invite any members of the core network. One exception was to secure the patient's permission to make a specific invitation to an agency or therapist that would be involved in postdischarge follow-up care. While such invitations were not always accepted, when they were the linkage provided positive gains for both the agency and the patient in continuity of care.

Included in the session would also be those members of the ward staff who had therapeutic contact with and responsibility for the patient during the inpatient stay. Pre- and postsessions with this staff facilitated planning the session and following through on any events that took place or on information gained from the experience.

The Patient Prior to First Network Session

The patient, Fritzie, was a 17-year-old woman recently graduated from high school. She had been admitted from the emergency room of the adjacent city–teaching hospital with suspected suicidal tendencies, confused mental state, and what was termed a drug overdose of unknown origin. During the first 3 days, as her symptoms stabilized, the following information was obtained. Fritzie was a twin, the pair being the oldest of a large but undetermined number of siblings. Names, ages, and gender of family members confused staff, who sometimes felt that an impossible number was being reported, and that genders were not always clear from the names used. Her father had died when Fritzie was about 9, apparently violently, and all the siblings except the youngest were born prior to this event. The youngest was born 6 weeks after the father's death. All lived together in the waterfront area, where a family business continued (junkyard and salvage operations) with one or more uncles and others as well as her mother involved.

Fritzie had a scar from a gunshot wound she claimed was inflicted by a lover when she was 16. She denied being closely involved with any one man at the moment but seemed to have some vague apprehensions about "Joe" wanting to marry her. Her talk was still somewhat confused or confusing. She reported some past, and occasionally current, clear visual and auditory hallucinations associated with a panic state. Her version of the incidents leading up to hospitalization varied from a feeling that her family might kill her to a sacrificial implulse on her part to die and "save" her twin. Her talk had an interwoven religious quality. All of these elements led to a tentative diagnosis of schizophrenic disorder.

As her condition stabilized, the confusion cleared somewhat and the staff discovered that Fritzie was the first in her family to graduate from high school and that she had ambitions toward college or business training, for which her academic record seemed adequate. It also appeared that her twin, called Francie, was a boy who had had academic problems and was considering dropping out of school entirely. She felt her mother would prefer her to marry Joe, who was an older man associated with the family business. The use of marijuana and other street drugs was said to be a family practice, with fear of informants to the police. A few of her family appeared during visiting hours. These were teenage boys and an older man. They were uncommunicative, and suspicious of staff. They spent little time "visiting," but sidled in and explored the whole ward, as though "casing the joint."

At this stage some of the therapeutic team began to doubt the diagnosis of established schizophrenia, and to consider the episode leading to hospitalization to be a combination of a "bad trip" and internal conflict over leaving home. Some rescue fantasies began to operate, and possible dormitory, halfway house, or other out-of-home placements that would further Fritzie's academic aspirations were being suggested.

First Network Session

At the end of the first week of hospitalization, on a Thursday, a family network session was scheduled. Fritzie was willing to see that the concerned persons came, interpreting this as "everybody in the family that lives together or is important to me." At the time arranged, 18 people showed up, including her mother, Mary, her mother's sister, Maggie (divorced with grown children out of the home), two uncles (her mother's brothers), all of her siblings, plus another boy who turned out to be an adolescent foster child of a neighbor who spent most of his time with her family and brothers, a pregnant woman introduced by one of the uncles as "my girl friend," and a 2-year-old boy. Four of the treatment staff also joined the group—a psychiatric nurse, a medical student, a psychiatric resident, and a psychology intern. The total number of persons to expect had been underestimated and there were insufficient chairs in the conference room, and as it turned out an insufficient number of ashtrays. Since the adolescent boys preempted chairs and ashtrays, the psychologist decided to sit on the floor to underline the informality rather than the anticipated formal style, which was making the family uneasy. Leonard, one of the uncles, immediately moved to dispossess some of the boys and allow staff to have chairs. The ensuing few moments of confusion quickly demonstrated his role as head of the clan. Additional chairs were secured and arranged in a large circle, and family relationships became apparent, including pecking orders and supportive pairings between siblings and particularly between the mother and her sister, Maggie.

As introductions proceeded, mystification about the number of siblings decreased. There were three sets of twins, and all were boys except for Fritzie, who with her brother appeared to be the only fraternal twins. This allowed for a normal spacing of children, and a total of 10 births in a 9-year period between Fritzie's birth and the time of the father's death. Many of the boys were known by nicknames, or by names that could have belonged to either gender—Billy, Gerry, Francie, and the like—but all were unmistakably young males. The only ambiguous person was the 2-year-old boy, Sonny. He seemed to be cared for by anyone and everyone, and who his parental figures were was not cleared up in any of the sessions.

Joe was not present, having gone off on a commercial fishing vessel at about the time of Fritzie's admission; he was not due back for a month or 6 weeks. One unrelated adult man was present, a friend of the uncles and probably involved in the family business. Simply clarifying the family relationships (and the fact that most of them lived either in the same big house or in other dwellings adjacent to both it and the junkyard) cleared up the confusion of the staff and made some of Fritzie's attempts to give family history seem more coherent and less of an indication of thought disorder.

As this phase of the session worked itself out, the staff also became accepted by the family network, who realized that they were not being judgmental about life-style and social drug use, and that Fritzie trusted them.

With therapist support, Fritzie then narrated her experiences that led to hospitalization. It became clear that the precipitating incident had been a family picnic, during which Fritzie began a "bad trip" that led her to think that somehow either she or her twin must die. The occurrence of some hunting nearby led her to panic, causing her to think that her family was about to actually enact her fantasy. This was news to most of the family network, who were able to reassure her—as did the staff—about the nature of the hallucinations. Watching and participating were also helpful to the clinical staff, who began to see the strains Fritzie suffered being the only girl with a large number of brothers, no father, and a submissive mother.

Fritzie's ideas of further school were not comfortable for her mother, who hated to see anyone leave the family circle, and had considerable anxiety over upward social mobility. It turned out that there was a third aunt, sister to Mary and Maggie, who had married a businessman, lived in a middle-class neighborhood, and apparently had been cut off from the tightly bonded group by self-consciousness about social differences. Maggie's two daughters had also disappeared from the clan in the same way. Fears that Fritzie would be lost to the group were palpable.

However, one of the uncles used himself as a model, pointing out that he had left in his teens, worked his way around the world, and done many things for about 10 years, and then returned quite able to resume a place in the family circle. He felt that several of the boys might want to do the same and that Fritzie, who "was as good as a boy any day," ought to have the same chance in her own fashion. None of the men and boys sensed the mother's separation anxiety over the loss of her first chick from the nest. All, including the mother, denied that her worries were because she needed Fritzie for household tasks and specific feminine role responsibilities. It seemed clear that the boys all cooked, cleaned, mended clothing, and so forth, just as the women were able and inclined to work in the junkyard and salvage business. Many of them read fairly widely in *Reader's Digest* and other magazines as well as paperback novels of adventure and fantasy, but only Fritzie seemed to have positive feelings toward schools and education.

Throughout the discussion the bonding of the network was apparent. With all of them together they revealed their attitude of cagey manipulation in a world of "us against them." Those facets of the establishment being "them," such as cops, courts, big business, schools, and social agencies, were to be used and manipulated, but not taken for granted at their face value. The ward staff's feelings of implied threats from the behavior of Fritzie's visitors was acknowledged: "We wanted to be sure you were treating her right. . . ."

Throughout the discussion there were many references to brotherly love and other religious notes, which revealed that the family group belonged to a primitive Christian sect that had little connection with the major denominations, and persisted mainly among this family and a few associates without the formal leadership of a pastor. The religious language, incongruous as it might seem, was an everyday part of the family's life-style.

The session concluded abruptly when Uncle Leonard, acting as head of the clan, announced that he had to go get his wife out of jail. The others trailed out as he departed.

Postsession Insights and Events

Debriefing with staff led to a marked change in diagnostic evaluations—with the schizophrenic underlay downgraded and the hallucinatory periods marked for exploration as being street drug related. The family life-style, composition, and religious persuasion made much that had suggested a serious diagnosis less confusing to staff, and the stresses on Fritzie were better understood.

The staff felt that a weekend at home could be risked as an appropriate next step, although they were still not completely at ease about the family setting. Probably the family network felt the same way about the staff, but there was enough trust in both groups for a more relaxed approach to problem solving.

During the weekend Fritzie joined the family in some after-dinner drug use, experienced adverse reactions including a "flashback" of the earlier bad trip, and returned to the ward in a panic state that subsided within 24 hours.

Second Session

Following the weekend pass episode, the staff decided to act on their feelings that the women in the family needed a stronger coalition, since Fritzie as the only girl had not experienced clear role models. The mother's anxiety over the change in the family as Fritzie became mature and independent also seemed important. The news about a third aunt was also exciting to Fritzie, and she suggested a meeting with her.

Fritzie, her mother, her Aunt Maggie, and Jessie, the upwardly mobile aunt, met with one of the family therapists and evolved a plan for Fritzie to stay in Jessie's middle-class home after leaving the ward. In this setting she hoped to learn a bit about how to be accepted in college or the business world over the summer, and to plan possible attendance at a local community college for business training in the fall. The reconnection of the sisters was tenuous. Considerable bargaining between adults about the conditions of the arrangement and Fritzie's ability to remain in touch with her own family was the main order of business.

The staff also communicated to the women, as they had to Fritzie, that her biological reaction to psychoactive drugs was apparently idiosyncratic but dangerous for her, and recommended abstinence from drugs and from alcohol. Fritzie acknowledged this intellectually, but was concerned that the symbolic identification of herself as a family member might depend on participation in their social drug usage. Nevertheless, as most of her immediate needs would be met in Aunt Jessie's home this was arranged as a discharge plan, and implemented.

Third Network Session

Since this family lived within the catchment area of our mental health center, follow-up postdischarge care was the responsibility of the center. At the time of her discharge from the inpatient ward—18 days after admission—Fritzie was asked to set a time for a follow-up meeting of the core network and chose to do so approximately 1 month later. This was held at the community mental health center and involved the same staff and the entire cast of characters from the two previous meetings.

Fritzie herself was free of symptoms, coherent, and unconfused. At her suggestion the rest of the network brought the staff up to date by telling about themselves.

Her twin brother had begun working as a short-order cook and was debating whether or not to continue working when school started. His alternative was to stay to finish high school in case he wanted cook and baker training either in the Navy or at a local trade school. No longer pressured by being paired with Fritzie, he could look at options and she could support independence.

Three of the younger boys had been involved in a minor delinquent escapade, and had been caught later. They had a juvenile court hearing scheduled. The family apparently did not want any help with this at the time, and the flow of the session at this point sounded quite like that of a middle-class family fighting the generation gap—the boys were proud of their survival skills, while the uncle and mother were upset about the inconvenience, concerned about not knowing what was going on at the time, and feeling unable to function effectively.

Fritzie had fled back to her own home once in indignation after Aunt Jessie reprimanded her for appearing too scantily clad in the front yard; however, she had returned to the aunt. There was a somewhat more comfortable relationship between the three adult sisters. Their earlier negotiations had been tested and the bonds were stronger.

Fritzie's greatest anxiety had expressed itself earlier around her nonparticipation in the family use of drugs, but she had been assured that her brothers and uncles still considered her a loyal member of the family and were not afraid she would "rat on them." Instead, her mother and her Aunt Maggie had established her in a useful neighborhood role as an unofficial drug counselor with other young teenagers. Her knowledge from the pharmacist's classes for patients and her own experience was being put to use within an expanding network. Some of the session was spent in clarifying her concepts and information, and providing her and the family with referral resources that might be of help to them and others at an earlier, less critical stage than Fritzie's own utilization of the hospital emergency room.

The case was closed at this point, not because everyone would live happily ever after, but because the task of this mental health unit was done.

Strengths of This Family

Although at first glance this seemed to the mental health center staff to be a family from which the patient should be "rescued," the series of network meetings revealed strengths within the family that could be utilized to establish a healthy context for Fritzie's continued growth and development without exacerbating the behaviors and anxieties that led to her hospitalization. First and foremost, the antagonistic "us against them" battle lines dissolved as both family network and staff appreciated the strength of mutual concerns for Fritzie. The core network's initial acceptance of the invitation to become involved was clearly based on a felt need to defend one of their own, and staff appreciated the strength of the bonds as they became allies.

Not surprisingly, once the alliance was established, the family's ability at flexible problem solving came to the fore. Given opportunities to understand Fritzie's problems and appropriate information, they evolved solutions beyond the staff's ability to prescribe them—as, for instance, in turning Fritzie's experiences into a resource for drug counseling in the neighborhood, and thus sanctioning her abstinence as a positive rather than a negative behavior. Patriarchally organized, and with a high premium placed on masculine values and activities, the head of the family acknowledged Fritzie as "as good as a boy any day." Nevertheless, her right to have her individual needs and interests was respected, once room was made for them to be both expressed and heard.

This combination of need for belonging and respect for individuality extended to the small group of involved women. The repairing of broken relationships among the maternal sisters brought out the strengths of each of these women as they negotiated with one another and then gained acceptance for their plans by the wider network. They were in fact capable of more functional roles than the submissive, passive–aggressive stance they at first publicly adopted.

While the narrative does not contain verbatim transcripts, and hence tends to focus on family issues, one should not discard the role of the nonfamily members—particularly the foster child neighbor and the other men engaged in the family business—in the therapeutic process. Indeed, they provided a different "community" perspective on the issues, and occasionally diluted the intensity of the family interactions by injecting their own experiences.

It has been the experience of the mental health center's staff that the patient's choice of persons almost always includes one or more who would be omitted by limiting sessions to biological–legal family, and that these individuals usually play roles of advocacy and broker between patient and family, and between family and staff. Staff involved in these sessions, once they entered the patient's world with respect, made an almost 180° turn, from feeling that this was a hopeless family situation to the appreciation of its depth of caring, its ability to utilize information, and its flexibility.

PRINCIPLES INVOLVED IN UTILIZING THIS TECHNIQUE

Patient Identification of Core Network

Persons belonging to the core network are primarily identified by the patient. Any ordinary limit setting on who should or should not have been involved—based upon conventional family descriptions, for instance—would have risked omitting one or more essential members of the patient's significant and intimately involved circle (Attneave, 1976, 1980; Henderson, 1980; Sokolovsky, Cohen, Berger, & Geiger, 1978; Speck & Attneave, 1973).

Techniques of network analysis can be used to help the patient in identifying these key persons in the Core Network (Cohen & Sokolovsky, 1979; Wellman). One useful aid for discussing the composition of the network and its core is a map developed by Attneave and published by the Boston Family Institute (Attneave, 1976). However, such a device seems to be of most use to help staff conceptualize networks, or for cases in which the network itself and its composition become an issue. In most instances at the mental health center, patients quickly grasped the idea of inviting the people that lived with them and others that were important in their lives without any lengthy discussion or technical jargon.

Short-Term, Crisis-Oriented Application

The short-term network style of approach may well prove to be an especially useful clinical tool in cases involving what Erik Erikson (1950) called epigenetic crises, or transitions in developmental life cycles for one or more family members. In these cases interventions in the relevant social network can appeal to the "natural healing forces" in the system, at a time when the system is in a state of crisis and thus more susceptible to making adjustments (Erickson, Rachlis, & Tobin, 1973; Speck & Attneave, 1973).

Similarly, the fact of involving the key persons in a patient's network in a process of demystification of professional attitudes, of prescribed changes in behavior, and of medical recommendations can spell the difference between sustained change after traditional clinical interventions and recidivism and failure (Brown, Birley, & Wing, 1972; Froland, Bordsky, Olson, & Steward, 1979). Therefore, the brief core network approach is probably most applicable to short-stay, crisis-oriented inpatient settings. Outpatient settings with similar crisis-oriented clientele will also find it useful.

Facilitating Solutions by Network Members

In whatever clinical setting social network intervention is applied, a cardinal principle must be to facilitate solutions of problems and resolution of stress by the network members themselves (Attneave, 1980; Collins & Pancoast, 1976; Rueveni, 1979; Speck & Attneave, 1973). The therapeutic gains from this type of empowerment contrast vividly with the dependency that forms a part of other clinical treatments. Furthermore, when continued therapy or use of other community resources is indicated, the network's understanding of professional goals and methods is a powerful aid to retaining the patient within the therapeutic system (Sarason, Carroll, Maton, Cohen, & Lorentz, 1977). For this reason, the participation of follow-up staff, as well as those involved in the original treatment setting, is an invaluable asset (Froland, Bordsky, Olsen, & Steward, 1979; Sokolovsky, Cohen, Berger, & Geiger, 1978).

Network Sessions as Sources of Diagnosis and Planning Data

Often network sessions provide data that aid diagnoses and planning (Attneave, 1976; Beels, 1979; Sokolovsky, Cohen, Berger, & Geiger, 1978). In this case example, the additional information from the sessions gave a context to the patient's behavior. Even though other gains had not been made in the case, the first network session was needed if appropriate case management and diagnostic evaluation were ever to be attained. This session helped untangle the complex relationships in which the patient was involved. The specifics of the relationship system had originally been obscured, not only by the patient's confusion, but equally by the staff's confusion in trying to understand a life-style quite foreign to their experience. Without this first-hand opportunity to experience the context, many idiosyncratic behaviors were seen as pathological and many strengths completely overlooked. The benefits of the network sessions for staff functioning and clinical training should not be undervalued.

Building Trust and Remaining Nonjudgmental

Trust between clinical staff and the family network is essential. In the case example, it was first established with the patient herself, then reinforced by her assuming responsibility for inviting the members to the network session. It was further strengthened by the fact that the staff (1) remained nonjudgmental about social and moral issues, and (2) stuck strictly to its tasks of facilitating better mutual understanding of Fritzie's problems, and of appropriate discharge planning. Indeed, at no time was responsibility for decisions and actions taken over by the professional members, although they offered the expertise, interpretations, and questions that are part of their normal role. Important also was the ability to remain nonjudgmental about issues such as the brothers' delinquency, the social use of street drugs, and the intricate sexual partnerships involved when one uncle appeared to have both a wife and a girlfriend—both pregnant. The staff discussions during pre- and post-network meeting sessions are valuable for sorting out case management priorities, and for dealing with the emotional reactions to the content of the network sessions.

Cultural Identities and Intercultural Understandings

Although this approach can be used effectively with "ordinary" middle-class patients, it is particularly suited to families whose social class, minority culture, or life-style do not parallel the experiences of the treatment staff. The sessions assist the clinician in ascertaining both the meanings of behaviors that are outside his/her usual experience, and their susceptibility to change. Furthermore, understanding of the patient is enhanced when staff discovers that the relationship patterns in a particular cultural milieu reflect rather common basic needs, aspirations, and conflicts. As for the patient, the network sessions often offer an experience that strengthens his/her sense of cultural identity and value vis-à-vis a potentially intimidating professional hospital milieu (Speck & Attneave, 1973).

Interstaff Respect and Cooperation

Throughout the implementation of this type of intervention, and especially as new information indicates a challenge to or reinterpretation of initial formulations of diagnosis and treatment plans, the same respect given to family and network members must include staff and trainees. Mutual problem solving, as opposed to power plays and fault finding, must be the prevailing theme. This enables everyone present to build upon strengths and to contribute appropriately rather than becoming involved in defending disciplinary loyalties and engaging in reductionist arguments (Leighton, 1983).

CONCLUDING REMARKS

The value of this type of intervention is twofold. First, it enhances family and patient strengths so that the patient returns to a context better adapted systemically to support healthy growth and change for its members. This has a real impact on feelings of successful case management and satisfaction on the part of treatment staff, as well as reducing the "revolving door" patterns mentioned earlier (Brown et al., 1972). This is a primary consideration in service-oriented agencies, and a major reason for providing this type of intervention as part of the inpatient setting.

The second major value of this type of intervention is its impact on the understanding and growth of those in training in a teaching hospital. By actually participating in the assessment of the strengths of the social context of a patient, and by observing how these elements can be coordinated with treatment goals, most trainees make a breakthrough from a narrow focus on individual pathology to the ability to develop realistic options in treatment planning and aftercare. The professional staff become consultants to the patient and to the patient's social support system in a manner that can be incorporated with prior training. Learning of a systems perspective occurs naturally rather than being presented as a dramatic and often polarized shift of theoretical position.

REFERENCES

Attneave, C. Social networks and clinical practice: A logical extension of family therapy. In D. S. Freeman (Ed.), *Perspectives on Family Therapy.* Vancouver: Butterworths, 1980, pp. 51–56.

Attneave, C. *Family network map.* Boston: Boston Family Institute (Harvard Street, Brookline, MA 02146), 1976.

Attneave, C. The social network as the unit of intervention. In P. J. Guerin (Ed.), *Family Therapy: Theory and Practice.* New York: Gardner Press, 1976.

Beels, C. C. Social networks and schizophrenia. *Psychiatric Quarterly,* 1979, *51* (3) 207–215.

Brown, G. W., Birley, J. L., & Wing, J. K. Influence of family life on the course of schizophrenic disorders: A replication. *British Journal of Psychiatry,* 1972, *121,* 251–258.

Cohen, C., & Sokolovsky, J. Clinical use of network analysis for psychiatric and aged populations. *Community Mental Health Journal,* 1979, *15,* 203–213.

Collins, A., & Pancoast, D. *Natural helping networks: A strategy for prevention.* Washington, DC: National Association of Social Workers, 1976.

Erikson, E. *Childhood and society.* New York: Appleton, 1950.

Erickson, G., Rochlis, R., & Toben, M. Combined family and service network intervention. *The Social Worker,* (Ottawa) 1973, *41,* 4, 276–283.

Froland, C., Bordsky, G., Olson, M., & Steward, L. Social support and social adjustment: Implications for mental health professionals. *Community Mental Health Journal,* 1979, *15,* 82–93.

Henderson, S. A development in social psychiatry: The systematic study of social bonds. *Journal of Nervous and Mental Disease,* 1980, *168*, 63–69.

Leighton, A. *The quest for synthesis in a splintered world.* Margaret Mead Memorial Lecture, presented at World Congress for Mental Health, Washington, DC, July 25, 1983.

Rueveni, B. *Networking families in crisis.* New York: Human Sciences Press, 1979.

Sarason, S., Carroll, C., Maton, K., Cohen, S., & Lorentz, E. *Human services and resource networks.* San Francisco: Jossey-Bass, 1977.

Sokolovsky, J., Cohen, C., Berger, D., & Geiger, J. Personal networks of ex-mental patients in a Manhattan SRO hotel. *Human Organization,* 1978, *37*, 5–15.

Speck, R., & Attneave, C. *Family networks.* New York: Pantheon, 1973.

Wellman, B. (Ed.). *Connections: Bulletin of the International Network for Social Network Analysis.* Department of Sociology, University of Toronto, Ontario, Canada. (This periodical is a continuing resource both for broad research and clinical applications.)

CHAPTER 9

Resources for Remarried Families

Jack O. Bradt
Carolyn Moynihan Bradt

The remarried family of today is often seen as a social problem resulting from the breakdown of the stressed nuclear family. This chapter focuses on the remarried family as a microcosm of current social conflicts—not itself a problem or a solution to the personal and family problems of the 1980s. Rather, to the extent that society does not support or couples do not negotiate changes in their life-styles or their relationships that will sustain ongoing family life with one marriage, new players are called in to replace or expand the number of members available to perform the tasks of family life.

The remarried family holds the possibility of containing and summarizing all that came before and moving ahead toward integration and change. Or it may be a structure that avoids change by avoiding the past and substituting new players to maintain the system without change until the new string of players wears out again.

Either way, the remarried family as a new social form is seen as itself a resource in the struggle for change in a social revolution—a resource of social adaptation as men and women flounder with new roles and old models of marriage in a society oriented toward achievement and consumption but unsupportive of family life.

OVERVIEW OF CHANGE

The remarried family is embedded in a matrix of societal change and has been called the family form of the future. It is estimated that by 1990 more people will be living in a single-parent or remarried households than in households of first

Jack O. Bradt, M.D. Department of Psychiatry, Georgetown Medical Center, Washington, D.C.

Carolyn Moynihan Bradt, A.C.S.W., Private Practice, Washington, D.C.

marriage (Cherlin, 1978). To assess the challenges of remarriage it is necessary to review the conditions of our times that *affect* marriage. Contemporary remarriage reflects several trends of social change affecting marriage:

1. The decreasing death rate (or increased longevity)
2. The increasing divorce rate
3. The increased participation of women in the work force
4. The decreased size of the family

Amid these changes the rate of adult participation in marriage is stable—people are still marrying (or remarrying).

Married is the customary state of adulthood. The national statistics on marriage extending back to the mid-1800s reveal that at least 90% of the population of every birth cohort on record have eventually married (Cherlin, 1981). What is new is not that adults will marry, but what they can expect in marriage.

Remarriage is not a new phenomena. Until 1970, the rates of remarriage had remained steady since 1860. What's new about remarriage is that it is now more often the outcome of divorce from a spouse than death of a spouse. New since 1970 is its increase in frequency (Cherlin, 1981).

Decreasing Death Rate, Increased Longevity

The expectation that early death for either spouse will end the marriage has been a declining possibility since the statistics on marriage have been kept (mid-1800s). In the past it was common for parents to die while their children were still young. Infectious diseases took a high toll. Perinatal sepsis and death were common for mothers, who often left young fathers with young children, often a surviving newborn. Sometimes christenings and funerals were juxtaposed. As mortality rates have fallen, a greater proportion of parental deaths have occurred when children have already reached adulthood (Cherlin, 1981). Consequently, the *life expectancy* of marriage as a *lifetime commitment* also increased.

Increasing Divorce Rate

It is also true that the expectation that the marriage will last until the death of one partner has been less true since 1860. Cherlin (1981) pointed out that the divorce rate (unlike the rate of remarriage) has had a steady and gradual increase since 1860—with certain peaks (notably after the Great Depression and in 1945 after World War II) and a valley in the 1950s, ended by a return to the gradual rise in 1962. However, the rise in the annual divorce rates in the 1960s and 1970s is much steeper and more sustained than any increase in the past century. By 1982 somewhere around 50% of all first marriages (and 60% of second and subsequent remarriages) were ending in divorce (Glick, 1982).

Since remarriage is a highly likely probability following divorce (75–80%;

slightly higher for men than women), the sustained rate of marriage increasingly has been the result of divorce and remarriage. What is different, therefore, about the marriage statistics of our time is the shift in the percentage of marriages that are remarriages. In 1971, 38% of all marriages were remarriages and 68% were first marriages for both. In 1981, 45% of marriages were remarriages of one or both parties and only 55% were first marriages for both (Monthly Vital Statistics Report, 1984).

Increased Participation of Women in the Work Force

At about the same time as the spike in the divorce rate the gradual rise of women in the work force also spiked. The expectations that husbands provide financially and wives care for the home, laundry, food, and children, free of work outside the home, have been changed by the increased participation of women in the work force. In 1977 the census data first recorded the majority of married mothers in the workplace with children under 18. In 1983, 59% of mothers were in the workplace; and for the first time a majority of mothers of children under 6 were in the work force—58% of all mothers of children 3–5 years old (U.S. Labor Dept. and Census Data). Cherlin (1981) suggested that the increased participation of women in the work force may be the single most important factor in the increased divorce rate. Another speculation is that the high divorce rate forces women's increased work force participation because of the lack of a stable marriage to assure financial dependency and shared economic fruits of the wage earner with his domestic partner.

Cherlin (1981) said, "The great increase in female employment has altered, perhaps permanently, men's and women's roles in the family" (p. 65). However, the alteration has not created a new definition. Currently observable are the social problems and personal conflicts as men and women approach a new marital reality with old role expectations. We believe the greater problem is that the change in how people live and exchange has not kept pace with the changed realities. For example, research indicates that as women take on an additional role as worker they do not redistribute household roles. Men and women do not yet expect to cohousekeep and coparent if they are coworking. Our notions of what a husband, wife, mother, and father is in our society are in great confusion, and that confusion spawns further confusions about other relationships—ex-wife, ex-husband, stepmother, stepfather, and so on. Family charts and reports often reveal marital chains that seem to be struggling with these issues as in a relay race—turning the baton over to the next runner.

The family and what it is about has changed drastically over the 200 years of our nation's existence. The complex of recent changes just described has been aptly called the "*Subtle Revolution*" (Smith, 1979), *subtle* because we live as if it isn't so, and *revolution* to designate such rapid social change in such a central core of social life in such a short period of time. Traditional societal responses no longer provide stability or support to marriage, but customs and emotionalized images are slow to change and new customs must be created.

CHALLENGES OF REMARRIAGE

Many social observers see marriage as a relationship within the institution of the family already overloaded with pressures to fulfill all of its members' emotional needs with less and less attention to extended kin, community, church, neighborhood, and friendships. Remarriages have even greater assignments. They are expected to correct. Expectations include a restitution of what has been lost—a marriage or an intact family (moreover a *new improved* version). If a marriage must affirm innocence or restore happiness, assuage guilt or fulfill dreams, relieve pain, undo wrong, exorcize stigma, provide structure or meaning, reorder the disordered, it is additionally burdened by the unresolved problems that preceded it.

Often there is also a denial of the complexities of previous histories and relationships, with their attendant loyalty conflicts. Especially when a spouse enters remarriage from a never-married history, there can be an unawareness of the heavy demands on time and energy that such complexity can create. There is the additional strain of creation as there are no readily available role expectations for how to live this different structure. Most people try to live their own version of husband/wife–mother/father roles as if the group will function like a nuclear family, but remarriage has some different challenges than first marriage.

Old Myths and Persistent Stigmas

Today marriage, divorce, and remarriage is a continuum, each a highly likely developmental stage of adult life. More than 90% of adults marry. One-third to one-half will divorce. Of those who divorce 75% will remarry; 60% of those who remarry will divorce and possibly remarry again (Glick, 1980).

The myths and stigmas of remarriage are inseparably related to the myths of any stage of the continuum, including the earlier stage of singlehood preceding first marriage. It is a myth that there is probably something wrong with someone who never marries. Still, being single beyond a certain age raises questions of excessive attachment to parent(s), sexual immaturity (hang-ups), sexual identity, narcissism, being too set in one's ways or marginally socialized, fear of commitment, fear of becoming a parent, undesirability . . . the wondering about the too-long-single is a long list.

The myths and stigmas of being single after divorce are more pejorative than those concerning the never-married. Start with personal failure. Even in divorce, which in part may be the outcome of better psychosocial maturity (clearer definition of self), the myth and stigma of failure abide. All of the questions about being single become applicable again, each now tinged with the attitude of failure, a heavy stigma in our success-oriented society. Add the real sense of loss to the myth about divorce and "divorced" is further stigmatized.

Perhaps there are more myths, and certainly less social stigma, about marriage than about singlehood or divorce. Most persons enter marriage with mythologies, ideologies, or expectations of what marriage is supposed to be or is desired to be. Most of these are romanticized notions of tender love exchanges rather than images of struggle for equality of status and power.

If not love, then gender ascriptions of role are supposed to keep marriages intact and satisfying. To be successful and desirable, a husband–father is to be a good economic provider; to be a successful wife–mother is to keep the husband happy with his domestic life and to raise successful children. Then there is religion. Marriages made in heaven are not to be judged by the home life and the work world. Marriage not blessed at home or at work is divinely blessed, not to be broken, but experienced or endured as one of God's mysteries. More contemporary myths about marriage (or one's partner) have to do with being sexy, communicative, self-actualizing. Regardless of which myths go unfulfilled, to choose to end a marriage is largely to be judged ethically or legally a transgressor, sexually or psychologically unstable or disturbed—in short, somehow a failure.

The Blight of Loss

Like death, divorce is a powerful social stimulus. Death reminds us of our individual vulnerability, divorce our institutional vulnerability. In general, we respond by avoiding whomever or whatever reflects our frailty, imperfection, immortality. We prefer to deny divorce just as we try to deny death.

Whether remarriage is less, more, or as difficult if preceded by death of a spouse rather than divorce from a spouse is not clear. Many factors enter into consideration: the social norm for a given age cohort, children from the previous marriages, ages of children, prior familial experience of loss whether from death or divorce, competence of family in reintegrating following loss, prior experience of remarriage, religious affiliation and attitudes, and response from extended families and other networks. Suffice it to say that remarriage is born of loss, sometimes minimal, sometimes profound.

The legacy of myths and stigmas about remarriage is in part a carry-forward of the myths and stigmas of earlier stages of the continuum. In addition are all or some of the following:

1. The first marriage should be the best, the only one. This is not their only marriage, therefore not what might have been—the best. Second marriage, second best.
2. Did he(she) break up the other's former's marriage?
3. Whose children are whose? Where's the *real* father(mother), the ex-husband(wife)?
4. It's understandable that the child is having trouble. He(she) lives with a stepparent.
5. They've had lots of martial problems, but this is a remarriage, so what can you expect?

Stigma and Passing

Better to have married once than never to have married at all.
Better to have stayed married than to have divorced.
Better to pass, as if married only once.
Simply put, when being different alienates it is a stigma.

Deviant behavior—divorce—threatens social stability. As long as the deviance is perceived as an exception rather than the rule, deviants can be ignored. It is when the deviance increases, threatening the traditional as well as the conventionally accepted, that the deviants are often stigmatized, encouraging compliance with tradition. If deviants are unrecognizable they avoid stigma.

We live in a culture where most aspire to better themselves, but at the casual level most of the time we prefer to be average, not different, middle class. Like most of the animal kingdom we are alerted by what is different, and usually respond by being both curious and threatened. It is less anxiety-provoking to be one of the masses, part of the mainstream, to pass.

A stepfather and his son, once a stepson, now adopted, go to the barbershop. When the boy's hair is cut, the barber, a woman, observes, "Your son has such curly hair. Nothing like yours. He must take after his mother." The father comments, "Yes, he's quite a curly-top."

Almost every remarried couple has wished or tried to live at some point as if the remarriage were the only marriage. For the remarried it is painful to acknowledge the past. The loss and stigma are easier to bear privately than to relate candidly to persons presumed to be keepers of the myths.

Isolation and Discontinuity

Optimally, in marriage one expects to maintain a continuity with those who have been part of daily life before marriage—one's family of origin, one's friends, one's colleagues. Even though marriage is a leaving, at its best it is not a discontinuity with one's past. Marriage is optimally a bridge between past and future for the individuals and a balance of membership and legacy between the partners. We have described marriage as needing an appropriate distance or tension between the two partners (lest they merge, or fuse, emotionally). This balance is partially maintained by the ongoing connections to the extended family and prior emotional network by each partner—the marriage being suspended between those. Therefore, a cutoff for either partner creates an imbalance of power or identity and increases the likelihood of one self becoming merged into the other or seeking extraordinary distance or conflict to maintain a sense of separate selves.

In first marriage there is often an expectation and offer of emotional support and an active participation from those who are part of one's intimate circle. The people from one's earlier life are looked to for psychological and at times financial support. They provide some continuity and lend some reality to the newly created family.

This is more complicated in second marriage. Depending upon how much or how little time has passed and how much or how little resolution and reconciliation has occurred, second marriage is more or less discontinuous with the past and in danger of isolation—emotionally, socially, and financially. If there is unfinished business there is a greater chance of the couple trying to protect their relationship by compartmentalizing it and by cutting off with the past—the very thing that is most likely to rob them of the acknowledgment and integration they will need to become real and rooted.

Moreover, remarriage can be an effort to seal off the past: "I try to think of my ex-spouse as dead." "I'm not part of that family anymore." "My kids are better off without me." "What's past is past." In some instances remarriage brings the finished and the unfinished business of the past into question to be emphasized or disrupted: "My parents (or in-laws) haven't spoken to me since the divorce—they wouldn't be interested in my wedding." or "Once we're married my family will get to know her(him) . . ."

Friendships and social standing are disrupted by divorce and again by remarriage. Friends often take sides in divorce or back away from both parties. Friends who have weathered death or divorce with a person may drop away in reaction to remarriage or from neglect during courtship. Some friendships in the crises of divorce depend upon not reconnecting (singles) or upon the victim status. Thus, the fewer the number of friends and family who give witness and affirm the undertaking when the remarrying couple make the commitment "for better or worse," the worse is the prognosis for the marriage.

Cherlin (1978) discussed the lack of institutional supports and the incomplete institutionalization of remarriage. This lack may explain the almost 60% divorce rate in remarriage. Remarriage is further complicated by a lack of comfortable social customs or courtesies and by difficult financial entanglements.

Financial Discontinuity

Financial support from those related to the previous marriage of either remarried partner is fraught with symbolic and real meanings. It is almost always less freely given. Financial exchange involves emotional conflicts that can lead to personal or legal struggles to redefine financial relationships.

> For example, a man who had always provided child support on time in the correct amount and usually without complaint or resentment becomes less reliable, stops payment, or asks for a reduction of payments when his ex-wife remarries.

> Or, a man who has always paid one-fifth of his income to his ex-wife for child support feels torn when his second wife (pregnant with their first child) objects to

his payments as necessitating her continued employment. She argues that the first wife didn't have to work.

Or, a woman who has always been considerate of the responsibilities that her ex-husband could assume before his remarriage requests that he assume greater financial responsibilities when he remarries.

Or, a man who is remarrying becomes erratic or stops his child support or alimony to his first wife.

Financial ties are very real binds and bonds with the past. Once-supportive in-laws may have questions about whether they are disloyal to their own kin if they relate (especially with money) to his(her) replacement. They may withdraw support even from their grandchildren so that they are not related to "that woman" or "that man" (the remarried spouse). The ex-spouse may see the same financial exchange differently (as supporting "that other man"). Financial relationships are treated by some as a form of intimacy and remarriage makes strange financial bedfellows.

Child support and alimony are more likely to be resented. In some instances the unrelated and unknown new spouse becomes in part the financial support for the new partner's ex-spouse, reversing the direction of the support more usual in first marriage, where the support is to be *given to* the newly married. It is more usual for remarriage to have support *required from* it to relationships of the past and to have past supports withdrawn. For the couple there is often a great discomfort about the balances and imbalances of financial responsibilities each brings to the marriage—debts, alimony, financial responsibilities for children (daily or by allotment). These imbalances can breed resentment.

Even folk wisdom alludes to the hazards of divorce:

Three kinds of people die poor: those who divorce, those who incur debts, and those who move around too much. (Senegalese proverb)

The remarried may risk all three in launching, and often are disadvantaged by their social network in trying to stay afloat financially.

Lack of Common Paradigm

The newly remarried family is immobilized as a group (and immobilizing for its individual members) because it lacks a family identity (Reiss, 1982), a central and shared concept of itself as a group—including common history, a family paradigm, and a core of ritual or ceremonies. The "we" of the family may refer more to descriptions of past structures than to the present group and be used more to distinguish subgroup memberships and paradigms in collision—as in "*We* never had to eat all at the same time in *our* family" or "*We* always open presents on Christmas eve." There is confusion about who are members of which group—a feeling of *Insiders* and *Outsiders*. Children sometimes behave as if they are prisoners of war in an enemy camp, spying and remaining loyal until reunited with the allies of original membership. A new spouse without children may feel outnumbered in the pulls to establish a new and common group identity and customs.

It is further complicating that people often divorce and remarry precisely *because* congruence of family paradigm broke down in the first marriage and they have found someone whose values and world view are more similar or more attractive—in an effort at change. Thus remarriage can be at once an effort at change and an effort to avoid change. This may create households with markedly different orientations and values connected in a chain and tempted to organize themselves in a *competitive* hierarchy—defined as "not that" or "better than" the previous household. This could lead to not exploring differences and/ or cutoff and ultimately to nongrowth and nonresolution. Acceptance and cooperation are more difficult than competition when people are without a secure membership bond and are threatened by loss.

Unrealistic Expectations

In this culture we see marriage as a *solution* to personal problems, as revealed in our music, drama, and myths. Thus we aren't prepared for it to be a problem we engage. The assessment of challenges and the search for resources are seldom part of the preparation for marriage or remarriage. As in first marriage, romantic myths, reinforced by the experiences of courtship, seem to assure the assumed future—"and they lived happily ever after." Few remarrying couples know what a different ball game remarriage is. There is nothing more commonly discussed in stepfamily literature than unrealistic expectations.

Romantic myths prevail, especially when the failed first marriage is considered only the ex-spouse's failure. If past losses, disappointments, and failures have been dismissed through blame and victim–villain equations, the ex-spouse always being "the villain," the remarrying couple has an alliance and can easily assume they need to look no further for change than to say "we're the good guys."

A man who used distance as a way of relating to his (alcoholic) ex-wife expects an easy togetherness that he has experienced in courtship with his second wife in their remarriage. He sees his own position in his first marriage as justified or coping when he overworked or avoided his wife. His second wife complains about his unavailability and distancing. He is surprised. He didn't expect to have to struggle with personal change.

Another unrealistic expectation is that of instant intimacy. The expectation that children will be enthusiastic and accepting of a new spouse or that a new spouse will replace or easily know and love a stepchild or other ex-relative leaves the couple unprepared for the reaction and hurt, guilt, and jealousy that can go along with the remarriage for the couple and for others in the system.

The previously unmarried or childless bride or groom may add new myths to the mix—signing up to become the "good spouse" and "good parent" for the child(ren)—to replace or outdo the ex-spouse. This fantasy is often reinforced by one or both of the parents. We have never heard more often than from remarried couples the wish that they had known, had been prepared for what their experiences in remarried life would be. Perhaps this need explains the proliferation of literature on remarriage and the large number of requests for "Survival Kits" (reprints) from the Stepfamily Association of America. As in most organizations, the limit of resources in remarriage is seldom recognized until problems are critical.

ASSESSING RESOURCES

Few individuals or families present with a complaint about their remarriage or their step relationships. They have concerns about their depression, their marriage, their family, their child, their symptom. However, the structural and historical issues of marriage–separation–divorce–remarriage (seen as a continuum) constitute the bulk of most clinical caseloads today. A truly systemic and multigenerational view of families reveals issues of remarriage and family reorganization in almost every clinical contact. As family therapists we touch hundreds of others for each client we contact.

Because a true systems perspective is rare in our institutions and classification systems in mental health agencies, many clinical contacts with issues of remarriage are mislabeled and misperceived as individual or couple issues. They appear as a school failure, an acting-out teenager, a depressed wife, a conflictual couple. If the clinician relies on the families' own presentation of the "symptom," she/he will have a very low count of "remarried" families. A systemic approach quickly reveals the facts of those family change points (nodal events) that leave members with acute or chronic loss issues and the system with a challenge to reorganize. Further questions of who is in contact with whom and who knows what about whom provide clues to ascertain whether resolution has occurred or denial prevails. In view of the fact that resolution is a process, most families will be somewhere in between crisis and resolution.

Family therapists have various ways of broadening the context from a focus on individual dysfunction toward the identification and mobilization of systemic resources. Operating in a multigenerational context, we see the assessment phase as an engagement of those family members motivated to make change. In the first phase of the joint effort the goal is to gather the facts in the context of the larger family and its history and in the process to lower the anxiety about the present. The complexities (see Table 9-1) of the structure of remarriage make it especially useful to actually map out the data rather than to proceed by simply considering the household to be the family.

The routine use of the poster-size drawing of the Family Diagram (Bradt, 1980; Bradt & Moynihan, 1971) in a history-gathering initial session does much to place the current situation into its historical context and provides a visual

TABLE 9-1
The Varied Origin and Structure of Remarried Households

	H never married before	H widowed, no C	H widowed, with C	H divorced, no C	H divorced, with C	H divorced, with some C	H divorced, all C elsewhere
W never married before		1	2	3	4	5	6
W widowed, no C	7	8	9	10	11	12	13
W widowed, with C	14	15	16	17	18	19	20
W divorced, no C	21	22	23	24	25	26	27
W divorced, with C	28	29	30	31	32	33	34
W divorced, some with C	35	36	37	38	39	40	41
W divorced, all C elsewhere	42	43	44	45	46	47	48

Note. W, wife; H, husband; C, child(ren).

There are 48 possible household configurations (varying in origin and/or membership) that are the initial outcome of remarriage; 33 of these will include one or more in-house children (those not underscored). The complexity is increased by (1) additional children born to the remarried couple (adds 48 more configurations); (2) parents who have been divorced and remarried more than once with children from more than one prior marriage; and (3) visitation and custodial arrangements.

presence of all the important characters. The family charting serves four general purposes (Bradt, 1980):

1. Shifting from a symptomatic individual to a family system conceptualization of both the problem and the solution.
2. Collecting, organizing, and integrating family data.
3. Lifting the mantle of mystery and fear about the emotional process by sticking with the facts of multigenerational family life.
4. Encouraging the identification of family resources for healing.

In addition, it serves to:

5. Clarify the distinctions between "household" and family memberships.
6. Define the number and longevity of relationships as resources.
7. Begin the exploration of household and family boundaries, locate members geographically, and review the development of present arrangements.
8. Identify relationship connections and cutoffs; elicit descriptions of the quality, current frequency, and changes in contact patterns.
9. Acknowledge previous relationships as important.
10. Suggest loyalty bonds and binds.
11. Provide data for defining important triangles.
12. Elicit the language of relationships as the family member(s) describe other members ("My father's new wife," or "My stepmother," or "My other mom").
13. Identify multigenerational experience with divorce, remarriage, and step-parenting issues.
14. Identify patterns of strength, weakness, and repetition of family themes over time.
15. Define the major family change points in time.

There are several other important areas of assessment in a remarried family that are not necessarily apparent from family diagram information. They include:

1. Relationship with former spouse(s). Has it progressed beyond blame? Is there an understanding of what happened, what went wrong, what was of value? Can they treat each other with respect and expect respect? Do they cooperate or compete? Have they "buried the hatchet" or is there still a hot or cold war going on?
2. History of financial arrangements, legal visitation and custody arrangements. History of disputes and court involvements.
3. Sex role expectations in various family units, i.e., both agree that "mothers care for children, but they're his children."
4. Spouse's knowledge and acceptance of the other's previous life as "real."

5. Balance and reciprocity of the visiting patterns between members of extended family and divorced family. Determine direction of contact—who calls, travels, writes, or visits whom, who adapts to whose schedule, and the like.

6. Where the family is in the process of remarriage according to usual developmental experiences (see description of developmental stages that follows).

7. Family ritual formation and areas of conflict. Who participates in designing shared family experiences? Do vacations, celebrations, meals reflect the varied histories or impose one past reality on the others?

RESOURCES

Since marriage and remarriage today occur without prescribed roles, in some ways the Subtle Revolution makes pioneers of us all. Pioneers struggle individually and collectively to maximize resources, and identify new ones.

Mind Set

The most sustaining and vital resource for successful remarriage is the paradigm or mind set of each member of the family about *who is the family*. This requires letting go of myths—some the myths of marriage (e.g., that the family living in one household is sufficient unto itself), and some the myths of role (e.g., that women take care of children and men supply the women from the world). The remarried father has to be a real functional presence with his children in the home, not simply the anachronistic male worker in the world. The stepfather needs to take time and energy from the world to get to know his stepchildren.

The conceptual leap for successful remarriage is to redefine the family as it is, not as it once was or was imagined to be. This redefinition establishes who is family. The new family is not only one's newly acquired spouse and in-laws with or without children, it is also the old family, one's former spouse and in-laws. The new family has enlarged; there are now more than two sets of grandparents or parents-in-law, more than one mother and father, more than his or her biological children, and often the potential of more children to be born.

Understanding the Concept of Triangles

Triangles are the smallest unit of both process and structure in the alliancing–skirmishing–loyalty processes of family life. Most family therapists have been introduced to the ideas of triangular functioning whether or not they learn to see all dyadic process as having visible or hidden third corners. Many family therapists regularly design their interventions on careful observation and strategic consideration of the triangular process of the family (Bowen, 78). A few family therapists not only inform their own moves but also inform or instruct their clients about triangular process. (These are usually Bowen-trained therapists who see their position as coach to the change efforts of individual members of family systems.)

The concept of triangular process is one that we consider a useful resource to teach families of remarriage. Directly or indirectly introducing the concept is often offering a new perspective for survival aiding both the understanding of what goes on and the strategy for change.

For example, a stepmother who is kind and experienced with children, loving and giving, and a favorite with nieces and nephews, is stunned by her stepdaughter's derisive and hateful presentation of her in the neighborhood and at school. "What have *I done* to her?" "Why does *she* hate *me*"? or "What's wrong with *her?*"

Such *her/me* questions are all on the individual or dyadic perceptual level. The periscope that the triangle concept provides and that this stepmother needs in order to cope more constructively is that their situation has more to do with the "important third parties" than with what *is* or *has been* between the two of them.

The Use of Triangles in Clinical Cases

Case Example 1

A father spent a lot of time with his daughter after his divorce and before his remarriage. At remarriage he shifted his energy and subtly expected "the little woman" (stepmother) to orchestrate, take over, or always be included. The stepmother sought the same goals as a sign of her acceptance and belonging in the system. The daughter is hostile toward her stepmother. The therapist proposed that hostility toward the stepmother would be most quickly reduced by the increase of individual relationship time and interest between father and daughter. There would still be the challenge to change and make room, but the change would not be so total. With less feeling of loss, the daughter is more able to explore the gains and possibilities for herself of having a relationship with her new stepmother. The stepmother will be more acceptable as an additional adult if she does not eclipse other historical relationships. The therapist also suggested that the stepmother develop a civilized contact with the biological mother. This would reduce the daughter's loyalty conflicts.

Case Example 2

A divorced mother with shared custody consults a family therapist about the anger, hostility, and clinging of her 9-year-old son, an only child. She could find nothing in the balance of her own relationship time and energy distribution with the child to explain this change. There were no significant changes in the school situation, residence, or contacts with extended family. There were no significant deaths. The child's adjustment to the divorce, custody, and his visiting situation had been smooth for 3 of the last 5 years since separation. The father had just remarried a woman with two teenagers. Although the child was not discussing the changes in his contacts with his father, the therapist decided to focus on the four potential triangles in the remarriage situation:

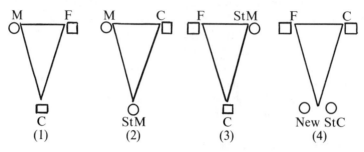

(M, mother; F, father; C, child; StM, stepmother; StC, stepchildren)

Triangle 1. A potential issue exists between the father and mother in facing or denying the realities of their divorce, the reawakening of loss. For women the feeling reaction tends to focus around security issues: "He'd be available as a backup financially" or "He'd come help me or fix things. If he's remarried he won't anymore." Others include: "She [2nd wife] has seven children. He won't send our child to college." Men are more likely to be concerned about losing contact or control of the situation with the child or to fear an increase or decrease of being needed. Often few interdependencies actually remain, but a spouse fears the loss of greater access in the relationship. The therapist might suggest that it is an excellent time for the original couple to review their own history together—especially acknowledging the positive and successful aspects. Divorced couples know better than most observers that which was of value between them. This seems to be a necessity for most couples to complete the "letting go" of the past. The failures of the relationship need not be the final or only definition. Most divorces are heavily assisted by lawyers, and some by mental health experts as well, in focusing on and examining and exaggerating the failures of the relationship so that the ending can be "justified." This promotes cutoff and negative interactions between biological parents. Many symptoms in children at the time of the remarriage of a parent relax with the easing of the feelings between the biological parents. Their better connection as parents also allows the mother to refer concerns about the son to the father by reporting them to him without assuming that solutions exist only in her household or in her relationship with the son.

Triangle 2. It is very common for the biological parent and the stepparent to be out of contact or even to have parented the same children without ever meeting. In this example the latter was true. The therapist assisted the mother in meeting and getting to know the stepmother, easing the tension and loyalty conflicts in the triangle for the child. He became free to spend time and even to like his stepmother when his mother was not seen as her enemy.

The other two triangles are not discussed because, in consulting with the mother about her moves in the system, those triangles will ultimately be dealt with in the other household. In good contact with the father, she could raise consciousness about their child's need to have some individual time with him, even with the presence of the stepmother or stepchildren. The useful thing about a systems perspective is that the therapist can more easily consult with any adult member of the remarriage chain and consider the best interests of all as the goal. She/he is ethically bound to do so.

Therapeutically, we have but to cast some light on what most people have available in their cultural experience of common wisdom. The magic of a technical name, "triangle," elevates it to a concept and possibly a tool. All of us grow up learning that: "Two against one is not fair"; "Fight your own battles"; "Two's company, three's a crowd"; "Don't get in the middle of a fight." If we add the therapeutic advice to "speak *to*, not *about*" or "if two people can't work something out, look for the triangles," or "speak for yourself, not for others," we can empower family members with some formulas for change. These relatively simple triangular moves are surprisingly unconsidered by families who have no script for their new relationships and fall into an adversarial enemy posture out of their awkwardness.

Realistic Expectations

In remarriage, becoming a family has no predictable time schedule. Like the process of differentiation, Bowen (1978) described, it is an ongoing project, often a lonely process, sustained by personal vision and challenge. In the remarried household the husband and wife who share this view of the possible, or sustain one another when hope flags, and value the pursuit of change, have begun the process of establishing a family identity. Knowing that remarital bliss does not come at the beginning, but is possible later, may sustain the couple through the adverse beginning so characteristic of remarriage. It is like the calmness with which the medical team reacts to the physical symptoms that signal rejection by the body of the organ in an organ transplant—expecting it and knowing that restored health lies on the other side of the struggle. It has been observed that remarriages that survive the first 3 years are less likely to end in divorce. Clinicians and participant–observers of remarriage recognize the fragility of the marital relationship in the initial months of remarriage.

Developmental Stages of Remarriage

Remarriage is a process more than an event. It is a process of becoming redefined that is noted for its *complexity* and often for its intensity. Observing families of remarriage, it is possible to describe some predictable developmental stages in the process. There already exist some useful developmental descriptions of the process in the literature as clinicians observe patterns of family experience. Most notable are McGoldrick and Carter (1980), Lewis (1980), and

Visher and Visher (1979) and Papernow (1984). The following list is derived from clinical observations and self-reports of remarrieds, and may serve as a guide to the predictable stages of becoming a stepfamily.

1. go back!
2. making room
3. struggles of realignment
4. (re)commitment
5. rebalancing relationships—acceptance
6. relinquishing feelings of deprivation and burden
7. growth toward integration
8. moving on

As in all developmental or life cycle thinking, progression from stage to stage is more or less difficult depending upon the successful completion of previous stages, in this case the definition of self and resolution of the tasks of separation and divorce or death. Understanding the stages of remarriage from the event itself to the integration and emergence of the unique new (and old) family and knowing what to expect becomes a resource, sustains hope, and guides clinical intervention.

Go Back!

As with all real change in a system, remarriage meets with an emotional reaction. The changes introduced or formalized by remarriage affect everyone and stimulate powerful feeling reactions in spouses, ex-spouses, siblings, grandparents, and children. The advent of remarriage of either of the original couple (re)awakens the feelings and unresolved experiences of *loss* for all family members and members of friendship and work networks, and sets off pressure for relationships to shift or resist change. Often the remarriage ceremony is the first formal ritual acknowledging the termination of the previous states of relationship. Many remarrying couples seem to unconsciously anticipate the act of remarriage as the kickoff of protest and therefore marry surreptitiously without much integration with their social networks.

Some children experience the impact of the loss of their intact family only when a parent remarries, others when a new child is born. Separated parents who have not yet reinvested energy in a new adult relationship often reinvest that energy in their child(ren). A new spouse can thus represent not only an additional adult but also a competitor for a resource. If the couple (who, after all, made the decision to initiate this merger) fail to experience their own jolt of "go back!" ("What have I gotten myself into?" "Is this a mistake?" "I never thought it would be like this"), they can count on the children's response to *go back*. Since their fragile loyalty bond to each other must be protected, it is infrequent for couples to be able to share and support each other in their fear. Depression may mask panic, promote withdrawal. Reports to each other to fear may stir panic or withdrawal rather than reassurance. Perhaps that is why it is so much more common for families to focus on the protest signals of the children launching a child focussing process in the marriage (Bradt & Moynihan, 1971).

Although some children are very protective of their parents, or deal with their own reaction indirectly—by finding allies outside the family who will feel sorry for them—it is common for children to engage actively in disruptive behavior, drawing focus to themselves by protesting in various ways and attempting to undermine the marriage. The form of the message to go back is different for different children at different developmental stages. Some children will deny the changes as long as it is possible.

Billy, the middle of three children and the only son, was 8 when his parents separated. His behavior went from tolerable to intolerable levels of infantile clinging and disrupting the household. His school performance deteriorated. His mother was overwhelmed and consulted a therapist. Family sessions with Billy, his siblings, and his parents brought about improvement. Through the family sessions Billy had been prepared for the remarriage of either or both of his parents. His father remarried when he was 10, his mother a year later. His stepfather moved into Billy's home. Billy protested only mildly, and mostly to the therapist, about his mother's remarriage.

His seeming acceptance was disrupted by the announcement of his mother's pregnancy, a year after her remarriage. His behavior exacerbated and he developed nightmares, going to his mother's and stepfather's bed for the remainder of any night they occurred. During the day he avoided his stepfather, with whom he had become companionable. In a tearful session with his mother, Billy, who seldom cried, explained that her pregnancy meant that she was not only sleeping with her new husband, but was also having sex. He revealed that he felt his mother had been unhappy in one marriage and would be unhappy again, and that having a child was "evidence" that she was married again. In his view he was no longer needed.

Research on remarriage reveals that the number one problem in second marriages is "the children" (Pasley & Ihinger-Tallman, 1982; Jacobson, 1979; Visher & Visher, 1979). Kay Pasley (1984) listed as among the research findings on remarriage and stepparenting that the quality of step relationships (between stepparent and stepchild) is a better predictor of family adjustment than the quality of the marital dyad. In the same report it is noted that custody arrangements change following remarriage, and contact with noncustodial parents decreases. This substantiates a wry cliche of stepfamily support groups that children are often the "wedding present" from the ex-spouse to the remarrying couple. The ex-spouse system sends powerful go back messages or actions. Geographic moves and changes of custody are extra possible adjustments to the already long list of changes.

"Go back" is an individual experience but also a social message from the persons closest to the remarrying family unit. If the support of family and community is sought, it is sometimes withheld.

A brother greeted his brother's report of a decision to marry his (now second) wife with "Why don't you just have an affair?"

Often close others have not been included in the courtship phase. Loyalty to the previous spouse, disapproval, or disrespect are more likely if the ending of the first marriage is seen in victim–villain terms and blame and guilt issues have not been resolved in selves and in the alliances of the system. We have often advised people approaching remarriage not to marry until they have met every significant family member and close friend of the spouse, including the ex-spouse and children. This is not primarily for investigative purposes, but for the connection of the couple to the important network of others. The more isolated the unit the more vulnerable to internal pressures to *go back. The more experiences of social context or social support the more the fragile remarried unit is fortified.*

Making Room

Territorial issues are universal and emotional experiences of redefining life in a remarried unit. This is true at many levels. At the literal level more people need more space and need to decide how the space is to be used. Are there enough rooms? Is there enough time? Do children have to give up or share their territory? Does the father's new household have space for visiting children?

Billy's father remarried a widow with a son about Billy's age. When he remarried Billy was pleased that his father would live in a house again—his new wife's house. He was not pleased about having to share a room with his new stepbrother when he visited his father. His mother readily agreed that this was not good for Billy or his sisters, who also had to share space with stepsisters. She looked to the therapist for sanction to put pressure on the new stepfamily that they should "do something about this." The therapist withheld approval of her triangling in the making room process. She was encouraged to exchange neutral or friendly reports on the children with her ex-husband, Billy's father, to get to know the new stepmother, and to support Billy in openly discussing his feelings with his father or father and stepmother.

Making room also applies to the emotional space. The couple may have established their own relationship without the presence or active involvement and responsibility for children, especially if they each had a separate household before marriage. Freedom to relate first without sharing household tasks, maintenance, and problems of marriage is often relinquished by living together. "Living together" is further crowded if household life includes children who live in or visit. A remarried couple with live-in children makes the old-fashioned rituals of courtship attractive again. People who quickly live together forego this privilege of unmarried relationship and curtail the private space around their relationship.

Making room also applies to the delineation of work/home time allocations. This balance is the central challenge for all intimate relating in the 1980s. Does she work? Does he share household and child care tasks? Does he/she expect to turn certain responsibilities over to his/her spouse? Are there feelings attached to whose children, or whose financial obligations, there are? Who has the options on time and monies? Who will shift their operation around these issues? Are these matters examined for planning, or do people drift into their automatic emotionalized notions? The fantasies or expectations are usually drawn from idealized images of "perfect" nuclear families where mothers don't work and/or the *Brady Bunch*, where there is a live-in maid, who reduces tasks, and no ex-spouses, which reduces complexity. Does the couple consider the families and spouses in their previous family units as resources in planning time, energy, and money problems? The cooperation of a team is not possible if people haven't resolved their previous battles and "buried the hatchet." Thus, making room may also include the further resolution of unfinished business in the separation and divorce, if further cutoff is not to result and resources are to be maximized by teamwork rather than competition.

Along with the demands of work on time and energy, the children will also actively compete for the couple's dwindling marital space. Children have had the experience of becoming the insider, first mate, or even parental partner in the prior marriage and separation and divorce. For children the remarriage does not always feel like a relief from those burdens and binds to normal growth. Moreover, the opportunity of another adult resource is more likely to be experienced as a usurption of position, status, and power.

A stepmother tells of her 13-year-old stepdaughter (who had lived in the home of her father for 2 years before the marriage) intruding herself physically between the couple's coming home greeting if the stepmother got there first. She would often wait outside long periods of time, rather than not be the first person to greet her father coming home.

Many a stepmother or stepfather moving into the other's territory has told of feeling the children's prior claim to the territory—a sense of being the intruder, the maid. Many a child has felt displaced by "*her*" rearranging "*our*" furniture.

This stage has encouraged much advice from stepfamily experts:

1. Move into a new common family home as soon as possible.
2. If this is not possible, redecorate, but with mutual participation and including the children.
3. If rooms must be shared, encourage participation in the problem solving.
4. Give visiting children a space of their own—a room, a bed, a shelf or drawer for belongings.

The process of making room is the first task around which members organize and proceed to the struggles that they must survive to become a unit.

Struggles of Realignment: Loyalty Conflicts and Power Struggles

Struggles, negotiations, protests, "finding the buttons and pushing them" are part of the triangular squirmishes as former relationship alignments break down and restructure. It is normal in stepfamily formation to proceed from protest to making room to confrontation of power and membership configurations. People fight to keep what they have when they feel they have little, and when they fear losing that. This stage could be visualized as a group of inhabitants of several small islands that have drifted closer together who become curious about the other islands and their inhabitants. They have constructed bridges to explore, but as they notice or become noticed by the alien inhabitants, they retreat to their smaller but safer spaces and join together to defend against invasion or to feel stronger on the next excursion. As long as fear persists, the possibilities of withdrawal to private space, tightening of boundaries, or takeover exist. However, withdrawal leaves very limited space, and patrolling boundaries or secret plans to take over consumes life energies and prevents growth or expansion. It is the possibility of gaining what new members have to offer—that by relinquishing space or easing access one might relinquish burdens or aloneness—that eventually encourages the risk. Taking the risks of sharing more people and more space and creating a more common territory to move back and forth brings up the potential of conflict and the need to settle disputes.

The struggles with one group could be avoided by alliances with old or "other outside" groups or by withdrawal, but the outcome is a stalemate of those new connections that create growth by hiding out in old alliances.

Billy (again) concludes: "My stepfather is different. He's interesting, but dangerous (to blame for all these changes). Dad doesn't know him. I won't get to know him either. Dad and I are together against him. It would be disloyal to get to know him. If he gets too close, I'll fight him."

A stepfather described his live-in 8-year-old stepson's participation in family life as: "It's as if we're the blue army and he's a hostage from the red army—here against his will, revealing nothing beyond name, rank, and serial number, spying when possible and remaining separate. If he were to deal with me not necessarily with affection, even with protest or negotiations, I'd feel like he'd taken off his uniform."

Secrets are essential to the boundary insulations that avoid new connections. For an excellent treatment of how secrets bond and bound, see Karpel (1980).

Intimate relationships survive only if intimates establish useful ways to deal with differences and anger and frustration. If members aren't willing to *risk* working out the tough issues at close range by revealing them to each other, they cannot proceed to intimacy. The fears resulting from previous loss or failure can result in an excessive conflict avoidance and a sense of threat if conflicts arise.

Reiss (1982) researched the problem-solving procedures as a measure of the family's orientation toward and sensitivity to its social world—its paradigm. The concept of common paradigm is useful in considering the often chaotic, conflictual experiences of members of remarrying systems and in assessing their development as a family. There are two important applications of this concept to the discussion of the defining–testing–struggle stage of remarriage. First, it identifies the chaos succinctly—How can the group relate without some shared structure? Struggles for *whose* (previous) structure and the obstacles (including time) to developing a new one bring up loyalty issues. (Boszormeny-Nagy & Spark, 1973). Second, it identifies more clearly the battleground for loyalty struggles. The struggle to hammer out a common paradigm and a common identity suggests betrayal of old ones.

If family units yield to the temptations to cut off from the other units in order to fortify group identity and tighten boundaries in the household group, the loyalties and conflicts may go underground and a pseudomutual, secretive, "as-if" household group will result.

To summarize the tasks and challenges of this stage, they are: (1) for members to stay connected enough with those elements of family who are important to each one's identity as an individual and as a member of subgroups; (2) to actively represent their positions, their histories, and their memberships in the new group; (3) to weather the conflicts that will arise; (4) to compromise when needed; and (5) to create new household definitions that integrate the richly diverse experiences of the varied pasts.

(Re)commitment—Budding of Family Feeling/Becoming Real

The reason that recommitment is the fourth stage of remarriage may have something to do with "becoming real," evolving a family mythology, paradigm, ceremonials, and definition that can coexist or compete with the strong emotional experiences of the past. The marriage ceremony does not do that for the interior (personal) experiences or the social identity of a couple or a family.

Wolin and Bennett (1984) discuss the importance of the creation of ritual in the establishment of family identity. The remarried family must create and define shared experiences. Rituals are useful in integrating and symbolizing the diverse past of each into shared events. These must reflect the needs of the present *and* the uniqueness of the group without denying or challenging past loyalties.

In the chaos of early remarriage, the therapist may be useful in assisting the family in defining simple repetitive actions and ceremonies of family life. The inclusion of the children in the wedding may not be as important as the recurring identifiable symbols and celebrations which are established in "redefining the family." Family meals, celebrations, holidays and vacations become patterned. An especially useful prescription is for family meetings, the ritual of a certain time for family business, planning and problem solving, complete with chairperson and minutes.

Becoming committed in remarriage follows the survival against pressures to go back, follows making space, follows struggles, redefinitions, and loyalty conflicts because only then are the dimensions of the membership and the commitment established.

Rebalancing Relationships—Acceptance

Once the stage of recommitment has been accomplished, the family members feel free enough to come and go, moving between old and new relationships and defining different memberships in each household. There is less threat and competition, more expectation of something to be gained by cooperation, greater understanding and possibility of trust. Sometimes this phase includes a rearrangement of custody, main residence, or visiting patterns. Legal rearrangements are seldom sought because trust is higher. Often it includes greater public acknowledgment of family members who are not present—"I have another sister in New York." "I have two fathers." It is now possible to acknowledge the richness of the potential resources of relationships without such pressure for "either-or" choices. Relationships are in the introductory phases of being personal, rather than categorical (the "wicked stepfather") or triangular ("we against her" or "us against them"). Relationships tend to become more private as opposed to secret. Children are uncomfortable reporting about all of their conversations with their stepmother to their mother or about their mother to their stepmother. There is much less "we" or "they" conversation, more "I" and "you."

Sometimes this is a phase in which unresolved issues of the previous marriage can be reworked and any old hatchets can be buried. The first marriage is not as threatening or denied in the second; the second marriage is neither going to disappear nor obliterate the past. The extended family can relate to new and older family members with the loyalties that are appropriate to the present, but without the need for brittle either-or choices that necessitate cutoffs. In the most ideal resolutions blame and defensiveness can be dropped as unnecessary. In others they can be diminished, greatly reduced, or held to a minimum.

Relinquishing Feelings of Deprivation and Burden

By this stage of the process in the separation–divorce–remarriage continuum many members can give up the burdens of their overresponsible, undercollaborating, isolated, or untrusting positions. There may have been some learned secondary gains of being "that poor child" or the woman (or man) "burdened" with his (or her) kids. There are always some available partners for "ain't it awful." Stepmothers are all aware of the skills that stepchildren can acquire in demonstrating her "neglect" by going without a coat or wearing the oldest clothes or failing to mention any attentions she pays. The family and neighbors need few cues to conclude that she's not being good to "the poor child." One stepdaughter had several prom dresses because she'd let relatives and friends "know" that "*she*" (her stepmother) wouldn't get her the dress she wanted—even though the stepmother had put that exhaustive search for the right gown in top time priority weeks before the occasion.

Most stepparents try *too* hard, bending over backward to please and demonstrate their good intentions and win approval from the child and the observing others. When the process reaches the stage of rebalancing and acceptance, they can usually define better their obligations to self and others and relinquish the burdens and deprivation of the "pledge" in a new sorority or fraternity. As a member the privileges and loyalty increase.

Growth Toward Integration

The paradox of the process of remarriage is that, once the differences are accepted, the challenges addressed, the complexity acknowledged, the commitment established, the relationships rebalanced, the feelings of deprivation and burden relinquished, the family emerges with an identity and cohesiveness that make it seem to its members (if not to outsiders) much like any other functioning family. The membership, broader than before, begins to be less self-involved and self-reflective.

Moving On

Through the previous stages the emerging remarried family is a system with sparse energy directed to the outside and much energy absorbed in its own growth. Being real is the arrival point of the process of remarriage. It is recognizable in the improved functioning of members—not only with each other, but in their own directions—away from family as well as among themselves. Members are free to move among established pathways in their complex network of relationships without major focus on the relationship, but rather upon problem solving, growth, and interaction with broader systems.

COLLECTIVE RESOURCES: CREATING A NONEXCLUSIVE FAMILY

The boundaries of a remarried family cannot be so exclusive of "outsiders" as an original family without severing important others from previous relationships.

A remarried wife finds herself entertaining her husband's ex-brother-in-law and his wife. Although she is somewhat uncomfortable at first, she recognizes that he once lived with her husband and related to him as an older brother. That relationship continued to be important to both parties after the first marriage ended by divorce. This contact by the new wife made it easier for the husband's ex-mother-in-law to come and stay as a houseguest when her granddaughter graduated from high school, allowing her to be present at this celebration.

Children probably cannot have too many people who care about them and offer them love and support. A family who has achieved a cooperative and accepting posture is capable of recognizing their importance in one another's lives or the lives of their children. They will find themselves able to provide what their children need most—continuity and reality in their present relationships. These people find themselves gathered for First Communions, Christmas, Bar Mitzvahs, graduations, or weddings with important members from all segments of the clan. On the other hand, grown children of parents divorced since their childhood often find themselves in anguish when one parent refuses to come to their graduation or wedding if the other attends. They dread those very celebrations that others anticipate with pleasure.

A remarried husband had custody of his son, Stan. They lived with his second wife, Jane, and their mutual son, Fred. Both of their extended families lived in distant cities. However, the biological, noncustodial mother, Eve, and her kin were local. After Jane bridged the cutoff from Eve, she eventually included all of that family with some welcome grandparents in their celebrations, especially those focused on Stan.

A first wife, mother of two teenage daughters, saw herself as victim of the divorce. The younger daughter began some serious acting-out, rebellion against rules, running away, and promiscuous behavior at the time of her father's remarriage—5 years after her parents' divorce. Landmark changes in family therapy included the original parents having a meeting (with the consent of the second wife and with the knowledge of the children). This reworking between them included a report by each to the other of the positive aspects of the other and of their history together. The therapist insisted that they do this privately as it was too personal to include any outsiders (even the therapist). The father spent more parenting time with the daughters. One came to live with him in the remarried household. This was difficult for the first wife, but increased her contact with the stepmother. The next tension arose when the second wife became pregnant. The first wife felt some grief because she'd always wanted a third child and was feeling some loss as her daughters distanced from her in the course of their developmental tasks of adolescence. By the time the son of the second marriage was born, the first wife reported that she'd been the first "babysitter" and the acting-out teenager was again appropriate in her behavior.

COMING OUT

Coming out is the opposite of passing. Passing "as-if" a first marriage household means to avoid acknowledging other family members, to pretend there is only one set of parents, to follow the convention of language of a first-marriage family. Coming out evolves as the remarried family moves through its stages of development.

Fred married Ellen. It was the second marriage for both. Their household consisted of Fred, Fred's daughter from his first marriage, Ellen, and Ellen's son from her first marriage. Initially in social situations Fred tried to pass by introducing Ellen's son as, "This is my son." Initially Ellen's son didn't like Fred calling him his "son." He missed his biological father and resented Fred's presumption or pretense. Ellen introduced Fred's daughter as "Fred's daughter" or as her "stepdaughter." Fred felt uncomfortable whenever Ellen did this. His daughter wished Ellen would just introduce her as "my daughter," but Ellen was determined to avoid making Fred's daughter feel what she knew her son felt whenever Fred called him "son." Fred felt hurt and angry anytime Ellen's son referred to his biological father as "my Dad," especially since Ellen's ex-husband had stopped sending child support a few months after Ellen and Fred's marriage and rarely saw him.

Fred and Ellen eventually changed their mind set but never got quite comfortable with step terms. The son became comfortable saying, "these are my two fathers." Eventually, when with Fred and Ellen, he referred to his biological father as his Uncle Joe, but when with Joe called him Dad. Ellen stopped using "step" in referring to Fred's daughter. She recognized that "stepdaughter" made her daughter feel excluded and disaffirmed their loving relationship. Both Fred and Ellen became comfortable introducing or being introduced by their children as "one of my parents" (mothers/fathers).

INFORMATION AND SUPPORT

There are several nontherapy resources that may preclude the necessity of therapy interventions or may be adjunctive to a course of treatment. The resources of *information* and *support* can be provided best in nonclinical interventions. Both come from primarily three sources: literature, networking, and own family (multigenerational) experience. The part of stepfamily formation that is pioneering and challenging, unexpected and isolating, is best addressed as a *social issue* rather than a personal problem. The social tools for solving social problems include a consciousness literature and group or collective action—a "movement."

Networking, Support, or Instructional Groups

There are many communities that have in place groups that bring stepfamily members together to exchange, learn, or socialize. Some churches have responded to the needs of members with groups of remarrieds. The Paulist Fathers have published a pair of booklets for parish use on Preparation for Remarriage (O'Brien and O'Brien, 1983). YMCAs, Family Service Agencies, individuals, and therapists have all been sources of organizing time-limited or ongoing groups. Schools have become increasingly concerned and provided Teen Raps on divorce and remarriage issues, or children's focus groups.

In existence since 1978, the Stepfamily Association of America Inc. (SAA) now has 62 chapters in 28 states and is dedicated to fostering chapter development wherever interested individuals or groups arise. They provide chapter development information, training manuals, an excellent newsletter, a resource list, and a sales program for the best stepfamily literature. They held their first positive, celebrating, informative, low-cost national annual meeting for stepfamilies in Colorado in 1982; since then, meetings have been held in Black Mountain, North Carolina in 1983, in Asilomar, California in 1984, and Washington, D.C. in 1985. Chapters and families network and exchange ideas in workshops on diverse topics—Sex in Stepfamilies, Discipline, Dealing with Conflict, Stepmother Burnout, and so on. It is interesting to note that although stepfather families are the largest statistical group, the membership of Stepfamily Association groups seems to be more often of the stepmother household. Speculations on the reason for this include that the stepmothers of live-in or visiting children are more centrally addressed with the primary parenting concerns. It is likely that in this culture mothers still have the most central role in family life, or that stepmother families more often consider themselves stepfamilies than stepfather families, who are more likely to "pass."

There is a body of knowledge accumulating from these groups on how to organize self-help efforts and community supports for families. The simplest wisdom about how to focus a group of stepfamilies in lively and productive exchange is to begin by asking, "What is *your* situation?" Remarried families usually have complex (and often amusing) descriptions of how they live, and when they begin there they are in the middle of a very personal exchange.

A common observation of SAA members is that the structure of a family does not determine its health or pathology. For many families the normalization, support, and information shared in literature or in group contacts prevents the intensification of problems or the development of symptomatology or anxiety about normal family events. For others it identifies more clearly those issues or patterns or binds that are in need of special focus with a therapist. Remarried families often seek therapists who are themselves remarried or have special interest in stepfamilies, because they have been misunderstood or discouraged when treated as "all families" (first-marriage families) by mental health professionals.

Literature

Ten years ago there was little written on remarriage in the professional literature and very little for popular consumption. *Living in Step* (Roosevelt and Lofas, 1976) was one of the earliest books available for those interested in remarriage. In the last 10 years, professional and popular resources have proliferated more rapidly than bibliographies are updated. The interest with which persons approaching or involved in remarriage seek written materials on their situation compares with the interest in books on pregnancy, childbirth, and infant development. These seem to be life stages so profound that seeking information and collecting opinions and experiences of others—lay or expert—is a common response even of those usually less "intellectual" in their approach.

Even therapists who would generally avoid directing clients to informational sources—assuming either that they have found them already or that "intellectual" approaches won't touch "emotional" issues—might do well to reconsider or experiment with that position in families approaching or involved in remarriage, especially if a social group is not available. The normalizing functions of information and the support of stories from other explorers make the map easier to design.

There are several highly informative and readable sources that clinicians would do well to screen for their own consciousness and for possible recommendation to client families. Some of the most concise *professional* overviews of theory and research, *must-reads* for consciousness of stepfamily issues, are:

- The chapter "Forming a Remarried Family" by Carter and McGoldrick (1980) in *The Family Life Cycle*.
- *Step-Families: Myths and Realities*, by Visher and Visher (1980).
- *Treating the Remarried Family* by Sager, C., Brown, H., Crohn, H., Engel, T., Rodstein, E., Walker, L. (1983).
- The *Stepfamily Bulletin*, a quarterly publication by the Stepfamily Association of America, Inc.

Some selected references of the popular literature for acquainting the professional and those most often recommended to clients are, for children:

- *What am I Doing in a Step Family?*, by Burman (1982).
- *All About Families the Second Time Around*, by Lewis (1980).
- *What's Special About Our Stepfamily*, by Burt and Burt (1983).

and for adults:

* *Second Marriage: Make it Happy, Make it Last!*, by Stewart and Jacobsen (1958).
* *How to Win as a Stepfamily*, by Visher and Visher (1980).
* *Making It as a Stepparent: New roles/new rules*, by Berman (1982).
* *Remarriage: A Family Affair*, by Messinger (1984).

Own Family History Experience

The third "nontherapy" resource is also a favorite "therapy" resource for certain groups of family therapists—most often those trained in Bowenian theory or by Boszormenyi-Nagy and Sparks, who emphasize the importance of the powerful ongoing concepts of a multigenerational family experience passed on in an emotional chain (of triangles or loyalty ledgers) in an evolutionary manner. This is the "Ask your Mother—or grandmother or Aunt Mabel" approach to normalizing or distinguishing the old and new of any life situation. Sometimes reviewing history is less face-to-face and more an examination of data or stories or folklore.

Both the wisdom and the pitfalls of the past generations' experiences can be consulted or considered with the outcome of greater freedom to accept and integrate or depart and change the patterns. Sometimes history will reveal "We have been here before and we're good at it," or "We've survived," or "In this family this is normal," or "It's a first." An event has contextual meaning in the family's history over time.

A bewildered stepmother of a 13-year-old daughter was encouraged to review the experiences of her broader clan for clues to her dilemmas. Her own parents had never been separated, divorced, or stepparents, nor had any of her father's siblings. Like her nuclear family, the extended family had been viewed as intact, having "no problems." Although several of the mother's siblings had experienced various family structures, only males had been divorced, remarried, or stepparents and all had been extruded or cut off. While not a resource for discussion without efforts to bridge these cutoffs, this review provided a clue that in this family those family relationships other than first-marriage families tended to be seen as "less real"—"not O.K."—and were distanced or cut off. It helped identify some of the fear and shame associated with her position. Also, she was the first *woman* in her family to be part of a multiple-marriage family.

Looking *more* closely, while it was true that her father's siblings had never experienced a divorce, he did have a brother whose wife had died of cancer, leaving him with a 9-year-old daughter and a 12-year-old son. These first cousins to the young stepmother had experienced the loss of their mother. There paternal grandmother had gone to care for them until their father remarried. He remarried a woman who had not been married before; they then had two more children. This aunt and uncle and grown cousins and the consideration of their lives provided insights, support, models, mistakes, and encouragement.

The female cousin revealed her feelings toward *her* stepmother, which gave the young stepmother insights about her stepdaughter's experience when more children were born.

Her male cousin reported the loss of his maternal grandparents after the remarriage, which alerted her to the pain, loss, and possible cutoff for her stepdaughter if she continued to avoid her natural mother's family.

There were many other examples and experiences available in this one family, but this glimpse is enough to illustrate the fruitfulness of discerning the antecedents.

COMMON CLINICAL ERRORS

Ten Ways to Fail as a Therapist to the Remarried Family

1. Overlook the difference between a first-married household and a remarried household.
2. Identify the membership accurately but get caught up in the focus on one member—treating the stepmother's depression, the adolescent runaway's behavior, the school failure.
3. Assume that past is past and has no bearing on the present.
4. (a) Join in the presenting member(s) emotional biases about who are the "good guys" and who are the "bad guys," the victims, and the villains.
   (b) Assume ex-spouses cannot do better negotiating a respectful relationship.
5. (a) Assume that any parent not present is not interested or powerful in the child(ren)'s lives.
   (b) Assume that any child not present is not powerful in the lives of presenting members.
   (c) Assume that the previous partners are inconsequential in the present marriage.
6. (a) Assume that extended clan members of divorced family systems are enemies.
   (b) Fail to consider positive relationships and possible losses of the ex-in-law systems.
7. Assume that, if people are cut off from each other, they are no longer important to each other.
8. Assume that the automatic (or present) patterns of visiting are the best for everyone; don't question these—if people are out of touch, they were never important.
9. Treat individuals or dyads; forget about triangles.
10. Consider the remarried structure to be the only possible problem and miss other normal problems of family life.

Examples of Clinical Failures

The scene is a large gathering of family therapists viewing a videotape of a well-known family therapist. The intervention was from a structural theoretical position. A father, Jim, a teenage boy, also Jim, and a depressed-looking mother, Ann, receive instructions that Ann should *look* at her husband this week rather than at her son. No one presenting the tape acknowledged the history that, although Jim and the son had the same name, they had only become related with the remarriage of the mother. A few in the audience revealed this later, and also that the couple separated the next week.

There are many family interventions that stimulate powerful changes without wasting unnecessary time in review of history. Behavioral and structural strategic approaches often provide shortcuts to families focused on a particular symptom. Two pitfalls of this approach with recently remarried families exist. First, failing to clarify and acknowledge the existing structure may lead to an intervention with little to do with the existing players and without requesting the significant absent others if a household group presents—as in this example. Second, the child-focused symptom will often be reinforced if an intervention is designed around the child's behavior. A couple in early remarriage is often already overfocused on the children and their needs or protests and underacknowledging of broader resources of family. The historical perspective may provide clues to broadening the focus and intervening in the most powerful triangles.

The scene is a supervision group of family therapists. They have not usually presented to a consultant using a family chart. Four of the eight cases they present are remarriages (or recouplings without marriage). In none was the whole marriage chain being explored.

Of these, one couple, Melanie and Eric (both with previous families that they left for each other), had been seen in this setting over a 3-year period. There was a romantic supportiveness of the couple relationship by the young, unmarried therapist. She had *never* inquired about Eric's contacts with his ex-wife and did not know the number or ages of his children, who were in the local area. Only one of Melanie's children was known, John, who was receiving treatment at this same family community health center. Melanie continued to serve her children in the home, which she left, continuing to do the grocery shopping and the laundry. The therapist presented this as inappropriate and threatening to the relationship between Eric and Melanie. The original couple (or family) had never been seen together. The "story" of neither first marriage had ever been reviewed.

It is surprisingly common for a therapist to "miss" a total picture of the situation by not asking the factual questions that go beyond the client's presentation of "who counts," "what hurts," or "what needs to change." It is our belief that if our clients knew the right questions or the helpful focus that might unlock situations, they would not need us.

The scene is a family therapist's office. A mother (divorced) and stepfather (widowed) are consulting about the acting-out behavior of one of her sons. They have recently tried to combine his four and her four children in one common household. They are referred by the psychologist at the son's private school. The therapist requests a joint meeting with the contacting couple, the son, the son's father, and his new wife. In that session he makes a suggestion that the son live with his father and new stepmother. The case explodes, with threats of lawsuits eventually resulting.

The therapist had not accounted for the fact that the second wife (step-mother) had never *met* the first wife until the joint meeting in the clinic and had not (recently) married prepared to take on another child. He had not accounted for the fact that the divorced couple had been involved in extensive custody battles to reach the present arrangement. He had not been supportive or even respectfully neutral about the ordinary struggles in the remarried household. Those who had come for help felt betrayed, delivered up to the "enemy" by an expert they were to pay. Thus, an ordinary move in resourcing a crisis from "extended" kin became an exaggerated crisis from failing to acknowledge the current loyalty structure of the family and their developmental stage, Going Back.

Another common error is omitting the remarried spouse from reworking of the original family issues without preparation or permission. A second wife or husband who comes to see that "they"—the original couple—need to sort some things out for the problems to settle down will often support or tolerate such meetings (alone or with the therapist). If the present relationship is not stable enough, it will need attention first or the present spouse will undermine any moving toward the original family because he/she views it as a threat of further loss.

The most frequent error of the literature and of clinical language is the perpetuation of the term "single-parent family." A household may have but one parent, but if we don't join in discounting the resource of the noncustodial parent, we will see "two-household families" and "resident and nonresident parents" where single parents used to be.

HOPE

Finally, becoming redefined as a family may result in symptoms and conflict that would indicate much more severe dysfunction in a first-marriage family. When crises in the early phases of remarriage in the system are presented to school or mental health agencies, it is extremely important that awareness of normative crises be provided by therapists and counsellors—lest they increase the anxiety of the family and destroy its most essential and fragile resource, hope. The therapist needs to be aware that this fragile resource is necessary for survival. It is the hope that pushes the family forward and that causes them to seek help. It is the hope that is most vulnerable when the normal chaos of adjustment ensues. ("We've failed before, we'll *never* make it" is the threat.)

Born of loss, the remarriage is a willingness to go on. Hope takes a leap of faith—a willingness to make another try at something that was probably a very painful or disappointing experience. Thus restitution is one of the goals of remarriage, a complicated goal because none of the members can ever replace the original family. The hope for renewal then rests on the possibility that all members can eventually become fully functioning family members willing to give and receive and build a common experience. If they succeed, they no longer exist as fragments but as part of a different kind of complete structure. Each gains additional people in his/her life as resources to continue to grow together.

For to him that is joined to all the living there is hope. (Eccles 9:4)

REFERENCES

Boszormenyi-Nagy, I. & Spark, G. M. *Invisible loyalties*. New York: Harper and Row, 1973.

Bowen, M. *Family therapy in clinical practice*. New York: Jason Aronson, 1978.

Berman, C. *Making it as a stepparent; New roles/new rules*. Garden City: Doubleday, 1980.

Berman, C. *What am I doing in a stepfamily?*, 1982.

Bradt, J. & Moynihan, C. J. Opening the Safe: A study of the child-focused family. In J. Bradt & C. J. Moynihan (Eds.) *Systems therapy*, Washington, D.C.: H/R Productions, 1971.

Bradt, J. *The family diagram*, Washington, D.C.: H/R Productions, 1980.

Burt, R. & S. M. Burt. *What's special about our stepfamily:* Garden City, N.Y.: Doubleday, 1983.

Cherlin, A. J. *Marriage divorce and remarriage*. Cambridge, Massachusetts: Harvard University Press, 1981.

Cherlin, A. J. Remarriage as an incomplete institution, *American Journal of Sociology*, 1978, 644–650.

Glick, P. C. Remarriage: Some recent changes and variations, *Journal of Family Issues*, 1980, *1*, 455–478.

Glick, P. C. Personal Comments: Masters lecture. The Annual Meeting of the National Council on Family Relations. Washington, D.C., 1982.

Karpel, M. *Family process*. Family Secrets: I. Conceptual & ethical issues in the relational context. II. Ethical and practical considerations in therapeutic management. 1980, *19*, 295–306.

Jacobson, D. S. Stepfamilies: Myths and realities, *Social Work*, 1979, *24*(3), 202–207.

Lewis, H. C. *All about families—The second time around*. Atlanta, Ga.: Peachtree, 1980.

Lewis, H. C. Clinical intervention with stepfamilies. Unpublished Paper, Lecture Groome Center, Washington, D.C., 1980.

McGoldrick, M. & Carter, E. A. Forming a remarried family. In E. A. Carter & M. McGoldrick (Eds.) *The family life cycle*. New York: Gardner, 1980.

Messinger, L. *Remarriage: A family affair*. New York: Plenum Press, 1984.

Monthly Vital Statistics Report, National Center for Health Statistics, 1984, *32* (11 Suppl).

O'Brien, J. T. & O'Brien, G. *A redeeming state: A handbook for couples preparing for remarriage in the church*. New York: Paulist Press, 1983.

Pasley, K. An overview of remarriage & stepparents: A summary of findings. Unpublished paper. Presented American Orthopsychiatric Association, Toronto, Canada, April 7–9, 1984.

Pasley, K. & Ihinger-Tallman, M. Stress in remarried families. *Family Perspectives*, 1982, *16*(4), 181–190.

Papernow, P. L. The stepfamily cycle: An experimental model of stepfamily development. *Family Relations*, 1984, *33*, 355–363.

Reiss, D. The working family: A researcher's view of health in the household, *American Journal of Psychiatry*, 1982, *139*, 1412–1420.

Roosevelt, R. & Lofas, J. *Living in step*. New York: Stein and Day, 1976.

Sager, C., Brown, H., Crohn, H., Crohn, T., Engel, E., Rodstein, E., & Walker, L. *Treating the remarried family*. New York: Bruner Mazel, 1983.

Stepfamily Bulletin, Stepfamily Association of America, Baltimore, Md., 1979–85.

Smith, R. (Ed.) *The subtle revolution*, Washington, D.C.: The Urban Institute, 1979.

Stewart, R. B. & Jacobson B. *Second marriage: Make it happy, make it last*. New York: W. W. Norton, 1985.

Visher, E. B. & Visher, J. S. Stepfamilies: A guide to working with stepparents and stepchildren. New York: Brunner/Mizel, Inc., 1979.

Visher, E. B. & Visher, J. S. *Stepfamilies: Myths and realities*. Seacaus, N.C.: Citadel Press, 1980.

Visher, E. B. & Visher, J. S. *How to win as a stepfamily*. New York: Dembner Books, 1980.

Wolin, S. & Bennett, L. Family rituals, *Family Process, 23*(3), 1984, 401–420.

CHAPTER 10

The Therapist's Personal Impact on Family Resources

Eric S. Strauss

Say these words out loud—closeness, trust, acceptance, belonging, loyalty, home. The ideas and associations sparked off by the sight and sound of these words convey the warm force of the idealized family life. We all possess an inherent desire for family, to belong to something bigger than ourselves, to be loved, to be able to make sacrifices for another, to have a sense of history and of the future. We are most fully ourselves within our families. There we experience our most intense emotions, from anguish to pride, and there we are offered the opportunity to succeed or fail in an arena of ultimate significance. We may discover our nobility or our culpability, or another's gentleness or their cruelty, and over time we encounter a wide range of human qualities in ourselves and other family members. Family life is fundamentally important to us and possesses a unique and penetrating power.

No wonder, then, that we have such high expectations of family life, and experience such bitter anger when disappointed. Much of the history of psychotherapy has been devoted to an examination of the family's failure, a form of grieving for the idealized family. One stage of such a process has been a rage directed at families, which were viewed as malevolent entities. Families have been thought of not as sanctuaries but as prisons, and the goal has been to escape. While these phobic attitudes toward families accurately express the dangers and destructive forces potentially at work in family life, they miss completely our inherent desire for the family and the family's own potential for good, for the expression of life-enhancing values, feelings, and behaviors.

CONCEPTUALIZING FAMILY RESOURCES

There are inherent healing properties within the family, which can simultaneously benefit the individuals who comprise the family unit and the family group

Eric S. Strauss, Ph.D. Private Practice, West Springfield, Massachusetts.

as a whole. When we think of family resources we are referring to these natural healing qualities within families. As clinicians, we see families whose resources or healing potential is buried under the debris of distress and unhappiness. Our task is to assess and treat the specific problem, to identify the family's potential resources, and to see if the family can be helped to encounter and experience these resources for themselves. We hope to create a set of conditions such that a natural healing process can occur within the family. We are catalysts for change and the moderators of change, but the potential and desire for change comes from the family's own needs, feelings, and beliefs.

A parallel exists between this family healing process and the principles of healing that apply to an individual's organic or psychological ills. In both family and individual healing, the clinician assumes that there are natural healing forces that can be mobilized by his/her correct therapeutic approaches. In 1888 Hippolyte Bernheim, a French physician, wrote an insightful book on the healing process and therapeutic influence titled *Suggestive Therapeutics*. Bernheim believed that:

> diseases are cured, when they can be cured, by their natural biological evolution. Our ordinary therapeutic methods consist in putting the organism in a condition such that the *restitutio ad integrum* may take place; we suppress the pain, we modify function, we let the organ rest, we calm the fever, we retard the pulse, we induce sleep, we encourage secretion and excretion, and, acting thus, we permit nature the healer, or, to speak in modern language, we permit the activity of the forces and the properties inherent in the biological elements to accomplish their work. (pp. 408–409)

Bernheim believed in the force of natural healing tendencies, but knew that the healer must play an active and crucial role in facilitating the healing process. So it is with families and the healing of families. The therapist tries to identify resources in the family as it is and to assess the family's ability to recognize and utilize these resources in their healing. The nature of the therapist's personal impact on family resources is the subject of this chapter, but before considering the therapist's role and style we should be more specific about the very nature of family resources.

The concept of the family's inherent healing properties is abstract, and each therapist must organize his/her thinking around the specific family resources that seem most significant, inclusive, and observable. It is not necessary for the therapist to consult a lengthy checklist of family resources, although such a catalogue could be compiled. Instead the therapist can identify for himself/herself those healing or life-enhancing properties of family life that seem particularly powerful and important. Different therapists concentrate on different resources, but my sense is that the roots of all resources can be traced to the soothing themes of home and belonging.

The family resources on which I concentrate include (1) shared history, (2) loyalty, (3) humor, and (4) hopefulness. History and loyalty are thematically joined by their emphasis on belonging or connectedness, on the establishing of a secure foundation. Humor and hopefulness, on the other hand, are both buoyant qualities, light in tone and aimed toward the future. This group of four major resources is balanced between the need to settle in and the need to venture forth, and so reflects both major movements of family life.

Shared History

A family gathers, two sons and a daughter, all grown with assorted spouses and children, to bury their mother. Also attending, at their mother's request, is their father, estranged from the family for over 30 years. The middle son, named Ezra, is unmarried, owns a restaurant, and is perenially trying to bring his family together (physically and emotionally) for dinners at his restaurant. Ezra arranges such a dinner after his mother's funeral, and for the first time his father also attends. This situation occurs at the conclusion of Anne Tyler's novel *Dinner at the Homesick Restaurant*, and throughout the novel Tyler's characters reveal the complex power of family life.

This family is by no means an idealized group. Beck Tull, the father, deserted the family with no warning. He subsequently sent occasional letters with news of himself to his wife Pearl, but maintained no contact with his three children. Pearl was a controlling, emotionally labile person; Cody, the oldest child, is bitter and resentful about his past; Ezra never marries but tries to provide the secure comfort of home for patrons of his restaurant; and Jenny, the youngest, marries three times and has great difficulty establishing her own sense of home. The one thing the Tull family does possess is a shared history, a history that is the fabric of family life and the setting for each individual's personal experience. " 'All we have is each other,' Ezra would say, justifying one of his everlasting dinners. 'We've got to stick together; nobody else has the same past that we have' " (p. 298).

Family memories, good and bad, provide us with a sense of belonging, of having roots in the past. We come to know ourselves and others through such memories, which build upon each other to form patterns, assumptions, and beliefs. Scenes of family life stand out in recollection, touchstones for our sense of self and the world. Tragedies, difficulties overcome, milestones, happy times, peaceful times—these all comprise the fabric of family life. A boy on vacation with his family wins a prize at a carnival game and proudly gives it to his younger sister. The memory becomes part of family lore, a source of pride for the boy, happiness and gratitude for the girl, and warmth and satisfaction for the parents over the happy moment and their son's generosity. These incidents create a world, a world that exists in each family member's mind, a world each person belongs to and is part of.

When the power and significance of a shared history is ignored or rejected, it is usually because painful memories predominate. A person tries to define himself/herself as totally distinct from the family and its history, but this proves to be impossible and the attempt severs the connection with the positive emotions that exist in some form in every situation. Turning again to *Dinner at the Homesick Restaurant*, we read of Cody's attempt to deny his family and categorize all its history as pathological:

> "You think we're a family," Cody said, turning back [to his father]. "You think we're some jolly, situation-comedy family when we're in particles, torn apart, torn all over the place and our mother was a witch."
>
> "Oh, Cody," Ezra said.
>
> "A raving, shrieking, unpredictable witch," Cody told Beck. "She slammed us against the wall and called us scum and vipers, said she wished us dead, shook us till our teeth rattled, screamed in our faces. We never knew from one day to the next, was she all right? Was she not? The tiniest thing could set her off. 'I'm going to throw you through that window, she used to tell me. I'll look out that window and laugh at your brains splashed all over the pavement.'"
>
> The main course was set before them, on tiptoe by Mrs. Potter and another woman who smiled steadily, as if determined not to hear. But nobody picked up his fork. The baby crooned softly to a mushroom button. The other children watched Cody with horrified, bleached faces, while the grown-ups seemed to be thinking of something else. They kept their eyes lowered. Even Beck did.
>
> "It wasn't like that," Ezra said finally.
>
> "You're going to deny it?" Cody asked him.
>
> "No, but she wasn't always angry. Really she was angry very seldom, only a few times, widely spaced, that happened to stick in your mind."
>
> Cody felt drained. He looked at his dinner and found pink-centered lamb and bright vegetables—a perfect arrangement of colors and textures, one of Ezra's masterpieces, but he couldn't take a bite.
>
> "Think of the other side," Ezra told him. "Think of how she used to play Monopoly with us. Listened to Fred Allen with us. Sang that little song with you—what was the name of that song you two sang? Ivy, sweet Ivy . . . and you'd do a little soft-shoe. The two of you would link arms and soft-shoe into the kitchen."
>
> "Is that right!" said Beck. "I didn't remember Pearl could soft-shoe." (pp. 294–295)

From the threat of "brains splashed all over the pavement" to a "soft-shoe into the kitchen," the Tull family's memories run the gamut. Ezra is able to preserve the good while acknowledging the pain that existed in the family's past. Cody desperately tries to renounce the family, but can never get distance from his resentment and disappointment with family life. He is as much a part of the family's history as anyone, but has denied himself access to the resource of a shared past. Like his father, who left the family but continued to try to impress Pearl with his history of accomplishments, Cody lives the illusion of independence but is not confidently rooted in the world. His momentum in the world is drawn from his bitterness, not from a personal direction or strength. Cody is never free of the past, yet can draw no comfort from it.

A shared history can contribute to one's sense of identity and identification with the larger family group. Feelings of belonging, pride in the family's past, warm memories can sustain family members through individual and family crises. Efforts can be made to overcome family problems because the family's history is respected and warrants a serious commitment to persevere. Perhaps a lack of shared history adds to the difficulties of recombined families, who are mixing separate pasts while simultaneously creating a new history of their own.

Loyalty

Each of us hopes to experience the loyalty of others close to us, and hopes as well to be able to demonstrate such allegiance and concern to another. Faithful, respectful concern and support are potential strengths of family life. Loyalty is thematically connected to the concept of a shared history, since both emphasize belonging and the intertwining of self and family. A parent risks injury to protect a child; a sister sacrifices a kidney so her brother can live; a child shows support for a parent who has lost a job; a girl respects her younger brother's privacy and does not tell her closest friend about his bed-wetting; members of the family support and defend each other against criticism or attack from outside the family—these are all expressions of loyalty.

While a shared history provides each family member with a factual basis for a sense of belonging and rootedness, loyalty is demonstrated by specific actions and behaviors. These experiences become part of our shared past and help cement relationships and family strength. The phrases "stick up for" and "count on" are colloquialisms based on the theme of loyalty. "Will you be there for me?" is the question to which loyalty responds "Yes!"

At the conclusion of *Dinner at the Homesick Restaurant*, the long-absent father, Beck Tull, sneaks away from the family dinner after being angrily confronted by his oldest son Cody. Ezra, continually working for family unity, insists that the whole family search for Beck. A sense of family loyalty prevents the acceptance of Beck's disappearance:

> "Please!" said Ezra. "Please. For once, I want this family to finish a meal together. Why, every dinner we've ever had, something has gone wrong. Someone has left in a huff, or in tears, everything's fallen apart . . . Come on! Everybody out, cover the area, track him down! We could gather back here when we find him and take up where we left off."
>
> "Or," Cody pointed out, "we could finish the meal without him. That's always a possibility."
>
> But it wasn't; even he could see that. One empty place at the table ruined everything. The chair itself, with its harp-shaped wooden back, had a desolate, reproachful look. Slowly, people rose. (p. 297)

The Tull family sets off to reclaim one of its own, and it is the family, not only Ezra or a collection of individuals, that moves out to find Beck. All the shared history, layers of relationships, and feelings of loyalty that comprise the family create an entity pulsating with life and movement. Anne Tyler evokes such an image of the family in one of the final scenes in *Dinner at the Homesick*

Restaurant. After Cody has been the one to locate Beck, he turns and sees the rest of the family approaching:

> Cody, searching for something to say, happened to look toward Prima Street and see his family rounding the corner, opening like a fan. The children came first, running, and the teenagers loped behind, and the grown-ups—trying to keep pace—were very nearly running themselves, so that they all looked unexpectedly joyful. The drab colors of their funeral clothes turned their faces bright. The children's arms and legs flew out and the baby bounced on Joe's shoulders. Cody felt surprised and touched. He felt they were pulling him toward them—that it wasn't they who were traveling, but Cody himself. (p. 302)

Cody and Beck, the two outsiders, unable to accept a lack of perfection in family life, are found, drawn back into an imperfect but vibrant network of lives.

Humor

Humor has recently been noted to play a salutary role in the process of physical healing (Cousins, 1979), helping to create beneficial chemical changes within the individual, and the therapeutic value of humor has long been acknowledged in folk wisdom. A person who demonstrates a capacity for humor often has a healthy perspective on life, can keep issues in proportion, be flexible, and retain some hopefulness in a difficult world. A sense of humor, therefore, is a good prognostic sign for individual functioning.

In addition to its individual benefits, humor helps bond people in a healthy manner. To appreciate another's sense of humor requires a shared world view and perspective on life. We all let our guards down and relax when laughing, and this trusting behavior, when not exploited, helps us build confidence in our relationships. We demonstrate loyalty when we allow another to laugh, and laugh with them, without thoughts of personal advantage or manipulation. The act of laughter, physically and emotionally confirming as it is, creates a connection between people that over time conveys trust, warmth, and loyalty.

The existence of humor in family life helps family members feel they are part of a group that is loyal, sees the world similarly, and has a history together. Families have shared jokes or favorite anecdotes or humorous experiences, a legacy of smiles that makes family members feel warmly connected to the rest of the group. This constructive or therapeutic humor is in marked contrast to the humor of ridicule, disparagement, or sarcasm, which expresses bitterness and alienation. More than the sound of laughter is required for humor to possess a joining and enlivening capacity.

Hopefulness

Each person and each family has to be able to aim toward the future, to persist even in spite of disappointments and setbacks. Being hopeful does not mean being Pollyannaish, since naive idealism is only the flip side of despair. Realistic hopefulness is both an individual characteristic and a family trait. The interactions between family members can build hope even if those same individuals have separately been disheartened. To see an expression of loyalty, to experience a sense of belonging, to recall a shared history are all relational moments that can contribute to the rekindling of individual hopefulness.

Likewise, one person's hopeful attitude and behavior can help create an atmosphere within a family where hope can arise. Ezra, in *Dinner at the Homesick Restaurant*, is a lone voice of hopefulness throughout much of the novel, continually planning family meals that end in disaster, but eventually he succeeds in influencing his family to accept and understand their relatedness and make the best of it. Hopefulness in a family implies energy or liveliness, and this is certainly conveyed in the kinetic image of family joining with which the book closes.

MOBILIZING FAMILY RESOURCES

When families come for therapy, the therapist must resist the tendency to focus exclusively on problems and conflicts. Every family possesses a shared history. Feelings of loyalty exist in all families at some level. Humor and hopefulness may be evident, but these qualities can be easily obscured or obliterated by conflict and dissatisfaction. The therapist should search out these family resources, and should try to create an atmosphere where latent strengths might be expressed. A structured family evaluation (Karpel & Strauss, 1983) provides the family with an opportunity to discuss their strengths as well as problems, since the therapist will be routinely inquiring about the facts of everyday life and positive family experiences. The therapist's active direction of this initial phase of treatment relaxes the family, balances the focus between the presenting problem and overall family functioning, and allows the therapist to observe the multiple facets of the family's interactions.

The therapist should be a careful observer of the family's strengths, and should provide the family with opportunities to describe its more successful and cohesive moments. In addition to being alert to the family's positive comments and directly inquiring about satisfying aspects of the family's life, the therapist also wants to establish an environment in which the family can feel safe, understood, and capable of being helped. In such an atmosphere, the family has an increased chance of discovering its strengths as a unit.

The therapist's style, personality, and presence have a powerful impact on the family's experience in treatment, and the concept of "therapeutic influence" is a relevant consideration for therapists of all schools. This chapter's primary focus is not on the therapist's theoretical orientation or specific interventions (*what* he/she does), but on general principles of therapy and the therapist's role that underlie effective treatment of any persuasion (*how* he/she does it).

Therapeutic Influence

The concept of therapeutic influence has a long tradition in the literature of medicine and psychotherapy. An individual's attitude toward self and others, his/her beliefs and fears about his/her illness or problem, can be largely responsible for the creation of the illness and can contribute to the exacerbation and intractability of such conditions. Healers of all types—spiritual, medical, or psychological—have through the centuries attempted to *capture the imagination* of their "patients" and thereby influence them to change their beliefs. An increase in hopefulness, faith in the treatment prescribed, or faith in the "doctor" himself/herself can create physical and psychological changes that lead to healing. Stressing the significance of the doctor–patient relationship in the healing process, Benson and Epstein (1975) commented that the most successful doctors are those who have faith in the effectiveness of their treatments, communicate their enthusiasm to the patient, have strong expectations of specific effects, are self-confident and attentive, and spend time with the patient. The literature on suggestion, the placebo effect, and the "doctor–patient" relationship deals specifically with these issues (Adler & Hammet, 1973; Cassell, 1979; Frank, 1978).

When treating a family, the therapist needs to carefully consider his/her professional stance, the type of impression he/she is making on the family. Once again the words of Bernheim, published in 1888, retain their relevance for a contemporary understanding of the doctor–patient relationship:

> To console a patient, to sustain his courage, to drive away from his mind the great anxiety which consumes him, is often to react efficaciously upon the disease. By the quiet persuasive voice of the physician the patient is restored as by a salutary balm, feels his confidence arise and his discomfort disappear. . . . Thus is explained, or rather conceived, the immense influence which a physician of tact may exercise over a patient by this moral medicine . . . (p. 412)

But what is therapeutic "tact"? What should the family therapist in particular keep in mind as he/she prepares to meet the family?

For the therapist to have a positive influence on a family a prime emphasis must be on the nature of his/her relationship with the group. Individual forms of treatment draw energy from the one-to-one encounter between the "doctor" and "patient," the intense and private interaction that the healer can employ therapeutically. The family therapist does not have this charged leverage available, but can carefully shape his/her professional stance so as to maximize alliance building with each family member and his/her consequent influence on the family.

The first contact with the family usually occurs when one family member calls to arrange an appointment. The therapist should take time with this call in order to learn about the presenting problem and to schedule the first evaluation session (Karpel & Strauss, 1983). Even on the phone, the therapist must be aware of the impression he/she is making. There is a risk in sounding either too "professional," formal, and abrupt or too casual and friendly. The overly professional approach, using technical terms and an impersonal tone of voice, may distance the therapist from the caller and impair alliance building. The overly friendly and flexible style may diminish the therapist's stature and cause the caller to lose confidence in the therapist's expertise.

The therapist should be alert to his/her tone of voice, language, and energy level on the phone. With a warm and pleasant tone, avoiding jargon or professional terms, the therapist can actively draw out the caller and effectively manage the phone call. He/she can sound alive and hopeful about the value of the meeting arranged with the caller's family, and strike an appropriate balance between expertise and approachability.

In the sessions themselves, the therapist wants to obtain the family's confidence in his/her professional expertise and personal trustworthiness. The family therapist must convey an air of competence and confidence, but the means of doing so can vary considerably. A charismatic personality, a warm and accepting manner, a precise and consistent theory, or an incisive ability to formulate the case and intervene in the family's functioning all may be components of an effective professional stance in family therapy. The key is that the therapist must be "alive" in the session, must have a presence; he/she must reach an accurate understanding of the family's issues and effectively communicate this to them. By his/her personality and ideas, the therapist must become an important person to the family. Without this entry into the family system, the therapist will be unable to successfully influence the expression and development of the family's resources.

Building Alliances

A core component of becoming a significant factor in the family's eyes is the therapist's ability to build alliances with family members. This skill brings to mind the circus performer whose task it is to keep six or eight of ten plates spinning on top of an equal number of tall sticks. He quickly sets them off, one by one, and by the time he's gone down the entire line the first plates are beginning to wobble. Off he goes to give them each a spin, and the next several minutes are spent in frenetic activity back and forth, with numerous close calls and gasps from the audience. Success is achieved when the performer decides to end the run, and one by one collects his props with a dramatic flourish.

In more subtle fashion, the family therapist faces a similar task. He/she must try to build some kind of working alliance with all family members, who are likely to be in conflict with each other. The principles of therapeutic neutrality and objectivity are clear and well established, but such an attitude is actualized by the therapist's concrete efforts, not inner intentions. Each family member must be carefully listened to, their opportunity to speak gently guarded by the therapist. Each participant must feel that he/she has been heard and understood.

The therapist should monitor each person's behavior and attitude, and be alert for signs of distress or dissatisfaction. If a plate is wobbly, the therapist can turn directly to it and give it a spin. Sometimes this can be accomplished within the flow of the session; at other times it requires that some special time be discreetly set aside for a separate conversation with the family member in question. The goal is to gain each family member's trust, or, short of that, to at least not have engendered their mistrust.

The W family—parents, three daughters, and one son, all in their 20s—came to therapy with a host of problems. Mrs. W was depressed; Mr. W was accused by his children of being verbally and at times physically abusive; one daughter was alcoholic and another had severe ulcerative colitis. There was a history of little intrafamily support and few wholesome alliances. Initial therapy sessions were seen by the family members as a chance to present their cases against others in the family.

Just from the standpoint of alliance building, the therapist worked hard to clear a space for each person's comments, and was respectful of all positions taken. At the same time, the therapist was quite active, preventing confrontations from going too far. Destructiveness was at least partially contained; the therapist appeared in charge and capable of dealing with intense emotion; each person's ideas were valued by the therapist; and any family member appearing distressed or confused received prompt support or clarification from the therapist.

Particular effort was placed on making a connection with the two "culprits" in the rest of the family's eyes, Mr. W and the alcoholic daughter. These two were often accused by the others of being insensitive, selfish, and hostile toward the family. They were by self-report the least enthusiastic about family treatment. The therapist listened supportively to their views of the situation, drew them out with interest and respect, and clearly showed that he assumed they were responsible adults who were concerned about their family. While doing this, he monitored the reactions of other family members, and drew them in when it appeared they were becoming anxious or angered by this sympathetic treatment of the problem members.

With the therapist's active assistance, both Mr. W and his daughter were able to make statements and express feelings that were "out of character" for them in the usual family scenario. They disclosed feelings of concern for the well-being of other family members, spoke positively about past family experiences, and expressed loyalty to the family. These two "identified patients" were thereby able to increase their own awareness of their caring and concern for the family, and the rest of the group had their negative assumptions about these two individuals challenged. The confrontational tone in the session eased with these disclosures, and the more relaxed atmosphere allowed some humor to enter the discussion.

This early shift in assumptions and atmosphere provided a positive basis from which the W family could respond to the therapist's recommendations and proceed with the work of therapy. The therapist stressed the need for strengthening the sibling alliance (specifically suggesting that the siblings arrange a time to get together as a group outside the home), and also encouraged Mr. and Mrs. W to go out as a couple and seek some relaxation away from the hurly-burly of the home. The therapist based these early recommendations on his perception of a marital rift, with each spouse having looked for allies among the children. The W family was more likely to be receptive to the therapist's suggestions because family strengths had been identified and acknowledged. The mutual expression and awareness of family resources helped create a more hopeful attitude within the family and increased the likelihood of change in their patterns of relationship.

The R family came for evaluation because of concern over the functioning of the only child, a 12-year-old boy. Mr. R was worried about the boy's serious demeanor and feared he was depressed. Mrs. R minimized this concern, and was troubled by the risk of creating a problem just by coming in for the sessions. Their son was noncommital about the therapy session and denied being depressed.

In view of Mrs. R's concerns and the son's apparent indifference, the therapist knew that alliance building was going to be a crucial early key to the therapy. He tried to acknowledge each parent's position, placing their feelings in the context of their concern for their son. One was worried about the boy's current condition, the other about the impact of the sessions on the boy's emotional state.

The therapist stated that he could not immediately resolve this difference of opinion, but could reassure Mr. R that the possibility of depression would be explored as well as reassure Mrs. R that this would be done in a delicate and sensitive manner that would not prove to be acutely stressful to their son. These statements were not made in a meek or defensive manner, but were expressed with confidence, energy, and hopefulness about the value of the assessment to the R family. By focusing on each parent's loyalty to the boy, the therapist avoided being trapped in an early argument about the value of treatment and set a more positive tone for the meeting.

Effective alliance building with each parent, aided by emphasizing their mutual concern for their son, allowed the therapist to gain a more complete understanding of the family's issues in subsequent sessions. Through an individual session with each spouse, along with a couples meeting, the therapist learned of the R's marital difficulties. Mrs. R was upset and worried about their marriage, feeling that Mr. R was emotionally unavailable to her. As a result, she felt especially hurt and slighted by his intense concern and sensitivity toward their son's emotional situation. Mr. R was dissatisfied with numerous aspects of the marriage, felt his wife blamed him for many of her own problems, and had directed most of his emotional energy toward his son.

The therapist was able to tell the R couple that their son, while not clinically depressed, was extremely worried about the state of their marriage and about his mother's emotional upset. Because of his feelings of loyalty, he put on a cheery front with her while appearing more somber and demoralized when alone with his father. He also felt some guilt as a result of Mr. R's being primarily involved with him rather than with Mrs. R. The therapist recommended that the most effective way of relieving the pressure on their son was for the R couple to deal directly with their marital problems. This would also be aimed at benefiting the couple, but the recommendation was accepted at this point largely due to Mr. and Mrs. R's concern for their son. Without this resource having been emphasized and utilized in the case formulation, the R couple would have been unlikely at that point to have agreed to marital therapy.

Humor

Another way in which the therapist gains the family's trust and creates a comfortable atmosphere in which resources may be uncovered involves the use of humor. We have noted that the family's humor is a major resource, but many families are initially unlikely to bring humor into the therapy sessions. They may be preoccupied with the problem situation, be out of contact with their potential for humor, or feel the therapist has no interest in the lighter side of family life. During the evaluation, the therapist's inquiries about routine or positive aspects of family life may draw out some smiles and laughter from the family. When this occurs, the therapist should respond in kind and create a lighter moment in the therapy. This may help the family capable of expressing humor to feel that it is permissible to do so even during the work of therapy.

When the therapist and family smile or laugh together, a sense of ease and relaxation, and a more trusting atmosphere, is created. Laughter is physically relaxing to the family and to the therapist. For the therapist working alone (without a cotherapist or observers), such moments can have a rejuvenating effect during a demanding experience. The solo practitioner usually has few opportunities for a relaxed deep breath or a moment off-duty, and so building some humor into the sessions can be particularly restorative. The therapist can join the family in this fashion, and be viewed as someone with whom family members can be comfortable. Even during these pleasant interludes, however, the therapist should remain aware of the need for a "proper professional stance." Should the therapist become too light in tone, laugh too long or too boisterously, or detour significantly from the family's agenda, he/she will lose esteem in the family's eyes and jeopardize their confidence in him/her.

Some families offer little in the way of levity to the therapist, and their grim and discouraged demeanor poses a threat to the treatment. A family therapy session without at least one good laugh or real smile is a difficult experience for everyone involved, and when this occurs the therapist can usually take the blame. The therapist may have been drawn into the family's morass of bitterness and been demoralized by the group's sense of hopelessness. Or the therapist may have hesitated in creating a lighter moment for fear of offending the family and being rejected by them. In either case, grim sessions can drain away potential resources, and humor and hopefulness may be especially difficult to rekindle down the road.

The therapist should try to shift the emotional tone of a too-grim meeting, and can do so in a way that is not disrespectful to the serious group before him/ her. These are not instances for one's favorite joke or anecdote, however, and the therapist should be sensitive to the subtle ways in which he/she can shift the group's mood. The therapist's smile alone can be an effective trigger for tension reduction. Smiling while responding to a benign remark made by a family member can encourage the family to relax.

A teenager might comment briefly that his daily chore is taking out the trash, and the therapist could say with a warm smile, "That definitely sounds like the highlight of your day." When a father comments on the fighting that occurs each morning between his teenage children while they wait for the bathroom, the therapist could say, again with a smile, "Ah, morning sounds like a lively time in your home. (*Turning to the mother*) What are you doing while the kids are stacked up like cordwood in the hall?"

In another family, all members had noted the father's recurrent use of the expression "police the area" when he wanted the house cleaned. After listening to this phrase repeated three or four times by various family members, the therapist said, "Well, we've clearly established that you have the most policed area in the neighborhood." In this instance, the therapist's smile was directed at the father, to diminish the possibility that he might feel offended or ridiculed by the therapist's remark. By relating in an appropriately humorous way with the family, the therapist puts them in touch with a family resource and becomes part of their experience of this positive quality. Humor is one resource that the therapist can become a small part of, and so is an especially effective area for trust and alliance building.

The Therapist as Editor

The therapist's personal impression on the family is one key to facilitating the expression of family resources. His/her tactfulness, energy level, tone of voice, alliance building skills, and humor all help establish a constructive atmosphere. Another key to the therapist's impact on family resources is his/her role as an editor of the content of the session. The therapist works to shape the session, to make things happen in a productive fashion. When the therapist becomes a figure of importance to the family, gaining their trust and confidence, his/her remarks will be taken seriously.

Most families do not present their strong points at the outset of treatment, and many are cut off from an awareness of their own resources. They often hesitate to admit their loyal or affectionate feelings, for fear of being disappointed or hurt, or because their anger dominates the moment. They may briefly touch on positive themes ("I used to enjoy our trips together . . .") but then back off abruptly into predictable resentment (". . . but that was before the kids lost interest in being with their parents"). The therapist can gently intervene here as editor, underscoring the initial fond reflection while diplomatically cutting short the return to dissension ("I understand how difficult things have been recently and how much this disappoints you, but tell me more about those trips in the past that went somewhat better"). While acknowledging the problems that exist, the therapist can follow any leads to areas of strength or good feeling and can make sure the family has the chance to discuss such positive features of their lives.

The experience of discussing family strengths—pleasant memories, warm associations, successful experiences, humorous moments—creates an immediate opportunity for family members to becomes reacquainted with these qualities in their lives. These moments in the session carry an experiential impact that can greatly enhance the family's awareness of the positive force of their shared history, mutual loyalty, humor, and hopefulness. The therapist as editor should nurture the family's efforts to describe its strengths and should prevent the family from squandering such experiences as a result of their too-rapid return to a discussion of problems.

Mrs. C and her 20-year-old daughter lived alone together and were seen as a result of their intense conflict over the daughter's life-style. Her mother felt she was irresponsible and immature in her reliance on a series of boyfriends and in her "neglect" of her family. The daughter felt mistrusted and rejected by her mother, and was out to prove her wrong. Their stalemated encounters quickly became loud and abusive. Both women would end up screaming at each other, punctuated by the daughter's running out of the house and not returning for several days.

In family as well as individual sessions, the therapist successfully built alliances with both women and came to understand the nature of their hurt feelings and vulnerability. Each felt unloved by the other, and believed herself to be guilty and deserving of such rejection. The therapist was soon able to orchestrate an opportunity for each to make this disclosure to the other. In a conjoint meeting, he said to each in turn, "You've had great doubts about your mother's/daughter's feelings and concern for you, but what clearly comes through in talking with you is your caring for your mother/daughter." Each responded favorably, with the therapist interrupting if they lost focus and slipped into the old argument or if there were interruptions or denials from the other. Making such honest and affiliative statements and hearing each other speak positively of family feelings helped move the case on to a more productive road. The issue had become "What went wrong?" rather than "Why don't you care?"

"Priming" the Clients

There are times when the therapist cannot rely on the family members to take advantage of the space created for disclosure of more constructive attitudes and feelings. If tossed the ball, as in our previous example, many mothers or daughters would drop it ("What are you talking about, my concern for her! That's long gone"). The therapist, in assessing the situation, determines how much prompting or priming the family needs. For many, it is useful if the therapist leads off by making the positive statement for them, an approach that can be subtitled, "I know the real you." Describing someone's true feelings to them when they are too guarded to express these directly is a risky manuever and must be done only when the therapist is confident of his/her assessment and of the family member's willingness to listen. Often, these moments are best reserved for individual meetings, in which the family member is less likely to be defensive. They are aimed at boldly uncovering a previously hidden realm of feeling, providing the family members with greater access to possible family resources, and lessening their self-consciousness about divulging such vulnerable feelings.

A family was evaluated in which the father was alienated from his children and wife. Mr. B was known for his explosive temper and irrational demands, which typically left his family huddled together for support until his raging blew over. He lived in his own room in the house, and felt himself to be a prisoner there. No one would listen to him, he said, and he spent less and less time at home.

Formulation and treatment planning for this, as for any, case is a multilevel process and is not our main concern here. However, it was essential that the therapist break through the rigidity of this group's hostility to allow the expression of more constructive emotions and interactions. The therapist had demonstrated concern and support for the feelings of all parties, but needed to actively change the tone of the father's usual presentation. Judging that the father respected the therapist and would listen seriously to what he said, and seeing evidence of the father's concern for his children, an individual session was arranged and the therapist described Mr. B's inner life to him:

I just want you to know that I understand your feelings, and I know how difficult it's been for you. What's been particularly hard, I feel, has been your having to cover up your real feelings for your family, your not being able to clearly show your concern and love for the kids. Every time you begin to let your guard down something happens to leave you feeling exposed and vulnerable. Usually it's some conflict with your wife. But I feel strongly that the kids care for you as well and need to be able to know more about how you feel. I'm not sure you'll agree with what I'm saying, but I'm confident it's correct. I just wanted you to be aware that I know.

In this case the father went on to describe his caring feelings about the family, and he and the therapist discussed ways of building these into the family sessions. A similar meeting was held with the two B children, who were in their teens, during which the therapist said he was aware of their concern and worry over both their parents. Acknowledging their as-yet unspoken concern for their father also helped to minimize the chances of the children becoming increasingly guilty over their criticisms of him. Mrs. B was also seen individually. Her feelings about her husband were listened to in a supportive fashion, and her loyalty and protectiveness toward her children was commented upon.

This concern for the children would be the leverage therapeutically employed to assist Mrs. B in cooperating with the rehabilitation of Mr. B's image in the family. Mrs. B could understand and accept that the children needed a healthier relationship with their father, that the therapist felt this might be attainable, and that these efforts would take nothing away from a consideration of the serious and heated marital problems. Such individual or subgroup meetings and "priming statements" by the therapist should take place whenever the therapist believes resources exist and feels the family members themselves will remain unresponsive to more subtle encouragements to disclose them.

Reframing

Reframing is another editorial technique the therapist can utilize to put the family in contact with their own resources. Usually with the whole family present, the therapist presents an alternate interpretation of the current problem that emphasizes mutual concern and loyalty, and adds an element of hopefulness.

The A family—parents, 10- and 13-year-old sons—were seen due to the parents' concern about the older boy's recent delinquent behavior. The parents said this behavior dated back about a year, which also happened to be the time that Mrs. A was diagnosed as having terminal cancer. Both parents saw little connection between the two facts, and said they felt they had been honest with their children about Mrs. A's illness. They stated that they were realistic yet hopeful about her response to some experimental treatments that were about to begin.

After a thorough evaluation, the therapist was able to offer the family a reframed explanation of the 13-year-old's behavior. He told them that theirs was an extremely caring family, and that Mrs. A's relationship with her sons had been very positive and important to them all. She had always had great confidence in the older son's ability to take care of himself, which was a comfort to her as she dealt with her own fears about dying and leaving the family behind. What their son was saying to them through his behavior, although he did not know this himself, was that he was not ready to let his mother go. He still needed her, and she had to know it. She could not die because she still had a job to do, and he was not faring well at all. Delinquent behavior was reframed to be an act of caring and loyalty, and the family could then reconnect with these positive resources and deal effectively with the major issue, Mrs. A's illness.

The "Fictional Dream"

The therapist as editor can appropriate some guidelines described by John Gardner in *The Art of Fiction* (1983). Speaking to young writers of fiction, Gardner stated that fiction is effective when it creates a dream in the reader's mind. For our purposes, his advice on how to create "the fictional dream" is directly relevant to the therapist's task as editor of the family session. Gardner stated that:

if the effect of the dream is to be powerful, the dream must probably be vivid and continuous—vivid because if we are not quite clear about what it is that we're dreaming, who and where the characters are, what it is that they're doing or trying to do and why, our emotions and judgments must be confused, dissipated, or blocked; and continuous because a repeatedly interrupted flow of action must necessarily have less force than an action directly carried through from its beginning to its conclusion. (p. 31)

The therapist, too, must attempt to keep the session "vivid and continuous." He/she should help family members to avoid vague or general comments or descriptions by encouraging and requesting more detailed statements. As an editor of the therapeutic process, he/she should work toward smoothing over any jarring notes and try to maintain an enlivening momentum or pace in the session. Some families enter treatment in an apathetic state, and the therapist must attempt to breathe life into these situations. By monitoring the pace of the session—making comments, drawing out family members, preventing destructive detours or long speeches—the therapist keeps a flow going that is lively and energizing.

The therapist's tone of voice should be varied and alive, not a whisper or monotone, and he/she must think about the impact that his/her remarks are having on the family: Am I being heard or listened to? Am I antagonizing anyone? By glancing at family members while speaking, by intentionally speeding up or slowing down or becoming louder or softer, the therapist should attempt to maximize his/her dramatic impact on the family. Just as with a trial lawyer addressing a jury, facts or theories alone are not usually sufficient to influence a family. The therapist, like the lawyer, must establish a personal relationship with the family, have an impact on them, capture their attention and imagination. Then perhaps he/she can increase their awareness and encourage development of their family's resources.

COMMON ERRORS

One common failure in family treatment can be termed "editor failure." If the therapist is inattentive to the need to control the session, to keep it moving "vividly and continuously," to build alliances and have an impact on the family, many families will quickly run out of steam or off the tracks. Repair work after such occurrences is difficult and frequently unsuccessful. The therapist may well miss his/her chance to be effective if these errors of omission occur.

Destructive Interactions

One such error involves letting resource-depleting interactions run on too long. The therapist can be lulled into sitting back and watching the events of the session, and can end up being a passive witness to a vicious and destructive interchange between family members. If this is allowed to continue for more than a brief time, the atmosphere may be tainted for future expressions of resources or positive feelings. Additionally, the family may have lost faith in the therapist's ability to protect them, to ensure that things do not get out of hand. If so, they may be very leery of letting down their guard and revealing any more vulnerable emotions. The therapist should make his/her presence known when conflict intensifies. Almost any comment could serve to interrupt a destructive family sequence, turn eyes to the therapist, and create an opportunity to redirect the session.

Deadly Pauses

Another example of editor failure is allowing too many pauses to occur during the session. Occasionally a family member will need to pause at some length before responding, and this is acceptable because it is a silence that is building toward a specific response. But pauses that just happen, that indicate a loss of focus or direction, that have a "what happens next?" quality are "deadly pauses." They increase the family's anxiety, shake their confidence in the therapist's ability, and drain energy from the session. When the therapist notices such a loss of continuity, almost any brief remark or comment can give the session direction and will be preferable to silence. It is important to keep in mind the expanded time sense that exists in therapy sessions. A 30-second silence is a significant and awkward gap and generally feels acutely uncomfortable.

Problematic Departures

Just as the therapist needs to orchestrate the family's experience in the session, he/she should also be sensitive to how the family feels upon leaving. The therapist is trying to help the family become more hopeful, at least about the value of treatment, and they should leave the session in an encouraged or, at worst, a neutral mood. To end the session, especially an evaluation session, on an unsettled, pessimistic, or intensely conflicted note is another instance of editor failure. If the family goes home in such a mood, the therapist will be unable to have any impact on the conclusions they may draw about treatment or family life. Having a bad taste in their mouths about the session, they might be less willing to risk further attendance. Finally, the therapist's passivity in letting the session develop to a painful conclusion reduces the family's confidence in the therapist's ability to help.

Editor failure at the close of the session implies that the therapist has let the family drift off into a negative departure. The therapist has become a witness to the family's conflict, and the session ends where it does simply because the therapy hour is over. This is a vastly different process from one in which the therapist decides to increase pressure on the family by leaving them stressed or confused at the end of the meeting. This might be done, for example, with an overly affable family who utilize heavy denial. When a therapist chooses to "shake up" a group, he/she is clearly in control of the session, has orchestrated the ending, and has a specific purpose in mind for his/her intervention.

The therapist should be very much aware of when the session has to end in order to allow himself/herself time to tie up loose ends, make an intervention, or provide the family with a brief summary of the issues. He/she can state that they will return to a particular unfinished area at the next session, demonstrating that he/she is in charge, is aware of the issues, and has a plan for dealing with them. At the conclusion of evaluation sessions and early in treatment, the therapist can also make a brief positive statement in closing, emphasizing the mutual concern demonstrated by the family's coming in together for therapy, or harking back to some more positive moments or discoveries within the session itself. Such positive comments should also be made when indicated in later phases of treatment, whenever the therapist has seen signs of family resources. Because the closing moments of the session are important and can have a dramatic impact, positive or negative, on the family, the therapist should thoughtfully manage this period in order to positively influence the family's attitude.

Tactlessness

An additional set of potential therapeutic errors occurs in the area of the therapist's actual comments or performance. These errors of commission can be described as instances of "tactlessness." Families will excuse therapists for not being brilliant at all times, but are far less forgiving when it comes to instances of the therapist's tactlessness, insensitivity, or thoughtlessness. If the therapist grossly misreads the family's concerns, listens poorly, and then boldly intervenes with a misinterpretation, the family will feel poorly treated and resentful. An attempt to infuse hope that disregards the depth of members' concerns and upset will also be resisted. The therapist must demonstrate he/she has heard the family, and must adequately prepare them for his/her interventions. To do less is a sign of disrespect for the family.

SUMMARY

Unless the therapist works at being aware of his/her impact on the family, he/she runs the risk of creating negative, hope-depleting reactions in its members. He/she may end up antagonizing or patronizing, overestimating or misleading the family, confusing or boring them. If the therapist views himself/herself as a key performer in the session, listens carefully and chooses words carefully, builds alliances, maintains a therapeutic tone and pace for the session, and gauges the family's reactions to his/her remarks and actions, then key errors of omission and commission can be avoided.

It is easy to underestimate what a difficult step a family takes when it comes in for treatment. Our most intense and important emotions are wrapped up in our family life. Our families reflect who we are, know who we are, and carry our dreams for the future. To be seen by a therapist with our family is more personally revealing and holds greater risk than being seen individually. Most families come into therapy carrying a sense of failure with them, and they then have to expose their perceived failure to the therapist. The family's vulnerability must be recognized and respected by the therapist.

The therapist must also recognize that crisis and conflict obscure strengths or resources in families. He/she has an obligation to appreciate how crucial family life is, and must help the family search out its own capacity for healing. Without such respect for the force and potential goodness of family life, the therapist will likely follow the family in its absorption in pathology. Effective technique must be based on the knowledge of what is important to people, and being attuned to a family's strengths can provide the foundation for therapeutic success.

When the therapist listens for signs of these resources, and describes them, he/she has made contact with the family on a powerfully significant level. He/she can help the family become more aware of their own healing potential, and can help them move from pain to possibility. Working as an ally, an expert, an editor, but most importantly as a person who is respectful of what is most human about his/her clients, the therapist can have an ethical personal impact on the family's life.

REFERENCES

Adler, H. M., & Hammet, V. B. The doctor–patient relationship revisited. *Annals of Internal Medicine*, 1973, *78, 4*: 595–598.

Benson, H., & Epstein, M. D. The placebo effect: A neglected asset in the care of patients. *Journal of the American Medical Association*, 1975, *232, 12*: 1225–1227.

Bernheim, H. *Suggestive therapeutics: A treatise on the nature and uses of hynotism.* Westport, CT: Associated Booksellers, 1957. (First published in 1888)

Cassell, E. J. *The healer's art.* New York: Penguin Books, 1979.

Cousins, N. *Anatomy of an illness as perceived by the patient.* New York: Norton, 1979.

Frank, J. D. *Persuasion and healing.* New York: Schocken Books, 1978.

Gardner, J. *The art of fiction.* New York: Knopf, 1983.

Karpel, M. A., & Strauss, E. S. *Family evaluation.* New York: Gardner Press, 1983.

Tyler, A. *Dinner at the homesick restaurant.* New York: Knopf, 1982.

PART FOUR

Challenge, Survival, and Healing

CHAPTER 11

Unexpected Resources in Treating Incest Families

Denise J. Gelinas

Families in which current or recent incest has been disclosed often present an urgent but seemingly intractable picture to the therapist and protective workers involved. These professionals are often frustrated by a set of forces that seem to make effective intervention very difficult, if not impossible. The seeming resistance of the victim herself, the persistence of the father's pursuit of the daughter, the apparent denial or passivity of the mother, and the sometimes tangled involvement of other agencies and professionals can conspire to frustrate efforts to prevent further sexual abuse and to modify the family patterns that encouraged the abuse in the first place.

This chapter tries to demonstrate that, in the face of the urgency and dilemmas inherent in these cases, there are powerful resources available that, if mobilized, can minimize or virtually eliminate these characteristic obstacles and can greatly facilitate change during family treatment. What is particularly striking is that *these patterns, which have until recently been seen as the major obstacles and problems encountered in working with incest families, are potentially the most powerful resources available for effective treatment.* In order to recognize and use these resources, the therapist requires a particular approach.[1] This chapter identifies four of these patterns. It describes how one set of assumptions and interventions on the therapist's part is virtually guaranteed to maximize the obstacles inherent in these patterns, and how different assumptions and interventions can minimize resistance and mobilize resources for change.

---

[1]The following resource analysis and treatment recommendations were developed primarily during the family treatment of *paternal* incest, that is, incest initiated by the father or stepfather, most usually toward a daughter. Such paternal incest can be seen as paradigmatic of male–offender incest with regard to roles, age and power dynamics, and needs involved. The present analysis and recommendations are also helpful, however, in treating other forms of male, or female, offender incest.

Denise J. Gelinas, Ph.D. New England Clinical Associates, West Hartford, Connecticut. Private practice and consultation, Northampton and West Springfield, Massachusetts.

Before a therapist can recognize and make use of family resources in the treatment of incest, he/she must be able to recognize and understand incest itself, a task that can be more difficult than it might seem at first glance. The following, greatly abbreviated, discussion is intended to familiarize the reader with some of the demographics, patterns, and consequences associated with incest, as an introduction to the analysis and practical recommendations that follow.

INCEST: PATTERNS AND CONSEQUENCES

It is important to emphasize that incest is not sex by mutual consent, but rather the exploitation of a relatively powerless person, almost always a child, by a trusted and more powerful family member. Although inception of incest can occur at any age, from only a few months to adolescence, the most common ages of inception are 4 and 9 years. The offender is almost invariably older than the victim and in a position of authority, trust, and affection vis-à-vis the victim. The role of offender is assigned according to the power dynamics involved. Female children constitute approximately 85-90% of the victims of incest, and male children approximately 10-15%. It should be noted that male-offender incest also predominates when the victims are male children; contrary to some popular fiction, boys are usually victimized not by mothers, but by fathers, stepfathers, or other male figures in their lives.

Prevalence and Persisting Negative Effects

Family theory and therapy have paid surprisingly little attention to incest, perhaps because incest has been considered by many family therapists, as by most of the mental health community, to be a relatively rare occurrence, or one that has little or random impact on the victim. However, research has indicated otherwise. The prevalence of paternal incest alone has been repeatedly documented at between 1.3% and 1.5% of the population (Finkelhor, 1979a; Kinsey, Pomeroy, Martin, & Gebhard, 1953), a figure that, as Finkelhor and others have pointed out, very closely approximates the prevalence of schizophrenia, although incest has received nothing like the research attention, monies, or concern devoted to schizophrenia. Yet the prevalence for all types of incest exceeds that of schizophrenia. Its effects on the victims constitute a persisting and recognizable syndrome. Victims of untreated incest tend to show three underlying negative effects that are *different* than their presenting problems and that emerge only *after* disclosure of the incest: underlying chronic traumatic neurosis (and the secondary elaborations arising from lack of treatment); a perpetuation of familial relational imbalances (with secondary effects); and an increased intergenerational risk of incest, by *spouse-initiated* sexual abuse of their children (Gelinas, 1983).

Recognition

Victims tend to seek treatment, usually without identifying themselves as such, and are well represented in clinical caseloads. Rosenfeld (1979) and Spencer (1978) found incest victims constituted 33% and 30%, respectively, of their caseloads. No such figures are available regarding family therapy caseloads. Presumably family caseloads that include referrals from certain sources such as children's protective services or runaway shelters would show quite a high proportion of families with incest. Yet other, more general family caseloads would tend to frequently include incest families as well. These can be somewhat difficult to identify. When seeking therapy, even adult victims rarely disclose spontaneously, and therapists rarely ask—thus the history of incest never comes to light and the underlying negative effects are rarely available for therapeutic work. This is particularly unfortunate because therapy directed specifically toward the incest tends to be successful, whereas treatment of incest victims in which the incest is not disclosed and dealt with directly tends to be unsuccessful and the victims tend to become repetitive treatment seekers. With inquiry by the therapist, however, incest victims *do* tend to disclose and the focus of treatment shifts over time to the persisting negative effects, that is, to the expression of the traumatic neurosis and to the relational imbalances in the family of origin that allowed incest to occur and continue, and that are often being recapitulated in the person's current relationships.

Fortunately some typical presenting problems can serve as "markers" to alert clinicians to the possibility of incest (whether as an ongoing problem in a family in treatment, or as an old untreated problem, for example, in a parent, that can mitigate against change in a therapy focused on more present-day presenting problems).

Adult incest victims very frequently show chronic depression and markedly poor self-esteem (Bernstein, 1979; Summit & Kryso, 1978), as well as marital and relational difficulties (Herman, 1981; Meiselman, 1978), sexual dysfunction (Giaretto, 1976; Meiselman, 1978), and increased risk of physical and emotional abuse toward their children (Summit & Kryso, 1978) and/or increased intergenerational risk of incest among their own children by their spouses (Gelinas, 1983).

Adolescent incest victims are *very* frequently encountered in runaway shelters and foster care systems. They are common among adolescent girls who have attempted suicide (Gelinas, Carr, Goodman, & Pastides, in review), or show a period of promiscuity (Gelinas, *et al.*, in review; Kaufman, Peck & Tagiuri, 1954; McCary, 1979) or prostitution and running away (James & Meyerding, 1977; Nakashima & Zakus, 1977). Adolescent boys with histories of sexually abusing younger children or histories of interpersonal aggressiveness show a high percentage of incest victimization.

Among *children*, any accounts or descriptions of sexual contact, fear of particular individuals, persistent "tummy" aches or headaches, enuresis, or encopresis should prompt inquiry. *Any* compulsive masturbatory behavior or any injuries (even slight) or infections of the genitals, anus, mouth and throat, or urinary tract are suspicious and should be investigated very directly.

Family Patterns Associated with Inception of Incest

To understand the negative consequences of incest, the characteristic problems encountered while treating incest families, and the treatment approaches that can use these patterns as resources, it is essential to look at the particular relational structure and roles often associated with paternal incest. Incest occurs because of combined individual and family processes, and attempts to understand the inception of incest by examining single factors in isolation miss the point. So do categorical schemata that suggest that incest occurs only in one type of family or only if certain events occur. Nevertheless, particular patterns do emerge repeatedly in families in which incest has developed. These characteristic patterns include bilateral parental estrangement, significant parentification, and relational imbalances.

In parentification a child is induced to assume, and does assume, premature excessive caretaking responsibilities in her family. Not only does the child perform certain task functions (e.g., cooking, laundry, house or garden work, and/or child care), she also has the responsibility for these functions. She doesn't help with the laundry, she does it, and if she doesn't do it, it doesn't get done. The parentified child *internalizes* her role of responsibility and begins to develop her identity around taking care of others. In time, she begins to meet the needs of other family members to the exclusion of her own. She forms her identity around the notion that she has responsibility for taking care of people, but they have no responsibility to care for her in return. Essentially, she has no rights to reciprocity. As an adult, the parentified child will continue to organize her life around caring for others and leaving her own needs unmet.

In families where incest has developed, the *mothers* have usually been parentified children and, as such, in young adulthood they are drawn to, and tend to attract, men for whom caretaking is important. Many of these men have experienced early maternal deprivation through death, depression, or divorce; they tend to be relatively dependent, needy, and insecure, and respond to the caretaking of the parentified woman they marry. Although each partner has carried relational imbalances from their families of origin into the new relationship, things go smoothly for a while because of the complementarities involved.

Obviously, the event that progressively disturbs that complementarity and initiates the *bilateral* estrangement is the arrival of the first child. Having already been a surrogate parent (to siblings, parents, and spouse), the wife may feel depleted and somewhat ambivalent about having a child. Nevertheless, at the birth of the infant, she focuses maternal caretaking on the infant. While this is obviously appropriate, it decreases the caretaking she can provide for the husband. Furthermore, because of the stresses involved during this time, she usually attempts to lean on her husband for support, only to find that he is unavailable. He, too, is in difficulty. His wife is providing less caretaking, *and* is attempting to lean on him for support; adding to the pressure, she is expecting him to assume responsibilities for a child. Not only is she "abandoning" him and placing new demands on him, but she is essentially producing his rival. Under these circumstances, it is nearly impossible for him to provide his wife with the support that she genuinely needs and the bilateral estrangement grows. As she tries to meet the growing demands of an infant with her limited emotional supplies she finds that he is more firmly unavailable, yet also more demanding. For him, relationships "give" and he will pursue her to get what he needs; as she increasingly avoids him, he escalates his demands for attention, affection, and nurturance. With time, and especially subsequent births and family demands, the systemic pattern progresses and the estrangement worsens.

The wife meets only the most pressing needs of the family; depleted and unable to gain assistance from her husband, she will attempt to gain assistance from a child as soon as possible and that child (usually the eldest daughter) will respond as best she can out of loyalty to her mother. With the pressure of his emotional needs unmet and his wife no longer available, the father may turn outside the family (if he has the contacts, self-confidence, and luck), or turn inside the family to someone besides his wife—usually the eldest daughter. Thus begins a second generation of parentification, by both parents.

A family with this pattern is at significant risk for the gradual development of incest. The inception of the sexual abuse occurs in the context of the father's pursuing his emotional needs, the mother's depletion and relational avoidance, and the daughter's parentification. In this situation, the daughter helps her mother with task functions (and often some emotional caretaking) and helps her father primarily with emotional caretaking (perhaps by listening to his day, or going to sporting interests with him, or sitting with him after dinner talking or watching TV). These are all appropriate, within bounds. But in families where the father is needy and shows poor judgment, impulsivity, alcohol abuse, or a heightened sense of entitlement, the pursuit of his emotional needs puts him at risk to gradually begin to slide from appropriate emotional and physical contact through sexually tinged contact to unmistakable sexual contact and thus abuse of his parentified daughter. The mother's relationally avoidant stance mitigates against her pursuing information to uncover the incest, or preventing it in the first place.

The daughter is sexually victimized by the father and is usually confused about this. Even if she is old enough to recognize that what is going on is sex, her rights as a child not to be abused by a parent are obscured by her parentified "lack of rights," and also the fear and the lowered self-esteem produced by the sexual abuse itself. She has an avoidant mother and an abusing but needy father, and is typically isolated from her siblings because the parentification is usually viewed by them as favoritism. None of these family members occupies an enviable position, and the incest victim has the worst place of all.

Some Common Variations in the High-Risk Family Patterns

Another family type at significant risk for the development of incest involves a dominant husband and a very inadequate wife. The incest again usually victimizes the eldest daughter and involves a good deal of coercion, if not outright violence; physical abuse of the victim and/or the other children may be present. Physical and/or sexual abuse of the primary victim by other, physically more powerful siblings may also be involved.

In these types of families, the incest is usually an expression of the offender's need for power and tenderness and his exaggerated sense of entitlement. It may involve a pursuit of his emotional needs through what can only be seen as a Sullivanian "malevolent transformation."[2] There tends to be a very strong patriarchal orientation, with a simultaneous need for, but contempt and devaluation of, women so that there are no balances to the exercise of practically absolute power.

In its more extreme forms the offender may in fact become quite malevolent—the town bully that one reads about in the newspaper who may come to grief legally or drive someone to injure him. He uses power in the family to control and to hurt. One such offender would shoot at the outhouse near their home in the country, his wife being the target. He beat the family dog to death and seemed to try to kill anyone or anything that the family cared for. His wife was not allowed to say anything, literally. He apparently used to threaten to chop her up when he was drunk. The family lived in a very secluded area and the wife could not readily obtain help. This offender had an alcohol problem and gave the children alcohol as rewards; most of the children were using alcohol regularly by age 11. There was a standing rule in the home that boys had to give this father money, alcohol, or food in order to date his daughters. His degree of control and violence and his predisposition to hurt anyone or anything that the family cared for certainly qualify him as a malevolent offender.

---

[2]"Malevolent transformation" is a process described by Harry Stack Sullivan (1953, especially pp. 201–202 and 213–215) in which a child's usual ways of expressing his/her need for tenderness elicit such rebuff, ridicule, or anxiety and fear-provoking responses that the child is essentially forced to substitute other ways of expressing this need.

During early childhood, this need for tenderness is usually expressed as desire for physical contact, then for interactive games with the parent, then for an audience. If these expressions consistently elicit ridicule, or responses that are anxiety or fear producing, the child's need for tenderness does not simply evaporate; he/she is forced to find other ways to elicit it. Sometimes some form of sublimation can once again summon forth that parental tenderness. If not, the child learns that it is "highly disadvantageous" to show these needs for tender cooperation to those around him/her, and so instead shows something else, a basically malevolent attitude—one that expresses the notion that one really lives among enemies. The malevolence hurts and provokes fear, as a preemptive protection from hurt and fear to the self.

A malevolent transformation is a persisting tendency, and can make a person difficult to like, but not necessarily difficult to love. This helps to explain why "malevolent offenders" are so interpersonally destructive yet their families maintain such strong loyalties to them. The family members can feel the deep needs and desires for tenderness, intimacy, and succorance that lie just beyond the very real malevolence.

Families that show these characteristics *do* respond to the following resource analysis and recommendations, sometimes with surprising readiness, but they generally require that the therapist be willing to adopt a fairly authoritarian stance, and be willing to include police and court involvement when necessary to maintain some controls in the situation.

Another situation that can be regarded as a variant occurs when the offender is what Groth (1982) has identified as a "fixated pedophile." Most incest offenders have a primary sexual orientation toward adult partners and the sexual contact with a child or children is a regression from this usual orientation. A fixated pedophile, however, has a primary sexual orientation toward children that is persistent and usually began during adolescence. Unlike the more usual regressed offender, there is usually no precipitating stress prior to the sexual contact with a child but rather a persisting interest and compulsive pedophilic behavior that is usually premeditated. Fixated pedophiles usually show considerable characterological immaturity. Also, they tend to choose male victims as primary targets. When seen in treatment (whether individual or family), the following recommendations remain applicable, but a great deal more emphasis on monitoring impulse control is required.

UNEXPECTED RESOURCES

Although some families and situations will obviously require certain special considerations, the four problems that follow are very characteristically encountered when treating incest families. When they are approached within a certain framework, these potential impasses can be avoided and then turned into important resources for therapeutic change. Each problem is briefly described, then some common therapeutic errors are reviewed; the recommended therapeutic approach follows.

The first and most important of these problems is the often flamboyant uncooperativeness of the victim toward those who are attempting to intervene in the incest.

CHOICE: Resistance and Uncooperativeness of the Victim or Filial Loyalty

Victims are well known for their resistance toward disclosing incest, their often adamant unwillingness to testify, their propensity for running away from foster placements, closing ranks with the rest of the family against helping agencies, therapists, or the courts, defending the offender, and often (erroneously) looking as if they desired, or at least actively allowed, the incest to occur. In short, they can be silent, stubborn, and resistant to influence or change, flouting all "logic" and further embracing the families in which they have been abused.

In a recent case in California, a 12-year-old girl allowed herself to be jailed and actually placed in solitary confinement for 1 week rather than testify against her stepfather. The obviously questionable judgment shown by the court in placing a 12-year-old child (the victim, no less) in solitary speaks perhaps to the frustration that legal and social service professionals can sometimes experience when faced with this seemingly inexplicable resistance of the victim.

On the other hand, all of the above problems can be better understood if viewed as expressions of loyalty toward the offender.[3] If this loyalty is explicitly acknowledged and actively supported by the therapist during treatment, the victim's stubborn defense of her father can take more appropriate avenues and work can begin.

Common Errors: Overlooking or Opposing Loyalties

For the family therapist, supporting the victim's loyalty to her father can be emotionally difficult because of feelings of sympathy for the child, and anger at the abuse, and because of the continuing protective concerns inherent in such a situation. Yet supporting these loyalties appears to be nothing less than essential to the therapy. One particularly striking example concerned a 17-year-old woman, the eldest of three daughters, referred for family work. Incest had begun when she was 8, and was discovered (not disclosed) when she was 12. I was told by the referring agency that the incest "had stopped," then resumed when she was 14 only to be rediscovered at age 17. During the first contact with the family, it rapidly became clear that the mother was angry and upset about the incest, the family was hostile and guarded about treatment, and the 17-year-old was saying nothing. During my attempts to understand their hostility toward being involved in family therapy, the mother stated that, when the incest was first discovered (when that daughter was age 12), they had been referred to family treatment. During the first session the therapist has referred to the father as a "creep" in front of the children; they subsequently refused to return for therapy. The mother then set up family therapy with a second therapist, who had the poor judgment to turn to her (also during the first session) and state, "Now we will see how you so failed your husband that he had to turn to one of your daughters." Said daughters refused to return to this therapist too, and here they were (5 years later) sitting in yet another initial family session, and just waiting. . . . A discussion of their route through earlier treatment highlighted how each of the two earlier therapists had inadvertently violated the daughters' loyalties, first to one parent and then the other. Placed by therapists in untenable loyalty positions, the girls simply refused to return.

The remainder of the session was spent exploring what that had been like for all members of the family, how it had affected their views of family therapy and therapists, and how it had made it essentially impossible for the sisters of the victim to disclose to their mother that their father was once again sexually abusing their eldest sister. During that session, it also became painfully obvious

---

[3]Since by definition *any* form of incest involves sexual abuse by a close family member, loyalty is a very significant issue in all incest situations. The closer the relationship (biologically and emotionally) the more important the loyalty considerations.

that the eldest daughter was quietly psychotic and had been unobtrusively hallucinating her way through high school. The point is simply that loyalty among family members exists, despite abuse, and it must be respected and supported by the therapist or treatment can barely commence, let alone produce change.

Ignoring or violating the victim's loyalty usually elicits protection of the abuser, regardless of age or circumstances of abuse. One 5-year-old boy, sexually abused by his father, was precipitously interviewed by a relatively inexperienced state trooper who was clearly horrified at the idea of incest and eager to get a conviction against the father. The boy immediately sensed this and began asking him questions about jail (Do inmates get snacks? Are there TVs? And then, more directly, could he stay with his father if the father went to jail?). The boy decided to disclose nothing, which is exactly what he did. Furthermore he retracted earlier statements to his mother, saying he had been dreaming, and essentially refused to discuss anything further.

His concerns that he might cause his father to be hurt by his disclosures, and the trooper's avidity for prosecuting without paying attention to the fact that this was the boy's *father* they were talking about, proved too much for this 5-year-old. He simply couldn't betray his father and thereby betrayed himself instead, a perfectly understandable choice for a 5-year-old. If this boy's obvious loyalties had been handled differently, there is every probability that he would have continued his descriptions of the sexual abuse. For instance, it would have been preferable to wait several days before the trooper interviewed him (which raised the spectre of jail). During this hiatus, the boy's mother and later the therapist could have helped the boy continue to disclose, begun to desensitize him to talking about sexual material, and "established" the descriptions of the abuse here in the world through his accounts, rather than simply in his memory.

At that point the boy would have been far better prepared for the police questioning and it would have been more difficult for him to retract such repeated and complete statements. If the police had supported his loyalty and concern for his father, the boy would not have felt so urgently that everything he said would place his father in jeopardy of jail.

This is not to imply that the adults concerned should have lied to the boy about prosecution. Yet, if the trooper had been less outraged and exclusively focused on jailing the father, he might have reassured the boy that they wanted the abuse stopped for good, that his father would go to court but that we couldn't know whether or not he would need to go to jail, and that even if he did, his father would be O.K. and the son would be able to visit him regularly. This approach would violate neither truth nor filial loyalty. In some cases, the abusers have eventually given their children *permission* to talk and reassured them of their continuing parental love. Even with this ideal situation, genuinely addressing the child's love, concern, and protectiveness toward the parent makes it more possible for the child to disclose, participate in treatment, or testify without overwhelming feelings of guilt.

In treatment, somewhat older children or early adolescents very often look depressed, dispirited, and distressed; in a misguided attempt to kindle a spark of life through anger, the therapist may pursue the child or adolescent with statements about what a serious thing incest really is, and what does she think of a 38-year-old man sexually abusing his 9-year-old daughter, and does this seem right or fair to her. This approach places the victim in a dilemma: if she admits how bad incest is, or how negative her experiences were, she indicts her father; if, on the other hand, she refuses to say anything to indict him, she tacitly denies how negative the experiences were for her and indirectly suggests that she was a willing participant. Placed in the dilemma of essentially denying her father, or her own experience, or accepting responsibility for what happened, a child, particularly one who has been an incest victim, will tend to deny her experiences ("Nothing happened; I lied." or "I was mad at my father so I said things—I was just kidding."); withdraw into surprisingly stubborn silence; or leave the field (e.g., leave treatment, run away, act out to divert attention, or show symptoms of sufficiently increased severity that she requires hospitalization).

Recommended Therapeutic Stance

Respecting Loyalties. If loyalty work is done the child can talk about the incest and still retain her love and loyalty for her father or stepfather. Respecting loyalty can take many forms. For instance, when initially attempting to ascertain what in fact happened (i.e., the specific acts involved in the incest), a therapist might inform the mother and victim (say, a 9-year-old girl) together that he/she wishes to speak with the girl alone for about 20–30 minutes to find out what actually happened. ["Alone" because children often feel inhibited discussing the sexual abuse in front of the nonoffending parent because: (1) it upsets that parent and (2) they fear "making" that parent angry at the offending parent. In either case they've "hurt" one parent or the other. If a very young child, 2–3 years old, is the victim, these considerations are usually outweighed by the reassurance the child can gain by the mother's presence.] It is often helpful to say that the mother knows and agrees that this needs to be talked about and that the father knows too. In early-phase family incest work, the offender often denies the incest; if this is the case, awareness of the father's denials are acknowledged, then followed by statements that that must be somewhat confusing for the child, that we hope that things get cleared up as quickly as possible, and that we want the child to tell the truth about what really happened.

When the therapist is then alone with the child, it is most helpful to talk about and have the child talk about how upsetting this kind of talking is, about whether she is afraid all this will get her father into trouble, about whether she feels badly talking about this, and about whether she loves her father, or loves and is confused about him at the same time. Within the context of supporting her positive feelings for her father and acknowledging her negative feelings and any confusion, the discussion is shifted to the acts involved ("And now, we need to talk for a bit about the things that daddy did, and even though it's upsetting you'll be alright and so will daddy and mommy.")[4] After the child's account, more work can be done on differentiating her distress from her continuing loyalty. Given this approach, a child or adolescent is much more likely to talk than if his/her loyalty has been violated.

Although is may be difficult to believe or to recognize in the face of some victims' denials, victims and other children are usually very loyal to dominant, even malevolent, offenders as well. Surprisingly, these loyalties can be particularly profound and tenacious, almost as if there were a relationship between how tyrannical the father had been and the degree of loyalty felt by the child. This is not to preclude the simultaneous presence of hatred and fear of the offender with loyalty, but the loyalty can require sensitive handling in such cases because it appears linked to some realization of how impaired or needy the offender is. The loyalty also relates to the degree of control he exerted over the children's world view, and that does not change overnight.

In therapy, the depth of this loyalty requires more delicacy on the therapist's part, but its tenaciousness and power can provide the needed emotional balance to the work on the father's malevolent activities. Without this loyalty as a balance, attempts to deal with the father's dominance or malevolence can veer decidedly toward the punitive or judgmental.

Accountability. When dealing with incest, issues of accountability also need to be addressed. Someone has sexually abused a child or sometimes a young adolescent. We need to remember that the most common ages during which children begin to be incestuously abused are 4 and 9 years old. The offender is typically about 20 years older than his/her victim, reinforcing the conviction of those treating incest that incest is abuse and not sex by mutual consent.

The optimal therapeutic stance supports the victim's loyalties while holding adults accountable for their behavior; this includes holding the offender accountable for the incest. Three "rules" have been particularly useful in helping therapists maintain this therapeutic position. They are particularly useful when introduced during the earliest phase of family work, because this establishes the therapist's stance and prepares the family for the basic parameters within which they can deal with the explosive, confusing, and painful situation of incest.[5]

The first rule informs all aspects of treatment, and is sometimes made explicit to the families. It is:

> *Any time there is sexual contact between an adult and a child, it is always the adult's responsibility.*

---

[4]If a statement is being taken for legal purposes a less leading question is necessary—for example, "And now we need you to talk a little bit about the things that have been happening to you."

[5]The following rules and techniques are applicable to the other problems/resources discussed later, as well as to the present issue of loyalty.

The adult has the knowledge, experience, and power in these situations, as well as the child's affection, trust, and dependency, all of which he then betrays; if anything in therapy can be said to be non-negotiable, it is this rule.[6] Besides its inherent truthfulness, this rule allows the therapist to support family loyalties without blaming the child for her own sexual abuse, and makes this clear to the family.

The second and third rules go together:

Children are intensely loyal to their parents, and that loyalty must be explicitly supported in treatment.

Adults are held accountable for the incest, but the therapist must never scapegoat, nor allow scapegoating.

These two rules respect the loyalty dynamics inherent in families, which are especially important when they perceive themselves as threatened by the child protective and criminal agencies, and initially perhaps by the therapist. At the same time, they hold the offender accountable without allowing the accountability process to slide over into scapegoating or character assassination; because of its unfairness, such scapegoating would eventually elicit protectiveness and loyalty toward the offender, which all too often is accompanied by illegitimate exoneration of his responsibility for the incest and the placing of that responsibility back on the child victim—putting therapy back to square one.

This therapeutic stance can be accomplished in a number of ways. For instance, at some points in treatment, the offender's wife or the police or social service agency may become very angry with him and begin to attack him in a number of ways, or hold him inappropriately accountable for family misfortunes or problems for which he was *not* responsible. When that happens the family's therapist can support the mother's anger at husband for those things for which he does bear accountability (e.g., the incest, and whatever else) while gently but firmly differentiating them from those things about which he doesn't bear responsibility (e.g., a son's driving accident, the wife's alcohol abuse, family money problems) or that didn't happen (e.g., unfounded assumptions that he has also had affairs, or been negligent at work, or stopped having feelings for his wife). By differentiating those things for which the offender is responsible from those for which he is not, the therapist begins to demonstrate to the family that holding the father accountable for the incest will *not* immediately implicate him in all sorts of other problems, nor, conversely will acknowledging one's love for him undo his responsibility for the abuse of the child. It makes it possible to deal with the complicating and bewildering aspects of the situation by differentiating love, abuse, and accountability from the chaos.

---

[6]For an excellent short discussion of the fundamental asymmetry of the adult–child relationship as it relates to sexual abuse, see Finkelhor (1979b).

Multilaterality. This therapeutic stance is best accomplished using the technique of "multilaterality."[7] Using multilaterality the therapist over time actively takes everyone's "side," genuinely attempting to understand the situation from each person's point of view and then representing each of their interests in the family. Multilaterality precludes the therapist's being any one family member's agent exclusively, which would violate that family member's loyalty concerns toward the other members of his/her family and would be a counterproductive therapeutic position since all family members do have legitimate interests in the family. Multilaterality is not objectivity or equidistance from everyone; it is rather an active process of recognizing, acknowledging, and balancing everyone's vested interest in their family. While it doesn't imply that everyone's agendas or interests should be accepted, they must be considered and taken seriously. Neither does multilaterality imply that all interests be forwarded during the space of one session. It means that over time the therapist must lift up each person's side and represent their interests so that no one is permanently left out or overlooked. As a matter of technique, if a person's side must be held in abeyance for whatever reason for many weeks it is very helpful to acknowledge this in the sessions; that way, that family member is reminded that his/her concerns have not been forgotten or discounted, and the other family members are reminded too.

Thus, for instance, if the district attorney's office has decided to prosecute and the father is currently on trial, he should be receiving a great deal of support from his family and therapist. While the rest of the family's needs should be addressed, and therapy proceed, their sides will perhaps inevitably be less vivid than the father's (and perhaps the victim's if she must testify), but this should be openly discussed to reassure them that things have not become too unbalanced. Interestingly enough, this open discussion usually provides added support for the father and then gradually reintroduces the issue of his accountability—a reality note that helps the family to deal with their anger at the courts and often at the victim for disclosing.

During the early phases of treatment, if the father/husband is spending considerable time on the stress "all this" is causing him—how his wife is angry and not speaking to him, his daughter has "betrayed" him (by disclosing), his other children are "different," he is having trouble sleeping, concentrating, and relaxing—a perhaps natural tendency here would be to "yes, but" him. He would be a relatively unsympathetic figure for many therapists, particularly if the sexual abuse of his daughter had been severe in acts or duration; yet simply falling back on his culpability or pointing out his abuse of his young child would tend to elicit loyalty toward him on the part of his wife and almost certainly on

---

[7]"Multilaterality" as a technique, and the issues of loyalty, accountability, and fairness in relationships, are based on contextual family therapy, originated by Ivan Boszormenyi-Nagy and developed by him and his coworkers (Boszormenyi-Nagy & Krasner, 1980; Boszormenyi-Nagy & Spark, 1973; Boszormenyi-Nagy & Ulrich, 1980; see also Gelinas, 1983; Karpel & Strauss, 1983).

the part of the victim—leaving the therapist in the unenviable position of attempting to induce some positive changes in a family that has closed ranks against him/her. The therapist could also be in the position of attempting to persuade people of the obviously rational truth (that the adult has the responsibility, the power, and the control in incest) in the face of the equally obvious and seemingly irrational refusal to see it. This refusal stems from their family loyalty toward the offender, and no amount of rational persuasion will convince them.

A multilateral intervention would be preferable here. It would include genuinely listening to his complaints, and acknowledging that he is having a very difficult time. Without detracting from this realization of how difficult it is for him, the family needs to *also* see that it has been very difficult for the victim as well as other family members. The victim is experiencing the multiple stresses of successive disclosures to the protective agency, the police, the pediatrician, and now the family therapist. Her father is angry at her for disclosing, her mother angry at her for the incest (!), and her sibs angry at her for "ruining the family name." The offender's wife is disbelieving, then shocked, not knowing who to believe, but feeling stressed and betrayed. Finally, the other children are experiencing radical shifts in their older sister's behavior as well as the multiple interventions in the family.

This represents everyone's "side" without negating his, and clearly it tacitly alludes to the issue of his accountability. Also during the course of the next few weeks, the offender and the family will see the therapist using this intervention if anyone else's interests become too exclusively the center of attention. Family members cannot count on the therapist to side with them *against* their family, nor to indiscriminately side *with* them *regardless* of what position they take; however, they can rely on the therapist to pay attention, to hold them accountable to be fair, and to hold others similarly accountable to fairness. The technique of multilaterally supporting all the family's loyalties while holding each person accountable for his/her own behavior helps the therapist demonstrate over time his/her trustworthiness—an important resource for working with families in which betrayal, secrecy, and abuse have occurred and have often been an integral part of family life for years. Scrupulous multilaterality is a resource that the *therapist* can bring to the work.

Addressing Protective Concerns. Another important technique for the early phases of treatment relates to the obvious protective concerns intrinsic to incest. The victim (or victims—in approximately 37% of cases there is more than one victim) must be protected from further sexual abuse during the course of treatment and during any legal interventions; this issue emerges almost immediately after disclosure or discovery.

Usually a protective agency or clinician, in an attempt to deal with the situation, will promptly remove the *victim*. Instead, it is far better to remove the *offender*. If it is necessary to remove someone to protect the child, the person to go should be the adult offender.

If the *victim* is removed, a number of negative consequences ensue, most of which render any therapeutic changes nearly impossible. First, the therapist and everyone else can talk until they are nearly blue about the *adult* bearing the responsibility for incest; but, if they then remove the victim, since actions do indeed speak louder than words, they reinforce the victim's and the family's ascription of responsibility for the incest. It reinforces their conviction that she is the problem. Removing the victim also essentially expels her from the family. Given the characteristic structure of incest families and the victim's usual position of responsibility without reciprocity, when she is removed the family tends to extrude her, then close ranks behind her. Their feelings tend to be that "the problem" is now removed, and they resist looking at the incest, its origins, and its consequences. Owing a debt to the now-invisible victim, they prefer not to be aware of this debt and so avoid the issues of incest and treatment; attempts to treat such a situation can be a very uphill proposition.

Families will tend to ignore their appointments or themselves select who "should" be included or not. They will tend to spend inordinate amounts of time externalizing responsibility and essentially scapegoating the victim—requiring the therapist to either try to correct this imbalance (thereby looking like she/he is exclusively on the victim's "side"), go along with it (accepting the family's pathology and thereby changing nothing), or attempt to stop it (thereby getting into a confrontation with the family's "resistance" that only the family can win). The family's motivation for therapy could not be lower.

However, if the *offender* is removed, a number of positive consequences follow; the issues of accountability and family loyalties become therapeutic assets, and motivation for change increases. First and most obviously, removing the offender protects the child and clearly and powerfully assigns responsibility, for all the family to see. It is often a revelation for family members that the offender and not the victim is being treated in this way, and that can only be a change in a positive direction for the family. This also contributes to the therapist's multilaterality, as it balances some of the support the offender has received, by supporting the victim *and* holding the offender accountable with a particularly real consequence.

This intervention also speaks to how seriously certain elements of society regard incest. It begins to legitimize the victim's need to have disclosed and also begins to explain some of her symptoms or previous acting out. This is a serious thing that has happened, and it will be treated as such. The siblings in particular seem to find this a novel notion and they begin to struggle with the issues of the offender's responsibility for the incest, the victim's having some rights and allies, and the cracking of the family's homeostasis, which was dependent upon the incest and the victim's parentification.

Removing the offender also significantly increases everyone's motivation for therapy. In most cases, the father will loathe living outside the home; if he can return only when the clinician and the protective agency (working cooperatively) feel that the risk of resumed incest is low enough to be tolerated (since both continue to monitor the situation), he will tend to be fairly cooperative with treatment. This early cooperation by the offender has a good deal of the manipulative about it, but that's alright initially. He is coming into treatment, being held accountable, and must make certain changes before being allowed back in the home; the path the offender needs to take is clear—ultimately he can either take it, or not return home.

The mother's motivation for treatment is also increased. Usually she will want the husband to be able to return and will therefore be more cooperative than not. Also the victim has been left in the home with the mother and the siblings. Usually the victim is seen as the problem, and often is blamed by the mother for the incest, almost as an adult rival. The siblings are angry with the victim and are in considerable turmoil with the father being out of the house and with the changes (that this implies) in the family's perception of itself. In short, the mother has her hands full, usually regards the victim as a thorn in her side, and turns to therapy to help herself out. With the breaking of the homeostasis that was based upon the daughter's parentification, and the incest, the mother has lost her primary support—that daughter—and will be searching for replacement assistance for tasks and caretaking. Once again she is carrying the full load of the family and appropriately looks to therapy to begin reintegrating her husband both for emotional and functional reasons.

The victim's motivation for therapy increases in part because of the difficulty of living in a home with an angry mother and siblings but also because removal of the father and assignment of accountability to him have probably been a welcome surprise to her. With early demonstration of therapeutic multilaterality, the victim may actually have some hope that the therapist can untangle the confusion and extricate her from the incest without destroying her family. The sibs merely want relief from the anxiety and confusion; they probably want their father back and usually want to see the therapist to "set the record straight." Over time the family structure shifts and they begin to understand things they had not even seen before.

Removing the offender also *prevents* a number of problems that tend to occur around the placement of the victim outside the home. It is much easier for an adult to find temporary housing (perhaps with friends, extended family, or in a rooming or apartment house) than for the protective services to find good foster placement. This is especially true if more than one victim is involved, or if the victim has been acting out. Also, incest victims show a marked tendency to run; they run even from their families of origin. When in placement the propensity to run is increased. So are their psychiatric symptoms and acting-out behavior. If the victim is removed—with all this implies about responsibility for the incest, isolation, and loneliness, her symptoms *can be expected* to increase. Of course, that affects the anxiety level and willingness of the foster family, introduces crises into the family therapy, and so on.

Placing the victim outside the home usually results in a number of all too real problems for the clinician and overlooks the family's resources. Removing the offender assigns responsibility, increases motivation for change, precludes a host of problems, and is really not that difficult to accomplish. Usually offenders will simply leave when asked to, especially when it is a strong recommendation from everyone concerned (clinicians, police or district attorney's office, protective service agencies, etc.). This clearly presumes prior contact and cooperation among agencies, a point to be reviewed later. Another factor is that his absence is temporary—only until the protective unit and the clinician together feel that the risk of resumed incest is low enough to be tolerated, given continued monitoring and a victim who now has allies who are readily accessible if any sexually tinged contact should resume.

It is, of course, quite difficult to remove the father if both he and the mother oppose this; this is particularly true in "malevolent" offender cases. During early phases of the family work, the assistance of protective and police services may be required. For instance, if the child has been removed, the wife and younger children may become targets for rage and battering; if the father is removed (the better alternative), a restraining order may be necessary to keep him from returning to the home. If the wife remains inadequate and allows him to return for visits despite the restraining order, the protective service needs to be notified and joint negotiations among protective service, family therapist, and family need to be instituted. Usually the situation can be stabilized if *both* parents and the children hear the unequivocal assurance that if the father continues to visit (and the mother allows this), the children will be removed. The obvious priority of physical safety for the children sometimes dictates this unpleasant and admittedly difficult intervention; when *all* family members hear this from the combined protective, clinical, and, if necessary, legal authorities, some sense of family loyalty and mutual protectiveness is usually generated, with the children enjoining father not to visit, *for his own good.* This can also take the onus of responsibility off the mother's shoulders and figuratively allow her to say, "Look what they will do; I have no choice—you had better not come by for a while." While not the optimal therapeutic stance for the long run, as a temporary, early-phase intervention this position has its legitimate role when used to stabilize the situation and physically protect the children.

There are some absolutely intransigent cases (usually with malevolent offenders, several victims, and a great deal of violence) where the coercive statutory powers of the legal system are the only possible interventions. These families are clearly less amenable to treatment. *If* this is the case the victims should be removed and treated on an individual basis, or as part of a sibling subsystem if several children have been removed. In these situations, children are often extremely loyal and protective toward their parents and so must be approached carefully, in an effort to use their loyalty as a resource. It is relatively unusual, however, to encounter these levels of intransigence and untreatability.

Since the formal avenues for removing an offender are so restricted, informal approaches have typically been more successful. The concerted, persistent, unified message from all concerned that the *offender* should temporarily leave is very effective. So is simply invoking routine—emphasizing that, on the whole, things work out much better if the adult rather than the child is the one to leave temporarily. (Using the terms "adult" and "child" allow the therapist to temporarily sidestep the issue of calling the offender an offender, a term that typically prompts him to see his voluntary leaving as an admission of guilt. Stating the issue in terms of an adult and a child puts pressure on the adult to be the one to leave.) If the wife is in agreement, or can be persuaded to be because of her concern for her child and the temporary nature of the separation, so much the better. Also, if prosecution is a probability, all gestures of cooperation by the offender are clearly advantageous to him and the therapist can make appropriate use of this situation to guide this potential cooperativeness with therapeutic directions.

There is, of course, an unmistakable coercive aspect to this intervention; for many clinicians this is distasteful. However, so is the sexual abuse of a child by his/her parent. The more readily the adult offender accepts responsibility for his abusing the child the less coercion enters the therapeutic picture. The less responsibility the offender takes the more psychologically damaged the child, and the higher the risk for resumed incest. During the early phases of treatment, control is an essential element that must be provided to the family in one way or another to prevent further abuse and to stabilize the situation while the therapeutic processes can begin. The techniques discussed here help to provide such control and are usually less coercive and preferable to those that might otherwise need to be employed by the relevant legal and protective agencies. It is perhaps understandable that some professionals find these control issues distasteful and may shy away from dealing with incest in part for these reasons. However, it does seem that, given the prevalence of incest and the seriousness of its consequences for the victims, professional distaste about temporarily using authority to protect the child is misplaced delicacy. Multilaterality and fairness demand that we not scapegoat the offender, but also require us to protect child victims until they can begin to protect themselves.

CHOICE: Father's Sexual Attraction to Daughter or Father's Needs for Relatedness

Incest is usually regarded as a situation where sexuality holds center stage—where sexual attraction or passion for a child can reach mythic or iconic proportions and where sexual stimulation is central to the heart of the matter. In the vast majority of cases, this is completely wrong; incest is most usually an expression of the search for interpersonal attention, affection, and nurturance by the adult offender. Its inception usually follows a long period of marital estrangement and often a recent narcissistic injury (such as an occupational injury, unemployment, or death of a parent). Incest is usually the result of a search for relatedness; it has been expressed in one of the worst possible ways, but holding center stage in incest is not sex, but need—and the need is usually for relatedness.[8] This is a rarely appreciated difference and certain common errors flow from this misunderstanding.

---

[8]One distinct exception to this is sadistic incest, that is, sexual abuse of a child that includes such formal sadistic practices as binding, whipping, humiliation, and cutting or burning of the sexual

Common Errors: Focus on Sex and "Perversion"

One common error is to condemn the father for any interest in his daughter or his children in the mistaken belief that sexuality lies at the origin of such interest. This misconception contaminates other aspects of the relationship, for the victim and other children as well as the offender, suffusing it with innuendo. It also contaminates the father–child relationship post hoc, calling into question even healthy aspects or interactions and essentially robbing the child of her past relationship with her father.

Another common error is to scapegoat the father by seeing his needs as some sort of fundamental perversion of character. This betrays everyone's loyalty to the offender, with all this implies about resistance in treatment. Futhermore, the father may either become angry because it's not true (which discredits the therapist and arrays the family's loyalty against the therapist) or he may accept this ascription and despair, which is likely to decrease his hope and motivation to change and increase the risk of any self-destructiveness or destructive acting out.

The very serious result of seeing his needs for relatedness as sexually perverted and sick is to isolate the father completely from his family. He is given no hope of returning to his family and denied *any* contact with his children, either in the present or in the future, and is often denied even supervised visitations. This absolutely violates the family's loyalty, and essentially punishes the victim for information she provides, increasing the siblings' anger at her because now they have lost their father because of her.

These points should not be seen as contradicting the earlier material about the advisability of removing the offender rather than the victim early in treatment. Removing the offender is *temporary*, holds no implications of character assassination, and makes no attempt to permanently isolate him or to prevent contact between children and father. Their rights to see each other must be explicitly supported by the therapist; if protective concerns necessitate that visits be supervised, that can be made explicit and the therapist can help coordinate the search for the appropriate supervisor. Interestingly, this is another example of therapeutic multilaterality—supporting both the children's (including the

---

areas. This is different from any violence that may occur in the more usual forms of incest while subduing a victim or gaining his/her "compliance"; such violence can be said to be "incidental" to the sexual abuse. In contradistinction, formal sadistic practices, when they occur, are intrinsic to the sexual abuse, and the goal of such violence is the increased sexual stimulation of the offender. The present discussion does *not* apply to treating sadistic incest, which introduces significant difficulties relating to family pathology, offender pathology, conditioning of sexual appetites, and consequences for the victims. While arguments could perhaps be made that sadism is also a very indirect search for relatedness, this seems to me an extremely tenuous position; classical conditioning and pathology appear more to the point here. The present discussion regarding needs for relatedness is therefore less applicable to the case of sadistic incest; however, loyalty considerations are not. Sadistically abused children usually show decided loyalty to the offender, often to the surprise of therapists.

victim) and the father's inherent right to see each other, while insisting upon the victim's rights to be protected from any further abuse.

This common misconception of the father's interest in his children as sexual and the resulting isolation of the father from family also can contribute to a process where the family's loyalty to the father turns him into a beleaguered hero, hounded by the minions of a punitive society. For the children he may become the knight in shining armor; they then firmly believe that he would visit them every day if he could, bring them presents, be much better to them than their mother, and so on. Essentially, preventing contact between offender and children fosters a split in which the father is illegitimately romanticized and the mother devalued: father can do no wrong, and mother no right. So much for issues of accountability, and fairness—and the family therapy will be preoccupied with the red herring of the all-good father and the rotten mother.

Recommended Treatment Stance:
Focus on Father's Capacity for Relatedness

Instead, recognition of the father's needs for relatedness and his relationally pursuant style can be used as the resources they are. He has the desire and capacity for relatedness and usually at least some of the skills to begin and maintain relationships. In the family the offender has often been the primary source of relatedness and warmth for the children (although not of caretaking, which has usually fallen to the mother and parentified daughter). His relatedness has earned him a type of emotional "credit," particularly with his children; he can be said to have accrued earned entitlement. This entitlement is a powerful resource to help temper the anger and the scapegoating of an offender after discovery or disclosure. His accountability for the incest is certainly not erased by this earned entitlement, but his entitlement does mean that he has earned the right to have his positive qualities and past contributions considered. His past appropriate warmth with the children, including the victim, is one of the reasons for their intense loyalty to him, and with assistance they learn to distinguish appropriate from inappropriate expressions of warmth and desires for relatedness.

The offender's drive for relatedness and his relationally pursuant style also function as resources in treatment because he will very usually *want* to be able to return to his family, and this increases his motivation to come to therapy and to eventually make the changes necessary to gain reentry into the family. While this motivation is often quite manipulative at first, his capacity for relationship can rapidly become more genuine. He begins to get very clear messages about his responsibility for the incest, information that incest is in fact abusive, exploitative, and destructive to his daughter. These messages *begin* to reorient him; coupled with increasing trust that the therapist will not scapegoat him nor allow scapegoating, he can begin to examine responsibility for the sexual abuse and its effect on his family. These changes would be much more difficult if there were no desire or capacity for relationship. His drives for relationship constitute a healing force in the family. These eventually contribute to the desire to make up for the destruction he's caused. Futhermore, they will help during the admittedly difficult phase of family work that addresses the marital estrangement and the need to improve that relationship if the risk of resumed incest is to remain as low as possible.

Finally, the offender's history of some form of relational life with his children can provide both a "predisposition" for them toward communication, caring, and contact and some of the vehicles for relationship. These are not necessarily always verbal interactions. In some families, the children may recognize their father's relatedness when he allows them to accompany and "help" him run errands, or do the yard work or grocery shopping; he may share an interest with the children, or be the parent who inquires about and scrutinizes their home-work. Whatever healthy vehicles for relatedness have existed in the past can be encouraged and used to foster appropriate relatedness in the family during treatment.

One family seen in therapy was comprised of a 40-year-old man, his 36-year-old wife, and their three daughters (ages 17, 15, and 11) and one son (age 9). The identified patient was the 15-year-old daughter, who had disclosed 4 years of sexual abuse by the father to her school counselor. During the family evaluation, it became clear that the 17-year-old daughter had been living with her boyfriend's family for 1 year, that she too had been sexually abused by her father for 3 years, and that the father was occasionally physically abusive to the 9-year-old son. The 15-year-old daughter was physically stunning, yet not especially bright intellectually. The mother and eldest daughter were literally not speaking to father, charges were pending, and the protective unit wanted the 15-year-old daughter and 9-year-old son placed outside the home. Everyone was angry at the father and scapegoating began; for example, threats had been made to inform his supervisors at work, which, due to the nature of his job, would have certainly meant his being fired. This was a very potent threat because this man had worked very hard and really achieved a position of respect and responsibility.

During the family evaluation it also became clear that the husband and wife's estrangement was long-standing and appeared to be exacerbated by their differ-ent life-styles. His was upwardly mobile; he had attended college part-time while working, graduated, and worked toward promotions. He wanted a social life with other couples, had become health/sports conscious, had cut back on his drinking, and, finally, had begun to have an interest in music. Her life-style was very different and she resented her husband's efforts to change himself and her; she worked as a cocktail waitress until 1 A.M. in a well-known lounge and would stay out until about 3 A.M. with her friends "drinking and just having a good time." She valued contact with her peer group and expressed loyalty to their values and to the ideas of relaxing and enjoying life in the company of her friends.

In the household no one was responsible for cooking, cleaning, child care, or general household organization. The mother worked nights and so slept from 4 A.M. to noon, and the father was out at work or in school. It gradually became clear that the father's physical abuse of his son was related to his frustrated attempts to actively parent in a chaotic household in which his son was relatively uncontrolled. His intermittent incestuous abuse of his daughters distressed him, and he described a feeling that an "undertow" pulled him in that direction despite his best efforts at resisting.

Working in cooperation with the protective services, the children remained in the home and the father voluntarily went to live in a coworker's basement apartment. The household became more chaotic in the father's absence; the son became reclusive and extremely irritable, the 15-year-old became depressed and angry, while the 11-year-old watched and the 17-year-old continued to live with her boyfriend's family in bitter isolation from her own. The father's and children's desires for contact were accommodated by *regular, predictable* visitation to the home; initially these were supervised weekly visits.

Over time the father began to provide long-distance, appropriate parenting for his children and he rapidly emerged as the primary caretaker. During his weekly visits, he insisted on a rudimentary schedule and list of chores. When problems arose, one of the children would usually phone him. With the new temporary living arrangements he could gain some control over the chaos, the mother felt less pressured by his particular aspirations, and (through lack of propinquity) the sexual and physical abuse dropped out.

Eventually, the parents initiated divorce; the father visited three times a week without supervision and provided the organizing functions of parenting (looking at chore lists, taking the children out each Sunday, providing telephone backup, checking on school work, and accompanying the children to buy school and winter clothes). The mother stopped staying out so late, became less bitter, and fought less with her former husband and the children. She provided the daily parenting presence, kept her job and her friends, and formed a close relationship with her 17-year-old daughter, who remained with her boyfriend's family.

Therapy continued for 18 months; at 6 months after termination, the father had found a more permanent place to live, and everyone involved (protective agency, family therapist, father, daughters, and mother) felt very comfortable with the idea of the children visiting him at his apartment, as a group or singly. He had taken full responsibility for the incest during treatment; with the increase in his abilities to parent and reduce the chaos, the "undertow" gradually disappeared and he felt very strongly (as did both his daughters) that the sexual abuse would not recur. His physical abuse of the 9-year-old boy dropped away immediately upon moving out of the house (besides the obvious factor of lack of propinquity, the boy began to miss his father and began to take advantage of opportunities to see him and to act in accordance with his standards).

The 15-year-old daughter's particularly strong loyalties to her father and her intellectual vulnerabilities gave some initial concern; during treatment in front of the whole family, her father told her that if *anything* happened that she felt uncomfortable or confused by, he wanted her to tell him immediately and then tell her mother and the therapist. They all agreed with this, including the 15-year-old, who recognized that these instructions were part of the new relationship with her father and that if any problems arose they would be dealt with fairly.[9] The father's needs for relatedness had paved the way for the sexual abuse, but also provided the pivotal concern, energy, and history of family ties that allowed change to occur. His efforts provided structure and warmth, and his history of relatedness with his children contributed to the loyalties they had for him, and their motivation to continue contact and to comply with his parenting efforts. His needs for relatedness also contributed to remaining too long in a marriage in which neither partner was happy, but that was gradually resolved, and his relational style was to serve him in good stead 2 years later when he began dating a woman whom he had met through work.

CHOICE: Mother's Depleted Parentification or Ability to be Responsive

Depletion and exhaustion cannot really be considered resources. The mother of an incest victim is almost always emotionally depleted long before the incest is ever discovered or disclosed, and this new information is hardly calculated to replenish her emotional supplies.

Common Errors

Three errors are commonly made in working with the mother of the victim/wife of the offender. First, her emotional depletion and passivity are often misinterpreted as lack of concern, and her relational avoidance mistaken for knowledge and collusion in the incest; some authors have gone so far as to blame wives for the incest.[10] Conversely, another common mistake is *not* holding the mother accountable for her role in the family structure and processes. While she is not responsible for her husband's sexual contact with a child, she does have some responsibility for participating in a family structure that is at high risk for incest, and some clear responsibilities in therapy for changing this structure.

Third, mothers of incest victims are often pushed too hard and too punitively to provide caretaking for everyone concerned, without some provision being made earlier to alleviate their significant depletion. Simply pushing or maneu-

---

[9]Some form of confrontation by the victim, with resulting acceptance of responsibility by the offender and a genuine apology, is a task toward the end phase of treatment. The success of this intervention, interestingly enough, is *not* dependent on the offender's response; it is dependent on the firmness and tenacity with which the victim asks her questions and makes her points. Most offenders respond well; a few do not, but the intervention succeeds nevertheless.

[10]It should be noted in this context that *some* mothers have in fact been knowingly and actively collusive in the incestuous abuse of their children and some have been actual participants, occasionally as primary offenders, although usually as secondary, recruited offenders. These situations of maternal participation are relatively rare, however. Maternal collusion is less rare, but still much less frequent than some authors have implied. The continuum of knowledge and collusion is very wide, with most mothers clustering in a region that can best be described as neither knowing about the incest or really pursuing the occasional odd statement or incident, but often being able to make better sense of certain situations or statements *after* disclosure or discovery has occurred.

vering the mother to provide caretaking might result in short-term improvements in this area, but these are usually rapidly overwhelmed by the mother's emotional exhaustion and needs, so that she becomes obviously or passively resistant to therapeutic influence. She was depleted and isolated before the incest was discovered or disclosed; at this point, she has also received very bad information, usually feels betrayed by both husband and daughter, has been separated from at least one of them, is facing protective and legal agency involvement, and is now in family therapy where the therapist is maneuvering to have her provide things she cannot and may even blame her for the incest or at least strongly suspect her of active, knowing collusion. The usual result of this is a family member who becomes *very* resistant to therapeutic intervention and clearly signals this to the rest of the family, who, operating from their loyalty positions, become resistant as well. The mother may resist by subtly undermining therapeutic efforts around protective concern, structural change, or issues of accountability; she may even become so resistant that she can deny the possibility of incest or refuse treatment whatsoever. Her self-esteem is badly hurt and she is in a no-win position, but is without the resources to extricate herself, or her family.

Recommended Therapeutic Stance

A potential resource in all this does exist, however. What underlies the mother's parentification and depletion is an *internalized*, felt responsibility to care for her husband and children, and this *is* a legitimate resource in treatment. The mother may or may not have been adequately taking care of herself and her family because of this depletion, but very probably has a strong sense of *obligation* to do so. This almost invariably allows her to have a renewed ability to respond to family members' needs *when she is no longer so depleted.*

Building Supports for the Mother. Alleviating the mother's emotional depletion can be depleting for the therapist as well if she/he attempts to do this from his/her own emotional reserves (a process that in any case comes closer to caretaking than therapy). Instead, it has been found very useful to assist the mother in developing a social support network. This should occur very early in treatment, during and immediately after the evaluation phase. Usually when asked about people with whom she can talk, a woman in an incest family will state that there is no one; however, with firm insistence and assistance by the therapist, the mother can generally identify some people that she can at least begin to cultivate as a potential social network. (During this cultivating phase, emotional support, encouragement, and sometimes insistence can be temporarily provided by the therapist.) These support networks of acquaintances, friends, extended family, clergy, neighbors, and the like tend to form slowly at first, and then coalesce more quickly once the therapist's insistence has generated some momentum in the process. It is helpful here to focus explicitly on the mother's isolation and her relational style, emphasizing that she expects to give but not receive, and that her caretaking capacity is now diminished because she has attempted to take care of everybody instead of herself and her family. The goal is to shift the mother's style of relating toward greater reciprocity, to help her differentiate those people who do deserve her caretaking from those who do not, and to clarify what kind of reciprocity she can legitimately expect from certain relationships.

A wide range of nonrelational supports outside the family can also be very helpful as sources of replenishment. For many people a reinvolvement in religion is extremely replenishing. Reinvolvement in an old interest, such as sports, knitting, woodworking, baking, gardening, or the like can be replenishing, especially when the time necessary for such involvement is discussed in the family work and validated by the therapist. This can help legitimize to the family that the mother literally *deserves* that time, and this shift in her position and in how she is perceived can be as replenishing as the actual activity. (Sometimes, in fact, the "activity" can be a nonactivity; one woman decided to hire a babysitter for 1 hour each day of the week. That way, she said, she knew from 11 to 12, Monday through Friday, she had time off. If she wanted to get her hair cut, run some errands for the house, read a book, or go for a walk, she could do so without having to take the children along. Even if running errands for the family, she said that getting away from the house and children for 1 hour each day was restorative, and helped her to be a better parent for the rest of the day. Besides the actual time spent away, the legitimizing of the fact that she had needs was a relief.)

The issue of *relationship*, however, remains very important here. The nonrelational sources of replenishment are useful but should not really be a substitute for establishing the relational support network. If the mother is extremely depleted and the network will take a lot of cultivating, it is helpful to use nonrelational sources of replenishment temporarily, or as a supplement, but always with the idea of emphasizing the relational issues as well.

Another interesting possibility in this realm involves the convergence of the mother's needs to establish relationships with reciprocity and the husband's relationally pursuant style (given added impetus by his obligation toward his children and his wife because of the incest). As treatment progresses the father will usually shift his focus from daughter to mother and will begin pursuing his wife relationally. Usually she is angry, hurt, outraged, and betrayed by the incest; these emotions can help fuel a new assertiveness in her to begin demanding some reciprocity in caretaking from her husband. His relational needs and remorse are almost always strong enough to tolerate these new demands for reciprocity and to begin to meet them. All of which begins to change the mother's unilaterally obligated, and depleted, relationships.

The Mother's Possible Abuse History. Finally, it is extremely important for the therapist to assess whether the mother was herself a victim of sexual and/or physical abuse. This is often the case in situations in which the mother is adamantly unwilling to deal with the possibility that incest has occurred in her family. In these cases individual therapy focusing on the mother's history of abuse is indicated, and it should run concurrently with the family treatment. The individual work usually moves more quickly than if she were not also in family work. Treatment should address her own victimization, in detail, and all the ways in which she feels her own victimization may have contributed to her daughter's. [Although the mother may have several exaggerated and/or erroneous concerns, it is clear that there is *some* intergenerational component to incest, with an incest victim growing up, marrying, and helping to establish a family structure in which her *husband* is at risk to sexually abuse one of their daughters (see Gelinas, 1983).] Treatment of the mother's incest history will often free up empathy for the daughter's experience of incest, as well as making available a great deal of energy, self-esteem, and assertiveness, and the family treatment tends to move rapidly from that point.

Support for the Mother's Motivation to Protect. When a family first presents for treatment, the mother's depletion is often easily assessed, but her potential for change is not. Some mothers look so depleted, bedraggled, or bitter that the problem seems intractable. Very usually it is not; in the overwhelming majority of cases, the mothers of incest victims do respond very well to treatment efforts, especially efforts that also address their own needs as well as their daughters' needs. They have often had little opportunity for someone to try to address their needs, and when the therapist does so as part of a multilateral position, they usually respond quite readily. For them a little goes a long way.

A *possible* exception involves the wife of a malevolent offender. The wives of malevolent offenders tend to be so cowed and inadequate that they will support their husband against their children regardless of the consequences and so are sometimes not really available for therapeutic work. Whatever the dynamics of these situations, and whatever the individual and systemic forces, the mother's abilities to respond to the manifest needs of her children are so submerged in her unilateral attempts to meet her husband's needs that they are essentially unavailable for *therapeutic* work; only legal intervention can begin to address, if not necessarily meet, the children's needs. However, these situations are in a distinct minority. Some wives of malevolent offenders do in fact take the opportunities offered by interveners, participate in setting legal limits on the husband, and begin to respond to the needs of their children. Also, most offenders are not malevolent.

For the overwhelming majority of mothers, their depletion is the result of continuous efforts on their part to provide caretaking in the context of a life in which no one has provided for them. If their depletion can be alleviated, they will begin to once again take care of their children because they have an internalized sense of obligation to do so—a recognition of the inherent entitlement of children to be cared for. For the therapist, it is incomparably easier to help encourage greater relational reciprocity than to attempt to graft on the ability to be responsive. These mothers already have that ability.

CHOICE: Multiple Agency Involvements or Therapeutic Network

Unlike many problems addressed by family treatment, incest usually implies protective and legal agency involvement. Whatever the propensity of mental health professionals to ignore incest, other professionals have taken positions on it. Incest is a crime as well as a therapeutic issue, and in most states legal and/or criminal issues are involved. Similarly, protective concerns (and the law) require the involvement of social service agencies. If these societal agencies are not initially involved in a case they soon will be, since therapists are "mandated reporters" and are required to notify the statutory agency in their state of the incest (even if it is supposedly no longer occurring).[11]

The inherent protective and legal issues have contributed to the reluctance of mental health professionals to treat incest (see Sgroi, 1982). Given its prevalence and seriousness, there are *very* few treatment articles, particularly in family therapy. This reluctance to get involved with legal and protective systems is perhaps understandable in that few therapists have received legal training, and the adversarial structure of the legal system is not particularly compatible with mental health concerns, cognitive styles of therapists, and the legitimate inability to predict human behavior. Nevertheless, the involvement of many agencies is practically a given when treating incest families. This multiple agency involvement can be a serious problem, and major irritation, if handled poorly, or it can be invaluable in changing families that have the powerful homeostatic set of forces found with incest.

Incest involves powerful forces intrinsic to its inception and maintenance (role assignments, relational styles, secrecy, isolation of the victim from her sibs, etc.); it can be difficult to stop and keep stopped. Other agencies can be invaluable in helping the therapist deal with these strong homeostatic elements.[12] They have the statutory powers to do things that are sometimes necessary on a temporary basis and that the family therapist cannot do. The protective and legal agencies can require a family to get therapy; they can get them started and usually keep them coming for their sessions during that early fearful and resistant phase. They can help get the offender out of the house, bring the child back in, and legitimize the notion that incest is harmful, shouldn't happen, and will be stopped. They can give, and enforce, a temporary restraining order if need be; they can help the family get temporary financial assistance, food stamps, and sometimes transportation. They can help monitor the family,

---

[11]There has been a very strong tendency in mental health and medical circles not to report child sexual abuse. The legal and ethical responsibility to make such a report undoubtedly contributes to patterns of professionals simply "not seeing" this abuse when it is manifestly obvious, or trivializing it (either as an issue or both in terms of its prevalence and consequences for the victim). It is a major *therapeutic* error to not make such reports.

[12]See Lustig, Dresser, Spellman, and Murray (1966) for more examples of homeostatic forces. Although this article comes far too close to blaming the victim, and the wife, its examples of homeostatic elements are valuable.

serving notice that the incest must not resume, and they can share responsibility with the therapist here.

Common Errors: Failure To Report and Isolation from Legal and Protective Activities

Not reporting incest to the relevant protective agency is a therapeutic error of major proportions. Keeping incest secret in this way is particularly tempting if the family involved is somehow financially, politically, or socially prominent, but it is an even larger error here because the power of these families will rapidly incorporate and entangle the therapist until he/she literally becomes part of the problem—another element in the pathological homeostasis and one who should have known better.

In reporting the incest, the therapist is notifying the protective agency of information strongly suggesting that a child is at risk of being abused or might have been abused; it is the responsibility of the *agency* to ascertain if abuse has or has not happened. Mandated reporters are legally protected from being sued in the event that they filed a report and it turned out to be unsubstantiated. Lack of substantiation can mean that no abuse happened, or that the investigator was not able to definitely establish that abuse occurred; it is no reflection on the mandated reporter. In short, the structure favors reporting and legally protects the reporter. It also keeps reports, including the unsubstantiated ones, on file for some period of time. More than one child has had abuse stopped because the unsubstantiated reports begin to accumulate, form a pattern, and point the way for a new and different investigation.

The family should be told immediately that the therapist is a mandated reporter, needs to file a report, and will do so immediately (or, *very* occasionally, as soon as clinically advisable, e.g., immediately after a suicidal offender has been hospitalized). This establishes the therapist's standing *outside* the incest, as not colluding in the continuation of either the abuse or the secrecy surrounding it. Filing unequivocally implies that incest is wrong—a revelation for many families—and serves notice that the therapist is not amenable to blandishments or threats of dire consequences (civil suit, suicide, etc.). It begins to open up the issue. It introduces the clearer light of reason, ethics, and the law into a secret, furtive corner of the family, and this is usually needed.

Offenders and families have a nearly infinite number of rationalizations about why the sexual abuse was not abuse. For example, one offender who sexually abused his daughter for 4 years, and, as reported by the daughter, never spoke to her during the abuse and physically subdued her when she resisted, said that "it was special" and so not abusive. Bringing the weight of societal agencies into this situation in this way unequivocally establishes that the sexual contact was illegitimate and abusive, that adults in society can and will intervene to protect children, and that the therapist will not be subdued by the family's rules.

If the therapist attempts to "protect" the family by not filing, he/she is siding with continued secrecy, a major homeostatic mechanism. Some might argue that it's not really secret anymore since the whole family now knows about it. All that has happened is that the family has told someone else (the therapist) about their secret and has now included him/her in it. The therapist is now inevitably colluding, siding with, and protecting the family's facade in the interest of the parents *to the exclusion* of the interests of the children because *incest can very rarely be stopped this way.* The victim begins to despair that any adult will (can) help her and either becomes more depressed, acts out, or quietly submits to resumed sexual abuse because she cannot tell the therapist. (She may fear that if she tells the therapist, he/she probably will again do nothing, her father will be angry, her mother will be angry at her father and the victim, and she'll make the therapist look foolish for having believed the father's earlier assurances.) The parents begin to see the therapist as a "buddy" and the children hold him/her in contempt. If the incest should be halted for the duration of the therapy, fine— but what happens after termination? Probabilities of resumption are quite high, and the therapist who knew of incest and didn't report it is in an extremely poor position professionally and legally, if the case later comes to the attention of an outraged protective service agency or assistant district attorney, particularly when severe incest is involved.

Recommended Therapeutic Approach: Advantages of Reporting and Working with Relevant Agencies

There is no substitute for filing. The protective service can help monitor the cessation of incest, and can often provide the therapist with information of a different sort than that to which we usually have access. For example, they can make home visits. One offender was quite cooperative in therapy and the family began to initiate some changes; however, protective service home visits found that all soap, light bulbs, and toilet paper were locked in father's bedroom, to which only he had the key. This degree of continuing, rather bizarre control by the father, lack of intervention or disclosure by the mother, and lack of disclosure by the children certainly suggests a high risk of the rapid resumption of sexual abuse once agency involvement was withdrawn.

The involvement of protective and legal agencies, if ignored by the clinician, can make therapy much more difficult and can allow a variety of difficulties to ensue. Conversely, actively cooperating with these agencies can reduce confusion and splitting, can help structure interventions to be mutually beneficial, can eliminate and reduce working at cross-purposes, and can share responsibility and improve monitoring. This is most easily accomplished by being active, rather than reactive. It is useful to contact the relevant agencies and individuals as soon as possible after opening the case. Typically families will provide the necessary releases of information when told by the therapist that it is usual to work in concert with case workers, pediatricians, attorneys, and the like. Time spent telling the involved professionals what the clinician needs and what he/she plans to do is time well spent. It is often helpful to cultivate "contact" people, to gradually establishing credit and trust with them. All systems have staff who understand the workings of their own systems and who can explain them to the clinician.

Continued, active contact is useful in reducing splitting and scapegoating of one professional or another; this also helps coordination of effort. Thus, if it is preferable to the family therapist to have the offender removed, he/she is wise to so inform the protective services to see if they will cooperate with that, rather than receiving a case that has met protective considerations (separating offender and victim) but has done so in a manner that makes the family therapist's task much more difficult. The other agencies have their own responsibilities and often the therapist is in a position to assist them as well. For instance, the clinician may have more experience with sexual abuse cases than another intervener and may be able to provide a steadying and supportive influence. As clinicians we can provide assistance regarding whether visitation should be allowed (it should) and whether it should be supervised (it may have to be). We can help negotiate custody issues and provide information to judges faced with these decisions. We can also help the agencies get information about the sexual abuse (and remind them that we occupy a multilateral position and will continue to hold the offender accountable but not scapegoat nor allow scapegoating).

All of these functions are obviously more easily accomplished with contact people that one knows. Sometimes, however, agency-level cooperation can be mutually beneficial. One local mental health agency had a contract with a protective service agency to provide therapy for referred sexual abuse family cases. These cases were proving somewhat intractable, however, and during review it became clear that the mental health agency was receiving the cases "too late." Invariably the families had been contacted by the protective services, had gone through several weeks of intake, the victim had usually been removed, and a new, ongoing (as opposed to investigative) case worker had been assigned, who *then* made the referral to the mental health agency. By then the family was no longer in crisis, the *victim* had often been removed, and the situation was not well structured for the family therapist. The protective agency was also concerned that the cases were not going particularly well. A short series of meetings shifted the referral process forward, so that the clinicians could recommend certain visitation and protective structures, both agencies' responsibilities were met, and the new cases began to progress reasonably.

Whether contact is at a formal agency level or person-to-person across agencies, active cooperation initiated by the family therapist usually results in reduced confusion, irritation, and anger, and quite often results in the case being structured so as to maximize our chances of getting needed changes in the family.

SUMMARY

Families in which incest has been discovered or disclosed are at risk of being broken and separated by protective, legal, and therapeutic error. Some families should appropriately experience divorce, dissolution, or the loss of their children, but these families are very much in the minority, and decisions of this magnitude (particularly loss of the children) should be made clearly and deliberately, not as the byproducts of error. Incest families have traditionally received no treatment, or court-ordered treatment with professionals known to the courts who may well have no expertise with either families or the treatment of incest.

Also, families with incest often have the reputation of being difficult, intransigent, or stuck, and sometimes they are. However, when therapeutic impasses with these families are examined, many of the problems cluster in the four areas just discussed: resistance of the victim, the father's desire for continuing relationship and intimacy, the mother's passivity, and multiagency confusion. Seen as expressions of filial loyalty, the father's needs for relationship, the mother's felt obligation to care for her family, and the possibility of establishing a coordinated therapeutic network around a family with an entrenched problem provides the therapist with therapeutic approaches that are very different from the "problem" orientation. The family's capacity for caring, and thus change, is mobilized; individual and family needs can be better addressed; and the family structures and incest, with its consequences, can be treated. The very process of discovery or disclosure contributes to this and functions as a hidden resource; it can provide therapeutic opportunities not available in other stuck family and marital situations. These opportunities, and the approach outlined here, draw on the positive resources of the family. The therapist, as well as protective and legal professionals, may well need to set limits and provide appropriate boundaries, especially early in treatment. Yet, if a resources orientation is also used, with its emphasis for incest on loyalty, accountability, relatedness, caretaking, and fairness, the family's strengths lie with, rather than against, the therapist.

REFERENCES

Bernstein, G. Office management of the incest victim. *Medical Aspects of Human Sexuality*, 1979, *3*(Nov), 67, 87.

Boszormenyi-Nagy, I., & Krasner, B. Trust-based therapy: A contextual approach. *American Journal of Psychiatry*, 1980, *137*, 767–775.

Boszormenyi-Nagy, I., & Spark, G. *Invisible loyalties: reciprocity in intergenerational family therapy*. New York: Harper & Row, 1973.

Boszormenyi-Nagy, I., & Ulrich, D. Contextual family therapy. In A. Gurman & D. Kniskern (Eds.), *Handbook of family therapy*. New York: Brunner/Mazel, 1980.

Finkelhor, D. *Sexually victimized children*. New York: Free Press, 1979. (a)

Finkelhor, D. What's wrong with sex between adults and children? Ethics and the problem of sexual abuse. *American Journal of Orthopsychiatry*, 1979, *49*, 692–697. (b)

Gelinas, D. The persisting negative effects of incest. *Psychiatry*, 1983, *46*, 312–332.

Giaretto, H. Humanistic treatment of father–daughter incest. In R. Helfer & H. Kempe (Eds.), *Child abuse and neglect: The family and the community*. New York: Ballinger, 1976.

Groth, A. N. The incest offender. In S. Sgroi (Ed.), *Handbook of clinical intervention in child sexual abuse*. Lexington, MA: Heath, 1982.

Herman, J., with Hirschman, L. *Father–daughter incest*. Cambridge, MA: Harvard University Press, 1981.

James, J., & Meyerding, J. Early sexual experiences and prostitution. *American Journal of Psychiatry*, 1977, *134*, 1381–1385.

Karpel, M., & Strauss, E. *Family evaluation*. New York: Gardner Press, 1983.

Kaufman, I., Peck, A., & Tagiuri, C. The family constellation and overt incestuous relations between father and daughter. *American Journal of Orthopsychiatry*, 1954, *24*, 266–279.

Kinsey, A., Pomeroy, W., Martin, C., & Gebhard, P. *Sexual behavior in the human female*. Philadelphia: Saunders, 1953.

Lustig, N., Dresser, J., Spellman, S., & Murray, T. Incest: A family group survival pattern. *Archives of General Psychiatry*, 1966, *14*, 31–40.

McCary, J. My most unusual sexual case: Nymphomania. *Medical Aspects of Human Sexuality*, 1979, *3*(May), 74–75.

Meiselman, K. *Incest: A psychological study of causes and effects with treatment recommendations*. San Francisco: Jossey-Bass, 1978.

Nakashima, I., & Zakus, G. Incest: Review and clinical experience. *Pediatrics for the Clinician*, 1977, *60*, 696–701.

Rosenfeld, A. Incidence of a history of incest among 18 female psychiatric patients. *American Journal of Psychiatry*, 1979, *136*, 791–795.

Sgroi, S. Introduction: The state of the art in child-sexual-abuse intervention. In S. Sgroi (Ed.), *Handbook of clinical intervention in child sexual abuse*. Lexington, MA: Heath, 1982.

Spencer, J. Father–daughter incest. *Child Welfare*, 1978, *57*, 581–590.

Sullivan, H. S. *The interpersonal theory of psychiatry*. New York: Norton, 1953.

Summit, R., & Kryso, J. Sexual abuse of children: A clinical spectrum. *American Journal of Orthopsychiatry*, 1978, *48*, 237–251.

CHAPTER 12

Family Resources in Coping with Serious Illness

Macaran A. Baird
William J. Doherty

When individuals experience serious illness, families experience equally serious stress. A serious illness in one family member requires a number of difficult reactions from the family, including shifting family roles, accepting individual mortality, relating successfully to the medical delivery system, integrating medical information into their own belief system, and understanding the implications of a life-threatening illness for the future of the family itself. In adapting to a stressful illness event or to the rigors of handling a debilitating chronic illness, families often are called upon to use every resource they possess. For purposes of this chapter, we define family resources as *characteristics of a family and its environment that positively influence the family's ability to cope with the health-related challenges it faces.*

This chapter offers a clinical discussion rather than a comprehensive review of the research literature on family resources in medical illness. For a more research-oriented discussion, see McCubbin and Patterson's (1983) Family Adaptation and Adjustment Model, which has family resources as a core component. The general family and health research literature has been reviewed by Pattison and Anderson (1975), and a conceptual organization of this area, along with recent representative studies, is found in Doherty and McCubbin (1985).

What family characteristics constitute resources in illness situations? What activities lead to their discovery and utilization? Who works with the family closely enough to encourage wise use of family resources? What roles do different professionals play in identifying and mobilizing family resources during serious illness? When is family therapy indicated as part of the medical

Macaran A. Baird, M.D. Family Practice Residency Programs, Department of Family Medicine, University of Oklahoma Health Sciences Center, Edmond, Oklahoma.

William J. Doherty, Ph.D. Department of Family Medicine. Presently Department of Family Social Science, University of Minnesota, Minneapolis, Minnesota.

treatment plan? This chapter deals with these and related questions. We begin with a discussion of how family resources are identified during different levels of interaction between health professionals and families, from simple information exchange to specialized family therapy. Next we describe ways in which family resources can be mobilized in health care interactions involving physicians, nurses, and family therapists. Finally, we discuss roadblocks to utilizing family resources and opportunities for overcoming these obstacles in the health care system.

IDENTIFYING FAMILY RESOURCES

When a family member is seriously ill, families are generally available and interested in contacting the health care team. It is expected that health care professionals will routinely have some contact with the families of seriously ill patients, even if only to briefly inform the family about the results of diagnostic procedures or surgery. Chronic illness generally means long-term contact with a health care team. It is through these interactions that family resources are discovered. Furthermore, different kinds of interaction reveal different kinds of family resources. Since family resources are identified by professionals primarily through talking with families, the following discussion describes family resources from the perspective of how they are discovered by the health professional—whether physician, nurse, therapist, or others—depending on the type of interaction the professional has with the family.

Table 12-1 outlines our model for delineating five levels of professional involvement with families in health care. Levels 1 through 4, described also by Doherty (1985), represent increasing degrees of sophistication in understanding and dealing with families from a primary care perspective. The role of a consulting family therapist is discussed for each of these primary care levels. Level 5 constitutes a greater degree of sophistication, normally characterizing only trained family therapists' interactions with families. At each successive level in the five steps, new family resources are more readily identified and mobilized by the health care professional.

Level 1: Minimal Emphasis on Family

At Level 1, family interaction with the medical team is scanty. The physician briefly informs the family about the outcome of surgery or the results of major tests such as those for cancer. Afterward, basic biological data are shared with the family if they happen to be available at the bedside when the physician sees the patient. No effort is made to contact the family except for emergencies or medical/legal decisions. In some cases the physician may view the family as an inconvenient appendage to the patient; the patient is seen as a repository for disease. This perspective is not stated openly, but is identifiable by observing the physician–patient interaction. Numbers from laboratory tests, medical abbreviations, and complex diagnostic terms and eponyms are the topics of importance. Rarely is there translation to nontechnical terms in language that the patient and family can understand. Rarely does the physician ask open-ended questions during a sit-down conference with the patient and family.

Family History

Under these circumstances only a few family resources are visible to the physician and other members of the health care team. One is a family medical history. This is a data bank of medical information that most physicians would utilize no matter how they view families in health care. This data bank may give diagnostic clues to inheritable diseases or uncover risk factors for disorders that cluster within families.

Economic Status

At level 1 *favorable economic status* may be recognized as helpful for a seriously ill patient. Sometimes being recognized as poor by state or federal standards is "favorable" since it permits the use of public resources to deliver health care services to a family. On the other hand, family wealth enables a patient to seek alternatives to the currently responsible health care team. This may be interpreted as a threat to the physician or institution unless families and their unique characteristics are viewed as important to the health care delivery process. At this level even assets as concrete as wealth may not be appreciated as resources by the health care providers. Family wealth is discussed again in the context of Level 2.

The Family Therapist as a Resource

How does a family (or systems) therapist fit into a health care system functioning at Level 1? Joining the system is the first task. In a teaching institution a therapist may be asked to be a consultant to a medical service team. For example, family medicine and pediatric residencies often have family therapists or behavioral scientists as part of their faculty. Internal medicine training also is beginning to emphasize behavioral skills for which family therapists and other behavioral scientists are needed (Lipkin, Quill, & Napodano, 1984). In this role the therapist may be part of the team that makes hospital rounds or interviews families in the office at times of serious illness. In a nonteaching setting a private physician with prior training in working with families may invite a family therapist into the medical system.

Once on the scene of action the therapist could model interviewing skills at discrete opportunities. Simply through recurrent exposure in the medical setting, the therapist would become a more understood entity. It is important to secure a physician ally who is able to provide a more family-centered role model for other physicians. The therapist needs that physician's credibility in order to

TABLE 12-1
Levels of Physician Involvement with Families

Level 1: Minimal emphasis on family	Level 2: Ongoing medical information and advice	Level 3: Feelings and support
This baseline level of involvement consists of dealing with families only as necessary for practical and medical/legal reasons, but not viewing communicating with families as integral to the physician's role or as involving skills for the physician to develop. This level presumably characterizes most medical school training, where biomedical issues are the sole conscious focus of patient care.	*Knowledge base:* Primarily medical, plus awareness of the triangular dimension of the physician–patient relationship. *Personal development:* Openness to engage patients and families in a collaborative way *Skills:* 1. Regularly and clearly communicating medical findings and treatment options to family members. 2. Asking family members questions that elicit relevant diagnostic and treatment information. 3. Attentively listening to family members' questions and concerns. 4. Advising families about how to handle the medical and rehabilitation needs of the patient. 5. For large or demanding families, knowing how to channel communication through one or two key members. 6. Identifying gross family dysfunction that interferes with medical treatment, and referring the family to a therapist.	*Knowledge base:* Normal family development and reactions to stress *Personal development:* Awareness of one's own feelings in relationship to the patient and family. *Skills:* 1. Asking questions that elicit family members' expressions of concerns and feelings related to the patient's condition and its effect on the family. 2. Empathically listening to family members' concerns and feelings, and normalizing them where appropriate. 3. Forming a preliminary assessment of the family's level of functioning as it relates to the patient's problem. 4. Encouraging family members in their efforts to cope as a family with their situation. 5. Tailoring medical advice to the unique needs, concerns, and feelings of the family. 6. Identifying family dysfunction and fitting a referral recommendation to the unique situation of the family.

Level 4: Systemic assessment and planned intervention	Level 5: Family therapy

Knowledge base: Family systems

Personal development: Awareness of one's own participation in systems, including the therapeutic triangle, the medical system, one's own family system, and larger community systems.

Skills:
1. Engaging family members, including reluctant ones, in a planned family conference or a series of conferences.
2. Structuring a conference with even a poorly communicating family in such a way that all members have a chance to express themselves.
3. Systemically assessing the family's level of functioning.
4. Supporting individual members while avoiding coalitions.
5. Reframing the family's definition of their problem in a way that makes problem solving more achievable.
6. Helping the family members view their difficulty as requiring new forms of collaborative efforts.
7. Helping the family members generate alternative, mutually acceptable ways to cope with their difficulty.
8. Helping the family balance their coping efforts by calibrating their various roles in a way that allows support without sacrificing anyone's autonomy.
9. Identifying family dysfunction that lies beyond primary care treatment and orchestrating a referral by educating the family and the therapist about what to expect from one another.

Knowledge base: Family systems and patterns whereby dysfunctional families interact with professionals and other health care systems.

Personal development: Ability to handle intense emotions in families and self and to maintain neutrality in the face of strong pressure from family members or other professionals.

Skills: The following is not an exhaustive list of family therapy skills but rather a list of several key skills that distinguish Level 5 involvement from primary care involvement with families.
1. Interviewing families or family members who are quite difficult to engage.
2. Efficiently generating and testing hypotheses about the family's difficulties and interaction patterns.
3. Escalating conflict in the family in order to break a family impasse.
4. Temporarily siding with one family member against another.
5. Constructively dealing with a family's strong resistance to change.
6. Negotiating collaborative relationships with other professionals and other systems who are working with the family, even when these groups are at odds with one another.

enter the world of acute medical care. After access is secured, the initial therapy is directed primarily toward the medical care system. Once a supportive environment is established (a process that could take years), the therapist could become part of the medical team. The remainder of this discussion assumes the presence of an environment supportive of involving the patient's family in the care of those who are seriously ill.

Level 2: Ongoing Medical Information and Advice

By including the patient's family as a part of the health care delivery process, family resources become more visible to health care professionals. At Level 2, the physician involves the family in a collaborative manner but still focuses on information and advice. Interactions typical of this level include communicating regularly with families, listening attentively to their questions, using key family members to assist communications, and referring families with gross levels of dysfunction for therapy. A basic family orientation to the care of seriously ill patients is possible when the physician is aware of the triangular nature of the doctor–patient–family relationship (Doherty & Baird, 1983). Those who act as advocates for the patient's family are more easily heard at this level of care than at Level 1. A variety of professionals such as nurses, chaplains, social workers, and therapists become viewed as potential family resources.

At Level 2, interaction with families of seriously ill patients occurs more regularly. Families are informed of minor and major changes in the patient's condition. The patient is seen as an individual whose life has been complicated by a disease. The clinical expression of that disease is uniquely influenced by the patient and the context in which the patient presents for care. Families are viewed as normally involved in the patient's care and recovery. Conversations are in a language intelligible to the family. A seated physician may ask open-ended questions. A general sense of collaboration pervades the interaction between the health care team and the family, and a number of family resources become visible.

Family Roles

From this perspective the family history reveals more than just a pattern of diseases. Basic family roles and their resource potential are now apparent to the health care team. The patient in the hospital can be recognized as a mother, father, sibling, income provider, or child. The impact of the serious illness may be different depending upon the patient's role in the family. Other family members may be identifiable as resources who are valuable during a hospitalization or after discharge from the hospital. With the current trend toward shorter hospital stays, these resources are more important than ever to help care for patients after discharge.

Family Economic Resources

The context in which the patient lives becomes more tangible to the medical care team at Level 2. Favorable family economic status is viewed as a resource that could allow the patient to purchase alternative medical care. Because the family has been incorporated into the medical team, the need for an occasional second opinion emanates from a shared evaluation of the patient's problem. Since neither physician nor family is threatened, existing family economic resources can be utilized more effectively.

Environmental Security

The environment in which the patient lives may now be understood as a potential resource. Some families reside, work, and play in an environment that is free from hazards such as air, water, and noise pollution. Relative freedom from violence and crime, storms, floods, fire, or other unpredictable environmental insults offers a secure base from which the family can struggle with serious illness. At Level 2, the health care team is aware of these resources in the family's environment.

The Family Therapist as a Resource

At this second level of involvement with families, the physician or other health professional may be able to diagnose gross family dysfunction that can interfere with medical treatment. For example, if frequent family arguments in the patient's room interfere with nursing duties or physician visits, consultation would be sought from a family therapist. This request for therapy would not be based upon a sophisticated understanding of family dynamics. It is done for practical reasons: the family discord is interrupting medical care. However, consultations with a family therapist would not be rare. The therapy would be directed primarily at the family but with an eye toward supporting and educating the medical team. At this level there would be some reluctance by the medical care team to eagerly involve the family therapist in a routine manner. Over time the medical team might come to a deeper understanding of the complexity of the interaction of the family with the health care system. However, such understanding by the medical team is evidence of a significant change in perspective and would move the interaction between the family and the health care team to Level 3.

Level 3: Feelings and Support

A health care team functioning at the third level of family involvment would have knowledge of normal family development, normal family reactions to stress, and the professional's own emotional reactions to patients and families.

Patients and families are viewed as having complex personal reactions to the stress of illness, reactions that the health care team tries to respond to in a supportive manner. The previously mentioned family resources would be identified with relative ease and efficiency at this level, since family resources would be a specific object of investigation and interview by the physician and health care team.

Family Role Performance

At Level 3, the health care team is aware that the patient's healing is likely to involve more than one person in an intimate way. For example, when Mr. X is admitted to the hospital with a large myocardial infarction (heart attack), Mrs. X may need to recover from the guilt she feels for not getting her husband to the hospital sooner. No matter that in reality he did not heed her earlier pleas for intervention. Just as he needs expert attention in the coronary care bed, she needs skilled help in the waiting room. At this level of family health care, she is recognized not just as Mrs. X but as a major supportive resource—the confidant, companion, and soon-to-be-home nurse. Recognizing the importance of her feelings in relation to her husband's illness as well as her role in the family is seen by the health care team as important in the treatment of Mr. X's illness.

Examples of interview questions at Level 3 are: "How do you, Mrs. X, feel about your husband's illness? I have seen his reaction to this diagnosis but I am not sure how you feel about it." "Mr. Y, what are your reactions to the idea that your son has a tumor? I know that we have explained our treatment plan and that we think we can remove the entire mass, but we haven't spent any time listening to your feelings about all of this." "Johnnie, what do you think about having to stay in the hospital for 2 weeks to get your medicine? We talk a lot each day about computer games but I don't know how you feel about all of this." Addressing the patient and the family about feelings is basic to Level 3. This sets the stage for discovering family resources.

Family Life Cycle Resources

Functioning at Level 3 is based upon an understanding of family and personal events in the context of family development and normal family reactions to stress. Knowledge of the family life cycle and of changing roles within developing families would be routine at this level of involvement. It is expected that young families often face different challenges and have different resources than do older families. Childhood diseases and adolescent adjustments to acute problems such as injuries and to chronic disorders such as diabetes and asthma are replaced with problems associated with occupational responsibilities, marital dissatisfaction, and adjustments of adults who are learning how to assist their less independent parents. At each stage of the life cycle, different kinds of resources become salient to the family and to the health care team—for example, good health and a large family support network during a couple's childbearing years, and adequate financial resources and supportive community services for a more isolated older couple.

Optimism

Interviewing the family at Level 3 offers more information about how the family feels about having faced previous challenges. How confident is the family of their survival skills? If this family has faced environmental hazards, serious illness, financial problems, or other stresses, how has it fared? In this manner the interviewer may uncover another family resource—optimism. The impact of patient and family optimism upon the health care team and the illness itself may be difficult to document. Research usually focuses on the effect of the antithesis of optimism—pessimism. Provided the health care team maintains a solid grip on medical reality, the family's optimism may be an important resource for both the family and the health care team.

Parental Authority and Decision Making

Families involved in medical crises demonstrate different degrees of the important internal resource of effective decision making, that is, the extent to which the family member(s) most responsible for a decision actually make it with support and input from other family members. This resource is visible to the health care team who interacts with the family at Level 3. For example, when parents are clearly in charge of major family decisions and are demonstrating leadership, then children in the family have more security in their roles. For a family possessing this resource, a serious illness in a child may not destabilize the parental (decision making) team, and children in the family accept parental leadership in making important decisions. When a child is seriously ill or injured, compliance with a treatment plan depends upon parental support for the treatment in spite of reluctance by the child. Absence of this parental leadership combined with the child's fear of a medication or treatment may result in a battle between frustrated parents, the frightened child, and the physician. Identifying this family resource of clear parental authority in the evaluation of serious and chronic childhood illnesses would improve the effectiveness of the treatment system.

Case Example. Twelve-year-old Mary has a severely fractured arm and will need surgery and prolonged rehabilitation for full recovery. During the preoperative discussion with the physicians, Mary's parents make a rapid decision in favor of surgery in spite of Mary's understandable reluctance. Postoperatively, Mary's discomfort does not trigger self-doubt and self-reproach by the parents over the initial decision for surgery. There are no subtle or indirect actions by the parents suggesting second thoughts over this action by the surgeons. Several months later rehabilitation exercises are begun in spite of Mary's pain upon movement. She has accepted that her initial treatment was necessary and does not undermine the physicians or her parents by unwarranted complaints about her serious injury and painful recovery. Mary was secure in her role in the family, as were her parents. She was reluctant to agree to reasonable medical treatment but accepted leadership exhibited by her parents. The result was a successful rehabilitation with minimal damage to the family system or the patient–family–health care team system.

If early assessment revealed weakness in this area, the physician functioning at Level 3 could intervene to reinforce the resource of parental leadership by focusing attention on the need for the parents to make the decision about surgery. Mary would be addressed with courtesy, respect, and gentleness but would not be asked to make the final decision. The physician would not coerce, beg, or play games with the young patient in order to get agreement. Recruiting this resource would involve demonstrating that the parents are in charge of this important decision. With most families, this effort would usually be successful. However, great difficulty with this task would be a warning that Mary may struggle to undermine the tenuous executive team in the recovery phase of her illness. Parents could be forewarned of this postoperative complication. Subsequent family meetings with the physician would be structured in a manner that would encourage discussion of this issue as well as the orthopedic aspects of the patient's serious injury.

Difficulty in mobilizing family decision making at Level 3 should make the health care team cautious about the family level of functioning. They would be likely to seek help from a family therapist if roles within the family could not be clarified. To a physician who understands how families respond to stress, nonacceptance of a rational treatment plan may trigger a consultation from a family therapist rather than consultation with another medical specialist (in our example, another orthopedist). This response would be more helpful to the family, to the medical specialist, and to the treatment system as a whole.

Family Health Expert

Because family roles are specifically noted at this level of involvement with families, a completely new type of family resource is available to the medical team: the family health expert (Doherty & Baird, 1983). This person is the internally recognized family authority on matters that relate to health. He/she is usually consulted before official medical advice is sought. This resource person passes judgment on the adequacy of current medical care and personnel. At Level 3 the power and authority of this family expert can be utilized rather than discounted. When major decisions are to be made, this expert resource can be consulted with the care that any other consultant would receive. This may mean that not only parents or spouses are involved in family discussions but also any other family member or friend who is the family health expert. The family health expert may be an aunt, cousin, or contact in the family's church. If this person can be included in the original educational process, the negotiated medical treatment may be able to avoid potential crises.

Clear, Direct, and Congruent Communication Patterns

Clear, direct communication patterns within a family and from the family to the medical system can be an important asset. In cases of acute serious illness, important decisions need to be made with dispatch. Delaying exploratory surgery or urgent treatment is awkward for both the health care system and the families involved. It is sometimes hazardous for the patient! When family members communicate their urgency clearly to one another and to the responsible physicians, their specific questions and fears can be addressed. Vague dissatisfactions expressed by family members and unclear statements by the physicians may confuse the important decision-making process.

In the course of treatment, especially when the patient outcome is not positive, the family's previously unclear communication pattern is likely to become even worse. Physicians who lack confidence in their decisions and are insensitive to family reactions to stress may simply avoid family members. Families may become diffusely angry. Discussion about the patient's diagnostic or care plan may deteriorate into arguments in which families, physicians, nurses, and other professionals may be used as scapegoats. Then the critical patient issues are avoided and decisiveness is lost. Clear, direct, congruent communication patterns within the family and between the family and the medical care team assist in decision making during urgent medical problems. This asset lies partly within the domain of the family and partly within the medical care system. By modeling effective communication patterns the health care team can strengthen this family resource.

Family Intelligence and Assertiveness

By using a more collaborative and sensitive style with families, the physician may discover another potential family resource—*intelligence*. Many families are endowed with levels of intellectual capacity that enable them to comprehend complex medical problems and management questions. An especially capable family may also *challenge* a diagnosis, treatment, or prognosis. This is an adaptive characteristic but may be threatening to the medical team and the physician. A collaborative spirit established early in the management of a case permits full use of these family resources without unnerving the professional half of the team. Families may appropriately question the need for surgery, the flow rates on intravenous fluids, the need for more or fewer consultants, more or fewer medications, and the occasional need for transfer of care to another institution. Fortunately, most physicians listen carefully to these bright and challenging families and either answer the queries appropriately or modify the treatment according to the families' suggestions. If a less family-oriented style of medical care is offered, then the family's ability to challenge the patient's care plan may become a major source of tension.

Family Medical Knowledge

An intelligent and observing family may have astute insight into acute medical care because of their intense concern for an ill family member. If involved in disease-specific self-help groups, these nonprofessionals may be well aware of current medical management issues. For example, Alzheimer's disease, diabetes, lupus erythematosis, arthritis, Down's syndrome, hearing impairment, and mental retardation and mental illness groups provide the most recent diagnostic and treatment data to the respective group members on a frequent basis. For these illnesses, educated family members may be better versed in their specific diseases than most general physicians. Accepting that reality and working with bright, educated patients and families can result in better care for the patient. It also demonstrates that health care is a shared responsibility. Such involvement by the physician requires a willingness to confront his/her own feelings of inadequacy in dealing with well-informed families as well as a sensitivity to their need to exercise some control over the treatment of mysterious chronic diseases.

Supportive Work Environment

Support for a family under stress from one member's serious illness may come from the workplace. Some work sites are conducive to sharing emotional support for coworkers under stress. Hallway chats and talks over the water cooler may let a person with an ill family member share feelings, test reality, and receive caring gestures from friends. Some employers sponsor health-related programs to assist workers in maintaining their own health or to adapt to illness in family members. Routine exercise programs, assertiveness training, wellness programs, and Employee Assistance Programs to help with substance abuse are becoming more common in the work environment. For many people the workplace has become a major source of support.

Level 4: Systemic Assessment and Planned Intervention

At Level 4 there is awareness of the complex interaction between the patient's family system, the medical system, the wider community, and the physician's own family system (Doherty, 1985). Typical behavior would include involving reluctant members in a family conference, conducting a conference in a manner that permits all participants to express themselves, avoiding coalitions, reframing problems to make them more resolvable, and making specific assessments of family function in order to organize primary care interventions and to assist in making referral for therapy uniquely suited to the family's needs. This level of interaction would require specific training in family systems and implies a close working relationship with a family therapist (Doherty & Baird, 1983).

All the resources identified at the previously mentioned levels of interaction would be available to the treatment team, plus new family characteristics uncovered by a more planned assessment. Although there may be infinite resources within families, these adaptive characteristics become visible to health care providers primarily through skilled interactions and observations. In families experiencing a serious illness, at least two new crucial resources may be identifiable—family adaptability and family cohesion, two core dimensions common to many theories of family functioning (Olson, Sprenkle, & Russell, 1979).

Adaptability

In the previous example of Mr. X's heart attack, adaptability (the family's flexibility in responding to demands imposed by stressors) becomes an important recognized resource. Will Mr. X be able to let go of critical decision-making powers in the family to allow Mrs. X to stabilize family financial matters during his illness? If not, how will the nurses react when the patient is constantly asking for phone privileges to handle family affairs? Reciprocally, Mrs. X must shift her role and become a family financial leader and spokesperson. Adaptability in the X family could be an important resource to be utilized by the health care team in the management of this seriously ill patient. A practical assessment of this family characteristic could be derived from observation of family interactions in the coronary care unit. A more rigid family would argue repeatedly over these role shifts. More adaptable families would be uncomfortable but would accommodate to the new situation. The atmosphere in the coronary care unit would be palpably different depending upon the presence of this family resource—*adaptability.*

Promoting this resource involves: (1) sitting down with the family and discussing the medical realities of Mr. X's condition, (2) listening to their reactions, (3) restating the problems in terms that are understandable to the family, (4) gently confronting unrealistic expectations that may be voiced by family members, (5) supporting family traditions that have encouraged adaptability in times of stress, (6) educating family members about new options in coping strategies, and (7) challenging the family with the task at hand—Mr. X is hospitalized and decisions must be made. This may also be called a primary care family intervention (Doherty & Baird, 1983).

This resource-mobilizing intervention may be done by a physician trained in working with families, by a nurse, social worker, or chaplain with special training, or by a family therapist. If there were no progress after two or three brief sessions, then referral for specialized family therapy would be considered. If formal family therapy were indicated, it might be most realistic to delay it until just after the patient is discharged from the hospital. The family's ability to shift some of their roles could be critical to the patient's health during this immediate postinfarction period. In ths setting, mobilizing family adaptability may be as important to Mr. X's long-term recovery as his discharge diet, exercise plan, and medications.

The level of family adaptability becomes especially salient when the family health expert does not agree with the medical care plan. An adaptable family would more easily modify their previous health beliefs and accept the professional definition of illness and treatment. More rigid families may undermine the professional definitions. Ultimately, a rigid family might demonstrate that the family's definitions are more valid by declaring the professional incompetent and/or inappropriate. Of course, if the medical team is wrong to begin with, such family rigidity may work out well in a particular situation.

Case Example. An 11-year-old girl, Amy, has just been diagnosed as having juvenile-onset diabetes mellitus. The health professional's perspective is that juvenile-onset diabetes is a metabolic disorder that requires the use of insulin injections and a modified diet and exercise plan. The health care team becomes involved in patient and family education about diabetic management. They discuss when to seek emergency assistance for a diabetic crisis for low or high blood sugar levels. Plans for careful follow-up are established. However, Amy's family believes that diabetes is created by improper vitamin intake. They plan to ignore the health care professional's input and treat their daughter with vitamin therapy and religious ceremonies. During the initial "honeymoon" of only mildly elevated blood sugar and minor metabolic problems, Amy does very well. The family's belief in their treatment plan is reinforced. Some months later Amy becomes seriously ill, with a very high blood sugar level, dehydration, and acidosis. A crisis has arisen.

A family with high adaptability would be more likely to accept professional help early on and temporarily, at least, modify their definitions of diabetes and its management. A physician who understands family adaptability could approach this preventable emergency with more compassion than anger. Rather than berate the family for irrationally ignoring medical advice, the professional could accept the immediate responsibility for acute medical care and congratulate the family for modifying their views enough to come *now* for help. Their current level of adaptability would be reinforced and their defensiveness and discomfort with the medical system minimized. This brief interchange would not postpone the urgent medical care that Amy would need. However, such an approach would lessen the energy wasted in anger by health care professionals and family members.

Cohesion

The family's level of *cohesion* (or emotional bonding) is also a resource with an important effect on the family's coping with serious illness. When one family member is hospitalized, the more cohesive family is easily visible in the hospital. The health care team has ready access to these family members to share in decision making and information transfer. At times of critical illness this contact assists both family members and physicians. The family's tightly woven interactional style is adaptive in a medical crisis. Rapid decisions can be made with a minimum of time lost due to absent family members. Family members' presence during times of critical illness offers love, warmth, and a caring atmosphere that cannot easily be reproduced by professionals in the health care system.

Of course, family therapists know there can be too much of a "good thing" such as cohesion (Minuchin, 1974). One family member may be hospitalized with a myocardial infarction while three or four family members are constantly present in the coronary care unit clutching their chests in pain! Promoting a functional level of cohesion would require the recognition of this enmeshment and efforts to help the family enforce more appropriate boundaries around this patient's illness. Then family members could concentrate on their realistic adaptation to the primary patient's condition. In this manner mid-range levels of cohesion (neither enmeshed nor disengaged) become a recruitable family resource.

Communtity Resources

Although community resources can be known to and accessed by health professionals at any level of involvement with families, they are most apt to be systematically assessed and mobilized at Level 4. Encouragement, economic support, and substitute people to fill vacant family roles are sometimes provided by extended family or close friends within the community. This form of community support may enable a family to adapt to one member's serious illness without the need for severe role shifts within the family. In addition, formal and informal community programs ranging from mental health center activities to self-help groups can strengthen families and enhance skills that assist in adaptation to a new stress. The medical care provider who is aware of these community resources can recruit them for a family even when the family is not aware of their existence.

Recruiting community resources to assist a family requires that at least one health care professional on the team has personal knowledge of and trust in these resources. This is often a social worker or discharge planning nurse. However, the physician functioning at Level 4 would also have a working relationship with frequently used community programs and be able to integrate them into the medical care plan efficiently. Getting to know the strengths and weaknesses of community resources would involve traveling to them and discussing common issues before a patient crisis occurs. This network-building activity would be recognized by the physician functioning at this level of involvement as an appropriate investment in developing family resources.

Level 5: Family Therapy

Even relatively sophisticated primary care family counseling at Level 4 generally is not adequate to handle chronically dysfunctional families who are difficult to engage in a cooperative treatment plan (Doherty & Baird, 1983). Here the primary care task is to make supportive contact with the family, assess the family's level of functioning, and refer to a therapist. Level 5, then, represents the distinctive involvement that family therapists have with families in treatment. It is conceivable that family therapy itself could be categorized into further levels of sophistication, but for our purposes one level seems adequate.

As Table 12-1 suggests, Level 5 begins at the point when the family is difficult to engage in medical treatment, whether because of the family's resistance, the physician's personal issues, or the influence of significant competing outside professionals or health care systems. In an analogy to biomedical health care, the primary care physician is trained to handle uncomplicated diabetes that responds readily to the standard treatment protocol. When the disease is recalcitrant to this "front line" treatment regimen, the physician refers the patient to an internist with more training and more treatment options in managing diabetes. Some of these treatment options will carry higher risks than the primary care protocol. In the same way, Level 5, family therapy, consists of more specialized—and sometimes risky—interventions that are deemed appropriate for more difficult cases in which simpler interventions have not been successful.

Although family therapy interventions differ considerably across different therapy models (Gurman & Kniskern, 1981), one common thread seems to involve techniques to help a "stuck" or rigid family get "unstuck." The skills listed in Table 12-1 are just a few examples of such techniques. Of particular importance in treating families with serious illness are skills in managing the complex and sometimes competing relations between the patient, the family, the health care team, and the therapist—the therapeutic "rectangle."

At Level 5, the therapist must be attuned to hidden or underutilized resources in the family. These might be healthy interaction patterns that the family experienced in the past before it got stuck, or potential leadership from a family member who has been disconfirmed in this role in the past. If an emotional cutoff from family of origin can be undone in therapy (Bowen, 1976), then an important new resource might be created where one was stifled in the past. The theme is that at Level 5 the therapist is skilled at ferreting out and catalyzing family resources that may have been invisible and inaccessible at prior levels of therapeutic involvement with the family.

In the example of the couple in which the husband has experienced a heart attack, Level 5 would be required if the couple were not able to take on new roles during the recovery phase, and thereby were experiencing continual conflict, emotional withdrawal, or life-threatening behavioral risks by the husband. Upon discovering this pattern, the primary care physician or visiting nurse refers the couple to the family therapist. The therapist learns that the infarction has exacerbated an already distressed marital relationship characterized by low levels of problem-solving ability and high levels of enmeshed conflict. In addition, the therapist finds that the husband has used his physician's admonition against "getting upset" to threaten his wife that she will kill him if she expresses disagreement with his behavior. The therapist's task is to help the couple turn two potential resources gone awry—their high level of cohesion, which has turned into overinvolved enmeshment, and their support from a concerned physician who has unwittingly colluded with one of them—into positive resources for the patient's recovery and the couple's happiness.

Finally, at Level 5 involvement with families in health care, the therapist's own resources are an important concern. These resources are both personal and systemic. Dysfunctional families highly stressed by physical illness can be terribly taxing to a therapist, particularly when medical emergencies or pseudoemergencies threaten the nonphysician therapist's sense of ownership of the treatment process, and when other health care professionals are involved as competing therapists for the patient and family. The dangers are legion: overprotecting the "sick" patient, taking health setbacks as personal failures, blaming the family for causing the patient's illness, and scapegoating the health care team. Therapists dealing with these challenges are well advised to surround themselves with trusted colleagues who can consult and provide cotherapy for the most difficult cases.

TECHNIQUES FOR IDENTIFYING FAMILY RESOURCES

During acute medical illness there are several types of interactions between the health care team and families that reveal family resources. We have already outlined the concept that these interactions occur at different levels of complexity. Keeping these levels in mind, we now discuss several potentially useful techniques for identifying family resources. We refer most often to physicians interacting with patients, but the same principles apply for any member of the health care team interacting with the family.

Using a Genogram

Physicians most often interact with the primary patient alone. This personal interview with the patient is useful in constructing a general picture of the patient's family as well as for obtaining the usual medical history. The family history may reveal genetic and historical influences on the patient's health. More specifically, the individual patient can help the physician or nurse construct a family genogram, which provides the health care team with a permanent record of family relationships and illness patterns (see Figure 12-1). Sometimes the graphic clarity of a genogram will provide diagnostic insight into the current patient's medical problem. If the individual interview occurs at Level 3 or above, the corresponding genogram may document important aspects of family roles and relationships. Resources that have been discussed previously may be recognized and charted along with standard family characteristics such as age and current location.

Using the Family Interview

A more potent assessment of family resources can be gathered through a family interview. The physician alone, nurse alone, physician and nurse, or physician

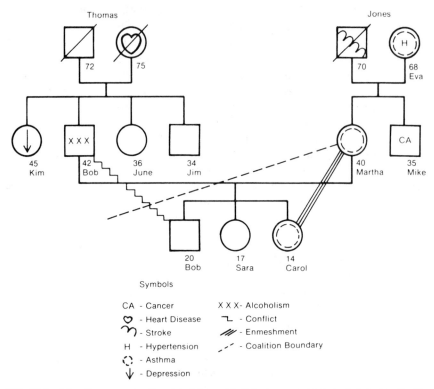

FIG. 12-1. A family genogram. Reprinted from W. J. Doherty and M. A. Baird, *Family Therapy and Family Medicine: Toward the Primary Care of Families.* New York: Guilford Press, 1983, p. 59.

and family therapist may choose to sit down and talk with the patient's family during an acute medical illness. At a minimum this could be done at Level 2 in order to share medical information with the family. More sophisticated interviewers may interact at Level 3 or 4 in order to assess family reaction to the medical problem or to help the family cope more successfully with this challenge. Through careful observation of the family's reaction to this process, a more formal evaluation of family adaptability, cohesion, and typical interaction patterns would be possible. The family health expert could be identified and asked for input. Family intellectual capacity, assertiveness, community support, environmental safety, family health assumptions, and the family's level of optimism could be evaluated.

Making a House Call

There are occasions when a visit to the patient at home is the most efficient way to assess and recruit family resources. The "house call" may be unusual from a family therapy perspective but is still part of the tradition of the primary care physician—especially the family physician. (In our setting all family practice residents are required to make periodic house calls on some of their patients.) Such out-of-the-office activity provides an intimate appraisal of the patient's milieu: economic status, environmental safety, community support, and general level of comfort available to the patient. A timely home visit may also demonstrate the health care professional's respect for the patient's own family and home environment. If this act raises *family self-esteem*, then another family resource has been enhanced.

THE ROLE OF THE FAMILY THERAPIST

During a family interview an experienced family therapist can help the physician or nurse by moving communication to higher levels of family involvement. We use here an example of a physician and a family therapist working with a family at the time of serious illness for one family member. The role of the family therapist and physician will overlap more with time as the team works together. This interaction is described from the perspective of primary care family counseling, which focuses on education, prevention, support, and occasionally challenge (Doherty & Baird, 1983). The goal is rarely to achieve far-reaching structural changes in the organization of the family. *The goal is to help the patient and family cope with a new crisis—an acute or serious medical illness in a family member.* Table 12-2 outlines the respective roles of the primary care

TABLE 12-2
Roles of the Physician and the Family Therapist

Goal	Physician's role	Family therapist's role
Engage the family	Display warmth and courtesy	Set the family and physician at ease with conversation
Education	Discuss all pertinent medical data and normal family stress reactions	Ensure that the family understands the medical data; help to normalize family stress
Prevention	Provide anticipatory guidance relating to the medical problem	Help generate adaptive role shifts and other coping activities
Support	Active listening	Reframe questions or statements to clarify meaning or impact of data
Challenge	Describe upcoming medical realities (death, disability)	Reinforce family resources, recruit new resources

physician and the supporting family therapist. The physician is assumed to be functioning with Level 3 skills, a level we would argue should be considered minimum competency for primary care physicians and other health professionals (Doherty, 1985). At Level 4, some of the therapist's role could be assumed by the physician.

At Level 3 and above, as exemplified in Table 12-2, it is routine to examine the patient's and family members' feelings in relation to the medical illness. If these feelings are potent and expressed congruently, the physician or other health care professional with less experience than the family therapist may need support. For nontherapists it may be unsettling to experience someone's rage or deep sorrow over a medical problem. The therapist can help by being present during potentially "hot" family interviews and by debriefing the nontherapist after the session. This type of support is invaluable in building a collaborative relationship between professionals with different skills and training.

When To Schedule a Family Interview

There are specific occasions when it is important to involve the patient's family in the care of the individual patient. Schmidt (1983) summarized the research support for the logic of holding family conferences for certain illnesses. We have proposed more general guidelines for deciding when to interview families at times of medical illness (Doherty & Baird, 1983). Figure 12-2 outlines these suggestions. The following discussion will emphasize the times when we believe a family conference should be an essential part of the treatment plan. It is at these times that family resources can be best assessed and mobilized.

Whenever Someone is Hospitalized

Hospitalization of a family member is a major event for most families. The hospital still is a place where most people go before they die. Some family members are recurrently admitted to the hospital for readjustments of chronic medications or for ongoing medical treatment. In those cases each hospitalization may not be a crisis but the chronic illness may be a major stress to the family.

When a Serious Chronic Illness is Diagnosed

For example, a new-onset adult diabetic patient who does not require hospitalization for initial management will benefit from a family meeting with the physician. Diet and life-style changes helpful for diabetic control usually involve everyone in the household. Minimally, a family interview demonstrates courtesy to those individuals involved in the recommended life-style changes. By enlisting their support, the physician begins the process of recruiting family resources.

Generally see Patient alone	Family Conferences Desirable	Family Conferences Essential
minor acute problems (e.g., common cold, contact dermitiis)	treatment failure or regular recurrence of symptoms	chronic illness (e.g., hypertension)
routine self-limiting problems (e.g., influenza)	routine preventive/educational care (e.g., pre-natal visits, routine child visits)	serious acute illness (e.g., myocardial infarction)
		psychosocial problems
		lifestyle problems (e.g., obesity)
		death

FIG. 12-2. When to assemble the family. Reprinted from W. J. Doherty and M. A. Baird, *Family Therapy and Family Medicine: Toward the Primary Care of Families*. New York: Guilford Press, 1983, p. 72.

When "Conservation" of Family Resources is Important

One way to avoid sacrificing family resources to the care of a chronic illness is to maintain an appropriate boundary around a medical illness. This is a complex issue. When a child is identified as asthmatic many changes are required of the patient and family. Adult members may be asked to abstain from smoking in the child's presence; houseplants and family pets may have to be removed; some kinds of family recreation may be unwise for the asthmatic child. In one sense everyone becomes the patient, yet only one person has the illness. The reality of this paradox must be understood by the entire group. It is easily lost in attempting to translate an interview for those who could not attend. The patient's family may have displayed a reasonable level of cohesion before this new medical problem was diagnosed, but the treatment of the problem may now create a risk of weakening interpersonal boundaries.

In this example, the challenge is to request these family changes in a manner that does not permanently set up the asthmatic child in a "sick role" for life. If the entire family is provided with accurate medical information, then the entire family can use its collective resources to cope with the problem. If key members are excluded from that session, then valuable family resources may not become available to assist the family in coping with this stress. Subtleties of communication are not easily grasped from "second-hand" information. Therefore, family resources are conserved: (1) if the paradox of other family members' involvement is understood and (2) if all participating family members receive the medical information directly.

When Medical Problems Are Related To Behavior and Life-Style

In chronic illness and disorders relating to behavior and life-style, family relationships and family resources are obviously of critical importance. In fact the adjustments of family members may be essential not only to the treatment of the problem but to its diagnosis as well. For example, in chemical dependency and substance abuse the diagnosis and management of the disorder relates directly to its impact on other family members (Barnard, 1981). If the physician is unfamiliar with gathering this type of data from the family, then a diagnosis may be very difficult until the problem progresses to a more obvious stage. Family reactions to one member's illness can be promoted to assist in the diagnosis and management of most chronic diseases such as eating disorders, spinal cord injuries, severe arthritis, diabetes, and chronic lung disease.

When Routine Medical Problems Become Unmanageable

Family resources are needed when routine medical problems become unmanageable for no obvious reason and when acute medical illnesses become unusually recurrent. For example, when a normal treatment plan for hypertension fails to remain effective, a family meeting is indicated. The family health expert or some other family resource may be recruited in order to improve compliance with the treatment protocol. Perhaps the family has new information at their disposal that would cause the physician to change the treatment plan in a way more compatible with the family routine, e.g., changing to fewer doses of medication per day might be easier for family members who assist the patient with daily medications before and after work.

When Acute Medical Illnesses Become Recurrent

Recurrent upper respiratory infections and streptococcal pharyngitis have been associated with high levels of family stress (Meyer and Haggerty, 1962). In this instance the medical symptom may be a reasonable entree into the family system. New resources could be found to deal with stress or existing coping mechanisms reinforced in order to reduce the medical complications. Without utilizing family resources the medical treatment team may be treating only part of the patient's discomfort, no matter how objective the evidence that it is a bonafide "biological" disorder.

ROADBLOCKS TO USING FAMILY RESOURCES IN HEALTH CARE

There are many obstacles to the regular utilization of family resources in health care. First of all, who has demonstrated its usefulness? There is a paucity of experimental research data to support a "family" approach to medical care. However, a few studies have demonstrated increased blood pressure control through involving the family in the treatment plan (Earp, Ory, & Strogatz, 1982; Morisky et al., 1983). If involving the family in the treatment and diagnosis is useful, it must be documented in carefully designed studies.

Second, recruiting family resources to deal with serious medical problems is most realistic when the physician recognizes families and family characteristics as relevant to the care of the patient. As we have outlined in this chapter, family resources only become available when someone looks for them with some level of sophistication and genuine interest. Skills in this area are only recently being taught in some medical schools and residency training programs. The best method of teaching physicians-in-training to work effectively with families and with family therapists is still uncertain (Glenn, Atkins, & Singer, 1984). To aid in training physicians to work with families, we have presented a model in which the level of involvement with the family can be identified. With this perspective the depth of physician interaction with a family can be gauged. Resources become more visible as the interaction becomes more sophisticated. Until reviewing the family system at least at Level 3 becomes a routine part of the medical "review of systems," family resources will be underrecognized and underutilized by physicians. However, as Doherty (1985) has observed, nurses have moved ahead of physicians in offering training in family-centered care.

Third, there is structural resistance to working with families in the health care system. There are few places one can *sit* and talk with families. Most clinics and hospitals are designed for one-to-one patient interviews. When family conference rooms are available they may have become crowded with stored hardware or there may be inadequate seating, ventilation, or privacy. Thankfully, that is not always the case, and many families have felt accepted in the medical setting.

Fourth, time conflicts often mitigate against involving the family at times of serious medical illness. Physicians, nurses, and other health care professionals may feel that working with the patient's family is not a high priority among the many tasks to be performed for a seriously ill patient. Family therapists and others experienced in working with families know the efficiency of this effort. However, until the benefits of this activity become apparent to the front line medical care providers, discussions with families will happen sporadically and after other priorities are addressed.

Fifth, reimbursement for working with families is unsatisfactory. Physicians are paid at a higher rate for surgical proceedures. Nurses are paid to care for patients in beds, not to talk with and listen to families in waiting rooms. Reimbursement patterns are unlikely to change unless the efficacy of involving families can be documented. If we do not satisfy this need for research, there may be little hope of financially rewarding health care personnel for utilizing families and their resources during the care of the seriously ill people.

Finally, fear of the unfamiliar may prevent health care providers from involving families. Therapists can alleviate this problem by becoming involved in the care of seriously ill and chronically ill patients. By working more closely with the medical care system, therapists can "join the family" and help physicians, nurses, and the entire health care team learn more adaptive patterns of interaction with patients and their families.

These barriers notwithstanding, we remain optimistic that the time for family-centered medical care is arriving. Doherty (1985) and Doherty and McCubbin (1985) offered documentation for the convergence of social, economic, clinical, and research forces toward a new consensus in the 1980s that rational, cost-effective, and humanistic health care must regard the patient as a member of a family or other supportive system whose resources are a core component of health care.

REFERENCES

Barnard, C. P. *Families, alcoholism and therapy.* Springfield, IL: Charles C. Thomas, 1981.

Bowen, M. *Family therapy in clinical practice.* New York: Jason Aronson, 1978.

Doherty, W. J. Family interventions in health care. *Family Relations*, 1985, *34*, 129–137.

Doherty, W. J., & Baird, M. A. *Family therapy and family medicine: Toward the primary care of families.* New York: Guilford Press, 1983.

Doherty, W. J., & McCubbin, H. I. (Eds.). *The family and health care* [Special issue]. *Family Relations*, 1985, *34*, 1.

Earp, J. A., Ory, M. G., & Strogatz, D. S. The effects of family involvement and practitioner visits on the control of hypertension. *American Journal of Public Health*, 1982, *73*, 1146–1153.

Glenn, M. L., Atkins, L., & Singer, R. Integrating a family therapist into a family medical practice. *Family Systems Medicine*, 1984, *2*, 137–145.

Gurman, A. S., & Kniskern, D. P. (Eds.). *Handbook of Family Therapy*. New York: Brunner/Mazel, 1981.

Lipkin, M., Quill, T. E., & Napodano, R. J. The medical interview: A core curriculum for residencies in internal medicine. *Annals of Internal Medicine*, 1984, *100*, 277–284.

McCubbin, H. I., & Patterson, J. M. The family stress process: The Double ABCX Model of adjustment and adaptation. *Marriage and Family Review*, 1983, *6*, 7–37.

Meyer, R. J., & Haggerty, R. J. Streptococcal infections in families: Factors altering individual susceptibility. *Pediatrics*, 1962, *29*, 539–549.

Morisky, H. J., Levine, D. M., Green, L. W., Shapiro, S., Russell, R. R., & Smith, G. R. Five year blood pressure control and mortality following health education for hypertensive patients. *American Journal of Public Health*, 1983, *73*, 153–162.

Minuchin, S. *Families and family therapy*. Cambridge, MA: Harvard University Press, 1974.

Olson, D. H., Sprenkle, D. H., & Russell, C. Circumplex model of marital and family systems: I. Cohesion and adaptability dimensions, family types, and clinical applications. *Family Process*, 1979, *18*, 3–28.

Pattison, E. M., & Anderson, R. C. Family health care. *Public Health Review*, *1975*, *7*, 83–134.

Schmidt, D. D. When is it helpful to convene the family? *Journal of Family Practice*, 1983, *7*, 967–973.

CHAPTER 13

Mobilizing Family Resources for Constructive Divorce

David N. Ulrich

CONCEPTUALIZING THE RESOURCES

"Family resources for divorce," sounds like a contradiction in terms. If the family is dissolving, what can the family's resources do but dissolve? Attention to the family from a systemic point of view makes it clear that resources do continue to exist and can be mobilized. Inasmuch as this happens, destructive sequelae of the divorce can be averted, and the prospects for a productive outcome can be significantly enhanced.

I present a point of view consistent with the systemic approach and with my own experience. The aim is to present a viewpoint, not to provide a comprehensive overview of the thinking and writing on divorce.

An inventory of identifiable resources could include such items as flexibility, willingness to approach stressful situations with humor, and ability to face reality. However, it does not seem to me that this provides a great deal of help to the family member, therapist, attorney, or mediator confronted with the task of helping a family to function, especially when that family is undergoing a crisis such as divorce. We prefer instead to take up certain basic concepts that we feel can help professionals identify and mobilize family resources during divorce.

Resources That Survive Divorce

Family resources available for divorce include the following.

Permanence

As Montalvo (1982) pointed out, virtually all societies have made a place for divorce as part of legitimate social process, but it is easy for us in our western

David N. Ulrich, Ph.D. Private Practice, Stamford, Connecticut.

culture, with its dispersed nuclear families, to think of divorce as a process whereby a family is taken apart. If there are no children, all the formal ties are severed by divorce. Once a child is born, the marriage can be taken apart but the ties formed by the child's arrival can never be broken. Grandfathers continue to be grandfathers and aunts go on being aunts. A genogram made a century later will, if it is faithful to the facts, record the divorced spouses as parents of the children, and it will also indicate that the children belong to both of the parents. In this respect, the family continues as a unit.

The Linkages

Once a child arrives, the families of origin of each spouse become formally linked. All four parents of the two spouses become the child's grandparents. With the child's arrival, the nuclear family now has two new subsystems: mother–child and father–child. These subsystems continue to exist following a divorce. Where children are involved, it is no understatement to say that the goal of all efforts toward constructive divorce is to preserve these subsystems as normal family units, occupying separate households but recognizing family ties. As Goldsmith (1982) pointed out, from a statistical point of view this kind of household is already normal. McGoldrick and Carter (1982) made the critical distinction that each of these households is a single-parent household, not a single-parent family. In their capacity as parents, neither ex-spouse can be said to be single until one of them is dead. The parent–child subsystem can represent a household whether the child is in full-time residence or not.

Synergism of Interests

Assuming that various family members have had access to each other, a deep synergism of interests may be evident, upon which the divorce itself may have little effect. A mother starts singing to her newborn child, and becomes aware that the words and cadences she is using are the very ones she heard when her grandmother sang to her. Even if these people have not had access to each other, the synergism exists—a grandfather is nevertheless a grandfather, who may hold the key to all kinds of family mysteries and treasures. These are facts; they cannot be dismissed, even if effort is invested in trying to dismiss them. This synergism of family interests is one of the basic premises of the contextual therapy of Boszormenyi-Nagy, as reported by Boszormenyi-Nagy and Ulrich (1981). When it is exploited, the adversary nature of divorce law can obscure these realities.

Of course, family ties do not necessarily point to the existence of active relationships. Yet within the nearby extended family, the absence of relationship can have as much emotional significance as the presence of one. To take into account the "operative emotional field," as McGoldrick and Carter (1982) put it, we are looking at a minimum of three generations on both sides. As Hareven (1982) pointed out, the modern family, because of extended life spans, is more likely than families of previous generations to have an effective three-generation overlap. We have spoken of the "synergism of interests" of these generations; for the child, a grandparent is a visible sign of, and spokesperson for, the forebears and everything they bring into the child's life. Goldstein, Freud, and Solnit (1979) suggested that the custodial parent should have the power to exclude the other parent from the child's life. In our view, one of the fatal flaws in this recommendation is that it fails to consider the child's basic right to have access to the families of origin of both parents, and the value accruing to the child of having this right realized.

Legacies

Another basic resource has to do with family legacies. As it is used here, "legacy" means the set of family expectations that impinge upon a given child. We are indebted to Boszormenyi-Nagy (Boszormenyi-Nagy & Ulrich, 1981) for this application of the term "legacy." The legacy for each child may be unique, varying according to sibling order, sex, the condition of the family at the time of birth, and the like. Yet the origins of the legacy reflect, so to speak, the snowballing effect of multiple generations of family experience. Also, as the term "legacy" implies, the expectations tend to be binding; they have the force and effect of a mandate. The legacy of one family may be: Any male who is a member of this family will be held to the utmost achievement. The legacy of another family may be: If you are a member of this family, you start here, you finish here, you don't change your place. Legacies can be either binding or potentiating; if the latter, they continue to serve as a resource for the parent and the children regardless of divorce. The children have the cost or benefit of the legacies from both families, unless the most strenuous efforts are made to break off their family ties, and even then the potential continues. For example, if the father's legacy was to favor the oldest son, while the mother's legacy was to regard males as vulnerable weaklings requiring direction, the oldest son might successfully join with his father, but the younger brother could easily be overlooked or even assigned a scapegoat role in the family.

Entitlements

Along with these legacies go entitlements. By virtue of being born into a family, a child is entitled to make certain claims on both parents and their relatives. As the child grows and starts performing acts of value to the family, he/she earns further entitlement to claim some return on their efforts. The marital partners, by virtue of the fact that each has consented to share parenting with the other, are also entitled to make certain claims upon each other. This includes the right to consideration as a parent. Because of whatever they have done for each other and for each others' families, they have also earned entitlement to make further claims for support and consideration. We believe that this is a healthy way to operate and that most people do operate this way. These claims continue to exist following divorce, whether they are acknowledged or not. In issues involving solely the marital pair, such claims may be wide open to dispute, but, where parenting is involved, we believe that the right to consideration is already established. This we see as a postdivorce family resource.

Trustworthiness

It is a rare marital breakup in which all trust between the partners is destroyed. The continuing existence of some degree of trustworthiness in the relationship between the ex-spouses in a resource. This residue of reciprocal trust can provide the necessary base for a willingness to give consideration to all of the significant people involved in the postdivorce family structure. A mother may, for instance, take into account the interests of the paternal grandmother, even if that grandmother's way of caring for her grandchildren may be somewhat intrusive and obnoxious at times.

The rare case in which all trust is lost may be one in which the bitterness of the breakup is exacerbated by the spouses' parents or by others. Yet, as Kressel and Deutch (1977) have suggested, the trouble may stem not so much from the actual meddling of the parents as from the internalized expectations of one or both spouses. The divorcing partner may be driven by the inner image of a parent who demands that trust be withdrawn.

Even when the trust base has been badly eroded in a marital relationship, the children still provide an input of loyalty and trust that may have profound value for both parents. The child does not easily give up his/her faith that the parents will care and cope. This is a continual reminder to them to keep functioning as adults. One divorcing father had the fantasy that he and his 9-year-old son would live an idyllic existence together on the other side of the country, in effect abandoning his daughter as well as his wife. In a family session, the boy said thoughtfully to his father, "I hope you don't make as big a mess of the divorce as you did of the marriage." The father heard the remark not as an insult but as an honest appeal. The experience served instantly to deflate the father's fantasy and bring him back to responsible consideration of how to parent both children.

The trust base also enhances the possibility that constructive dialogue can take place. For instance, the mother who feels that she can openly negotiate with her ex-spouse's mother about what kind of gifts she will give the children has a chance to shape the outcome in a way helpful to everybody concerned. Openness to negotiation therefore appears to be a family resource that does not terminate with divorce.

A System in Flux

The capacity of families to change may be considered a resource. This capacity is heightened during crisis, and divorce is one of those crises in which the capacity for change is the greatest. Goldsmith (1982) pointed out that the crisis of divorce can lead to growth and development in ways that were not available within the marriage, and that the relationships between parents and children may improve with the divorce.

Capacity to See Divorce as a Constructive Solution

Systemic family therapy theorists suggest that the capacity to see divorce as a constructive solution, rather than as a litigious approach to a failure, may be one of the most critical resources available to families confronted with the reality of divorce. Because the capacity to see divorce as constructive is crucial to the outcome of divorce, the next section is devoted to a fuller consideration of this topic.

The Definition of Divorce

As Walsh (1982) pointed out, the difference between coping and dysfunction may depend on how a crisis is explained. As with other crises, depending on how the event is defined families can find or fail to find a variety of coping strategies. Beavers (1982) noted that shared meanings can render stress more understandable and acceptable, or less so, in divorce as elsewhere. While most professional mental health workers are committed to the task of looking for positive outcomes in divorce as in other crises, some professionals still decry divorce as an irreversible destructive force. Statistics appear in *The New York Times*, for example, having to do with how many children of divorced parents go to child guidance clinics, as if this were evidence that the divorce had damaged the children. The same statistics could be used to argue that both the divorce and the children's disturbance are evidence of the preexisting parental conflict. Or they could be used to argue that divorced parents are more attentive to their children's needs. (Perhaps the only valid way to assess the effect of divorce on children would be to set up a comparison with the children of likewise conflicted parents who had not divorced). Hareven (1982) pointed out that divorce can be a sign of enough human concern to pay the cost of correcting a hopeless situation. Such issues of cause and effect are extremely difficult to assess. Our point here is that the mental health professional should scrutinize with the greatest care any statement that pathology *results* from divorce.

According to the Committee on the Family of the Group for the Advancement of Psychiatry (1980), divorce "belongs to a class of changes of family relations for which there is no good way to prepare . . . divorce is an especially unmanageable catastrophe." In contrast, Cotroneo, Krasner, and Boszormenyi-Nagy (1981) affirmed that predivorce counseling can help to reinforce the capacity of the family to foster the children's growth and to avert the depletion of parental resources. The degree of readiness to perceive divorce in workable terms will have a critical effect on the outcome for all concerned, including the extended families.

The Conventional Assumptions

In order to help people find the potential for constructive meanings in divorce, some of the conventional assumptions about marriage must first be examined. Although society at large gives little or no thought to preparing people for marriage, it is a conventional assumption that marriage should be forever. This is a natural hope. We start life with the experience of a permanent bond in the family of origin, and this provides us with our basic reference point in life. In planning to share life with a partner, one's deepest yearnings have to do with a permanent place, with the closeness and continuity that provides. In extreme situations, the desire for a permanent place takes the form of ownership, which can be deadly for the spouse.

It is also the conventional wisdom that every couple starts marriage with a clear slate, so anything that happens afterward is their own fault. In fact, the reefs and shoals they encounter may have been in place long before the couple got there. Yet they will be ready to blame themselves and each other if they get stuck. It is also conventional to see marriage as a static condition rather than as a situation that provides people with an opportunity for change that they may or may not put to use.

These conventional assumptions all point toward the catastrophic view of divorce. This can block off any hope of understanding. Instead, the accumulation of pain, blame, resentment, rage, and the like, leads to a sense of hopelessness, sometimes expressed as a feeling that divorce is worse than death. If spouses do not understand what has happened to them, they may not understand how any part can be saved or any resource can be utilized. Sometimes, therefore, one of the therapist's earliest and hardest tasks is to try to avert or mitigate the doomsday process and its effects.

It is not surprising that divorce is sometimes described as worse than death. When a loved one is lost through death, grief is connected with positive memories. Family and friends do what they can to support this way of looking at it. The funeral service usually contains a eulogy. The divorce court does not. In divorce, the thrust is to look on the bad side of the other person. Family and friends may reinforce this outlook, and legal events may make it virtually mandatory. Meanwhile, the bad other remains on the scene, providing fresh reminders of his/her badness, which are hard to bear, and of his/her goodness, which are intolerable. The normal ambivalence of marital partners gets suppressed; only the bad is retained in awareness. This malignant process makes it harder to retrieve any image of the good other that would facilitate the continuation of coparenting.

The Alternative View

An alternative kind of awareness of marriage is necessary if one is to be ready to mobilize for divorce. The hope of "forever" is profoundly human and powerful, but it does not offer a guide to marriage. Marriage can be seen as an effort to create a situation where each spouse can get on with his/her life tasks and pleasures with help from the other. As an attempt to resolve previously unresolved developmental issues and move on toward new tasks, it may be better than doing nothing. Yet it may turn out to be a partially or wholly maladaptive solution. In this case divorce may be the solution of last resort. Thus it stands as an alternative route to mobilization of resources, a bypass around the inability of two spouses to help each other get things done.

What turns a marriage into a nonsolution is much too complex a topic to cover here. What needs more general recognition is that there are factors outside the control of either spouse that can prevent fulfillment. As Boszor-menyi-Nagy and Spark (1973) pointed out, invisible loyalty to the family of origin may dictate to one spouse or to both that he/she remain uncommitted and ungiving to the other. Or the marriage itself may be a protest, so the spouse has served his/her purpose when the protest has been made. Or the needs and interests of the couple may, in reality, diverge to such a degree as to make the unit unworkable. The point to be made by these examples is simply that in some cases divorce can be a legitimate alternative, and a couple looking at it this way does not need to pull the house down around them on their way out the door.

We are addressing here a kind of awareness that can apply to many life situations. It involves the ability to see the full dimensions of reality, to recognize the extent to which others have become enemies, yet to recognize, and make no move that would foolishly jeopardize, such commonality of interests as still remains. If common interests and aims can be identified, the classic examples being the welfare of the children and the continued growth of the parents, then these can offer leverages toward a constructive outcome. The children's presence may help the parents restrain their enmities; this in turn leaves each parent freer to pursue his/her own life. The therapist needs to be careful not to confuse the ex-spouses' willingness to deal with each other, and to show some empathy for each other, with an inability to terminate the marital relationship. The pathology-seeking approach to marital and divorce issues can, for example, result in the therapist's automatically perceiving good will on the part of one ex-spouse toward the other as vacillation. Also, while indignation may spur people on to mobilize for divorce, I do not perceive blanket condemnation of the other spouse as a sign of health.

Paradoxically, willingness to see divorce as a constructive solution could in the long run lower the divorce rate, because openness to the consideration of the variables that produce a constructive divorce might also result in better understanding of situations in which divorce might not be a constructive solution.

IDENTIFYING RESOURCES

A major part of the therapist's work consists of identifying the resources available to a particular couple. However, this cannot be simply a matter of taking inventory. In two crucial respects, assessing resources involves the process of therapy, not just its contents. The first of these is the attitude of the therapist toward the task. The second is the degree of readiness of each ex-spouse to move toward the mobilization of resources. We need to pay attention to each of these factors.

The Therapist's Orientation

Multidirectional Partiality

The extent to which resources can be identified and mobilized will depend in considerable measure upon the attitude of the therapist. In traditional one-to-one therapy, it was considered appropriate for the therapist to become the advocate for a single client. This was easy, as the therapist was not required to take anybody else's interests into account, regardless of what impact the therapy had on them. The therapist could let his/her own rescue fantasies flourish—for example, the sense of saving the good client from the bad spouse. However, family therapy in general, and couples therapy in particular, requires a balancing of the therapist's point of view. In the past, the attempt was made to adopt "neutrality" in order to preserve balance, but neutrality is a myth, because the therapist cannot possibly avoid having his/her sympathies pulled one way or another, and the attempt to deny this can result in a flat, sterile approach.

Boszormenyi-Nagy and Spark (1973) suggested that the therapist may engage in "multidirectional partiality." The therapist attends first to the side of one client, then the other, making it clear that each will be heard in turn and that the interests of each will be recognized. This approach takes self-discipline. The therapist will sooner or later feel an active pull to share one spouse's indignation at the other. In one instance, a father showed the therapist a note from his ex-wife about his daughter that was so curt the therapist felt it like a slap in the face. He said to the father, "I have to struggle not to feel biased by something like that," thus admitting his reaction without yielding to it. There are various ways to avoid getting terminally locked in. If a parent denounces the other parent, the therapist can ask questions like, "Was it always like this? Were there times when things were better? Can you try to remember ways he was good with the children? Have you looked for signs that the children still care for him? Are you sure you can seriously say that he has been of no help at all since the separation? Is it possible that some of the things you are complaining about are beyond his power to fix?" While attempting to be fair, the therapist is also eliciting important information about both of the spouses.

Siding

Of course, siding with one parent is a necessary part of the therapeutic process in the sense of giving that person the opportunity to vent his/her pain, or resentment, or despair, or whatever it may be. Until that is done, the client will have no confidence that the therapist has any grasp of his/her predicament, and as a result there may be great reluctance to share important facts and feelings. However, the rule of siding is that any siding with one spouse has to be balanced by equal siding with the other, no matter how hard that seems, and the opportunity to do so must never be foreclosed.

It goes without saying that this means having access to both parties or at least making the attempt. A misuse of professional expertise occurs when a therapist sees only one spouse and then sizes up the parenting resources of both spouses. In one situation, a therapist interviewed only the children and their mother, without letting the father know about it, and then recommended against overnight visitations with the father. The father accosted the therapist in the lobby of the courthouse and accused him of being a "hired gun." The therapist's defense was that he had based his report upon "all the information available to me." It seemed evident that the therapist felt constrained by the same rules of adversary proceedings that might apply to the mother's attorney. Once he had been retained by the mother, he did not believe it would be proper to contact the father. I see no reason for any mental health professional to hobble himself/ herself with any such restriction. The therapist should spell out this distinction to all parties when accepting a case. Otherwise, the professional is vulnerable to the accusation of being a "hired gun," and crucial material about the resources of the other spouse may be lost.

One way to avoid the pitfalls of terminal siding is to have cotherapists. This provides each therapist with a check against the impulse to take a side and stay on it. Also, it appears likely that each of the spouses will tend to perceive at least one of the therapists as a source of support, and this will work against the mobilization of distrust.

Readiness to Mobilize

The degree to which each spouse is ready and willing to mobilize resources, and the degree to which this can be enhanced by the therapist, are of course crucial. The central thesis of this chapter is that therapists are concerned not so much with a checklist as with questions about readiness to mobilize resources. The stages of the individual life cycle can be conceived of as recurring mobilization of resources for more advanced tasks. A key example is the effort toward individuation as preparation for the tasks of marriage and parenthood. Marriage, in turn, does not advance the couple to the next step. It simply provides a situation in which each spouse may or may not take the next step with help from the other. Thus, with both marriage and divorce, the question has to do with how resources can be mobilized.

As soon as we speak of mobilization of resources in the context of divorce, we will encounter resistance. In some quarters, any mobilization of effort that is linked to divorce is seen as immoral and destructive of family values. Also, for many of the people undergoing it, divorce is experienced as a period of pain and turmoil, emotional and physical as well as financial exhaustion, and incapacity to feel or to be very reasonable about much of anything. In this respect, then, we as professionals are working against the tide when we talk about mobilizing for a productive outcome, yet this is what is called for. In the next few decades it may come to pass that spouses who treat the custody issue as a pitched battle, rather than seeking for a constructive way of handling the issue, will be looked upon with about as much favor as parents who beat their children.

In the following sections, I deal with this question of the spouses' readiness to mobilize resources by pinpointing specific areas the therapist can explore. This exploration is not, of course, distinct from the therapeutic process, because the very act of exploring attitudes can serve to get the mobilizing process under way.

Willingness To Face Issues without Deviation

A basic factor is whether each spouse has the capacity to stick to an issue and deal with it on its merits. A father may, for instance, show perfunctory interest in his child's school problems, then become animated as he denounces the mother's views about education. The therapist is thus provided with a clue that it may take considerable work, or prove impossible, to get the father to become effectively involved with school issues, or possibly any real issues concerning the child's welfare.

Negative Feelings

The extent to which the negative feelings of each spouse interfere with cooperation between them is, of course, a crucial question for the therapist. One encounters a wide variety of emotional states. In one case, the bitter and unyielding resentment of one spouse toward the other may originally have been dictated by a parent and remained unchanged from the beginning. In another case, with the passage of years there may have been a gradual accumulation of resentments that has finally become overwhelming and has led to a frenzied, repetitive, unchanging litany. In yet another case, the full realization of the breakdown in the relationship may result in acute panic and rage that will prove transient. In each case the therapist must probe for clues that something positive is salvageable. It is essential to ask, for instance, "How long have you felt this way, and are there any times when you feel differently?"

Various factors help determine whether the spouse is in a state of transient upset or committed to a lasting vendetta. The legacy of each spouse may have a profound effect on whether they can mobilize useful effort. In one situation, for example, a mother sought to deny the father any visitation rights, clutching at trivia to prove his unfitness. It quickly emerged that she was in the midst of a bitter standoff with her father, had not spoken to him in months, and had also refused to let him see the children. She was, it seemed, acting out a multigenerational legacy of parents being split off from children. Her attitude toward her father provided, in this case, an accurate gauge of what her attitude toward her husband would be.

The Sense of Injustice

A related issue is how deeply one spouse feels "ripped off" by the other, how legitimate the complaint appears to be, and how the person can be helped to deal with this now. It seems quite possible that in many cases where one spouse appears to be unable to let go of the marriage, what he/she may actually be clinging to is an unresolved sense of injustice. This can be the cause of lasting stagnation if it is not identified, faced, and worked through.

Suspicion

Another way to assess the degree of immobilization is to look at the extent and quality of suspicion. One parent may express a good deal of suspicion and fearfulness over how well the other will take care of the children. The documentation for these fears may make them seem genuine, or they may begin to look manipulative, or they may begin to reflect the parent's own fearfulness about life. It is important to explore whether the parent can begin to distinguish between genuine fears about the children's welfare and fears that really attach to what went on between the adults, or between a spouse and his/her own parent. The answer will show at what level the therapist will have to work to begin to restore vestiges of trust in the other spouse.

Attitudes toward the Separation

Another avenue of assessment has to do with whether each spouse accepts the separation as legitimate. Either spouse may reflect genuine grief and anger, which are the prelude to acceptance. Or there may be an obsession with the power aspects, who is winning or losing (e.g., "I feel I'm a loser, there's nothing I can do, I have to put up with whatever he/she gives me."). Or there may be an obsession with who was right or wrong, or who is the "better" parent. In some cases, spouses may still argue that the person who was "wrong," or to blame, does not deserve to get the children, as if the custody of the children were a matter of reward and punishment for the parents. The attitude of the parent will influence their response to the therapist. For example, if the client's attitude is that the bad parent does not deserve the children, the therapist's efforts to deal realistically with the custody issue may be seen as a betrayal. If the client's concern is with being a loser, then the therapist's attempts to establish that there is anything good about the other spouse may, at least initially, be heard as proof that the therapist regards the other spouse as the winner.

Capacity for Differentiation

It is important to know how well one parent can distinguish between the marital and the parenting qualities of the other parent (e.g., "He takes a lot of his work frustration out on me, but I don't see him doing that to the children.").

Acknowledgment

As already indicated, an important issue is whether each spouse can see the contribution he/she has made to the difficulties in the marriage, and whether each spouse can acknowledge the positive contributions made by the other to the marriage or to the children. In one situation, a husband was able to recognize that his alienation from his mother had led to his alienation from his wife; his reworking of his relationship to his mother prepared him for new approaches to his wife. Even though she rebuffed these efforts and went through with the divorce, he had become free to acknowledge her value both as a person and as a parent. He was also able to acknowledge the sadness he felt at the hurt caused to each by the other. Closely related to this is whether the individual is able to make an assessment of the marital situation that is clearly separate from what others (e.g., parents and friends) think about it.

Another perspective from which assessment can be made is that of whether the parent can recognize that the issues created for the children, and their ways of experiencing the separation, will be different from the parents'. A basic distinction here is whether the parent is primarily concerned with the narcissistic issue of winning the children's support. For instance, if the children seem upset when they return from a visit to their father, their mother may choose to assume that this is proof of the father's unfitness, or she may realize that the upset could be an unavoidable result of the separation. Another critical instance is when either parent pushes the children too rapidly to accept a new marital partner. Another, of course, is when the parent regards the children's continuing affection to the other parent as an act of disloyalty, or demands that the children act as spies or messengers. A parent's response to efforts at constructive intervention by the therapist will soon show how much that parent can be expected to change his/her outlook. This, of course, is one of those situations where the therapist needs to show awareness of the parent's needs before seeking to effect change.

Access

Another factor has to do with the general question of access. This includes a parent's willingness to give access not only to the other parent, but also to the other parent's relatives, any one of whom may have special significance for a child. A critical access issue is whether the parents are still willing to allow the children to have access to both of them at the same time. For the parents to see the children together, even on a very limited basis, can have enormous significance for the children. One boy expressed his pleasure and relief at seeing his mother and father dance together at his older brother's wedding.

Support Networks

How ready the client is to mobilize constructive efforts may depend a great deal on the nature of his/her support networks. These can include the family of origin, one or both extended families, friends, work associates, and religious and community entities. To some extent this is a matter of taking inventory, but simultaneously the therapist may be looking for ways that unused supportive contacts can be restored. This is especially meaningful when there have been cutoffs that can be repaired. It is also important to detect any negative inputs, such as a parent maligning the ex-spouse.

Assessment with Children

A particularly elusive aspect of assessment has to do with sorting out children's attitudes toward parents. I do not believe that children should be put in the position of having to make decisions about custody. They are not generally equipped to do so, and the stress of being disloyal to one parent may be severe. In practice, however, situations do arise where it is important to know whether children's reactions to certain events (e.g., overnight visitation) are genuine or whether they are assumed out of loyalty or fear. In one case, for instance, it became evident enough that the children were parroting their mother's views about overnight visits with father; they spoke in a repetitive, elocutionary style, stumbling over some of the big words, and glancing nervously toward the waiting room where she was sitting. It should never be overlooked that under layers of overtly expressed hostility, the child usually has a reservoir of love and concern toward the denigrated parent.

Some, but not all, of the points covered in the sections on assessing adults may also be appropriate for children. The ones that seem natural to consider with children include ability to face issues between them and their parents, nature and degree of negative feelings, and feelings of injustice and suspicion. To put it the other way round, the question with children has to do with how much remains of their trust and positive regard.

MOBILIZING RESOURCES FOR CONSTRUCTIVE DIVORCE

The Therapist

As Goldsmith (1982) observed, the divorce crisis means a system in flux, hence open to change. This offers the therapist the opportunity to help rearrange things. I have already mentioned what I regard as the most desirable baseline for the therapist's approach: the maintenance of an attitude of multidirectional partiality, showing equal concern for the interests of everyone involved. This helps to reclaim whatever vestiges of trust remain in the broken relationship. The cultivation of trust, in turn, provides the underpinnings for constructive change.

Timing

Concerning the timing of the therapist's intervention, the ideal time for therapeutic intervention to begin in a divorce case is before the children have heard about the impending divorce. Unfortunately, people who have been in marital therapy prior to the decision about divorce are usually reluctant to look at the need for further therapy once the decision has been made; they seem more inclined to run than to talk. Divorce therapy as such has not so far become a generally recognized process. Steinberg (1980) proposed attorney–therapist teamwork, with the therapist "absorbing" the emotional issues aroused by the legal events. It is to be hoped that, as more attention is paid to what can be accomplished, the utility of divorce therapy will become more widely recognized. Even now there are individual spouses or couples who want help in going through the divorce process so as to find a productive outcome.

Whom To See

Concerning whom to see, it is desirable, if not always possible, to have at least one session at which all family members are present. This is in keeping with the idea that it is better if the parents can be together when the children are told about the divorce. The basic structure of the new family system can be defined and supported in a joint session—for example, the role the father will play in maintaining discipline. Both parents can be helped to recognize and address the children's anxiety (e.g., when it turns out that a child is afraid to go on vacation with one parent because the other parent might be gone when the child gets back). The joint session can serve as a vivid reminder to the parents that the children still need both parents. The children can even provide comfort or call for accountability, as when one teenager remarked, "I've worked with both mother and father, I see both, I recognize both, it's two people that have different worlds. And I hope you're not going to let this wipe everybody out."

There are no intrinsic limitations on whom the therapist may see. The therapist can function better with the freedom to talk to anybody and everybody by prior agreement—the extended family, the judge, and the attorneys, especially the attorney of a parent who refuses to be seen. One therapist suggested, "Take a lawyer to lunch." In the event that the therapist is aware that the lawyer retained by one spouse is out for a killing, it is permissibile to suggest to that spouse that another legal opinion might be helpful. It helps to know someone to recommend. It is also essential for the therapist to realize that the client is not only entitled to retain control of the legal process, but responsible for doing so. It simply is not enough for a client to fall back on, "My lawwyer told me to do it." One therapist suggests that his clients view their lawyer like a builder engaged to build a house. The builder is not responsible for the design. Taking steps like these helps free the therapist to function in a nonadversary role, as advocate for everyone whose basic interests are at stake.

Focus

As the therapist proceeds with the divorcing spouses and the people close to them, focus on concrete issues may prove more rewarding than relatively vague moves—for instance, toward "improved communication." Riskin (1982) spoke of the importance of helping the family move toward specific positive goals. I believe the best way this can be done is to identify, and preserve the focus upon, specific issues, no matter how trivial they may on the surface appear to be, with the emphasis always upon the family members' finding ways to resolve or bypass these issues and move on. The very reluctance of family members to stay on a specific issue, no matter how unimportant it sounds, may be an index of how deep the issue really is. In one case, a mother's complaint about her adolescent son's refusal to go look for a lost dog led quickly into her fear that her son did not care for her; this, in turn, proved to be a displacement of her belief that her ex-husband had never cared for her. Having brought this much out, it was not hard to help the mother see how she was displacing her fear onto her son.

Therapy and the Law

As divorcing spouses become involved with the legal system, it may be necessary to clarify the difference between the lawyer's role, which may be adversary, and the therapist's role, which should not become adversary. This explanation may have to extend to the entire courtroom procedure, the requirements of which may turn out to be not only adversary but also irrelevant to, or inimical to, the preservation of existing family resources. For example, the client may be encouraged to go into court prepared to do everything possible to destroy the credibility of the other spouse. The client's attorney may ask from the therapist only such information as can be used to damage the other spouse. It may be necessary to make the simple distinction for the parent that, while it may become imperative to fight over such issues as money and residence, a line must be drawn between this and fighting over the children or using the children in the fight.

Review

In helping to establish the postdivorce family structure, it is important for the therapist to realize that time is of the essence. What seems most appropriate now may change sooner than anyone expects. For instance, both extended families may agree that the mother gets sole custody of an infant son, but when the son is ready for his training wheels the need for this arrangement may have been outlived. Also, the ex-spouses may continue to war over the initial agreement. Accordingly, it is valuable if opportunities for periodic review can be built into a separation agreement. The review may be automatic or on request. The mechanism for the review can be specified: counseling, mediation, even the appointment of a respected family member as arbiter. If this provision is made, then one parent will not be so likely to be perceived as launching an attack on the other when he/she raises fresh issues about custody, visitation, or care.

The Client

Among the tasks with which the therapist will help the divorcing clients are the following.

Working through the Loss

An early and major task for each spouse is, of course, working through the loss. Goldsmith (1982) spoke of the "death of the marriage" and the working through that must follow. We have noted how, for the person experiencing it, the loss of a spouse through divorce can in some respects be more devastating than loss of a spouse through death. We have seen few marriages so devalued by their partners that their loss did not provide cause for grieving. Concurrent with, and distracting from, grief is the damage to self-esteem. For people whose parents never validated their passports to enter the human race, the marriage may have been a second try at validation, and its collapse can throw one at least temporarily into a frightening void. This is reinforced, of course, if one spouse relied upon the other as the sole source of self-validation. As one client put it, "I lopped off chunks of myself to be with him. I only related to others through him." McGoldrick and Carter (1982) spoke of the "retrieval of self." This could mean getting back the "lopped-off chunks," opening access to other sources of recognition for the self, from family, friends, and work associates. Montalvo (1982) suggested that mobilizing indignation can help get a divorcing spouse to claim that to which he/she is entitled. This may be the spark that gets someone going again, provided it does not lead merely to a litany of grievances.

Perspective on the Spouse

Providing therapeutic support through controlled siding can enable the client to experience enough sense of trust to begin to reopen the positive side of the ambivalence toward the ex-spouse. Many ex-spouses go through this process on their own with reasonable success. When they cannot do so, support via therapeutic siding may be a necessary preliminary.

Recognition of the positives about the ex-spouse must not be taken to mean that the divorce has "failed." Recognition of the spouse's positive contributions to the marriage and one's own contribution to its breakdown is a valuable step for numerous reasons. Paradoxically, a consideration of the justice adhering to the other party is essential to the retrieval of the self. Until the value of the other is acknowledged, the client is not fully in touch with his/her own feelings.

Facing how the breakdown came about means facing the ledger of relational accounts, that is, recognizing what one owes to the other as well as what is owed from the other. When ex-spouses fail to achieve a separation, this can mean that one (or both) spouses feels profoundly "ripped off" and are still looking for reparations without knowing how to get them. Such claims need to be identified before people can begin to face how they wish to deal with them, perhaps simply by marking them "uncollectable" and writing them off.

As the perspective on the ex-spouse changes, the client may begin to restore some confidence in how the ex-spouse will function as a coparent.

Mobilizing Networks

The client will usually need to work at mobilizing the surrounding subsystems that can give support to the self as well as to the children. The postdivorce period may be an especially good time to tackle this task, since the emotional reworking that accompanies the divorce can include the removal of old obstacles and the opening of new doors. The momentum of breaking out of the marriage can carry over to renewing old contacts and reexamining old conflicts that stood in the way of contact. New questions can be opened about jobs or careers or volunteer opportunities. Maintaining or restoring connections with the extended family of the ex-spouse can be supportive for the client and may hold great value for the children.

The work of improving ties with family members can become quite intensive, as the therapist encourages explorations in new attitudes and new trial actions designed to renew contact. In one situation, the therapist worked with the husband to relieve a severe cutoff between him and his mother, which had been keeping him emotionally isolated from other people. He reached the point where he was able to observe, "I've thought of telling her I love her, but I'm afraid of the two of us crying in the car and I couldn't handle it. If I cried in front of her, she might not think I'm strong, and that's what she wanted." His working this through was a crucial factor in his handling his divorce in a responsible way and in making new attachments. Such efforts bring an increase in stability and a decrease in anxiety for everyone concerned. As Kressel and Deutch (1977) observed, family and friends can serve as allies and provide support where it is most needed.

Continuing the Work of Individuation

The self one "retrieves" following separation is not likely to be a fully matured self. Another major task of the separating adult is usually going "back to the drawing board" and working again at individuation from the family of origin. Some people may be tempted to flop back into dependency on the family; others may be so afraid of doing so that they fail to use the family as a resource. However, if one can say, "I have to make use of this experience in order to move on; please help me make the move," someone in the extended family should be able to respond to this appeal. If there is no one who can respond, then this deprivation must itself be faced as part of the individuation process.

In its fullest sense, we see individuation as considerably more than becoming separate from, and independent of, the family. Individuation is one of those life tasks that builds on earlier skills and in turn provides the base for further realization of life tasks. These include responsibility as an adult toward those who have a legitimate claim for consideration and help. Thus individuation seems to us, in its broadest sense, to be a mobilization for providing resources to others as well as to the self.

Parent–Child

There is now general agreement that the children are better off if both parents have meaningful participation in the ongoing daily life of the children and vice versa, even though this cannot be full-time (in most cases it never was) and even though the involvement of the children in two households may cause stress. As various studies have pointed out (Goldsmith, 1982; Jacobs, 1982; Wallerstein, 1980), the father is still critically important to the family and is still able to fulfill his functions as father, provided that insurmountable obstacles are not put in his way. Needless to say, the same is true for the mother, even though circumstances such as economic hardship may interfere.

Informing and Explaining

One of the early and major tasks of the divorcing parent is informing the children about the divorce and providing them with explanations. There is a good deal of disagreement on how parents should initiate the talk with children about divorce. A psychoanalytically oriented therapist might want each parent to talk to the children alone, so there will be a chance to start structuring the new, exclusively one-on-one relationship. Family therapists point out that, however awkward it may be when both parents address the children together, the children have an immediate, living demonstration of the continuing ability of the two parents to work together—a demonstration that may preserve the children's sense of trust that their world is not being hopelessly split down the middle. There is, of course, no reason why it cannot be done both ways, but I suggest that the initial message should come from both parents in order to protect the child's sense of trust in the parental relationship. This is a resource too valuable to be casually dissipated.

Concerning the reasons given to the children for the divorce, this, too, may have a significant effect both upon the children's sense of trust and upon their level of anxiety. An amorphous explanation ("We just don't love each other anymore") leaves the children prey to all kinds of anxious fantasies about the real reasons—including fantasies of being to blame. To go to the other extreme and insist on telling the children the whole "truth" may turn into something of an exercise in sadism. Neither parent is able to tell objective "truth" about the other at this point, and the effect may be to make the children a captive audience of one parent's venom toward the other. The best reasons to give are those of which the child is already aware: "You know how daddy and I are always fighting." These reasons can be summarized by the statement that the parents have decided together that everyone's lives will work better if the parents live apart. Reassurances for the child at this time should include the clear statement that the child is not to blame.

If the children seem to have great difficulty accepting the reasons for the divorce, it may help to point out that this may become clearer as the children get older, when they are better able to understand that both parents can have legitimate reasons for separating and no one needs to carry blame. It can even help to remind the children what the parents originally saw in each other. One of the greatest reassurances that can be given the children is that they will be free, from the very first moment of being informed about the divorce, to express positive feelings toward both parents. In one situation, a mother and her two children were discussing various aspects of the divorce with a therapist when the girl remarked, "I'm glad I'm going to be living with mother." The boy, whose need to defend his father was evident, instantly responded, "I'll tell daddy you said that." The mother promptly intervened to explain that it was all right for either of the children to say good things about either of their parents. This provided immediate reinforcement of the network that would hold this mother–daughter–son trio together as a unit and preserve a continuing link to the father.

By extension, of course, the reassurance that is given the children about their access to the other parent applies as well to that parent's family. As I have already pointed out, the children's right of access to their relatives is inalienable, and one of the basic merits of protecting this right is that the network of trustworthy relationships is thereby considerably extended and reinforced.

Working through the Loss

Unlike their parents, one of whom at least has assessed the pros and cons and decided that divorce is the answer, children seldom arrive at a total acceptance of divorce. Even if intellectually the children can grasp the need for the separation, it is not so easy to come to grips with the awareness that the two crucial supports of their life are now splitting apart. The children's emotional burden can be relieved if they can at least occasionally see their parents united in coparenting tasks. It will of course be greatly relieved if the parents do not bring the children into the conflict by criticizing the other parent or by seeking to restrict the children's emotional or physical access to the other parent.

No matter how much they may be distracted by the onslaught divorce makes on their own self-esteem, it is essential for both parents to recognize that the early phases of the divorce also have a heavy impact on the children's self-esteem. Not only may they have specific fantasies about being at fault ("Dad told me he couldn't stand it any longer if I kept asking for new skates"), but in a much more diffuse way, the children may feel the divorce is proof that they just weren't good enough to be worth staying together for. It is very hard for the parents to give direct reassurance about these matters to children, yet the adversary aspect of the divorce process need not become so debilitating to the parents at this stage that they cannot find some ways of restoring the children's sense of value. After all, the children are usually still able to find some ways of restoring a sense of value to the parents.

Turmoil

In helping the parents with the children, it may sometimes be necessary to remind them that the children did not choose the divorce, and that children, as Wallerstein and Kelly (1980) pointed out, do not usually look on divorce as a relief or a solution. One child provided a clue about her feelings by saying to her father, "I can't feel your kiss on the telephone." Anyone choosing divorce may expect that there will be turmoil for the children, as when they return from visitations with either parent. If acting out occurs, it needs to be understood in the context of the stress to which the children have been exposed. For instance, a child may "lie" in order to protect one parent from the other, and to treat this as grounds for punishment would be inappropriate.

Timing

Also, as Montalvo (1982) pointed out, children's emotional progress following a divorce may move at quite a different pace than their parents'. It may take a long time before they can accept a parent's having a new partner. These feelings may even serve as a guide to the parent who is trying to move too fast, and they must be taken into account if traumatic results are not to occur. For instance, it is usually a guarantor of trouble when a parent becomes engaged simultaneously with the divorce.

Parent as Executive

The divorcing parent is in a different position than ever before. Somewhat like an executive who has been given sole responsibility for setting up a new division of a company, the parent is now in a solo position, drawing on the resources of the extended families and of the children as well as seeking, if matters have not become too acrimonious, to bring in the ex-spouse at critical support points having to do with the children. A corollary to the above is making room for the other spouse to do likewise, that is, to set up a household in which the children are also meaningfully involved.

Boundaries

The task of setting up a separate, one-parent household requires new boundaries and definitions. The parent may have to find new ways to make the generational boundaries distinct, that is, helping the children to recognize that the adult must have a kind of authority which they do not. Minuchin (1974) spoke of the necessity for firm but flexible boundaries in any family. Thus, the mother may only create confusion if she appeals to her son to be the "man of the house" in the father's absence. At the same time, since there is one less person to administer or to do the work, it may become necessary to define the children's responsibilities much more distinctly than before. Here, too, negotiating skills can be a help. The parent may, as Montalvo (1982) suggested, have to create more distance from one of the children, because if they have been overly close, this may disrupt the attempt at establishing parental authority over all the children. The issue of authority may also have to be worked out with overly intrusive grandparents or other relatives; this may be the crucible in which the issue of individuation heats to a critical point. Hard decisions may also have to be made about how permeable to make the boundary of the household to the other parent, how to accept his/her help without permitting him/her to intrude so much that the household unit cannot take shape.

Keeping Siblings Together

It is generally recognized that one crucial component of the single-parent household is the continuity of relationship among siblings. Tessman (1978), for example, pointed out that children can best cope with the distress about parental separation when other meaningful relationships remain uninterrupted. Bank and Kahn (1982) showed what vicissitudes such sibling bonds can suffer when parents divorce; yet their examples equally demonstrate the importance of the bonds to the siblings. At a time when the family is being so radically altered, the siblings, even if their overt relationship to one another seems to be full of rivalry and conflict, provide each other with more stability then they may be getting from their parents. Together, the children can split up among them some of the emotional load; for example, if one has to go through a rebellious phase, another may ease the burden on the parent by being extra compliant. Together, they can confirm one another's perception of reality, defend one another to some extent, and create an atmosphere of fun to penetrate the onset of parental gloom. Misguided efforts to balance things out for the parents by splitting up the children between them may be enormously costly in terms of the children's development.

Tug-of-War

If the parent wants the therapist to join him/her in pulling the children away from the other parent, it may become necessary to clarify not only that this creates turmoil for the children, but also that the result is likely to be precisely opposite from the one desired, that is, the children will move toward the other parent. Even if they appear to be throwing their loyalties entirely to one parent, this will be costly later, when they reassess their loyalties and their identities. It may also be necessary for the therapist to point out that he/she, by declining to join in binding the children, is actually serving the best interests of the parent, whether it looks that way or not.

Criticism of the Other Parent

It may prove useful to instruct the client, with whatever degree of emphasis is required, that criticizing the other parent, or their life style, to the children can only create serious tension between the children and the attacking parent. One father reported a radical change in his children's behavior toward him as soon as he stopped trying to educate them about the shortcomings of their mother's way of life (e.g., how wrong of her it was to keep an unlisted phone number).

Narcissistic Injury to a Parent

The therapist may have to intervene in situations where one parent indicates that he/she feels wounded by the children's attitudes toward the separation. In one family, a father seemed deeply hurt because his daughter announced that she wanted to live with her mother just after he had bought a big house for himself and the girl to live in. He was evidently suffering a severe narcissistic wound, and he was not paying attention to what might actually be happening to his daughter. The therapist pointed out that the situation was not of the daughter's making, and she was already victim enough of it; that it was not fair to treat a positive wish toward her mother as a negative wish toward her father, and that it might be important to explore why she had been unable to express her wish sooner, instead of simply blaming her for the delay. It seemed important to make this intervention in order to get the father past his narcissistic wound and help him to restore his parental function.

Parent–Parent

Coparenting

The most arduous task, one for which closure never comes, may be that of establishing and maintaining the coparenting connection. Even in an extreme case where the other parent refuses to have any part in this process, it is important to the children's sense of trust that the effort be made and the offer kept open. If the other parent has totally withdrawn from the children, it is essential to make whatever effort can be made to help the children reconnect with the missing parent. Otherwise, the children will believe that there is no one in their lives who cares about the preservation of the most basic ties.

Assuming that the other parent is available, many situations can be identified in which it is better if the children can see that the parents are both working together, even if working together does not mean that they agree on everything. In one situation, a 14-year-old son chose to move to his mother's and the court supported his wish. Since this put them a continent apart, the father tried to keep up contact with his son by phone. Believing that his ex-wife would do nothing about it, the father routinely admonished the son about wearing his braces, getting to gym, and so on. When asked why he did not direct his questions to the mother, he replied that he had no respect at all for his ex-wife. The therapist suggested that this might be about all the son was able to hear. Given that the father's concerns were genuine, it might help if the father could say to the son. "I discussed this with your mother," or at least, "I tried to."

Joint Custody

Concerning the issue of joint custody, it is obvious by now that my bias is in the direction of helping parents do everything they can to function as coparents. Joint custody can serve to make this official without necessarily imposing a rigid symmetry of time spent with each parent. The essence of joint custody is to make it clear that both parents continue to take responsibility for the children's welfare. Not only is this important in principle, it can have practical sequelae; for instance, it avoids such situations as the noncustodial parent being unable to get access to school records or to authorize emergency medical care.

Fighting between the parents may not be a contraindication for joint custody, if it is not the children they fight about. Whether joint custody is officially established in every case or not, it is important to realize that the principle underlying joint custody may be on its way to becoming universal. The Committee on the Family (1980) recommended that, in situations where the parents are equally adequate but are unable to work out a custody agreement, the custody preferentially should be assigned to the one who is more likely to provide access to the other. As Cotroneo *et al.* (1981) put it, "*The best custodial parent is the parent who can most fully tolerate and cooperate in helping children maintain contact with all significant persons in their relational context.*"

Regularity of Visitation

A crucial issue that may need much working through with the parents is the children's right to regularity in the visitation schedule. Neither parent is entitled to belittle the children's right of access to the other parent by acting casually or negligently to undercut agreements about visitation. In some cases, the court will use its authority to defend this principle, but in many cases it does not. Alterations can, of course, be made in the schedule when this makes room for a legitimate activity that conflicts with the schedule. There are no clear-cut rules, but great care should be taken to weigh whether the activity in fact deserves priority over the visitation. When it begins to look as if the activity was an excuse for preventing the visitation, it is time for the therapist to intervene.

Risk to Children

In cases where there is a real issue of risk to the children, this risk should be quite specifically defined, and specific measures adopted for dealing with it—measures that will not be unduly divisive between the children and the parent. In a case, for instance, where the mother is afraid of the father's drunken driving, it may be legitimate to rule that he cannot take the children out in his car, but it is not valid to say that he cannot see the children. As the Committee on the Family (1980) suggested, the distinction must be drawn very carefully between what has proven to be harmful to a child and what one spouse finds offensive in the other (e.g., an alternate life style). Also, it is essential to take into account the point emphasized by Cotroneo *et al.* (1981), "From the child's side, a bad or distorted relationship to parents is better than no relationship at all."

Generally speaking, the therapist helps to clarify and reinforce the structure. It may involve practical assistance with the specific details of visitation arrangements. In the extreme situation, when the parents have fallen into the pitfall of communicating with each other only through the children, the therapist may even choose to step in and become a liaison person until the parents are capable of resuming direct contact. Otherwise, the children may be drawn into the center of the parental conflict.

In his *Guide for the Divorcing Parent*, Gorman (1980) advised separating couples to have the minimum necessary verbal contact with each other, in order to reduce the level of conflict. I prefer to base my intervention on a more optimistic view: that in many cases, people can develop a new structure that works. A better way for the therapist to reduce the conflict may be to take the firm position that both parents are equally essential. To the extent that each spouse is relating to the therapist like a competing sibling, the reassurance that nobody is going to get bumped out of his/her place can help reduce fear and acrimony. The therapist may find it possible to say to one or both of the ex-spouses, "Can you see him (or her) also suffering over this? Could he (or she) also be acting out of fear of losing the children?" In ways such as these, the therapist can assist the parents in their quest for a constructive outcome.

CONCLUDING OBSERVATIONS

Don'ts for the Therapist

In order to highlight some of the points I have made about working with divorce, I will review some of the errors therapists can make. It can be seen that these errors have to do with reducing, or failing to enlarge upon, the residue of trust between the divorcing spouses, as well as between them and the members of their families. If only by silence and inaction, the therapist can unwittingly condone attitudes or actions that work against the marshalling of resources.

Using Conflict as the Baseline

The therapist may assume without question that what is basic between divorcing spouses is conflict. This may be a fallacy. Regardless of the evidence of hostilities, one or both of the divorcing spouses may be holding onto the hope that good can be salvaged from the wreckage and put to use. They may adopt adversary roles partly, at least, because no one has offered them a better model. Some individuals do find it hard to cope with the emotional work of divorce. However, if the therapist views vestiges of trust between the separating spouses as evidence of "failure of the divorce" or "neurotic delaying," the therapist may be doing the couple a profound disservice.

Splitting the Family

Accepting conflict as the baseline may predispose the therapist to condone splitting up of the family as well as of the marriage. The therapist may permit the exclusion of noncustodial grandparents to go unchallenged ("Why not? It's obvious that they are dreadful people."). Or the therapist may condone the separation of siblings, or stand by while the newly divorced custodial parent plans to take the children to live at a distance. The distress thus generated may not surface for years. Worst of all, one parent may simply regard the other as expendable, and resist even vigorous efforts of the therapist to preserve the other as a parent. Yet this can never be regarded as a working solution.

Taking Sides

Accepting the conflict as basic can also lead the therapist to feel that he/she must, or is permitted to, take sides ("Sure, the other party may have a point, but what can I do about it? My hands are tied."). Or the therapist can play the good parent who rescues the favored client from his/her evil spouse.

Of course, it is sometimes impossible to listen to a spouse's indignant outpourings without feeling a rush of sympathy. The client indeed may be telling exact truths. However, often one needs only to bring in the other spouse to fill in the *missing* pieces of truth that give a critically different perspective. When the other spouse is unavailable, it becomes the therapist's job to construct out of whatever clues are available a mental model of what that spouse feels and thinks. Otherwise, it is easy to become merely a dupe of one's sole informant.

The therapist must not permit allegations of one spouse concerning the irresponsibility of the other as parent or provider to go unquestioned. Hard and unrewarding as it may sometimes be to the therapist, the therapist's job is to go the extra mile to ensure that he/she has not ignored some basic interest, or claim, of one of the spouses.

Parent–Child Conflict

The therapist need not assume that severe conflict between a child and a separating parent is evidence of a lack of mutual trust or caring. Instead, the therapist can seek to identify the actual causes of the conflict.

Pseudoguidance

The client may seek to enlist the therapist against the children as well as against the other parent. The client usually believes that he/she is only seeking guidance for the children, while actually engaged in exploiting them. A rather flagrant example is the client who asks the therapist for advice on how to make the children stop lying about the other parent. The therapist may wonder why the interrogation is taking place. Or the parent may want help in squelching the rebellion of a child, whose disruptive behavior may be traced to the parent's attempt to use the child as a substitute spouse. As with the spouse, the therapist cannot allow the child's interest to be defined solely by the parent.

Summary: The Resources and How to Mobilize Them

If kept in perspective, divorce itself can be seen as a family resource, an alternate route to getting on with life when the marriage has put an unmanageable obstacle in the way. Properly handled, divorce takes a marriage apart without damaging family networks. When there are children, the ex-wife is still connected to the husband's family through the children and vice versa. The children still share in the sometimes profound synergism of interests of each of their parent's families of origin. They are still able to benefit from both families' legacies and entitlements. There is nothing inherent in the divorce process to devalue grandparents, aunts, uncles, cousins, and so on. The children have an inalienable right of access to these people. The presence of other members of the extended families can also be a source of strength for the separating couple, when they are not cut off from these benefits.

Likewise, there is nothing inherent in the divorce process that destroys the potential for continued coparenting when this has already existed. Each ex-spouse has earned the right to consideration from the other, by virtue of having entered into parenthood together and of having contributed something to each other's welfare. Divorcing couples may keep the residue of reciprocal trust hidden from themselves and each other, but divorce seldom destroys all of this residue, and from it a measure of trustworthiness can usually be restored.

When divorcing parents are able to see divorce as an alternate route to the mobilization of resources for ongoing life tasks, they are free to develop new skills, not only as individuals but also as parents. The work of parenting may in fact become better balanced between the two parents than it was before.

The reward of the parents for their exertion on behalf of the children is the children's continued appreciation of their parents' efforts. This goes on even when the surface atmosphere is one of misconduct and conflict. When children express hatred for one or both divorced parents, close inspection will usually show that they feel they have been assigned this task. The children are usually willing to make their reservoir of trust and caring available to the parents. The parents can draw on it to make up for their own depletion, provided they do not deplete the children's resources by doing so.

Since the publication in 1980 of a similar service in a religious format, I have not yet heard of any instance of its actual use as a service. I have encountered opposition from a few people who were disposed to see it merely as a slick way of condoning divorce and did not recognize that it had to do with parenting. I have had many requests from people who wished to use it as a guide in their own divorce. I have used it as an adjunct to counseling and have heard from others who also used it this way.

The resources I have identified are relational resources. I have spoken not merely about the preservation of relationships, but more specifically about the preservation of whatever residue of reciprocal trust still exists and can be renewed in these relationships. To carry out these functions, the therapist must be in touch with both parents or at least make it clear that there has been a persistent effort to be in touch with both. If one parent refuses to have any contact with the children, the remaining parent is encouraged to keep trying to restore contact and to let the children know this is going on.

Essentially, then, I believe the task of the therapist is to provide enough multilateral support so that trust can reemerge and open the door for resumption of growth.

The Appendix, "A Statement for Children When Parents Are Separating," provides an example of a secular ritual of separation. Each parent affirms not only his/her own continuing role as parent but also a continuing regard for the parenting role of the other. The statement is designed to be used as a brief service, with or without a formal conductor, in the presence of the children.

APPENDIX: A STATEMENT FOR CHILDREN WHEN PARENTS ARE SEPARATING

HUSBAND OR WIFE: [*addressing children by name*] You may be afraid that because we are going to read this out loud to you, it is not really our own ideas. But your mother [father] and I went through it before we all met here, and we are going to read only what we truly could agree on.

WIFE: We are meeting here today to put into words for our children and for each other the meaning of the changes we are going through.

HUSBAND: As husband and wife, we did all we could to make our marriage work. It has been costly to us to admit that we have been unable to succeed. There is no hiding the loss that each of us suffers. We had hoped to be able to stay close to each other, to support each other, to cherish each other. Now, for each of us, the future must rest on the hope that what we could not do together, each of us will be able to do separately.

WIFE: But that is only part of the story. We are here because we did succeed together in one way that was, is, and always will be central to our lives. That is in our having you children. The failure of our marriage does not mean, and nobody should take it to mean, that we have failed in being parents. And of course the ending of our marriage does not mean that there is any ending to our being parents. If your great-grandchildren someday draw a chart of your family, it will show us as your parents.

HUSBAND: [*addressing children by name*] Your mother and I have this understanding: I will continue to respect and support her mothering of you. I will be glad to have you go to her. You may find that she and I are fighting about other things, but about this we agree.

WIFE: And I will continue to respect and support his fathering of you, and I will be glad to have you turn to him for that. He is right, you may find that he and I are fighting about other things. But about you, we agree: you need and deserve two parents, to see each of them enough so that you can share the everyday work and joy and trouble of your lives with each of them.

HUSBAND: And it is understood that in matters concerning you, your mother and I will try to work together as a team. This means that when there are important decisions to be made about your welfare, we will, whenever possible, consult each other. We will try to plan together so that the schedule of your daily lives will go well. If there is an event that calls for both parents to be present, we will accept each other's presence. We promise to do all we can to keep bad feelings about each other from getting in the way.

WIFE: This is also understood: belonging to two parents means that you belong to both of the families your parents came from. If your lives are to be full, if you are to keep in touch with your own roots, you need full freedom to see and to care about the people both in your father's family and in mine. I will respect the ties you have to your father's family.

HUSBAND: And I will respect the ties you have to your mother's family.

WIFE: [*addressing children by name*] At a time like this, there are some things that children need to understand. Your father and I hope [or know] that it will be easy for you to understand that you are not to blame for what went wrong between the two of us. Of course, there are times when parents blame children. But we cannot, and do not, blame you for what went wrong between us.

HUSBAND: It may be very hard for you to understand why your mother and I are not staying together. Even if you can understand, we know you will be unhappy about it for a long time to come.

WIFE: You may blame one of us, or both of us, for letting it happen. As time goes by, you may learn more about what each of us has gone through. If you blame us now, perhaps someday you will find that you do not have to blame us any more.

HUSBAND: Then it is understood that this marriage is coming apart, but let's see who's here.

WIFE: [*says all first names*] [number of] children [or child], and two people who will always be your parents.

REFERENCES

Bank, S. P., & Kahn, M. D. *The sibling bond.* New York: Basic Books, 1982.
Beavers, W. R. Healthy, midrange, and severely dysfunctional families. In F. Walsh (Ed.), *Normal family processes.* New York: Guilford Press, 1982.

Boszormenyi-Nagy, I., & Spark, G. *Invisible loyalties.* New York: Harper & Row, 1973.

Boszormenyi-Nagy, I., & Ulrich, D. Contextual family therapy. In A. S. Gurman & D. P. Kniskern (Eds.), *Handbook of family therapy.* New York: Brunner/Mazel, 1981.

Committee on the Family of the Group for the Advancement of Psychiatry. *New trends in child custody determinations.* New York: Law & Business, Inc./Harcourt Brace Jovanovitch, 1980.

Cotroneo, M., Krasner, B. R., & Boszormenyi-Nagy, I. The contextual approach to child-custody decisions. In G. P. Sholevar (Ed.), *The handbook of marriage and marital therapy.* New York: Spectrum Publications, 1981.

Goldsmith, J. The postdivorce family system. In F. Walsh (Ed.), *Normal family processes.* New York: Guilford Press, 1982.

Goldstein, J., Freud, A., & Solnit, A. J. *Beyond the best interests of the child.* New York: Free Press, 1979.

Gorman, I. *A guide for the divorcing parent.* Self-published, 1980.

Hareven, T. K. American families in transition: Historical perspectives on change. In F. Walsh (Ed.), *Normal family processes.* New York: Guilford Press, 1982.

Jacobs, J. W. The effect of divorce on fathers: An overview of the literature. *American Journal of Psychiatry,* 1982, *139* 1235–1241.

Kressel, K., & Deutsch, M. Divorce therapy: An in-depth survey of therapists' views. *Family Process,* 1977, *16* 413–444.

McGoldrick, M., & Carter, E. A. The family life cycle. In F. Walsh (Ed.), *Normal family processes.* New York: Guilford Press, 1982.

Minuchin, S. *Families and family therapy.* Cambridge, MA: Harvard University Press, 1974.

Montalvo, B. Interpersonal arrangements in disrupted families. In F. Walsh (Ed.), *Normal family processes.* New York: Guilford Press, 1982.

Riskin J. Research on "nonlabeled" families: A longitudinal study. In F. Walsh (Ed.), *Normal family processes.* New York: Guilford Press, 1982.

Steinberg, J. Toward an interdisciplinary commitment: A divorce lawyer proposes attorney–therapist marriages or, at the least, an affair. *Journal of Marital and Family Therapy,* 1980, *6,* 259–268.

Tessman, L. H. *Children of parting parents.* New York: Jason Aronson, 1978.

Ulrich, D., Bender, F., & Whitfield, F. A service of affirmation when parents are separating. Cincinnati: Forward Movement Press, 1980.

Wallerstein, J. S., & Kelly, J. B. *Surviving the breakup.* New York: Basic Books, 1980.

Walsh, F. Conceptualization of normal family functioning. In F. Walsh (Ed.), *Normal family processes.* New York: Guilford Press, 1982.

CHAPTER 14

Families and Abuse: A Contextual Approach

Margaret Cotroneo

This chapter focuses on a resource-oriented approach to abusive families, the contextual approach. This approach, developed by Ivan Boszormenyi-Nagy and colleagues, serves as both a theoretical framework and an action strategy. It considers the individual and systemic dimensions of human relationships to be dialectically related within a given relational context. The goal of contextual work is to help family members find a balance of giving and receiving that leaves no family member in a condition of permanent benefit or burden. This balance enables family members both to live as separate persons and to remain available to each other as resources. It accounts for the trustworthiness of relating among family members and between the family and its social context.

A contextual approach to intrafamilial abuse means acknowledging and working to rebalance a situation of injury and injustice while simultaneously attempting to move each family member toward a more trustworthy position. This chapter offers a theoretical framework and practical applications of contextual work with families who present with problems of abuse.

RELATIONAL CONTEXT

An understanding of the major concepts of the contextual approach is contingent upon an understanding of the notion of relational context. Each person is born into a complex network of relationships—familial, personal, social, and environmental. This relational context shapes the nature of future relationships. It includes the individual's legacy or the facts, events, and circumstances that a person inherits just by being born to a particular family, society, and culture. It also includes the resources and limitations naturally found in relationships with family members, friends, colleagues, and the world at large. Finally, there is a connective relationship to the next generation. This connection is built up

Margaret Cotroneo, R.N., Ph.D. School of Nursing, University of Pennsylvania, Philadelphia, Pennsylvania.

through the consequences of actions or behaviors. Context, thus understood, conveys both what is unique to the person and what is actually and potentially shared in common with others.

This use of the word context differs from the usual, more limited meaning of the term as "circumstance" of an action or behavior. The term "circumstance" generally refers to something outside the person. The term "context" denotes what constructs, humanizes, and personalizes action or behavior. It denotes the "*is*-ness" that weaves together the threads of one's relational world into a coherent, expressive whole.

Context is the fullness of relational reality—the whole cloth of relationship— whether viewed individually or systemically. It is woven from the interactions, concerns, and commitments shared by relating partners in a process of relating over time. Once woven, a relational context can be reduced neither to the terms and conditions of any single person or idea, nor to any system of persons or ideas. To summarize, context is the whole of any relational situation—an integration of past and present relating that shapes the future. Its dimensions are factual, psychological, systemic, and ethical.

A contextual approach to intrafamilial abuse assumes that abusive actions or behavior are shaped by a person's full relational context and cannot be understood outside it. Two major guidelines for intervention emerge from this assumption:

1. The resources for intervention and healing exist within a given relational context. Put another way, the hand that hurts is also the mediator of healing in the sense that healing cannot be freeing for growth if the source of injury or injustice is avoided or protected from the rightful claims of an injured party. (Cotroneo, 1982).

2. Holding people to some method of accountability for the nature, kind, quality, and consequences of relating is freeing rather than burdensome. To the degree that people are able to actualize a balance of giving and receiving care and due consideration in their relational world, injustice and exploitation are diminished and trust building is enhanced.

The emphasis is on creating a climate in which each person's side receives due consideration. Judgment or blame is deferred in the interests of eliciting an accountability that places the abuse in its full relational context. The substance and energy that builds, shapes, and moves a relational context is trust, the next major concept of this approach.

DYNAMICS OF TRUST

A resource orientation seeks to build relationships of trust even in the midst of pervasive mistrust, without endangering the rights or welfare of individual family members, particularly those who are most vulnerable.

It would be well to examine how the term "resource" is used here. In the contextual approach, the term denotes options for trust. Trust is defined as a stance toward reality, shaped by a balance of giving and receiving that enables a person to discern, in every concrete situation, what is authentically and normatively human and helps her/him to respond in that situation with care, competence, and an attitude of fairness. Trust is the fundamental resource of all human relating, binding people to each other in a thread of continuity that can be positive or negative for purposes of growth. Trust resources lie in reciprocal care and the capacity to acknowledge reciprocal care no matter how seemingly minimal its manifestation. The nature, kind, quality, and consequences of relating form the basis of care. Care or its lack shape the dynamics of trust, justice, growth, and human solidarity. Contextual resources, therefore, are relationships, both actual and potential, in which caring is invested, reinvested, or exploited, resulting in a reserve of trust or mistrust for future relating. From birth onward, care sets the stage for the availability of options for trust in the future.

In a resource orientation to intrafamilial abuse, the commitment to trust building serves as the framework for action. Functional trust, that is, trust that can be activated in the situation, enhances one's capacity to handle inevitable failures and disappointments, to rework unrealistic expectations, to integrate complexity, to make new claims on relationships, and to sustain ongoing commitments. It shapes the ability to act with responsible care when responsible care is called for. Functional mistrust, on the other hand, results in stagnation. Stagnation is a condition of disengagement from the process of reciprocal care through the inability or unwillingness to give and to receive due consideration. It is born of injustice in one's relational world in the sense that a person is cheated or deprived of care they rightfully deserved or in the sense that their caring was exploited. Stagnation is often manifested by a destructive form of entitlement; that is, a fixation on one's own needs and expectations that serves to extinguish the obligation to consider the needs and expectations of others. Persons so entitled tend to deny responsibility and to indulge in blame, fault finding, and competitive power struggles. They may also become very protective and demanding in close relationships. They are often more rigid in their expectations of themselves than of others and their behavior is isolating. Their personal pain is often unbearable as they search for someone who will extend unilateral care to them.

To summarize, trust is shaped by reciprocal care and made concrete in actions of giving and receiving. The intergenerational balance sheet of giving and receiving is elicited by such questions as: Who was available to take care of the children? Who turns to whom in time of need? How are expectations of care and devotion managed in the family and outside the family? Who is entitled to care by virtue of having been cheated, deprived, or in some way exploited? Who is most vulnerable to the loss of care? How have the resources for care been shared between the generations?

Resources in the contextual approach are always linked to care in the family. Care manifests itself in the physical and emotional tasks of caretaking. It is the fundamental experience that elicits responsibility. Someone's concern for us is the magnet of our reciprocal concern. When we do not experience another's concern for us, we tend to withdraw from the attempt of reciprocity in order to "take care of ourselves." We pull back to onesidedness and trust is diminished.

Although trust is presumed to be present in all relationships, life experience informs us that sometimes people are unwilling or unable to receive care or to extend it appropriately, signaling mistrust. However, in any given relational context, so long as people continue to interact with each other resources can be presumed. Even destructive acting-out behavior can be a signal of care if one looks beyond the event to the relational context. The following vignette serves to illustrate this point.

John, age 16 years, lived with his mother and two siblings in a low-income housing project. He was truant from school and a substance abuser. He was constantly in difficulty with the police for theft and street fighting. John's mother had never married; the children had different fathers. She was illiterate. In the course of her life she had been exploited by males who later abandoned her. She manifested a childlike need to please people in order to be cared about, a fact that neighbors exploited. Her behavior was characterized by helplessness, anger, depression, suspiciousness, and combativeness toward others. In the course of working with this family it became clear that John responded to his mother's helplessness with his aggressive acting-out behavior. It was his attempt to advocate for his mother in the only way he could be effective. He was doing something to rebalance the exploitation in his mother's life. While John's behavior expressed a lack of concern for himself or society, it signaled his overriding concern to obtain justice for his mother.

Cases of this nature are common in family life. The family has its own terms and conditions for trust building. For that reason trust cannot be prescribed. Instead, investments and reinvestments of care are needed. If the resources of relationships are maintained from generation to generation, it is because people have sufficient reserves of trust both to repay past investments and to reinvest in future relationships. Eliciting this intergenerational balance sheet of resources requires a practical grasp of the fundamental methodology of the contextual approach: multilateral advocacy.

MULTILATERAL ADVOCACY

This process of eliciting the family's own balance sheet of giving and receiving care and due consideration I refer to as multilateral advocacy. Because it extends beyond decision making to an exploration of the benefits and burdens of ongoing relationships, multilateral advocacy can be distinguished from the notion of advocacy in the legal sense. Multilateral advocacy is a process of finding and utilizing resources of relationships through establishing reciprocal accountability. It is an intervention strategy as well as an assessment process. For example, in any given situation each person has a perspective on the merit of his/her position as well as a perspective on the merit of the positions of others. By eliciting and acknowledging these positions and asking each relating partner to take some responsibility for responding to the positions of others, a climate of trust is built through mutual accountability. This sets the stage for coresponsible decision making.

Family members and legal and social service interveners are more inclined toward resources when they feel their own side has been fairly considered. Moreover, in a climate of reciprocal accountability, people are free to challenge myths, distortions, and denials. This is especially important in situations of abuse in which decisions have to be made that involve the safety and welfare of vulnerable persons. Creative options for a comprehensive treatment plan are more likely to emerge in a climate in which one can expect fair consideration. Multilateral advocacy, therefore, is not simply a tool of the expert; rather it is an instrument for healing relationships that family members and those who try to help them can implement outside the therapy room. (Cotroneo, 1979).

In working with intrafamilial abuse, multilateral advocacy is characterized by six guidelines for trust building:

1. A subjective assessment by relating partners of what each has invested in the relationship and gained from the relationship (position of entitlement).
2. The expectation that one's side will be fairly considered.
3. The understanding that no one side, whether one's own or someone else's, can ever function as an adequate explanation of the whole situation.
4. The realization that resources and limits that are absent at one moment in a relationship may be present at another.
5. Resolutions that leave no relating partner in a condition of permanent benefit or burden.
6. A presumption that all who are affected by decisions will share in the process of decision making.

Clearly, as a methodology, multilateral advocacy includes the techniques of asking good questions and putting back on the family the burden of examining their situation and finding options for what to do about it. Beyond these considerations, however, it places a responsibility on the therapist to be sufficiently free from the burdens of exploitation in his/her own relationships to be able to advocate for each family member from a position of fairness. The therapist's capacity to extend trust and consideration is crucial to work with families in situations of abuse. In my experience, family-of-origin work is an essential part of the training of therapists who want to do this kind of work.

ASSESSMENT OF RESOURCES

Having briefly presented the notion of multilateral advocacy, I now turn specifically to an assessment of resources. In the first instance, an assessment of relational resources means a full assessment of the event of abuse: What happened? What immediate factors led to the abuse? What can be done both to protect the injured party and to help other family members? What does the law require? Next, an assessment of relational resources also includes consideration of the relational configurations of abuse: (1) the justice system of the family, (2) entitlement, and (3) parentification. The discussion of these configurations of abuse is followed by a discussion of a case, the C family, to illustrate the application of theory to practice.

The Justice System of the Family

The first of the relational configurations that shape abusive situations is the justice system of the family. The justice system of the family is the configuration of giving and receiving that takes its shape from family relating, either through actions that benefit others or actions that exploit them. An adequate assessment of justice issues requires an exploration of a minimum of three generations of family relating. In terms of simple justice, each of us is required at times to be giver, at times receiver. People cannot give of themselves indefinitely without receiving in like measure. Nor can they receive indefinitely without experiencing an imbalance in relationship that must be reworked through giving.

Actions, unlike feelings, have factual consequences. In a largely invisible process of family accounting, the actions of giving and receiving are registered and synthesized as resource (benefit for the future) or as burden (sources of exploitation). Chronic imbalances in giving and receiving care and due consideration shape abuse in families. When persons are deprived of care they rightfully deserved they emerge from childhood inclined to rebalance the injustice through attitudes and actions designed to obtain justice. If some reciprocity is not forthcoming from the injuring parties, the person will tend to seek caretaking from mates, children, colleagues, and the world at large. Moreover, there is a tendency to accept injustice as a norm for relating outside the family.

Depending on the nature, kind, quality, and consequences of the injustice a person has experienced, she/he may simply use others as objects of exploitation. Ordinarily, when the exploitation is acted out in this substitutive relational context, a person feels no guilt. In terms of his/her personal context justice is being done even though the consequences may be utterly destructive for others. This dynamic is called destructive entitlement (Boszormenyi-Nagy) and is discussed under the next heading. The term means that injured parties are "entitled" to receive care rather than give it. This entitlement is not a feeling or perception. It is a fact of life that is acted on in a destructive manner in other relationships.

Entitlement

Entitlement is a relational configuration that shapes abuse in families. Essentially entitlement is the freedom to give and ask in trust. It is earned through investments of care and due consideration in relationships. To the degree that a person makes caring investments from which others benefit, he/she gains freedom to claim reciprocal care in that relationship. To the degree that a person invests in exploiting others, her/his freedom to give and claim care is diminished as trust is eroded. In assessing each family member's position of entitlement, the therapist seeks to understand the balance between self-care and care for others. These two aspects of the individual are not viewed as mutually exclusive but rather as dialectically related. One of the central tasks in shaping responsibility is the capacity to integrate concern for individual rights and personal options for growth with a concern for obligations and being available to others as a resource.

As applied to abuse, entitlement issues surface in the context of a person's capacity to manage the demands of caretaking, both with regard to care of themselves and care extended to others. The following case may serve to illustrate entitlement issues in abusive families:

Ms. R sought help, complaining of depression, resentment, and anger directed toward her children, ages 4 and 2. She felt she could not tolerate even their ordinary demands for parenting. What finally compelled her to find help was a recent incident in which she stood at the top of the stairs with her 2-year-old son in her arms fighting an angry wish to throw him down the stairs. At the time Ms. R entered therapy she was 30 years old. She stated she had no energy to invest in the marriage or in parenting her children. She described her husband as tolerant, giving, and available both to her and to the children. His behavior, however, did not mitigate her chronic sense of anger, resentment, and loneliness.

As a young person, Ms. R was overavailable to her parents, who were in conflict. She was expected to tend the house for her mother and provide intimacy for her father as a way of bridging the gaps in their marriage. Inevitably Ms. R failed in her efforts. Instead, she became an object of her mother's disappointment and rage and her relationship to her father culminated in incest from her 13th to her 18th year.

An analysis of her parent's legacy indicated that her mother's marriage to her father was viewed as an act of disloyalty by her maternal grandparents. In fact, when her mother conceived her, the pregnancy was kept secret from her mother's parents to avoid their disapproval. From the other side, Ms. R's father had been forced into the position of protecting his mother from an abusively controlling stepfather. Both of Ms. R's parents brought a sense of personal depletion into the marriage, resulting in excessive demands for parenting from the spouse relationship. When they could not meet each other's expectations for care and devotion, they each turned to their eldest daughter.

Eventually Ms. R came to feel exploited, although she remained loyal to her parents. She never told her mother about the incest even after her parents divorced. She continued to phone and occasionally visit them, although she would never permit her daughter to be alone with her father. Both of her parents remarried. Burdened by resentment, guilt, and unmet longings in her relationship to her parents, Ms. R stood on the edge of either taking her own life or replicating an abusive situation with her children. Unable to abandon her parents or to evade her legacy with them, Ms. R chose to return to the source of her injuries. Although afraid, she seemed compelled to face her parents, understand their motivation, and hear them express at least a modicum of regret for their treatment of her.

Over a period of 6 months, Ms. R incorporated her husband, her father, and her mother in the therapy sessions. She voiced her injuries and listened to their side. Her parents were unable to find the courage either to face each other or to face their joint culpability in their behavior toward their daughter. They continued to scapegoat each other and to try to entrap their daughter in split loyalties. On the other hand, they did travel several hundred miles to be available to her, they told their own stories, and they listened to her. While Ms. R was disappointed on her own terms, she was finally able to let go of her responsibility for their well-being and to claim consideration for herself. In claiming consideration for herself, she was freed from guilt and resentment to a degree sufficient to reinvest in other relationships.

Through the mystification or denial of entitlement issues, a family legacy of injustice is protected. In cases of abuse, this protection is extended to relationships a person wants and needs. The claim for consideration or the failure to claim consideration in an injured relationship is an expression of a problem of entitlement. What is the basis for protecting a legacy in which one has been deprived of care or exploited? From a contextual perspective, loyalty and legacy form the matrix of entitlement and help to shape the dynamics of protectiveness that characterize many families in situations of abuse.

Legacy

The legacy is a configuration of facts, events, circumstances, and commitments linked to a particular family and culture. Persons inherit their legacy by the facts of birth and upbringing. Unlike perceptions, which may or may not be factually based, the legacy is rooted in facts and is transmitted to each generation through a process of interactions, expectations, and commitments. In addition to family constellation, life-style, and roles, it includes communal and societal events such as war, persecution, famine, oppression, and survival experiences. It also includes ethnic, racial, and religious roots. The legacy likewise includes personal-familial events such as illness, birth and death, loss and abandonment, divorce, suicide, experiences of success and failure, and endured injuries and injustices. Legacy is not simply a record of facts and events. It is also a record of needs, resources, and commitments. It serves as a vessel of all the actual and potential sources of trust and mistrust in the family and society.

The facts of one's legacy affect relationships in two ways: (1) in the sense that they define reality (e.g., being the firstborn in a family), and (2) in the sense that they shape our perceptions and expectations of reality (e.g., through experienced injustice). By virtue of her/his legacy, a person stands in continuous relationship to others—past, present, and future. Through the process of live relating with family and community, legacy is transmitted and tradition is personalized. As we care about, examine, correct, and make sense out of our legacy, we claim it as our own. Our ability to be at home in our legacy is finally what enables us to say "I am history, I am tradition" in the sense that we take responsibility for our part in shaping the future.

Loyalty

Loyalty (Boszormenyi-Nagy & Spark, 1973) can have many meanings ranging from individual feelings of devotion to forms of social solidarity like national allegiance. In relational terms loyalty refers to commitments born of direct experience. These commitments primarily take the form of expectations of devotion and due consideration, held in common by people in the family, community, or society and transmitted intergenerationally. Thus each person is born into, develops, creates, and transmits loyalty expectations.

The relational basis for loyalty is care. In fact, loyalty is like an invisible intergenerational tapestry woven from the fibers of caring relationships. Loyalty expectations can be freeing or enslaving. For example, in the family, the investments of care that parents make in their children from birth onward form the basis for the parental expectation of filial devotion. When parents can make appropriate investments in parenting, their children are free to reciprocate by caring about their parents and by investing in their own mates and children. This kind of commitment is growth producing (positive loyalty). When parents, for whatever reason and regardless of fault, cannot invest appropriately in their children, the children tend to react to the loss with greater emotional attachment. Because all children are deeply committed to a continuing relationship to their parents, they take on parental failures as their own and react to them with emotions of shame, guilt, and resentment. Thus emotionally bound, they are not free to invest appropriately in relationships outside the family unless and until they can come to terms with the loss or deprivation they have experienced in relationship to their parents. This kind of commitment is growth inhibiting (negative loyalty).

Loyalty commitments form the basis of justice and entitlement in the family. Loyalty expectations are framed in terms of an indebtedness that begins with the fact that we are born in need of care. Whether or not we are cared for and how we are cared for construct and shape lifelong obligations toward significant other people. These obligations are expressed in terms of our expectations of other people and our availability for meeting the expectations of other people. To the extent that people are able to find ways to discharge their loyalty obligations, past relationships can be utilized as trust resources. To the extent that people are enslaved by unreworked obligations, past relationships become sources of mistrust. Thus loyalty represents a claim on the future that carries with it a "governing obligation" to care about the sources of one's life. Because it shapes future commitments, loyalty is a powerful intentional force in all relationships.

From a contextual perspective, abusive behavior is viewed as an affirmation of loyalty to the family of origin. The abusive parent protects the family of origin by substituting the marital and parenting relationship as the context for rebalancing relational injuries. The expectations for care and devotion that were not met in the family of origin are assigned to the spouse and children, tending to overburden these relationships and distort their reality. The loyalty dynamic is manifested in child abuse in the child's tendency to protect the needy parent. It is also manifested in situations of incest, in the tendency to blame the child victims, thus avoiding an examination of the adult context and the families of origin. Protectiveness in relationship is a signal of loyalty conflict. Protective behaviors are a constant presence in intrafamilial abuse.

Parentification

Parentification (Boszormenyi-Nagy & Spark, 1973) is the last relational configuration that is significant in shaping abuse in families. Parentification is defined as age- and context- inappropriate expectations for care and devotion from children. It is a consequence of the justice system of the family. Children who are parentified live under a burden of responsibility for the well-being of their parents. The more at risk the health and welfare of the parent(s), the more the obligation to extend care is assumed by the child. In essence, parentification is a manifestation of loyalty in the sense that the obligation to care about one's parents overrides one's own entitlement to receive care and devotion.

The parent's role in parentifying a child is not always intentional, although it can be, nor is it always pathological. Indeed, a certain amount of parentification is intrinsic to every parent–child relationship in the sense that each child sometimes serves as an object for meeting parental needs and for taking on the burdens of parental hopes and failures. Every child is a new resource for parents, providing them with an opportunity for growth. Such a child can be strengthened by a deepened sensitivity to needs of others and may be less self-centered and consequently more responsible for their own actions. However, whenever a child is required, intentionally or unintentionally, to be available to parents to the exclusion of consideration of their own growth and success, the parentification can be said to be destructive. This child becomes a primary caretaker, assuming a counterautonomous position in family life. They experience abandonment and failure of parental advocacy, rendering them vulnerable to exploitation in other relationships.

In my experience, the dilemma of the parentified child is seldom acknowledged from the vantage point of the child. The development of assessment and intervention tools that family therapists might employ in listening to children on their own terms goes largely ignored in the field. Often the interpretation of parents is accepted as baseline for understanding a child's side of a family situation. Systems theory itself would lead us to believe that intervention in the relationship between parents will handle the child's dilemma. Yet, when we make the investment of time to try to help children express their worries and struggles, we find that their experience and the significance that they attach to events in the family may differ in very important ways from those of their parents. For example, in one family I treated, a father considered it to be in his son's best interest to implement a separation from his wife after his son's Bar Mitzvah. His son, however, attached the greatest significance to the convergence of events. He concluded that his Bar Mitzvah was the precipitating event in his father's leaving.

Given the tendency of children to assign responsibility to themselves for any loss or deprivation of parenting they experience, the failure to actively elicit and acknowledge their side constitutes a further burden for them. This issue may well be a matter for ethical reflection.

In work with families in situations of abuse, three primary manifestations of parentification can be identified. The first is the fostering of dependency in children through the transmission of parental fears and anxieties, thus encouraging children to turn exclusively to parents for protection from an alien outside world. The child's moves toward independence are met with hostility and fear. This dynamic is evident particularly in families in which the parental legacy is marked by loss or abandonment. A cycle of relating is established that takes this shape: the greater the fear of loss or abandonment, the more intense the mode of relating to the child, the stronger the loyalty expectation, and the more frequent the tendency of the child to behave counterautonomously in order to confirm his/her commitment to the parent(s). As a consequence of this kind of relating, the child often takes increasing responsibility for the well-being of the parents.

The second significant manifestation of parentification is that of split loyalties. A child's devotion or care for one parent is maintained at the cost of his/her relationship to the other parent. Children who are caught in split loyalties carry a huge burden of guilt for abandoning one or the other parent. Chronic conflicts between parents in which there is no closure or resolution leaves a child vulnerable to split loyalties. These children express confusion about what to do, and no matter what they do, they lose.They may dissociate from the traumatic events in the family. Becoming sponges for failure, they tend to perceive themselves as incompetent and manifest self-destructive behavior. Suicide may become an option for these children. In my experience, split loyalties is a major contributor to depression in children and is the form of parentification that has the most severe consequences for future trust and accountability.

The third manifestation of parentification that appears in abusive families is the failure of parents and other significant adults to acknowledge what the child has given, particularly in the areas of care and devotion. Instead the child is often criticized for not meeting expectations that are frequently inappropriate and perhaps even impossible to meet. Such children believe themselves to be unworthy of trust. They grow up with a sense of never having been significant enough to deserve a place in the family. They tend to expend their life energies attempting to root themselves in relationships by trying to please others, often self-sacrificially. Failing to please, they build a destructive entitlement to claim the consideration they deserve in a substitutive relational context.

It is important to remember that no dynamic in family life is predictive of future relating. However, the trust resources in one generation can be so used up as to render the next generation severely deprived of even the minimal resources necessary for quality living. The case discussion that follows illustrates the dynamics of justice, entitlement, and parentification in a single family that presented itself with both spouse abuse and child abuse.

CASE EXAMPLE: THE C FAMILY

Mary and her four children were referred for family therapy by her lawyer. She had sought legal advice after she fled her home subsequent to the abuse of one of the children. She went to the home of her parents who learned, for the first time, what had been going on in the marriage. The parents advised Mary to see an attorney. They also encouraged her to bring her 15-year-old daughter to the emergency room for treatment. The child had been severely beaten with a strap and could not walk. Her legs and back were painfully swollen. The medical staff of the emergency room filed a report of abuse with the county child protective services unit. The father was served with a subpoena to answer charges that he had abused his daughter. As the case unfolded, it was learned that there was a systematic pattern of both spouse abuse and child abuse in this family that extended back over 19 years, beginning just prior to the birth of the first child. All of the children were victims except the youngest who, nevertheless, suffered from many fears. The eldest, Ralph, a 19-year-old, had been the most severely abused. The second child, 15-year-old Ann, was the victim of the abuse that served as a catalyst for the outside intervention. The third child was a 13-year-old son named Joseph. The youngest child was an 11-year-old son, John. The sons were more severely abused than the daughter.

The family was, by all material standards, successful. The father owned his own business. He was a college graduate, and his income was in the range of $80,000 annually. The mother was a housewife who was very active in her children's school life. It was learned later that no one except for the elementary school principal and one of the teachers had any suspicion of problems in the family. Except for occasional fighting between the youngest and his peers, and a recent drop in his grades, the children were high achievers who were polite, respectful, and well regarded by the teaching staff. They had many friends and were very active in after-school activities. The eldest was in college and reportedly doing well.

Mary's Side

The conflicts in the marriage centered around Mary's management of money and her disciplining of the children. The family lived on a strict budget and Mary was anxious about overspending. She wanted to avoid her husband's harsh criticism of her competence. She feared his violent reactions. Therefore, although she needed more money, she never asked and fell behind in bill payments. The same was true about problems with the children. She was expected to enforce the rules of discipline but could not control the children's behavior. Eventually she and the children collaborated in hiding information, such as a poor school grade, from father. Thus, in addition to being parent and wife, Mary held a position as one of the children. The family lived in fear of the father's long interrogations once his suspicions were raised. These interrogations, usually culminating in physical violence, had lasted as long as 6 hours. Outside the violent episodes, Mary described her husband as "gentle, kind, considerate, and a terrific father." He expected a great deal from her and she felt as if she could never measure up to his requirements. She questioned whether he cared about her because she never managed to do anything "right."

John's Side

John's first response was to deny that the abuse was as serious as Mary described. He said she had become so fearful that she no longer knew when he was angry and therefore "overreacted." He felt excluded from the family because no one was "truthful" with him. In John's view, he had to carry the entire responsibility for the family. His wife was not assertive and depended on him for even small details. It was like "having another daughter." If he wanted to know what was going on he had to probe until the truth came out. He was tired and no one acknowledged how hard he worked. He felt taken for granted. The children were good children, and he was proud of them, but he wanted them to be strong and to be assertive. The interrogations were designed to teach them how to face things rather than run away. He minimized the abuse and felt that dwelling on the facts of the abuse did not reflect the whole of the marriage and parenting situation. He thought his wife was very competent but she would not be truthful. She avoided conflict. Moreover, it seemed that nothing he did could inspire her confidence in him. She always delegated responsibility to him and never faced her own contributions to problems. Instead she ran away. In his view, his efforts to care for the family weren't acknowledged and he felt abandoned.

The Children's Side

Ralph, 19, went to live with his father when the family separated. He felt protective of his father and took his side. He felt his father had not been treated fairly by his mother and the children. He acknowledged that he had been abused but said he "deserved it" and that his father was trying to help him become a stronger person. He insisted that the family get back together again.

Ann, 15, was fearful that, in going to the emergency room, she had alienated her father. She felt guilty. She did not ever want to face her father again. She did not want to talk about what happened. She didn't know what was going to happen to her life now and felt adrift. She advocated for mother's position and did not want the family reunited.

Joseph, 13, was anxious and torn between his parents. He was afraid of making his father angry and he was not entirely comfortable with his mother. He had been close to his father but could acknowledge that the interrogations were something he did not want to go through again. He thought maybe his father could change now that the whole thing was out in the open, but he didn't know who to trust and didn't have anyone to talk to.

John Jr., 11, was angry and silent. He refused to comment on what had happened. He put his fist through a door at home and was fighting almost constantly with Joseph and his mother. He did not want his mother to go back home again. He wanted her to stay away from his father. John Jr. was the most direct in holding the father accountable for hurting him and the whole family.

The Families of Origin

John is an only child of immigrant Italian parents. His mother did not want any more children. There is no history of abuse in the family. He describes his mother as hard working, with "old-world values." She was very "cold" and didn't express any affection. Although he was successful she would never allow him to help her or to give her anything to make her life easier. She lived alone in a small rural community with her siblings, and she never initiated any contact with him. On the other hand, he never shared much with her because he felt he couldn't burden her. She had had a hard life. He felt she was a "good" woman but she never understood him.

John was closer to his father, who encouraged and supported him. His father believed he could succeed and was very proud of him. John's father tried to protect him from his mother, whom the father viewed as inadequate. The father wanted his own mother to raise John. John's father died when John was 10 years old. In John's view, there was always a wedge between his parents, and when his father died, John was alone with a mother to whom he never felt close. John's mother had no objection to his choice of mate that he recalls. She always liked Mary, and Mary became a primary link to his mother. Mary often called his mother to extend invitations and the like. John thought that in Mary he had found a warm, affectionate, giving wife who could create a loving home and family and make him a priority in her life. He asked nothing more of her and in exchange he could offer security and stability, someone she could rely upon.

Mary was an only child of a mother described as fearful and protective. Mary never felt close to her mother, who tended to "react" with blame to any problem. Mary learned to be selective in what she revealed to her mother so as not to elicit her blaming. She describes her mother as unhappy and impossible to please. She describes herself as preoccupied with placating her. On the other hand, her father was patient and understanding, and Mary turned to him for comfort when she was in conflict with mother. Mary's father would listen to her and try to help her avoid her mother's blame. Mary knew very clearly that her father was unhappy in the marriage and she felt great sympathy for him. Mary tried to help him. Mary's father would never take up issues with the mother directly but would try to find ways to "avoid problems." Mary sometimes felt her father could do more when her mother's reactions were unfair, but for the most part she saw him as compassionate, self-sacrificing, and deserving of consideration.

She did not know why her parents stayed together, and she could never talk with her mother about anything important because she was afraid of her criticism or rejection.

Mary was happy to marry and leave the family, although she still felt responsible for caring about her father. Her parents were unhappy with her choice of partner. They found John dominant and arrogant and felt he would try to control Mary's life. For her part, Mary found him to be strong, sensitive, and someone she could depend upon. Initially she felt attractive and appreciated by her husband—on a "pedestal." She wondered what she had going for her that he would want to marry her.

Neither Mary nor John described a social network with whom they interacted as a couple. Friends were made primarily through his professional contacts, the exception being a close male friend of John's who lived in another city and in whom he sometimes confided. Mary did not describe any close female friends. She began to avoid visiting her parents early in the marriage because she felt her mother and her husband were uncomfortable in each other's presence. For the same reason her parents seldom came to her home. Mary did not visit them alone because she felt caught between her mother and her husband.

John's mother visited only when invited for a family occasion. While the social network of the children was larger, their friends usually did not come to the house. Because of John's anger and the fear of doing something for which they could be blamed, Mary and the children cut themselves off from friends and family. John, on the other hand, did not trust his associates, most of whom he felt were competitive with him. He could not let down his guard with them. He wanted the family to be a place where he could retreat from outside pressures.

The Dynamics of Abuse

The violence began immediately after marriage, first verbal and then punching, usually over "some little thing." It was frequent. Later the violence took the shape of episodes of rage with escalation of physical displays of force. In Mary's words "many times there would be a friend, relative, or a client in the living room and I would be getting hit upstairs. I was expected to carry on as if nothing was wrong. Many a dinner I cooked and served after one of these episodes. The shame was tremendous. I thought we were the only 'nice' people in the world with this sort of problem." The violence occurred even during the pregnancies.

The first reported incident of child abuse occurred when Ralph was 4 years old and John was trying to teach him not to suck his thumb. Ralph didn't understand and he couldn't comply. He was slapped. When the children did not do what was expected, Mary was blamed for not being a strong enough parent. Eventually she began to wonder about her own capabilities. She began to think that she could not handle the children's behavior so she began to try to hide from John anything, large or small, for which she could be blamed. As the children grew older, they joined her in withholding information from John.

"I always felt so sorry for the children that I started keeping secrets from him. For instance, if they broke something at home, like a window, I would fix it before he found out. It wasn't that he would get angry over what they had done but, with his constant questioning, he would make it seem like they were lying or hiding part of the truth, and that's what he would beat them for." As the children got older, John began to use a belt in disciplining them. Mary began to identify a pattern to the violent behavior.

The first person in whom Mary ever confided was a teacher at school, and Mary only told her about one episode of child abuse and about her fears. This was 4 years before the abuse was publicly exposed. Mary tried short separations twice but always returned. The violent episodes were less frequent but more severe after her return. Three years before the event that exposed the abuse, John began to have an affair. He began to think about getting out of the marriage. He wanted to give up his business and have more time for himself. He couldn't tolerate the pressures at work or at home. He felt trapped. In many ways, he gave Mary the message that he wanted her to take responsibility for leaving the marriage.

Mary went to see a clergyman, who told her that her husband needed help and that she should take her children and leave until he got help. The clergyman referred her for counseling but she never went.

The violence toward herself and all of the children intensified, and on several occasions Mary called the police. On each occasion they separated John from the family and advised Mary to take legal steps to protect herself. However, Mary was afraid to embarrass her husband and harm his business.

The final episode involved Ann, who was caught in a "lie" about her schoolwork. She was slapped across the face and beaten "thirty or forty times" with a leather belt. While John was asleep, Mary drove to her parents' house and told them the whole story.

Although this family had many material resources, the facts and events they report are not significantly different in their dynamic configuration from those abusive families in which lack of parenting skills and resources, unemployment, lack of education, poor housing, and inadequate material resources intensify the relational stress factors. The more one experiences injustice in family life, the greater is the tendency to tolerate it in subsequent relationships.

The next section of this chapter focuses on the therapeutic work with the C family.

RESOURCES FOR TRUST BUILDING

As defined earlier in the chapter, resources in the contextual approach are relationships, both actual and potential, in which caring is invested, reinvested, or exploited. What happens to resources in a multigenerational context? Relational resources are used primarily for nurturance, trust building, rootedness, relatedness, and growth. Each generation both inherits and creates resources and thus becomes the mediator of care for the next generation. When one generation, for whatever reason, must use up what is available from past and present relationships without reinvesting, the next generation is significantly deprived. The case of Mary and John, which has been described above, serves as a focal point for discussing contextual work with an abusive family.

Identifying Resources

The first task of contextual assessment is to work with the family to build a climate of trust by differentiating the relational contexts. This means eliciting an entitlement position from each family member—what is each member's burden? How can burdens be converted into options for strengthening the caring in the family? The primary resource of the therapist is an attitude of fairness, or what Boszormenyi-Nagy has described as multidirected partiality. The therapist turns first to each adult family member, asking them to respond to the factual agenda, the situation of abuse, from their own vantage point. What happened? What do you think about what happened? How have you been affected? Is there something more you could have done to help? Is there some way others could be more helpful to you? How do you feel about what's been said by other family members? In appropriately modified fashion the children are asked about how they see things, what they are worried about, how they have been affected, and what would help them. They are also asked about ways in which they have tried to help their family.

Simultaneously the therapist both elicits entitlement from each family member and holds each one accountable to take responsibility for presenting his/her side of things and for responding to the concerns raised by other family members. The initial focus is the event of abuse, but the message the therapist directs to each member is one of acknowledging that there are many sides and that each person deserves to be heard first on their own terms without prejudgment. Parents are asked to help their children express their worries and they are asked to address those worries as they surface.

Resources in the Initial Sessions

The referral for the C family was made by Mary's attorney, who was clearly her advocate and strongly defended her entitlement to redress. Actually it was Mary herself who asked for help for her children. Typically, I indicated that if I took on the family as clients, I would also want to see John, initially by himself but at some point together with Mary and the children.

In the first meeting, the children's split loyalties were most manifest. Their pain was intense, and it was this pain to which their mother was responding. I sided with the children and their pain born of caring for both parents. Except for the oldest son, Ralph, who wanted the family together again under any circumstances, the other children were clear that things could not remain the same, but they wanted the family together. Ralph's position was especially difficult. Other family members indicated they could no longer trust him because he was such a strong advocate for father. Mary felt betrayed by Ralph because she had taken his side so often in disputes with his father. I acknowledged Ralph's loyalty and pointed out that he was taking responsibility to keep the family together at any cost. I tried to support him by indicating my need to hear from his father directly and also by raising up the children's concerns: on the one hand, the violence could not be tolerated; on the other hand, they wanted the family together. At the same time I sided with their mother's entitlement to consider her own terms and conditions in making decisions about her life. Simultaneously each family member was asked to try to think through how they could help each other, including the father. I asked the family to talk in detail about the abuse and how they understood it.

The clearly identifiable resources were Mary's overriding concern for her children and the children's ability to speak openly about their caring for both parents. Ralph's position as his father's advocate was converted into a resource in the sense that it was put in the context of Ralph's taking responsibility for the family. The other children were then freed to care about Ralph's burden. As a severely parentified child, Ralph felt responsible for keeping his parents together, whatever the cost to himself.

The initial work went on for two sessions as part of discussions about parenting decisions, large and small, that Mary was trying to make. She was also helped to think through what she wanted on a day-to-day basis. The question, "What do you want?" is a very important one for all family members. It is especially crucial in abusive families because everyone is suffering under a burden of parentification that mimimizes their ability to ask for what they need and want from others. The abuser also carries this burden and uses force to make his/her claims. In this climate, the overriding concern of the family is to be protective of relationships. Protectiveness closes off the family system to the reality testing of new information. Instead family members recycle old information, which soon becomes distorted.

To summarize from a contextual perspective, the initial sessions with an abusive family have several purposes: (1) to create a climate of trust through implementing multidirected partiality; (2) to maintain the vantage point of the whole relational context while attempting to help family members respond to their immediate situation; and (3) to keep open the lines of relationship by directing family members toward rather than away from relationships that can be helpful.

Extended Family Resources

There is a strong tendency on the part of abusive families to isolate themselves. The avoidance of extended family serves to perpetuate the abusive situation. For example, in the C family, it was very helpful to Mary when her parents were brought into the situation. Their advocacy of her at the initial stages enabled her to consider herself and her own needs as a priority. Later on it helped her examine the unresolved loyalty conflicts that emerged in her relationship to her own parents. She was able to understand the strength of her inclination to get entrapped between opposing sides: her mother and her father, her husband and the children, the children themselves. John was encouraged to tell his mother about the abuse and he did so. Thus, his mother became a potential resource rather than one more person in his life before whom he had to be "perfect." Facing his mother with his limitations enabled him to confront the destructive tendencies in himself. It also opened up the possibility that John might be able to look at his anger at the mother who had failed to acknowledge anything he had ever tried to do for her. This is quite different than the insight that is part of the therapist–client relationship that is implemented as an exclusive contract with an individual client.

Facing a parent with one's own failures frees one from the burden of expectation that shapes abusive behavior. Studies of abusive families have shown that one of the recurring variables that shape parenting behaviors is that of high expectations. One of the most significant tasks of the contextual therapist is to work with the burden of expectations of the abuser. Severely high expectations of oneself, born of relationships to parents in which there was a high degree of parentification and split loyalties, shapes the destructive entitlement to receive caretaking that is so evident in abusers. Moreover, it contributes to the lack of guilt that is characteristic of abusers. The entitlement to receive care overrides the obligation to extend care to those who need it. The abuse is a settling of debts, a matter of justice, and where there is justice there is no guilt.

Family-of-origin work is done simultaneously with the management of the exposure of abuse and its aftermath. If the couples' parents are alive, it is important to ask whether they are aware of what has been happening in the family. Frequently, as in the case of the C family, the therapist finds that both parents are cut off from their own parents and siblings. Since there is an unbroken dynamic connection between the generations, it is important to make these lines of continuity explicit early in the therapy. Frequently, I will bring the grandparents into the early sessions, and I consider it a positive sign for future therapeutic work if the abuser is able to discuss the abuse with his/her own parents. Moreover, grandparents who are available to parents can relieve the burden of responsibility from the children. If grandparents are dead or unavailable, it is still important to reconstruct those relationships and to try to help family members understand what was given and what was gained or lost in those relationships.

There is no attempt to wipe the slate clean in the event of destructive parent–grandparent relationships; rather, there is an attempt to humanize the relationships; so that loyalty commitments can be redistributed. Unresolved loyalty issues between the generations tend to make those relationships "larger than life," and they become destructively empowered in people's lives. To be able to reinvest in those relationships on a more adult basis, that is, from a position of accountability rather than blame or avoidance, helps a person earn some constructive entitlement for growth, and success. Sometimes therapists too readily accept limited material resources of a family as sufficient reason to postpone or even ignore family-of-origin work in order to focus on "here and now" issues. In my experience, this devalues the legacy of those families and contributes to the overburdening of the nuclear family group, most especially with single-parent households.

Ecosystem Resources

Abuse has implications for the social solidarity of a community. Social solidarity refers to the capacity of a society to maintain a balance between the welfare of individuals and the welfare of the whole. The family is the major resource for effecting this balance. The family functions as a mediator of trust and mistrust. It is the family that helps its members manage and overcome the chaotic tendencies of social change; it is society that provides individuals with the resources of a larger context in which they can rebalance the limitations of their familial legacy with fresh options for growth and success. Abuse undermines the trust base of the family unit and of society as a whole because it converts trust resources into sources of mistrust. In a climate of mistrust patterns of exploitation develop.

In situations of abuse, it is important for the therapist to remember that both the family unit and the social network of the family need to be strengthened simultaneously if intervention is to be sustained over time. Early and direct contact with school personnel, self-help groups, and social service and legal resources is helpful in identifying resources. Unfortunately, in my experience, it is precisely these ecosystemic resources that are unavailable, either because they are polarized by the mistrust of mental health practitioners and/or family members or because they are fragmented due to the lack of a clear mandate on anyone's part to develop a comprehensive treatment plan for the family as a whole and for any individual members requiring attention and care. In the absence of a coordinated and comprehensive treatment plan, the resources of the ecosystem become fragmented and thus unavailable to each other and the family. The earlier the contact with those agencies that have contact with the family the greater the capacity to work on the basis of trust rather than mistrust.

After hearing from the family, I generally invite into the second or third session those persons in the social network of the family that have contact with them. In situations of family violence, the responsibility for intervention must be a shared responsibility from the beginning. No therapist is in the position of being able to function as a sole outside resource to the family. Unfortunately, by their unwillingness to build trust with those who differ in their approach to families, therapists stand in danger of promising more than they can deliver. In my view, in situations of family violence, therapeutic intervention is only as effective as the therapist's capacity to share responsibility with family members and the family ecosystem.

In the C family, the primary resources that the family members moved toward were the school system and the legal system. During the course of therapy, Mary also sought out the resources of a local self-help group for abusive parents. This was helpful to her in being able to place her situation in the context of other parenting situations. John opposed this contact, fearing that, as Mary gained a clearer sense of their situation, she would be less likely to want to return to the marriage. Frequently, in situations of abuse, the abuser feels threatened by the family's contact with outsiders and moves to distort and undermine that contact. John was committed to quickly getting beyond the abuse into the future of the family, again a typical position. He feared confrontation with his own side. Taking responsibility for his own side would force him to confront the consequences of his behavior and thus his own failures. This was intolerable to him, and he spent much of his early participation in therapy criticizing Mary for her need to focus on the facts of abuse and the consequences.

Mary selected an attorney on the recommendation of her father. The attorney was a strong advocate of Mary's side and emphasized Mary's entitlement to make a new life for herself. Mary was very resistent to this message and developed a strong mistrust of her attorney. She began to feel caught between her attorney and John, who had taken the position that Mary's attorney was only interested in finances. John selected an attorney whom the couple had known socially. He selected the attorney because it was someone "Mary trusts." It was very clear that neither John nor Mary had the resources to confront each other. Thus third persons, including the therapist, stood in danger of being used as parents who would then compete with each other. I insisted that the couple and their attorneys meet together with me so that each person could give some assessment of their own position. That meeting, though difficult, finally made explicit the view that John and Mary needed to take more responsibility for their own situation. The care of the children was the issue for which everyone could be held accountable. I articulated this position and, in advocating for the children, had some leverage to engage the adults on the basis of trust rather than power.

The other resource with which Mary made contact was the school system, primarily the principal and the children's teachers. They proved very supportive to the children and in this way were helpful to Mary. It is clear that the school personnel were very uncomfortable in handling their relationship to John as he continued to have contact with his children. I took the position with John and Mary that the teachers and principal were being helpful to the children and that the children would lose valuable resources if John or Mary tried to engage school personnel in choosing sides. This position served to strengthen Mary in taking responsibility for her own parenting of the children instead of investing in the approval or disapproval of others to shape her decisions. John needed to be held accountable for his tendency to scapegoat as a way of avoiding taking his own position.

The goal of therapeutic trust building is not to wipe the slate clean and ignore the long history of abuse. Rather, it is to help the couple come to terms with those modes of relating that might serve to reengage them in violence. If Mary could not be freed to act on her entitlement, she would eventually move back into the relationship with John motivated by caretaking behaviors that serve to obliterate her side. From his side, the more John was able to discuss his behavior and make his concerns explicit in a climate in which they would be fairly considered the less his motivation to scapegoat.

After about 12 sessions, it was possible for John and Mary to deal with each other directly without involving the children in their conflicts. This was a major therapeutic goal for the early sessions. In the course of working with them, it became clear that neither John nor Mary wanted to terminate the marriage. However, with therapeutic guidance Mary was able to remain firm in her resolve that the issues of parenting the children, decision making around finances, the quality of their availability to each other as adults, and their capacity to face and manage conflicts over differences would have to be fully addressed before she would consider reconciling the family. John continued to pressure Mary primarily by eliciting her acknowledgment that he "had changed."

The couple continued in therapy and, as some very concrete concerns were surfaced and addressed, the major entitlement issues became more pronounced. Mary continued to get stuck at the level of her inability to ask for something for herself. The less she was able to do this, the less she was able to view herself as a person of merit who deserved consideration. She became hesitant and indecisive in the relationship. On his part, John also continued to get stuck at the level of his inability to manage multiple commitments. He felt "trapped" because he was never able to do what he "wanted." His life was built around a strong system of indebtedness. His merit as a person was linked to meeting obligations. Thus, he needed to maintain the position of overresponsible, overfunctioning caretaker in his relationships. This required that others, particularly Mary, remain in the position of "weak ones."

Mary's strength was in direct proportion to her entitlement. Her entitlement was diminished every time she failed to please the significant people in her life. She was always vulnerable to criticism. John's strength was also in direct proportion to his entitlement, but this took another form for him. As Mary became less entitled and more burdened by feelings of inadequacy, she withdrew from John. He reacted to her withdrawal with overfunctioning behaviors at home and at work. Using denial and projection, John attempted to reassert some control in a situation in which he was threatened with loss of relationship.

Neither John nor Mary had ever learned to advocate for themselves in a relationship. They had never learned to ask for what they needed or wanted. Both required frequent acknowledgment of the effectiveness of their caretaking behaviors, yet this left them empty and without adequate resources to get unstuck. They expected perfection in themselves and in their relational world, yet each of them longed to be relieved of this burden by the other. They were relationally crippled by the burden of expectations, an indication of strong loyalty bonds to their families or origin. The marriage and the parenting of the children had become a substitutive context for rebalancing issues of care, devotion, and acknowledgment in the family of origin.

In the middle phase of therapeutic work with this family, the focus was on the simultaneous consideration of the issues of justice, entitlement, and parentification in the family of origin and the nuclear family in an effort to differentiate the contexts and help family members free some creative options for relating. The children were periodically included in this work. After one year, the family moved back together in a new home. The physical abuse did not recur and the children were able to reinvest in their own development. At this point, only Ralph showed signs of inability to manage relationships outside the family. He suffered with depression, which John refused to acknowledge. He fused with Ralph and could not distinguish between his own needs and those of his son.

The couple continued in therapy on an intermittent basis. It was clear that, although the physical abuse ceased, the psychological abuse continued. Mary felt that the children had decided to care about their own lives and no longer wanted to get caught in the marital struggle. She began to confront a future without children at home to parent and at the same time began to see John "as he really is." She worked on defining and claiming a self that she could trust in relationships. John immersed himself in his work, moving from one consuming obligation to another, creating siuations in which clients were almost totally dependent on his ability to rescue them from crises. Thus he continually reengaged others at the level of his own loyalty conflict—rescuing his mother from the hard life she had endured and being strong for his father. While the physical abuse had been terminated and the children had been freed from a large share of the burden of parentification, John and Mary continued to struggle at the level of their own entitlement. Eventually, the children would also have to face issues of entitlement as a consequence of their experiences in the family. This family, however, has learned to identify, activate, and use relational resources in the course of their therapeutic work.

In summarizing the therapeutic work with the C family, it is important to point out that, once violence has been used as an instrument for reestablishing the balance of care in a family, there is no guarantee that it will not recur. Care shapes the loyalty dynamic and therefore it is a powerful motivator of human relating. The therapist who works with such families from a resource orientation is ethically bound to support the family members in their inclinations toward trust even in the face of evidence of pervasive mistrust. However, the therapist is only free to do so if the abuser demonstrates the capacity and willingness to abstain from all forms of violence. That proviso, in my experience, can only be implemented when the legal interveners, the family members, and the therapist share responsibility for the development and management of a comprehensive treatment plan. By its very nature and consequences, family violence requires coresponsibility as an operating principle of intervention. The final section of this paper addresses the intersection of family systems and legal systems.

THE INTERSECTION OF FAMILY SYSTEMS AND LEGAL SYSTEMS

In situations of intrafamilial abuse, the best interest of the individual is often used as the standard for legal intervention. From a contextual perspective, the best interests of family members are interlocked on the basis of loyalty commitments and expectations, shaped over time and manifested as reciprocal care. Persons who are significantly deprived of parenting they rightfully deserve remain bound, for good or ill, to the source of their deprivation until they find some way of rebalancing the injustice. The loyalty dynamic is powerfully shaped in childhood by a child's growing responsibility for the well-being of parents. Abusers present a legacy of being parentified, overresponsible children who strengthened their parents through the sacrifice of their own growth. As adults, their close relationships become a substitutive context for reconciling a legacy of imbalanced giving and receiving. It is in this realm of relational justice that the legal system and the justice system of the family collide.

The legal system, adversarial in nature, is useful in making the social and legal side of abuse—the rights and responsibilities of individual family members and of society—more explicit. However, the lines of relationship are rendered invisible. Isolated from a relational context, fairness is defined in terms of one person's side at the cost of another. Thus the abusive relationships can become the standard by which all relationships in the family are judged. In an adversarial context, there is a tendency to fracture the whole, thus obscuring relational resources.

The justice system of the family, on the other hand, is relational in nature. It demands a balance of the vantage points of each family member in coming to a resolution in which no relating partner is left in a condition of permanent benefit or burden. However, a family systems orientation, with its traditonal bias in favor of the whole, may fail to account for differences in resources and in entitlement among family members, particularly as regards children.

Neither the adversarial perspective nor the family systems perspective, taken alone, has been effective in helping families who struggle with abuse. When one family member uses force to impose his/her terms and conditions for relating on another family member, often the most vulnerable, a structure of accountability outside the family, which also includes the family, is required. In my experience, social and legal accountability for abusive behavior is the first step toward therapeutic intervention in family violence. The failure to address the question of accountability in clear terms from the outset continues to privatize the abuse. The privatization of abuse undermines and distorts the basis of trust between family and society. The foundation of that trust in the family is personal responsibility shaped by reciprocal care. The foundation of that trust in society is the capacity of its members to balance personal freedom with the obligation to care for those who are in need of care.

Addressing the question of intervention in intrafamilial violence requires a reworking of the relationships between legal interveners and family therapists, beginning with identification of the ways in which they can function as resources for each other. Self-critical thinking is required on both sides. Family therapists need to critically examine family systems theory and its ideology, particularly with regard to gender-related issues and the family. For example, in families in which incest is the presenting problem, a mother is defined as collusive when she does not function as a responsible caretaker. By virtue of this definition, the therapeutic work is designed around getting her to undertake the caretaking function without due consideration being extended to the whole of her side. This reflects the gender-related presumption that women are defined by their relationships. I believe this bias in family therapy is one of the reasons why we know so little about the mother's side of the incest configuration, particularly as it relates to her entitlement position. As the demography of contemporary family life changes, the quality of the relationships between men and women and the question of who will care for children in our society are irrevocably linked.

On the other side, legal interveners need to pose critical questions to each other about the adversarial model and its long-term consequences for family relationships, particularly with regard to children. The present system of intervening in family disputes in our courts has proven inadequate to the task from every vantage point from which we examine it. When children are involved, they are frequently left permanently disadvantaged by legal resolutions that focus on the blameworthiness of their parents.

As a beginning step, in cases of intrafamilial violence a family-based evaluation can offer a baseline of intervention upon which all sides can build, providing, that is, that family therapists are willing to take the initiative in bringing together the family and the legal and social service resources in the early sessions. This kind of conjoint evaluation provides a forum for coresponsible decision making in which family members can be guided toward resources by taking more responsibility for their own situation. It also provides an opportunity for the sharing of resources among participants with the possibility that creative options for intervention can be shaped.

As family therapists, we know a great deal about the dynamics of abuse. We have also learned a great deal about what is genuinely helpful to families from an individual and systemic perspective. Now, I believe it is time to direct our energies toward interdisciplinary assessment and intervention in family violence so that interveners can begin to use each other as resources. A resource orientation rooted in the realities of family life is, in my view, family therapy's major contribution to the field of mental health in situations of intrafamilial violence.

REFERENCES

Bozormenyi-Nagy, I., & Spark, G. M. *Invisible loyalites: Reciprocity in intergenerational family therapy.* New York: Harper and Row, 1973.

Cotroneo, M. M. At the intersection of family systems and legal systems: Child custody decisions in context. *Connecticut Bar Journal*, 1979, *53*, 349–355.

Cotroneo, M. M. The role of forgiveness in family therapy. In A. S. Gurman (Ed.), *Questions and answers in family therapy* (Vol. II), New York: Brunner/Mazel, 1982, pp. 241–244.

CHAPTER 15

Death and Dying and the Multigenerational Impact

Norman L. Paul
Shel J. Miller

> I think that the material presented has adequately dem-
> onstrated that the majority of British people are today
> without adequate guidance as to how to treat death and
> bereavement and without social help in living through
> and coming to terms with the grief and mourning which
> are inevitable responses in human beings to the death of
> someone whom they have loved.

This statement by English anthropologist Geoffrey Gorer, published in 1965, concluded his well-known survey, entitled *Death, Grief, and Mourning*, about reactions to bereavement. We feel that it can be regarded as a statement equally relevant to American people in 1986.

Kubler-Ross (1969) and Becker (1973) each elaborated on this focus in their outstanding books. Kubler-Ross (1969), in *Death and Dying*, highlighted the sequential and recursive phases of the process of dying that attracted the attention of both caretaking professionals and the public at large. Becker (1973), in *The Denial of Death*, addressed himself to the problems resulting from one's heroic attempts to transcend death. That failure of denial touches those of us who believe we have, in fact, transcended mortality. His book won a Pulitzer Prize. Although there have been a number of inquiries since these publications (e.g., Aries, 1974; Stannard, 1975; Fulton & Markuson, 1978), the impact of loss through death has barely begun to show up as a major focus for the well-intentioned and well-informed psychotherapist.

Norman L. Paul, M.D. Department of Neurology, Boston University School of Medicine, Boston, Massachusetts.

Shel J. Miller, Ph.D. Harvard Community Health Plan, Boston, Massachusetts; Private Practice, Brookline, Massachusetts.

GRIEF AND LOSS: A THERAPEUTIC FRAMEWORK

One has the impression, given the earlier works by Bowlby (1961, 1980) and Lindemann (1944), that, coupled with the above-mentioned books, mental health professionals would have now gone beyond merely reflexively citing the import of loss issues as a key problem in both individual and family dynamics. When it comes to the actual process of therapeutic change itself, such application of this intellectual knowledge withers in the face of the challenge of using these notions experientially. Part of the problem involved is not only the timing, but also the manner, of inducing and encouraging the grieving process. One of the things that family systems has revealed is that grief work confined to an individual and his/her therapist may actually deaden the relational possibilities for the client in his family. This tends to happen when the affects of grief are confined within the therapist–client relationship and excluded from the family.

It is curious how the application of a general systems format to the family and its many processes more often than not tends to exclude the area of death and dying. Such neglect vitiates the obvious intent of a theoretical perspective that professes to be all-inclusive. In part, this avoidance extends to the reverberation of affective forces in general in human systems. Such theories profess to thereby dodge the client's or family's emotional resistance. It is not clear, however, whether this represents a new way to promote "discontinuous" change, or an old way of simply giving up in the face of the challenge of enhancing experiential awareness of self, both of the therapist and of each self in the family being treated.

The continuing quandry as to how to cope with affects is well summarized by a Rochester, New York, psychoanalyst, George Engel, who, in his efforts to evolve an adequate classification of the phenomenology of affects, readily acknowledged the total inadequacy of our language: "We still recognize not only that in nature affects do not exist in pure unalloyed form, but also that to deal with affects in written, verbal, or conceptual terms is fundamentally inconsistent with their nature and can succeed only at the expense of their over-simplification and impoverishment" (1963, p. 267). Perhaps caregivers should turn to the masters of expression of affects, the poets and playwrights, who are light years ahead of us in this domain. Surely authors such as Shakespeare, O'Neil, and Shepard are no strangers to the enormity of affect that death and dying generates in the lives of individuals, the family, and indeed the nation.

Despite the constraints of language, as far as the therapist is concerned, one must continue in the exploration and assessment of such intense affective experiences as grief, because of its critical importance in the human experience. The theme of grief associated with death is clearly one that is too often regarded as unnecessary (Toynbee et al., 1969). This conception of death as essentially unimportant precludes the consideration of resources for coping with death. Often when a death has occurred in a nursing home or hospital, there are social agents that are mobilized to assist the bereaved, including extended family members and friends, to cope in a manner that enables them principally to avoid or ignore what they have lived with or through. Such social agents include morticians and clergymen. The first of these social agents assist in the disposition of the physical remains of the deceased. The latter are expected to provide some quality of comfort to those family members and friends who have witnessed the dying and have become part of the death experience. Yet, how many of these helpers are specifically trained to meet the experiential needs of children and adults for information about death and grief? Family members of all ages need to know these facts, and such information will vary, for example, depending upon the type of death in question.

We think it would be useful at this point to provide an abbreviated typology of dying experiences as they are related to different kinds of bereavement (a complete typology would require a book in itself):

1. *Expected death: Terminal diseases and cancer.* The level of guilt associated will be reflected in the relationships between the parents and children, and relationships between spouses. Guilt develops in bereaved young children who often blame themselves for the death of their parents because of a concrete event (such as having left out the toy that mother collapsed upon). Guilt develops in the bereaved young adult who may have had a destructive fantasy wish toward his parent just prior to the elder's death. Guilt develops in the young parent who loses a child often to the point of avoiding the dread act that eventually led to the tragedy: sexual intercourse. Thus, guilt is often expressed in the acknowledged sexual dysfunction between spouses. Guilt can be expressed insidiously in the apparent appearance of serious psychosomatic illnesses such as ulcerative colitis, heart attack, and cardiovascular disorders such as strokes. The anticipatory grief (Fulton & Gottesman, 1980) available in these instances is illuminated in the final (nonpsychiatric) case example below of the Saroyan family.

2. *Unexpected deaths: Traumatic accidents and sudden physical deaths, also murder, stillbirths, and suicide.* These situations are much more difficult for the survivors to resolve, especially if they are young children as in the case example of Tom below.

3. *Combination of numbers 1 and 2 above.* Such situations include holocaust and terrorist actions such as kidnapping situations where people are held as hostages. Soldiers during wartime (Freud, 1915) are another example of both expected and unexpected death. They have a practical expectation that they could die, but at the same time they have an illusion of invulnerability.

In thinking about death from a family point of view, one becomes aware that the same death, such as a suicide or a murder, may be expected by some family members, yet wholly unexpected by others. The uncertainty of how expected one's own or a family member's death may be gives rise to the need for the unwitting utilization of many different brands of numbness. There are basically two types of numbing addictions in our culture. One is the so-called negative category, which includes things such as drugs, food, and promiscuous sex. The other, so-called positive category involves workaholism, addictive physical fitness, hasty remarriage, and prolonged and continuous psychotherapy.

The task of the therapist, then, is to help clients find a safe manner in which to break through these numbing endeavors and develop the courage to face the avoided pain. Since such affect is anathema to most people, the therapist must often enlighten the client as to the consequences of avoiding his/her gut feelings and thoughts. The consequence of avoiding pain is quite simple: more pain is created—in the self (e.g., somatic or psychotic breakdown), in the relationship with a spouse (conflict avoidance in a marriage inevitably leads to interpersonal incompatability), and in the parent–child relationship (children learn from their parents' model the lie of invulnerability borne of suppressed feelings). The avoidant character becomes more machine-like and less human each day. This situation heightens the likelihood of further social isolation whether because of one's chronic whine or perpetual hostility or occasional explosiveness. In general, such unfinished business with grief supports the formation of an emotionally overreactive response style (cf., Bowen, 1972). Logical decision-making function becomes impaired in the seemingly cool, collected, machine-like personality that is often associated with being "rational."

As the client faces pain, the benefits from so doing become intrinsically rewarding. First, the client develops a confidence that he/she can cope with the sense of loss and grief without falling apart or crying forever. The client develops an appreciation for the power in drawing on his/her inner resources—that which may bubble up while alone facing his/her loneliness. At the same time the benefit of such soul-searching and sustaining of the emotional self leads to increased potential for successful relating to significant others. The others may be appreciated as is rather than blamed for being different; the others will be perceived more accurately once the unfrozen self becomes more open and less in need of disowning (via projection onto the others) unwanted affects in the clients.

It may be hard to conceive that the concept of health and pathology should be related to either the areas of dying or death, so intense is the allergy to these entities! Death is part of nature's way of telling us to slow down, insofar as in the quest toward immortality one is confronted by physical evidence of an aging process in a body that is vulnerable to a variety of internal and external stresses. To focus on death requires a broadening of our discussion to include paradox and existential confusion as concurrent elements.

The paradox herein involves the fact of birth as being the commencement of one's own death. Existential confusion enables one to deny that this is true. The challenge become how to live one's life within the framework of this quandry. One solution, elucidated by Becker (1973) in *The Denial of Death*, is becoming a hero who conquers death through the illusion of immortality. It is the fame in posthumous immortality that often inclines the common man, with easily concocted images, to believe he can follow in the footsteps of a William Shakespeare or a John F. Kennedy. A diametrically opposite solution was carried out by Reverend Jim Jones: escape by mass suicide (Naipaul, 1982). Of the myriad solutions within this range, Norman Cousins (1983) has given us an apparently more moderated solution: the use of laughter as a healing tool for the confusion. Of course, religions such as Christianity claimed to have solved the problem by promising true believers life after death. Their belief that Christ rose from the dead makes death irrelevant for them.

The therapeutic crux of the paradox is in conceiving and creating simultaneous opportunities for both individual and family growth in the crisis of bereavement. One of the major difficulties in addressing this subject is that we believe that humans require a validation of the actual experience of dying and grief as being real, the essence of which is impossible to convey in words. Such comprehensive reality testing affirms the social and relational importance of each individual as a self, and at the same time, as a member of a family. If the therapist conceives of each individual as a fragment of a family, his/her ethical responsibility extends beyond the person(s) sitting in his office. One realizes the opportunity in the tragedy to further the growth of the larger system involved in letting go of one of its members. From this perspective, the larger family is always a potential resource to the identified patient seeking therapy. By requiring a genogram, for example, from day one the therapist begins the process of identifying these resources, as well as of mapping out the generational "changing of the guard" as new births replace sequential death. Laura Perls (1961) makes clear, in her humanistic comments, the need for a naturalization of death as well as of childbirth:

Real creativeness . . . is inextricably linked with an awareness of mortality. The sharper this awareness, the greater the urge to bring forth something new to participate in the infinitely continuing creativeness in nature. This is what makes out of sex, love; out of herd, society; . . . out of sound, music; . . . make life liveable . . . and therapy possible. (p. 129)

To practice within such a theoretical frame, the therapist must have faced his own feelings regarding his mortality. An awareness of one's own changing genogram and of one's own pockets of unresolved grief can only enhance one's availability to one's clients. The therapist inexperienced with such powerful affects and their power, of avoidance of them will be more likely to overlook the inherent capacity of his client family to abide the existential terror in themselves. They would all simply be aligning themselves with the more traditional cultural pattern of denial. Active, continuous work on his/her own extended family attachments will permit the therapist to suggest meaningful and practical maneuvers to clients regarding their extended kin network. *Selective* and *relevant* sharing of one's own vulnerability within one's own family also helps the client family to realize that we are all in the game of life and death, joy and guilt, confidence and terror together, like it or not. As it becomes at least covertly clear that the therapy itself is a joining of the therapist's and client's own family systems in a new human system, the family is led to feel like part of a team working on universal issues. When such a sense of togetherness is appropriately and professionally conveyed, the process of diagnosis in therapy is demystified. The journey is then one of discovery of strengths and acknowledgement of mortality, vulnerability, and courage.

THE USE OF VIDEO- AND AUDIOTAPE

The obvious constraint of words to reevoke all of the heretofore multiple attachment and detachment processes inherent in life can begin to be superseded by the use of video- and audiotape materials. Furthermore, these modalities can enable clients to achieve a sustained and repeatedly reinforced level of affective empathy regarding themselves and the other(s), that is, whether living, dying, or dead. By reviewing the videotape of himself/herself over a proper time sequence, which may be 10 minutes, or several weeks, or even several years later, a client is confronted with evidence of his/her physical being, own visibility, and obvious mortality. The anxiety that most clients have in anticipating such feedback seems to be related to the general human aversion to finding out how little one knows about oneself. To know thyself as visible suggests that one exists fully, which of course brings up the alien terror of being alone in the world, for a finite period of time, in a vulnerable body. The latter is regarded generally as all too mortal. Also, the client can begin to see the extent to which one has unwittingly numbed himself/herself in the interest of survival. On videotape, the client may see it in his/her own eyes, physiognomy, or posture.

The incongruity between the client's inner life and that which can be seen on the television monitor (i.e., the credibility gap regarding one's being) can finally be discovered. In many cases, the individual may watch and actually remain numb the first time. In such cases, sufficient awareness may be attained with the help of other family members who have the history of seeing what the self cannot. A spouse, for example, will usually be more naturally attuned to the familiar visual cues of the other, now objectified on tape. When seeing his/her own cues, the client will often betray his/her total unconsciousness, as in the case of a husband who didn't know how angry he looked. Recognizing this will provide much relief to the wife who has previously perceived her partner as *willfully* provocative or unavailable.

Given the appearance of being an unbiased observer, the television begins to slowly stir the sleeping self. Repeated reviews are usually necessary to challenge the strength of the client's denial system (numbing). This reinforcement can be accomplished not only in later therapy sessions, but also at home by the client reviewing tapes of his/her sessions. All sessions are also audiotaped for later use by the client, who often may share them with his family.

Each of the following techniques are used in conjunction with video and audio recordings:

1. The use of a *genogram* filled out by the client and elaborated with the therapist. Its contextual value is reflected back in bold relief to the family from a large easel pad during every session. The genogram is a map that leads to the delineation and discovery of people who were important, who died, and who have not been recognized as having lived heretofore. The genogram is an introduction to a sense of generational time.

2. A *visit to a grave site* or to the area where the ashes may have been spread (Williamson, 1978). Such a journey graphically confronts the individual with the

reality that someone important had died, as well as with the lingering existence of some powerful affects within himself/herself. The individual is given concrete evidence, necessary in many instances, to provide access to the previously sealed over feelings. The client who begins this journey emerges slowly from an emotionally embalmed state, and emotional support is always necessary. The client is exhorted to record this experience on audiotape in order to be able to review as much as possible about what happened on the visit and with family members in later discussions with the therapist.

3. *Videotaping of a picture of the deceased.* In a paradoxical fashion, the perception of a videotaped large picture of the deceased on the monitor very often will provoke a sense of that person being alive. The television picture will actively stimulate intense memories and feelings about the client's experience with that person. The anticipatory sense of being overwhelmed by this experience is generally short-lived and does not extend much beyond the initial moment of viewing.

4. *Role-play involving the image of the deceased.* Much can be accomplished in simple role-playing where there is some unfinished business between the bereaved and the departed. The client may be encouraged to compose a letter to family members or to close friends of the deceased. This approach is often used as a stepping stone to technique 2.

5. *Sending actual letters* to family members or to close friends of the deceased. The experience of inquiring of others regarding their experience, often unshared with the client, can open doors to forgotten memories as well as to new positive behaviors and relationships. The thrust of such a letter is to fill in the vacuum of knowledge about the deceased's long and short-term history prior to the death. In the heat of the blackness immediately surrounding the death, shock about the details and the context of the death are often misperceived or colored with unnecessary blame, such as toward a relative, friend, or physician attending the event. Such blame then serves to distract the bereaved from the anger or sadness necessary to move himself/herself towards resolution.

6. A *visit to the place of death*, such as the hospital, home, or accident scene. This refresher can graphically reconnect the client with fragments of a rarely recalled earlier experience, and enable him/her to move further through the grief process. It is surprising how often one hears from clients about how they have avoided such places for many years previously. Sometimes they have confusedly forgotten why they avoided such places.

7. A *review of hospital records, obituaries and other details* of the death. This may include accounts of an individual's hospitalization before death. These details will enable the client to emerge from a previously disconnected sense of relatedness to the bereaved. Additional sources of data are newspaper accounts, including obituaries, death certificates, and details of the physical ambience surrounding the death event (e.g., a flood, a snowstorm, or a myriad of other mundane accidents). Helene Deutsch (1937) stated, "The process of mourning as reaction to the real loss of a loved person *must be carried to completion.*" This clinical mandate is most challenging in its implication for both clients and

therapists alike. We believe that there is no such viable goal as total completion, but rather a discontinuous movement both toward and away from recognition and acceptance of the death.

8. The *inclusion of friends, relatives, and/or other informants* regarding the deceased in the therapy sessions themselves. Of particular value here are grandparents and elderly friends. People in their 70s, 80s, or 90s represent vital data sources that can enable the client to have a sense of continuity with his/her parents and grandparents in a way that had never been achieved before. Other informants may include a salient person present on the occasion of the relative's death, such as the housekeeper, or the driver of the other car that killed that relative.

9. The use of *evocative music*. There is a wide range of evocative music that can be played in a session at a crucial moment. It could be a piece such as "Kol Nidrei," the somber Hebrew melody chanted on the Day of Atonement, which can stimulate a mourning experience. It could be a piece that had been playing at the moment one had been told of the parting of the loved one. Often, evocative music serves a dual purpose in a paradoxical fashion: on the one hand, being used to enable the bereaved to heal the wounds of grief; on the other hand, being used to allow the therapist to gain entry to the grief residue.

These techniques are vehicles to facilitate access through the client's sensory modalities to primary experiences or pictures of himself/herself in relation to the bereaved. They are employed to stimulate the experience of the hitherto unrecognized pain, tears, anger, and rage about the fact that someone who was so close and important has disappeared. In a sense, the unrecognized numbness concealing powerful emotions can now thaw, after which the client can return more fully to the world of the emotionally alive. Whereas these techniques depend on visual and auditory sensory modes, the therapist may, in the future, devise other adjunctive techniques that will directly stimulate other senses, such as the kinesthetic or olfactory.

CASE EXAMPLE

The experience of the survivor of an unexpected death is characterized by the absence of any kind of anticipatory grief or preparation. This unprepared situation gives rise to a greater sense of guilt because of the lack of external reality inputs that could verify that one is not responsible. In addition to self-blame, there occurs a greater sense of powerlessness. Thus, one is paradoxically in the bind of feeling alternatively to be at the source of the externally caused event, or to be the helpless bystander to the "act of God."

Tom's stepmother, Helen B, called for help with her husband's 23-year-old son, whom she said was "hardly talking to me." Furthermore, Tom appeared to be closed off, reclusive, and painfully confused. Mrs. B elucidated the family context for her stepson's misery. His father had divorced his mother when he was 5. He and his sister, Jeanette, lived with their mother until the first Mrs. B died soon after an automobile accident when Tom was 7 and Jeanette was 4. The father then moved in with his kids and a year later remarried. (See Figure 15.1.)

Tom's father and stepmother had had two more children: Angela, age 14, and Benjamin, age 10. Tom had just completed his first year of graduate school in a nearby state and was living at home for the summer. The mother emphasized her difference from Tom, and hinted at the chronic, intense strife in their relationship.

Knowing that there were 2 months before Tom would be scheduled to leave the state, the therapist encouraged him to be in touch for a series of meetings (Table 15-1) that would end up with his resuming graduate school in the fall. At that time he would continue with the therapist for monthly meetings, at most, when he could commute from school. The therapist shared his expectation that some family development issues were ready for resolution and planned to address those issues. The therapist had in mind to look at Tom's conflicts with his stepmother in the context of his prior losses: of his own mother in his original nuclear family through divorce, and later by death. In the therapist's first contact with Tom on the telephone, Tom quickly noted that "for so long I've repressed my feelings about everything: since my mother died everything

TABLE 15-1
Chronology, Membership, and Focus of Sessions

6/25/82	Tom alone—history of losses and present concerns.
6/28/82	Tom alone—focus on grief, numbness and fear of intimacy.
6/29/82	Tom, Mr. B, and Jeanette—permission granted by father for Tom to open a discussion regarding his mother, whom his father had divorced.
7/ 2/82	Tom alone—information from maternal grandmother, who helps with the denumbing of memories of just after his mother's deathh.
7/11/82	Tom alone—recognition of rage toward stepmother.
7/19/82	Tom alone—reaction to Haas tape and recognition of the editing and displaying of self-rage.
7/26/82	Tom and Helen B (stepmother)—stepmother watches Tom's videotaped reaction to Haas tape followed by a joint review.
7/27/82	Tom and maternal grandmother—Tom's fears about his earlier guilt regarding mother's death; makes a commitment to visit her grave.
8/ 2/82	Tom alone—a review of a newspaper account of his mother's accident and further grief work.
8/ 6/82	Tom and Jeanette—a review of changes in Tom as the siblings share previous modes of denial of loss.
9/15/82	Tom alone—he reviews course of treatment and plans some further work on extended family.
3/11/83	Tom alone—a review of grave visit and reaction to videorecording of an enlarged candid of mother.
3/25/83	Tom and Mrs. B—a joint review of videotaped reaction (previous session).
4/ 8/83	Tom and maternal Aunt Mary—same material reviewed.
4/15/83	Tom alone—a respite as previous session is reviewed and his mother's hospital records are present and avoided.
4/22/83	Tom alone—a review of his mother's hospital records.

Family Tree

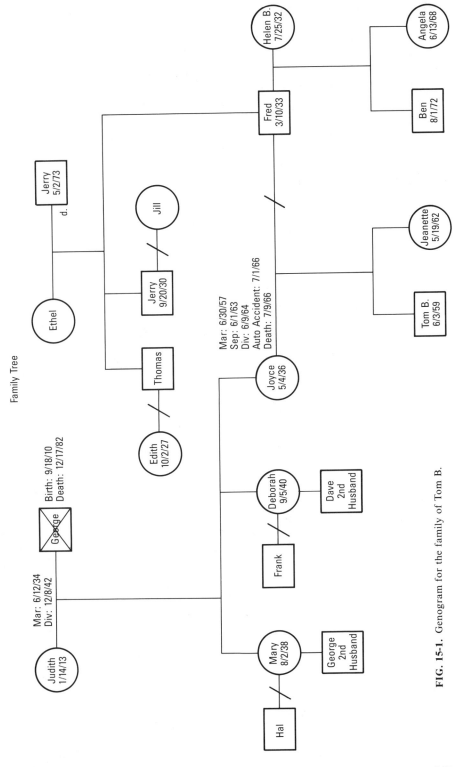

FIG. 15-1. Genogram for the family of Tom B.

changed." Apart from the minor pathology hunt for a diagnosis to satisfy the family's insurance company, the view taken over the next 12 sessions was from the perspective of Tom's and his family's strengths. These included his loyalty to all of his family (and theirs to him), his ability to use imagery and metaphor, his connectedness with his family and the potential empathy among his biological sister and maternal grandmother, his and the family's values of openness and honesty, and his courage to face both his rage and the years of denial of his pain.

In the first session on June 25, 1982, Tom repeated his concerns about having lost his mother, and noted that he had never gone to his mother's funeral. The groundwork for visiting his mother's grave was quickly seeded. The therapist conveyed his belief in Tom's potential to further complete his relationship with his mother as a major task of the brief consultation. Tom's emphasis was on the difficult relationship with his stepmother, and his growing ambivalence about the type of friends he had selected in the past year of school. He had sensed a certain distance from them and an inability to open up.

In order to pave the way for identifying as many family resources as possible, the therapist had already spoken not only to Tom at this point, but also with both his stepmother and father on the telephone. Furthermore, the therapist conveyed to Tom the importance of eventually having a session with his sister since she too had sustained a major loss, and could be of great support to him. The importance of having contact with his maternal family, especially his mother's mother, was also suggested.

The therapist was intentionally taking on the role of the family practitioner, available and impartial to all members of both the nuclear and extended family as necessary. The therapist knew that there were other members of Tom's family that would help to identify resources for healing both his look of fear and his tendency to quietly withdraw into himself. He hoped to bring out the latent vitality from behind that veneer of earnestness with which Tom approached his story. As Tom spoke, one could practically see the cloud form over him to separate his inner self from that of the therapist. It seemed that he had the courage to be himself more fully, and to reach inward to the emptiness that he would slowly go on to describe while displaying that characteristic numbness that comes with the shock of learning that one's mother has died.

Despite Tom's complaints about his difficult stepmother, it was clear that he was quite loyal to her, even to the extent of wanting to protect her from both his displaced and real rage. Among his complaints concerning the second Mrs. B were the facts that she was a member of a fundamentalist church, and that she lived in a very different social world from himself. Tom had grown up in a family that had among its values a basic respect for one another with a tolerance for differences in people. The therapist was able to cash in on these values and thereby help Tom to sidestep further blaming of his stepmother. Tom had the growing capacity to take responsibility for his own actions, and this was a theme that could also be milked. For example, he made it clear in the beginning that "My main problem is not with my family; I'm really closed up in general."

In the second session, he was able to provide an artistic description of his closed-up self. It was like a gray, compressed ball that he experienced as an enemy that produced a cloud of fear, anger, and sadness. It was suggested that such feelings could be a great resource to him if he could experience that compressed ball as his friend instead of as an enemy. He quickly realized that it was forming in his chest to keep him out of touch with his inner experience. He then went on to share his memories of the bad blood that existed between his father's extended family and his maternal family. He also revealed his fear of intimacy, his exhaustion at having been closed, and his being flustered by the expectation of unresolvable conflict in relationships. He decided that his major goal in therapy was to be able to feel more comfortable and trusting with intimacy in general. His father and his sister were invited to a session in order to reproduce the family existing at the time of Tom's mother's death. His confusion about his parents' divorce could also be addressed as well.

On June 29, 1982, his father and sister attended the session with Tom. The father emphasized his lingering pain over being wrenched apart from his children by his first wife, Joyce. Tom expressed his chronic hesitation to refer to that pain, and his need to protect his father from all of those awful memories. His father, thereafter, was able to quickly give the permission Tom ostensibly needed to ask more about his mother. It was noted that the three of them had always avoided that subject in the past. Tom was encouraged to talk more between sessions with both his father and sister about these topics. It was emphasized that the more people in his extended family that he reached out to, and talked to, the greater sense of security and continuity he would be able to create for himself.

Before the next meeting on July 2, 1982, he approached his maternal grandmother. In this session, he started talking about his problem with role models, and how that was related to his difficulty with women. He also remembered that he had developed a significant mysterious blood disease after his mother had died. By the next session, on July 11, 1982, the ball in his chest was now like "an angry blackness surrounded by a dirty gray confusion." As he stayed with the phenomenological description of his inner state, he gradually recognized that he was feeling neglected, unheard, and misunderstood. He realized how much he was afraid of hurting his stepmother if he expressed the rage that he felt toward her. It was suggested to Tom that he was now ready to bring in his stepmother to share some of these feelings directly with her at a future meeting. Two weeks later, he did bring in his stepmother to a session.

In the interim, Tom had an individual session in which he expressed his frustration with himself at his constant editing of his own anger. Tom talked about a significant triangle in his life at school, which involved the loss of a potential girlfriend to a roommate. He discussed how he had handled the situation in total silence. This train of thought led to his expressing his concern that he might be abandoned by the therapist. Rather than focus on the transferential aspects of these ideas, the therapist suggested that a similar concern might have arisen in his original family in the triangle between his mother, father, and himself. Since he had mentioned that he and his father have secrets from his stepmother, Tom was concerned about the consequences of really talking it all out with her. He felt conflicted between wanting to talk openly to her on the one hand, and to protect her by being polite and distant on the other hand.

To further mobilize that part of Tom ready to be denumbed, a stressor tape was played. This audiotape of a 64-year-old mother and her 42-year-old daughter addressed the problem of conflict and unresolved grief. Here is Tom's response and elaboration with the therapist:

TOM: Um, I was jealous of the daughter because here she was telling her mother all of this stuff, and her mother was actually listening. The mother was interested in what the daughter had to say even though she may have felt like defending herself. She was interested, so I was jealous of that. I feel like if my stepmother sat here, or my aunt, or whoever, that they wouldn't be as interested. Um, and combined with the jealousy, I was like annoyed with the daughter, and it's a very familiar feeling that I get every time I see a mother and her child where the child is yelling at the mother, because I always feel that he/she doesn't know how lucky they are. She actually has a mother, and so I get angry and jealous. The daughter seemed to just need to get stuff out, and to make a person understand what it has been like all along if you have been holding these feelings in, but I feel that there should be more to it than that. She didn't seem to want to work something out with the mother. She just seemed to say, you know, "You fucked me up, and that's that. I just want you to know that you did." I don't know . . . I know that that is hard for me to do. I don't know why, but I feel that it was too much, and it was just too hard to get out, and she wasn't receptive at all to anything coming in.

THERAPIST: Can you say anything more about the anger that you felt about not having someone to be there for you, to listen?

TOM: Um, it's just something that I have always felt not just when I see people being mean to their parents, but when I see them being nonchalant about their parents. It makes me feel really mad because they have them and it looks like they don't appreciate them, and I want them, and I don't have them.

THERAPIST: What is it like not having it?

TOM: Well, like she said, it's lonely, and you feel like an orphan, and it's tiresome. It makes you mad, and it makes you sad, and it makes you tired. It makes you, um, feel like everything that you do in life you have to do alone. It makes me feel like I am handicapped, like I am missing something, and like there are things that some people learn from their parents that are almost like secrets. I feel like I am definitely missing out on something good. There is something good that must go on that I am not getting.

THERAPIST: What kind of secret?

TOM: I don't know. I mean it's silly, but that is the way I feel. I know that it sounds silly, and I know that it's probably not true at all, ever.

THERAPIST: Maybe it is!

TOM: Maybe it is, but I mean, it's true that, it's true for me that whatever it is, I feel like it's not around. I don't know what kind of secrets, secrets about life, about um, secrets how to get along in life.

THERAPIST: Who in particular do you feel held out from you in sharing these things?

TOM: Um, I don't know, I am not sure that I feel like anyone really held out, I just feel like my mother left, so she couldn't, and my father was unavailable. He was preoccupied, he couldn't. He was too busy. It always seemed to me that he was always into himself, he was doing it because he needed to do it for himself. He wasn't thinking about me. I don't feel like the daughter felt when she said, you know, 'I feel like you never cared about me.' I don't feel at all like my father never cared about me, or my stepmother, or anyone really. I just feel like they, like my father, um, was too involved in his own life. I know that he cares about me. Also, my mother. If my mother was alive, I would probably hate her.

In the next session, with Tom's stepmother, after a preliminary orientation this videotape was played for her alone (the therapist was in the room with her). Then, Tom joined the session. Spurred on by Helen's calm acceptance, and resonance with that material, Tom led up to his rage and sadness in relation to both his mother and his stepmother. Then he was able to tell his stepmother how painful it was that she was not in fact his real mother. Having said this, he was able to share his fear of being abandoned by her for expressing such anger. He went on to admit to her that, despite having distanced her repeatedly for self-protection, he really did need and love her. Mrs. B was quite thoughtful in listening to Tom's concerns. Since this meeting was videotaped, Tom was able to watch himself as a more objective witness to his strong expression of pain and hurt. He was impressed with how much feeling he could safely experience, express, and modulate.

Two days later, we had another session because Tom's maternal grandmother was visiting Tom from out of state. She had come armed with pictures and letters written by Tom as a child. His maternal grandmother then filled in more details about Tom's biological parents, and revealed to him that, at the age of 9, he had blamed himself for his mother's death because of an argument that had occurred just prior to the accident. Encouraged by his maternal grandmother's concern and openness, Tom went on to ask her more about her own family and life, focusing especially on the events leading up to his maternal grandmother's own divorce, which had occurred many years before. In this session, Tom made a commitment to visit his mother's grave.

Tom was encouraged to get a copy of a newspaper account of his mother's accident. This material was forthcoming from his maternal grandmother. It was while reading that account in the next session alone, on July 18, 1982, that much more of his sealed-over sadness erupted. The deepening of his affect was further facilitated by playing somber sounds of music taken from a "Kol Nidrei" service. On August 2, 1982, his imagery once again was reviewed regarding his having been told of his mother's death. He also shared an essay describing the emptiness that he felt. He found himself remembering two of his mother's boyfriends, and with some encouragement, he went back to his imagery. As his sadness deepened, he described the dull grayness in his chest becoming clear and misty. He noted a continuing image of white noise in his stomach, and understood the suggestion that he could take that particular experience as a signal from his body that he was feeling psychological stress, and that he was being called back by his body to be healed by it from within. His sister, Jeanette, was invited to have a session with him alone to get an expanded validation of his sadness, as well as for his sister to receive support for *her* loss.

Prior to the session on August 6, 1982, he invited his sister down for the weekend to his university. In that session, for the first time ever, they exposed and shared with one another much of the sadness that they both had felt. The sister described how she dealt with her sadness by putting a lot of time into athletics, which allowed her to distance herself from her feelings of loneliness. She also said that she used the defense of perfectionism in overidentifying with their father. She talked about having cried once very much, and then another time just a little, after their mother's death. She noted that she stopped crying after that lest she cry in front of their stepmother. Jeanette was impressed by the changes in her brother and was really surprised when he burst into tears on a couple of occasions when they were together over the weekend. Furthermore, she was able to give him some valuable feedback about his previous years' friends, whom she met and characterized as "cool but numb." Tom returned from school for what was planned to be the final session on September 15, 1982. He noted that the sadness was still there, surprising him at various intervals, when he was alone in his room, and that he would just burst into tears. He also noted that there was a certain high that he experienced with each such recognition of his sadness. He asked for a copy of his genogram in order to work on further hypotheses about the origin of his clouds, his guilt, and his fear of being a fickle and unmarriageable person. We also discussed the possible denial of loss existing on his father's side of the family regarding a second cousin that had committed suicide at the age of 24. His plan was to call after a trip to his mother's grave in the event that he got more information from his maternal grandmother about his maternal grandfather. The latter had long been cut off from his family.

Tom noted that he was quite happy at school now, and that he would be in touch when necessary. Three weeks prior to the September 15th meeting, I received a phone call from Mrs. B thanking me for the work that I had done with her family. She thought that there now was a greater understanding among them, and that her stepson was feeling very positive about himself, and behaving more independently. She further pointed out that Tom was now reaching out to more types of friends than he had before. She said that she appreciated that Tom had not been given answers, but that as a result of the consultation he had found the ways to his own answers.

A few months later, Tom returned after having visited his mother's grave on the occasion of his maternal grandfather's recent death. He spent no time alone there, and so little time that he avoided making an audiotape, as had been previously requested. A portion of that interview follows:

THERAPIST: What was the thought you had when you first got here?

TOM: It is just that feeling, that empty feeling to be abandoned. [*He is tearful here*] An angry feeling, a frustration, because there isn't anything that I can do about it . . . I mean, there isn't anything I can do to change it. I can just try to understand it better, or something . . .

THERAPIST: Well, I imagine that you could have shared that anger with her when you were at her grave. How do you think that you would have put it?

TOM: Well, I did tell her that I was mad about the fact that she knew that she was going to die at some point, or at least I think that she did, and she didn't leave anything behind.

THERAPIST: Say some more about that as if you were talking directly to her.

TOM: "If you knew that you were dying then you must have thought about us, and why couldn't you even write a letter? Why couldn't you have just passed on a message if you didn't have the strength to write a letter? Why couldn't you catch a word with us? You just left nothing! You just left a space." [*He is crying off and on*] I always feel guilty when I feel that way because it is demanding. Here was a 30-year-old woman with two children, dying, and I'm saying why couldn't you leave something, why couldn't you do . . . [*He is crying again*] I brought a big picture of her. [*He takes the picture out*]

THERAPIST: Reply to your demand, and put it in her words.

TOM: [*Speaking as if he were his mother*] "That's why I feel so guilty, because the reply would be something like, 'You know, I feel terrible, and I wish that I could have been able to think about something like that, or be able to handle something like that, but there was no chance.' "

THERAPIST: What if she had said those things to you that you just said, what would be the first response that would pop into your mind to say back to her?

TOM: "I'm sorry to be so demanding." It must have been awful, the poor thing.

THERAPIST: Ask if she left any word or things for you kids, or for your father to pass on to you that he may have been too guilty to deal with.

TOM: "Did you leave anything? Anything at all? Even the tiniest message?

Tom was asked to review the video recordings of the above, and then to view a picture of his mother about to be recorded for video playback.

TOM: I still am angry. [*He says this whispering, with disbelief*] I look many times older than my mother, and uglier. I always look like a forlorn character.

THERAPIST: Can you hold it next to you, the picture? Put it a little closer to you. Put it down a little, closer to your face by an inch.

TOM: Does this get recorded?

THERAPIST: Yes. For a little bit more sense of completion, we could send for the hospital records.

TOM: I have all the bills. [*He laughs*] My father put them in a chest, the records. I don't know how much they would keep after all of these years.

THERAPIST: But, they might say something essential.

Tom had brought in an enlarged picture of his mother which was placed on the video screen. Because it had been blown up to 2 by 3 feet, there was an increasing approach to a more real-life representation of his mother. He was allowed to review this session on playback with his stepmother a couple of weeks later, and they were able to acknowledge the unspoken pain that had existed. A couple of weeks later, much of this material was reviewed with Tom's maternal aunt. It was a very difficult session for him, followed by a session of planned review of his mother's hospital records just prior to her death. This was difficult for Tom to do, so the session was postponed until the next week.

TOM: How should I do this? What should I do, just read it? Can you tell me why you want me to do this?

THERAPIST: Yes, because I want to see which particular phrase or sentence affects you in which way.

TOM: Why?

THERAPIST: Because people normally have certain things that they react to more than others in such records.

TOM: Well, she had more surgery than I thought. Okay. I don't want to do this!

THERAPIST: What are you feeling?

TOM: I don't know. I just, I don't know if it's different today than any other day. I don't want to break down.

THERAPIST: You don't want to cry?

TOM: Right.

THERAPIST: Because of what you are feeling toward me?

TOM: No, I don't think so.

THERAPIST: Because of . . . ?

TOM: I don't know.

THERAPIST: Because of what is going on outside of here?

TOM: I am just moody this week. It's partly because I was ill this week. [*He is crying*]

A week later, Tom took another look at the hospital records. After reviewing them completely, he found himself leaning back and sobbing.

THERAPIST: What do you imagine saying?

TOM: Saying to her? That I wish that she didn't have to suffer so much, and that I didn't want to see her go.

THERAPIST: Imagine that you are only 7 years old, what do you think of how it would come out? That statement to your mother just before she died.

TOM: "Why do you have to go? [*Sobbing*] Why can't you get better?" I guess I might ask if, I might wonder if my father was going to do the same thing, or if he was going to stay around. I might ask her, "What should we do about him? Who is going to take care of us?" I guess that she didn't take care of us for a pretty long time before she died.

THERAPIST: You mean June, 1966?

TOM: I don't remember, I think it was people with a large family. [*that took care of him and Jeanette*] I would have wanted to, you know, just ask her a lot of questions about how she felt, and tell her a lot about how I felt. You know, tell her that I was really mad, and that I was really sad, and scared.

THERAPIST: See if you can visualize that, doing that now, and say it as if she were here now for a moment.

TOM: I feel like it is so redundant. I have already done it. I did it at the grave. I believe that I have done it here.

THERAPIST: Do you feel those experiences are complete for you now that you have experienced it fully?

TOM: Experienced what fully?

THERAPIST: Your anger and sadness.

TOM: I don't know. I thought that I had. I think that the anger is gone, at least it's not around.

THERAPIST: Big difference?

TOM: I was wondering yesterday about anger and how when I am angry I think now that I was angry then, and I didn't know it. I was very angry, I think, and I didn't know it at all. Now I am just not angry anymore. I hardly ever, although I can't say I hardly ever get angry, but it's just not the way it used to be. I kept going around being angry all of the time. I think that is replaced with anxiety. I don't know if that makes sense, but I think that it probably does.

This approach comprises the dual perspective of family system and family development. The family system approach emphasized the interlocking aspects of a family member's belief system, and the behaviors from one generation to another. Family development reminds us that this system is changing all the time rather than being static. In order to fully understand what is important for an individual in the family, one must always link one's observations about individual self-growth with what is happening in family evolution. The filling out of the genogram was an indispensable part of working with Tom and his family.

It allowed us, once potential resources were thereby mapped out, to proceed with the process of joint self- and family actualization. In dealing with the devastating impact of death on the child, and the consequences of unresolved grief many years later, one must be concerned with how to facilitate a denumbing that is mutually supported not only by the major client, but by the whole family. One must assume that the identified client is not the only numbed person, but that they are all potentially capable of developing in the direction of greater healing. The concept of family actualization is based on the notion that greater development is possible by family members in tandem than separately, and that such development is greater than the sum of each family member's self-actualization.

If the therapist plants the seeds for recognizing the many resources available to the client within his/her own family, the client grasps the optimistic view about the benefits that will be reaped. It is thus much easier for the client to, over time, approach and invite family members to a session. One lays the groundwork for the client to proceed further beyond therapy, to getting to know himself/herself through the family. What is mobilized here is a process of creating greater intrafamilial empathy. There is a great deal more of a payoff in the creation of this type of ability to share pain and increase perspective on one another in the family, than in the development and nurturance of a therapist–client transference and countertransference relationship with all of the intensity and time commitment involved therein. One of the major pitfalls in the more traditional therapeutic process is that the affect between client and therapist is heightened.

In our approach that affect is better directed between the client and significant others in his/her own family. If Tom had been encouraged to share on and on about the extent of his feelings about his stepmother only with the *therapist* rather than with her directly, it might have been more difficult for him to access the extent of his pain or the nature of its displacement. A significant pitfall that was avoided was to have invited the whole current nuclear family in from the start. Tom himself had warned indirectly against this approach by telling the therapist that he had met with a woman (counselor) and his stepmother and father when he was in the 10th grade, and "it was a horrible experience." As a therapist, one must carefully assess the timing and sequencing of certain sharing of experience. The powerful affect is best shared in the context that would be safe to *all*.

In this case, Tom needed to be assured that he was sufficiently denumbed and clear about his own rage that he could safely express it in a controlled situation rather than being expected to test and risk his loyalty to both parents by dealing with his feelings earlier about his stepmother in the presence of his father. It was important that he access the sealed-over shock about the loss of his mother before dealing with the problem of having to reattach to his stepmother. He had clearly suffered an interruption of his and his family's development through the divorce and the death, and had not had the emotional support he needed at the time to fully experience all of the vicissitudes of his blocked love. It was essential to say a more complete goodbye to his mother first, before he could say hello to improved relationships with his stepmother, other family members, and the rest of the world.

The family practitioner model in this instance is quite consistent not only with brief intermittent therapy through the life cycle, but also with a situation where the therapist as a resource is limited, as in a health maintenance organization, or in any community mental health center. This long-term brief therapy model fits nicely with the importance of facilitating family resources as discussed elsewhere in this book. The sooner the therapist engages the family in helping him/her become obsolete as their helper, the sooner the family may mobilize over and over its talents for helping themselves.

As those who have done child work have long known, it is very important that parents be present to participate in a brief treatment contact. The therapist must seize on the initial therapy encounter and encourage the whole family to be active, if necessary, tapping everyone's capacity for problem solving, which in the case of death and dying involves gaining access to the important affects that have been mutually and multiply denied.

For a child experiencing the loss of a parent, the departing parent and the other parents can be major resource leaders. The child needs the modeling by a parent of vulnerability in saying goodbye and in evidencing a sense of completeness in reviewing his/her life at an age when he/she was just becoming psychologically clear about his/her own mortality, and of object inconstancy, that is, that he/she too must die eventually. Tom had to face a death, so sudden and unexpected, in a family already distressed by divorce. As a result, neither parent could provide the necessary leadership in facilitating the grief process. It should be no surprise that forces of the incomplete grief became reactivated at a critical time in Tom's and his family's development. First, Tom was the first child to test the waters of the separation process in the current nuclear family. Second, his initial push for more autonomy (moving out of the family home 5 years before) had occurred at the same time that his half-siblings were close to the age that he and his sister were when they were abandoned by their mother. Thankfully, their mother was buried rather than cremated. So, in both a spiritual and concrete sense, Tom was able to gain access to his feelings about her at the cemetery.

Tom would have to take the responsibility to fill out both sides of the dialogue, just as he took the responsibility for gathering information from many living family members about his family. In addition to owning the major responsibility for gathering data, he collaborated with the therapist in a major way in calibrating the process of dialoguing with his significant others. He was thoughtful and loyal in sharing his confusion, fear, anger, sadness, and numbness, all in a moderate degree, at an appropriate pace and place. In this way, he himself became a model to the rest of his family, bestowing upon himself the competence to become that significant other to himself and to the others that he so dearly missed. Where numbness existed in the form of negative identification with the deceased, aliveness took over in the form of positive identification with the deceased to challenge that formerly too-dominant deadness. Tom could experience many members of his family as more available than ever before, and he could experience himself as more resourceful than ever before.

Such is the paradoxical task of the family therapist, who must guide the self from death back to life, from external nurturance back to self-support, and then back again cautiously to the ever-connected family environment for more self-sustaining feedback in the direction of self-support. Perhaps the most self-nurturing asset lies in the individual's acceptance of his/her own mortality after having faced fully the death of a loved one; that is, the acceptance of what he/she can *not* give to himself/herself: the fountain of youth.

A "NONPSYCHIATRIC" CASE EXAMPLE

After-the-fact therapy is, of course, only one royal road to the truth of the dying and letting-go experience. Many families take heed of and work hard to overcome the numbing process on their own. One marvelous self-documented example is the public case of Aram Saroyan. Buoyed by a journalist's perspective, Saroyan summoned the "courage to be" resource within himself in the anticipatory mourning of his dying father, William Saroyan, in *Last Rites* (1984). Aram Saroyan has written a chronicle of the highly charged period of his life when his father died. Over a period of five weeks, the reader is led to experience the demise of one tortured life (his father's) and the rebirth of another's (his own) (see Figure 15-2).

The son of the famous writer came to know a man "very different from the one that the world at-large seemed to insist he was." As the book opens, the elder Saroyan, at age 72, who seemed to have had a good and strong life, was now succumbing to prostate cancer. Aram had been entirely out of touch with his father for about 4 years at this point. This rupture stemmed from his father's blaming reaction toward Aram's auto accident when Aram had felt adamantly that he was clearly a victim, and could not have been culpable.

The younger Saroyan understood the fact that the last episode of his father's life could be an important one for him to live through completely in order to learn and perhaps grow beyond the point at which he was stuck with his distant father. Attentive to the intergenerational ripplings set off by a grandparent's death, Saroyan includes in his chronicle the effects of the impending death of his own children, as well as the circular effects of his children's grief on him. It was the tears expressed by the older daughter, Strawberry, aged 10, which made him realize how much "death brings back the most important things you have shared together, the moments of truest intimacy, perhaps because death itself is so intimate."

The reader is eased into the nature of the conflict between father and son from the vantage point of what happened between Aram's sister, Lucy, and William on the occasion of Lucy driving up from Los Angeles to Fresno with a basket of fruit and good wishes for her father. In Aram's words, on this visit,

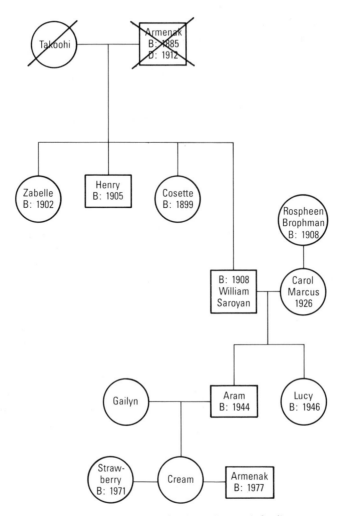

FIG. 15-2. Genogram for Aram Saroyan's family.

their father "had abused her viciously and kicked her out of the house." William's reaction to seeing his daughter for the first time in several years was that "her perfume was such a stink, that it was killing him faster." With that point of departure, Aram makes it clear how well he, himself, has known the "black poison of his father's soul that has engulfed her that day," and "how hard it was for me to forgive him even so that I understand him." Because of the "toxic, paralyzing air that at any moment may replace the real air between us," it is "only because he is now dying" that Aram would even conceive of seeing his father again.

Aram Saroyan well understands the effect of living with a numb parent who himself has never been able to accept the early death of his own father. Aram's numbing stemmed from a situation where "one knows when there is no way in the world to reverse the tide of hate, and brutal hysterical anger coming from a parent, and knowing that it has nothing whatsoever to do with the child." Now, at age 37, Aram Saroyan reviews the context in which his father never liked him, his sister, *or* his mother, whom he divorced twice. He clarified the peculiar but predictable way in which his father could never like anyone after an hour or two, unless they were a stooge or a lacky for him, able to be seduced and controlled in their worship of him.

William Saroyan never recovered from the rage he experienced at the death of his own father just before he was 3 years old. He transferred that rage to his children, who clearly felt that William would have just as soon killed them, which he did not do physically, but did in other ways. "He initiated and carried out a long psychological war against us, so that we went numb with disbelief and sorrow, and deep murderous anger." So, the rage was mindlessly transferred at least over three generations. The father took great pleasure in releasing his rage against not only his children, but against many people, especially potential intimates. Lucy and Aram were careful not to release their anger out of fear that they literally might murder their father.

William Saroyan's father died prior to his third birthday of a ruptured appendix, and William was taken by his mother to an orphanage where he lived for the next 5 years. So, the irrevocable loss of his father was further amplified with the sudden loss of his mother as well. By the time the elder Saroyan was 8 years old, he had acquired the irrevocable impression, "like a mirror with a slight warp in it which gives everything back slightly changed in the reflection. That warp in my father was *loss*, pure and simple." This loss for William came to a head at age 35, the age at which his father, Armenak, had died and the father–son war was on. "When everybody got ready to fight the war, to kill, he, William, felt at a sudden loss."

When William Saroyan fell in love with Aram's mother, he was a man in love while dying, the way he had been dying as a child when he quite literally "froze his losses." Aram's parents were married and divorced twice each by the time he was 8 years old, so for most of his life Aram was aware of the death and poison inside his father, and therefore better able to understand, on the occasion his father's literal dying now, why his father told his sister, Lucy, that the "son is not to come, not to write, and not to phone lest he kill me if he does." The son realized that it was William's fear of feeling strong emotion that a visit from Aram and his family might kindle. Aram could see how the tantrum that his father had just thrown at his sister, Lucy, was the tantrum of the 3-year-old, the one that he couldn't throw at the time that his own father had died. It was a tantrum that would clearly prevent any possibility for intimacy or for gratefulness on his father's part, because his father could not afford to have any emotional needs. These needs died long ago, and William hadn't been able to recognize any emotional need since those devastating losses before he was 3, of a dead father and a mother who was separated from him, and who placed him in a new home, in an orphanage. Time stops here, but the body lives on. Aram saw clearly how his father hated his family *because* he loved them. He could also see that no matter how hard his mother tried, she could never succeed with his father because of all these complicated dynamics. William, in becoming a famous man, acquired a touch of the divine, of the immortal.

Ironically, people love William Saroyan for the sweetness of his books. He became the most famous Armenian of all time, and when he would come to a moment of complete terror, pain, and madness, he would simply remember that he was a famous writer loved by Armenians. Finally, William Saroyan could not afford any more demanding entanglement except that with Fame itself, and that became his only love. William Saroyan himself is quoted as saying in a note that his son found in his house one day during the writing of the book called *Not Dying*: "The only person I have ever really loved is Saroyan, and all that I really love now is the little of Saroyan still left in me."

The younger Saroyan realized that the father didn't want to see Aram's family because it reminded him of Mrs. Saroyan and she reminded him of the "death" inside of him all of his life. These were the thoughts in Aram's mind as he tried to sort out his guilt in musing about the will that his father might leave. He recurrently suspected that his father would freeze his assets and very little money would pass down to the family. He certainly wouldn't be able to discuss these matters with his father in the weeks that William had left to live. Sounding himself like a family therapist, Saroyan goes on to explain, "The whole terrain is about to be closed, to become finite and I find myself grappling to discover its basic order. I must do this less for his sake than for my own. If I can understand him, and myself in relation to him, I can spare myself the anger and resentment that is so much a part of what is between us." It is the order of that terrain that Saroyan goes on to learn to fathom in the rest of the book. He already had learned that as long as he remained in any contact with his father, he would be the subject of periodic and unpredictable attacks of psychological violence. He knew that his father was a confirmed physical coward, who had never had a fist fight in his life, but was compelled to be verbally vicious to his family whenever they spoke on the phone. He knew that his father was a man who never had a single serious affair, but who frequented prostitutes so that he could have a form of sexuality that reduced his intimate experience "to the impersonal level of a financial transaction." Aram believed that his father could not break down and admit human frailty and accept human succor.

One of William's acts of "deep psychological violence by a father against his son" involved telling Aram horrible, untrue things about Aram's own mother when Aram was a sexually impressionable 13-year-old. The "evil" things for which the father could not forgive his wife involved the fact that she was not an heiress; that she was Jewish and had lied and said that she wasn't, out of fear; and that she hadn't told him that she was illegitimate. Yet, William Saroyan himself had insisted, to be sure that his wife could bear him children, that they conceive a child out of wedlock. Aram was that illegitimate child. From the inhumane and outrageous claims that William Saroyan made against Aram's mother to his son, it becomes clear how much the man had to displace his rage, and pain at the loss of his own parents onto his own marriage partner. Furthermore, whenever Aram himself tried to show his father that he was a man, his dad's typical response would be, "you are a horse's ass." This would be screamed at his son at the top of his lungs in a murderous rage.

In the second week of these reflective last rites, Aram was to learn from William's doctor that his father "didn't want to see you." This occurred after his father had a stroke. At this point, it became clear to Aram that if he were to go to visit his father, he would ironically have to do it when his father was unconscious, lest his father be aware of his presence and reject him once more. His father's plan was to arrange his death in such a way as to make it appear that he had no son.

It would seem that there was no father–son relationship existing here. Aram had not seen his father's two houses in Fresno, California, for about 16 years. These houses were filled with memorabilia, and collections of all the man's writings and doodlings. This was a man who collected almost everything that he could, and had come up with a way to hold onto all of his money and collections even after his death. This was done so that for all intents and purposes "he will still be not dying," so that he, himself, by the force of his own will, can "guarantee himself immortality." Aram knew that all his father's properties were to become part of the Saroyan Foundation. The son's last direct communication with his father, he now realizes in the third week of his father's dying, occurred 3½ years before, after which time he never saw or spoke to his father again. At that time, he had been attempting to help his father with one of his real estate properties, which had been mismanaged and resulted in loss of income to the family. The son had offered to oversee the repairs of his father's Malibu property because it was in almost total disrepair, but it was then that father had called him "a horse's ass, without any business sense."

As the younger Saroyan writes, he tries "to break down what is happening to me, sometimes reaching into the past, to give a name to the deep restlessness I feel when I am not, in fact, going numb again. And in naming it, I do, in fact, find some relief from it." As his father lies dying, Aram realizes that he is "once again, and, in fact, for the final time, in the palpable grip of William's nervous system." Part of being in that grip involved creating a distrust toward people, much in the way his father was an emotional grandstander who "played for the gallery." He was "the whore with the heart of gold—in the deepest sense an emotional impossibility."

One might think, from reading Saroyan's books, that he was one of the most wonderful and understanding fathers of all time, but, in fact, those sweet books were written when William Saroyan was still single, and "before he tried, and in fact, did not succeed, at becoming a family man himself." After conveying these important ironies about his father's life and writings, it became clear to Aram that, as his father was dying, his own link in the mortal chain would open and hook into oblivion. He realized that his father's "just barely begun mortal link" had been abruptly and finally truncated with the early death of his own father, so that instead of existing at the birth end of the chain, William's link hooked into the abyss at both ends, on the one side being birth, and on the other side being death, with his then 2-year-old father in-between. It is this process that caused his father to go into an "involuntary, and in fact, pre-rational freeze that he might still be in 69 years later."

That is to say, words cannot delineate the experience that so profoundly affects the human being who is unable to complete his relationship with a parent or loved one, or to understand the intensity of the experience of interrupted grief. Yet, Aram is able to go on, and almost approximate with words how he was emotionally forced to absorb the guilt, the self-consciousness that he must have had as a child living in a situation in which he felt emotionally thwarted. It became increasingly difficult for him to accept his own emotional impulses. He began, he realizes now, to lower the "invisible shield" in his own emotional reality. He goes on to note, "In the child that I was, there was only the most natural sense of acceptance and love from my father. If he looked at me funny, I looked at me funny, too." Thus, the younger Saroyan begins to explain the process by which children absorb the contagious feelings of their parents, especially the numbness.

Four weeks into the chronicle, Aram's sister, Lucy, was able to share with her brother how terribly alone she felt. She moved more deeply into her grief, fearing that she would be unable to stop the crying: "I was really scared, Aram, you know? I mean, I really thought it was never going to end." One sees here the good sense that brother and sister had in supporting each other, rather than to have allowed the misery of their parent to affect their needed sibling bond.

Here is a pivotal paragraph from the fourth week of the chronicle:

> It is a last reprisal of all that has gone before and I find myself alternately murderously angry and helplessly fascinated to notice the very depths to which his condition reaches me, as well as remembering earlier moments in my life when I became seized by the dissociation in ways that have remained vivid. . . . My father has refused to accept me emotionally all of my life and this has had a profound impact on that life, encompassing in me at times the very character of perception itself. (pp. 120–121)

Aram goes on to explain how this affected his mother after his parents' second divorce. She lived for several years in a state of "sustained distraction." Aram continues, "I mean that my eyes, ears, nose, sense of touch and taste, all of my senses, were out of precise harmony, the physically synchronized harmony that is supported and ultimately enforced by a favorable emotional environment. My father's inability to accept emotion, either in himself, or from others, created an environment that involved a sort of continual short-circuit."

In the fifth week of this chronicle, the younger Saroyan finally is clear that he wants to see his father one more time before he dies. The emotional vacuum of having remained at a distance throughout the experience put him in a postition of accepting his father's own emotional block. He could not grow himself as a person by responding in kind to his father. He hoped that his father would not "feel deeply humiliated to see me in the condition he was in now."

"That first look he gave me was both more naked than any I have ever seen from him before, and at the same time more defiant. 'Hi, Pop' I said, finding my voice already almost choked with emotion, the emotion I had been having so much trouble keeping track of during all the days before I had seen him." Again, the continuity of life and the natural aspect of death becomes clear for Aram as he sits in the hospital room with his dying father and his young daughter, Cream. He notes, "Some newly emerged electric particle of our whole unit, danced between us—the *new generation*—of our matter itself, as Pop lay dying, and I sat, at 37, in the middle of the process he was ending, and she was beginning." Suddenly, he realized that in the last moments of his father's life,

> we were linking up with me in the middle from child to father, to father's father despite the fact that emigration and the American experience had eliminated the second and third links until this point. . . . "It was almost as if he were both dying, and being born too. . . . We were, in this moment, all at once, it seemed to me, the family we had never been. . . . I moved toward his forehead and said, "Good-bye, Pop", just before kissing him [and then] without hesitation, he flung his arm over my shoulder as I leaned over him, and the kiss turned into a hug. Suddenly, I found myself holding my dying father. "Thank you, Aram", he said, his voice deep with emotion, the long-withheld words suddenly real now on the air. "*Thank you*, Pop", I answered, feeling my own emotions swell. I felt instantaneously that we were speaking both in the moment and at the same time saying good-bye for our whole lives. "It is the most beautiful time of my life. . .and death". "For me too, Pop", I answered, now literally crying.

Outside in the corridor, as he closed the door, Aram heard his father saying loudly, "It's unbelievable! . . . It's unbelievable."

"The fact that he could surrender to me as he did was something very like a miracle to me. It was as if he were saying, at long last, you're a man, I love you, let me give you the legacy of my emotion, let me melt and merge into you, my son and my heir." The son realized that once he could let his father go, the father could in earnest begin to die. William knew that he had done his job, not only as an artist, but as a father as well, at that point, and the son had released him now from any burden of parental obligation. William Saroyan died a few days later, and thereafter the following message was allowed to be made public from the elder Saroyan. "Everybody has got to die, but I have always believed an exception would be made in my case. Now what?" This literary perfectionist, this man who believed in his immortality, had to deny the possibility of his death right to the end, lest it touch him before he was ready to be connected with his children. And what his son has been able, so eloquently, to explain to the rest of us is something about the mystery and majesty, as well as the "potential for healing in the experience of dying." As Aram goes on to explain, "It is a passage we are only now beginning to recognize in all its wonder and power, as only a few years ago we began to realize natural childbirth."

The partially numbed son of the numbed father has the most difficult chore. It is so much harder to grieve the loss of the hated parent. When there is so much unfinished business with the deceased, to make one's peace and place becomes a potentially overwhelming, but necessary task. Having been taught all one's life to be overreactive and yet sealed over, the out-of-touch child needs both much distance and emotional support. Such a paradoxical challenge demands the active empathic participation of his nuclear family or other responsive reference group. The singular task involves the exoneration or forgiveness of the rejecting/abandoning parent. He must walk a narrow line, tempted by total emotional cutoffs on one side and overinvolved fusion on the other.

It is obvious that much transgenerational research is required to make this challenge more possible for all of us. The successful Saroyan created for himself and future generations of Saroyans a link from natural childbirth to natural death so as to recreate the formerly *lost* and biologically *imperative* generational continuity.

CHALLENGE OF FORGIVENESS

Last Rites, an invaluable resource for both individuals and families, can be regarded as Aram Saroyan's symbolic expression of achieving a reciprocating forgiveness between himself and his father. The healing consequences of this are obviously critical for his own relationship to both his wife and their children. The healing thwarts the existence of a grudge.

Grudges are emotionally laden entities generally not addressed in descriptions of the grief or mourning process. It appears that both grudges and the process of forgiving are regarded as not relevant to psychology, but rather more appropriate to the domain of theology. A cursory review of the scientific literature on grudges and forgiving affirms the absence of this obviously vital alternative to the numbing process and numbness.

The New York Times, 27 December 1982, devoted a column to "Forgiving: A Kind of Freedom" in the weekly *Relationships Section*. This unusually interesting column was stimulated by the then recently released movie, *Ghandi*. As Glenn Collins, the *Times* writer, stated, "Ghandi's message is unequivocal: 'If everyone took an eye for an eye, the whole world would be blind!' "

Dr. Doris Donnelly, a visiting lecturer at Princeton Theological Seminary in New Jersey, was quoted in the same article as saying, "To a victim of battered-wife syndrome, advice to turn the other cheek seems a bit ludicrous . . . but ultimately, when that battered wife is out of danger, at some point, she is going to have to address the question of forgiveness, or hang on to her outrage for the rest of her life." Dr. Donnelly added, "Schiller said that 'hate is a prolonged form of suicide.' " She said that forgiveness has had a bad press and a poor image problem, underscoring her belief that one can't ever underestimate the power of love. She believes that real forgiveness is rare and is too often preempted by a mere pretense for reconciliation. Real forgiveness is a process, a gradual thing, that emerges only after we have affirmed the hurt and pain to those who have wronged us. It can only develop after we realize that we do not "want to be in bondage to the person or event that hurt you." Here begins the process of freedom from the grudge.

An old Chinese proverb states, "The person who pursues revenge should dig two graves." A comprehensive family systems approach must include attention to these spiritual and experiential issues in helping both the dying and the bereaved. To neglect any of these is to encourage numbness. By contrast, empathic attention to these areas, especially forgiveness, can restore a client's lost vitality.

> Bury something—
>   under the ground
>   in your heart
>   in your head
>   under the bed
>   in a closet
>   under your hat
>   inside your soul . . .
> What are the consequences?
>   Dead & buried?
>   Gone & done for?
>   Never.
> Something lives on—often against our will—but it lives on.

America has become a nation of gravediggers. Repression and denial of self, past and truth have become dangerously ingrained in the fiber of life. . . . Whether it's the simple process of denying a feeling and moving on, or the difficult grappling with death and burial, we as a people are getting quite adept at purposefully forgetting and moving on. However, the damage done to the human heart is insidious and irreparable. (Judy Braha, Director, 1985, of New Erlich Theatre's *Buried Child* by Sam Shepard)

APPENDIX: RESOURCES

Apart from the bibliographical references, there are a variety of resources that have been created around the country. They include, among others, hospices and educationally oriented organizations devoted to providing information, both cognitively focused and experientially directed, for the public and caregiving professionals.

HOSPICES

Hospices represent a badly needed development. The hospice movement stemmed principally from Dr. Cecily Saunders's efforts in England to care for the terminally ill and their next of kin. Generally, the care and involvement with the bereaved is limited and restricted because the need for hospices has outstretched the available resources. The family-oriented arrangement is suited to acquaint and support new families with both the challenges and options confronting a family with a dying member. They also assist a family who wishes to have the dying member die at home.

A guide to locating the hospices extent in the United States has been published (*1984 Guide to the Nation's Hospices*). The publisher is: The National Hospice Organization, Suite 402, 1901 North Fort Myer Drive, Arlington, Virginia 22091.

Memberships in this national organization are twofold; one for the hospital providing hospice care, at $500 per year, and one for the nonhospice-providing hospital, at $250 per year. To locate a hospice in your community, one can either write the national organization or call the local General Hospital Oncology Department, or call OMEGA (listed in your telephone directory).

INSTITUTIONS

Organizations devoted to enabling families to be better informed about the dying process and grief in both the dying and potentially bereaved are few and far between because in many ways they are regarded as counter cultural in nature.

The Grief Education Institute, located in Denver, Colorado, was organized in December of 1976 specifically to meet currently expressed needs of the bereaved. Their goals are fourfold:

1. To provide education and support services to the bereaved.
2. To disseminate information to the general public on grief as a normal process.
3. To provide education on grief to health care professionals and others who work with the bereaved.
4. To conduct research on grief.

They have had well-attended local conferences to further the cause of death education and have produced for sale a well-thought out and superbly useful manual for interested citizens: *Bereavement Support Groups: Leadership Manual*, written and compiled by Dr. Alice Demi. It can be obtained for $10 plus $1 postage from: Grief Education Institute, 2422 South Downing Street, Denver, Colorado 80210. Membership applications for both individuals and agencies can be obtained by writing to the Grief Education Institute at the above address.

The National Center for Death Education, located in Boston, Massachusetts, represents an exciting development in the area of death and dying. It was established in 1984 and is the public window, as it were, of the New England Institute, a professional college for educating students for the funeral service profession. The National Center was dedicated in June 1984 with keynote speaker, Dr. Herman Feifel, a nationally known thanatologist. His speech included the interesting statement, *"It is a historic phenomenon that consciousness of death becomes more acute and center-stage during periods of social disorganization, when individual choice tends to replace automatic conformity to consensual social values.*

The National Center has an academic program that includes such courses and institutes as:

- Helping Children Cope with Death and Aging
- Grief Conseling and Grief Therapy
- Clinical training program at Children's Hospital Medical Center

The National Center for Death Education also offers a certificate program for caregiving professionals interested in becoming more expert in the area. It also has available a very useful "Annotated Audiovisual Bibliography." Inquiries about this center should be directed to: Gail Gruner, Director, New England Center for Death Education, New England Institute of Applied Arts and Sciences, 656 Beacon Street, Boston, Massachusetts 02215.

EXHIBITIONS

The Children's Museum of Boston, Massachusetts in August 1984 presented a thought-provoking and moving exhibition of "Endings: An Exhibition on Death and Loss." It was designed to explore the difficult feelings and ideas that children and adults experience when confronted by irreversible loss. The range of focus included "Learning About Death," "Experiencing Death," and "Dealing With Death." There was a difficult and disturbing segment involving a video presentation that examined the difference between make-believe death and "real" death on TV by contrasting repeated takes of an actor's gory death, complete with gallons of fake blood, with newsreels footage of Beirut. The Children's Museum is to be admired for offering a compassionate and realistic view of a painful subject.

ACKNOWLEDGMENT

Editorial review by Betty Byfield Paul, L.I.C.S.W., Counseling Associates, Lexington, MA.

REFERENCES

Aries, P. *Western attitudes towards death: From middle ages to present* (P. M. Ranum, Trans.). Baltimore: Johns Hopkins University Press, 1974.

Becker, E. *The denial of death.* New York: Free Press, 1973.

Bowen, M. Towards the differentiation of self in one's family. In J. Framo (Ed.), *Family interaction.* New York: Springer, 1972.

Bowlby, J. Processes of mourning. *International Journal of Psychoanalysis,* 1961, *42,* 317–340.

Bowlby, J. *Attachment and loss* (Vol. III). New York: Basic Books, 1980.

Collins, G. Forgiving: A kind of freedom. *The New York Times,* Relationships Section, December 27, 1982, p. B10.

Cousins, N. *The healing heart.* New York: Norton, 1983.

Deutsch, H. Absence of Grief. *Psychoanalytic Quarterly,* 1937, *6,* 12.

Engel, G. Toward a classification of affects. In P. H. Knapp (Ed.), *Expressions of the emotions in man.* New York: International Universities Press, 1963.

Freud, S. Thoughts for the times on war and death. In J. Strachey (Ed. and Trans.), *The standard edition of the complete psychological works of Sigmund Freud* (Vol. 14, pp. 289–300). London: Hogarth Press, 1957. (Original work published 1915)

Fulton, R., & Gottesman, D. Anticipatory grief: A psychosocial concept reconsidered. *British Journal of Psychiatry*, 1980, *137*, 45–54.

Fulton, R., & Markusen, E. In G. Owen & J. L. Scheiber (Eds.), *Death and dying: Challenge and change*. Reading, MA: Addison-Wesley, 1978.

Gorer, G. *Death, grief, and mourning*. Garden City, NY Doubleday, 1965.

Group for the Advancement of Psychiatry. Death and dying: Attitudes of patient and doctor Vol. V, Symp. New York: Brunner/Mazel, 1965.

Kubler-Ross, E. *On death and dying*. New York: Macmillan, 1969.

Lifton, R. J. *The broken connection: On death and the continuity of life*. New York: Basic Books, 1983.

Lindemann, E. Symptomology and management of acute grief. *American Journal of Psychiatry*, 1944, *101*, 141–148.

Naipaul, S. *Journey to nowhere: A new world tragedy*. New York: Penguin, 1982, p. 885.

Osterweis, M., Solomon, F., Green, M. (Eds.). *Bereavement: Reactions, consequences, and care*. Committee for the Study of Health Consequences of the Stress of Bereavement Institute of Medicine. Washington, DC: National Academy Press, 1984.

Parkes, C.M. *Bereavement: Studies of grief in adult life*. New York: International University Press, 1972.

Paul, N.L. The use of empathy in the resolution of grief. *Perspectives in Biology and Medicine*, 1967, *11*, 153–169.

Paul, N.L. The need to mourn. In E. J. Anthony & C. Koupernik (Eds.), *The child in his family: The impact of disease and death*. New York: Harper Colophen Books, 1970, pp. 219–224.

Paul, N. L., & Paul, B. B. *A marital puzzle*. New York:

Perls, L. One Gestalt therapist approach. *Annals of Psychotherapy*, 1961, *1*, 125–129.

Saroyan, A. *Last Rites*. New York: William Morrow, 1982.

Stannard, D. E. *The Puritan way of death: A study in religion, culture, and social change*. New York: Oxford University Press, 1975.

Stannard, D. E. *Death in America*. Pennsylvania: University of Pennsylvania Press, 1975.

Toynbee, A., Mant, A. E., Smart, N., Hinton, J., Judkins & S. Rhode, E., Heywood, R. & Price H. H. *Man's concern with death*. London: Hodder & Stoughton, 1968.

Williamson, D. S. New life at the graveyard: A method of therapy for individuation from a dead former parent. *Journal of Marriage and Family Counseling*, 1978, *4*, 93–101.

Index